RURAL ENGLAND
1086–1135

RURAL ENGLAND
1086–1135

A Study of
Social and Agrarian Conditions

BY

REGINALD LENNARD

Sometime Reader in Economic History in the
University of Oxford

OXFORD
AT THE CLARENDON PRESS

Oxford University Press, Great Clarendon Street, Oxford OX2 6DP

Oxford New York

Athens Auckland Bangkok Bogota Bombay
Buenos Aires Calcutta Cape Town Dar es Salaam
Delhi Florence Hong Kong Istanbul Karachi
Kuala Lumpur Madras Madrid Melbourne
Mexico City Nairobi Paris Singapore
Taipei Tokyo Toronto
and associated companies in
Berlin Ibadan

Oxford is a trade mark of Oxford University Press

Published in the United States by
Oxford University Press Inc., New York

British Library Cataloguing in Publication Data
Data available

Library of Congress Cataloging in Publication Data

ISBN 0-19-821272-0

3 5 7 9 10 8 6 4 2

Printed in Great Britain by
Bookcraft Ltd
Midsomer Norton, Somerset

PREFACE

THIS book is an attempt to describe the social and economic conditions of rural life in England during the Norman period, when the country was under the impact of an early and somewhat indeterminate form of feudalism. But its scope is limited. On the one hand, it is not concerned either with the juridical concepts that were implicit in the manifold bonds of the social complex, or with the nature and extent of the changes that occurred between the coming of the Normans and the compilation of Domesday Book. To survey everything related to my subject was impossible, and it seemed best to omit these topics because they have already received much attention from historians and in particular occupy many pages in the works of Maitland and Vinogradoff. On the other hand, matters of agricultural technique—field systems, cropping, methods of tillage, and the like—have been omitted because of the scantiness of strictly contemporary evidence. It is indeed probable that much of what is revealed in later sources was also the practice of the earlier generations to which my book is devoted; but there is no lack of wide-ranging descriptions of medieval agriculture and I preferred to confine myself to material that is demonstrably relevant to my restricted period and to shun the perils of anachronism.

To what extent the results of my researches will seem new to others I do not know. Having spent the best part of a good many years in these studies, I find it difficult to estimate the degree to which my own views have been altered by gradually increasing familiarity with my subject. I have certainly learnt that money played a larger part in agrarian affairs than I had supposed and that the farming-out of manors on stock-and-land leases was so common that this mode of estate management, which was inherited from Anglo-Saxon England, must at least rank in importance with the system of tenure by knight-service introduced by the Normans. I have also come to recognize Norman England as a land of greater local variety, and rather less-marked regional contrasts, than I had previously conceived it to be. And I have found that the peasants differed from one another in economic standing much more than I had thought.

Two points of detail call for a word of explanation. It was not until this book was already in proof that Professor Raftis's monograph on *The Estates of Ramsey Abbey* (published in Toronto with a preface dated November 21, 1957) came into my hands. Secondly, I have followed the practice of my old friend Adolphus Ballard in rendering the *villanus* of the Domesday period as 'villan' in order to avoid the associations of developed serfdom which belong to the word when it is spelt 'villein' or 'villain'.

My obligations are many. Sir Ernest Barker—once my tutor —kindly read the original draft of my first chapter and gave me encouragement. Professor Cheney—once (I am proud to think) my pupil—has enlightened me on numerous points and saved me from several blunders. Among others who have helped me I have especial reasons to be grateful to Sir Charles Clay, Professor Galbraith, Miss N. D. Hurnard, and Mr. P. H. Sawyer, and, for much-needed aid on Anglo-Saxon matters, to Professor Dorothy Whitelock, Miss Harmer, and Mr. Alan Ward. Finally, it is both a duty and a pleasure to acknowledge with gratitude that my researches have been greatly facilitated by grants from the Leverhulme Trust in 1945 and 1946 and from the Houblon-Norman Trust during the years 1953–8.

                                                            R. L.
Lower Heyford
17 *January* 1959

CONTENTS

CONTENTS

I

AN OLD COUNTRY

WHEN William the Conqueror seized the English Crown, he became the ruler of an ancient realm. England was already an old country. The civilization of Roman Britain had, it is true, evaporated without leaving any appreciable mark upon the new and vigorous communities which the Anglo-Saxon invaders established within the boundaries of the former province; and little connexion can be traced between the institutions of those communities and the institutions of that older Celtic Britain which outlasted Roman rule in the hilly regions of the west. But Anglo-Saxon England had now a long history of its own and one that told of a remarkable continuity in development. Though the Scandinavian invasions and settlements had rudely interrupted this history and wrought lasting changes in its course, the England which the Norman duke subjected to his rule had its roots firmly and deeply set in a distant past.

Edward the Confessor, whose heir William claimed to be, was the direct descendant, through six generations of English kings, of Egbert of Wessex; and early Saxon genealogists traced the royal pedigree beyond Egbert to Ceawlin, who had ruled over the West Saxons five centuries before the Norman Conquest, and was believed to be the grandson or great-grandson of Cerdic, the traditional and perhaps historical leader of a fifth-century invasion of Britain. Archbishop Ealdred, who crowned William King of the English on Christmas Day, 1066, was the twenty-fifth occupant of the see of York. Of the fifteen bishoprics that then existed in England, ten dated from the seventh century, while the archiepiscopal see of Canterbury could trace its history back to the time of St. Augustine who was consecrated in 597. And though the continuity of monastic history had been broken in the ninth century by internal decay and Danish invasion, many of the houses that were restored in the last sixty years of the tenth century regarded themselves as the successors of much more ancient foundations. At Glastonbury a dim period of legend precedes the abbey's first appearance in history in the seventh century; and, among other monasteries that were not cathedral monasteries, Abingdon, Malmesbury, and Chertsey, and the nunnery of Barking, could look back to seventh-century predecessors. Even in those parts of England where the destruction wrought by the Danes had been most complete, the reformers of the age of Dunstan had shown a desire to maintain a link with the past by their choice of old monastic sites for the abbeys they established at Peterborough and Ely.

With regard to the continuity of secular institutions, other than the monarchy, we are in some particulars less well informed. Historians today would not assign either to the office of sheriff or to the administrative districts known as 'hundreds' the high antiquity that was claimed for them by Stubbs. But the national assembly or *Witan*, which under Norman rule grew into the feudal *Commune Concilium*, was essentially the same institution as the assemblies that we find already established in the Kentish and Northumbrian kingdoms four centuries earlier. The shire system, upon which Norman administration was to depend so much, can be discerned in Wessex about two hundred years before the Norman Conquest. The method of assessing property for purposes of taxation in fiscal 'hides' was certainly of old standing when the Conqueror made use of it for his exactions; and it had a predecessor, though not, it would seem, a direct ancestor, in the mysterious 'Tribal Hidage' which most scholars assign to the seventh century. In the matter of currency, the silver penny had been the basis of English money ever since the time of Offa of Mercia who reigned from 757 to 796; and the diplomatic forms employed for solemn charters by the Confessor, and for a short time by King William, have a continuous history on English soil that goes back at least to the year 679. In the sphere of law, it would be a tedious and hazardous task to seek for early evidence of specific usages that were still being observed under the Norman kings, but there can be little doubt that a great part of the body of law known to men of the Conqueror's day as the *laga Edwardi* was in fact very ancient.

To the political historian the annals of Anglo-Saxon history may sometimes appear to be a dreary waste of futile and disastrous conflict. For the historian of institutions, however, the lights and shadows of the picture fall very differently; and none can question the toughness and vitality of a society which maintained so large a measure of institutional continuity throughout so many generations and across the scorching ordeal of the Danish onslaughts. But it is, perhaps, in the economic sphere that the solidity of the old English achievement is most remarkable. When we speak of an 'old country' we usually mean something more than one whose political and constitutional history extends over a long period. The term seems to imply a country more or less fully settled in an economic sense and to indicate that the peaceful energies of men have extended their beneficent sway over all parts of it, turning the wilderness into ploughed fields and utilizing the resources of the land, according to the measure of knowledge and skill then obtaining, for the fulfilment of human purposes and the maintenance and betterment of human life. And England was an old country in this further sense when the Normans conquered her. Anglo-Saxon society had passed beyond the colonial stage. Though, judged by modern standards, the population was, no doubt, very scanty and the area of wood, waste, and marsh very large, Anglo-Saxon farmers were not nibbling the edges of a wilderness that was still unsubdued. The villages were small; and we may well believe that the village fields were in many cases severed from those of neighbouring villages by a thin belt of land that remained in a wild state. But villages, hamlets, or farmsteads were to be found throughout the length and breadth of the country, and even the waste and wood were not wholly unutilized, but provided supplies of firewood, timber, and game and were to some extent a source of food for sheep and pigs. In some parts there were blocks of untouched woodland and marsh larger by far than anything to be found in modern England apart from Dartmoor and Exmoor and the moors and fells of the north. But the framework of rural England as we know it was already laid out. Except perhaps in the four northern counties and southwards along the ridge of the Pennines, it is probable that even in the reign of the Confessor there was no spot in England from which half a day's walk would not bring one to an English home.

The agrarian history of medieval England is preserved in an incomparable series of records; and it is with Domesday Book, the great survey of the country made by the Conqueror in the twentieth year of his reign, that the English historian first acquires an instrument of knowledge superior to anything that is available for any other land. The four northern counties are, it is true, almost entirely excluded from its scope. It contains no information about London and some other important towns. It is hard to interpret and easy to misunderstand. It is not always accurate. It baffles all attempts to make a satisfactory estimate of the population upon the basis of the data that it supplies. But, in spite of these defects, Domesday Book tells us more about the human geography of the country in the eleventh century than will ever be known about the condition of any other part of the world in that early period. On the basis of the facts which it records we can speak with some confidence about the degree to which the land of England was occupied and even make an approximate estimate of the extent to which it was utilized for agriculture. A modern traveller who disembarks at Plymouth, if he goes by railway through Bristol to London and then takes a train from King's Cross to York and beyond York to the southern boundary of the county of Durham, will at every point of that journey of 500 miles be within 5 miles of some place that is mentioned in Domesday Book. Nor is it otherwise if one follows the main-line route from Dover to London and from London through Rugby and Crewe to Chester and Birkenhead.

In regard to the state of tillage it is necessary to speak with caution. But the evidence unmistakably suggests, if it cannot be said to prove beyond all doubt, that the area under the plough in the country as a whole (exclusive of Middlesex and certain northern regions for which the evidence of Domesday is either wanting or misleading) was not much less, and may even have been somewhat greater, than the extent of arable in the early years of the twentieth century. This can be affirmed of an area comprising twenty-eight modern counties.[1] Yet such a statement, if made without qualification, might well give a very wrong impression. We have to remember that in modern England the area available for farming has been reduced by the immense expansion of the towns, while the arable forms only a part, and in the period chosen for comparison comprised much less than half, of the land devoted to agriculture. The England of which Domesday Book tells us lacked the fine fields of permanent grass that are such an important element in modern English farming and today form so conspicuous a feature in the English landscape. In the eleventh century the meadows were scanty in the extreme; and, apart from them, we are probably justified in suspecting

[1] See Appendix I.

that the pastures consisted mostly of very rough grazing grounds, which must have been infested with scrub, and the insufficiency of which is reflected in the utilization of woodlands as swine-pastures and in the medieval practice of turning out beasts to graze over the stubbles and upon the extensive areas that were left each year under bare fallow by the prevailing systems of cropping.[1] At the same time, we should form in our minds an erroneous picture of the country which William the Conqueror ruled if we failed to recognize that the total extent of the arable fields was very large, and that in general the proportion of the land which was under the plough varied less from one district to another than it does under modern conditions of agricultural specialization and urban development.[2]

But general statements about the condition of the country need to be supplemented by a more detailed examination of particular districts; and in the first place I choose for the purpose the neighbourhood of my own home.

The little river Cherwell, from its source in Northampton-shire to its junction with the Thames at Oxford, touches or traverses thirty-seven parishes.[3] The names of all but five of these are to be found in Domesday Book. Nor must we conclude that the omitted parishes lay in a wild condition. Woodford Halse is one of them; and the presence of human dwellings and cultivations within its bounds is proved by entries in Domesday relating to its hamlets, West Farndon and Hinton.[4] Warkworth, another of the five, contained within its former boundaries the

[1] Of scrub-infested pasture there is some indication in the fact that Domesday uses the expression *silva minuta*, and the Exon. text the word *nemusculum*, for land on four Somerset manors which is described as *pascua* in the satellite text of the Bath Cartulary: *E.H.R.* lviii (1943), 37.

[2] Apart from regions with an exceptional amount of woodland or fen, the proportion of arable must have varied much less than it did in 1914, before the changes induced by war. In thirteen eastern and midland counties for which the Domesday figures have been adjusted in Professor Darby's volumes to the modern county areas (excluding Shropshire and Staffordshire which were in an abnormally wasted condition in 1086) the ratios of Domesday ploughs to areas varied from one per 211 acres in Gloucestershire to one per 371 acres in Cambridgeshire, or indeed only to one per 287 acres in Leicestershire, if we exclude Cambridgeshire and Lincolnshire on account of their fenlands. The percentages of the same county areas which were under the plough in June 1914, ranged from over 67 in Cambridgeshire and nearly 60 in Suffolk to 18 in Leicestershire, 22 in Warwickshire, and 23 in Herefordshire.

[3] In reckoning the number of parishes I have counted Banbury and Oxford as one each, and have excluded a few places which were only made into parishes since the beginning of the nineteenth century.   [4] Dd. i, ff. 223, 227.

hamlet of Grimsbury, which appears in Domesday as already in existence on the eve of the Conquest and was in 1086 the home of 18 peasant households and 4 slaves, while its land was tilled, and tilled to the limit which the Domesday commissioners judged to be practicable, by 6 plough-teams.[1] Souldern, again, which lies in Oxfordshire, close to the Northamptonshire border, cannot be identified with any place that is mentioned in Domesday, but some Saxon graves have been found in the parish and Souldern church possesses an early Norman tower. Marston, near Oxford, seems to be referred to in a charter of the Confessor; and its exclusion from Domesday is probably due to its being already (as it certainly was in the thirteenth century) a member of the manor of Headington, the account of which in Domesday may include the facts relating to Marston. Even in the case of the remaining parish—Wardington—one can point to its apparently Old English name and the fact that the church contains some work which appears to be of early Norman date.[2]

Besides the villages from which the parishes take their names, the Cherwell valley contains a number of hamlets. Seventeen of these are mentioned in Domesday as inhabited places possessing one or more plough-teams in 1086; and it is clear from the references to former values, if not from some more precise statement, that none of them had come into existence after the Conquest.[3] Since the source of the Cherwell is less than 33 miles distant from its confluence with the Thames, these facts imply a pretty thorough settlement of the district, even though the course of the stream is very tortuous.

It is impossible to make any summary statement about the population of this valley or about its agricultural development, chiefly because the descriptions of certain manors appear to have included statistics of detached properties that were treated as portions of these estates though geographically separate from them, with the result that the local facts cannot in these cases be isolated. But the number of mills is significant, for the mills of Domesday were undoubtedly flour-mills. Even in this matter

---

[1] Dd. i, f. 227b.

[2] For Souldern see *V.C.H. Oxon.* i (1939), 355. The charter which refers to Marston is *Cod. Dipl.* 862, which is also in Thorpe, *Diplomatarium* (1865), pp. 368–9: the identification is accepted by Stenton, *V.C.H. Oxon.* i. 375.

[3] Among the hamlets I include Bodicote which was made a separate ecclesiastical parish in 1855. One, if not more, of the hamlets is now represented by an isolated farm.

exactness is precluded. More than fifty mills are mentioned in entries relating to the Cherwell valley, but probably some of them lay outside it and we cannot say precisely how many did so. Yet it may be taken as virtually certain that there were some thirty or forty within the bounds of those parishes that today touch the river at some point, though the wheels of a few of these mills may have been turned by the waters of tributary streams like the little river Swere. It is clear too that some of the settlements in the valley were substantial villages. Kidlington, for example, was the dwelling-place of 32 *villani*, 8 bordars, and 2 serfs; and, as in the case of the two former classes it seems that only the heads of households were enumerated, this may perhaps imply a population of some two hundred souls.[1] In this village the contrast presented by modern conditions is striking, for by 1841 Kidlington, apart from its hamlets, had a population of over a thousand, and during the present century it has developed rapidly as a detached suburb of Oxford. But Water Eaton, now a hamlet in the ecclesiastical parish of Kidlington, contained in 1086 33 peasant households, which would mean 165 persons if we reckoned 5 to a household; and 8 centuries later (1891) its population was 161.[2] A few miles higher up the valley we find at Shipton-on-Cherwell another little village which cannot have been much smaller, and may have been larger in the Conqueror's reign than it became towards the end of the nineteenth century when its population sank to half what it had been in 1871. The census of 1891 showed a population of 71, and 30 years later this had only increased to 84. The Domesday figures point to a population of between 60 and 70 if we take the serfs to be isolated individuals and multiply the number of *villani* and bordars by 5; but if we allow the serfs to have families like the others, that will bring the estimate up to 95. There were 5 plough-teams at Shipton in 1086: on the assumption that 120 acres were tilled by each team, it would appear that the arable amounted to nearly 60 per cent. of the present area of the parish.[3] Of the larger villages it is hazardous to speak; for it is in the descriptions of them that there is most reason to suspect the inclusion of non-local matter. That is especially the case with the royal manors of Kirtlington and Adderbury and

---

[1] Dd. i, f. 158.   [2] Ibid.
[3] Ibid., ff. 156, 224*b* (the latter entry being one of those Oxfordshire descriptions which were incorporated in the Northamptonshire section of Domesday Book).

the Bishop of Lincoln's manors at Deddington, Banbury, and Cropredy. But there seems no ground for doubting that Tackley, apart from its hamlets, had nearly 150 inhabitants and could show perhaps as much as 1,200 acres under the plough.[1] About 6 miles farther north, Somerton appears in Domesday as a village whose inhabitants may be estimated at about 130, while its 10 plough-teams would, on the usual reckoning, point to an extent of arable slightly exceeding the 1,119½ acres of arable that were to be found in the parish exactly 8 centuries later.[2]

A single region chosen at random is not necessarily representative, so further samples must be examined. But it will perhaps be sufficient to apply the rough and summary test afforded by the proportion of the parish names that are to be found in Domesday or earlier records in the first hundredal district dealt with by the *Survey of English Place-Names* in each of the counties of Domesday England for which the results of that survey have been published. The figures are given in the following table:

County	Hundred or wapentake	Number of parishes in the survey	Number of parishes in the survey which are mentioned in Domesday, the Exon. Domesday, the I.C.C. or earlier sources
Bedford . . .	Stodden	14	14
Buckingham . .	Bunsty	14	11
Cambridge . .	Armingford	15	12
Devon . . .	Braunton	21	21
Essex . . .	Waltham	5	4
Hertford . .	Hitchin	11	7
Huntingdon . .	Normancross	21	20
Middlesex. . .	Spelthorne	12	12
Northampton . .	Fawsley	21	20
Nottingham . .	Bassetlaw	85	70
Oxford . . .	Langtree	6	6
Surrey . . .	Brixton	17	15
Sussex . . .	Easebourne	14	10
Warwick . . .	Hemlingford	53	38
Wiltshire . . .	Highworth	7	5
Worcester. . .	Doddingtree	40	32
Yorks. E.R. . .	Holderness	45	38
Yorks. N.R. . .	Bulmer	27	27

In all but one of the samples the parish names which are recorded in 1086, or earlier, form more than 71 per cent. of the total. The exception is the hundred of Hitchin in Hertfordshire which can show only 7 early parish names out of a total of 11—or an equivalent of some 63 per cent. But 3 of the other parishes in this hundred contain hamlets which are mentioned in Domesday as inhabited places.[1]

These facts seem to justify the conclusion that the picture presented by the Cherwell valley is not untypical of Domesday England. That pleasant and friendly district may well have been somewhat more fully settled and tilled, and less thickly wooded, than was usual even in the regions most suitable for agriculture. Oxfordshire appears to have possessed more ploughs in proportion to its acreage than any other county could show in 1086; and even in Oxfordshire the Domesday map reveals some bare patches. But it is surely significant that chance samples taken from various parts of the country point to conditions of settlement not radically different from those obtaining in the Cherwell valley, while a sharply contrasting state of things can only be discerned if we turn deliberately to regions of fen or forest which long after the Conqueror's day were still distinguished as such from the norm of rural England.

We must not be too ready to fill the vacant spaces of the Domesday map with imagined woodland or marsh. In a corner of south Oxfordshire, near the junction of the Thame and the Thames, there are four parishes which Domesday seems to ignore. Neither their names, nor any of the subordinate names that the modern map shows within their limits, can be found in the great survey. Unless we accept some rather doubtful identifications, the same may be said of their neighbours Stadhampton and Chislehampton. Yet there is little doubt that this blank patch, so far from being uncultivated, was no less developed agriculturally than the rest of the county. One of the unmentioned places, Culham, is referred to in a tenth-century charter as an estate of 15 *mansae* or hides.[2] Of the others, Clifton Hampden, Drayton, Chislehampton, and Stadhampton appear in later

---

[1] They are Almshoe in Ippollitts, Minsden in Langley, and Temple Dinsley in Preston. The argument in the text would be strengthened if account were taken of hamlet names. In Doddingtree Hundred, Worcestershire, the *Survey of English Place-Names* mentions twenty-one minor names as recorded in or before 1086. But statistical presentation of such material is hampered by the fact that some places mentioned in Saxon charters may have been only landmarks and not inhabited places until later.

[2] Birch, *Cartularium Saxonicum*, No. 759. Culham belonged to the abbey of Abingdon; see Stenton, *V.C.H. Oxon.* i. 393.

days among the endowments of the bishopric of Lincoln, being closely associated with the nearby manor of Dorchester-on-Thames, which had been the seat of the bishopric until it was transferred to Lincoln in 1072; and it is more than probable that (apart from the entries that possibly relate to Stadhampton and Chislehampton) they are all really covered by the Domesday description of Dorchester, which is credited with far more ploughs than could possibly have found employment within the modern bounds of the parish. In the same way Warborough—the remaining parish of those which Domesday fails to notice in this part of Oxfordshire—would seem to have been included in the account of Benson, for it subsequently appears as a member of that royal manor, and Benson, like Dorchester, is assigned an excessive number of ploughs. The ploughs enumerated in the Dorchester and Benson entries are in fact sufficient to have provided the whole of the area which was thus dependent upon those manors (including the distant parish of Epwell which is unmentioned in Domesday and was reckoned to be an outlying member of Dorchester in the thirteenth century) with a larger equipment of teams in proportion to the total acreage than is found in Domesday Oxfordshire taken as a whole.[1]

On the other hand, in another part of Oxfordshire, the Domesday map reveals a blank space which without doubt represents an extensive area of ancient woodland. There is more than a hint of this in Domesday Book itself. 'In Shotover, Stowood, Woodstock, Cornbury, and Wychwood', we read, 'the king's demesne forests have nine leagues in length and the same in breadth'; and though agriculture had intruded even here upon the huntsman's realm it was apparently limited to the tillage accomplished by 6 *villani* and 8 bordars with $3\frac{1}{2}$ plough-teams.[2] Sir Frank Stenton remarks that 'these meagre details conceal

---

[1] For the association of Clifton, Drayton, Chislehampton, and Epwell with Dorchester see *Rotuli Hundredorum*, ii. 748–51. For Stadhampton see H. E. Salter, *V.C.H. Oxon.* ii (1907), 4. If the entry relating to *Hunesworde* (Dd. i, f. 157*b*) really refers to a holding in Chislehampton, as Stenton suggests (op. cit., p. 428 n.), and if the *Survey of English Place-Names* is right in identifying one of the *Hentone* entries with Chislehampton, and *Hantone* with Brookhampton, which it regards as a hamlet of Stadhampton (*Place-Names of Oxfordshire*, pt. i, pp. 154–5), this would substantially strengthen the evidence for the cultivation of the area in question. But indeed the difficulty is not to find enough Domesday ploughs to till the fields of the unmentioned parishes, but enough land to employ the 69 ploughs assigned to Dorchester.

[2] The 'league' of Domesday is usually reckoned to be a mile and a half; but Round thought that in Worcestershire the evidence suggested that it was only half a mile in length: *V.C.H. Worcs.* i (1901), 271–2: cf. ibid. Northants. i (1902), 279–80.

rather than express the fact that in the eleventh century the open country to the north of Oxford between the lower courses of the Evenlode and the Cherwell formed the only considerable interruption to a thick belt of woodland extending from the hills above Burford to the forest of Bernwood in western Buckinghamshire'.[1] It is in the western part of this area that the emptiness of the Domesday map is most apparent; and, among the names unknown to Domesday that are to be found there today, a good number seem to incorporate the word *leah* which is usually associated with forest clearings. Thus, between Charlbury on the Evenlode and Witney on the Windrush, we have Crawley, Hailey, and Delly End; and a little farther west, between the same rivers, Langley and Asthall Leigh and Widley and Tangley, while other names reminiscent of the forest are Minster Riding in Minster Lovell and Field Assarts near Leafield. Moreover, an unusual amount of wood is mentioned in the Domesday accounts of villages lying on the edge of the bare patch and this is clearly additional to the woods of the king's demesne forest. At Witney the wood is described as 3 leagues in length and 2 leagues in breadth (perhaps 4½ miles by 3 miles) and ten other places had woods not less than a league in length and a third of a league in breadth.[2] All this is very different from the Cherwell valley where no wood at all is recorded for most of the villages except on the east of the river from Islip downwards, and it is only at Islip and far up the river in the neighbourhood of Adderbury that we find woods comparable in extent with those possessed by many villages in the valleys of the Evenlode and the Windrush.[3] Yet the contrast between the condition of the Wychwood area in the eleventh century and its aspect in modern times may easily be exaggerated. The largest area of continuous woodland in the county is still to be found here and still bears the name of Wychwood Forest. Even now it covers some 3 square miles; and it was evidently a good deal larger than that until the middle of the nineteenth century when much

---

[1] *V.C.H. Oxon.* i. 375.

[2] The ten villages are Spelsbury, Combe, Bladon, Northleigh, Taynton, Asthall, Minster Lovell, Cogges, Eynsham, and Stanton Harcourt.

[3] Below Islip we are in the neighbourhood of Stowood and Shotover. On the king's manors of Bloxham and Adderbury (which are reported on jointly) the wood was 13½ furlongs in length and 9 furlongs in breadth, and at nearby Hempton (in Deddington) there was woodland 1½ leagues long and 3½ furlongs wide: Dd. i, ff. 154*b*, 157*b*.

belated inclosure took place in the district.[1] It is, moreover, probable that in the Conqueror's reign the uncultivated area was not
quite so extensive as would appear from the lack of names on
the Domesday map, for there is evidence which suggests that
Charlbury, though unmentioned in Domesday, had been in
existence for centuries and that the particulars relating to it lie
concealed in the description of Banbury.[2] And after all the bare
patch was not very big. It was only 11 miles right across it from
the large and important royal manor of Shipton-under-Wychwood to Eynsham with its 18 ploughs and 67 peasant households,
while only 7 miles separated Spelsbury in the north, where the
land was tilled by 16 ploughs, from Minster Lovell in the south,
where there were 6 ploughs and 2 serfs on the demesne, and 17
villans with 10 bordars had 7 ploughs besides.[3]

In some parts of England there were stretches of wood and
waste far larger than anything of the kind in Oxfordshire. Between the North Downs and the South Downs lay the Weald,
the 'mickle wood' which a ninth-century chronicler described
as 120 miles long from east to west and 30 miles broad.[4] This
great woodland belt, of which Ashdown Forest and St. Leonard's
Forest are surviving remnants, had been reduced from its former
size by the middle of the eleventh century; but it was still very
large. The Domesday map, as Professor Darby has remarked,
shows that in 1086 only the southern part of Sussex was 'closely
occupied': he considers that 'at least one third of the county was
part of the wild and wooded district that extended into Surrey,
Kent and Hampshire'.[5] For more than 30 miles westward from
the hundred of East Grinstead in Sussex, over a belt of land
straddling the then undetermined border of Surrey and varying
in depth from some 8 miles to more than 20 miles, the only places
mentioned in Domesday are Ifield, where there were 9 peasant
households and a single plough-team, and Worth with one villan and half a team. In Surrey only two named settlements

---

[1] Mary Marshall, 'Oxfordshire', in *The Land of Britain* (The Report of the Land
Utilization Survey), 1943, p. 226; *V.C.H. Oxon.* i. 1; ii. 209.
[2] *V.C.H. Oxon.* i. 378, 393. Charlbury and its hamlets are included in the hundred of Banbury in the Hundred Rolls.
[3] Dd. i, ff. 154b, 155, 157b, and 238b (the Spelsbury entry being included in the
Warwickshire section of Domesday).
[4] Early references to the Weald are collected in Mawer and Stenton, *The Place-
Names of Sussex* (English Place-Name Soc., 1929), p. 1.
[5] *An Historical Geography of England*, ed. H. C. Darby, 1936, p. 166.

are situated on the wealden clay.[1] And if, in the hundred of East Grinstead itself, a cluster of names seems to carry the Sussex settlements right up to the present border of Surrey, the entries relating to these places show that they possessed only thirteen ploughs between them. Brambletye alone, with a priest and fifteen peasant households, deserves to be regarded as a village: the rest were tiny hamlets where a little cultivation had developed mostly in connexion with woodland swine-pastures belonging to some distant manor in the agricultural south. At one of these hamlets there was an iron-working (*ferraria*), while at Walesbeech, another member of the group, traces of a Roman bloomery have been discovered, so it seems possible that the penetration of the forest in this direction may have been stimulated by the presence of the iron ore and facilitated by two Roman roads which struck through the Weald within a few miles of Walesbeech.[2] Farther east, until one reaches the neighbourhood of Ashford and Mersham in Kent, the emptiness of the Domesday map is conspicuous over a large area. But appearances are here deceptive. A number of small unnamed settlements—outlying members of southern manors—are described in Domesday as situated in the Sussex hundreds of Hawksborough and Shoyswell (*Essewelle*); and the fact that 94 ploughs and over 300 peasant households are assigned to the manor of South Malling near Lewes makes it almost certain that the description of this place, like the description of Dorchester in Oxfordshire, incorporates the particulars of a number of unmentioned places in the hundred to which the manor gave its name. As the hundred and manor both belonged to the Archbishop of Canterbury and extended over a large piece of the apparently vacant area between South Malling and the Kentish border near Wadhurst, there can be little doubt that the unnamed villages or hamlets lay in this district.[3]

Composite entries of this kind have also to be reckoned with

[1] *V.C.H. Surrey*, i (1902), 320 n. 6. The places are Ockley and Hartshurst. Hartshurst (*Arseste*) is now represented by Hartshurst Farm in Wootten near Ockley: see Gover, Mawer, and Stenton, *The Place-Names of Surrey* (English Place-Name Soc., 1934), p. 279. Two tiny unnamed properties will have to be added to the settlements on the clay if the suggested identification of them with Horley and Gosterwood is accepted.

[2] *Historical Geography of England*, pp. 39, 71–72; I. D. Margary, *Roman Roads in Britain* (1955), i. 28, 53–57.

[3] Dd. i, ff. 16, 16*b*. For the area covered by the manor and hundred see *V.C.H. Sussex*, i (1905), 373, 388 n. 1, and the map between pp. 386 and 387.

in the Weald of Kent. On the eastern edge of the vacant area, Aldington with 240 peasant households, 13 *servi*, and 83 ploughs must have included subordinate villages or hamlets whose existence is concealed by the silence of Domesday.[1] Moreover, the virtually contemporary lists preserved in the Domesday Monachorum show that to the west of Aldington a number of places which are unmentioned in Domesday were in fact already sufficiently well developed to possess churches of their own.[2] These facts cast a shadow of doubt over Mr. Jolliffe's estimate that uncultivated woodland covered something like a third of Kent.[3] There can be no doubt, however, about the importance of the woods in the economy of the county. Domesday mentions nearly fifty 'denes'; and we know from Saxon charters and later documents that such denes or denns were woodland swine-pastures lying at a distance from the manors to which they belonged, like the Sussex swine-pastures in the hundred of East Grinstead. Moreover, not all the denes of Kent were entered in the survey: that is evident, as Miss Neilson has pointed out, because the Archbishop of Canterbury possessed, both before the Norman Conquest and in the thirteenth century, a 'very much larger' number of denes than are assigned to him in Domesday Book.[4] But if the denes tell us of the presence of woodland and of its profound influence upon agrarian organization, they also are a sign that the forest had been penetrated and to some degree utilized. The denes were swine-pastures; but they tended to

---

[1] Dd. i, f. 4.

[2] *The Domesday Monachorum of Canterbury*, ed. D. C. Douglas, 1944, pp. 77–79. Bethersden, High Halden, Woodchurch, Headcorn, Smarden, Biddenden, and farther to the west, Marden, Goudhurst, and Cranbrook all occur in the lists of churches and not in Domesday. The church of Bethersden 'cum masagiis et bosco ipsius denne' is mentioned in the foundation charter of St. Gregory's, Canterbury issued by Lanfranc in 1086–7: *Cartulary of S. Gregory*, ed. A. M. Woodcock (Camden Soc., 1956), p. 2. The frequent occurrence of the suffix *denn* in the names of these places is significant. The lists of churches in the Domesday Monachorum also help to correct the impression given by the scarcity of Domesday names near the Kentish coast, both near Folkestone and also in Sheppey and in the low-lying district between the North Downs and the Medway estuary. But here Domesday itself supplies a warning in the obviously composite character of the entries for Folkestone, Hoo, and Milton and its assignment of a number of unnamed churches to these places.

[3] J. E. A. Jolliffe, *Prefeudal England: The Jutes*, 1933, p. 6, cf. p. 54. Perhaps the same should be said of Darby's similar estimate for Sussex cited above (p. 12). Besides the case of Malling, suspicions are aroused by the 99½ ploughs and 180 peasant households recorded at Ditchling, a manor which we know to have possessed swine-pastures in the Sussex Weald: Dd. i, ff. 26, 22b.

[4] *V.C.H. Kent*, iii (1932), 182.

develop into something more. As the swineherds felled trees to build their huts and provide themselves with fuel, the clearing would tend to grow and tillage might begin. Domesday Book itself, though it has little to say about the denes, can show us at least one in Kent that had grown into a substantial village. If we may judge by its name, Newenden on the banks of the Rother, was a dene of comparatively recent origin; but by 1086, though the woods still provided pasturage for a considerable number of swine, a market was held there and there were twenty-nine peasant households in the place and five plough-teams.[1]

Compared with the Weald, the wooded district of Warwickshire known as the Forest of Arden might almost be described as a cultivated area. It is true that in the northern part of the county, particularly on the heavy clay, Domesday Book reveals extensive woods in manor after manor. But it is of woods subordinate to agricultural villages that we read; and only a narrow belt of land running westwards for 19 miles from Coventry to Alvechurch in Worcestershire appears altogether bare of settlements. Tillage had made extensive inroads within 'old Arden's ancient bounds'. Weston-in-Arden, now a hamlet of Bulkington near the Leicestershire border, possessed 4 plough-teams in 1086, while those of the modern parish as a whole amounted to more than a dozen.[2] Away to the west, Hampton-in-Arden, though it contained woodland 3 leagues long and 3 leagues broad, had 66 peasant households, a priest, 2 serfs, and 2 bondwomen, with a total of 15 ploughs and a mill.[3] And though Henley-in-Arden is not to be found in Domesday and may not have come into existence before the twelfth century, the parish of Wootton Wawen, of which Henley was formerly a hamlet, was already fairly populous. Wootton itself is mentioned in an eighth-century charter; and Domesday tells us that in 1086 there were there 45 peasant households and a priest, with 6 ploughs and 2 mills, while several places within the bounds of the parish were also quite considerable villages.[4] It is noteworthy that one of these

---

[1] Dd. i, f. 4. For the derivation of the name Newenden see J. K. Wallenberg, *The Place-Names of Kent* (Uppsala, 1934), p. 342.

[2] Dd. i, ff. 240 (Weston and Bulkington), 240*b* (Barnacle and Marston), 244*b* (Bramcote). Whether the *Brancote* of f. 242*b* relates to Bramcote in Bulkington is doubtful.

[3] Ibid., f. 243*b*.

[4] Ibid., f. 242*b* (Wootton, Edstone, Offord, Ullenhall, Whitley).

places bears the name of Whitley, which probably indicates
a clearing in the wood. The word *leah* seems to have meant
originally 'woodland' and later a 'clearing', and in time it came
to be used rather loosely for almost any kind of open land or
meadow, so that 'one would not be justified in assuming that
every *ley* was really one-time forest-land'.[1] But in a wooded
region its significance can scarcely be mistaken. In Warwickshire some eighty-five place-names incorporating this element
have been noted; and a considerable intrusion of Saxon settlement upon the forest may legitimately be inferred from the fact
that twenty-six of these *leah* names are the names of Domesday
manors.[2] Some of them were already large villages. Stoneleigh,
which in the thirteenth century was known as Stoneleigh-in-
Arden, is credited in Domesday with 68 *villani*, 4 bordars, 2
priests, a serf and a bondwoman, 2 mills and 35 ploughs.[3] Such
numbers may well indicate that unnamed hamlets of Stoneleigh
were included in the statistics; but in any case they point to
a notable expansion of tillage at the expense of the forest. In
addition, Domesday shows us 15 other Warwickshire places with
names ending in *leah* which possessed 3 or more ploughs apiece
in 1086; and in 7 out of the 15 the inhabitants included a priest.
Moreover, 2 Warwickshire *leah* names—Aspley and Ragley—
appear in Saxon charters though they are not to be found in
Domesday Book.[4]

The legend of Robin Hood has given to Sherwood Forest
a celebrity exceeding even that of Shakespeare's Arden; and

---

[1] *The Chief Elements in English Place-Names*, ed. A. Mawer (English Place-Name
Soc., vol. i, pt. ii, 1924), p. 45. See further: A. H. Smith, *English Place-Name
Elements* (ibid., vol. xxvi, pt. ii, 1956), pp. 18–19.

[2] Gover, Mawer, and Stenton, *The Place-Names of Warwickshire* (English Place-
Name Soc., vol. xiii, 1936), p. 316.

[3] Dd. i, f. 238.

[4] The Domesday *leah* names of Warwickshire mostly occur in one or other of two
groups—either in the angle formed by Watling Street and the line of the rivers
Blythe and Thame, or in the district drained by the Alne and the Arrow. This
suggests that the forest had been penetrated in two directions—from the north-east
and from the south-west—and it is tempting to see in the former the advance of the
Anglian Mercians and in the latter that of the Saxon Hwicce. There is much
interesting information about Arden in the Introduction to Gover, Mawer, and
Stenton, *The Place-Names of Warwickshire*, and in P. A. Nicklin, 'The Early Historical
Geography of the Forest of Arden', *Trans. Birm. Arch. Soc.*, vol. lvi, for 1932, but
published in 1934. The latter contains a map illustrating the distribution of woodland in Domesday: the former work contains a map showing the distribution of
leah names: cf. Darby and Terrett, *Domesday Geography of Midland England* (1954),
pp. 290–4.

a modern writer describes this region as still possessing 'some of the finest primeval woodland in Britain'.[1] It is therefore not surprising that Domesday entries are comparatively scanty for a large portion of western Nottinghamshire, while in a map that shows the parish boundaries the forest area can easily be distinguished by the size of its parishes and the sharp contrast it presents in this respect to the huddled mass of small parishes in the eastern and southern parts of the county.[2] Yet nowhere in Nottinghamshire do we find any large space for which evidence of occupation is wholly lacking in Domesday Book; and on the eastern edge of the most notable bare patch the 90 ploughs credited to Southwell and its 12 'berewicks' or hamlets (some of which are unnamed in Domesday Book) suggest that this patch was not wholly uncultivated.[3] Even in western Nottinghamshire some manors were centres of considerable agricultural activity. Worksop had 54 peasant households and 23 plough-teams; Kirby-in-Ashfield had 15 teams; and the royal manor of Mansfield together with its berewicks of Skegby and Sutton could boast 5 sokemen, 35 *villani*, 20 bordars, and 2 priests, with 21½ teams, 2 churches, and a mill.[4] In these western wooded parts, moreover, Domesday reveals 9 places whose names incorporate the word *leah* and thus point to the extension of cultivation by clearing: between them the 9 possessed 43½ plough-teams.[5]

It is to Arden or Sherwood rather than to the Weald that we should look for a typical example of the woodland regions of England in the eleventh century. We cannot, of course, picture the condition of the four northern counties which Domesday omits. We must renounce any attempt to speak positively about Yorkshire, Lancashire, Cheshire, Derbyshire, Staffordshire, and Shropshire, for these counties had all, in greater or less degree, suffered punitive devastation at the hands of the Conqueror; and we can neither regard their wasted condition as normal, nor discern with sufficient particularity what their state had been before that great disaster. But, these regions apart, it can be affirmed with some confidence that the Weald is without parallel in the

---

[1] Professor J. W. Carr in *V.C.H. Notts.* i (1906), xxviii.

[2] See the Domesday map in *V.C.H. Notts.*, vol. i, and the map of wapentakes and parishes in Gover, Mawer, and Stenton, *Place-Names of Nottinghamshire*, 1940.

[3] Dd. i, f. 283.　　　　　　　　　　　　[4] Ibid., ff. 285, 289*b*, 281.

[5] Six of these nine settlements are situated in the district between the Erewash and the Leen.

rest of England. Nowhere else was there so large an expanse of
untamed woodland that has disappeared from the modern map
through the subsequent development of tillage. The New Forest
is no true parallel, for its woods and thickets and heaths are to
this day approximately as extensive as they were after King
William had enlarged its bounds.[1]

It is not in the forests but in the fens that we find something
really comparable with the Weald. Round about the Wash, for
mile upon mile of what is now rich farming land, the absence of
Domesday settlements seems to speak to us of watery desola-
tion. The human geography is here fully explicable by physical
circumstances. Man seems to be debarred from the fertile black
soil of the marshland and obliged to confine himself to island
sites like Ely or to the strip of silt that lies along the seaward edge
of the fen. Yet agriculture was practised in these sporadic settlements. At Ely there were nineteen plough-teams.[2] And the
waters themselves were made to contribute to human needs.
Enormous numbers of eels were due from the fisheries to the
great monastic landowners, and numerous salt-pans show that
use was made of the special facilities of the silt zone for the
manufacture of a commodity that must have been particularly
needed in these parts for the curing of fish. Whether the piece-
meal reclamation of marshland of which we read in the twelfth
century had already begun, it is impossible to say; and neither
from Domesday nor from any other reliable sources can we learn
whether the drier portions of the peat were as yet utilized to any
extent as summer grazing grounds for sheep or cattle. But just
over the Norfolk border, where the fuller detail supplied by
the Little Domesday becomes available, we find that Walton,
a village on the silt, was maintaining two large demesne flocks,
one of 800, the other of 1,300 sheep.[3] In view of that fact it is
scarcely credible that there had been no similar development in
any part of the neighbouring Lincolnshire fenlands, for which
Domesday Book, in accordance with its usual practice, records
no livestock other than the ploughing oxen.[4]

---

[1] Baring estimated that in the New Forest area the Conqueror found 75,000
acres 'practically uninhabited', and that he 'enlarged this forest' by taking in
village lands amounting to from 20,000 to 25,000 acres, thus forming the 'main
forest', whose limits 'corresponded roughly to the outer boundary of the present
forest'. F. H. Baring, *Domesday Tables*, 1909, p. 202.
[2] Dd. i, f. 192.   [3] Dd. ii, ff. 160b, 213.
[4] For the fens see H. C. Darby, *The Domesday Geography of Eastern England*, 1952,

Some general conclusions must be attempted. Beyond all doubt, England was an old and settled country at the time of the Norman Conquest. But it is also certain that Nature in a wild or almost wild condition lay near at hand in almost every part of the kingdom. The wilderness had been subdued and mostly reduced within narrow limits, but it was not extirpated, nor wholly rid of danger. Horses and pigs might be turned out in the woods to graze; but as late as 1209 at Mardon in Hampshire two foals belonging to the Bishop of Winchester were devoured by wolves.[1] In many districts there was in 1086 enough untamed waste and woodland to provide opportunities for generations of pioneering effort directed to the enlargement of the cultivated area. Among the most notable differences between one region and another were those due to the absence or presence of extensive woods. Norfolk was one of the most highly-developed counties. The evidence suggests that it was second only to Suffolk in density of population, and that all other counties were considerably, some greatly, inferior in this respect. No part of Norfolk seems ever to have been under Forest Law. Yet Domesday Book shows us that in the centre of Norfolk the amount of woodland was sufficient to mark off the centre from the rest of the county as a region in which swine were numerous and demesne sheep-farming was little developed.[2]

In general rural England in the eleventh century was a land of variety. But the varieties were limited in range. This is true not only of the economic geography and the proportions between arable farming and other branches of agriculture, but also of certain social conditions of fundamental importance. Here and there, in the wilder parts of the country, there were indeed a few

and *The Medieval Fenland*, 1940, also the same writer's article on 'The Fenland Frontier in Anglo-Saxon England' in *Antiquity*, vol. viii, 1934, and his paper on 'The Domesday Geography of Cambridgeshire' in *Proc. Cambridge Antiq. Soc. for 1934–5*, vol. xxxvi (published in 1936). All these contain admirable maps. In Lincolnshire, Domesday refers casually to a shearing-house (*lanina*) at Stallingborough near Grimsby (f. 340) and to a flock of sheep of unspecified size at *Sudtone* near Great Sturton (f. 354*b*); but these facts have no bearing upon conditions in the fenlands about the Wash. As regards Cambridgeshire, the I.C.C. with its crop statistics fails us for the fen country: the Ely Inquest reveals flocks of moderate size in the neighbourhood of Ely itself, but includes no sheep among the stock of Wisbech, which, as Darby points out, is the only place in the Cambridgeshire silt area mentioned in Domesday.

[1] *The Pipe Roll of the Bishopric of Winchester*, ed. Hubert Hall, 1903, p. 36.

[2] See H. C. Darby, 'The Domesday Geography of Norfolk and Suffolk', in *The Geographical Journal*, lxxxv (1935), 439–43.

people living rather isolated lives, as there are to the present day. At Eardisley in Herefordshire, on the skirts of Radnor Forest, there was a patch of cultivated land 'in the middle of a certain wood', where the Domesday commissioners found only one house worth the tax-collector's notice, with one plough and two serfs and a Welshman who paid 3s. in rent.[1] For all we know, the swineherds of the Sussex 'denes' may have lived apart from their fellows and have visited their parent manors but seldom. In Derbyshire we may suspect that life was pretty lonely at some of the little 'berewicks' of the Peak district such as Edale. Yet the remoteness of such places must not be exaggerated. Though Edale lay deep among the hills and was backed by a wide expanse of desolate moorland, it was scarcely more than an hour's walk down the valley to Hope, which to all appearances was a regular village with a church and a priest.[2] And of England as a whole, apart from the unsurveyed northern counties, the unassailable evidence of Domesday Book enables one to assert without hesitation that the great majority of Englishmen lived in villages—or hamlets that were probably associated to form village-townships for administrative purposes —and also that these villages were nearly all within easy reach of other villages. To those familiar with the English countryside today and inclined to take its layout for granted, this may seem a trite conclusion. But these conditions have great sociological significance. They meant that most Englishmen were in the daily affairs of life brought into contact with others besides the members of their own families. They meant that men lived in communities. They meant also that the range of acquaintance-ship could easily extend beyond the limits of a single village— that the English villager could easily get to know people who belonged to another parish. It is easy to see how this would tend to prevent close inter-marriage; and in relation to that matter a precious glimpse of concrete reality is afforded us by the chance survival of an eleventh-century memorandum about some peasants at Hatfield in Hertfordshire. From it we learn that Dudda, a Hatfield *gebur*, had three daughters: one of these was married to a Hatfield man, but another was married to a certain Ælfstan who lived 7 miles away at Datchworth, and the

---

[1] Dd. i, f. 184*b*. This case is cited by Vinogradoff, *English Society in the Eleventh Century* (1908), p. 265.
[2] Dd. i, ff. 272*b*, 273.

third was the wife of Ælfstan's brother. We learn too that Lulle, a grand-daughter of the Hatfield 'bee-master', was married to Hehstan of Walden; that three other women of Hatfield origin had found homes respectively at Watton, at Wymondley, and at Essendon; and that the daughter of one of them had a Munden man for a husband.[1]

Moveover we cannot doubt that the same conditions which had these consequences in the domestic sphere had also a potent influence in promoting the vitality of institutions such as the hundred court and shire court, which involved men in the concerns of communities wider than the village, so that they could reach out beyond the family, the manor, and the village or parish, to form 'habitual provincial connexions' such as those to which Burke attached so much importance. The world of rural England in the early feudal age was a small world and its denizens were mostly poor and ignorant folk. But it was, in its humble way, a world of neighbours. That men were not always good neighbours to one another goes without saying. It has been so in all ages. But the conditions of human geography made better things possible.

[1] Thorpe, *Diplomatarium*, pp. 649–51; Earle, *Land Charters and Saxonic Documents* (1888), pp. 275–7; cf. Seebohm, *English Village Community* (4th ed.), p. 139 n. Wymondley and Great Munden, the most distant of these places, are about 12 miles from Hatfield, though if either Little Munden, or Munden in Watford is meant the distance would be less. It is noteworthy that the abbey of Ely, to which Hatfield belonged, does not appear to have had property in any of the other places, but one cannot feel sure about Essendon, the nearest of them, which does not seem to be recorded in Domesday.

II

THE GREAT LANDLORDS AND THEIR ESTATES

NORMAN England was a country of great estates and great landlords. The term 'landlord' is indeed more appropriate to the conditions of that feudal age than the term 'landowner', for the latter word, if strictly interpreted, suggests ideas somewhat different from those which prevailed in medieval England after the Norman Conquest. Under Norman rule Englishmen were learning to think of all land, except the royal estates themselves, as being held ultimately of the king by some species of permanent tenancy which involved the obligation to perform certain services and make certain payments to the Crown. Moreover, the 'tenants-in-chief', who thus held property directly from the king, did not keep all this property in their own possession, but commonly granted out some of it to sub-tenants whose rights and duties in relation to their lords were of a similar nature to those of the tenant-in-chief in his relation to the king. This process of 'sub-infeudation' often led to the development of a series of tenancies, one below another; and, though we may well doubt whether such elaboration was carried very far during the first generation after the Conquest, one case of a four-storied tenancy is to be found in Domesday Book.[1] It must be remembered too that even on the lowest story of the specifically feudal tenures, the lord of a manor who kept that manor in his own hands—holding it, as the technical phrase goes, 'in demesne', and receiving directly the produce of his home farm and the customary services and payments of the peasantry—was himself the landlord of peasants, whose rights in their holdings, however much they might be challenged by developments in legal doctrine or impaired by high-handed action, had some of the qualities of permanence that we usually associate with the idea of ownership. For these reasons the question who was the 'owner' of a particular piece of land does

[1] Lubbenham, Leicestershire: Dd. i, f. 230b; see Stenton, *William the Conqueror*, p. 447.

not admit of a simple answer in a society dominated by feudal ideas. In all ages the ownership of land has meant in fact the possession of rights over land, but in modern times the rights involved have been so commonly concentrated in the hands of one person that we inevitably think of him as the 'owner', whereas in the Middle Ages they were normally divided, some being held by one person and some by another.

On the other hand, the word 'landlord' has implications for a feudal society that sharply distinguish the conditions of the feudal age from anything with which we are familiar. Governmental authority, like ownership, was divided. Property in land was associated with some measure of jurisdiction over those who dwelt upon it. For centuries before the Norman Conquest Englishmen had been familiar with the conception of 'lordship'. Authority in local matters of jurisdiction and police, which we should consider to be functions of government, had not uncommonly been exercised by local magnates whose aristocratic prestige was enhanced by wealth derived from their lands; and it would be anachronistic to regard such lords as officials of the State. Whether all rights of private jurisdiction before the Norman Conquest originated in a royal grant, as was the case with the more far-reaching of such rights, is uncertain; but when an Anglo-Saxon king conferred 'sake and soke' or any other jurisdictional privilege upon a thegn, he was not appointing an official, but conferring a piece of property. It has been said of the old English hundred that 'for the bulk of the population it was the most common and active of the public institutions they had to deal with'.[1] And yet many hundred courts passed into the hands of private lords. The right to receive taxes could also be granted away. Edward the Confessor gave or confirmed to the abbey of Bury St. Edmunds the privilege of taking a geld from the men of the township for itself, whenever other men had to pay an army geld or a ship geld to the king; and it is probable that in other cases where a monastery was granted exemption from taxation this really involved the privilege of intercepting the taxes which the tenants of the monastery would otherwise pay for national purposes.[2] There could be property, as it were, in pieces of governmental authority as well as in pieces of land.

---

[1] Vinogradoff, *English Society*, p. 97.

[2] Thorpe, *Diplomatarium*, p. 417; Maitland, *Domesday Book and Beyond* (1907), pp. 272-3; Vinogradoff, op. cit., p. 192.

It is hard to say whether before the Norman Conquest property in land was in itself considered to imply any jurisdictional power; but under the Normans it was clearly recognized that every landlord had the right to hold a court for his tenants, whether they were humble manorial peasants or men of rank possessed of large estates as the feudal sub-tenants of a great baronial 'honour'. Conversely, we seem to discern through the obscurities of Domesday Book some tendency for lordship over men to be transformed after the Conquest into a lordship over their land—a tendency for peasants who in the days of King Edward had been distinguished from their fellows in being free to sell their holdings, and might be bound to a lord by nothing more than the personal, voluntary, and sometimes revocable bond of 'commendation', to become regarded by 1086 as tenants holding their lands from the Norman successor of their former lord.[1] In general a blending of public and private, of governmental authority and proprietary right, is a fundamental characteristic of feudalism. Owner and ruler are merged; and we may do violence to the facts and ideas of the time if we try to distinguish precisely between official positions and hereditary possessions, or between a tax and a rent.

Without some appreciation of the nature of feudal landlordism any attempt to assess the distribution of landed property in Norman England is bound to be misleading. The complexities that I have tried to describe are puzzling and tedious; but they can only be avoided at the expense of truth. Yet three facts of great importance stand out in stark simplicity. First (to repeat what I have already indicated), great landlords and great estates were predominant. Secondly, the great landlords were foreigners. By 1086, indeed, almost all the important lay landlords were men of continental origin—Normans, Bretons, or Flemings for

---

[1] Thus at *Estone* in Bedfordshire we find in 1086 four sokemen holding 3 virgates of land as tenants of the Bishop of Coutances—*de episcopo*. They had held the same land before the Conquest 'et cui voluerunt dare potuerunt'; but they were then the 'men' (the commended men, we must suppose) of Burred, the pre-Conquest magnate to whose rights the Bishop of Coutances succeeded both in Bedfordshire and Northamptonshire (Dd. i, f. 210). At Maldon in Essex Rannulph Peverel was entitled to a payment of 3s. a year from a certain sokeman, 'sed in tempore regis Edwardi non habuit ejus antecessor nisi tantum modo commendationem' (Dd. ii, f. 6, quoted by Maitland, op. cit., p. 68). But it would be rash to infer legal principles from the methods employed by Norman lords in the treatment of Saxon peasants. For further illustration of these matters see the accounts of *Invasiones* in the Norfolk and Suffolk sections of Domesday Book.

the most part—men, or the heirs of men, who had either been the companions of the Conqueror in his great adventure or had joined him subsequently. As Sir Frank Stenton has pointed out, in the whole of England south of the Tees—that is in the whole country covered by Domesday Book—there were only two Englishmen 'holding estates of baronial dimensions directly of the King'; and even if we take account of sub-tenants, it is still true to say that 'with less than half-a-dozen exceptions, every lay lord whose possessions entitled him to political influence was a foreigner'.[1] The great ecclesiastical estates also were now almost entirely in the hands of aliens. Worcester alone among English sees had still an English bishop; and 'Ramsey and Bath were the only abbeys of more than local importance which remained under the authority of Englishmen.'[2] Thirdly, landed property, and indeed property in agricultural land, if we include the rights that were then bound up with land or conferred only upon landlords, was in Norman England so much more important than all other sources of wealth that its distribution may not unfairly be taken as almost equivalent, for broad statistical purposes, to the distribution of wealth in general. The towns were few and tiny. Industry and commerce were on a small scale. The rich man was a landlord, and land was the source of his riches.

The predominance of great estates that marked the England of Domesday Book is indicated in a rough, general way by some statistics patiently compiled by Corbett for the lands held in chief by certain classes of landlords. The total annual values which Domesday attributes to rural properties throughout the country in 1086—exclusive of those northern counties which were not covered by the survey—were reckoned by Corbett at about £73,000. Of this total, the royal estates, including the lands assigned for her life to the Confessor's widow, account for about 17¼ per cent., and the lands of the bishoprics and religious houses for some 26¼ per cent., while nearly 54 per cent. represents the value of lay fiefs whose tenants-in-chief were less than 190 in number. Further, it appears that twenty of these

---

[1] Stenton, *Anglo-Saxon England* (1943), pp. 618, 671.

[2] Ibid., p. 671. Besides Wulfstan of Worcester, Giso of Wells had held his see since the Confessor's reign, but he was not an Englishman. The complete displacement of the old English aristocracy was not, however, an immediate result of the Conquest: in the text I am describing the conditions when Domesday Book was compiled.

lay fiefs, together with a dozen of the greater episcopal and monastic estates, comprised between them something like 40 per cent., in value, of all the rural land in Domesday England.[1]

The general impression that one gets from these figures is probably not unjust. But the position of the landlords cannot fairly be assessed on the basis of statistics relating to the value of the lands they held as tenants-in-chief. We have to remember the effects of sub-infeudation. A baron might have granted out many of his manors to sub-tenants; and, on the other hand, he might himself, as the sub-tenant of another lord, be receiving rents and produce from estates that did not belong to the honour he held as tenant-in-chief of the Crown, while if he were acting as a 'farmer' of some royal manors he would receive additional revenue from lands over which he exercised control without being in any sense their owner. Since the great ecclesiastical landlords commonly granted out part of their estates to knightly sub-tenants, but very rarely held land as sub-tenants themselves, Corbett's figures probably exaggerate the proportion of the land that was actually controlled by the bishops and monasteries. But precise knowledge of the position is not attainable. It would be an enormous task to sort out and tabulate the information supplied by Domesday Book with a view to compiling statistics of the estates the various landlords held in demesne, whether directly from the Crown or as sub-tenants; and in the end the results could scarcely be satisfying, for the farming of royal estates is a matter on which Domesday tells us little, and an attempt to estimate at all closely the relative wealth of individuals would be frustrated by lack of adequate information

[1] The figures in the text are inferred from those given by Corbett in *Cambridge Medieval History*, v (1926), 507–11. I have counted the fiefs granted to the king's half-brothers, Odo of Bayeux and Robert, Count of Mortain, along with the baronial, not the royal, estates. Corbett's references to Queen Edith and Stigand show that the situation he describes was not that of the year 1086: he seems to have been trying to describe the various estates at the time they were granted out, which is rather unsatisfactory. His figures illustrate the great differences between the greater and lesser tenants-in-chief. For example, among ecclesiastical estates, we have the sees of Canterbury and Winchester with lands valued at about £1,750 and over £1,000 respectively (without counting those of the cathedral monks), while the figure for Chichester is £138. Of the lay baronies Corbett says that they comprised 'fiefs of all grades, starting from quite modest estates producing incomes of only £15 a year or less and gradually advancing in stateliness up to two princely fiefs with revenues of about £1750 a year each' (p. 510). He reckoned that there were between ninety and a hundred baronies valued at less than £100 a year.

about the charges incumbent upon each estate in the way of military service.[1]

An example may illustrate the degree of importance attaching to these baffling complexities. Hugh de Port was in 1086 the greatest lay lord in Hampshire and he also held a few manors in some other counties. He was undoubtedly tenant-in-chief of lands valued in Domesday at approximately £250, but, of these, manors worth some £73 were held of him by sub-tenants. In addition he may have been tenant-in-chief of thirteen other manors in Hampshire and of the manor of Snailwell in Cambridgeshire, but the peculiarities of the Domesday entries make it uncertain in these cases whether he had succeeded to estates formerly held by Odo of Bayeux or was holding them as Odo's sub-tenant.[2] These lands were valued at £47. 11s., and of them the amount held by Hugh's sub-tenants was worth £7. 6s. If we regard Hugh as tenant-in-chief in all these cases, we may say that the sub-infeudated part of his estate was worth £80 or rather more than a quarter of the whole. But against this we must set the fact that he was himself a sub-tenant on a large scale. In Hampshire he held land in nine places as the tenant of five different lords; and he was also a sub-tenant in Kent, Surrey, and Berkshire. The value of all these lands amounted to more than £170; so that the lands he held in demesne, in the two capacities of tenant-in-chief and mesne tenant, considerably exceeded in value the whole of the fief he held directly from the Crown, in spite of the fact that so much of the latter had been granted out to sub-tenants.[3] In addition Hugh had 'received' and was perhaps 'farming' a couple of royal manors in Hampshire and he certainly farmed some lands that had belonged to Queen Edith in what is now the county of Rutland.[4]

[1] We should need to know what we cannot know, in order (i) to set off against the deduction of a sub-infeudated estate the amount of knight service that became the responsibility of the tenant through its sub-infeudation, and (ii) in assessing the wealth of a baron who kept an abnormally large part of his honour in demesne to allow for the cost of maintaining knights in his own household.

[2] Round, from whose account of Hugh de Port I have derived much of this information, says that he held the thirteen Hampshire manors 'practically in chief' though 'nominally from the Bishop of Bayeux': V.C.H. Hants, i (1900), 422.

[3] The excess would be greater than the figures in the text suggest, if Hugh de Port was, as Round thought possible, 'identical in some cases with one of the under-tenants entered simply as "Hugh"': op. cit., p. 422. On the other hand, it is not impossible that the Domesday scribes may occasionally have omitted to mention a sub-tenant and so have made a sub-infeudated manor appear to be held in demesne.

[4] Dd. i, ff. 38b, 39, 219. In the Hampshire cases, the statements are made quite

Though in one capacity or another Hugh de Port was a landlord in seven counties, the fief that he held in chief of the Crown
lay almost entirely in Hampshire. It thus fails to illustrate one
of the best-known features of the land system of Norman England. The great estates were curiously widespread. King William
himself had a large amount of agricultural land reserved as
Terra Regis in every Domesday county except Cheshire, Shropshire, and Middlesex. About a score of the tenants-in-chief had
estates extending into ten or more counties.[1] At least fourteen
lay lords held in chief both north of Trent and south of Thames.
Of the landlords of Gloucestershire, Somerset, Devon, and
Cornwall at least fifteen had lands in one or more of the counties
of the east coast. The Count of Mortain figures as a tenant-in-
chief in twenty counties—Hugh, Earl of Chester, in nineteen
besides his palatine earldom.[2] For a man to hold land in four or
more counties was very common. Nor was it only tenants-in-
chief who had geographically dispersed estates. The nine manors
which a certain Oidelard held as a mesne tenant from Ralf de
Mortimer lay in Hampshire, Berkshire, Wiltshire, Oxfordshire,
Herefordshire, and Shropshire. Robert de Vals held land of
Robert Bigot in Norfolk, Suffolk, and Essex. A man named
Saswallo was a tenant of Henry de Ferrers in Northamptonshire, Warwickshire, Derbyshire, and Lincolnshire.[3] Within
the several counties estates were very frequently scattered. In

casually, so it would be rash to conclude that these were the only manors Hugh
held to farm in that county. The entry relating to lands now in Rutland runs: 'Has
terras tenuit Eddid. Modo tenet Hugo de Porth de rege.' But we are left in doubt
how much was meant to be included in 'these lands'. I mention these details to
illustrate the impossibility of compiling exact statistics.

[1] That is without taking account of anything they held as sub-tenants. If house
property in towns is included there were certainly over a score of them. The figures
given by Stubbs, which show only sixteen landlords holding estates in ten counties
or more, are for lay fees only: *Constitutional History*, i (5th ed.), 296 n.

[2] The statement of Stubbs that Hugh of Chester had estates in twenty-one
counties besides his earldom seems to be an error: ibid. 296 n.

[3] These three men were not tenants-in-chief anywhere. It was quite common for
a tenant-in-chief also to hold land as a sub-tenant in several counties; but it is
uncertain whether there were more than a few cases of such dispersion among
sub-tenants who were only sub-tenants, for the Domesday descriptions frequently
leave us in doubt whether we have to do with different persons of the same name.
Stenton (op. cit., p. 621 n.) says that Henry de Ferrers 'gave land in six counties to
Saswallo'; but I can only find him holding of De Ferrers in the four counties mentioned. The name Saswallo occurs among the tenants of the Count of Eu in Sussex
and among those of Geoffrey de Mandeville in Oxfordshire and Berkshire. For
Oidelard see Stenton, *V.C.H. Oxon.* i, 385. A man named Oidelard was a tenant
of St. Augustine's Abbey in Kent.

Buckinghamshire, for example, the thirty-odd villages in which the Count of Mortain was tenant-in-chief, so far from forming a compact group, lay 'in fourteen out of the eighteen hundreds into which the county was divided'.[1] There appears, moreover, to be no contrast in this respect between the baronial estates and those of the Crown. The royal manors in Hampshire, apart from the Isle of Wight, were even more widely dispersed than those which Hugh de Port held in chief, being strewn round the edge of the county, while many of the latter fall into one or another of three definite though widely separated groups.[2]

It is important to appreciate the significance of these remarkable features of Anglo-Norman tenurial geography. But first one must emphasize the fact that the scattered estate was no novelty introduced by the Conqueror. Nearly a century before the Norman Conquest we find wealthy Anglo-Saxon nobles disposing by will of properties that extended into several shires. The estate bequeathed by Ælfheah, ealdorman of Hampshire, who died in or about the year 971, included lands in Somerset, Wiltshire, Hampshire, Berkshire, Buckinghamshire, and Surrey —perhaps also some in Middlesex and Oxfordshire.[3] At the beginning of the next century, Wulfric Spot, the founder of Burton Abbey, certainly had possessions in nine counties stretching from Yorkshire to Gloucestershire, and, if some suggested identifications are correct, in three others too.[4] The existence of similar conditions on the eve of the Conquest is revealed in Domesday Book. The Norman barons were often enfeoffed with the lands of particular Saxon landlords; and not uncommonly it was a dispersed estate that was taken over. Thus Alestan of Boscombe in Wiltshire, who is described as a king's thegn, had apparently been succeeded by William d'Eu in nine counties ranging from Bedfordshire to Somerset; while the fief of Geoffrey de Mandeville included elements in eight counties which had formerly belonged to Ansgar the Staller or his 'men'; and Geoffrey Alselin had a certain Tochi as his *antecessor* in Yorkshire, Lincolnshire, Nottinghamshire, Derbyshire, Leicestershire, and Northamptonshire.[5] Particularly far ranging had been

---

[1] Ballard, *The Domesday Inquest* (1906), p. 98.
[2] This is clearly shown on the map in *V.C.H. Hants*, i, between pp. 448 and 449.
[3] D. Whitelock, *Anglo-Saxon Wills* (1930), pp. 22–25, 121–5.
[4] Ibid., pp. 46–51, 151–60.
[5] The fact that their lands passed to the same Norman lord gives ground for identifying the 'Alestan' of the other five counties with the 'Alestan de Boscumbe'

the interests of Merleswein, who was an important personage under the Confessor. He was a landlord not only in Lincoln-shire and Yorkshire, but also in Gloucestershire, Somerset, Devon, and Cornwall.[1] Wulfward White, again, one of King Edward's thegns, had possessed a very widely dispersed estate: he was before the Conquest a landholder in nine counties, in-cluding Lincolnshire, Somerset, and Kent; but Domesday shows that his lands were divided up among a number of new lords.[2]

There were probably other scattered estates in the Confessor's realm besides those which Domesday Book enables us to dis-cern.[3] But undoubtedly this kind of thing was carried much farther under the Conqueror. The great estates increased in number, in size and in geographical range. On the other hand, we should seriously misunderstand the nature of these estates if we failed to appreciate the fact that their general dispersion was compatible with a considerable degree of local concentration. Stenton has pointed out that, though many of the great estates, or honours as they are sometimes called, 'consisted entirely of isolated manors or groups of manors scattered widely over the country', it was nevertheless 'by no means unusual for the bulk of an honour to be concentrated in a particular district'. William fitz Ansculf, for instance, held an honour extending into twelve counties; but 'its core was a large block of villages around his castle of Dudley'.[4] As he is stated to hold one of the more distant

and 'Alestan Boscomme' of Somerset, Wiltshire, Hertfordshire, and Bedfordshire, particularly as the forms 'Alestan' and 'Alestan de Boscumbe' are clearly used for the same person on f. 71b. Similarly there can be little doubt about the identity of Asgar the Staller, Esgar the Staller, Asgar, Ansgar, and Esgar, whose lands were obtained by De Mandeville. See Ellis, *Introduction*, ii. 43; Ballard, op. cit., pp. 99–100. Stenton (*Anglo-Saxon England*, p. 618) says that 'the entire fief' of Geoffrey Alselin consisted of lands that had belonged to Tochi with the exception of 'two small properties'; but this is not quite accurate, for Geoffrey had other *antecessores* at Etwall in Derbyshire (f. 276b), at North Muskham and Barton in Nottinghamshire (f. 289), and for a small manor situated either at Branton or Cantley in the West Riding of Yorkshire (f. 326).

[1] Except in Cornwall, Ralph Paynel was Merleswein's successor; and there is nothing to suggest that the Merleswein of the Cornish Domesday was not the same person.

[2] Cf. Round, *V.C.H. Somerset*, i (1906), 399, and *V.C.H. Bucks.* i (1905), 216–17.

[3] Except where the Saxon landowner was succeeded in various counties by the same Norman lord, it is, as a rule, only in the rare cases of Saxons with a distinctive 'surname' like Wulfward White that we can be at all sure that we have to do with the owner of a scattered estate and not with a number of distinct individuals of the same name; and the fate of Wulfward's lands shows that great Saxon estates were sometimes divided up by the Conqueror: hence some pre-Norman dispersed estates may be concealed from us.   [4] Stenton, op. cit., p. 619.

of these villages *in castellaria sua*, it is probable that the concentration had a military purpose, for *castellaria* was 'the contemporary term for a district within which the distribution of land has been planned for the maintenance of a particular fortress'.[1] Historians have indeed long recognized that on the frontiers of the Conqueror's realm the feudal geography was largely determined by strategic considerations.[2] On the Welsh border this is exemplified by the strong earldoms of Chester, Shrewsbury, and Hereford (though the last of these had been suppressed after the rebellion of Roger, the second earl, in 1075); while the operation of similar motives in regard to the coasts of the channel is to be traced in the great power given to Odo of Bayeux in Kent, and to the king's other half-brother, Robert of Mortain, in Cornwall, and also in the establishment of compact baronies, associated with important castles, in the probably ancient divisions of Sussex known as 'rapes'—perhaps too in the striking concentration of royal manors in the Isle of Wight. On the side of Scotland, there was the earldom of Northumbria and there was the bishopric of Durham (though the omission of these regions from Domesday Book prevents our knowing anything about their tenurial organization at this time), while the large and compact estate in north-west Yorkshire which formed the *castellaria* of Richmond is also to be explained by the needs of border defence, for the King of Scots appears to have been in possession of the northern part of Westmorland, as well as of Cumberland, during the greater part of the Conqueror's reign.[3] The history of that reign, however, makes it abundantly clear that it was also necessary to guard against internal danger and indeed that foreign foes were particularly to be feared because it was so easy for an invader to win the support of the English against their Norman oppressors. Hence castles were built throughout the length and breadth of the land; and the *castellaria*, like the castle itself, is a Norman innovation.[4]

A good example of a compact estate that was newly created

[1] Stenton, op. cit., p. 619.

[2] Stubbs, op. cit., i. 294–5.

[3] For the castlery of Richmond as a means of border defence see Stenton in *Inventory of the Historical Monuments in Westmorland* (Historical Monuments Commission, 1936), p. liii.

[4] A few castles—half a dozen, it seems, at most—had been built in England before 1066; but they appear to have owed their origin to the Norman favourites of the Confessor: see A. Hamilton Thompson, *Military Architecture in England during the Middle Ages* (1912), pp. 33, 37–38; cf. Stenton, *Anglo-Saxon England*, p. 554 and n.

for military purposes within the interior of the country is to be found in Derbyshire and extending over the Dove into the adjacent parts of Staffordshire. The feudal geography of Derbyshire in 1086 provides an instructive contrast to that of Hampshire. In the latter county, apart from the Isle of Wight, both the royal estates and those of the leading baron of the county were, as we have seen, scattered, the royal lands being the more completely dispersed of the two. In Derbyshire, on the other hand, there was a marked concentration of royal estates in the north of the county, along the valleys of the Wye and the upper Derwent, with a smaller group, beyond the high moorlands of the Peak, in the neighbourhood of the River Etherow. But alike in economic resources and in geographical compactness the king's lands in Derbyshire were surpassed by those of Henry de Ferrers, the lord of Tutbury Castle. South of the hills, throughout a block of country between the lower reaches of the Derwent and the line of the Dove—a block that extends some 18 miles from east to west and occasionally attains a depth from north to south of about 13 miles—there was hardly a village in which De Ferrers did not possess some property, while in a great part of this district there was no other tenant-in-chief at all.[1] On the other side of the Dove, too, this compact estate spread into Staffordshire, being rounded off by a little group of manors which lay in the near neighbourhood of Tutbury itself and covered practically all the low-lying land between the river and the high ground of Needwood Forest.[2] It is true that Domesday Book does not employ the word *castellaria* in connexion with any part of this concentrated complex of property; but that it was recognized as such seems to be indicated by the name 'Castillar' attached in later days to a Derbyshire rural deanery which consisted almost entirely of parishes comprised within the bounds of De Ferrers's fee.[3] And Domesday shows clearly that it was after the Norman Conquest that all these lands became the possessions of a single landlord: in the days of King Edward they had belonged to a great number of owners, many of whom seem to have been little more than peasants.[4]

---

[1] This is well illustrated by the map in *V.C.H. Derby.* i (1905), between pp. 326 and 327.
[2] Dd. i, f. 248b.
[3] Stenton, *The First Century of English Feudalism* (1932), p. 194.
[4] Two of De Ferrers's predecessors in this district—Siward and Gamel—were apparently thegns of considerable property (unless indeed we have to do with

In spite of his compact castlery in Derbyshire and Stafford-shire, Henry de Ferrers is no exception to the rule that the great landlords had widely dispersed estates. He was a tenant-in-chief in no less than fourteen counties, ranging from Lincolnshire to Herefordshire and Wiltshire, and from Derbyshire to Essex. In Berkshire and Leicestershire he figures as a great landlord, but in Lincolnshire and Nottinghamshire, in Wiltshire, and in the counties of Buckingham, Gloucester, and Hereford he had no more than an odd manor or two. Yet only in Lincolnshire and Warwickshire does it appear that all his property was granted out to sub-tenants; and of his five Essex manors four are definitely stated to be held in demesne.[1]

The geographical dispersion of the great estates, which was very much more pronounced at the end of the Conqueror's reign than it had been in the days of King Edward, may well be regarded as the most remarkable feature of the Anglo-Norman land system, for it seems legitimate to attribute to these conditions a profound and far-reaching influence upon the course of English history. We cannot, indeed, measure the importance of this factor in comparison with that of other fac-tors which contributed to the same results. But there is good reason to see in it one of the causes that eventually combined to make the English realm united and centralized beyond all the other feudal states of medieval Europe, except, perhaps, the Norman kingdom of Sicily.

Having solid economic interests in so many parts of the coun-try, the English baronage were less inclined to make provincial separatism the goal of their ambitions and better able to ap-preciate the advantages of a central government that was strong enough to provide some degree of nation-wide security. The

different men of the same name), but most of the others, if thegns, were thegns of a humble type. At Doveridge, however, De Ferrers had succeeded Earl Edwin; and at Brailesford his predecessor was *comes Wallef* whom Stenton identifies with Waltheof. There were a few De Ferrers manors on the east side of the Derwent.

[1] Precise statements as to manors being held in demesne are common in the case of Essex; but in general they are so rare in Domesday that nothing can be argued from the absence of such a statement. As a general rule it is probably safe to regard manors as held in demesne if nothing is said about a sub-tenant; but it would be rash to conclude that there are no exceptions to this rule. The case is clearest when the description of a fief contains an unbroken series of manors without any mention of a sub-tenant, followed by a series of manors that were clearly sub-infeudated. The account of Henry de Ferrers's Leicestershire estates affords a good example of this arrangement though the series of sub-infeudated manors is broken by an entry about Sheepy which *ipse Henricus tenet* (Dd. i, ff. 233, 233*b*).

story of baronial rebellion, on account of its dramatic quality, is liable to obscure this aspect of the situation. And that story is easy to misread. It is perhaps significant that, in the two revolts in which separatist aims can most readily be discerned, a leading part was taken by one of the highly privileged earls of the western marches—by Roger, Earl of Hereford, in 1075, and by Robert of Bellême, Earl of Shrewsbury, in 1102.[1] Of the anarchy of Stephen's day a chronicler certainly tells us that 'there were as many kings or rather tyrants as there were lords of castles, having each a mint for his own money, and the power of doing judgment in royal fashion on those subject to him'; but, as Stenton has suggested, this baronial autonomy 'was the result, not of any deliberate opposition to royal power, but of the unprecedented situation created by a disputed succession to the kingdom itself'.[2] And there can be no doubt that in the thirteenth century the aim of the rebellious baronage was not to escape from the authority of the national government, but to control its actions.[3] In any case the geographical layout of the baronial honours made rebellion more difficult. 'An insubordinate baron', says Stubbs, 'whose strength lay in twelve different counties would have to rouse the suspicions, and perhaps to defy the arms of twelve powerful sheriffs, before he could draw his forces to a head.'[4]

But it was probably in more indirect and subtle ways that the system of dispersed estates did most to promote the unification of the country and to increase the power of the monarchy. It helped to whittle down the diversities of manorial custom, for it meant that the steward of a great lord might have to travel

[1] In 1075 the other two rebel lords were, as Stenton remarks, 'survivors from the Old English order'—Earl Ralf, whose father was probably a Breton and had held high office under the Confessor, and the Anglo-Danish Waltheof.

[2] William of Newburgh, *Historia Rerum Anglicarum*, Lib. i. c. 22, Stubbs, *Select Charters* (9th ed., 1913), p. 139; Stenton, *First Century of English Feudalism*, pp. 216–17. Stenton adds: 'Many features of the time which are often regarded as illustrations of baronial independence were really the baronial response to a condition of civil war.' William of Newburgh was writing half a century after the time he describes.

[3] Even in Stephen's reign 'one main object of the greater barons was to obtain positions in which they could exercise the royal power in the shires in which they had territorial influence'; and this object 'often led to antagonism between different families' which formed an element in the civil war (Stenton, *First Century*, pp. 223–4). Scattered estates must have helped to make a baron seek the office of sheriff as a remedy for insufficiency of territorial influence: their intermingling led to the local antagonisms.

[4] Stubbs, *Constitutional History* (5th ed.), i. 296. The theory that estates were deliberately scattered in order to weaken the barons is, however, quite untenable.

over a great part of England 'holding all his lord's courts, reducing their procedure to uniformity, and completing in a humbler sphere the work of the King's itinerant justices'.[1] It contributed powerfully, if indirectly, to the triumph of royal over feudal and franchisal jurisdiction. But this is a matter that calls for some explanation. According to a recognized feudal principle every lord could hold a court for all his men—not merely a court for each of his manors, but one for the whole honour; and it was the duty of the vassal to attend, if he was summoned, however distant his dwelling.[2] Potentially such an honorial court was a very dignified and important body: its suitors would include men of rank and wealth who were regarded as barons. But in England feudal geography prevented these courts from becoming serious rivals of the royal courts. It was difficult for the lord of a widespread honour to enforce the attendance of his more distant tenants, especially as the courts commonly met every three weeks and as some of the suitors might be tenants of more than one lord and owe suit to several honorial courts.[3] On the other hand, if there were local sessions for different parts of the honour for the convenience of the suitors, the lord would be involved in much trouble and expense, and when the court met there might be little business for it to do. As a result the honorial courts languished. In the words of Holdsworth, 'great feudal courts for a large dominion were made infrequent, and in the long run impossible by considerations of time and space'.[4] But similarly the geographical factor

---

[1] Pollock and Maitland, *History of English Law* (2nd ed.), i. 185.

[2] 'Omni domino licet submonere hominem suum, ut ei sit ad rectum in curia sua: et si residens est ad remotius manerium ejusdem honoris unde tenet, ibit ad placitum, si dominus suus submoneat eum' (*Leges Henrici Primi*, 55 (i), Stubbs, *Select Charters*, p. 126).

[3] In later days we find the Earls of Oxford owing suit to the Abbot of Ramsey's honour court of Broughton and also to the court of the Honour of Clare. Both obligations seem to have been consistently scorned, if we may judge from the rolls of numerous sessions at Broughton between 1255 and 1295 and from the Clare Rolls for 1308 and 1309: see W. O. Ault, *Court Rolls of the Abbey of Ramsey and of the Honor of Clare* (1928), pp. xvi, xxvii and *passim*; Maitland, *Select Pleas in Manorial Courts* (Selden Soc., vol. ii), pp. 57, 62, 68, 72, 77, 79–80, 84.

[4] *History of English Law* (3rd ed.), i. 177. For some illustrations of honorial courts which languished see N. Denholm-Young's article on 'Eudo Dapifer's Honour of Walbrook', *E.H.R.* xlvi (1931), 623–9. Mr. Denholm-Young speaks of 'the shadow-life of the Court of Walbrook'. The difficulties and expense occasioned by a session of a great honorial court are well illustrated by the customs of the court of the Honour of Lacy as described in the history of Gloucester Abbey: *Historia et Cartularium Monasterii Sti Petri Gloucestriae*, ed. W. H. Hart (Rolls Series), i. 36.

helped to limit the growth of franchisal jurisdiction—that is to say, of the jurisdiction which came into private hands, not as part of the authority of a landlord as such over his tenants, but by a definite or implied delegation of royal rights by the Crown.

In Cheshire, where the Earl of Chester was the only lay tenant-in-chief, the development of franchisal privileges had full scope; and the earldom became virtually an independent feudal principality like the duchy of Normandy. But throughout the greater part of England the intermixture of estates was a barrier against such things, and those same 'considerations of space and distance', which, as Holdsworth observes, 'limited the purely feudal jurisdiction', operated also in the franchisal sphere, so that 'the average baron had the opportunity to exercise only the humbler class of franchises'.[1]

To put it short and plain, we may say that a franchise might either give a man a right of jurisdiction over lands that were not his and over persons who were not his tenants, or it might give him over his own men and his own manors (or some of them) a more ample and far-reaching right than that which belonged to him merely because he was their lord. The hundred courts in private hands are the outstanding example of the former kind of privilege; and in some few cases—particularly in the great monastic 'liberties' of Peterborough, Ely, and St. Edmunds, which were of pre-Norman origin—the same lord possessed a group of contiguous hundreds and could thus exercise jurisdictional rights over a large part of a county. Because of the intermingling of estates, however, the feudal principle and the sentiments that favoured it must have operated in a way that tended to prevent the private hundreds from becoming sufficiently important or sufficiently independent to withstand the centralizing forces of the royal system of justice. Since the hundred usually contained the manors of various lords, the franchise by which the jurisdiction of its court came into the hands of a private individual offended against the feudal idea that justice should be done to a man either by his lord or by that lord's overlord. An indication of the way things might work out is provided by some records of the hundred court of Clackclose in Norfolk for the year 1284. This court belonged to the Abbot of Ramsey, and his franchise included the right of 'view of

[1] Holdsworth, op. cit. i. 27.

frankpledge'.¹ But the rolls show that the court did not in fact exercise the last right; and it seems clear that this was because the lords of many manors in the hundred had obtained the same privilege for themselves, with the result that, in those manors which were not thus privileged and also in his own manors, the abbot held the 'view' in the manorial courts instead of in the hundred court.² Furthermore, these Clackclose rolls illustrate the tendency to seek royal justice in preference to that of the franchise-holder. In a case of assault brought before the hundred court on 23 March 1284, the Prior of Shouldham was involved. Whether this was because the offence was said to have occurred on a manor belonging to the priory or because the accused were the prior's men is not clear; but at all events the prior repudiated the jurisdiction of the hundred court and claimed that by royal charter he and his canons had the privilege of not being bound to answer in any plea except before the judges of the king.³

It is impossible to assess the importance of factors such as these in determining the actual course of development, but it can scarcely be doubted that the influence they exercised was considerable. And the result to which they contributed, in greater or less degree, is apparent from the fact that Henry II, the great architect of centralized royal justice, 'saw no inconsistency between the extension of the scope of royal jurisdiction and the granting of hundreds with their courts, to subjects'.⁴ In the thirteenth century many lords of hundreds were without the privilege of 'return of writs' which would enable them to prevent the sheriff, the representative of the central government, from

¹ That the 'view' was included is shown by an agreement of 1236 between the Abbot of Ramsey and the Prior of Shouldham, which incidentally suggests that the prior had tried to escape from the abbot's jurisdiction: see *Cartularium Monasterii de Rameseia* (Rolls Series), ii. 321–2.

² For all this see W. O. Ault, op. cit., pp. xli–xlv. A similar conflict of interests is illustrated by a dispute between the Abbot of St. Edmunds and Richard, Earl of Gloucester, which ended *c.* 1260 in the recognition of the latter's jurisdiction over his own tenants within the liberty of St. Edmund: see *Rotuli Hundredorum*, ii. 172, 178, cited by H. M. Cam, *The Hundred and the Hundred Rolls* (1930), p. 208.

³ 'Et prior venit et dicit pro se et pro canonicis et fratribus suis quod non tenentur respondere eidem Henrico in isto hundredo quia clamat habere libertatem per cartas regum Anglie quod ipse et canonici sui non tenentur respondere de nullo placito coram quocunque nec aliq' nisi coram iusticiariis domini regis' (Ault, op. cit., p. 154).

⁴ Cam, op. cit., p. 138. Henry II 'can be shown to have made at least fifty-two grants of hundreds, and the list is certainly not complete'.

interfering in the affairs of the hundred.[1] The private hundred in fact came to be regarded by its lord 'primarily as a source of revenue rather than a source of political prestige or public authority'; and in most cases the lord 'seems to be little more than a sleeping partner, drawing his share of the profits of government but leaving his officials . . . very much under the orders of the sheriff in actual governmental work'.[2]

In regard to the other type of franchise—that which gave its possessor an amplified jurisdiction over his own tenants—the tenurial geography was also a powerful limiting factor. Since large compact estates were so rare, the number of cases coming within the ordinary franchise-holder's competence, and involving his more exalted powers, would usually be too few to make the franchise either very valuable to its owner or a really important element in the national system of justice. It is with their neighbours men quarrel and go to law, and generally against neighbours that crimes are committed; and the geographical intermixture of estates meant that a large proportion of the population had as neighbours living in nearby villages, or even in the same village as themselves, the tenants of another lord than their own. But in cases involving the men of different lords the court of neither lord could be regarded as a wholly satisfactory tribunal, and the multiplication of such cases must have provided increased opportunities for the jurisdiction of the royal judges and sheriffs. Though the *Leges Henrici*, which is the best of the early Norman law books, seems to show that petty criminal cases of the kind would be dealt with either by the lord of the accused or by the lord of the manor in which the offence was committed, the well-known ordinance regarding local courts, which Henry I issued between 1109 and 1111, required actions between the vassals of different lords to be tried in the shire court if the plea was concerned with land ('de divisione terrarum vel de preoccupatione').[3] And a little later the so-called *Leges Edwardi Confessoris*—however sceptical we may be about

---

[1] H. M. Cam, op. cit., p. 138. In Wiltshire 16 out of 28 private hundreds had return of writs, in Devon only 2 out of 33.

[2] Ibid., pp. 141–2.

[3] *Leges Henrici Primi*, 25 (2) ('respondeat accusatus in curia domini sui de causa communi'), 20 (2), 27, 94 (2), in Liebermann, *Gesetze*, i. 562, 560, 611; and Henry I's Ordinance ('Et si [placitum] est inter vavassores duorum dominorum, tractetur in comitatu'), ibid. i. 524, and Stubbs, *Select Charters*, p. 122; see also G. B. Adams, *Origin of the English Constitution* (1920), pp. 380–4, and Liebermann, op. cit. iii. 301.

accepting its statements at their face value—bears an unmistakable witness to the trend of things by its assertion that if a plea regarding the men of different barons arises in a baronial court, a royal judge must be present 'since without him it ought not to be decided'.[1] It seems indeed clear that, as a result of the tenurial mosaic, cases which would otherwise have gone to feudal or franchisal courts were, in one way or another, brought within the sphere of royal justice. And this had consequences of far-reaching importance. The history of the judicature in medieval England is largely an exemplification of the principle that 'to him that hath shall be given'. Only busy people become business-like; and an increase in the business of the royal courts would tend to make them more efficient and therefore more attractive to litigants. It must also have assisted the development of the common law itself and have helped to make it more logical and systematic. For the greater the number of cases, the better the chance that they will include cases closely resembling one another and therefore capable of facilitating the growth of something like case-law and of promoting the rational development of legal principles by analogical reasoning.[2]

---

[1] 'Et si placitum de hominibus aliorum baronum oritur in curiis suis, assit ad placitum justicia regis, quoniam absque eo finiri non debet' (*Leges Edwardi Confessoris*, 9 (2), in Liebermann, op. cit. i. 633, and Stubbs, op. cit., p. 127).

[2] That such methods were consciously applied in the thirteenth century is shown by the statement of Bracton: 'Si autem aliqua nova et inconsueta emerserint, et quae prius non fuerint usitata in regno, si tamen similia evenerint per simile judicentur, cum bona sit occasio a similibus procedere ad similia' (*De Legibus*, i. 2, ed. Woodbine, ii. 21; Stubbs, op. cit., p. 412).

III

ESTATES AND LANDLORDS: A SAMPLE COUNTY IN DOMESDAY ENGLAND

I F the material provided by Domesday Book were more susceptible of statistical treatment than it is, so that the distribution of landed property in Norman England could be
set forth in a neat series of averages and percentages, descriptions of particular districts and individual estates would still be
required to clothe the statistical skeleton with flesh. In fact, the
obstacles that withstand comprehensive statistical summarization of the Domesday evidence are so great, that such descriptions afford the only sure road to an appreciation of the actual
condition of affairs in 1086. Some generalizations were attempted
in the preceding chapter; but these must now be supplemented
by a closer approach to concrete realities; and the present
chapter is devoted to an examination of the situation in Oxfordshire—a county not unfitted to be chosen as a sample because
it lies in the heart of England, remote from the influence either
of Welsh or Scandinavian usage, unharmed by the vindictive
devastation with which so much of the north was punished by
the Conqueror for its rebellion, unaffected by the special conditions incident to frontier defence or the traffic of seaports, and
dominated by no abnormal elements of physical geography such
as fen, forest, or moorland. The description itself will be twofold,
being concerned, first, with the distribution of the land among
the tenants-in-chief, and, secondly, with the results of sub-
infeudation, or, in other words, with the estates actually held
in demesne either by the tenants-in-chief or by mesne tenants.
Finally, from the estates we shall turn to the landlords, and,
so far as the frustrating poverty of the evidence will allow, en-
deavour to see what sort of men owned the land of Oxfordshire in 1086.

I

The king himself was one of the greatest of Oxfordshire landlords. From the fact that the royal manors provided a revenue

of some £481 a year, it might easily be supposed that he was the greatest of all; but this figure is deceptive, for the soke of nineteen hundreds was attached to these manors and much of the king's income must have been derived from the profits of jurisdiction in the hundred courts.[1] Actually there were two tenants-in-chief—the Bishop of Lincoln and the Bishop of Bayeux—whose fees contained more plough-teams, more *villani*, more bordars, and more serfs than were to be found on the estates of the king. The bulk of the royal estates was comprised in six large and very valuable manors scattered about the county from Bloxham to Benson and from Kirtlington to Bampton. In all we read of 215½ plough-teams on the Crown lands in Oxfordshire, and 68 of these belonged to the demesnes or home farms, but a considerable addition ought to be made to the total figure, for Domesday omits to give the number of the tenants' teams on the combined manor of Bloxham and Adderbury, where there were 72 villans and 16 bordars.[2]

The enumerated population on the royal estates amounts altogether to 323 villans, 202 bordars, 78 serfs, 17 *buri*, and 5 'radknights'. Of the management of these estates Domesday Book tells us little, but it seems clear that most if not all of them were let out at farm for fixed money rents.[3]

Besides the king, there was a handful of tenants-in-chief whose estates greatly exceeded those of other Oxfordshire landlords. But here we are faced by problems of interpretation, and must recognize that the tenurial pattern presented in Domesday Book was not wholly up to date in 1086. The Oxfordshire section of Domesday concludes with an account of the lands belonging to the 'fee of Earl William'. This was William fitz Osbern, Earl of Hereford; but he had fallen in battle in 1071 and his second son Roger, who succeeded to his English title and estates, had forfeited these after the rebellion of 1075. As Stenton observes, it is a peculiarity of the Oxfordshire Domesday that it describes the Fitz Osbern lands under a separate rubric, whereas 'in most parts of England' this fee 'was incorporated into the royal demesne, or granted out to different tenants-in-chief'.[4]

Disaster had also overtaken Odo, Bishop of Bayeux, in

---

[1] See Stenton, *V.C.H. Oxon.* i. 374–5.

[2] Dd. i, f. 154*b*.

[3] Langford, Shipton-under-Wychwood, and Shenington are described as held *ad firmam*, and all the other royal manors rendered fixed sums of money.

[4] *V.C.H. Oxon.* i. 388.

1082; but though, like Roger of Hereford, he was in prison in 1086, he is still regularly treated as a tenant-in-chief in Domesday.[1]

Another kind of difficulty is presented by the estates of the Bishop of Lincoln, for they include several manors which to most intents and purposes belonged to the abbey of Eynsham. It seems that the monks of Eynsham had fled in a panic about the time of the Norman Conquest; that some of the lands of the deserted monastery were granted to the bishop of the diocese, Remigius; and that Remigius subsequently revived and re-endowed the house. In consequence, the manors of Eynsham, Shifford, and Little Rollright occupy a rather anomalous position in Domesday Book, for they are treated as part of the fee of the Bishop of Lincoln but are described as held of him by 'Columban the monk', who was perhaps already Abbot of Eynsham and seems to have returned there later after migrating for a few years to Stow in Lincolnshire.[2]

Since all three manors, along with Mickleton in Gloucestershire and other properties, were made over to the house at Stow by Remigius in 1091 and were recognized to belong to the abbey of Eynsham by Henry I's charter of 1109, and since Domesday itself treats the church of Eynsham as the tenant-in-chief of Mickleton, the inclusion of the Oxfordshire manors in the bishop's fee is rather misleading or perhaps reflects a merely temporary condition.[3] For these various reasons the Domesday account of three of the greatest estates in Oxfordshire—the Fitz Osbern fee, the fee of Odo of Bayeux, and the fee of the Bishop of Lincoln—cannot be regarded as wholly satisfactory and

[1] Occasional varieties seem to reflect the uncertainty of Odo's position. In Hampshire and Cambridgeshire he does not appear among the tenants-in-chief, but Hugh de Port is described as holding land of him, or (in the latter county) of his fee: cf. D. C. Douglas, *Domesday Monachorum*, p. 28.

[2] The evidence, which is inconclusive, is given and discussed in H. E. Salter, *Cartulary of the Abbey of Eynsham* (Oxford Hist. Soc.), i, 1907, ix–xii, 32–37 (Nos. 4, 5, 6, 7), 50–51 (No. 28); cf. *V.C.H. Oxon.* ii (1907), 65, and E. K. Chambers, *Eynsham under the Monks* (Oxfordshire Record Soc.), 1936, pp. 2–3. Dom. David Knowles, referring to the Domesday entries, says 'presumably a single monk was holding what had been the abbey of Eynsham': *The Monastic Order in England* (1940), p. 81 n. 4.

[3] *Eynsham Cart.* i, Nos. 5 and 7; Dd. i, f. 166. Yarnton is in much the same case, for though we are told that Roger d'Ivry holds it 'of the bishop', Domesday adds that it belongs to the church of Eynsham—*est de aecclesia Eglesham* (f. 155b). It was in fact one of the original endowments of the abbey and along with the places mentioned above was transferred to Stow in 1091 and confirmed to Eynsham in 1109.

probably approximates more closely to the actualities of the situation in the county before the rebellion of 1075 than to those of the year 1086. Yet we cannot now hope to substitute a more accurate picture for that which Domesday gives us. The best we can do is to take the Domesday data as they stand, but recognize that they incorporate some features that were already superseded and others that either to some extent misrepresent the facts or were of temporary character.

Subject to these qualifications, the general position is clear enough. The fees of six tenants-in-chief, if we include the fee of Earl William, must have covered something like half the agricultural land in the county. About half the plough-teams, more than half the peasant householders, and nearly half the serfs were to be found on these estates, and their total annual value was over £1,400 while that of all the other tenants-in-chief put together was not much more than £1,000 and the renders of the royal manors, including the profits of jurisdiction in the courts of nineteen hundreds, amounted, as we have seen, to some £481.[1] Of the six estates, those of Odo of Bayeux and the Bishop of Lincoln were much superior to the others, and all the figures indicate that the fees of Robert d'Oilly and Milo Crispin were more extensive and more valuable than the fees of Roger d'Ivry and Earl William.

Markedly inferior to these great estates, but markedly superior to all others in the county, were the Oxfordshire estates of Abingdon Abbey, Earl Hugh of Chester, and Walter Giffard. The three were very similar in value and extent. There were, it is true, 79½ plough-teams on the lands of the abbey as compared with 66½ on those of the earl and 65 on the manors of Walter Giffard; and the abbey could boast a somewhat more numerous peasantry and a greater number of serfs; but the Domesday commissioners reckoned the values of the three estates to be nearly identical—the figures being £71. 10s. in the case of Giffard, £70. 10s. for Abingdon Abbey, and £70 for Earl Hugh. Next in order of magnitude come 11 tenants-in-chief whose estates ranged in value between £20. 5s. and £45. 10s., while the number of ploughs varied from 18 to 48. A classification by values would mark off from these a group of 21, each of whom held of the king in Oxfordshire lands worth

---

[1] Some uncertainties in the account of the Bishop of Lincoln's fee make precise figures unattainable.

less than £20 but not less than £10, the total value being
£291. 10s. as compared with a total value for the group of 11 of
about £340. If, however, we base our classification upon the
plough-team figures, the distinction between these two groups
loses its sharpness, for on 11 estates belonging to the latter group
we find 18 plough-teams or more, the largest number being 24½
on the fee of Richard Puingiand.

The great estates, and those which one might describe as
moderate, together account for more than nine-tenths of the
agricultural property in the county. About 93 per cent. of the
plough-teams are to be found on the 42 estates which were
valued at £10 or more, and the value of these lands exceeded
92 per cent. of the total manorial values.[1] Yet small estates were
numerous. Of the 91 Oxfordshire landowners whom Domesday
seems to treat as tenants-in-chief, 14 held in that capacity lands
worth between £5 and £10 and 36 had lands valued at less
than £5.[2] It must not be assumed, however, that the owners of
these small properties were all people of modest wealth. Probably some of them were. Aretius, for example, who was one of
the king's 'ministers' or servants, appears to have had no other
land than a little manor at Lew in this county which was valued
at 35s.[3] But in many cases it is impossible to determine whether
a small Oxfordshire landowner should or should not be identified with a man of the same name who figures as a landlord
elsewhere. And certainly some great landlords are to be found
among those tenants-in-chief whose property in Oxfordshire
was quite insignificant. The Count of Mortain himself appears
here only as the owner of a manor at Horley worth £5 and a

[1] The royal manors are included in this statement (though in their case it is of
'renders' and not 'values' that we read) but I have made no allowance for the
tenants' ploughs that are omitted in the entry for the royal manor of Bloxham and
Adderbury: the introduction of a hypothetical figure for them would of course
increase the percentage of the total ploughs to be credited to the larger estates.

[2] Ellis gives eighty-four as the number of tenants-in-chief in Oxfordshire, but
that is for the Domesday section devoted to this county and does not include the
Oxfordshire manors that were entered under other counties—manors which give
us six more tenants-in-chief. The discrepancy between this total and mine is no
doubt due to the difficulty of identifying the king's 'ministers'. Probably Ellis
identified the William of Rollright with the William of Benson: I have not done
so. I have, however, tentatively assumed that the Lewin who owned Chinnor and
Cowley was the same man as the Lewin who held Hanwell, though, like the two
Williams, they are separated by other names in the list of the king's 'ministers'. Both
had held the same lands before the Conquest and it seems rather unlikely that two
Englishmen of the same name were thus fortunate.

[3] Dd. i, f. 160b.

hide of land worth £1 which was held of him by the 'monks of St. Peter'.[1] The tenants-in-chief whose Oxfordshire lands were valued at less than £5 include Eustace, Count of Boulogne, and William fitz Ansculf, each of whom had possessions in eleven other counties.

In general the Oxfordshire landlords afford an excellent illustration of the tenurial geography that was characteristic of Norman England. There is definite evidence that 55 of the 91 tenants-in-chief also had property elsewhere than in Oxfordshire. Thirty-four of them were tenants-in-chief in five or more counties.[2] Within the county itself the manors of the great lords were widely dispersed. If much of the Bishop of Lincoln's land lay near the old site of the bishopric at Dorchester and in the neighbourhood of the little river Thame, he also had a group of manors on the northern edge of the county. The fee of Odo of Bayeux sprawled over almost the whole of Oxfordshire apart from the Chiltern district and the area to the south of it. Robert d'Oilly's estate included manors on the county boundaries at Goring in the south-east, at Hook Norton to the north-west, at Stratton Audley to the north-east, at Bampton in the south-west. Roger d'Ivry, too, held Mixbury on the borders of Northamptonshire and Buckinghamshire and, 28 miles away, Clanfield, which looks across the Thames into Berkshire—also Fulbrook which is only severed from Gloucestershire by one intervening parish. On the other hand, the manors of Milo Crispin were mostly concentrated in the part of Oxfordshire which lies nearest to his castle of Wallingford; but even he had property at Alkerton far away to the north on the edge of Warwickshire. A good deal of the fee of Earl William, again, lay, like Milo's, in the Chiltern area, but it also included property at Milton-under-Wychwood and Cornwell in the west of the county and a manor at Fritwell which borders on Northamptonshire.

Some of the smaller estates also consisted of widely separated manors. That of Geoffrey de Mandeville comprised three elements—a considerable manor at Kingham, a smaller manor at Wendlebury, 19 miles away, and some land worth 5s. at Rycote,

[1] Dd. i, f. 157.
[2] I have taken no account of the 'fee of Earl William' in these figures. If we confine ourselves to the tenants-in-chief who have separate rubrics in the Oxfordshire section of Domesday and leave out the king's ministers and the 'Canons of Oxford and other clerks', as well as the fee of Earl William, we are left with 55 leading tenants-in-chief of whom 46 were also tenants-in-chief in at least one other county.

which is over 11 miles from Wendlebury and 28 miles from Kingham. The two manors of Gilbert de Gand were at Hanborough and Ewelme, 19 miles apart. Hugh de Grentemaisnil had four manors in Oxfordshire—at Cottisford, Sibford Gower, Shipton-on-Cherwell, and Charlton-on-Otmoor. Shipton is only 5 miles or so from Charlton (though separated from it by two other parishes), but Cottisford is nearly 10 miles from Charlton and over 11 miles from Shipton, and Sibford Gower is more than 15 miles from any of the other places.

These features of the tenurial geography of Oxfordshire were not entirely the result of Norman innovation. There had been some dispersed estates in Oxfordshire before the Conquest. The fief which the Bishop of Coutances held in 1086 included the dispersed members of two Saxon estates; and in this case the Norman rearrangement had led to a little consolidation. As the successor of a certain Ulward, who was probably the same person as the great thegn Wulfward White, the bishop had obtained manors at Glympton, Wootton, Finmere, and Hethe. Glympton and Wootton are contiguous, but Hethe, the nearer of the other two, lies 11 miles away, and it is separated from Finmere by the parish of Shelswell. Shelswell, however, had formerly belonged to Edwin, son of Burred; and the bishop also succeeded to his property both here and elsewhere so that by 1086 Finmere, Shelswell, and Hethe formed a compact block held by the same tenant-in-chief.[1]

Another pre-Conquest example of dispersed ownership is provided by the estate of Abingdon Abbey. Though most of the abbey's Oxfordshire property lay within easy reach of Abingdon, it had two isolated possessions—a valuable manor at Tadmarton, more than 25 miles away, and some land worth 30s. at Arncot which is situated on the Buckinghamshire border, some three miles south-east of Bicester. It is indicated in Domesday that both these places had belonged to the abbey before the Conquest; and it was claimed that they had been given to it during the tenth century.[2] A considerable distance, again, separated

---

[1] This was apparently an accidental result of transfers that were on too large a scale to have been made in order to effect this small consolidation, which indeed seems to have been without practical consequences, for each of these manors was held by a different sub-tenant in 1086: Dd. i, f. 221.

[2] Dd. i, f. 156b; *Chronicon Monasterii de Abingdon* (Rolls Series), i. 191–200, 370–1; G. B. Grundy, *Saxon Oxfordshire* (Oxfordshire Record Soc., 1933), pp. 4, 68 n.; D. Whitelock, *Anglo-Saxon Wills*, pp. 106–7.

the manors which Lewin, one of the king's 'ministers', had held
before the Conquest and still retained in 1086. One was at
Cowley, close to Oxford; another was at Chinnor, 13 miles from
Cowley on the Buckinghamshire border; and, unless the king
had two *ministri* of the same name, who were equally fortunate
in keeping their lands, he had a third manor at Hanwell which
lies on the border of Warwickshire, over 25 miles from Cowley
and more than that from Chinnor.[1]

II

It has seemed right at the outset to describe the distribution
of the land of Oxfordshire among the tenants-in-chief, for that
is the first step to an appreciation of the tenurial geography of
the county; and the pattern of property which such a description reveals comprises what the king and his clerks may well
have considered to be the essential features of the situation. But
we need to go much farther if we are to form a true picture of
the Oxfordshire landlords and their estates in 1086. And the
next step is to take account of the modifications produced by
sub-infeudation.

The immediate lord of a manor might be, not the tenant-in-
chief, but a sub-tenant; and among the various persons who
had rights over the land in a feudal society it was the immediate
lord who came nearest to the modern conception of a landowner. As we shall see later, even he often let the manor on
lease to a *firmarius* and so abstained from direct control of the
demesne farm. But, unless he did this, it was he who received
the produce of that farm, to him that the peasants paid their
rents, and for him that they performed the labour services that
were incumbent upon them. And if he let the demesne for a
fixed amount of produce or money, it was his authority that
settled the terms of the lease, and, like a modern landlord, he
could at his discretion farm the land himself when the period

---

[1] Dd. i, f. 160b. Probably the owner of these manors was the same person as
'Lewin of Neweham', a tenant-in-chief in Buckinghamshire, who had retained since
the days of King Edward several manors in the north of that county (Dd. i, f. 153).
The mother of 'Lewin of Niweham' had in 1066 held Mollington in Oxfordshire
which is less than 3 miles from Hanwell (ibid., f. 244); that he is so described in the
entry about his mother, but not in the entries relating to Hanwell and the other
Oxfordshire manors, does not imply a distinction, as at first sight it might seem to
do, for the Mollington entry occurs in the Warwickshire section of Domesday: see
Chron. Abingdon, ii. 9.

for which it was let came to an end. With matters of this kind, and indeed with all purely manorial affairs including the jurisdiction of the 'hall-moot' or manorial court (where such existed), his overlord had no concern. We must therefore re-examine the tenurial geography of our sample county, and, so far as the evidence will allow it, describe the distribution of the land, not, as before, between the tenants-in-chief as such, but between the immediate lords, whether they held their manors in chief of the king or as feudal sub-tenants.

The Oxfordshire estates of the tenants-in-chief varied greatly in the degree to which they had undergone sub-infeudation by 1086. In some cases the whole property had been disposed of in this way. Thus the five manors of Hugh, Earl of Chester, had all been granted out, though unfortunately we cannot be sure whether the earl's tenants were five distinct persons or whether the Robert who held South Weston should be identified with the Robert who held Tackley, or, again, with the Robert who was the earl's tenant of Ardley but had granted it out in his turn to a certain Drogo.[1] It was the same with the estate of the Bishop of Coutances: all his six Oxfordshire manors, and the bit of land he held at Worton, were in the hands of tenants.[2] Robert de Statford, too, had apparently enfeoffed the whole of his Oxfordshire property to various tenants, though Domesday is not clear on the point as regards a manor at Great Rollright.[3]

The lords who acted thus ceased to be Oxfordshire landowners in any effective sense. They no doubt required military service from their tenants, and suit of court, and incidental payments such as aids and reliefs; but they would take no part in the management of the land unless a tenant died leaving an heir who was a minor and even then the right of wardship would end when the heir came of age. On the other hand, some tenants-in-chief kept all their Oxfordshire lands in demesne.[4] Among the more considerable landowners, the Bishop of Winchester, Richard de Courcy, Cristina (the sister of Edgar the Ætheling) and the Saxon Lewin appear to have done this. It is perhaps

---

[1] Dd. i, f. 157. Stenton identifies the Roberts of S. Weston and Ardley with Robert d'Oilly.   [2] Ibid., f. 221.   [3] Ibid., f. 158.

[4] In regard to all that is said about manors held in demesne it must not be forgotten that there is some room for error, because if Domesday happened to omit mention of a tenant, an enfeoffed manor would appear to be held in demesne: it follows that the statements in the text err, if at all, on the side of understating the land enfeoffed to tenants.

significant that the estates of each of these four, though valuable,
consisted of a very small number of manors. Cristina indeed
had only one. Yet the Count of Evreux, whose eight modest
properties were together worth only half as much as Cristina's
manor of Broadwell, had, so far as we can tell, retained
them all in demesne.[1] Of those tenants-in-chief who had only
one manor in the county, a good many kept it in demesne:
apparently this was the case with the Bishop of Salisbury at
Dunsden, with the abbey of St. Denis at Taynton, with Hugh
d'Ivry at Ambrosden.[2] But Ralf de Mortimer's single manor
of Idbury was held of him by Oidelard, and the Bishop of Worcester had enfeoffed Urse d'Abitot with the manor of Spelsbury
which was all that he had in the county.[3] Several of the lay lords
had retained a single rich manor and enfeoffed all the rest of
their estate. Thus Walter Giffard kept the valuable manor of
Caversham, but granted out all his other Oxfordshire lands,
which comprised five substantial manors besides Caversham
and also some other property.[4] William de Warenne, similarly,
kept Mapledurham (worth £12) but granted Caversfield and
Gatehampton (worth £5 and £2 respectively) to a tenant.[5]
Geoffrey de Mandeville kept Kingham (worth £15); but his
property at Rycote and Wendlebury (together worth £5. 5s.)
was held by his tenant Saswallo.[6] Richard Puingiand, again,
held Middleton Stoney (worth £10) in demesne, but his other
manor of Godington (worth £5) was enfeoffed; and in the same
way Ernulf de Hesdin retained Chipping Norton (worth £22),
but his other Oxfordshire property—a manor at Black Bourton
(worth £4) and some land at Ludwell in Wootton (worth £2)—
was held of him by two tenants.[7] Hugh de Grentemaisnil, however, kept Shipton-on-Cherwell, a small manor which was
valued at only £4. 10s., though his three other Oxfordshire
manors, which were enfeoffed to tenants, included two worth
£10 and £8 respectively.[8] It may be conjectured that where a
single valuable manor was held in demesne it was in some cases,

---

[1] Dd. i, ff. 155, 159, 160, 160b, 157.
[2] Ibid., ff. 155, 157, 157b.   [3] Ibid., ff. 159, 238b.
[4] Ibid., f. 157b. Some of the entries are not quite free from ambiguity.
[5] Ibid., ff. 157b, 148. It seems likely that Brien, the tenant of Gatehampton, was
the same person as the Brienz who was tenant of Caversfield.
[6] Ibid., f. 159b.   [7] Ibid., ff. 159, 160.
[8] Ibid., f. 224b. The hidation figures show that Shipton was in proportion to its
value considerably less heavily burdened with taxation than the other manors.

perhaps usually, one in which the lord had a place of residence. We can be sure that this was so in the case of Ernulf de Hesdin's manor of Chipping Norton, for, as Stenton remarks, it was at his house there that Ernulf executed a charter in the presence of his wife and children and many knights of his household (*familia*).[1] The extensive earthworks still to be seen immediately to the north of the church may well be the remains of his castle, or of a castle erected later on the site of his hall. At Middleton Stoney, too, the surviving remains of a motte-and-bailey castle near the church are suggestive, for even if the castle itself was built in the reign of Stephen, a manor where the lord had a house would be a natural place to choose for such a fortification.[2]

The extent of sub-infeudation on the really great estates of the county must be considered without regard to the 'fee of Earl William'. The whole of that was in 1086 in the hands of various tenants, but it is impossible to know whether this had been the case before the forfeiture of 1075 or whether things had been radically altered since that event; and it might well be argued that the tenants of this fee whom we meet in Domesday were virtually tenants-in-chief. On the other five great estates however, the position is clear. They differed comparatively little from one another in the matter of sub-infeudation. Whether we measure things by the valuation figures or by the number of plough-teams, it is true to say that, in each of the five, between one-third and two-thirds of the estate had been granted out to tenants by 1086. Moreover, all the five lords had adopted a general policy of enfeoffing their least valuable and retaining their most valuable manors. Though some of the enfeoffed manors were worth much and some quite small properties were retained, the general tendency is unmistakable. On the estates of Robert d'Oilly and Roger d'Ivry the average value of the manorial units held in demesne was more than twice that of the enfeoffed units; and with Milo Crispin the ratio was more than three to one; but it was greatest of all on the fee of Odo of Bayeux. In the case of the Bishop of Lincoln the same policy is no less evident, but here it would be rather misleading to employ this simple method of exhibiting its working, for many of

---

[1] *V.C.H. Oxon.* i. 384, citing Round, *Calendar of Documents preserved in France*, pp. 481–2.

[2] That the castle at Middleton Stoney was built 'early in King Stephen's reign' is asserted by J. C. Blomfield (*History of Middleton and Somerton* [? 1888], p. 8), but he gives no evidence.

the bishop's knights had been enfeoffed with lands that were reckoned to be members of the great manors which are characteristic of this fee, and we are told nothing about the geographical situation of these knights' lands and are only given the 'hidation' (that is, the taxation assessment), and not the value, of what each individual possessed. Where distinct manors were enfeoffed, however, their value was very much less than the value of those portions of his great manors which the bishop kept in demesne.[1] In general it seems clear that with all these great tenants-in-chief the value of the individual manors was a governing consideration in the selection of the places to be retained and that little effort was made to keep in demesne the manors that were geographically concentrated. Milo Crispin, it is true, includes in his enfeoffments the more isolated portions of his fee. But Robert d'Oilly keeps Bicester (worth £16) and, 7 miles away, Kidlington (worth £14) while he grants out the intervening manors of Weston-on-the-Green (worth £12) and Bletchingdon (worth £5), as well as Stratton Audley (worth £3) and Bucknell (worth £7)—places which lie near Bicester on the other side. On the fee of Odo of Bayeux, again, the very valuable manors of Deddington and Great Tew are in demesne, and several less valuable manors, lying between these two places and linking them together, are enfeoffed. In much the same way, Roger d'Ivry, among his more valuable manors, retains Asthall and Fulbrook, which are close neighbours, but grants out Brize Norton, though it adjoins Asthall and is worth rather more, and keeps in demesne Mixbury, a still more valuable manor, 24 miles away.[2]

---

[1] The estates of Abingdon Abbey afford a particularly clear example of the policy: each of its three demesne manors was much more valuable than any of the properties it had enfeoffed to tenants. At Tadmarton it had enfeoffed part of the land worth £6, but the part it kept in demesne was worth £12. These Oxfordshire facts are in accordance with Mr. Painter's observations as regards the country in general: he remarks that to a baron 'one manor yielding £20 was far more useful than ten worth £2 each': Sidney Painter, *Studies in the History of the English Feudal Barony* (Johns Hopkins Press, Baltimore, 1943), p. 22.

[2] Over the Buckinghamshire border Roger had three manors within 5 miles of Mixbury, but all these were enfeoffed to tenants, and the most valuable of them (Radclive) was worth only £5, while Mixbury was worth £15. Of his Oxfordshire demesne manors, Beckley, some 14 miles distant, is the nearest to Mixbury. Whether the castle at Mixbury (which became known as Beaumont Castle) had been built by 1086 we cannot say: its remains, suggestive of a motte with double bailey, are still to be seen just north-east of the church, which contains some twelfth-century work. For Roger's position as a mesne tenant see below, p. 53.

II

In the extent and layout of the estates held in chief of the Crown we see, as it were, the work of the Conqueror as an architect of Anglo-Norman landlordism. In the enfeoffments made by the tenants-in-chief we trace the modifications introduced by the barons themselves, mainly, no doubt, with the object of making permanent provision for the knights that they had to furnish for the feudal host.[1] And it is only by exposing the results of all the enfeoffments and sub-enfeoffments down to the lowest stage of the feudal structure that we can appreciate the realities of the agrarian situation.

Unfortunately, at this stage mists of uncertainty drift over the scene and obscure the historian's vision. Many of the immediate manorial lords of whom Domesday tells us are dim figures named Robert or Richard, Godfrey or Gilbert, and in the absence of more specific designations it is usually impossible to know whether we have to do with a single individual or with two or more persons of the same name. Such uncertainties for the most part concern the lesser manorial lords—the sort of men who were not tenants-in-chief anywhere and as mesne tenants had only very modest possessions. But the man who appears to be a humble knight holding perhaps one small manor if we regard him as a distinct person from those of the same name who are mentioned in other entries, will assume very different proportions if he is identified with the others, and may on that hypothesis become an important 'honorial baron' holding from his lord a number of manors in several shires. Even a great tenant-in-chief may lie concealed under a false appearance of poverty and humility in an entry which relates to some land that he held as a sub-tenant and refers to him only by his Christian name. The chance which occasionally reveals the identity of an

---

[1] Round, *Feudal England*, p. 247; Stenton, *Anglo-Saxon England*, p. 627. Professor D. C. Douglas considers that 'the Conqueror on occasion intervened directly in the subinfeudations at least by ecclesiastical tenants-in-chief' (*Feudal Documents from the Abbey of Bury St. Edmunds* (1932), pp. xcv–c; cf. *Econ. Hist. Rev.* ix (May 1939), 130–1). It would be rash to assert that this never happened; but, in some cases supposed to afford examples of such action, it seems that the king was really dealing with the problem of confiscated lands, which, after they had been granted out, were found to have been held before the Conquest by the lessees of some abbey—or under its lordship—and that he solved it by requiring the new Norman tenants to hold these lands as tenants of the church in question, so that the knight service owed for them would form part of that church's quota; see E. Miller, *The Abbey and Bishopric of Ely* (1951), p. 67, especially n. 2.

individual shows that such cases are not imaginary. For example, a certain Roger was mesne tenant of half a hide of land at Yarnton on the fee of the Bishop of Bayeux. It was an extremely modest property containing land sufficient for a single plough, tilled by two villans and a bordar, and valued at 20s.[1] But the rest of Yarnton, a manor worth £14, was held of the Bishop of Lincoln by no less a person than Roger d'Ivry, one of the greatest landlords in the county.[2] It seems very probable that the apparently humble tenant of the Bishop of Bayeux was in fact the same man. The Domesday scribe happens to have written the name *de Ivri* over the line in the one case but not in the other.[3]

The uncertainties make it impossible to compile complete tenurial statistics. Portions of the tenurial map of Oxfordshire are, as it were, illegible in regard to the details of ownership at the manorial level. None the less a good deal can be discerned; and there is no reason to suppose that the ascertainable facts are unrepresentative.

In the first place the net result of sub-infeudation has been to reduce, but not to destroy the predominance of the great tenants-in-chief. Even the greatest of them now sink below the king, but otherwise their position is unchallenged. Though the Bishop of Lincoln had granted out lands worth £156, and had received nothing as a sub-tenant, he held more in demesne than anyone else in the county except his royal master; and Odo of Bayeux, Milo Crispin, Robert d'Oilly, and Roger d'Ivry stand out above all the rest of the Oxfordshire landlords, although each of them had enfeoffed a large portion of his fee and only the last two had acquired any Oxfordshire land as a mesne tenant. If we accept Stenton's well-grounded identification of certain Roberts and Rogers with Robert d'Oilly and Roger d'Ivry, and include what these two lords held as the tenants of others, it is safe to say that the royal estates and the estates held in demesne by the five great tenants-in-chief comprised between them well nigh a third of the entire agricultural resources of the county. Nearly a third of the ploughs, more than a third of the peasant households, and more than a quarter of the serfs were to be found on these lands. If we take account of the valuations—excluding the royal manors because these were not valued in the same way as the others—the result is much the same. The

[1] Dd. i, f. 156.   [2] Ibid., f. 155b.
[3] The identification is made by Stenton, *V.C.H. Oxon.* i. 405 n. 5.

value of the estates held in demesne by these five landlords amounted to something between one-fourth and one-third of the total value of all the manors in Oxfordshire apart from the *Terra Regis*. Comparisons with modern conditions are liable to be misleading; but it illustrates the significance of these facts to note that in 1873 the six largest landlords in Oxfordshire owned in all less than one-seventh of the county area.[1]

Next to the really great estates in order of magnitude, Domesday Book reveals a group of seven—those of the Bishop of Winchester, Abingdon Abbey, Hugh de Bolbec, Richard de Courcy, and three tenants of the Bishop of Bayeux.[2] In scale these differed from one another within comparatively narrow limits. Their values ranged from £40. 10s. to £54. 10s., while the least valuable of the greater estates—that of Roger d'Ivry— was worth more than £92. Their plough-teams varied in number from $31\frac{1}{2}$ to 56, while in the group previously considered these ranged from 79 to 180 among the tenants-in-chief, and the king was credited with $215\frac{1}{2}$.[3] Elements that were geographically more or less widely dispersed were a feature common to all seven estates. In some other respects, however, the differences between them are strongly marked. The Bishop of Winchester, Abingdon Abbey, and De Courcy were tenants-in-chief of all their Oxfordshire property; but Wadard, Ilbert de Lacy, and Adam, son of Hubert, had nothing in the county except what they held as tenants of Odo of Bayeux, and, apart from a very small property at Rycote which he held in chief, Hugh de Bolbec's Oxfordshire lands consisted entirely of those he held as the tenant of Walter Giffard. Again, the Winchester and De Courcy estates were each concentrated in two, and the Abingdon estate in three, valuable manors; but each of the other four landlords, along with a couple of valuable, or at least substantial, manors, had a number of much smaller properties. Altogether, though precision in such a matter is unattainable, we shall probably not be far wrong if we estimate that between

[1] My authority for this statement is the *Return of Owners of Land*, published in 1875 and commonly known as 'The New Domesday'. In any comparisons of this kind, it must not be forgotten that the relation of modern tenant-farmers to their landlord is very different from the relation of medieval peasants to the lord of the manor: some of the latter had a right in the land which approximated to a property right.

[2] Again I accept the identifications made by Stenton.

[3] The figures include both demesne ploughs and those of the peasants, but on the royal estates the enumeration of the latter was, as we have seen, incomplete.

one-eighth and one-ninth of the farm-lands and agricultural resources of Oxfordshire was in the hands of this group of seven landlords. Some small addition would have to be made to the class of estates just considered if we assumed the identity of all, or nearly all, the Williams, Gilberts, or Ralfs who appear among the mesne tenants of the county. But, with names as common as these, such an assumption would be very improbable in the absence of any other reason for the identification; and we shall in fact leave a generous margin of error for the bare possibility of what is unlikely, if we conclude that quite half the agricultural property in the county consisted of estates smaller and less valuable than any of those in our group of seven. Statistical classification of these lesser estates is, however, impossible. Among landowners bearing the same name some may very well be identical, especially if they are tenants of the same lord, even if their names are common ones; and though we can rule out as too improbable identifications sufficiently far-reaching to build up a large estate out of entries that may for all we know relate to different individuals, the assumption that every such entry does in fact concern a distinct person would clearly be unjustifiable. We may be pretty sure that no large estates are concealed from our view by these uncertainties; but the number of the smaller properties and the extent of a good many of them must remain unknown. At the same time the proportions and character of some of the lesser estates can be clearly discerned; and there is no reason to suppose that the samples are unrepresentative. The bearer of an unusual name is as likely as anyone else to be the owner of a very ordinary estate.

Even a few examples are sufficient to show that the estates which were inferior in scale to those already described were exceedingly various. The Saxon princess Cristina had only one manor in Oxfordshire, but it was worth £31, its arable was tilled by 30 ploughs, and the enumerated population comprised 52 villans, 8 bordars, and 14 serfs.[1] If William fitz Nigel the tenant of Earl Hugh was really a distinct person from all the Williams we meet on other fees, his estate was somewhat similar to that of Cristina—a manor worth £30 with 26 ploughs, 42 villans, 4 'free men', 2 bordars, and 8 serfs.[2] But he was a mesne tenant,

[1] Dd. i, f. 160.
[2] Ibid., f. 157. For the identification of William, the earl's tenant, with William fitz Nigel, constable of Chester, see Stenton, V.C.H. Oxon. i. 382.

while Cristina was a tenant-in-chief. In sharp contrast to them, the Count of Evreux held in chief, and in demesne, eight small and widely scattered properties whose total value was £15. 10s.[1] The chance that they had uncommon names enables us to distinguish some very modest landowners. Wenric, a tenant of Abingdon Abbey, though he also had a small manor in Berkshire, appears in Domesday as holding nothing in Oxfordshire besides some land at Sandford-on-Thames which was worth £5.[2] That was also the combined value of the little manors which a Saxon named Orgar continued to hold at Gangsdown in Nuffield and at Berrick Salome.[3] A certain Benzelin, though a tenant-in-chief honoured with a rubric to himself, had only some land at Lillingstone Lovell that was tilled by two ploughs and valued at £2.[4] Very similar to this was the property at Bainton held by Erchenbald as the tenant of Ghilo, the brother of Ansculf.[5] Yet some of those who had only a little property in Oxfordshire were great landlords elsewhere. Among the landowners who in this county held in demesne lands worth £15 or less we find the names of the Archbishop of Canterbury, the Bishop of Salisbury, the abbey of Battle, the Countess Judith, Henry de Ferrers, Hugh de Grentemaisnil, Geoffrey de Mandeville, William and Rannulf Peverel, and William de Warenne.

The geographical intermixture of property which marks the layout of the fiefs of the tenants-in-chief was intensified by subinfeudation. Here and there, it is true, that process had resulted in some local concentration. But this was on a small scale. At Yarnton, as we have seen, Roger d'Ivry appears to have held as a mesne tenant both the manor held in chief by the Bishop of Lincoln and the half-hide of land that belonged to the fee of Odo of Bayeux.[6] Probably Rainald, the tenant of a manor at Fritwell on the fee of Earl William, should be identified with the Rainald who held some land of Milo Crispin in the adjacent vill of Somerton; and an ambiguous entry in Domesday seems to indicate that he also held for a time a manor at each of these

[1] Dd. i, f. 157. Grafton, one of his possessions is more than 30 miles from Mollington where he had land tilled by a single plough and valued at £1.

[2] Ibid., f. 156b.

[3] Ibid., f. 159b. He is entered as a tenant of Milo Crispin, but Domesday adds: 'Has duas terras quas tenet Orgar de Milone de rege deberet tenere. Ipse enim et pater suus et avunculus tenuerunt libere T.R.E.'

[4] Ibid., f. 160. Apparently the only other Benzelin to be found anywhere in Domesday is one who held Standen in Wiltshire (worth £2) as a tenant of Ernulf de Hesdin: ibid., f. 70.   [5] Ibid., f. 159b.   [6] Above, pp. 52–53.

places as a tenant of Odo of Bayeux.[1] At Ludwell both a hide
of land held in chief by Ernulf de Hesdin and 2 hides held in
chief by 'the son of Turstin' were in the hands of a tenant named
Osmund.[2] At Northbrook again, we find a certain Rainald
holding some land of Robert de Statford: he was presumably
the same person as the Rainald who held some other land at
Northbrook as the tenant of Roger d'Ivry.[3]

Yet in general the effect of sub-infeudation was to increase
the dispersion and intermixture of estates. The sub-infeudated
portions of the great fees were divided among a number of
tenants. Sometimes indeed a particular tenant would receive a
scattered property, although his lord had the power to give him
one that was comparatively compact. Roger d'Ivry was tenant-
in-chief of the neighbouring manors of Holton and Horspath,
but the former was granted to Godfrey and the latter to Gilbert,
while Godfrey (if he is the same Godfrey) received from Roger
a manor of precisely the same value as Horspath farther away
at Wolvercot.[4] In a number of cases we find that land in the
same vill has been distributed to different mesne tenants by the
same tenant-in-chief. On the fee of Odo of Bayeux, for example,
though two valuable and contiguous, or almost contiguous,
manors at Barton and Sandford St. Martin were held by Adam,
the son of Hubert de Ryes, a small part of Barton was held by
Wadard.[5] In another part of the county, Tythrop, a 5-hide vill
belonging to Odo, had been divided between his tenants
Wadard and Ilbert de Lacy in equal proportions.[6] Most of
Stoke Lyne had been granted by Walter Giffard to the 'Hugh'
whom Stenton identifies with Hugh de Bolbec, but 3 virgates
in the same place were held of Giffard by a certain Turold
together with another 3 virgates in nearby Tusmore.[7] On the
fee of Robert de Statford, part of Middle Aston was held by
Goisbert and a larger portion by Gilbert.[8] At Garsington the
land that belonged to the abbey of Abingdon was divided
between two tenants.[9]

[1] Dd. i, ff. 161, 159b, 155b. The identifications are made without hesitation by
Farrer, *Honors and Knights' Fees*, iii (1925), 234.
[2] Dd. i, ff. 160, 160b. [3] Ibid., ff. 158, 158b. [4] Ibid., ff. 158b, 159.
[5] Ibid., ff. 156, 156b. Adam, the tenant of Sandford St. Martin and Barton Ede,
has been 'definitely identified' by Round with Adam, son of Hubert de Ryes and
brother of Eudo the king's *dapifer*: *V.C.H. Oxon.* i. 380, citing Round, *E.H.R.* xvi
(1901), 728.
[6] Dd. i, f. 155b. The identification of *Duchitorp* with Tythrop is made by Stenton.
[7] Ibid., f. 157b. [8] Ibid., f. 158. [9] Ibid., f. 156b.

A highly instructive example of the diverse effects of sub-infeudation is afforded by the entries in Domesday relating to *Tewa, Teowe, Teoua,* and *Tuua* which apparently cover the three villages now known as Great Tew, Little Tew, and Duns Tew. Those which in Stenton's judgement refer to Duns Tew show us that no less than four lords were tenants-in-chief in this vill. Of the four, the Bishop of Lisieux retained his land in demesne, while Odo of Bayeux had enfeoffed his portion to Wadard, but the other two lords, Robert d'Oilly and Robert de Statford, seem to have granted their lands to the same mesne tenant, a man named Euruin, so that here sub-infeudation had involved some measure of consolidation. On the other hand, at Great Tew there had been no sub-infeudation, the whole place being held in demesne by Odo as tenant-in-chief, while at Little Tew all the land had been enfeoffed; a portion which the Bishop of Lisieux held in chief there had been granted to a tenant of his named Rotroc, and the rest of the vill, which belonged to Odo, had been divided between Wadard, Ilbert, and Humfrey. Even if we abandon the attempt to distinguish the various vills named Tew, it is clear that four lords between them held all these lands in chief, but that the immediate lords were seven in number, two of the seven being identical with two of the tenants-in-chief.[1]

What the intermixture of feudal estates really came to, and what it might involve for the social relations of men, can perhaps be apprehended more readily if we take our stand, as it were, at one or two arbitrarily selected spots in the Oxfordshire of 1086 and look about us upon the tenurial landscape of the immediate neighbourhood. And first let us make our observations at Lower Heyford in the Cherwell valley about mid-way between Oxford and Banbury. Within three miles of this place the modern map shows us (besides Lower Heyford) 12 villages which we can recognize in Domesday; and we find that 11 different tenants-in-chief have property in this small area and that the land is divided among at least 16 immediate lords.[2] There is more than one lord in 5 out of the 13 vills; and only at Duns Tew, Middle Aston, and Middleton Stoney has any tenant-in-chief retained his land in demesne.[3] If we move south-eastwards

---

[1] Dd. i, ff. 155*b*, 156, 156*b*, 158, 158*b*.

[2] Here and in the other groups I give the minimum number to avoid uncertainties due to identity of names.

[3] The *village* of Middleton is more than 3 miles from Lower Heyford, but I have

for some 20 miles to Cuxham, near the western escarpment of the
Chilterns, a somewhat similar picture meets the eye. A three
miles radius gives us 15 Domesday vills, including Cuxham: in
these vills there are altogether 12 tenants-in-chief or perhaps we
should say 11, if we regard the fee of Earl William as no longer
in being; and the immediate lords cannot be less than 17 in
number. Six places are divided between two or more immediate
lords; and though Milo Crispin is the sole tenant-in-chief in 4
villages, he holds only Chalgrove in demesne and each of his
remaining properties is in the hands of a different tenant.[1]
Besides Milo, 5 other tenants-in-chief have retained some land
in demesne in this little district. Then we make a journey of
25 miles to the west and pause at Alvescot a few miles from
the Gloucestershire border. Within three miles of us there seem
to be 11 Domesday sites besides Alvescot: some of the land belongs to the king; and the tenants-in-chief are 13 in number
or 12 if we reckon Roger d'Ivry to be really the tenant-in-chief,
and not a mesne tenant, of the part of Black Bourton that belonged to the 'fee of Earl William'.[2] With the king the immediate
lords number at least 15: Black Bourton and Brize Norton are
each divided between 3 lords, Bampton between four. Six of
the tenants-in-chief have retained their land in demesne and
though the royal manor at Bampton has apparently been let
for a fixed rent, neither it nor the king's other manor at Langford is enfeoffed.

An intermixture of property such as we find in these three
sample groups of villages would not necessarily be incompatible
with the predominance of one or two landlords possessed of
estates much larger than the others in the group. We must
therefore take a glance at the distribution of property in each
group in order to see how things really stood in this matter. If
we confine ourselves to the immediate lords and use the hidation
figures as the most convenient means of comparison—though
that is certainly a very rough method of measurement—this is

included it as the church is less than that distance from Lower Heyford church: the
parishes are contiguous.

[1] Chalgrove is rated at 10 hides: each of Milo's 3 sub-infeudated manors is rated
at 5 hides and his land at the hamlet of Watcombe (reckoned as one of the 15
vills) at 2 hides.

[2] Roger d'Ivry was a tenant-in-chief at Clanfield and Brize Norton and is therefore already counted. Similarly in the Cuxham group the Robert who held the
portion of Watlington that belonged to the 'fee of Earl William' was probably Robert
d'Oilly the tenant-in-chief of 8 hides in Watlington which he kept in demesne.

what we find. In the Heyford group five lords have 9 or 10 hides each, and even if we were to assume the identity of the two Roberts and all the Rainalds among the local landowners, that would only give us 13 hides and 17¾ hides respectively as the assessments of the two largest complexes of property in the group. In the Cuxham group the situation is rather different. Here William fitz Nigel holds a 40-hide manor at Pyrton as the tenant of Earl Hugh, and this greatly exceeds any other estate in the group. Yet there are four other lords with 10 hides each and Robert d'Oilly probably had about 20 hides—perhaps even more.[1] In the Alvescot group the royal estates predominate, the king having 42½ hides out of a total of less than 130. But the Saxon princess Cristina has 24¼ hides; Fulk, a tenant of Roger d'Ivry, has over 14 hides, Pagen, another tenant of Roger d'Ivry has nearly 10, and if the Roger who is Robert d'Oilly's tenant at Bampton is the same person as the Roger who holds of d'Oilly at Kencot, he must have 8 hides.[2] It is important too to notice that the lords who have only a little land in these groups of villages include some wealthy and powerful people—the Count of Evreux and the Bishop of Hereford in the Alvescot group—Rannulf Peverel in the Cuxham group—and, in the Heyford group, Wadard, who was a tenant of Odo of Bayeux in six counties and is represented on the Bayeux tapestry.[3]

Our sample group may probably be regarded as fairly representative of conditions in the county as a whole. It is true that the description of some large manors on the *Terra Regis* and on the fee of the Bishop of Lincoln justifies the conjecture that several unnamed vills may here lie concealed under a single comprehensive heading, and that in these cases what is treated as a single manor may really be a complex of property involving a geographical extension of unified landlordly authority that went far beyond anything we have found in the sample groups. But outside the estates of the king and the diocesan bishop there is nothing to suggest this kind of thing.[4] And as we have seen,

[1] The vagueness in Robert d'Oilly's case is due to uncertainty of identification.

[2] The hidation figures underrate the importance of Cristina's estate, on which, there were 30 ploughs as compared with a total of 32 on the two royal manors. In the Cuxham group too, Pyrton was heavily assessed; there were 26 ploughs there as compared with 13 on Milo Crispin's 10-hide manor of Chalgrove and a like number on the 8-hide manor which Robert d'Oilly (in this case certainly) held at Watlington. [3] But perhaps Wadard had 9 hides at Somerton (Dd. i, f. 155*b*).

[4] Of course manors on other estates may well have included an unnamed hamlet or two besides the vill named in the Domesday entry. We know that the 6-hide

the great manors of the bishop had been largely cut up by sub-
infeudation, so that as regards the immediate lords there was
even here much tenurial heterogeneity. Unfortunately, we are
not told where the lands of most of the bishop's knights were
situated. We know, however, that three of them were given
properties rated at 10 hides or a little more and that at least
seven others had between 5 and 10 hides apiece.[1]

Historians have in the past had much to say about the
scattered fiefs of the tenants-in-chief in Norman England, which
according to a familiar but now quite discredited theory were
formed after this fashion by King William with the object of
weakening forces that in fact were necessary to the maintenance
of his rule over the conquered people. They have also, with good
reason, exhibited the prevalence of villages of divided lordship
in a number of eastern counties; and have rightly emphasized
the greater liberty and independence that must have been enjoyed, and the larger measure of responsibility for the management of their own affairs that must have been exercised, by the
inhabitants of villages where 'no one has a manor which contains the whole vill' and three or four lords hold property side
by side.[2] Yet too little attention has been given to the social and
political significance of such an intermixture of estates, intensified by sub-infeudation, as the foregoing analysis of Oxfordshire
conditions has revealed in a county that lies well outside the
region of Scandinavian settlements and does not appear to have
been at all peculiar in its tenurial geography. In the preceding
chapter an attempt was made to show that the dispersion of the
great fiefs contributed to the development of royal justice and
the unification and centralization of the Anglo-Norman state.
But in the light of the Oxfordshire evidence it is perhaps permissible, though no doubt hazardous, to advance somewhat
farther upon the path of speculation. The great paradox of
English medieval history lies in the fact that it shows us an
unusual concentration of authority and power in the monarchy,

manor of the Bishop of Exeter at Bampton included the hamlets of Aston and
Chimney which are not mentioned in Domesday: see A. J. Robertson, *Anglo-Saxon
Charters* (1939), pp. 226, 475–6; Stenton, *V.C.H. Oxon.* i. 377–8.

[1] Dd. i, ff. 155, 155*b*.

[2] See Maitland, *Domesday Book and Beyond*, pp. 129–50; Pollock and Maitland,
op. cit., pp. 605–34; Vinogradoff, *Growth of the Manor* (1905), pp. 304–6, and
English Society in the Eleventh Century, pp. 390–8; F. M. Stenton, *Documents Illustrative
of the Social and Economic History of the Danelaw* (British Academy, 1920), Introduction, pp. lix–lxii.

and yet, as it unfolds, discloses a landed gentry distinguished for its political capacity and exceptionally ready to assume political responsibilities. May it not be that this development was promoted by tenurial conditions such as those revealed by the Domesday account of Oxfordshire? The conduct of local affairs in hundred court and shire court must have been profoundly affected by the circumstance that in every part of the county the interests of a number of lords were involved. No considerable area lay under the dominant shadow of a single will. Moreover, the landlords differed greatly in rank and wealth. A man's local position was often far from commensurate with his importance in the state. A leading magnate like William de Warenne might have an interest in the county and its affairs, yet hold only a modest position among its landowners. On the other hand, Richard de Courcy was not one of the greater landlords of Norman England but his was among the more considerable of Oxfordshire estates.[1] Against such a social background it requires no unwarrantable stretch of imagination to picture the suitors of the hundred and shire courts as including lords, and stewards of lords, who, having varying grounds for their sense of self-importance, were not likely to feel cowed or submissive, but could boldly stand up for their rights and opinions in the face of their fellows. One cannot but suppose that in consequence of such conditions local government would be to a large extent a matter of discussion rather than of dictation. The discussion may often have become a wrangle, punctuated by threats and explosions of anger; but even in a politically mature society, deliberative assemblies witness occasional 'scenes'; and even in the assemblies of the eleventh century, men who were proud, selfish, and violent might now and again, perhaps not infrequently, discover that their interests could be advanced more effectively by persuasion and compromise than by reliance upon force. Discussion is the great political educator.

III

The landlords who in 1086 held land in demesne in Oxfordshire, and were therefore Oxfordshire landlords in the sense that they had a direct and controlling interest in the economy of manors within the county, included many sorts and conditions

[1] It is what a man held in demesne that one must reckon in estimating his importance as a local landowner.

of men.[1] Among them were a number of great ecclesiastics. The Conqueror's half-brother, Odo of Bayeux, should no doubt be regarded rather as Earl of Kent than as a bishop; and neither his great estates, nor the small property in north Oxfordshire held by the king's physician Gilbert Maminot, Bishop of Lisieux, belonged in any sense to their Norman sees.[2] But the Archbishop of Canterbury, the Bishops of Winchester, Salisbury, and Lincoln—perhaps also the Bishop of Hereford who held a manor at Bampton of the Bishop of Exeter—were ecclesiastical landlords in the proper sense of that term; and besides Eynsham Abbey (which lurks ambiguously behind the figures of the diocesan bishop and the monk Columban), we find that the old Berkshire abbey of Abingdon, the old Gloucestershire abbey of Winchcombe, and the new abbey of Battle in Sussex all possessed property in the county, while the abbey of St. Denis of Paris had a valuable manor at Taynton, and the Norman houses of Bec and Préaux had a little land at Swyncombe and Watlington respectively.[3] In addition, the list of Oxfordshire landowners includes the impoverished Canons of St. Frideswide and a few 'clerks', one of whom, Rannulf Flambard, the owner of a small manor at Milton-under-Wychwood, was destined for greatness stained with infamy. Altogether, though no precision in the matter is possible, we shall not be far wrong if (excluding the Bishops of Bayeux and Lisieux and also the 'clerks', whose land was probably their personal property, but counting the land held by Columban as monastic) we reckon that about 16 per cent. of the agricultural resources of Oxfordshire belonged to estates that in 1086 were held in demesne by bishops and monasteries as part of their endowments.[4]

[1] Much of what follows is derived from Stenton's Introduction to the Oxfordshire Domesday in *V.C.H. Oxon.*, vol. i.

[2] The same might be said of the lands of the Bishop of Coutances, but all his Oxfordshire estates were sub-infeudated.

[3] The abbey of Bec held Swyncombe as the tenant of Milo Crispin. Stenton thinks that the 'monks of St. Peter' who held a hide of land (apparently at Horley) of the Count of Mortain were probably the monks of Préaux: *V.C.H. Oxon.* i. 381 n. 6.

[4] The estimate is based on my own calculations. Ballard's figures for church property in Oxfordshire (23·2 per cent. of the hidage and 22·5 per cent. of the teams) are for lands held in chief and for the area covered by the Oxfordshire section of Domesday, so that they exclude the Oxfordshire manors that were entered under other counties: see his *Domesday Inquest*, map facing p. 88 and table on p. 262. Of any glebe that may have belonged to parish priests we know practically nothing so far as Oxfordshire is concerned; but in general such holdings would be comparable with those of peasants and would not justify the inclusion of the

That the lay landlords were a very heterogeneous group will have become apparent from the account already given of their estates. We know but little about them as individuals; and can only make guesses as to their personal relations with their Oxfordshire property, for, as Stenton says, 'Ernulf de Hesdin seems to be the only Oxfordshire tenant-in-chief who can be seen in residence at one of his manors within the county.'[1] Some of the great men who had lands in other parts of England were probably 'absentee landlords' in the fullest sense of the term, or at most visited their Oxfordshire manors only occasionally. Robert d'Oilly, however, had charge of Oxford Castle and was probably sheriff, while Milo Crispin held the castle of Wallingford just over the Berkshire border and the bulk of his Oxfordshire property lay in the neighbourhood. That a good many of the less exalted lords had a permanent residence in the county seems in the nature of things probable; but a number of them were servants of the king and as such may have had duties that would often call them away. Names like 'Rainald the archer', 'Siward the huntsman', and 'Teodric the goldsmith' are suggestive; and Stenton has ascertained that Richard Ingania, who had some property at Lillingstone Lovell, was 'one of the king's chief huntsmen'; and that Hervey, the owner of land at Bix and Ibstone in the Chilterns, was 'a king's messenger'.[2] Yet some Norman families had apparently begun to take root in the county. Barford St. Michael belongs to Ilbod, the brother of Ernulf de Hesdin, whose home at Chipping Norton was only some 8 miles away. Wigginton belongs to Guy, the brother of Robert d'Oilly.[3] A few family connexions can be discerned. Milo Crispin appears to have married a daughter of Robert d'Oilly; and Roger d'Ivry was the son-in-law of Hugh de Grentemaisnil.[4] This last connexion is reflected in the tenurial

priests among the landlords. The bishops and monasteries would of course derive some advantage from the sub-infeudated parts of their estates, which in particular would relieve them of some, or all, of the burden of knight service. My object in limiting consideration to lands held in demesne is to show the part played by ecclesiastics as immediate lords directly concerned with manorial economy, or, in other words, to estimate the range of their landlordly authority and activity, and not to attempt the impossible task of comparing their wealth with that of other landlords.

[1] *V.C.H. Oxon.* i. 384.

[2] Ibid., pp. 382, 386–7. Possibly some of the 'ministers' may have retired before 1086; the name of a man's former office would easily, one imagines, adhere to him.

[3] Ibid., p. 386 n. 1.

[4] The evidence for Milo's marriage is the verdict of an Oxfordshire jury of 1183:

geography of 1086. Among the manors which Roger held in chief, and retained in demesne, were Mixbury in north Oxfordshire and Beckley in the neighbourhood of the county town; but he also held, as his father-in-law's tenant, both Cottisford which adjoins Mixbury and Charlton-on-Otmoor which is only 3 miles from Beckley, while his wife possessed the manors of Oddington and Islip which form a connecting link between Beckley and Charlton.[1] Friendship as well as kinship seems to have influenced the distribution of land. There was a bond of close comradeship between Robert d'Oilly and Roger d'Ivry: a tradition that is preserved in the thirteenth-century cartulary of Oseney Abbey, and is generally accepted as true, tells that they took part in the Conquest as sworn brothers—'fratres jurati et per fidem et sacramentum confederati'—and traces of this alliance can be discerned in their joint tenancy of lands at Arncot and Sandford-on-Thames.[2]

Besides Roger d'Ivry's wife, two other ladies are included by Domesday in the list of Oxfordshire tenants-in-chief. One was the king's niece, Judith, widow of Earl Waltheof, who had been executed for his complicity in the rebellion of 1075: her two manors of Merton and Piddington were both held in demesne.[3] The other was the Princess Cristina, already mentioned. Whether she ever lived at her manor of Broadwell, which she held in demesne, we do not know. Less than a year after the Battle of Hastings she had gone to Scotland with her mother and brother and her sister Margaret, and in the year of the Domesday inquest, if not before, she took the veil in the old Saxon nunnery of Romsey, where later she had charge of her niece Matilda, the future queen of Henry I.[4] Yet another lady, whose name, Bristeva, shows her to have been an Englishwoman, appears in Domesday as a tenant of the Bishop of Lincoln: she rented 20½ hides that were reckoned to be part of

see Stenton, ibid., p. 383. For the marriage of Roger d'Ivry we have the authority of Orderic who also tells us that Robert, son of Richard de Courcy, married another of Hugh's daughters: *Historia Ecclesiastica*, viii, c. 16.

[1] Dd. i, ff. 158b, 224b, 160, 160b.

[2] Ibid., f. 156b; *Chron. Abingdon*, ii. 25. As tenants-in-chief, each of the friends held a very similar 10-hide manor in Shirburn and also some land at Rousham: Dd. i, ff. 158, 158b, 159. Probably they were the Robert and Roger who had a half-hide of waste at Noke: ibid., f. 161. Cf. f. 155 (Newington).

[3] Ibid. i, f. 160.

[4] Ibid., f. 160; *Anglo-Saxon Chronicle* (E), A.D. 1067 and 1085 (a scribal error for 1086); Ordericus, *Hist. Eccles.* viii, c. 20, cf. Knowles, *The Monastic Order*, p. 137.

the manor of Dorchester and also held 2½ hides, apparently at
Marsh Baldon.[1] Compared with the property of these two
Anglo-Saxon women the 5-hide manor which 'Turchil' held in
chief and in demesne at Drayton, near the Warwickshire border,
was in itself insignificant; but the subsequent history of Drayton
proves that its owner was Thurkill of Warwick, sometimes
known as Thurkill of Arden, a man equivocally distinguished
as the only Englishman, except Colswein of Lincoln, who appears in Domesday as holding in 1086, as a tenant-in-chief of
the Conqueror, an estate that can justly be described as 'of
baronial dimensions'.[2] Thurkill was the son of Alwine (Æthelwine) the Sheriff; and his great estate in Warwickshire included
a few manors inherited from his father and some land at Ashow
and Brandon that he had himself held 'freely' in the time of
King Edward.[3] He was a benefactor of Abingdon Abbey and
is described in the history of that house as 'dwelling in the parts
of Arden'—*in partibus Ardene mansitans*—and as *valde inter suos
nobilis*.[4] Far inferior to Thurkill in wealth and importance, the
king's minister Lewin, whose Oxfordshire property has already
been mentioned, was yet exceptionally prosperous for an Englishman of the year 1086; and in this county he had much more
land than Thurkill. His three manors, which had all been his
before the Conquest, were together worth £22: there were
29 ploughs on them, 6 of which belonged to the demesne farms;
and Lewin's tenantry consisted of 66 villans and 9 bordars, and
he possessed 12 serfs.[5] The smaller landowners too included a
few men of the conquered race. Besides Orgar with his 5 hides
of family property, of which something has already been said,

[1] Dd. i, ff. 155, 155b. The *Bristeva* of Domesday represents the Old English
Beorhtgifu: see O. von Feilitzen, *Pre-Conquest Personal Names of Domesday Book*
(Uppsala, 1937), p. 194.

[2] Dd. i, f. 160b; Stenton, *V.C.H. Oxon.* i. 386, 422 n. 4; *Anglo-Saxon England*, p. 618.

[3] Dd. i, ff. 240b, 241, 241b.

[4] *Chron. Abingdon*, ii. 8, 20, 21, quoted by Freeman, *History of the Norman Conquest*,
iv (1871), 782. Freeman paints Thurkill as an astute traitor (or 'collaborator' as
we should say nowadays), and says that his lands 'were largely increased by royal
grants out of the confiscated estates of less lucky Englishmen' (ibid. 189). We may
applaud the historian's refusal to regard success as always justified of her parents
and yet feel that we have too little knowledge upon which to base a moral judgement in such a case. It would indeed be possible to argue that Thurkill had pro-
tected some of his fellow countrymen, for an unusually large number of Englishmen
who had held land freely in Warwickshire before the Conquest retained the same
property in 1086 as Thurkill's tenants.

[5] Dd. i, f. 160b. If Lewin was the same person as 'Lewin of Neweham', as suggested above (p. 47, n. 1), he had also a substantial estate in Buckinghamshire.

a man named Toli retained, as the tenant of Milo Crispin, some land at Cowley which he had held freely in the time of King Edward; and, among the royal servants or ministers, who in 1086 are holding their land of the king, we find that Siward the Huntsman has 2½ hides, and Sawold, along with other property, 3 hides, which they had respectively owned before the Conquest, while 3½ hides out of the 5½ hides possessed by Teodric the Goldsmith had previously belonged to his wife. It is somewhat hazardous to infer a man's origin from his name; but Alfred, 'nephew of Wigot', who held Stoke Marmion and Checkendon in chief as well as in demesne, was probably an Englishman and his uncle was probably the great thegn Wigod of Wallingford.[1] Among the more modest landowners there are, in addition to those already mentioned, some six or eight whose names suggest that we have to do with men of English birth: several of them were *ministri regis*. Finally, on the Bishop of Lincoln's great manor of Dorchester some English freemen seem to be reckoned among the bishop's enfeoffed knights. We are not told how many of them there were, but as they are described as *Angli liberi homines* and their combined holdings amounted to only 3½ hides, they were probably not much superior to peasants such as the *liberi homines* whom we find at Church Enstone, Pyrton, Goring, and Aston Rowant.[2] All told the native landowners other than peasants were in 1086 an insignificant element in the county. Few in number and mostly poor, they were the flotsam and jetsam of an aristocracy that had been wrecked in the storms of the Conquest. One of them, the above-mentioned Sawold, appears to have been in difficulties at the time the Domesday Inquest was taken: his property was worth £10 in all, but more than half of it was held in pledge—*in vadimonio*— by Robert d'Oilly.[3]

The wealth of Oxfordshire was in alien hands. But not all the foreign landlords were Normans. William fitz Ansculf and Ernulf de Hesdin belonged to the lands which neighbour Normandy on the north; and Robert, Bishop of Hereford, who held a manor at Bampton as tenant of the Bishop of Exeter, came of

[1] Dd. i, ff. 159b, 160b, 160. The identification of Wigot with Wigod of Wallingford is made by Freeman, op. cit., p. 736.

[2] Dd. i, ff. 155, 157, 158, 159. Of the 26 *liberi homines* enumerated in the county, all but 4 occur at villages within 10 miles of Dorchester. Stenton, who gives the number as 23, appears to have overlooked the 3 at Goring: *V.C.H. Oxon.* i. 392.

[3] Dd. i, f. 160b.

Lotharingian stock; while, among the less important landowners, Conan, who as one of the Bishop of Lincoln's knights
held 7¾ hides of the manor of Dorchester, bears a name that is
suggestive of Breton origin. Yet a great majority of those whose
continental antecedents have been traced derived from Normandy and these Normans include the greatest of the Oxfordshire landlords—Odo of Bayeux, Remigius the Bishop of
Lincoln, Milo Crispin, Robert d'Oilly, and Roger d'Ivry.[1]
There can be little doubt that Norman blood was similarly
predominant among the lesser lords, many of whom must have
been vassals of the greater men before they set out for England.[2]

Apart from the few whose names are writ large in the pages
of English history—Lanfranc, Odo, Flambard, in particular—
we have little means of knowing what manner of men these alien
landlords were. Some of them played an active part in the
administration of the conquered realm. The four commissioners
who conducted the Domesday Inquest in the county of Worcester were all Oxfordshire landlords.[3] We must remember, however, that the possession of demesne manors does not necessarily
imply even temporary residence within the county; and it seems
that some of the greater people continued to regard Normandy
as their homeland. Roger d'Ivry, though 'an occasional witness
to the English charters of the Conqueror' was 'more particularly
a Norman figure'.[4] In 1078 he had charge of the tower of Rouen
and, after the Conqueror's death, he appears to have held the
office of Butler (*pincerna*) under Robert of Normandy.[5] Aubrey
de Couci, who in Oxfordshire held Iffley and Minster Lovell
in chief and Burford as the tenant of Bishop Odo, resigned his
Northumbrian earldom and retired to the Continent.[6] And near
the end of the century, when the aged Hugh de Grentemaisnil
lay dying in England, the Prior of St. Evroul was sent over from

[1] For these matters of derivation I rely on the conclusions of Stenton and
Douglas.

[2] This seems clear in the case of Odo's tenants, Wadard and Adam, son of
Hubert: the former is represented in the Bayeux tapestry and Adam came from
Ryes which is 4 miles from Bayeux: see D. C. Douglas, *Domesday Monachorum*,
Introduction, p. 29.

[3] See the passage from Hemming's Cartulary printed by Ellis, *General Introduc-
tion*, i. 20. The four were Bishop Remigius, Walter Giffard, Henry de Ferrers, and
Adam, brother of Eudo Dapifer, who is the same person as Adam, son of Hubert,
Odo's tenant.

[4] D. C. Douglas, *Domesday Monachorum*, pp. 56–57.

[5] *V.C.H. Oxon.* i. 383; Davis, *Regesta*, No. 308.

[6] Stenton, *William the Conqueror*, p. 353.

Normandy to give him spiritual comfort; and his body was taken to that house for burial.[1]

Except for those who were national figures and are unlikely to have had much personal contact with their Oxfordshire estates, very little can be discerned about the character of individuals. But the chance that they formed the subjects of edifying stories does enable us to catch a glimpse of two men who were Oxfordshire landlords in the fullest sense of the term.

Because he could cite him as an example of the miraculous powers of St. Aldhelm, William of Malmesbury has some interesting things to say about Ernulf de Hesdin, the lord of Chipping Norton. We are told that he suffered from a sore disease which deprived him of the use of his hands, and, having sought the aid of a celebrated physician at Malmesbury, was cured, not by medical skill, but by a balsam taken from the saint's tomb. The account of this marvellous occurrence is introduced by a brief but vivid description of Ernulf. He was a distinguished man—'vir inter optimates Angliae opinatissimus'—and was remarkable alike for his skill in agriculture and for his bounty to the poor. He was so careful about the payment of tithe that, if a barn was filled with corn that had not been tithed, he would order it all to be turned out and tithed without delay.[2] The implication that he was both pious and business-like and took a close personal interest in the management of his estates is made more acceptable by his numerous and munificent gifts to monasteries—which are well documented—and by the striking increase in values which Domesday reveals on many of his manors.[3] Moreover, there can be no doubt that he is the person referred to in a Hyde Abbey chronicle as *Ernulfus de Hednith* (or *Hedinth*); and that chronicle not only mentions his wealth and his outstanding 'industry' (describing him indeed as *industria summus*), but clearly indicates that he was a man of scrupulous honour and sensitive conscience, for it says that he was wrongly accused of complicity in the rebellion of 1095 and, though vindicated in a trial of battle, was so deeply mortified by the unjust charge, that he abandoned his English estates and went on the Crusade. He died at Antioch.[4]

[1] Ordericus, *Hist. Eccles.* viii, c. 27.
[2] *De Gestis Pontificum* (Rolls Series), pp. 437–8.
[3] See below, pp. 210–12.
[4] 'Chronica Monasterii de Hida ab anno 1035 ad annum 1121', in *Liber de Hyda* (Rolls Series), pp. 301–2 ('tanto dolore et ira est commotus, ut abdicatis omnibus

If the story of Ernulf was one of piety rewarded by a miraculous cure, that of Robert d'Oilly provided a salutary lesson of repentance induced by a marvellous dream. For many years Robert played a part of some importance in the government of Norman England. He witnesses a charter as *minister* as early as 1067 and a quarter of a century later appears among the witnesses of a charter issued by Rufus.[1] He was, it seems, one of the royal constables under William I, as well as constable or castellan of Oxford Castle.[2] He was almost certainly sheriff of Warwickshire before 1084, and probably also sheriff of Oxfordshire.[3] An Abingdon chronicler describes him as wealthy and avaricious, sparing neither rich nor poor in his efforts to heap up riches. He persuaded the Abbot of Abingdon to grant him the manor of Tadmarton, and even when he was forced to give it up—apparently by a judgement of the king's court—managed to exact an annual payment of £10 as the price of peace. But what most distressed the Abingdon monks was his seizure of a meadow outside the walls of Oxford for the use of the knights of the castle. This, however, led indirectly to his change of heart. He fell seriously ill and in his illness dreamt that the Blessed Virgin, at the prayer of two of the Abingdon monks, caused him to be brought into that very meadow and there mocked and tormented by some filthy lads—*turpissimi pueri*—who, setting alight wisps of hay from the meadow, threw them in his face and burnt his beard. Moved by this experience and his wife's persuasions, he went to Abingdon, renounced his claim to the Tadmarton rent, and contributed more than a hundred pounds to the building operations upon which Abbot Reginald was then engaged. Nor were these the only fruits of his contrition.

quae regis erant in Anglia, ipso rege invito et contradicente, discederet; associatus autem Christianorum exercitui. Antiochiam usque devenit, ibique extremum diem clausit'). The identification with E. de Hesdin was made by Freeman, *William Rufus* ii. (1882), 65; and the Keeper of MSS. at the British Museum informs me that in the manuscript of the chronicle (Domitian A. xiv, f. 10*b*) the name could easily be read as HEDINTH. E. de Hesdin's own name occurs as *Hedyng* and *Hesdich* (*Gloucester Cart.*, Rolls Series, i. 93, 223), as *Hesdinch* and *Hodine* (*Calendar of Documents in France*, pp. 108, 364), and as *Heding* and *Hedinc* (Delisle et Berger, *Recueil des actes de Henri II*, i. ccccxxxiii). I am indebted for this last reference to Sir Charles Clay. That E. de Hesdin set out for Jerusalem is stated by William of Malmesbury who implies that he never returned (*De Gestis Pontificum*, p. 438).

[1] Davis, *Regesta*, Nos. 10, 319.

[2] Ibid., No. 270; *Chron. Abingdon*, ii. 7; cf. G. H. White in *Trans. Royal Hist. Soc.*, 1948, pp. 149–51.

[3] Davis, *Regesta*, No. 200; *Chron. Abingdon*, ii. 12; *V.C.H. Oxon.* i. 382 n. 4.

Henceforward he promoted many good works, befriending the poor and repairing churches both within and without the walls of Oxford.[1] Yet he remained, it would seem, the efficient Norman administrator. He never gave up the castle meadow; and it was towards the end of his life that he built the 'Great Bridge' at Oxford.[2] On the other hand, one must note that, ten years or more before the change of which the chronicler makes so much, he and his comrade Roger d'Ivry had founded the church of St. George within his castle.[3]

On the whole, history has been kind to the barons and knights of the Conqueror's realm, for, of all their acts, the most faithfully recorded are those upon which they themselves would have relied to win them abiding merit—their gifts to churches and monasteries. The landlords of Oxfordshire were not backward in the prevailing form of pious generosity. The abbeys of Ivry-la-Bataille and St. James by Northampton, and the priories of Lewes, Castle Acre, Lenton, Colne, Longeville, Tutbury, Hurley, and Runcorn all owed their foundation to men who held land in the county in 1086.[4] The nunnery of Elstow in Bedfordshire was founded by the Countess Judith.[5] Hugh de Grentemaisnil took a leading part in the restoration or re-foundation of the abbey of St. Evroul.[6] Seven of the landlords of Domesday Oxfordshire figure among the benefactors of the abbey of Abingdon.[7] In many cases entire manors were given away; and such gifts, unlike the gift of tithes or churches, were made at heavy cost to the donors. The abbey of Bec received the manor of Swyncombe in Oxfordshire from Milo Crispin,

---

[1] *Chron. Abingdon*, ii. 12–15, 24–25.

[2] Ibid. ii. 15, 25, 284. The *Magnus Pons* was evidently Folly Bridge and the cause-ways leading to it, as the name 'Grandpont' was in the Middle Ages 'often used of the part of Oxford between South Gate and Folly Bridge' and the sentence in the chronicle which describes the bridge as *ad septemtrionalem plagam Oxoniae* (p. 15) must be a slip for *australem plagam*: H. E. Salter, *Medieval Oxford* (Oxford Hist. Soc., 1936), p. 15.

[3] Ibid., p. 29; cf. Salter, *Early Oxford Charters*, No. 58. Salter accepts the date 1074 and Robert's repentance is placed in the time of Abbot Reginald who became abbot in 1084.

[4] The founders were, respectively, Roger d'Ivry, William Peverel (St. James by Northampton and Lenton), William de Warenne (Lewes and Castle Acre), Aubrey de Vere, Walter Giffard, Henry de Ferrers, Geoffrey de Mandeville, and William fitz Nigel.

[5] Dd. i, f. 217; W. Farrer, *Honors and Knights' Fees*, ii (1924), 401.

[6] Ordericus, *Hist. Eccles.* iii, c. 2, ed. Le Prevost, ii. 18.

[7] They were Thurkill, Robert d'Oilly, Henry de Ferrers, Saswallo, Drogo, Adelina d'Ivry, and Milo Crispin: *Chron. Abingdon*, ii. 8, 24, 32, 67–68, 72–73, 97.

that of Blakenham in Suffolk from Walter Giffard, that of Monxton in Hampshire from Hugh de Grentemaisnil, and that of Ruislip in Middlesex from Ernulf de Hesdin.[1] Eye in Middlesex was given to Westminster Abbey by Geoffrey de Mandeville.[2] Abberton in Essex was given to St. Paul's Cathedral by Rannulf Peverel.[3] Richard de Courcy gave some of his continental property to the abbey of Marmoutier at Tours.[4] Besides Bec, the abbeys of Cluny and Gloucester and Préaux and the priory of St. George at Hesdin benefited from the liberality of Ernulf de Hesdin.[5] The benefactions of Ilbert de Lacy were also wideranging. In Oxfordshire Ilbert figures only as a tenant of Bishop Odo, but he was an important tenant-in-chief in the north of England. He founded a church within his castle at Pontefract and among the endowments which he conferred upon it were some tithes on his lands at Lyneham and Stanton St. John in Oxfordshire.[6] He gave the manor of Hambleton to the abbey of Selby, of which his son afterwards became abbot, and other Yorkshire lands to the abbey of St. Mary in York.[7] He gave the manor of Tingewick in Buckinghamshire to Holy Trinity of the Mount at Rouen.[8]

Of the motives which inspired all these actions no one can speak with confidence. In some cases, perhaps, the impetus was merely a crude fear of hell or the hope of securing supernatural aid to recovery from illness. It is rather significant that the history of Abingdon Abbey, which often mentions the circumstances in which the gifts were made, tells us that four of its benefactors were stricken with illness at the time.[9] Not improbably some pious donors did what they did mainly because it was the thing to do. Their royal master and his queen had set the fashion. But an example may be followed because it is believed to be good and not with the object of winning credit in the eyes

[1] M. Morgan, *English Lands of the Abbey of Bec* (1946), pp. 145–9.

[2] Davis, *Regesta*, appendix no. LXV.

[3] M. Gibbs, *Early Charters of St. Paul's* (Camden Soc., 1939), No. 61.

[4] Round, *Calendar of Documents in France*, No. 1194.

[5] Ibid., Nos. 1386 (cf. Dd. i, f. 205*b*), 318, 1326; *Gloucester Cart.*, i. 93, 223 (cf. Dd. i, f. 43).

[6] Farrer, *Early Yorkshire Charters*, iii, No. 1492.

[7] Ibid. iii, No. 1414; i, No. 350.

[8] Ibid. iii, No. 1483.

[9] The four are Robert d'Oilly, Milo Crispin, Drogo de Andelei, and Adelina d'Ivry. Milo's gift, however, was made in return for the medical treatment he received from Abbot Faritius, who was celebrated as a physician: *Chron. Abingdon*, ii. 97.

of men; and it would be unreasonable, as well as ungenerous, to assume that the barons of Norman England were never moved by a feeling that the peaceful and studious routine of the cloister, and the solemn grandeur of the great churches they were helping to build, represented in some way a nobler ideal than the turbulent life of feudal society. The emotions that Canute is said to have experienced when he heard the chanting of the monks of Ely were perhaps less unusual in the days of the monastic revival which followed the Norman Conquest.[1] Yet many Norman landlords enriched themselves by the appropriation of monastic property. In Oxfordshire the notorious Urse d'Abitot held some land in 1086, and the Hervey who held four manors as a tenant of Bishop Odo has been traced in Yorkshire and identified with Hervey de Campeaux who encroached upon the lands of Selby Abbey and died excommunicate in consequence.[2] On the other hand, it was apparently this same man who gave two houses with their tofts to the monks of St. John at Pontefract.[3]

[1] *Liber Eliensis* (1848), i. 202.
[2] Dd. i, ff. 155*b*, 156, 156*b*, 157, 238*b*; Farrer, *Early Yorkshire Charters*, iii, No. 1547.
[3] Ibid., No. 1475.

IV

SOME SPECIMEN ESTATES

THE feudal topography of a single county, such as that of Oxfordshire described in the last chapter, illustrates the incidence of Norman landlordism upon the land and its inhabitants and reveals conditions that must have had a profound influence upon social life and upon the spirit and vitality of local government. But from a picture thus restricted in geographical scope little or nothing can be learned about the scale and nature of a system of ownership whose most striking characteristic is the prevalence of estates that were dispersed among several counties. An attempt must therefore be made to elucidate this aspect of the matter by examining in some detail a select number of these. Like the description of a particular county, the description of specimen estates is open to the objection that the patterns which emerge from a study of this kind may not be typical of the country as a whole. But at least it can be claimed that the five estates chosen for examination represent different types and are various in origin, in size, and in geographical distribution. Three of them are ecclesiastical, two of them lay estates. The former were all in existence before the Norman Conquest; but that of the Bishop of Winchester and his monks—one of the largest and most ancient in England— had been built up during many generations and lay mostly in the south-west; while that of Ramsey Abbey had been acquired since the latter part of the tenth century and was situated in the eastern and east midland counties; and that of Burton Abbey— small in extent and comparatively recent in origin—was confined to Staffordshire, Derbyshire, and Warwickshire. Of the two lay estates, Ralph Paynel's consisted almost entirely of lands which had belonged to a single Saxon landlord before the Conquest, and was of modest proportions, but contained elements geographically remote from one another; while that of Eudo Dapifer included lands that had belonged to a great number of Saxon proprietors, and was at once much larger than the Paynel fee and (though it extended into a larger number of counties) less widely dispersed.

I. *The Estates of the Bishop of Winchester and his Monks*

The wealth of the Bishop of Winchester and his monks, in spite of losses incurred since the Norman Conquest, was still in 1086 fully commensurate with the dignity and importance of their venerable church. Domesday Book shows that a distinction was made between the lands of the bishop and those of the convent; but, as it describes both under the rubric of the bishop's fee, it seems legitimate, in the first place, to consider them as a whole. They were of vast proportions and included elements in nine counties. Yet these counties are all contiguous; and the great bulk of the Winchester estates lay in Hampshire, Wiltshire, and Somerset. They included, however, three valuable manors in Berkshire and a single very valuable manor at Farnham in Surrey. North of the Thames the church of Winchester possessed estates at Witney and Adderbury in Oxfordshire and at Wycombe and Ivinghoe in Buckinghamshire; and it had a cluster of four manors in the south-western corner of Cambridgeshire and a small manor at Cottered in Hertfordshire; but the total value assigned by Domesday to all the Winchester lands in these four counties is scarcely more than half the value it ascribes to the Winchester estates in Somerset, while the Somersetshire estates themselves were worth less than those in Wiltshire, and far less than those in Hampshire.

In addition to these rural estates the bishop owned Taunton with its 64 burgesses; and he had 9 houses (*mansiones*) in Oxford and 27 'fenced tenements' (*hagae*) in Wallingford. A reference in the Domesday account of Meon reveals the fact that he also possessed 8 *hagae* in Winchester which were apparently dependent upon that rural estate; but as Domesday Book contains no survey of Winchester itself, we cannot tell whether he already received the extensive income from house property in the cathedral city which is recorded as belonging to the see in the survey of 1148.[1]

The most ancient endowments were situated in the heart of the old kingdom of Wessex. The great estate of Chilcombe in

---

[1] The early twelfth-century survey which is bound up with that of 1148 in the *Liber Wintoniensis* refers to conditions in the time of the Confessor, but appears to be confined to properties which owed land-gafol and 'brug' to the king, and presumably excludes any that paid these dues to the bishop. The text of the *Liber Wintoniensis* is printed in the fourth (*Additamenta*) volume of the Record Commission edition of Domesday, and both surveys are discussed by Round, *V.C.H. Hants*, i. 527–37.

Hampshire was reputed to have been given by King Cynegils to St. Birinus in the first half of the seventh century 'when Christianity first began' in Wessex, and, if this was so, it must have belonged to the West Saxon bishopric even before the bishop's see was established at Winchester.[1] In Somerset, the huge manor of Taunton is said to have been given by Queen Frithegyth who went to Rome in 737; but possibly the queen's grant was really made to a local monastery whose lands were transferred to the church of Winchester in 904.[2] In Surrey, the estate at Farnham, where the Bishop of Winchester had his official residence until 1927, was already the property of the see in the middle of the ninth century and may possibly have been acquired originally through a grant which King Caedwalla is said to have made in 688 for the building of a monastery.[3] According to the *Annales de Wintonia* Brightwell in Berkshire had been given by King Æthelwulf, the father of Alfred the Great; but such evidence as is available suggests that the Winchester lands beyond the Thames were obtained at comparatively recent dates. Adderbury in Oxfordshire and Morden in Cambridge-shire were both bequeathed by the Ætheling Athelstan in 1015, and Witney was given to Bishop Ælfwine by the Confessor about thirty years later.[4]

The geographical layout of the Winchester lands varied a good deal from county to county. In Hampshire they included elements in more than half the hundreds into which that county was divided, but lay mostly to the east and north of the cathedral city—indeed between the upper waters of the Itchen and the Meon almost everything belonged to the bishop or his monks.[5] In Somerset some sort of parallel to this concentration is afforded by Taunton and its appendages along with nearby

[1] B.C.S. 620 (a suspect charter of Edward the Elder) and 1147 (a confirmation by Edgar). The Anglo-Saxon version of the latter (Robertson, *Anglo-Saxon Charters*, No. xxxviii) does not mention Birinus. All these texts associate Cenwalh as donor with his father Cynegils.
[2] B.C.S. 475 (dated 854) and 612. Miss Robertson appears to accept both these charters: op. cit., pp. 339–40.
[3] B.C.S. 495, 72. The grant by Caedwalla, which Stenton accepts as genuine (*Anglo-Saxon England*, p. 69), does not indeed mention Winchester, but is preserved in the same cartulary as that which includes the ninth-century document by which Swithun granted Farnham to King Æthelbald for life.
[4] 'Annales de Wintonia', in *Annales Monastici* (Rolls Series), ii. 9; D. Whitelock, *Anglo-Saxon Wills*, pp. 57, 167–9; Kemble, *Cod. Dipl.*, No. 775.
[5] There was one valuable manor in the Isle of Wight (Cauborne = Swainston in Calbourn).

Pitminster; but the estates of Rimpton on the border of Dorset and Bleadon near the Bristol Channel were isolated. Of the Wiltshire manors much the most valuable was Downton, which probably included several distinct vills.[1] Away to the north-west were the manors of Stockton and Fonthill Bishop, between the Wylye and the Nadder, and farther still a little manor at Westwood on the edge of Somerset; but with the exception of Enford on the Salisbury Avon, some 20 miles north of Downton, all the rest of the Wiltshire property was situated beyond Salisbury Plain in the north-eastern quarter of the county—mostly among the downs on both sides of the Kennet. Farnham was the only Winchester possession in Surrey, but it seems to have included the whole hundred of Farnham, which contains several parishes unmentioned in Domesday, and as it marched with Crondall in Hampshire it formed part of a large block of Winchester estates which straddled the county boundary at this point. There was nothing corresponding to such concentration either in Berkshire or beyond the Thames, though the four Cambridgeshire manors formed a small contiguous group.

Omissions and ambiguities in the statements of Domesday Book make it impossible to present an exact statistical account of this great complex of property, but it can safely be said that the estates which appear to have been held in demesne, either by the bishop or the monks, comprised lands that were tilled by some 970 plough-teams, and that at least 210 of these were demesne teams belonging to the landlord. Some 500 *servi* were employed on these demesnes and the peasant tenants included more than 1,300 *villani* and more than a thousand bordars and cottars.[2] The mills numbered over a hundred. And the total valuation amounts to £1,325 odd.[3]

[1] The land boundaries given in Saxon charters indicate that it included Bishopstone, Nunton, Charlton (in Standlynch), and Redlynch: see W. H. Jones, *Domesday for Wiltshire* (1865), pp. xx, 213; cf. G. B. Grundy, *Saxon Land Charters of Wiltshire* (1st series, reprinted from the *Arch. Journal*, 1919), pp. 145–50; and Darlington, *V.C.H. Wilts.* ii (1955), 84. None of these places is named in Domesday.

[2] I have included some *coscez* with the *cotarii*. We are also told of 40 *coliberti* and 17 *porcarii*. Burgesses are excluded as not belonging to the rural population: owing to the absence of any survey of the cathedral city their enumeration in Domesday must be incomplete.

[3] The figure is probably somewhat excessive for the rural property. It includes the render of £154 for Taunton and that figure may include the renders of the burgesses, the market, and the mint which amounted to £6. 12s. Perhaps the total of £1,325 should also be reduced by £15 which is the value of a manor at Twyford (Hants), for it is doubtful whether this was a demesne manor. Domesday says of it:

In addition to the demesne manors we have to reckon with lands that were 'sub-infeudated' or at least held by free or named tenants, or, in the case of two Hampshire manors by the *villani*. The valuation of all these lands comes to about £338; but except in Hampshire the data in regard to other matters are inadequate. The Hampshire values, however, amount to about £205, or more than 60 per cent. of the total; and the estates to which this figure applies comprised lands tilled by at least 158 teams and included 15 mills, while their enumerated population consisted of some 227 *villani*, some 257 bordars, and some 136 *servi*.[1]

The Winchester estates in general were very largely composed of entire villages in which no other tenant-in-chief had as such any part. But there were exceptions to the general rule. In Cambridgeshire all the four Winchester manors lay in vills of divided lordship.[2] Adderbury in Oxfordshire belonged partly to the bishop and partly to the king, while Robert de Statford also had a hide of land there.[3] Even within the bounds of the old West Saxon kingdom, divisions of this sort are discernible here and there—for example, at East Meon, Binstead, Polhampton, Boarhunt, and Brockhampton in Hampshire.[4] Moreover, though in most places where it had property the church of Winchester was tenant-in-chief of the whole village, this does not mean that in all such villages there was only one landlord. In many entries we read not only of a manor held in demesne by the church, but also of subordinate estates in the hands of its mesne tenants, who in a few cases are specifically described as knights. Indeed on the Winchester estates it is unusual to find a single tenant holding an entire village that is separately described in Domesday; and some of the subordinate tenements

---

'Eldred femina Oswold tenuit de episcopo. Wlfricus tenuit T.R.E.' (i, f. 40), and Round conjectured that the first *tenuit* was a mistake for *tenet*. Of the figures given above, only the valuation total is really affected by these uncertainties.

[1] These figures do not include those for Eldred's manor at Twyford mentioned in the last note, and I have also taken no account of the small estate of *Burnewic* (Brownwich in Titchfield) as the bishop held it *de rege in feudo* and *non est de episcopatu* (Dd. i, f. 40b). In any case the figures should be regarded as minima, for even in Hampshire particulars are not given for all the tenants' holdings. On the statistics of these lands see further Appendix II.

[2] I.C.C., ed. Hamilton, pp. 51–52, 55, 60–62.

[3] Dd. i, ff. 154b, 155, 158.

[4] Ibid., ff. 40b, 41b, 43; cf. ff. 38, 44b, 45b, 46, 47. For all places in Hampshire I rely upon Round's identifications in the Victoria County History.

are so small that a division of the village lands must be assumed.[1] More than a dozen separately valued tenements (other than the lands of the village churches) are valued at £2 or less. Some others, to which no separate value is assigned, were of small dimensions. On the large manor of *Elendune* (now Wroughton) in Wiltshire, an unnamed knight was tenant of a hide and a half, and at Wanborough in the same county a man named Richer held a single hide.[2] In general, however, there is ground for thinking that villages where either the bishop or one of his tenants was the sole landlord were a good deal commoner than appears on the surface of the Domesday descriptions. In many cases the size of the manors makes it probable that we have to do with composite entries covering more than one village; and many of the subordinate holdings were on a scale which would suit the supposition that each of them comprised an entire vill. On the great manor of Downton, where the lands which the bishop held in demesne were valued at £80 and those of his knights at £23, William de Braose was mesne tenant of 14 hides, and two other knightly tenants are credited with 5 hides each.[3] Since villages assessed in 5-hide units are remarkably common in Wiltshire it seems likely that these last holdings represent either distinct villages or a 10-hide village divided between the two tenants. On the manor of Enford in the same county, most of which was held in demesne, a tenant named William, who was evidently a knight, had a 5-hide estate which may reasonably be identified with the hamlet of Fifield (formerly *Fifhide*) in the same parish, so that, though undistinguished from Enford in the record, it affords a close parallel to the 5-hide village of *Fifhide* (probably Fyfield on the Kennet) which was held of the bishop as a whole by a man named Edward, but (unlike *Fifhide juxta Enford*) is named and separately accounted for in Domesday.[4] Occasionally the sites of subordinate holdings are mentioned in composite entries, and the account of Overton in Hampshire includes a statement that the 5-hide holding of a certain Geoffrey lay in Bradley.[5] As there is no other reference

<hr>

[1] West Tisted and Chilton Candover in Hampshire (Dd. i, f. 40b) and Fyfield in Wiltshire (f. 65b) are examples of separately described vills that were each held by a single mesne tenant.

[2] Ibid. f. 65b.   [3] Ibid., f. 65b.

[4] Ibid., f. 65b. Cf. Gover, Mawer, and Stenton, *Place-Names of Wiltshire* (1939), pp. 328–9; *V.C.H. Wilts.* ii. 201.

[5] Dd. i, f. 40. The words *in Bradelie* are interlinear, and were perhaps added

to Bradley in Domesday, this mesne tenant may well have been the immediate lord of the whole of that place. In contrast to this, one of the tenants of the manor of Hurstbourne Priors in the same county is described as holding 5 hides in the village itself—almost as if the contrary would normally be expected in such a case.[1] And however these things may be, the Winchester estates in Hampshire certainly included a good many villages which were entirely retained in demesne.

As the enfeoffments made on the Winchester estates before 1135 were sufficient to provide for an amount of military service exceeding the *servicium debitum* of 60 knights, there can be little doubt that many of the bishop's tenants in 1086 held their lands by knight service.[2] But in a great majority of cases Domesday tells of Englishmen who had preceded them; and its record in this respect is not complete, for a charter of the Conqueror refers to a certain Wilward Belgisone as the former holder of some land at Alton Priors which was granted by the bishop to William Escudet, and though Domesday duly reveals William 'Scudet' holding 3 hides at that place as the bishop's tenant, it makes no mention of any predecessor.[3] Of the bishop's former, presumably pre-Conquest tenants, a few in Hampshire are described as thegns.[4] Both in these cases, and in some others, the holdings of two or more had been combined by 1086.[5] It is much more usual, however, to find that the new tenant's holding corresponds with that of a single predecessor.[6] And though a few new holdings had been created out of land previously occupied by peasants, it would seem that the imposition of knight service had not by 1086 involved any considerable reduction in the

because the place is 9 miles from Overton. Round notes that 'the parish of Bradley is still a detached portion of the Hundred of Overton': *V.C.H. Hants*, i. 461 n. 3.

[1] Dd. i, f. 41 ('De hoc manerio tenet Goisfridus de episcopo v hidas in eadem villa').

[2] H. M. Chew, *The English Ecclesiastical Tenants-in-Chief and Knight Service* (1932), p. 19.

[3] Davis, *Regesta*, No. 270; Dd. i, f. 65*b*.

[4] Dd. i, f. 41 (*Widenaie* = Witnal in Whitchurch, and Hurstbourne Priors); cf. Crondall, where Lewin and Vlward, the predecessors of German, and Justan and Lefsi, the predecessors of Turstin had each a 'hall'.

[5] For examples see Chilton Candover, Wield, and Crondall (ibid., ff. 40*b*, 41).

[6] See Easton, Crawley, Fareham, Chilcombe, Freefolk, Hurstbourne Priors, Farnborough (sub Crondall), Droxford, Alverstoke, and (apparently) Alresford and Overton in Hampshire; also Fyfield, Ham, Wroughton (*Elendune*), and East Overton in Wiltshire (ibid., ff. 40, 40*b*, 41, 41*b*, 65*b*). But some of the former tenants held *in paragio*.

area which the bishop and his monks held in demesne, but that the knights' fees, if such they were, had mostly been formed out of lands that were already in the hands of tenants.[1]

The tenants of 1086 included three important barons— William de Braose, Roger d'Ivry, and Hugh de Port. They also included Ralf, son of Seifrid, who occupies a modest place among the tenants-in-chief of Berkshire; William Escudet, the king's cook; and Hugh the Butler, who can hardly be any other than Hugh d'Ivry.[2] Most of them, however, bore such common names that it would be profitless to speculate about their identification. But it is noteworthy that in Hampshire three Englishmen were still in possession of lands they had held before the Conquest, that an unnamed Englishman appears as tenant of 3 hides on the manor of Enford in Wiltshire, and that at Taunton several of the tenants have English names.[3] At Milbrook in Hampshire the whole manor was still held, as formerly, by *villani*; and this was also the case at Alverstoke in the same county, except for a single hide that was held by an unnamed knight.[4]

Of the demesne farms on the manors that were retained in demesne little can be said. There were just 2 demesne ploughteams on 19 of them, 3 teams on 11, and a single team on 8. On 6 manors no such teams are recorded. On one there was only a team and a half and on another there were 2½ teams. There were, however, 8 manors which had 4 demesne teams, and 10 with 5 or more; but in most of these cases there are clear indications that we have to do with the combined figures of several vills.[5]

[1] On the Hampshire estates tenants whose land was previously held by *villani*, or whose predecessor held it *quasi villanus*, occur at Bishops Waltham, Stoke Charity, Fareham, Chilbolton, and Whitchurch (ibid., ff. 40, 40b, 41) and there is no reference to predecessors in the case of certain tenants at Houghton, Abbotstone, Bentley, and Polhampton (ff. 40b, 41b); but on the other hand 5 hides at Kilmiston, previously held by a tenant, were in demesne in 1086 (f. 40).

[2] That the Hugh who held Abington Pigotts in Cambridgeshire of the bishop was Hugh the Butler is revealed by the Cambridgeshire Inquest, see I.C.C., p. 60; cf. Dd. i, ff. 190, 216; Davis, *Regesta*, No. 55; and G. H. White in *Trans. Royal Hist. Soc.*, 4th series, xxx (1948), 141.

[3] Dd. i, ff. 40 (Easton), 41 (Chilcombe), 41b (Exton), 65b, 87b. Round thought it probable that the Cheping who retained his holding at Chilcombe was identical with the formerly wealthy 'Cheping de Ordia', most of whose lands passed to Ralf de Mortimer. *V.C.H. Hants*, i. 428.

[4] Dd. i, f. 41b.

[5] Only the great manors of Alresford, Chilcombe, Downton, and Taunton had more than 6 ploughs *in dominio*; of the 3 which had 6, Easton and Bishop's Waltham

The ratio of demesne teams to peasant teams varies greatly. In Hampshire, for example, the places with a couple of the former include Wootton St. Lawrence and Fareham where the peasants had 15 and 14 teams respectively, and, on the other hand, Hoddington with 2 peasant teams and Stoke Charity with only one.[1] In Wiltshire the variations are much smaller; but even in this county the peasants possessed 10 ploughs at Enford and a single plough at Westwood though there were 3 ploughs *in dominio* on each of these manors.[2] In view of the effect which such differences may have had upon the proportion of the demesne arable that was tilled by the ploughing services of the manorial tenants, it is impossible to treat the numbers of the demesne ploughs as an index to the extent of arable land comprised in the various home farms. But it is not unreasonable to suppose that, as a general rule, manors with a large amount of demesne arable would tend to keep more demesne ploughs than those with a small amount.

Since the bulk of the Winchester lands lay in a part of the country in which slaves were numerous, it is not surprising that servile labour played a substantial part in the economy of the demesne manors on these estates. Apart from a few tiny properties valued at 25*s.* or less and a few places where indications of a demesne farm are wanting, there are, among all the manors which the bishop or the monks retained in their own hands, only three in Hampshire, two in Cambridgeshire, and one in Wiltshire where no *servi* are recorded.[3] Compared with the total number of *villani*, bordars, cottars, and the like, the proportion of *servi* was on the Winchester demesnes considerably larger in Wiltshire and Somerset, but slightly smaller in Hampshire, than it was respectively in each of those counties taken as a whole. Hampshire, however, contained more than half the total number of the Winchester slaves.

In conclusion something must be said about the division of the estates between the bishop and the monks of the cathedral priory. We hear of lands given specifically for the maintenance

had each 2 churches; and, of those with 4 or 5, Houghton and Overton (Hants) had similarly 2 churches, while at Whitchurch, Hurstbourne Priors, and Crondal the size of the enumerated population seems to indicate a composite entry.

[1] Dd. i, ff. 41*b*, 40*b*.

[2] Ibid., f. 65*b*.

[3] Domesday Book also records no slaves at Pitminster in Somerset, but the Exon. Domesday (p. 161) mentions four on this manor.

of the monastic community long before the Norman Conquest, but such allocations were not always lasting.[1] It was apparently between 1070 and 1082 that steps were taken to make a comprehensive arrangement. An early twelfth-century charter informs us that Walchelin, who had become Bishop of Winchester in the former year, assigned half the property to the convent; that his brother Symeon, who was prior, gave up to the bishop all the knights belonging to the convent's share *pro diversis expensis*; and that the bishop temporarily appropriated 300 'librates' of the monks' land to the building of the cathedral church on the understanding that restoration would be made when the work was completed.[2] The vagueness of the last two statements frustrates any attempt to relate these transactions to the statistics of Domesday Book; but there can be no doubt that in 1086 the bishop had much more than half of the total complex of estates. His demesne manors were then worth about £800 and those of the convent not much more than £500; but the plough-team figures are more favourable to the latter, for it appears that some 440 teams found employment on the demesne manors of the monks as compared with some 530 on those of the bishop. Nor is the contrast much altered if we include the estates granted out to knights or other tenants of non-peasant character, and the two manors that were held by *villani*. If allowance is made for a considerable margin of error, we may perhaps conclude that the total value of all the rural property of the bishop was about £1,000 and that the total value of the monastic lands (including those which the monks held *de episcopatu*) was in the region of £660.[3]

---

[1] A charter attributed to the year 909 asserts that Whitchurch had been given *ad refectorium*, but was afterwards appropriated to the bishops: B.C.S. 624; cf. Robertson, *Anglo-Saxon Charters*, p. 305. Yet it appears among the monks' lands in Domesday (i, f. 41). Alton Priors appears to have been given to the community at Winchester 'for their refectory' early in the tenth century and was still *de victu monachorum* in 1086: B.C.S. 566; cf. Robertson, op. cit., pp. 30–31, 291; Dd. i, f. 65b.

[2] *Registrum Johannis de Pontissara* (Canterbury and York Soc.), pp. 621–2. I am indebted to Professor Cheney for calling my attention to this charter, which may be dated between 1115 and 1129, but is only preserved in this late copy. Walchelin is said to have started rebuilding the cathedral in 1079, and Symeon became Abbot of Ely in 1081 or 1082: *Annales de Wintonia*, pp. 32, 33.

[3] I use round figures to avoid a misleading appearance of exactness where exactness is really impossible. In fact I make the total value of the monastic lands (inclusive of the subordinate estates but exclusive of those the monks held *de episcopatu*) to be £627. 5s. 6d., and it is reassuring to find that this figure is so nearly midway between Professor Knowles's figure of £600. 1s. and the £640 of Corbett.

Geographically, as between county and county, the partition was very uneven. In Somerset the monks only possessed the manor of Bleadon, which, together with the land held by a tenant, was valued at £16, while the episcopal estates in this county were worth more than £210.[1] In Hampshire, on the other hand, the monastic lands were worth not much less than those of the bishop, and in Wiltshire actually exceeded his in value. In Berkshire the monks had only Woolstone and in Buckinghamshire only West Wycombe, neither of which was very valuable; but the bishop had not much more in these counties. Elsewhere the monks possessed nothing. Within the bounds of Hampshire each of the two parties had some of the manors that lay in the neighbourhood of the cathedral city between the Itchen and the Meon.

II. *The Estates of the Abbey of Ramsey*

The Benedictine abbey of Ramsey in Huntingdonshire owed its origin to the monastic revival of the tenth century. Founded about 970 by Oswald, Bishop of Worcester, with the active co-operation of Æthelwine, the ealdorman of East Anglia, it soon became a notable home of learning and in the reign of William the Conqueror was still one of the most important monasteries in England. Though it suffered some loss of possessions as a result of the Conquest, it was a rich house in 1086. Ambiguities and omissions in the figures supplied by Domesday Book make exact statistics unattainable, but the margin of error in the following tables cannot be large and they may be taken as a general indication of the extent of the Ramsey estates, of their distribution as between one county and another, and of the degree to which they had been sub-infeudated. The total of all the valued items comes to £365. 16s. 4d., but, compared with other rich monasteries, Ramsey was richer than this sum suggests for the amount of knight service that it owed was exceptionally small.[2]

Though they included lands in eight counties, the Ramsey estates were fairly well concentrated. A ride of about 40 miles

---

[1] The value of the episcopal estates includes the render of Taunton.

[2] My total may be compared with the corrected figure of £358. 5s. in the revised edition of Knowles, *Monastic Order*, p. 702. In making my calculations I have treated the figures of subordinate entries as additional to those of the main entries in the absence of evidence to the contrary.

from the abbey would have sufficed to reach even its most distant properties, with the exception of a little group which lay some 50 miles away near the Norfolk coast. Most of the Ramsey manors were indeed much nearer than these limits would suggest. Measured by the Domesday valuations, half the abbey's property was situated in Huntingdonshire and more than 65 per cent. of the remainder in the adjacent counties of Cambridge and Bedford. Moreover, more than half its Huntingdonshire lands lay in the hundred of Hurstingstone, in which the abbey itself stood, and most of its Cambridgeshire estates were closely bunched near the Huntingdon border.

In twenty-two substantial villages the abbey was the sole tenant-in-chief and seventeen of these appear to have been retained entirely in demesne in 1086.[1] In some other places too it was much the largest landlord. In Huntingdonshire it possessed 23 of the 40 hides at which the two Hemingfords were assessed and in Cambridgeshire it held 9 hides in the 10-hide vill of Elsworth, nearly 11 of the 15 hides at Over, 10¼ out of 15 hides at Burwell, more than 8½ of the 15 hides at Girton. Immediately to the south of the abbey, in the hundred of Hurstingstone, the concentration of its estates is especially remarkable, for here Upwood, Wistow, Warboys, Broughton, Abbot's Ripton, Wyton, Houghton, St. Ives, and Holywell formed a series of contiguous vills which belonged wholly to Ramsey, and, with the exception of 3 hides in St. Ives and a single hide in Holywell, were wholly retained in demesne.

On the other hand, Ramsey had property in some vills of divided lordship in which it was far from occupying a dominant position. At Offord, in the county of Huntingdon itself, besides the 10-hide manor which came to be known as Offord Cluny because Ernulf de Hesdin had given it to the great Burgundian abbey of that name, we find that Ramsey has 4 hides while the Countess Judith and Eustace the Sheriff have 3 hides each. In Cambridgeshire, examples of such intermingling of lordship are frequent and striking. At Boxworth the abbey was the least of 5 landlords—at Bourn, the least of 4. In Bedfordshire too it appears as one of the smallest of 6 lords at Wyboston; and at

---

[1] The least considerable of the 22 vills were rated at 4 hides: 12 of them were rated at 10 hides or more, and Lawshall (the only Ramsey possession in Suffolk), though not hidated in Domesday but assessed at 'eight carucates with the soke', was in later days reckoned as a 10-hide manor: Dd. ii. f. 378*b*; *Cart. Rams.* (Rolls Series), iii. 213, 222.

THE ESTATES OF RAMSEY ABBEY IN 1086

A. Lands apparently held in demesne

County as in Domesday	Ploughlands (i.e. the number of ploughs for which there is said to be land)	Plough-teams on demesne	Tenants' plough-teams	Villani	Bordars and cottars	Servi	Other classes	Value £ s. d.
Huntingdon	255⅞	43	197	455	70	None	14 priests 10 sokemen	161 15 0*
Cambridge	74½	14	48½†	108½	54	24	1 'franc' 4 sokemen 8 fishermen	59 7 0‡
Bedford	56½	9	45⅛	110	22	20	...	45 15 0
Norfolk	Not stated	10	11¼	65	72	13	1 liber homo 29 sokemen	24 1 8‖
Suffolk	Not stated	3	10	16	10	5	1 Frenchman	12 0 0
Hertford	20	2¼	11	27	14	4	1 priest	11 0 0
Northampton	20	6	16	47	17	6	1 priest 3 sokemen	9 12 0¶
Lincoln	2¼	1	1½	4	2	..	1 sokeman	4 5 0
Total	...	88½	340¾	832½	261	72	1 liber homo 2 Frenchmen (?) 16 priests 47 sokemen 8 fishermen	£327 15 8

B. Lands apparently enfeoffed

County as in Domesday	Ploughlands	Total plough-teams	Villani	Bordars and cottars	Servi	Value £ s. d.
Huntingdon	Incompletely stated	26	26	15	..	16 8 0
Cambridge	6	5	5	9	..	3 0 0
Bedford	Incompletely stated	5½	9	4	3	4 11 4
Norfolk	Not stated	2	..	18	..	10 0 0
Suffolk, Hertford, Northampton, Lincoln		No enfeoffments recorded				
Total	..	38½	40	46	3	£24 9 4

C. Sokeland where separately described

Huntingdon. 8¼ ploughlands.

Lincoln. 7 ploughlands, 4 plough-teams, 12 sokemen, 2 villani, 3 bordars.

* The figure does not include the *piscariae et marae* which were valued at £10 (Dd. i, f. 205).
† At Knapwell, where there were 4 sokemen and 8 *villani*, no tenants' plough-teams are mentioned, so this figure must be too small.
‡ The 8 fishermen at Wisbech who rendered 5,260 eels are unvalued.
§ Including half a plough-team at Standon though it is uncertain whether this belonged to the demesne or the tenants.
‖ This figure does not include the £3. 10s. at which the soke of the hundred and a half of Clackclose was valued.
¶ This figure does not include a house of 16d. which the abbey possessed in Northampton.

Clifton, where there were five tenants-in-chief, Ramsey Abbey and the Countess Judith, with a single hide each, were of little importance in comparison with the other three.

Several vills were divided between Ramsey and some other monastic house. Thus Ramsey and Peterborough had each $2\frac{1}{2}$ hides in the 5-hide vill of Hemington in Northamptonshire while Chatteris in Cambridgeshire was almost equally divided between Ramsey and Ely, and, of the 10 hides at Holywell in Bedfordshire, Ramsey had $3\frac{1}{2}$ and Westminster Abbey the rest.[1]

Very little of the Ramsey land appears to have been sub-infeudated by 1086. Two motives for creating military sub-tenancies were here lacking. The military service required from the abbey was singularly light in proportion to its wealth, being limited, it seems, to 3 or 4 knights, whereas the neighbouring foundations of Ely and Peterborough had to provide 40 and 60 respectively.[2] Hence the Abbot of Ramsey had no need to sub-infeudate a great deal of property as a remedy for what Round calls 'the standing entertainment of a roistering troop of knights'.[3] And since the monastery continued to be ruled by Saxon abbots until after the date of the Domesday inquest, its policy had not been affected, as that of some religious houses was affected, by the inclination of a Norman abbot to treat the imposition of knight service as an opportunity for giving his lay kinsmen a share in the spoils of the conquered country.[4] In any

[1] In this and the preceding two paragraphs no account has been taken of sub-infeudation: the statements refer only to the distribution of the land between the tenants-in-chief. There is a table setting forth the position as regards the latter in N. Neilson, *Economic Conditions on the Manors of Ramsey Abbey* (Philadelphia, 1899), pp. 10–12, but it is not quite accurate.

[2] That at one time Ramsey owed a service of 13 knights for certain purposes may be inferred from the fact that Rufus between 1091 and 1100 released the abbot 'de servitio decem militum in festis' and ordered that in future he should provide three 'sicut antecessores sui faciebant in septentrionali parte fluminis Tamesiae' (*Cart. Rams.* i. 235). But from this it would seem that the heavier obligation was only maintained for a short time; and even 13 knights were a light burden in comparison with that imposed upon Ely and Peterborough. In 1166 the *servitium debitum* of Ramsey was stated to be 4 knights.

[3] *Feudal England*, p. 301.

[4] As regards improper enfeoffments see ibid., pp. 301–3; Chew, op. cit., pp. 116–18. Professor Knowles seems to me to underestimate the force of the evidence: *The Monastic Order* (1940), p. 118. Besides the cases usually cited, there is the Conqueror's instruction to sheriffs to restore to bishoprics and abbeys lands given away by bishops and abbots, which surely implies that improper alienations had been numerous; and two spurious charters in favour of Battle Abbey witness to the apprehensions felt by the monks: Davis, *Regesta*, Nos. 50, 113, 271. It is significant too that chroniclers sometimes praise abbots for not acting in this way:

case tenancies, other than peasant holdings, were as yet few and unimportant on the Ramsey estates. They included three 5-hide manors. Two of these were in the county of Huntingdon—one being held by a man named Suin and the other by Aubrey de Vere who had granted out 2 of its 5 hides to an unnamed knight.[1] The third was at Little Barford in Bedfordshire, and is described in Domesday as held by Eudo Dapifer 'of the abbot's fee', and as held of Eudo by Osbern.[2] All the other tenancies were smaller than these; and, though in a few cases the tenants bear names that suggest a native origin and a hide at Clifton (*Clistone*) in Bedfordshire remained in the possession of a man named Lewin who had held it before the Conquest, 8 tenants are described as *milites*. Only 2 of these knights are named—Richard and Hugh who held 3 hides worth 30s. at Stukeley.[3]

It may well be that some of the Domesday tenants of the abbey, including even some of the *milites*, held their lands in accordance with old English custom rather than by any feudal tenure of Norman pattern. The knight's fee was, in a twofold sense, a thing of gradual growth. Not only was the actual progress of sub-infeudation largely haphazard and uneven: there was at first a good deal of vagueness and variety in the nature of the tenures that were created.[4]

The Ramsey records throw a little light on these matters. In Domesday Little Barford appears to be an ordinary example of sub-infeudation, with Osbern holding the manor as sub-tenant of the mesne tenant Eudo. But Eudo had made an agreement with Abbot Ailsi by which he was to hold the Ramsey property in Barford for half a knight's service for the benefit of his sister Muriel, who was evidently married to Osbern: the tenancy was to continue for the lives of Eudo and his sister, and thereafter not only this land, but also some property which Eudo had in his own right in the same place, was to belong to the abbey free of all claims on the part of Eudo's successors.[5] Whether this

---

Evesham Chronicle (Rolls Series), p. 95; *Liber Eliensis*, i. 275. On the other hand, allegations against early Norman prelates made in the reign of Henry II were perhaps tendentious attempts to counter the king's case for increasing knight service on the basis of the *Cartae* of 1166.

[1] Dd. i, f. 204b. [2] Ibid., f. 210b. [3] Ibid., f. 204.

[4] See Vinogradoff, *English Society*, pp. 74–89; Stenton, *First Century*, pp. 152–4; D. C. Douglas, *Econ. Hist. Rev.* ix (May 1939), 135–8.

[5] *Chron. Rams.*, pp. 207–8. Though Abbot Ailsi seems to have survived until 1087, the agreement must be earlier than the Domesday inquest. Osbern witnesses it as

arrangement was superseded by a regular enfeoffment before 1086 we cannot say; but in the reign of Henry II the 5 hides were held for the service of one knight due to the abbey by Hugh de Beauchamp to whom many of Eudo's Bedfordshire estates had been granted, and a fine of 1193 seems to indicate that both this manor, and also 3 hides at Barford which are described as *de feodo Eudonis Seneschalli*, were then held by one Peter de Leiham, who seems to have been a descendant of the Domesday sub-tenant Osbern.[1]

Another example of change in the nature of a tenancy is provided by Dillington in Huntingdonshire. In 1086 the abbey held this manor in demesne; but Abbot Aldwin (who was abbot, it seems, from 1091 to 1102 and again, after a period of deposition, from *c.* 1107 to *c.* 1112) granted it to R(annulf), brother of Ilger, for life at a rent of £3 a year.[2] Then in another, and presumably later, document we find the same abbot granting Dillington along with Stow to 'R' the Dapifer, nephew of 'R'(annulf), brother of Ilger, and granting it *in feoudum* for the service of one knight.[3]

Again, from the text of yet another *conventio* made with Abbot Aldwin we learn that one of the Domesday tenants of the abbey subsequently obtained an alteration in the conditions of his tenure, the most natural interpretation of which is that it converted a life interest into an hereditary estate. Pleines of Slepe was one of three *homines abbatis* who appear in Domesday as holding between them 4 hides on that manor, and the agreement into which he entered provided that, of the hide and

sororius Eudonis. Eudo's own property in Little Barford must be identified with the 3 hides at *Bereforde* (in Biggleswade Hundred) which Domesday represents as held in chief by Osbern, son of Walter: Dd. i, f. 216*b*. Besides that relating to the Ramsey 5-hide manor, this is the only Domesday entry for Little Barford, and the 3 hides had been held formerly by Eudo's antecessor Vlmar of Etone, while in the fine of 1193 referred to below, 3 hides are distinguished as of Eudo's fee.

[1] *Cart. Rams.* iii. 48; Madox, *Formulare*, p. 218 (No. ccclix). In the fine Hugh quitclaims the homage of Peter and 5 hides to the abbey, which in return gives him 11 marks and renounces its claim in the 3 hides and in the service owed for them—'in servicio earum quas Petrus de Leiham tenet quae hidae sunt de feodo Eudonis Seneschalli'. G. H. Fowler (Bedfordshire Hist. Record Soc. ii. 67–68) applies the last words to the 5 hides too, which is surely wrong. For evidence connecting Peter de Leiham with Osbern see Farrer, *Honors and Knights' Fees*, iii. 177–8; but Farrer failed to point out that, in the agreement with Abbot Ailsi, Osbern's name in the list of witnesses is followed by that of Walger his son ('Osberno sororio Eudonis et Walgero filio ejus').

[2] *Chron. Rams.*, p. 234; *Cart. Rams.* i. 128.

[3] *Chron. Rams.*, p. 257. The cartulary text (ii. 259) is clearly corrupt.

28 acres that he held, he should give 18 acres to St. Ives and should hold the remainder by hereditary right (*jure hereditario possidebit*), so that after his death whichever of his sons he might name should possess it without paying a relief.[1]

As regards the abbey's demesne manors, the outstanding fact is that demesne plough-teams, the sure indication of a home farm, were maintained on almost all of them. On no less than 24 these were just 2 in number, and only at 3 places do we find as many as 4. Of the total number of teams on these manors rather more than a fifth belonged to the demesne, but the proportion varied greatly from place to place. Upwood and Offord in the county of Huntingdon were alike in having 2 demesne teams, but on the former manor there were 32 *villani* and 2 bordars with 14 teams and on the latter only 4 *villani* and 2 bordars with a single team.[2]

In spite of the fact that so much of the Ramsey property lay in Huntingdonshire, a county in which no *servi* at all are recorded in Domesday Book, members of this class formed part of the enumerated population on 19 of the demesne manors. They occur in groups of from 2 to 8; and in Cambridgeshire we may perhaps infer that they were ploughmen, for on 6 of the 8 manors where serfs are recorded there were just 2 to each demesne plough, but in the other counties this ratio is found only at Shillington in Bedfordshire.

Of the demesne stock-farming we get an occasional glimpse where the evidence of the Little Domesday or that of the Cambridgeshire Inquest is available, and, exiguous as the data are, they suffice to indicate that sheep-farming had been developed to a considerable extent on the Norfolk coast, for the abbey had a flock of 600 at Brancaster.[3]

III. *The Estates of Burton Abbey*

The abbey of Burton in Staffordshire was somewhat younger than Ramsey and was not a wealthy house. It had been founded

---

[1] Dd. i, f. 204*b*; *Chron. Rams.*, pp. 235–6; *Cart. Rams.* i. 129. The agreement was made 'de feudo suo id est terra unius hidae et terra viginti et octo agrorum quos ipse ante hanc in suo possederat dominio'. If the gender of *quos* is to be taken seriously, this would imply that the 28 acres, from which the gift was to be made, were not part of the fee. Probably they were Pleines's 'allodial' property.

[2] Dd. i, ff. 204, 204*b*.

[3] Dd. ii, f. 215*b*.

at the beginning of the eleventh century by a rich thegn named Wulfric Spot; and in 1086 it owned 10 manors in Staffordshire, 7 in Derbyshire, and 1 manor at Austrey in the county of Warwick, while, appended to its manor of Mickleover in Derbyshire, were 3 'berewicks' and the soke of 8 other places. It also possessed 5 houses at Stafford, and a mill, 3 houses, and some meadow at Derby, and was entitled to receive 40 sheaves of corn every Martinmas from the burgesses of the latter town. Of the handsome endowment bequeathed by the founder much had passed into lay hands by the end of the Confessor's reign, but the remainder still constituted the bulk of its property in 1086.[1]

A large part of the Burton land was concentrated in the near neighbourhood of the abbey, and Darlaston, its most distant possession, was less than 25 miles away. The Domesday valuation of the whole—exclusive of the properties in Derby and Stafford to which no values are assigned—amounts to £39. 8s. 8d.; and the total number of plough-teams is 61½, or 62½ if we include a team belonging to some sokemen at Wins-hill. The recorded population comprised 115 *villani*, 26 bordars, 1 priest, 1 *liber homo*, and 6 sokemen, without counting the individuals who held certain manors at farm. These figures may serve as a rough indication of the extent of the Burton estates, but are probably slightly smaller than they should be. No plough-teams are recorded for Darlaston, Okeover, and Bed-dington, though there was land sufficient for two teams in each of these places.

In thirteen out of the eighteen vills in which it had property in 1086, the abbey appears to have been the only lord: in other words, manor and vill were in these places identical.[2] At Burton

---

[1] Wulfric Spot's will is in D. Whitelock, *Anglo-Saxon Wills*, pp. 46–51, and with a commentary on it by C. G. O. Bridgeman in *Collections for a History of Staffordshire* (William Salt Soc.) Vol. for 1916, pub. 1918, pp. 1–66, which also contains a translation of King Æthelred's confirmatory charter (pp. 115–19). For the Domes-day account of the Burton estates see Dd. 1, ff. 239, 246, 247b, 273, 280. Bridgeman (op. cit., pp. 293–4) suggests that, besides the lands credited to the abbey in Domesday, it already possessed Willington in Derbyshire, as it certainly did in the early part of the twelfth century. According to the *Chronica Abbatum*, Willington was given by Edward the Confessor (*Mon. Ang.* iii. 47), and though it appears in Domesday under the lands of Ralph FitzHubert (f. 277), it is said to have been formerly held by Leuric, whom Bridgeman would identify with the recently deceased abbot of that name. The manor was only worth 20s.: no demesne ploughs are recorded, but there were 4 *villani* and 2 bordars with 4 ploughs.

[2] I have included Winshill among the thirteen, although the king appears to

itself the position is uncertain because of the difficulty of distinguishing entries relating to Burton from those relating to Barton-under-Needwood.[1] Stapenhill and Ticknall in Derbyshire, Austrey in Warwickshire, and Appelby, which was then reckoned to be partly in Derbyshire and partly in Leicestershire, were vills of divided lordship, the abbey being the principal landlord both at Stapenhill and at Appelby.[2]

It seems that Burton Abbey owed no knight service at all, and though some of its estates were let out to tenants in 1086, there is no evidence of real sub-infeudation.[3] Of Okeover we are definitely told that Eddulf was holding it for a rent (*ad censum*), and though Domesday says nothing about the nature of the tenures by which a certain Nawen held Whiston and two unnamed 'men' held Darlaston, both these places, as well as Okeover, were *ad firmam* in the reign of Henry I, and Nawen was then still the tenant of Whiston. It is perhaps significant that Darlaston and Whiston were the farthest from the abbey of all its estates, and that Okeover was also among the most distant.[4]

Demesne plough-teams are recorded on 14 manors, but 7 of these had only 1, while 5 others had 2 each, and Branston a team and a half. Mickleover is credited with $5\frac{1}{2}$ demesne ploughs, but probably some of them belonged to its berewicks.[5] These small numbers, however, merely reflect the small size of the manors, for the demesne ploughs formed a far larger proportion of the total number than was the case either on the Winchester estates or on those of Ramsey Abbey. There were altogether 24 of them as compared with $36\frac{1}{2}$ belonging to the peasants.[6] The excess of the latter was greatest at Stretton and Leigh, where in each case there was 1 demesne plough to 5 tenant ploughs. On 6 manors the 2 classes were equal and at Appelby and Winshill there was an excess of demesne ploughs.

have retained some rights over the six sokemen pertinent to Repton whom he had placed (*apposuit*) in Winshill.

[1] Dd. i, ff. 246b, 247b, 250b. That the first entry relating to the abbey's estates on f. 247b refers to Burton and that *Stadford* was written in error is clear from the version in the Burton cartulary: *Staffordshire Collections*, v (1884), pt. i, pp. 3, 7; ibid. for 1916, p. 170.

[2] Dd. i, ff. 273, 278 (Stapenhill), 273, 231b (Appelby).

[3] For Burton's freedom from knight service see Chew, op. cit., p. 8.

[4] Dd. i, f. 247b; *Staffordshire Collections* for 1916, pp. 224, 228 (Survey A).

[5] No ploughs are mentioned at three places, and it is doubtful whether the plough recorded at Whiston belonged to the demesne or not.

[6] These figures are exclusive of the doubtful Whiston plough and of the sokemen's plough at Winshill.

This relatively large development of demesne farming is especially remarkable because no *servi* or *bovarii* are recorded in Domesday on any of the Burton estates. Perhaps one should suspect that it has omitted to mention them contrary to its usual practice; but much of the Burton land lay sufficiently near the abbey to be worked by household servants who would normally go unrecorded like the monks themselves.

IV. *The Estates of Ralph Paynel*

In one respect the fee held in 1086 by Ralph Paynel resembles the ecclesiastical estates already described, for though its lord was a layman and an intruder from Normandy, the fee itself consisted almost entirely of lands that had been in the possession of a single landlord before the Conquest. Ralph Paynel had stepped into the shoes of Merleswein, a man of note under the Confessor, who had been entrusted with high responsibilities by Harold and had served as sheriff, apparently in Lincolnshire, for a short time in the Conqueror's reign, but took part in the Northumbrian rising of 1069 and disappears from history in the confusion that followed its suppression.[1] Much of Merleswein's land, it is true, fell to other people; but Ralph Paynel was his real successor; and almost all that he held in chief at the time of the Domesday inquest had belonged to Merleswein in 1066.[2]

Geographically, however, the Paynel estates stand out in sharp contrast, not only to the comparatively compact domains of Ramsey and Burton, but even to the wide-ranging estates of the see of Winchester. The most northerly possessions of the Bishop of Winchester lay in the south of Cambridgeshire, some 90 miles from his cathedral city and about 150 miles from

---

[1] *Early Yorkshire Charters*, i. 27; Thorpe, *Diplomatarium*, p. 386; Dd. i, f. 37*b*; Davis, *Regesta*, No. 8; Gaimar (Rolls Series), i. 222; Symeon of Durham (Rolls Series), ii. 187, 190.

[2] The only certain exceptions are I think Burton Coggles in Lincolnshire where he succeeded Earl Morcar (Dd. i, f. 362*b*) and his little unnamed manor in Northamptonshire which had belonged to Turchil (ibid., f. 225*b*). Grinchel is named as the former owner of some land at Broughton, Scawby, and Sturton (Lincolnshire), but the proximity of these places to Merleswein's estate at Broughton makes it probable that this was the land which the Confessor, in the last year of his life, gave to Merleswein after Grinchel had incurred forfeiture (ibid., ff. 362*b*, 363, 376). Farrer suggested this conclusion though he failed to identify *Bertone* with Broughton, *V.C.H. Yorks.* ii. 173, where he misleadingly implies that all Merleswein's lands, except three Yorkshire manors, were obtained by Paynel, and also that the latter's Northamptonshire manor had belonged to Merleswein.

Taunton which was the centre of his Somersetshire lands. But a distance of 280 miles separated some of Ralph Paynel's Devonshire lands from his manor of Nunnington in the North Riding of Yorkshire.

The general layout of the Paynel fee can best be appreciated from the following table which shows county by county the extent of the estates as measured, on the one hand, by the Domesday valuations, and on the other, by the number of ploughs for which there was reckoned to be land available:

The Estates of Ralph Paynel in 1086

County	Total (lands in demesne + lands enfeoffed)		Lands apparently held in demesne	
	Value	Ploughs for which land was available	Value	Ploughs for which land was available
	£ s. d.		£ s. d.	
Devon . . .	44 5 0	65	38 15 0	53
Somerset . .	21 10 0	37	None	None
Gloucestershire* .	5 0 0	Not given	None	None
Northamptonshire .	10 0	4	None	None
Lincolnshire† . .	43 6 8	63¼	36 10 0	53½
Yorkshire‡ . .	6 2 8	50	4 2 8	46
Total . . .	£120 14 4	219¼+	£79 7 8	152½

* A virgate and a half in *Langetrewes* Hundred is unvalued.

† A messuage in the city of Lincoln and lands estimated to be sufficient for twelve teams and held mostly by sokemen were unvalued.

‡ About half the land was waste and is unvalued.

In addition to the lands of which he was tenant-in-chief (as shown in the table) Ralph Paynel held a manor at Sturton in the West Riding of Yorkshire as the tenant of Ilbert de Lacy. This was valued at 40s. and credited with land for 3 ploughs.[1]

In Yorkshire the Paynel estates were far from being geographically concentrated, though those in the North and West Ridings fall mostly into fairly definite groups. Of his Lincolnshire lands, most lay in the north of the county in the contiguous wapentakes of Manley and Walshcroft, but a substantial portion of them were situated in the south of Kesteven, while the manors

[1] Dd. i, f. 315. That the Radulfus of this entry was Ralph Paynel is clear from the reference to Sturton in Paynel's charter of *c.* 1090–1100: C. T. Clay, *Early Yorkshire Charters*, vi. 68.

of Dunham and Ashby de la Laund lay like stepping-stones between these groups. Only in the Walshcroft wapentake was there any close concentration. Both in Devon and in Somerset the layout was very different from that in the north. In the former county everything lay within 15 miles of Exeter, except the manor of Edginswell which is only a few miles farther away, but within this limited range the Paynel lands were scattered, the ten places named in Domesday being actually in seven different hundreds. In Somerset everything was situated within 8 miles of East Quantockshead. For the rest, the fee included a manor at Tarleton (*Torentune*) in Gloucestershire (with perhaps an odd virgate somewhere in Langtree Hundred in the same county) and 2 hides at an unnamed place in the hundred of *Stoc* (now part of Corby Hundred) in Northamptonshire.

It is hard to say whether Ralph Paynel was the lord of many entire vills. In Lincolnshire he seems to have held the whole of Broughton and Irnham; but the fifteen other places where he had land in that county were all vills of divided lordship. Of the position in Yorkshire nothing definite can be determined, for the Domesday entries frequently lump several places together and, though no other lord can be traced in a good many cases, their vagueness makes it hazardous to draw positive conclusions. Difficulties of another kind meet one in Devon, for since Devonshire parishes commonly include a number of hamlets, it is improbable that every place with a distinct name in Domesday was sufficiently independent to justify its being considered a distinct vill. At Dunchideock and at Throwleigh Ralph Paynel was the sole lord, but, though no one else is named as a landlord at Ilsington (*Lestintone*), there were other lords at Bagtor and Ingsdon which are now hamlets of that parish, while Edginswell, which appears to have belonged entirely to him, is included in the parish of Cockington, which was a manor of William de Faleise.[1] In Somerset, the Paynel lands, though geographically concentrated, seem to have a good deal intermingled with estates of William de Moion and Roger de Corcelles; but, though Domesday represents both Ralph Paynel and William de Moion as having manors at *Cantocheheve* or *Cantocheve*, it is clear that these were respectively East Quantockshead

---

[1] Dd. i, ff. 113*b*, 117, 111. For the identification of *Ainechesdone* with Ingsdon, and of *Wille* with Edginswell, see *Place-Names of Devon* (English Place-Name Soc., 1932), pt. ii, pp. 476, 511.

and West Quantockshead, which in all probability were already distinct vills held each by a single lord.[1]

A large proportion of the Paynel fee was sub-infeudated. Measured by the Domesday valuations, more than a third of it was in the hands of mesne tenants in 1086. Some land had been granted out in each of the six counties into which the fee extended, and in the counties of Somerset, Gloucester, and Northampton none of it was retained in demesne. More than half of the sub-infeudated portion consisted of the Somersetshire manors held of Ralph by Ralph de Rouellé, and it has been conjectured that the Ralph who was mesne tenant of the Paynel manor at Tarleton in Gloucestershire was the same person.[2] None of the other mesne tenants had received more than a single manor of small value. Roxby in Lincolnshire, held by a man named Herbert, was valued at £4: the others were worth less. Ralph Paynel evidently followed the usual practice and kept his most valuable manors in demesne. He had two in Lincolnshire worth £10 each, and two worth £9 each in Devon, while the most highly valued of the sub-infeudated manors was East Quantockshead which was worth £8. In the whole fee fourteen manors were valued at £4 or more and ten of these were held in demesne. There is nothing to suggest that any of the under-tenants belonged to the conquered people.

Apart from the wasted lands in Yorkshire, and a tiny 'bere-wick' and 5 places classed as 'sokes' in Lincolnshire, all the estates that Ralph Paynel held in demesne were equipped with one or more demesne ploughs.[3] But in 9 cases there was only one and in 6 cases two of them, while 2 Lincolnshire manors are credited with 3½ and 4 respectively. The only other place with more than 2 demesne teams is Sturton in Yorkshire, where the association of 5 with a single peasant team combined with a statement giving 3 as the number of 'possible' teams on this manor, compels one to suspect some error in the text.

The proportion between demesne ploughs and peasant ploughs varied from manor to manor, the former providing from one-eighth to one-half of the total ploughing strength,

---

[1] Dd. i, ff. 96, 96b. There were nine plough-teams at each.

[2] Ibid., f. 168; Clay, op. cit. vi. 63. Even in Somerset he is only called *Radulfus* in Domesday, but the Exon. text supplies the name *Radulfus de roileio*. The *Torentune* of Domesday is identified with Tarleton by Ekwall.

[3] No account has been taken of Tealby (*Tavelesbi*) in Lincolnshire, as the Domesday text is evidently defective on this point: Dd. i, f. 362b.

apart from the doubtful case of Sturton. There were some *servi*
on each of the Devonshire manors. They occur in groups ranging from two to seven, but there is no relation between their
numbers and the numbers of the demesne plough-teams.

The following table shows how the enumerated population of
the demesne manors was divided between the various classes:

The Enumerated Population on the Demesne Manors of Ralph Paynel in 1086

County	Villani	Bordars	Servi	Sokemen	Others
Yorkshire* . .	38	3	..	2	2 priests
Lincolnshire . .	123	22	..	128	5 censarii, 2 priests
Devon . . .	96	30	32	..	..
Total . .	257	55	32	130	5 censarii, 4 priests

* Including Sturton.

The subsequent history of the Paynel fee, which has been
traced with admirable fullness by Sir Charles Clay, provides
a salutary warning against any tendency to regard the baronies
of Norman England as completely formed by 1086. During
Ralph Paynel's lifetime great additions were made to the lands
that he held at that date. In Yorkshire he doubled his possessions
by acquiring, probably through marriage, a share in the lands
which at the time of Domesday were held of the Count of
Mortain by Richard de Surdeval.[1] Nor were these his only
acquisitions in that county. In addition, the Lindsey Survey of
1115–18 shows that since 1086 he had become tenant-in-chief
of a number of small estates in Lincolnshire. But if the history
thus witnesses to the continuance of change, it also provides a
remarkable example of agrarian continuity and reminds us that
this was not confined to the estates of the Church. East Quantockshead was one of the manors that had belonged to Merleswein before the Conquest and had passed into the hands of
Ralph Paynel before 1086. Though granted out, as we have
seen, to Ralph de Rouellé, it subsequently reverted to the
family of the tenant-in-chief, and in these mid-years of the
twentieth century it belongs to Mr. G. F. Luttrell, who is a
lineal descendant of Ralph Paynel.[2]

[1] The assessment in carucates of the lands thus obtained was practically the same
as that of all the estates Paynel held in the county in 1086.
[2] For all this paragraph see Clay, op. cit. vi. 56–61, 65.

V. *The Estates of Eudo Dapifer*

The estates that Eudo Dapifer held in 1086 were an amalgam of properties which before the Conquest had belonged to a number of Saxon landowners. His chief predecessor was Ulmar of Etone, a thegn of King Edward, whose designation was derived from Eaton Socon in Bedfordshire.[1] Most of the land which Eudo held in that county had previously belonged to this man, and he had also owned Gamlingay, which was Eudo's most valuable manor in Cambridgeshire, and one of the three houses that the latter obtained in the town of Hertford. Whether he should be identified with any of the persons named Ulmar who appear as the Dapifer's predecessors at half-a-dozen places in Essex may, however, be doubted, for the name Ulmar (*Wulfmaer*) was very common.[2] In general a plurality of origins is the mark of Eudo's fee. The list of his predecessors contains more than a score of unmistakably distinct names as well as some unnamed thegns, *liberi homines*, and sokemen. As a good many may well have been peasants, one cannot rule out the possibility that they included the commended men of some Saxon magnate whose forfeiture led to the incorporation of their lands in the same baronial estate after the Conquest. But the names of those whose men they were are sometimes recorded and they too are various—King Edward, Harold, Earl Waltheof, Earl Ælfgar, and Robert, son of Wimarc, besides Ulmar of Etone. Moreover, Eudo's specified predecessors include several Saxon landowners who were men of rank and substance—Ælfric Camp; a king's thegn named Godwin; another named Aschil, who is usually identified with 'Anschil of Ware'; and, in the case of three small properties in Cambridgeshire, no less a person than Earl Gyrth, the brother of King Harold.

Some of Eudo Dapifer's lands had not come to him when they were forfeited by their Saxon owners, but had previously been granted to Lisois de Moustiers, the 'bold knight', whose

---

[1] Dd. i, ff. 212, 212*b*; cf. ff. 132, 197*b*. Some of Ulmar's property passed to others.

[2] Round confidently identified them all with Ulmar of Etone: *V.C.H. Essex*, i. 492 n. 7; cf. 351–2. Ulmar 'of Etone' is, however, described as a king's thegn and never as a *liber homo*, while in Essex the latter description is employed in several cases and the former in none, though one of Eudo's other predecessors in that county was *Goduinus teinnus regis* (Dd. ii, f. 49*b*). Four clearly distinct persons named Ulmer appear among the inhabitants of Hesset and Tostock in Suffolk in the early Norman lists of Abbot Baldwin's 'Feudal Book' (D. C. Douglas, *Feudal Documents*, pp. 31, 33).

gallant enterprise at the crossing of the river Aire in 1069 or 1070 is commemorated by Orderic.[1] This man's fee certainly included elements in Norfolk, Suffolk, Essex, Cambridgeshire, and Bedfordshire, and the references to him in Domesday are so casual that he may well have owned other lands besides those in connexion with which he is mentioned.[2] He was living at the time of the Ely land-plea which took place between 1071 and 1075, but presumably died or incurred forfeiture before 1086, and probably Eudo received the whole of his English property.[3]

Though destined to attain to yet greater wealth before his death in 1120, Eudo Dapifer already figures in Domesday as a great landlord. The total value of his fee exceeded £380 and, besides the rural estates which are thus accounted for, he had 5 houses in Colchester, 3 in Hertford, and no less than 23 in Stamford.[4] He may therefore not unfairly be ranked as a landowner with the abbey of Ramsey, but there is no reason to suppose that the burden of knight service was particularly light in his case, and the contrary is suggested by the extent to which his lands were sub-infeudated.

The fee included elements in eleven counties, but the portions which lay in Norfolk, Northamptonshire, and Huntingdonshire were small, and those in Berkshire and Hampshire almost negligible in amount, while in the county of Lincoln there was nothing except the houses in Stamford. Measured by the Domesday values, more than half of the whole lay in Essex and Suffolk, and a third of it was contained in Bedfordshire, Cambridgeshire, and Hertfordshire. The Dapifer was thus essentially a landlord of the eastern and east midland counties. It is tempting to conjecture that his two outlying manors, Ashe in Hampshire and Losfield in Berkshire, were intended as convenient resorts for one whose official duties involved frequent attendance at court. Losfield was close to Windsor, where he held 2 hides of the royal manor; and Ashe, though 13 miles from Winchester, may have been one of the nearest places available since the environs

---

[1] *Hist. Eccles.*, ed. Le Prevost, ii. 195.

[2] Dd. i, ff. 197b, 212b; ii, ff. 49b, 239b, 240, 279b, 403.

[3] I.C.C., pp. 192–5. For evidence that he was regarded as Eudo's *antecessor* see Dd. i, f. 212b (Beeston); ii, ff. 240, 279b, 403; and, for the identification with Lisois de Moustiers, Dd. i, f. 197b (Gamlingay).

[4] The valuation figure in the text is exclusive of an ounce of gold entered as part of the value of Weeley in Essex: Dd. ii, f. 51. The house property is unvalued: ibid., f. 106; i, ff. 132, 336b.

of the city were so largely covered by the estates of the bishop and the monks of St. Swithun's.[1]

The lands of the fee were in general less widely dispersed than one might expect in view of the fact that it extended into so many counties. There was, it is true, no close concentration of manors comparable with that adjacent to Ramsey Abbey or with the block which Henry de Ferrers possessed near his castle of Tutbury. But in Bedfordshire Eudo had lands which he held in demesne in five contiguous parishes near the north-eastern border of the county, and though his Essex property included something in twelve different hundreds, the bulk of it lay in the north-west, dotted here and there from Arkesden and Radwinter in the north to Harlow and Shellow in the south.

The cases in which manor and vill coincided were comparatively few in number. There were not more than 19 of them, and 3 of these were probably mere hamlets that may well have been members of villages in which more than one tenant-in-chief had a part, while the estate clearly included land in between 50 and 60 villages where the lordship was divided. Yet a mere enumeration of this kind is rather misleading for it takes no account of the greater value and importance of the larger manors. And though various obscurities make exactness unattainable, it is probably safe to say that, apart from the house property in Stamford, Colchester, and Hertford, nearly half the entire estate, measured by the Domesday valuations, consisted of villages in which Eudo was the sole tenant-in-chief.

A large proportion of the whole was sub-infeudated. If some ambiguities in the Domesday text for Norfolk and Suffolk are interpreted in their most probable sense, it appears that the value of the lands granted out to tenants amounted to 38 per cent. of the total value of the fee, and if the East Anglian estates are excluded the figure works out at 44 per cent.[2] In Cambridgeshire and Northamptonshire rather more was sub-infeudated

---

[1] For the situation of Losfield see Farrer, *Honors and Knights' Fees*, iii. 268. The holding in Windsor is mentioned along with the holdings of other court officials: Dd. i, f. 56b. There was an orchard (*virgultum*) at Ashe which perhaps suggests a place of residence: *Cartularium Monasterii Sti Johannis de Colecestria*, ed. S. A. Moore (Roxburghe Club, 1897), i. 2.

[2] The figures may be compared with those for the estates of Ralph Paynel (some 33 per cent.), and the Winchester estates (20 per cent.). The chief difficulties arise from entries in which the scribes of the Little Domesday failed to distinguish between *tenet* and *tenuit*. No account has been taken of 2 hides at Hamerton in Hertfordshire which were held by 2 knights and are not separately valued.

than was retained in demesne, but in Suffolk nearly everything was retained.

The most valuable manors were not granted out. Of those that were, only Knebworth in Hertfordshire was worth as much as £10. But a few of the tenants had received lands in several places which together made a considerable estate. Difficulties of identification preclude certainty in the case of Richard de Sackvill, but if Farrer's conclusions are accepted, his holdings had a total value of some £54.[1] Those of Humphrey de Anslevill, which lay partly in Cambridgeshire and partly in Hertfordshire, were worth just over £23; and a man named Pirot appears as Eudo's tenant for lands in Cambridgeshire, Essex, Suffolk, and Bedfordshire which altogether were worth more than £19.[2] Only three of the named tenants seem to have belonged to the conquered people.[3]

The diminution of Eudo's estates through sub-infeudation was not balanced by his holdings as a mesne tenant. What he occupied in this way is indeed almost negligible; and even if one assumed that every mesne tenant in Domesday Book who is called Eudo was in fact the Dapifer, it would make no appreciable difference. The cases are few and the holdings minute.

Yet the lands retained in demesne were worth altogether about £227; and they appear to have been tilled by $185\frac{1}{2}$ plough-teams of which at least $57\frac{1}{2}$ were demesne teams, while the enumerated population consisted of 274 *villani*, 139 bordars, 19 cottars, 2 *rustici*, 101 serfs, some 35 *liberi homines*, 25 sokemen, a couple of knights, and 3 priests.[4] Ten substantial manors, each worth £12 or more, account for more than two-thirds of the total valuation.[5]

---

[1] Round points out that De Sackvill must have come from Secqueville-en-Bessin which is only some 7 miles from Eudo's ancestral home at Ryes.

[2] De Anslevill also had lands in Cambridgeshire worth nearly £15 as the tenant of Guy de Raimbercurt: they were in the near neighbourhood of Wimpole, where some of the land he held of Eudo was situated. Pirot, again, held lands worth £10 on the fee of Nigel de Aubigny.

[3] The only man of substance among these was one Turgis, who was Eudo's tenant at one of the Rodings and at Harlow in Essex of lands worth £8 in all, and also held at Latton, which adjoins Harlow, a little manor worth £3 as the tenant of Eudo's brother-in-law, Peter de Valognes.

[4] The enumerations are certainly not quite complete; but the number of serfs is probably too large, for at Newsells we read of *xxi servus* (Dd. i, f. 139), and the false concord, together with the disproportionately large number, points to textual error.

[5] *Cocclesworda* in Suffolk, though described as a berewick of Eriswell, is here reckoned as a separate manor: it was worth £24 (Dd. ii, f. 402b).

In 12 cases the demesne ploughs were 2 in number; but on 3 manors there were 3 of them, and on 4 manors (including the so-called berewick at *Cocclesworda* in Suffolk) there were 4, while Newsells in Hertfordshire could boast of 5. At several places there appear to have been no demesne ploughs at all.[1] Their absence, however, does not necessarily mean that there was no home farm. At Barley in Hertfordshire the only plough was one belonging to 4 *villani*, but there was a manorial demesne rated at more than a hide and a half, and we are told that this was tilled with the ploughs of Newsells, to which place it is closely adjacent.[2] On the other hand, at Brettenham in Norfolk the lord's interest was apparently limited to what he got from the *liberi homines* who occupied the land.[3]

The ratios between the demesne plough-teams and those of the peasants varied widely. At Tuddenham in Suffolk there were 2 of the former while the peasants had only a team and a half, but at Gamlingay the peasants had 15 teams as against 3 on the demesne.[4] In most cases a majority of the teams belonged to the peasants, but only at 5 places were they more than twice as numerous as the others.

From the livestock statistics provided by the Little Domesday for the counties of Norfolk, Suffolk, and Essex we learn that demesne sheep-farming on a large scale was practised at Eriswell in Suffolk and its unidentified berewick of *Cocclesworda*. Together, these two places maintained 1,680 demesne sheep, which is rather more than half the total number Eudo possessed in the three counties. But this was not a result of Norman enterprise, for their combined flocks had declined by more than four hundred since the Conquest.[5]

Such, in rough outline, were the English estates of Eudo Dapifer in 1086. But even more decisively than in the case of Ralph Paynel, the process by which he became a great English landlord was by no means complete by that time. He lived until 1120; and during the intervening years the misfortune of his brother Adam combined with royal favour to augment his wealth. Besides succeeding to most of Adam's lands, he acquired

---

[1] At Weeley in Essex the ploughs were evidently omitted in error (Dd. ii, f. 51).
[2] Dd. i, f. 139.   [3] Dd. ii, f. 239b.
[4] Ibid., f. 403; i, f. 197b.
[5] Perhaps the long hundred was employed in the enumeration: if so, the true figures would be larger than those given in the text. I can find no justification for Farrer's identification of *Cocclesworda* with Chelsworth.

many of the estates of Roger de Aubervill and of Sasselin.[1] William II gave him several manors.[2] Henry I gave him the castle and town of Colchester, a royal manor at Witham, and the three magnificent manors of Great Waltham, Saffron Walden, and Sawbridgeworth which had formerly belonged to Geoffrey de Mandeville and were valued in Domesday at sums amounting to £160.[3] On the other hand, Eudo did not retain everything that he had held in 1086. Besides a mass of tithes, several manors were included among the endowments he conferred upon the abbey of St. John at Colchester, which he founded—or refounded—in the last decade of the century. In particular he gave the abbey Weeley and Mundon, which were the most valuable of all the manors he had held in Essex at the time of the Domesday survey.[4] He died without heirs, and his fief, though long referred to as the Honour of Eudo Dapifer, was, as Round says, 'dislocated at his death', for, after reverting to the Crown, its constituent manors became the subjects of diverse new enfeoffments.[5]

[1] Farrer, op. cit. iii. 166.

[2] Davis, *Regesta*, Nos. 399, 435, 442; *Colchester Cart.* i. 18, 28.

[3] *Colchester Cart.* i. 22, 27; *Regesta*, ii, ed. C. Johnson and H. A. Cronne, 1956, Nos. 519, 552, 661; Round, *Geoffrey de Mandeville* (1892), pp. 328–9. The Mandeville manors were granted subject to the proviso that William, son of Geoffrey de Mandeville I, might recover them by paying Eudo the sum of £2,210. 3s., which he owed the king.

[4] *Colchester Cart.* i. 5. This is the inflated confirmation charter of 1119, but there is no reason to doubt what it says about these two manors. The early charters of the abbey are discussed by Round, *Geoffrey de Mandeville*, pp. 424–5; *E.H.R.* xvi (1901), 721–30, and in J. Armitage Robinson, *Gilbert Crispin* (1911), pp. 158–66.

[5] Round, *V.C.H. Essex*, i. 347–8, 491 n. 10. The subsequent history of the honour is traced in detail by Farrer, op. cit. iii. 164–295.

V

ESTATE MANAGEMENT I:
THE FARMING-OUT OF MANORS

No one can read even a few pages of Domesday Book without becoming aware of the distinction between manors which the tenants-in-chief held in demesne and manors held of them by their tenants. For the allocation of feudal rights and obligations this distinction was of fundamental importance; and the language of Domesday Book compels us to make it the basis of any descriptions of estates such as those attempted in the last two chapters. Moreover, though the survey seems primarily to be concerned with the fiefs of the tenants-in-chief inclusive of the manors they had granted out to tenants, and though this treatment of the material may well have been the most appropriate to the needs of a feudal monarchy, the historian of Anglo-Norman landlordism is bound to look, as it were, upwards rather than downwards, and to regard the land as divided among those who held the manors in demesne. To lay the emphasis in any other way would be to misrepresent the agrarian realities. For whether the immediate manorial lord was a humble knight, a great baron, a monastic corporation, or the king himself, it was this lord—the one holding the manor in demesne—whose will was dominant in its affairs. Whatever his position in the feudal hierarchy—whether he held the manor in chief of the Crown or was separated from the king by one or more stages of sub-infeudation—the primarily economic rights of a landlord belonged to him and he was the lord of the peasants who tilled the soil. In the mature jurisprudence of thirteenth-century England he could be regarded as the *verus dominus*, the real owner of the land, while his lord and that lord's lord were regarded as owning not the land itself, but 'seignories' over it.[1]

Yet to impose the legal conceptions of the thirteenth century, or even those of the age of Glanvil, upon the inchoate feudalism of the early Norman period would be highly anachronistic.[2] The

[1] Pollock and Maitland, op. cit. ii. 2–6.

[2] Stenton, *First Century*, pp. 9, 151–2; Galbraith, *E.H.R.* xliv (1929), 354–5
D. C. Douglas, *Econ. Hist. Rev.* ix (1939), 128–43.

brief statements of Domesday Book are liable to deceive us by their simplicity and uniformity. They tell us so little about the relations of lords and overlords, or about the relations of a lord to the peasantry on his demesne manors, that it is scarcely possible to understand what they say without amplifying and explaining it in the light of later evidence. But the danger of anachronism constantly threatens such a process. In particular, two tempting assumptions must be avoided. We must not assume that every lord who appears in Domesday as holding a manor held it by an hereditary title or with the precise rights and obligations that belonged to one or other of the free tenures recognized a century or so later—knight service, sergeanty, fee farm, or, in the case of church lands, frank almoin[1]. The systematic classification and definition of those tenures and their incidents were only gradually worked out in legal thought between the accession of Henry I and the death of Henry II. Secondly, we must not assume that the manorial lords of Domesday Book usually managed their estates by a system of demesne farming through bailiffs such as was common in the thirteenth century. In fact there is good reason to believe that many manors definitely described in Domesday as held in demesne were let out to a farmer on lease, and, further, that a sub-tenant who is referred to in Domesday in terms identical with those it employs about tenants by knight service might actually occupy a position which differed little, if at all, from that of such a farmer. This means, of course, that some shadow of doubt is thrown over the descriptions of estates given in previous chapters. It remains true, however, that the distinction between demesne manors and sub-infeudated manors is one of fundamental importance, that this distinction must be allowed for in any account of the distribution of landed property in Domesday England, and that there is no other way of allowing for it than by accepting the statements of Domesday at their face value. Nor is there any need to doubt the substantial truth of the statistical and geographical picture which is then presented to us. At the same time it must be recognized that the distinction between manors retained in demesne and those granted out to feudal

[1] I speak of fee farm and not of socage, for it was only in the later Middle Ages that the latter term (which properly belongs to the tenure of free peasants) was extended to include the tenures commonly described in the twelfth century by some variant of the term *feodifirma*: Pollock and Maitland, op. cit. i. 293; Holdsworth, *History of English Law*, iii (3rd ed.), 52–53.

sub-tenants was not in 1086 as definite and profound as it subsequently became; and also that, even where the intention of the scribe is free from obscurity, one cannot rely upon Domesday for absolute precision and consistency in the allocation of individual manors to one or the other class. In this matter, indeed, as in many other matters, the critical study of Domesday leads to the conclusion that it is in general trustworthy, but that one can seldom be quite certain whether a particular detail is accurate or not.

When we read in Domesday Book that a manor is held of X by Y we should no doubt as a rule understand this to mean that the manor has been sub-infeudated, or, in other words, that it has been granted to Y on a tenure which obliges him to perform services for X of the type ordinarily understood as feudal. Further, in view of the evidence collected by Round and the strong confirmation this has since received from other sources, it cannot be disputed that the service owed was very commonly some form of knight service.[1] As a general rule, again, we may take it that the tenures in question were, if not hereditary, tending in fact to become so. But that tenurial conditions had not yet settled down into regular forms, and that the bare statements of Domesday conceal a good deal of variety, clearly appears from the cases of two Domesday sub-tenants whose position is illuminated for us through the fortunate survival of documents giving detailed information of a kind that is not to be found in Domesday itself.

Roger de Lacy was an important baron with lands in several counties. At Holme Lacy in Herefordshire and at Onibury in Shropshire he appears in Domesday as a tenant of the Bishop of Hereford; and there is nothing in the entries recording these two tenancies which distinguishes them from innumerable other entries, or suggests that there was any difference between the two cases.[2] In fact, Roger had only a life interest in both these manors and he held Holme Lacy for the service of 2 knights and

---

[1] Round, *Feudal England*, pp. 295–308: for additional evidence see D. C. Douglas, *Feudal Documents*, especially pp. lxxxii–xcv.

[2] Of Holme Lacy we read 'Hanc terram tenet Rogerus de Laci sub episcopo', Dd. i, f. 181b; of Onibury, 'Isdem episcopus tenuit T.R.E. Aneberie et nunc tenet Rogerus de Laci de eo', ibid., f. 252. No significance should be attached to the use of the word *sub*, in place of the more usual *de*, in the former entry: see Jolliffe, *Constitutional History*, 1937, pp. 81, 140. Perhaps the scribe avoided *de* because the word formed part of Roger's surname, which in the Onibury entry was interpolated above the line.

Onibury for an annual rent of 20s., which is the figure given in Domesday as the value of that manor. It is indeed hard to see how Roger's tenure of Onibury differed from a farm for life. Yet at both places forces making for inheritability were clearly at work. Holme Lacy had been held by Roger's father, Walter de Lacy, before him, apparently on the same terms; and though Roger had to pay money and employ the influence of friends to get it regranted to himself, it subsequently became hereditary in his family.[1] It was much the same with Onibury though we are not told that Onibury had previously been held by Roger's father. Nearly a century after the two places were granted to Roger for life, we find one Hugh de Lacy acknowledging that he owes the service of 2 knights for Holme and a rent of 20s. for Onibury.[2] Even Walter, the original tenant of Holme Lacy, appears to have enjoyed rights of disposing of the land, which seem extraordinary in the case of a life tenant, for apparently he gave a *villanus* along with two-thirds of the tithe at Holme Lacy to the church of St. Peter at Hereford of which he was the founder.[3]

The other case comes from Wiltshire. In the Domesday account of Alton Priors in that county we are told that William Scudet holds 3 hides of the Bishop of Winchester.[4] But chance has preserved a notification from the Conqueror himself, from which we learn that William Escudet was the king's cook, that the Bishop of Winchester had at the king's request granted him the land in Alton Priors previously held by *Wluuardus Belgisone*, that William is to do service for this land to the bishop, and that after his death it is to revert to the monks of the cathedral— 'sine calumpnia alicuius hereditatis redeat in victum predict (orum) fratrum'.[5] What sort of service William had to render

---

[1] Galbraith, 'An Episcopal Land Grant of 1085', in *E.H.R.* xliv (1929), 353–72; and for the subsequent history of Holme Lacy see H. M. Colvin in *Medieval Studies Presented to Rose Graham*, ed. Ruffer and Taylor, 1950, pp. 15–40. The means that Roger employed to obtain the grant are described in these words: 'Hanc predictus miles videlicet Rogerus per amicos et per pecuniam requisivit.' Professor Galbraith remarks that Roger was really 'redeeming' his father's land in the way that was to be denounced in the second clause of Henry I's coronation charter.

[2] The text of this document, which is dated 1177, is printed by H. M. Colvin, op. cit., pp. 36–37.

[3] *Gloucester Cart.*, i. 85. Mr. Colvin is, I think, almost certainly right in identifying the *Hamme* of this text with *Hamme* (= Holme Lacy) in Herefordshire.

[4] Dd. i, f. 65b.

[5] 'Royal Charters to Winchester', ed. Galbraith, *E.H.R.* xxxv (1920), No. v, p. 387.

we do not know: perhaps he only took over the obligations of his Saxon predecessor. But here, again, we clearly have a tenure for life recorded in Domesday in terms which might easily be supposed to imply a permanent sub-infeudation; and in this case the tenure did not in fact become hereditary. Another document in the cartulary of Winchester Cathedral announces that William Giffard, Bishop of Winchester, has reseised the prior and monks of 3 hides in Alton and Patney which King William 'who conquered England' had borrowed for William Escudet so long as he lived.[1]

It would be easy to overrate the significance of these two cases for the general interpretation of Domesday Book. Though providing a salutary reminder that conditions were more various than the phraseology of Domesday suggests, they must not be regarded as typical. The lands in question were church lands earmarked for the support of the cathedral clergy, or, in the case of Onibury, of the bishop.[2] But there is reason to think that the churches were particularly reluctant to alienate such lands by permanent enfeoffments, while to most of the lay lords, on the other hand, the hereditary fee must have been familiar before they left their continental homes.[3] Moreover, it is generally believed that the earliest enfeoffments in England after the Conquest were made without the issue of a charter recording the conditions of the grant.[4] The written record would be most obviously needed if the conditions were in some way exceptional; and for this reason also it would be hazardous to regard the terms on which Holme Lacy and Alton Priors were granted as typical. In any case the emphatic language employed to limit those grants to a single life witnesses unmistakably to the strength of the tendency to inheritability.[5] In spite of that

[1] *Chartulary of Winchester Cathedral*, ed. A. W. Goodman, 1927, No. 220, which may be dated 1111–14: cf. No. 42 and Galbraith, *Royal Charters*, No. xxvi (op. cit., p. 392). Patney is not, I think, mentioned in Domesday: it lies within a mile or two of Alton Priors, but the parishes are not actually contiguous.

[2] Holme Lacy is described as *de victu canonicorum* in Domesday, Onibury as *de victu proprio episcopi* in the *Privilegium* of 1085, and Alton Priors as *de victu monachorum episcopalis ecclesie* in the Conqueror's charter.

[3] Galbraith, *E.H.R.* xliv (1929), especially pp. 353–5, 363–8; cf. Douglas, *Econ. Hist. Rev.* (May 1939), pp. 136–7.

[4] Round, *Feudal England*, pp. 257, 305; Vinogradoff, *English Society*, p. 227; Stenton, *First Century*, p. 152.

[5] The grant of Holme Lacy was made 'eo insuper adhuc tenore si Rogerus monachus efficiatur vel moriatur quod neque mater neque uxor neque filii neque fratres neque aliquis parentum suorum de hac terra supradicta se intromittant sed

emphasis the De Lacys managed to make their tenure of Holme Lacy and Onibury inheritable; and, as we have seen, a similar process of development can be discerned in the case of some of the tenants of Ramsey Abbey.[1] From the cartulary of Shrewsbury Abbey, again, we learn of several attempts to turn life tenancies into estates of inheritance; and a striking testimony both to the forces pulling in this direction and to the anxiety of the abbey to resist them, is provided by the account of a certain Rainald, son of Elieth, who voluntarily returned a hide that his father had held at farm and was given £10. 10s. by Abbot Godfrey as a reward for doing so.[2]

As a rough and ready generalization—subject to the warning that any statement of the kind is really an over-simplification— one might say that a feudal landlord could deal with his manors in one or other of three ways. He could grant them out to a feudal sub-tenant. He could manage them more or less directly and cultivate the demesnes for his own profit through his bailiffs. He could 'put them to farm', or, in other words, let them out to a *firmarius* for a rent. In feudal jurisprudence the important distinction was that between the first of these methods and the other two. When a lord sub-infeudated a manor he ceased to be its immediate lord; but if he leased it to a *firmarius* he still remained the lord of the manor and it continued to be one of his 'demesne manors'—as much so as if it was managed directly for his profit by his bailiff. But as regards the everyday social and economic relations of the peasantry to their superiors the important distinction was rather that between the second and third form of estate management. When the lord farmed his own

episcopus quicunque tunc erit ad proficuum sanctae ecclesiae et sui absque ulla contradictione qualis tunc fuerit recipiat'. For the Conqueror's charter about the reversion of the land at Alton Priors, see above, p. 108.

[1] Above, pp. 89–91.

[2] 'Rainaldus filius Elieth reddidit huic Ecclesiae et nobis unam hidam quam pater ejus aliquando habuerat ad firmam ex hac ecclesia. Et quia hoc spontanea voluntate fecit sine omni retractatione vel calumnia sui aut alicujus heredis dedit illi Godefridus Abbas Xli et Xs coram multis testibus' (*Collectanea Topographica et Genealogica*, i. 24–27). According to the *Monasticon* Godfrey was the second Abbot of Shrewsbury and died in 1128: *Mon. Ang.* iii. 514. Mr. Colvin (op. cit., p. 17 n. 3) has called attention to the memorandum containing this passage in connexion with the case of Rainer of Thonglands who had received some land from Fulchered the first abbot for life, but whose son tried to retain it. For an earlier and very striking illustration of the forces at work see the story of Ryhall and Belmesthorpe in Rutland as revealed in Kemble, *Cod. Dipl.*, No. dccccxxvii, with the sequel in Dd. i, f. 228.

demesnes he stood in a direct relation to the peasants and their affairs. When the manor was put to farm, the *firmarius* stood between them and their lord.

To grasp these distinctions, and to appreciate the difference of emphasis that should be attached to them by the student of feudal jurisprudence and by the social historian, is a necessary preliminary to an understanding of the historic realities. But we shall do violence to those realities if we rest satisfied with these facile classifications and fail to notice that in the early Norman period matters were in a state of flux. The distinctions were not sharply drawn. One type of estate management shades off into another; and the vagueness and hesitancy of Domesday Book may be closer to the actual facts than the attempts at clarification which the historian is bound to make in his effort to render the past intelligible. A life interest and an estate of inheritance are very different things; but, when a life interest is renewed in favour of the first tenant's son as was the case at Holme Lacy, the distinction loses some of its importance. Land granted in fee farm was to the lawyers of the Angevin period granted on an hereditary tenure for a perpetual rent just as land granted for knight service was granted for the perpetual obligation to perform that service: there was a world of difference between the legal position of one holding per *feodifirmam* and that of a *firmarius* who was a mere lessee.[1] But a *firmarius* might hold a lease for life and Roger de Lacy had but a life interest in Onibury for which he paid a money rent like any *firmarius*: none the less Onibury, as well as Holme Lacy, became hereditary in his family. We even find that Domesday, contrary to its usual practice, can come very near to implying in a Gloucestershire entry, that a manor ceased to be *in dominio* when it was put *ad firmam*.[2]

Occasionally a twelfth-century charter will even describe a tenancy for life or lives as a fee farm. Between 1113 and 1130

---

[1] That fee farm implied an heritable tenure is definitely asserted by Pollock and Maitland, op. cit. i. 293; by Holdsworth, op. cit. iii. 52; and, for Normandy, by Delisle, *Études sur la condition de la classe agricole et de l'état de l'agriculture en Normandie au Moyen-âge* (reprint of 1903), p. 45. Jolliffe (op. cit., p. 95) translates the term *feudofirma* as 'heritable farm'.

[2] Dd. i, f. 164 (Hempstead): 'Hoc manerium cepit W. comes in dominio et non fuit ad firmam. Sed modo vicecomes posuit eum ad lx solidos numero'; cf. f. 14*b* (Newington, Kent): 'Terra quae fuit in dominio est ad firmam pro lx solidis.' Henry I, in a charter of 1107-23, granted St. Suithun's 'theloneum de omnibus dominiis suis sive sint ad firmam sive in dominio', 'Royal Charters to Winchester, No. xxi', *E.H.R.* xxxv (1920), p. 393.

the Abbot of Gloucester granted Brampton in Herefordshire to
William Brito and his wife for their two lives *ad feodi firmam*.[1]
Sometime between 1153 and 1168 Abbot William II of St. Benet
of Holme granted the vill of Potter Heigham in Norfolk to a
tenant ' in feudo firma . . . quamdiu vixerit'.[2] And though tenure
by knight service and tenure in fee farm came to be sharply distinguished, Domesday itself is witness that in the Conqueror's
reign it was possible for a man to hold land by a tenure which
required him both to render knight service and to pay a money
rent.[3] For the purposes of economic analysis (to take another
point) there is a fundamental contrast between a system of demesne farming, in which the chances of profit and loss remain,
with the direct management of the estate, in the hands of the
lord, and a system in which these things passed to a *firmarius*
holding the demesne in lease while the lord received a fixed
rent. Yet the methods of demesne farming that obtained in the
thirteenth and fourteenth centuries on the estates of the Cathedral Priory of St. Swithun's at Winchester afford an example
of an intermediate condition, which meant that much of the
'risk-bearing', along with at least some chance of half-illegiti-
mate profits, was transferred to the reeves or sergeants who acted
as farm-managers.[4] Whether methods of this sort were ever
employed in the early Norman period we cannot say; but the

---

[1] *Gloucester Cart.*, ii. 113.

[2] *Register of St. Benet of Holme*, ed. J. R. West (Norfolk Record Soc., 1932),
i. 105–6, No. 190; cf. No. 257. What appears to be another example comes from
another manor of the same abbey. Between 1127 and 1134 Richard Basset was
granted the manor of Heigham next Norwich *ad firmam* for life (ibid., appendix E),
but in a deed by which he surrendered his right, some time before 1154, he speaks
of 'Hecham quam tenebam de eis in feodo ad firmam' (ibid., No. 157). For what
may be a later literary employment of the term fee farm in the case of a grant for
two lives, see *Gesta Abbatum* (Rolls Series), i. 72. But the writer may be quoting from
a twelfth-century document.

[3] The Domesday account of Long Ditton in Surrey which was held by Wadard
of Bishop Odo concludes with the statement: 'Ille qui tenet de Wadardo reddit
ei l solidos et servitium unius militis' (i, f. 32). At *Cumbe* in Kent, which was also
held by Wadard of Odo, a similar tenure is probably implied by the statement that
the place was worth £4 and the service of one knight (f. 10b). Sundridge, in the
same county, 'reddit xxiii libras et unum militem in servitio Archiepiscopi'
(f. 3). For what appears to be another case of slightly later date see *Chron. Rams.*,
pp. 234, 257 (Nos. 241 and 282). But such mixed tenures are not confined to the
early Norman period: for a Lincolnshire example from Henry II's reign see the
charters of Walter and Hugh Bek printed by Miss D. M. Williamson, *Lincolnshire
Archit. and Arch. Soc. Reports and Papers*, iv (new series), pt. i (1951), p. 49.

[4] J. S. Drew, 'Manorial Accounts of St. Swithun's Priory, Winchester', *E.H.R.*
lxii (1947), 20–41.

possibility should not be ignored. In the alternative case of leasehold farming, the evidence, as we shall see, suggests that the early leases were of the type known as the 'stock and land lease'—the lord providing some of the working capital in the form of stock and thus being more deeply implicated in the business of farming than is suggested by the modern associations of the term 'leasehold'.

The study of estate management in Norman England is not an easy matter. Floating mists often obscure the historian's vision of the landscape. But a cautious exploration of the ground is possible. And the Kentish lands of the Conqueror's half-brother, Odo, Bishop of Bayeux, afford a good starting-point. The description of these estates occupies nearly six folios of Domesday Book; and Kelham, rashly venturing on a count, reckoned that they comprised 184 distinct properties.[1] In fact the elements they included are too various for a satisfactory enumeration to be made. Small tenements assessed at a *jugum* or less and worth only a few shillings cannot properly be counted as units along with the great manor of Folkestone which was valued at more than £145. It is clear, however, that a great majority of the manors and other properties had been granted out to tenants: only in seven places is the bishop described as holding in demesne.[2] But Domesday fortunately enables us in this case to get beyond the simple division into demesne manors and sub-infeudated manors and not only shows us that many of those granted out to tenants paid a fixed rent—so that we must regard them either as held of the bishop by a tenure approximating to fee farm or else as being farmed out by the mesne lords —but also makes it clear that nearly all those described as held in demesne were in fact put to farm. These two points must be considered separately.

In the first place, of 14 substantial manors held by named tenants we are told that they render a sum of money—or at least a sum expressed in money terms—and this sum is in every case

[1] Robert Kelham, *Domesday Book Illustrated* (1788), p. 25. Miss Neilson considers this figure to be 'probably too low': *V.C.H. Kent*, iii. 188.

[2] Neilson (op. cit., p. 190) says: 'Eight manors were held in demesne; in the rest tenants were enfeoffed by the bishop.' I suppose that she made the number eight by including *Dene* (Dean Court) which was in the king's hands in 1086, though Adelold had previously held it of the bishop (f. 10b). The seven demesne manors and their values were as follows: Hoo, £60 (f. 8b); Bilsington, £50 (f. 10b); Elham, £40 (f. 9b); Wickhambreux, £30 (f. 9); *Burnes*, £12 (f. 9); Hardres, £7 (f. 9); and Stelling, £2 (f. 9).

greater than the value assigned to the estate.[1] The tenant of one
of these manors—Lessness—was Robert Latin (or Latimer as he
is called in the Domesday Monachorum), and this man also
appears as Odo's tenant in respect of 5 other manors, which,
unlike the 14 just mentioned, are described as held *ad firmam*.[2]
In the case of two of them—Tottington and Bromfield—the
present and former values are given in the ordinary way and
nothing is said about the amount of the farm or rent; but for the
others the amounts due are stated and are in each case greater
than the present value.[3] Again a man named Robert, who is
evidently the same person as Robert Latin, is stated to hold both
Teston and Bensted *ad firmam*: we are told the values of both,
but no figures are given for the rents.[4] Yet another manor,
Ringleton, is described as held *ad firmam* by Herbert: it is valued
at £8 yet renders £13.[5]

Now it is hard to say whether the statements about these 8
manors being at farm should be understood as indicating tenurial conditions materially different from those obtaining on the
14 other rented manors. Perhaps they were let on a less per-

---

[1] The fourteen manors are Lessness, Plumstead, and Chelsfield (f. 6b); Peckham
and Leeds (f. 7b); Allington (ff. 7b–8); the two Suttons and Turnham (f. 8); Chalk
(ff. 8b–9); the two Ewells, Swanton, and Knowlton (f. 11). Their renders range from
£4 to £35. Usually the phrase employed is 'et tamen reddit', but in four cases
'et tamen qui tenet reddit'. Besides these manors, a *jugum* in *Pinpa*, held of the
bishop by Adam and valued at 10s., pays 15s. (f. 8b). In addition, similar statements relating to former conditions are made in regard to three manors of which
Fulbert is described as tenant: Barham was worth £40 when the bishop received it
'et tamen reddebat ei c libras' (f. 9b); Chilham is worth £30 'et tamen reddebat
episcopo baiocensi quater xx libras et xl solidos' (f. 10); and Eastling is worth
£4 'et tamen episcopus habuit viii libras' (f. 10b). Of *Dodeham*, also held by
Fulbert, we read: 'T.R.E. valebat x lib Episcopus misit ad firmam pro x libris
quando fulbertus recepit vi lib et modo similiter' (f. 10b).

[2] The five manors are Tottington (f. 7), Bromfield and the lost Harbilton (f. 8),
Chatham and Boxley (f. 8b). Robert Latin also held some land in Summerdene
Hundred 'et inde reddit Rotbertus de firma vi libras' (f. 11b). Of this land, or
some of it, we are told 'De novo dono episcopi habet in manu regis de Ricardo
filio Gisleberti comitis'. This puzzling statement invites comparison with the entry
about Tottington: 'Rotbertus Latinus tenet ad firmam de Rege Totintune de novo
dono episcopi'—also with the entry 'Herbertus tenet ad firmam de rege Ringetone.
De feudo est episcopi' (f. 11).

[3] The variation in the terms employed should be noted—'et tamen est ad
firmam pro iiii libris' (Harbilton); 'et tamen Rotbertus reddit lv libras' (Boxley);
and the ordinary formula 'et tamen reddit' (Chatham).

[4] f. 8b. That the tenant was Robert Latin is made almost certain by the fact that
both places had previously been held of Bishop Odo by Adelold, who was Robert
Latin's predecessor at Harbilton and Bromfield.

[5] f. 11.

manent tenure. Perhaps, on the other hand, it is only an accident of Domesday phraseology that has vouchsafed a more precise description in their case.[1] But it is at least certain that 22 of the manors held by Odo's tenants were let for a fixed rent, which, in 18 cases, is at least expressed in money. Of this we have direct evidence; and indirect evidence carries us some way farther. There is some ground for thinking it probable that other tenanted manors besides these were in fact let in the same way. Tottington, Bromfield, Teston, and Bensted, as we have seen, were all held at farm; but Domesday gives us no information about the amount of the rents for which they were let. For the 18 other manors, 4 of which are described as held at farm, the amount of the rent is stated, and on all 18 exceeds the valuation. The compilers of Domesday were evidently interested in recording the rents where this was the case: it was a matter with a possible bearing on the taxability of the estate. It seems probable that the rents are not stated for Tottington, Bromfield, Teston, and Bensted because they did not exceed the valuation. But manors which resemble these in being described as held at farm form a minority of those whose rents are stated. Hence it is unlikely that these four manors were the only rented manors on Odo's Kentish estates on which the relation of rent and value was not such as to lead to the amount of the rent being recorded, and we may therefore regard it as probable that the rented manors, besides the 22 for which we have direct evidence, included some of those whose descriptions in Domesday make no reference either to a rent being due or to the manor being held at farm, but are as reticent on these matters as the Domesday description of Onibury. As we have seen, it is only the grant of 1085 which tells us that Onibury was rented and that the rent was the same as the Domesday valuation.[2]

For Odo's demesne manors the evidence is clear and compelling. Of the 7 manors which he is stated to hold in demesne, 5 are described as rendering a specified sum: in the case of one of the 5—Hoo—we are told that 'he who holds it' makes this render, and another—Bilsington—is said to render £70 *de firma*. On all 5 manors the rent exceeded the value. Moreover, between the descriptions of two of them—Hardres and *Burnes*—there

---

[1] As we shall see later, there is in fact reason for thinking the latter alternative the more probable.
[2] Above, pp. 107–8.

is an entry relating to Stelling: the bishop holds it in demesne and it is worth 40s.; but nothing is said about any render. Yet these three entries are immediately followed by the statement: 'Haec tria Maneria episcopi Baiocensis tenet Rannulfus ad firmam.'[1] It is therefore certain that all but one of the manors which Odo held in demesne in Kent were in fact let for a rent; and we have further confirmation of the conclusions suggested by the evidence from the manors held by named tenants—that the rents are only stated where these exceeded the value, and that some manors were let for a rent though Domesday says nothing about it. We also have here additional grounds for thinking that when Domesday tells us that a place renders so many pounds, it means much the same thing that is meant by saying that the manor is 'at farm'.[2]

The normality of conditions on the lands of the Bishop of Bayeux must not, however, be too readily assumed. Odo had been in disgrace since 1082 and there can be little doubt that his estates, if not actually forfeited, were at least, as Ellis says, 'under sequestration'.[3] It would therefore be plausible to suppose that the arrangements obtaining in 1086 were partly of the nature of temporary expedients and in particular this might not unreasonably be suspected in regard to the farming out of demesne manors. But such considerations cannot diminish the value of the evidence cited above for the interpretation of Domesday terminology. And in fact, when we turn from Odo's fee to the *Terra Regis* and the great ecclesiastical estates which

---

[1] f. 9. There can be no doubt that the sentence refers to the manors dealt with in the three preceding entries: a reference to what follows seems to be precluded by the fact that one of the three following entries relates to some houses held by Adam, son of Hubert.

[2] Since the argument in the text is based partly on the contention that the renders of manors are only given where they exceed the valuation, it should be noted that this refers only to properties which are valued. Renders only are sometimes given for house property, for lands held by *villani*, and for subordinate holdings which are not separately valued: e.g. Luddlesdown (f. 7b), Buckland (f. 10b), Barfreston (f. 9b). Throughout the description of Odo's Kentish estates the rule holds good that renders and values are both given for manors only when the render is greater than the value. The nearest approaches to an exception are provided by entries relating to a *jugum* at Oare (f. 10) and to 40 acres in Bewsborough Hundred (f. 11b). The first contains the statement 'Hanc tenent iii villani ad firmam et reddunt xx solidos et tantundem semper valuit.' The second says: 'Ibi est unus villanus reddens v solidos et tantum valet.' But neither concerns a whole manor: both relate to small properties rented by *villani* and similar to those for which renders only are given.

[3] Ellis, op. cit. i. 5. The evidence is inconclusive.

occupy nearly all the rest of Kent we find a very similar condition of affairs.

It is true that on the lands of the four lay tenants-in-chief—Hugh de Montfort, Count Eustace, Richard, son of Gilbert, and Haimo the Sheriff—there is no trace of manors being at farm or paying a rent.[1] But of the four large royal manors, three were evidently let out at fixed rents.[2] And a 'farm system' was widely employed on the estates of the Church of Canterbury. Though the archbishop is represented as tenant-in-chief of all of them, the Domesday description is divided into three portions—the demesne manors of the archbishop, the lands of his knights, and the lands of the monks. The first section comprised some two dozen distinct estates (besides the borough of Sandwich, some burgesses in Canterbury and Romney, and certain subordinate properties); and in this section we find twelve or, if we include a subordinate estate at Lympne, thirteen cases of renders exceeding the valuation, while for *Nortune* and Aldington renders are mentioned in place of any present values and Sandwich is described as paying a 'farm'.[3] In the other two sections values only are given in most cases, but at three places belonging to the knights and five places belonging to the monks we read of renders exceeding the valuations and at Adisham, which was one of the monks' manors, we are told the present render but only the former values. On the lands of the Bishop of Rochester, which afford a striking contrast to those of Odo of Bayeux in that none of the manors appears to have been sub-infeudated, values only are stated in most cases, but for Southfleet, Stone, Bromley, and Stoke renders are also given which at each place exceed the valuation. It is much the same with the abbey of St. Augustine: most of its manors are merely valued, but renders as

[1] I am not taking into account small subordinate holdings such as the mill in Bewsborough Hundred for which Fulbert rendered 24s. to Hugh de Montfort (f. 13b). Apart from that of Odo, which should no doubt be regarded as a lay estate though he happened to be a bishop, none of the lay estates in Kent was very large.

[2] At Aylesford the render exceeded the value, but at Milton it was apparently less than the figure given as the value of that manor. Of Dartford we read that the English valued it at £60 but that the French reeve 'who holds it at farm' put the value at £90 yet paid sums which add up to £87. 13s. 2d., though as £70 of this was paid in weighed money it may represent rather more than the reeve's valuation.

[3] That the first section comprised only demesne manors is clear both from the arrangement which separates this section from the *Terra Militum*, and from the lack of all reference to named tenants except in the case of subordinate holdings. But it may also be noted that nine of the estates which paid renders are specifically described as held by the archbishop *in dominio*.

well as values are given for three of them (the renders being in every case greater than the values) and at *Platenort* a valuation, past and present, of 20*s.* is followed by the statement 'tamen appreciatur XL solidis eo quod sit ad firmam'.[1] The estates of St. Martin of Dover present a different picture. We are told that the 'prebends' were held in common in the time of King Edward and had then paid £61 *inter totum*, but were divided by the Bishop of Bayeux; and the descriptions that follow show them in the hands of individual canons and give their values without any reference to renting, though rents instead of values are given for some miscellaneous properties. Nowhere in the Kentish section of Domesday is a render as well as the present value stated for a manor except where these differ; and then the render is almost invariably greater than the valuation.[2]

Some more light on these matters can be obtained from a comparison of Domesday with the alternative text contained in the so-called Domesday Monachorum of Canterbury—a text which deals with the Kentish estates of the archbishopric, the monks of Canterbury, and the bishopric of Rochester.[3] In this the render of Domesday is frequently described as a *firma*.[4] But, further, the Domesday Monachorum sometimes tells us about the farm in cases where Domesday Book says nothing to suggest that the manor was at farm. Thus Brook, valued at £4 in both texts, is described in the Domesday Monachorum as held *ad firmam* by Robert of Romney.[5] For Appledore, again,

---

[1] Dd. i, f. 12*b*.

[2] There were three tenants-in-chief in Kent besides those dealt with in the text, but each had only one manor. Values only are given for Lewisham, which belonged to St. Peter of Ghent, and for the Battle Abbey manor of Wye, but the Wye values are stated with a precision that suggests actual renders, the current value being defined as £100 *ad numerum* (ibid., f. 11*b*). Of Albert the Chaplain's manor of Newington, we are told that the land which was in demesne is at farm for 60*s.* (ibid, f. 14*b*).

[3] *The Domesday Monachorum of Christ Church, Canterbury*, ed. D. C. Douglas. The text in question extends from f. 2*v* to f. 5*r* of the manuscript (pp. 81–98 of Professor Douglas's edition). It is a contemporary Domesday 'satellite' and the existing manuscript is dated *c.* 1100 by the editor.

[4] Malling, Wrotham, and Gillingham (Dd. i, f. 3, 3b; Dd. Mon., pp. 87, 85) are examples of this among the archbishop's demesne manors, while the estates of his knights and of the monks provide instances at Lenham (*Lerham*), Orpington, and Westwell (Dd. i, ff. 4, 4*b*, 5; Dd. Mon., pp. 93, 94, 91), and we find the same thing on the estates of the bishopric of Rochester at Southfleet, Stone, and Bromley (Dd. i, f. 5*b*; Dd. Mon., p. 96). The references for the Domesday Monachorum are to the pages of Professor Douglas's edition.

[5] Dd. i, f. 5; Dd. Mon., p. 92.

Domesday Book gives only a valuation of £16. 17s. 6d., but the Domesday Monachorum states that Robert of Romney holds the manor at farm and that it is worth £12 but renders £16. 16s. 7d.[1] For Boughton under Blean, Domesday provides a *valet* of £30. 16s. 3½d.; the Domesday Monachorum speaks of its rendering a *firma* which together with the archbishop's *gablum* amounts to £30. 15s. 3d.[2] Yet the Domesday valuation of a farmed manor was not always a comprehensive figure including, as in this last case, other payments besides the farm if such were due. The survey which supplies the facts just noted is followed in the Domesday Monachorum by a schedule of manors and the farms and other payments that they owed. This schedule is a baffling text, for there are numerous and large discrepancies between its figures and those given by the survey which precedes it and by Domesday Book.[3] But a few manors exhibit some correspondences which seem to indicate that Domesday is not always consistent, either in its valuations or when it tells us that a manor renders a certain sum; the content of both sets of figures apparently varied, more being included in some cases than in others. Thus for Wingham both Domesday and the Domesday Monachorum survey give a value of £100 and say nothing about the manor being at farm, but the schedule mentions a *firma* of £100, *gablum* of £29. 10s., and 'customs' amounting to something over £3.[4] For Northfleet, again, Domesday Book gives a render of £37. 10s. and the survey says that he who holds this manor renders £37 *de firma*, while the schedule tells us of a *gablum* of more than £10 and of a payment of 20s. due to the archbishop as well as of the farm of £37.[5] A similar state of affairs is revealed at Pagham in Sussex. Domesday values this manor at £60 and states that it renders £80 *sed nimis grave est*: in the schedule we read of the farm of £80, *gablum* of £8, and

---

[1] Dd. i, f. 5; Dd. Mon., p. 91.

[2] Dd. i, f. 3b; Dd. Mon., p. 85.

[3] The schedule is confined to the demesne manors of the archbishop and includes all those which he held (wholly or partly) in demesne in Kent, Surrey, Middlesex, and Sussex, with the exception of Pluckley and Mersham in Kent. Manors that were *de victu* or *de vestitu monachorum* are not included; and it is noteworthy that the Domesday Monachorum survey describes Mersham as a manor of the monks (p. 91) though Domesday treats it as a demesne manor of the archbishop. Perhaps the exclusion of Pluckley is due to a sub-infeudation subsequent to 1086; but the schedule is in a hand of c. 1100—the same hand as the survey. There is another copy of it in Lambeth MS. 1212, pp. 353–4.

[4] Dd. i, f. 3b; Dd. Mon., pp. 83, 98.

[5] Dd. i, f. 3; Dd. Mon., pp. 86, 99.

'customs' of £3.[1] On the other hand, both Domesday and the survey in the Domesday Monachorum say that Bexley renders £30. 8s., while the schedule puts the farm at £26 but mentions three other payments, which, added to this farm, make the total precisely £30. 8s.[2] One is tempted to speculate whether these puzzling variations are merely due to careless inconsistency or whether they reflect actual differences in the terms on which the manors were farmed—such payments as the *gablum* being in some cases included in the farm and in others paid directly to the lord—but there is nothing in the schedule itself to support the hypothesis that real differences are involved. As regards the question with which we are mainly concerned, however, its testimony is perfectly clear. It shows that the farming-out system was much more extensively employed on the archbishop's demesne manors than we should gather either from Domesday Book or from the survey in the Domesday Monachorum. The schedule consists of twenty-six items and these cover a somewhat larger number of manors as several of them relate to a pair of manors.[3] In twenty-five items a farm is specifically mentioned, and as the remaining case is precisely similar in all other respects, it seems likely that the difference is due to omission of the words *de firma* by a scribal error. But what is really significant is that a farm measured and apparently payable in money, was due from sixteen places in regard to which no mention either of a farm or of a render is to be found in Domesday Book or in the survey of the Domesday Monachorum. And it is the same story with the manors of the monks. For these, additional evidence is supplied by another Canterbury manuscript which contains a schedule of the farms of the monks 'quas bone memorie lanfrancus archiepiscopus sic constituit et ordinavit tam de maneriis que reddunt bladum et denarios quam de illis que reddunt denarios tantum'.[4] I have not been able to identify all the places in this list; but it unmistakably indicates that, among manors

---

[1] Dd. i, f. 16b; Dd. Mon., p. 99.

[2] Dd. i. f. 3; Dd. Mon., pp. 86, 99. The entry in the schedule runs: 'Bixle de firma xxvi libras et xx solidos archiepiscopo. Gablum lxiii solidos. Ad elemosinam v solidos.'

[3] The division into twenty-six items is obscured by the way the extended text is printed, but is obvious in the manuscript, as the facsimile shows (f. 5v).

[4] Canterbury Register K, ff. 69v, 70r. I owe my knowledge of this text to the scholarship and kindness of Mr. P. H. Sawyer. There is another copy of the schedule in Lambeth MS. 1212, p. 344.

for which neither Domesday nor the Domesday Monachorum
gives any hint of a farm or render, farms measured in months,
weeks, or days and paid largely in kind were paid by at least
7 manors in Kent, 3 in Essex, a couple in Surrey, and a couple
in Suffolk, and further that money farms were received from
2 such manors in Kent, 2 in Essex, 2 in Buckinghamshire, and
1 in Surrey.[1]

Wherever one can bring these matters to the test the evidence
points to the same conclusion. According to a well-known list,
preserved in two versions in the muniments of St. Paul's Cathedral,
farms measured in months, weeks, or days were in the time of
Wulman, the first post-Conquest dean, payable to the canons
from 16 manors, of which 10 were in Essex, 3 in Hertfordshire,
2 in Middlesex, and 1 in Surrey.[2] All but one of these can be
identified in Domesday Book, but Domesday, while telling us
the value of these estates, says nothing to suggest that any of
them owed farms.[3] Again, a collection of miscellaneous memoranda relating to the abbey of Bury St. Edmunds and apparently
dating from the latter part of the eleventh century, provides us
with two accounts of food farms due to the abbey from a number
of its estates in East Anglia and shows these estates combined in thirteen groups, each of which rendered a month's
farm.[4] But the descriptions of these places in Domesday contain
no reference to these arrangements: we read in them of values
not of renders. And the examples from Essex and East Anglia
prove that the Little Domesday, in spite of its greater detail, is
like the Great Domesday in this respect. At the other end of

[1] Of these manors those paying food farms were Hollingbourne, East Farleigh,
Peckham, Meopham, Ickham, Monkton, and Mersham in Kent; Lawling, Milton
Hall, and Bocking in Essex; Merstham and Cheam in Surrey; and Hadleigh and
Monk's Eleigh (?) in Suffolk. The money-paying manors were Preston and Cliffe
(Kent); Stisted and Southchurch (Essex); Halton and Monks Risborough (Bucks.);
and Walworth (Surrey). The sums stated to be due from Halton and Monks Ris-
borough exactly equal the Domesday valuations of those places.

[2] *Domesday of St. Paul's*, pp. xxxix, 152. Caddington, one of the Hertfordshire
manors, has been transferred to Bedfordshire. In the list Luffenhall is combined
with Sandon.

[3] The unidentified manor, Sutton in Middlesex, is probably that which Domesday describes as held by the canons *de victu* in the vill of Fulham (i, f. 127b); in
this case too it gives only valuations.

[4] D. C. Douglas, *E.H.R.* xliii (1928); A. J. Robertson, *Anglo-Saxon Charters*,
No. civ, pp. 194–7, 198–201. Professor Douglas, to whom we owe the first publication of this important text, speaks of the manors as arranged in twelve groups, but
both the lists in the document in fact contain thirteen groups. Presumably the
months were months of four weeks.

southern England additional evidence is supplied by the Exon. Domesday. In that text the word *reddit* is not infrequently employed where Domesday Book uses the word *valet*. Cornwall and Devon, Somerset and Dorset all provide examples not only from ecclesiastical but also from lay estates.[1] Since the similar cases cited from the south-eastern counties were necessarily limited to church lands—because the texts which provide the alternative readings relate only to ecclesiastical estates—this south-western evidence for manors in lay hands deserves emphasis. In Somerset I have noted cases where Exon. has *reddit* in place of the *valet* of Domesday on the estates of thirteen lay tenants-in-chief.[2] Especially interesting is Exon.'s account of one of the lesser landowners of Somerset, a certain Eschelin or Schelin, who had a small *mansio* at Foddington; for while Domesday merely tells us that this was formerly and is now worth 20s., the Exon. text is 'reddit per annum XX solidos et quando Escelinus accepit ad firmam de rege valebat tantundem'.[3] It is also noteworthy that in the Exon. text an original *valet* has sometimes been altered into *reddit* or an original *reddit* altered into *valet*.[4] If we could be sure that these were intelligent corrections, their occurrence would indicate that the compilers of Exon., unlike the compilers

---

[1] For Cornwall, see, for instance, *Pavtone*, Dd. i, f. 120b, Exon., p. 181 (Bishop of Exeter), and Stratton, Dd. i, f. 121b, Exon., p. 216 (Count of Mortain)—for Devon, *Hame*, Dd. i, f. 103b, Exon., p. 165 (Abbot of Tavistock), and *Tresetone*, Dd. i, f. 108b, Exon., p. 294 (Judhael of Totnes)—for Somerset, Pitminster, Dd. i, f. 87b, Exon., p. 161 (Bishop of Winchester), and Lydiard Punchardon, Dd. i, f. 96, Exon., p. 342 (William de Moion)—for Dorset, Bloxworth, Dd. i, f. 77b, Exon., p. 34 (Cerne Abbey), and *Waia* (? Broadway), Dd. i, f. 83b, Exon., p. 48 (wife of Hugh the son of Grip).

[2] These are William de Moion, cited in the preceding note, Count Eustace (*Contitone*, Dd. i, f. 91b, Exon., p. 263), Earl Hugh (Henstridge, Dd. i, f. 91b, Exon., p. 264), the Count of Mortain (Shepton Beauchamp, Dd. i, f. 91b, Exon., pp. 245–6), Baldwin of Exeter (Hemington, Dd. i, f. 93, Exon., p. 294), Roger de Corcelle (Idson in Stogursey, Dd. i, f. 93b, Exon., p. 397), Roger Arundel (Hewish Champflower, Dd. i, f. 94b, Exon., p. 412), Ralph de Mortemer (Walton in Gordano, Dd. i, f. 96b, Exon., p. 416), Alured de Ispania (Quantock, Dd. i, f. 97b, Exon., p. 352), Turstin, son of Rolf (Compton Pauncefoot, Dd. i, f. 97b, Exon., p. 359), Eschelin (Foddington, Dd. i, f. 99, Exon., p. 432), Edmund, son of Pagan (*Picote*, Dd. i, f. 98b, Exon., p. 444), and Gilbert, son of Turold (Ubley, Dd. i, f. 98, Exon., p. 415).

[3] Dd. i, f. 99, Exon., p. 432. My attention was called to this case by Professor Galbraith.

[4] For example, Horwood, Devon, p. 315; Westowe, Somerset (p. 400), where *reddit* is substituted for *valet*, and Nether Stowey (*Estalueia*) and Ely (*Illege*) in Somerset (pp. 350, 398), where *valet* is substituted for *reddit*. In the description of the Cerne Abbey estates in Dorset, *valet* has been altered to *reddit* in every case except Poxwell (pp. 33–36).

of Domesday Book, intended to make a real distinction between the terms and were interested in recording renders where these were due. In that case we might be able to set an approximate limit to the practice of letting manors for fixed rents in these south-western counties. But it is impossible to exclude the possibility that the corrections were made by a clerk of greater accuracy than intelligence who was checking the existing manuscript of Exon. with an original in which the terms were employed indifferently, so that the copyist who wrote Exon. was really justified in a literal inexactness which the checker thought it necessary to correct.

For the greater part of the country only the evidence of the Exchequer Domesday is available. But that evidence can now be interpreted more surely. For it is now clear, first, that the *reddit* of Domesday indicates the payment of a definite rent or farm and not the actual or estimated profits of direct exploitation by the lord, and secondly, that the renting of manors must have been a good deal more prevalent than we should gather from the specific references to it in the Exchequer text. Owing to variations in Domesday terminology and the difficulty of drawing a line between estates that might properly be regarded as small manors and merely subordinate holdings, the Domesday evidence is scarcely susceptible of statistical summarization. On the royal estates, manors clearly described as being at farm or as owing a render can be found in twenty-five out of the thirty-four counties surveyed; and in several of these counties—for example, in Buckinghamshire, Worcestershire, and Devon, all, or almost all, the royal manors are described in this way.[1] Of the remaining nine counties, Cheshire and Shropshire contained no royal estates; and in Middlesex the king had only a few acres of 'No man's land' (*nanesmaneslande*), a vineyard, and a few rent-paying cottars; while the wasted condition of Yorkshire makes it an exceptional case. Besides little Rutland and partly-wasted Staffordshire, the only other counties in

---

[1] Some doubt may be felt about Warwickshire, which I have included among the twenty-five. But Domesday tells us what that county renders 'inter firmam regalium Maneriorum et placita', and a render seems to be implied by an entry about Brailes—'T.R.E. reddebat xvii libras et x solidos. Modo valet lv libras et xx summas salis'—while of *Cotes* we read: 'Haec terra cum burgo de Waruuic et tercio denario placitorum sirae reddebat T.R.E. xvii libras. Quando Robertus recepit ad firmam valebat xxx libras. Modo tantundem cum omnibus quae ibi pertinent.' Dd. i, f. 238.

which precise statements about renders or farms are lacking from the description of the *terra regis* are the counties of Lincoln, Nottingham, and Huntingdon, and in each of these one or more entries may well be regarded as implying that a render was due.[1] It is in fact generally accepted that a system of farms prevailed on the demesne manors of the Crown; and the real problem is concerned with the lands of others. For them the information supplied by Domesday is curiously uneven. In eight contiguous counties—those of Worcester, Warwick, Leicester, Rutland, Nottingham, Lincoln, Northampton, and Huntingdon—unequivocal statements about farms or renders appear to be wholly wanting, and this is also the case with Hertfordshire, while in several counties which are neighbours of this central group the evidence is very scanty.[2] On the other hand, references to farms or renders are comparatively numerous in each of the counties surveyed in the Little Domesday—Norfolk, Suffolk, and Essex—and also in Shropshire, in Surrey, and Sussex, and, to an exceptional degree, both in Hampshire and, as we have seen, in Kent. In view of the geographical dispersion of the greater fees it is perhaps permissible to conjecture that this grouping of the evidence reflects differences in the amount of information which different groups of Domesday commissioners decided to record rather than regional differences in estate management. In Domesday itself, in spite of all its deficiencies in this matter, we find references to farms or renders on a great variety of estates. If we rigidly exclude all cases where there seems any room for doubt as to the meaning of the entries, as well as all cases where the rent is less than 20s., we can still point to examples of farming out for a fixed rent on the lands of 75 tenants-in-chief of whom 28 were ecclesiastical lords; and the information supplied by the Exon. Domesday enables us to add

---

[1] In Lincolnshire, the present values of Kirby and Kyme are particularized as *cum pondere et arsione*, Dd. i, f. 337b. In Nottinghamshire, Dunham 'T.R.E. reddebat xxx libras et vi sextaria mellis modo xx libras cum omnibus quae ibi pertinent', ibid., f. 281; see also *Ernehale*, i.e. Arnold, f. 281b. In Huntingdonshire, the value of Godmanchester is given as £40 *ad numerum*, ibid., f. 203b.

[2] Outside the royal estates (including those of Queen Matilda), I have noticed only one case in Buckinghamshire (Marsh Gibbon? f. 148b), Bedfordshire (Stotfold, f. 213), and Derbyshire (Osmaston, f. 275b); and the last is rather doubtful as it depends on the statement 'Horum denariorum duae partes sunt regis tercia Henrici' (de Ferrers) which follows the valuation. Of Stotfold we are told that it was at farm for £30 on the day Ralf Taillebois died. I have taken no account of farms or renders due from boroughs, or from Newark, which, though called a manor, contained 56 *burgenses*.

another 20 names to the list.[1] Among the ecclesiastical lords we find, along with the two archbishops and a number of bishops and abbeys, a couple of *capellani*; and the list of lay lords includes many of the greatest barons and also a few quite humble people such as William Corniole, who is classed as one of the king's sergeants and appears to have held only two small manors in Wiltshire.[2] But, further, the evidence of Domesday cannot be fully appreciated unless some account is taken of entries which, though they fail to tell us unequivocally of manors at farm or owing a render in 1086, yet more or less definitely indicate that an estate had formerly been put at farm and leave room for supposing that it was still treated in this way, or, again, make some statement which would be hard to account for unless this were the case. Thus, for example, we read that Deerhurst in Gloucestershire used to give a farm of £41 and 8 sextars of honey in the time of King Edward and is now worth £40; and that Eyton in Shropshire was worth £21 in the Confessor's day and rendered £14 when Earl Roger gave it to Shrewsbury Abbey.[3]

Similar statements are made about the estate of Westminster Abbey at Pershore in Worcestershire; about the Bishop of Chichester's manors of Henfield and Preston in Sussex; about Chipstead (*Tepestede*) in Surrey, which William de Watevile formerly held of the Abbot of Chertsey; about Great Baddow in Essex which belonged to the *Abbaye aux Dames* at Caen.[4] Then

---

[1] I have reckoned as tenants-in-chief not only those allotted a special rubric in Domesday, but all who had no lord between them and the king such as those classed among the king's 'thegns' or the king's *servientes*, and also four Shropshire lords, who in this 'palatine' county held their lands of Earl Roger, as well as Richard Pincerna, who similarly held of Earl Hugh in Cheshire. Odo of Bayeux and Geoffrey of Coutances have been reckoned with the ecclesiastical lords though their English lands cannot be regarded as belonging to their churches. I have also counted Walter the Deacon and Albert and Girold the chaplains among the ecclesiastics.

[2] In some cases the named tenant may himself have been the 'farmer' and the render may be what he owed the king not what he received from some unnamed 'farmer' to whom he had leased the land. We know that this was so with Eschelin the tenant of Foddington in Somerset.

[3] Dd. i, ff. 166, 252b.

[4] Ibid., ff. 175, 16b, 17, 33; ii, ff. 21b, 22. One cannot exclude the possibility that some estates may have been put to farm as a temporary expedient before a permanent grant was made. Perhaps that was so with the Warwickshire lands of the Countess Godiva of which we read 'Has terras Comitisse Godivae tenet Nicolaus ad firmam de rege' (Dd. i, f. 239b); cf. the statements about some lands in Northamptonshire and Leicestershire which had belonged to Queen Edith (ibid., ff. 219, 230b).

we have entries of various types which contain no express statement that the place was at farm but are most readily explained as implying that it was, especially when we remember that Domesday unquestionably gives only a valuation for many manors that we know to have been at farm. Thus Holworth in Dorset, which belonged to Milton Abbey, is valued at £3 and a sextar of honey; and it seems unlikely that this indicates anything different from the entry which tells us that William de Braose's land at *Ristone* in the same county 'renders thirty shillings and four sextars of honey'.[1] Again, manors are sometimes valued at a certain sum 'and an ounce of gold' and these cases invite comparison with those of the type represented by a Berkshire entry which states that Hanney 'valet VI libras et tamen reddit VI libras et unciam auri'.[2] Similarly, a rent rather than a mere valuation is surely implied when the sum mentioned is described as 'blanch' or we are told that the manor is worth so many pounds 'by weight and assay', 'by tale', or 'by weight'. It is indeed only in relation to royal estates in Norfolk, and, to a less degree, in Suffolk, that valuations expressed in such terms are of frequent occurrence.[3] But here and there we find a suggestive particularity of this kind employed in the description of

[1] Dd. i, ff. 78, 82. Cf. Little Witley (*Witlege*), Worcestershire, where 'Arnuinus presbiter tenuit redd' (? reddens) aeclesiae omnes consuetudines firmae et i sextarium mellis' (f. 172b); also Fleetham, Yorks., valued at 40s. and a sore falcon (f. 310b); and the church of *Warverdinestoch* (Stogumber), Somerset, valued at £3 and four cows (f. 91). As Stenton observes, 'no one would express a valuation in the modern sense in terms of pounds and honey': *V.C.H. Notts.* i. 215.

[2] For examples of manors *valued* in this way see Miswell (*Mascewelle*), Herts., Dd. i, f. 138; Weston Colville (*Westone*), Cambridgeshire, ff. 196, 196b; Weeley, Stevington (*Steintuna* in Record Commission edition = ? *Steuituna*), Thurrock (Grays Thurrock), and Walthamstow, Essex, ii, ff. 51, 82, 90, 92; and Cretingham (*Gretingaham*), Suffolk, ff. 406b, 407. For Hanney see Dd. i, ff. 61b, 62, and, for other *renders* of the kind, Southfleet and Stone, Kent, f. 5b; and Lugwardine, Herefordshire, f. 179b. Of Blakenham (*Blacham*), Suffolk, we read 'hoc manerium ad firmam per tres annos unoquoque xii lib. et in tribus annis simul i uncia auri de gersuma', Dd. ii, f. 353b.

[3] For example, Ellingham, Norfolk: 'Tunc et post val. iiii libras modo iiii libras blancas et iiii solidos', Dd. ii, f. 126b; cf. Kimberley, f. 121; Bowthorpe, f. 121b; Flockthorpe, f. 122; Cantley, f. 123; Aylsham, f. 132; Palling, f. 134; and, in Suffolk, Thorney, f. 281b, and Norton, f. 286. Of Ormesby, Norfolk, we read: 'Tunc totum val. x libras modo xxi ad numerum', f. 115b; cf. Mildenhall, Suffolk, f. 289; and Godmanchester, Huntingdon, i, f. 203b. Hintlesham, Suffolk, is valued at £22 *ad pensum*, ii, f. 289; cf. Bramford, f. 289b; and Barrow, f. 289b. On the *Terra Regis* in Lincolnshire, the values of Kirkby Laythorpe and South Kyme are described as 'cum pondere et arsione', which Foster translates as 'by weight and assay', i, f. 337b, while Blackpool, Devon, 'valet xx solidos ad pensam et arsuram', f. 101.

manors that were not part of the *Terra Regis*. Several estates of
Count Eustace in Essex and Hertfordshire are valued in assayed
money.[1] Nutfield in Surrey, which belonged to his wife, is said
to be worth £15 *de viginti in ora*.[2] Kingsbury, a manor on the
Terra Comitissae Godevae in Warwickshire, is worth £13 *ad
pondus*.[3] For Wye in Kent a valuation in pounds *de viginti in ora* is
given for the date at which Battle Abbey received the estate,
while its present value is put at £100 *ad numerum*.[4] Particularly
suggestive are the entries for several royal manors in East Anglia
which give the value as *x* pounds 'blanch' and a *gersuma* of *y*
shillings *ad numerum*.[5] Even more compelling are the descriptions
of Assington in Suffolk and Rainham and its members in Norfolk. Assington, a manor of Rannulf Peverel, is valued at £20
'sed non pot' reddere de C solidis'.[6] Rainham, which belonged
to Hugh de Montfort, is said to be worth £8. 10s. *cum magna
pena*.[7] Clearly these 'values' are in fact rents; and we are meant
to understand that in the opinion of the Domesday Commissioners a rent of £15 was the most that ought to be expected in
the first case, and that the rent of Rainham could only be maintained with great difficulty.[8] Finally, in Essex, as Round pointed
out, large increases are frequently recorded in the values of
manors 'where the stock remains unchanged, if indeed it has not
decreased'; and this is, in Round's words, 'a strong reason for
believing that "valet" meant the actual sum received', for it is
hard to see how the commissioner or the jurors can have reached
such results under these conditions by an actual appraisal of the
value, and there is ample proof in Domesday itself that Norman

---

[1] In Essex, Great Tey 'valet xxii libras candidas', Dd. ii, f. 29*b*; cf. Laver
(*Lagafara*), f. 30*b*; while Boxted 'tunc et post val. viii libras modo xii blancas',
f. 30; cf. Stanford, f. 30*b*. Tring, Hertfordshire, 'valet xxii libras de albis denariis
ad pensum hujus comitis', i, f. 137.

[2] Dd. i, f. 34.   [3] Ibid., f. 239*b*.   [4] Ibid., f. 11*b*.

[5] See Bedingham, Norfolk, 'Tunc totum val. iiii libras post et modo viii blancas
et xx solidos ad numerum de gersuma', Dd. ii, f. 131; cf. Sall, Thurning, Lessing-
ham, Hempstead, in Norfolk, ff. 131*b*, 134, and Parham, Suffolk, f. 285*b*. The
argument in the text is not, I think, shaken by an entry like that for Godalming
which runs: 'T.R.E. valebat xxv libras et post xx libras modo xxx libras ad
numerum et tamen reddit ad pensum et arsuram xxx libras', Dd. i, f. 30*b*.
Particularity of description is here certainly applied to the value as well as the
render, but how else could the real point of the statement be made clear as the
sums were nominally the same?

[6] Dd. ii, f. 416*b*.   [7] Ibid., f. 237*b*.

[8] Similar statements about *renders* are of course common: see, for example,
Sculthorpe, Norfolk: *sed non potuit reddere*, ibid., f. 168; Cambas, Suffolk: *sed vix
pot' reddere*, f. 291.

landlords often demanded excessive rents for manors that they put to farm.[1]

Of the tenurial arrangements that lay behind the farms and renders of Domesday Book and its satellite texts less can be discovered than one would like to know.

In some cases we can clearly perceive the vestiges of an ancient system of food rents originating in an obligation to provide for the needs of a peripatetic court or noble household. Food rents were deeply rooted in old English usage. They are mentioned in the laws of Ine of Wessex which appear to have been issued in or about the year 694, and gifts to monasteries in the form of a food rent chargeable upon some estate of the donor are recorded in several documents of the first half of the ninth century.[2] In the following century we sometimes find such renders described as the *feorm* or provision for one or more days—'æne dæg feorme' or 'twegra daga feorme'—and in these terms we obviously have the Old English equivalents of the farms of one or more days or nights of which we read in Domesday, the relation between the Saxon word *feorm*, provision, and the word *firma*, farm, a fixed payment, being so close that philologists consider it possible to regard them as really identical, the former being not improbably derived from the late Latin *firma* and having the primary sense of a 'fixed portion of provisions'.[3] In Domesday a considerable number of royal manors or former royal manors, together with a few that had belonged to some great Saxon earl, are described as rendering farms of this kind, either singly or in groups. Examples occur in eight contiguous southern and western counties—Sussex, Hampshire, Dorset, Wiltshire, Somerset, Gloucestershire, Herefordshire, Shropshire—and also in Cambridgeshire, Bedfordshire, Norfolk, and Essex; but the system

---

[1] *V.C.H. Essex*, i. 364–5. In Lincolnshire, Domesday Book again and again mentions a *tailla* in addition to the 'value'; and Stenton suggests that in these cases the 'value' should be regarded as the actual rent and the *tailla* as 'a sum of money paid directly to the lord by both free and unfree tenants, and standing outside the sum for which the lessees of the manor answered to him': *Introduction to the Lincolnshire Domesday* (Lincoln Record Soc.), pp. xxii–xxiii. This interpretation would carry us far, for the *tailla* is mentioned in more than 200 Lincolnshire entries in relation to lands belonging to 7 ecclesiastical and 42 lay lords.

[2] Ine, c. 70, i; F. E. Harmer, *Select English Historical Documents of the Ninth and Tenth Centuries*, 1914, Nos. i, ii, v; cf. Nos. iv and vi, which are little, if at all, later.

[3] See *O.E.D.* sub 'Farm', and, for tenth-century examples of 'feorms' measured in days, D. Whitelock, *Anglo-Saxon Wills*, Nos. viii and xi, and A. J. Robertson, *Anglo-Saxon Charters*, No. xxxii. A night's food rent—*niht feorme*—is mentioned in Edgar's Charter to Ely: ibid., No. xlviii, p. 100, cf. p. 347.

was not confined to the places where Domesday refers to it in specific terms.[1] Sometimes the render was a fraction of a night's farm—at Linton in Herefordshire only a fourth—but usually it was a farm of one or more days or nights, and Writtle in Essex, which had belonged to Harold in King Edward's day, was then bound to furnish a farm of ten nights as well as £10 in money.[2] The unit of measurement, however, was evidently a local and not a national unit. In Cambridgeshire a farm of three nights was commuted for £13. 8s. 4d., and Great Baddow in Essex (which had formerly belonged to Earl Ælfgar of Mercia) owed eight nights' farm before the Conquest and was rendering £17 in 1086; but in Wiltshire and Somerset farms of a single night appear to be equated with sums ranging from £100 to £110.[3]

We have no means of knowing to what extent payments from the royal estates continued to be made in kind in 1086. Stenton considers that many of the food rents had been commuted for money payments before the Conquest; and by the time of the Domesday survey money rents had undoubtedly taken the place of the three days' farm of corn, malt, and honey which certain royal estates in Cambridgeshire had rendered (along with some money) in the days of the Confessor.[4] But change did not always take this direction. On several Gloucestershire manors we find on the one hand that a due of 3,000 dog-cakes has been commuted for 16s. but on the other hand that King William is exacting a render of cows and pigs which appears to be an innovation.[5] And the evidence suggests that in many places the

---

[1] The farms of Neatham and Broughton (*Brestune*) in Hampshire are not described as farms of a day or a night, but, as Round pointed out, their T.R.E. value (£76. 16s. 8d. in each case) was exactly double that of Barton Stacey and Eling which owed half a day's farm each: *V.C.H. Hants*, i. 401. In Cambridgeshire several manors, in regard to which nothing is said about the farm being reckoned in time, owed 'for honey, corn, and malt' precisely the same sum of money which other manors in the county rendered in lieu of a farm of three nights consisting of the same commodities: Dd. i, f. 189b. In Oxfordshire and Northamptonshire the counties as a whole rendered a commuted (?) farm of three nights: ibid., ff. 154b, 219.

[2] Ibid., f. 179b (Linton); ii, f. 5b (Writtle).

[3] Dd. i, ff. 189, 189b; ii, ff. 21b, 22; i, ff. 64b, 65, 86, 86b. See Round, *Feudal England*, pp. 110–12. Cf. *V.C.H. Hants*, i. 401. R. L. Poole, with reference to the Hampshire and Somersetshire evidence, says 'it appears that in certain definite instances the farm of one day or night amounted before the Conquest to something like £80, and after to something approaching £100': *The Exchequer in the Twelfth Century*, 1912, p. 29.

[4] Stenton, *Anglo-Saxon England*, p. 476; Dd. i, ff. 189, 189b.

[5] Ibid., f. 162b. Nothing is said about the renders of these manors being assessed in nights' farms.

old system was maintained in its old form whatever that may have been. Domesday employs the present tense in regard to a number of the nights' farms in Hampshire, Wiltshire, and Dorset; and of Bitton (*Betune*) in Gloucestershire we are told precisely that it rendered a night's farm in the time of King Edward *et modo similiter facit*.[1] Change, moreover, did not necessarily imply any Norman preference for a different mode of exploitation, for it might well be induced merely by the alienation of some of the land. The case of Westbury-on-Severn is instructive. Here the pre-Conquest render of a night's farm was continued for four years under King William. After that, much of the land passed into the hands of the abbey of Cormeilles and two lay lords, and yet such was the tenacity of custom that the sheriff was still finding the whole farm from the remainder in 1086, though perhaps the word *tamen* in the Domesday entry that tells us of these matters was intended to indicate that this was scarcely justified.[2] A century after the Conquest, the author of the 'Dialogue on the Exchequer' reports a tradition that only payments in kind had been made from the Crown lands under the first two Norman kings, and though we know that this tradition was untrue, it may well reflect a considerable movement towards commutation in the reign of Henry I, while there is no reason to doubt the author's assertion that he had himself known men who had seen provisions brought in to the court from the Crown lands at stated times.[3]

Parallel to the farms of nights and days on estates of the Crown are the farms usually measured in weeks or months which are recorded for ecclesiastical estates. In Domesday Book we catch a glimpse of the system in Cornwall where the Canons of St. Pieran had lost two estates from which they formerly received a farm of four weeks.[4] But it is from other sources that we learn with what elaboration some of the greater ecclesiastical communities had planned a scheme of farms to provide for their needs throughout the year, and gather that arrangements of the kind were a normal feature of estate management in such cases.

---

[1] Dd. i, ff. 39, 64*b*, 65, 75, and, for Bitton, f. 162*b*. In the Dorset and Wiltshire examples the contraction *redd* is used, but the context makes it, I think, certain that this stands, as usual, for *reddit*, and not for *reddidit* or *reddebat*. Awre in Gloucestershire rendered half a night's farm T.R.E. and, like Bitton, *modo similiter facit* (f. 163).   [2] Dd. i, f. 163.

[3] *Dialogus de Scaccario* (ed. Charles Johnson, 1950), p. 40.

[4] Dd. i, f. 121.

The monastic cathedrals of Canterbury and Rochester, the Dean and Canons of St. Paul's, the abbeys of Ely and Ramsey, Bury St. Edmunds, and St. Albans all employed this system; and signs of its presence can also be discerned at Westminster and Worcester and Abingdon.[1] In some instances the evidence is of comparatively late or uncertain date; but for Bury St. Edmunds we have the authority of an apparently eleventh-century memorandum, and the schedule of archiepiscopal manors (which, by its twenty-six groups, seems to hint at an organization of farms to cover a year) can be little, if at all, later. Elsewhere we find tradition assigning the arrangements to a similarly early period. At Ely the abbey chronicler even supposed them to have been devised in the reign of Canute. The scheme for the monastic manors of Canterbury Cathedral is ascribed to Lanfranc. That for St. Paul's is stated (in a text of

---

[1] For the *firme monachorum* of Canterbury Cathedral (covering apparently 387 days reduced by commutation to 366) see Canterbury Register K, ff. 69*v*, 70, and Lambeth MS. 1212, p. 344: that a similar system was applied to the archbishop's demesne manors is suggested by their division into 26 groups in the schedule following the survey in the Domesday Monachorum (ed. Douglas) facsimile f. 5*v*. For Rochester ('firma tocius anni per xiii currentes menses') see *Custumale Roffense*, ed. J. Thorpe, 1788, pp. 12, 20, 35. For St. Paul's (nearly 53 weeks) see *Domesday of St. Paul's* (Camden Soc.), pp. xxxix, 152. For Ely see *Liber Eliensis* i. 201–2, where an item has perhaps dropped out of the text, since the listed farms of days and weeks only amount to 51 weeks, though the author speaks of the farms 'quae per annum ecclesiae in cibum sufficerent'. For Ramsey ('tredecim quindenae firmae divisae per abbatiam ita ut unaquaque quindena firma a cellerario protendatur per quatuor septimanas') see *Cart. Rams.* iii. 230–6, cf. 160–5. For Bury St. Edmunds (13 months' farms) see Robertson, *Anglo-Saxon Charters*, No. civ and *E.H.R.* xliii (1928), pp. 382–3. For St. Albans ('Tot ergo habemus firmas quot sunt septimanae in anno et unam in antecessum') see *Gesta Abbatum* (Rolls Series), i. 74. A Westminster Abbey document which 'appears to have been written in the first quarter of the twelfth century' and is printed by J. Armitage Robinson (*Gilbert Crispin*, pp. 41–42), describes a *firma monachorum in septimana* and states that the distant manors paid money instead—'reddunt pro tota septimana viii libras et x solidos'. For Worcester Cathedral a memorandum of similar date, inserted into the earlier part of Hemming's Cartulary, describes the 'firma que datur per annum' and lists certain supplies which the cellarer received *in septimana*, though every *villa que firmam dat* made what appear to be additional renders at Christmas, Easter, and the Feasts of the Assumption and Nativity of the Virgin, while at Martinmas the *firmarii* gave the suggestive number of 52 pigs: see *Hemingi Chartularium*, ed. T. Hearne, 1723, pp. 98–100; Thorpe, *Diplomatarium*, pp. 447–8; N. R. Ker in *Studies in Medieval History Presented to F. M. Powicke*, 1948, p. 54. In the Customs of Abingdon, which are said to have been exhibited to Rannulf Glanvil during the vacancy that followed the death of Abbot Roger in 1184–5, reference is made to Cumnor and eight other places 'qui faciunt unum mensem de firma' along with Cuddesdon 'qui dimidium mensem de firma facit', and in another passage to the manors 'quae faciunt ix menses et dimidium': see *Chron. Abingdon*, ii. 307, 326.

the middle of the twelfth century) to belong to the time of Dean 'Wulman' who appears to have been dean when Bishop Maurice confirmed the privileges of the chapter between 1091 and 1107.[1] At Ramsey, though the schedules which show what farms the various manors paid throughout the year are undated, a *statutum* laying down the constituents of a full farm was attributed to Abbot Aldwin who held office from 1091 to 1102 and again from 1107 or 1108 to about 1112.[2] At St. Albans, Matthew Paris writes of the system as one that had been improved through the addition of a supplementary allowance by Abbot Geoffrey who ruled that monastery from 1119 to 1146. In the case of Rochester, the elaborate schedules of farms in the *Custumale Roffense* cannot be earlier than the last decade of the twelfth century; but more than two hundred years before that the right to receive some farms measured in days had been bequeathed to the cathedral; and Lanfranc, when he recovered Fawkham for Rochester, arranged that it should supply a fifteen days' farm *ad victum monachorum*; while some time between 1094 and 1098 Bishop Gundulf imposed the obligation of providing a farm of eight days upon the newly acquired manor of Aston in Gloucestershire, and Haddenham is said to have owed two months' farm in Gundulf's time.[3] On the whole there can be little doubt

---

[1] According to Hales Wulman was 'the first Dean of St. Paul's after the Conquest': he appears to be the same person as 'V', the dean to whom Bishop Maurice's charter was addressed: *Early Charters of St. Paul's*, ed. M. Gibbs (Camden Soc., 1939), No. 59, cf. p. xxiv.

[2] *Cart. Rams.* iii. 163. That the Ramsey manors were paying farms of some sort before the end of the eleventh century may be inferred from a writ of William II which makes the abbey's claim to Isham in Northamptonshire turn on the question whether that estate had rendered a farm to the monks in the Conqueror's reign: ibid. i. 233–4; cf. Dd. i, f. 228.

[3] Whitelock, *Anglo-Saxon Wills*, No. xi, pp. 26–27; *Textus Roffensis*, ed. Tho. Hearne, 1720, pp. 144–5, 220, cf. p. 157. The schedules of the *Custumale* include Darenth, which Hubert Walter gave to Rochester, in exchange for Lambeth, between 1196 and 1198: *Registrum Roffense*, ed. Thorpe, 1769, pp. 270–1. It is true that Darenth was originally bequeathed to Rochester in the tenth century: Whitelock, op. cit., pp. 28–29; but it had come into the hands of the archbishop by 1086—'quod manerium quomodo ad archiepiscopatum pervenerit ignoratur' says the *Textus Roffensis*, p. 153—and the schedules cannot belong to the period before that happened. They include (with the exception of Lambeth) all the manors which, according to a charter of Archbishop Theobald, were assigned to the monks by Gundulf and he did not become bishop until 1077: *Textus Roffensis*, p. 206. Among these manors is Haddenham which appears to have been given by Lanfranc after 1086: Dd. i, f. 143*b* (Nedreham = Hedreham = Haddenham); *Textus Roffensis*, pp. 215–16, cf. pp. 145–8; Davis, *Regesta*, No. 301. For the farm of Haddenham in Gundulf's day see *Registrum Roffense*, p. 119.

that farms of this type had been a common feature of monastic estate management in England before the Norman Conquest, just as farms of nights and days had been a common method of providing for the needs of the royal household; but much re-organization and systematization must have taken place during the early Norman period. The traditions point towards that conclusion; and powerful factors were making changes necessary in various ways. There was the movement towards separation, or more definite and permanent separation, between the property of the bishop or abbot and that of the convent or chapter—a movement which owed part of its force to the need of securing the latter against royal claims to enjoy the revenues of the see or abbacy during a vacancy.[1] In some monasteries the number of monks altered so much and so rapidly that the amount of provisions required must have been utterly trans-formed in a few years.[2] The imposition of knight service, again, was a new factor. It was extremely unequal in its incidence, and, where it was heavy, would either involve a serious addition to the number of mouths to be fed (if the knights were main-tained, as they were for a time at Ely, *infra aulam ecclesiae*) or else lead to a sub-infeudation of manors which might well disturb an antecedent arrangement of farms.[3]

[1] The influence of this motive is apparent in the writ of Henry I which confirms the division made at Bury by 'Abbot Robert' (before 1112?) and provides that 'regales ministri tempore vacantis abbacie nullam potestatem sibi attrahant in maneriis predicti conventus' (*Feudal Documents*, ed. Douglas, No. 35, p. 69). For the move-ment in general and the connected development of separate establishments for the abbots, see Knowles, *The Monastic Order in England*, 1st ed., pp. 404–6, 434–6, 612–15, 625–6. That division was not uncommon before the Conquest is main-tained by E. John, *Journal of Eccles. Hist.* vi (1955), 143–55.

[2] For changes in the numbers of monks see Knowles, op. cit., pp. 126–7, 713–14. The Abingdon Chronicler says that the number of monks in that house increased threefold under Abbot Faricius (1100–17) and quotes the abbot's own assertion that 52 brothers had been added to the number he found there: it is significant that both statements occur in passages concerned with the supplies of food: *Chron. Abingdon*, ii. 49, 147–9. According to the *Textus Roffensis*, there were only 5 canons at Rochester when Gundulf became bishop (1077) but when he died (1108) he left there more than 60 monks, having, it seems, introduced 22 at the outset: op. cit., p. 143. The reaction of numbers upon estate management is illustrated by the statement in Domesday Book about a hide of land at Knightwick in Worcestershire belonging to Worcester Cathedral: 'est de dominico victu monachorum sed praestita fuit cuidam Edgidae moniali ut haberet et deserviret quamdiu fratres voluissent et carere possent. Crescente vero congregatione tempore regis Willelmi reddidit', Dd. i, f. 173b.

[3] For the household knights at Ely see *Liber Eliensis*, i. 275. At Worcester, Wulfstan 'habebat in curia sua milites multos', *Vita Wulfstani*, ed. Darlington (Camden Soc., 1928), p. 55. See also Douglas, *Feudal Documents*, pp. cvi–cvii.

The descriptions of ecclesiastical farms that have come down to us exhibit both variety and marks of changing conditions. Those recorded in the early memoranda of Bury St. Edmunds consisted entirely of provisions but in this case the greater part of the food-rents seem to have been commuted for money before the end of the eleventh century.[1] The farms of which we read in the *Gesta Abbatum* of St. Albans were money payments and of the 33*s*. a week received by the cellarer of the monks, 3*s*. was allotted to the nine *sarcinarii* or carriers 'who have the duty of bringing our food from London or elsewhere', the rest of the money serving *pro victu nostro*. From this it seems clear that, in the thirteenth century, St. Albans normally obtained provisions by purchase; but it would be rash to conclude that it did so in the first half of the twelfth century, though indeed that appears to be implied by the statement that Abbot Geoffrey had augmented the monks' allowance by 5*s*. a week 'ita ut cotidie ad coquinam nostram quinque solidos haberemus'.[2] At Worcester and Rochester, and apparently at Ramsey, the regular farm included a certain amount of money along with the supplies of provisions; and in the case of Ramsey, money seems to have been a possible alternative to some of the payments in kind.[3]

Of the 32 Glastonbury Abbey manors unequivocally stated to have been at farm in the reign of Henry I, 29 were then farmed for money rents, 2 owed (respectively) 4 and 5 'great farms' valued at £5 each, and 1 had to pay £60 and 4 such farms as well; while, among the manors which are not specifically described as *ad firmam*, Pennard owed 1 'great farm' and 36*s*. and Lyme a weekly render of fish. The document from which we learn these facts was compiled by Hilbert the Precentor after the death of Henry of Blois which occurred in 1171;

---

[1] Douglas, op. cit., p. cxxxiii.

[2] *Gesta Abbatum*, i. 73–74. Besides the money farms, St. Albans received certain offerings in kind (ibid., pp. 74–75); and outside the scheme of farms at Bury the memoranda mention some small money payments earmarked for the purchase of extra supplies such as fish and mead at certain anniversaries. The abbey of Abingdon seems to have obtained some of its food supplies by purchase in the latter part of the eleventh century for a writ attributed to William the Conqueror grants freedom of tolls in respect of 'omnia quae ministri monachorum Abbendoniae ement ad victum monachorum in civitatibus et burgis et omnibus mercatis': *Chronicon*, ii. 2. Apparently the farms only covered 9½ months at Abingdon: see above, p. 131, n. 1.

[3] See the *Statutum* attributed to Abbot Aldwin: *Cart. Rams.* iii. 163–4.

but by that time several changes had taken place on the Glastonbury estates. A render of 'small farms', valued at 33s. each, now
formed part of the obligations of 4 manors which had apparently
paid only money in the time of King Henry; but, among other
changes, the manor of Brent-Marsh is described as rendering £80
instead of £60 and 4 great farms, and at Pennard the money
rent had been more than doubled while 3 small farms (together
worth £4. 19s.) had taken the place of the great farm (worth £5)
which it had previously owed.[1]

The monks of Canterbury Cathedral and the Canons of
St. Paul's still received farms consisting largely of provisions in
the thirteenth century; but in both cases the system had been
a good deal modified since the time to which the oldest descriptions refer.[2] At Canterbury alteration appears to have begun
early and at first to have proceeded bit by bit. Indications of its
advance can be discerned in the two texts of the arrangements
attributed to Lanfranc which have come down to us.[3] In each
text of the schedule we read first of manors which rendered
farms measured in months, weeks, or days; and each concludes
with a list of manors and money rents which in the Canterbury
manuscript is distinguished by the heading *Firme in denariis
tantum*. The basis of this grouping was evidently the allocation of
manors in the first group to the feeding of the monks and of
those in the last group to the provision of money for the purchase
of clothing.[4] But some money payments appear to be included

---

[1] Trinity Coll., Cambridge, MS. R. 3.33, ff. 115–16A. This important text was
discovered by Dom. Aelred Watkin, but is still unpublished: Professor Postan has
given some account of it in *Econ. Hist. Rev.* (1953), p. 358 et seq. Postan is inclined
to identify the 'Lym' of this *Inquisitio* with Lympsham in Somerset, but I think it
must be Lyme on the Dorset–Devon border. In what I say above I have taken
no account of the *gabulum assisum* or of small renders of honey.

[2] R. A. L. Smith, *Canterbury Cathedral Priory*, 1943, pp. 129–33; *Domesday of
St. Paul's*, p. xxxix.

[3] Canterbury Register K, ff. 69v, 70; Lambeth MS. 1212, pp. 344–5. Smith
(op. cit., p. 129 n. 3) says that 'these arrangements replaced the *institutio antiqua*
of the Saxon period', for which he refers to Lambeth MS. 1212, f. (really page) 346.
This is an error: this *institutio antiqua* is the same as that in the *Domesday Monachorum*, ed. Douglas, p. 79 and is not concerned with the monastic manors at all,
being an (apparently fragmentary) account of payments, including chrism-money,
due from churches: see Douglas, op. cit., pp. 5–7.

[4] Of the 26 places in the first group, one can, I think, identify 20, perhaps 21,
with places which are either described specifically as *de cibo* or *de victu* in the
Domesday Monachorum or the Great Domesday, or else are (in six cases) included
in the Little Domesday under headings describing them as *ad victum*. The most
doubtful case is *Bertona*. Dr. Urry tells me that Barton was a manor less than

in the 'farms' of the first section along with renders of grain and malt, pigs and cows, cheese and honey, firewood and salt, and *luminaria* for lamps in the dormitory. The month's farm is set forth in detail in the case of Hollingbourne, and among the items are £8 *in denariis* for the kitchen, a *gersuma* of £11 and some payments in the way of wages to the servants in the brewhouse.[1] But, further, there was a tendency for the money element to increase and it seems pretty clear that this development proceeded by stages, though unfortunately no dating of the stages is possible. In the first place, in the description of the month's farm we read that each of the pigs must be worth 2s. and that the reeve can at his discretion take either the money or the animals.[2] Secondly, this first section of the document ends with a list of four places, which, like the manors in the last section, are described as rendering money only, without anything being said about their owing farms measured in months or days. Thirdly, in the earlier part of the first section, among the manors definitely stated to owe such farms, we find Appledore which 'non aliter firmat nisi tantum XV libras et III uncias auri et III bindas anguillarum', Preston which 'solebat firmare XIIII dies sed nunc reddit pro omnibus rebus XVI libras', and Little Chart which 'reddit X libras pro firma VII dierum'. Moreover, from the sums thus mentioned as payments in commutation of the original farms we can draw some conclusions about the

---

a mile from Canterbury beyond the north gate; and it is identified by Somner with the manor variously called *Nordwda* (*Nordeude* in Domesday) or *Norgate*, which is described as *de cibo* both in the Domesday Monachorum and in the 'Excerpts' of St. Augustine's (*Domesday Monachorum*, ed. Douglas, p. 88; Ballard, *An Eleventh Century Inquisition*, British Academy Records of Social and Economic History, iv (1920), 12). One of the 26 places is an exception to the rule—Merstham in Surrey, which is described as *de vestitu* in Domesday, (i, f. 31). But in both manuscripts of the schedule Merstham and Cheam are linked together as owing one month's farm and Cheam is stated in Domesday to be *de victu* (i, f. 30b). As regards the 14 items of the second group, 9 are described as *de vestitu* either in the Domesday Monachorum or in Domesday, and the only exception is Southchurch in Essex, one of a list of manors headed *ad victum* in the Little Domesday (Dd. ii, f. 8).

[1] I feel doubtful whether the payment of £8 to the kitchen was really part of the regular month's farm. An entry near the end of the first section states that 'Herebertus dei inimicus reddit viij libras pro quadam terra que pertinet ad Holingebourne id est Godintune'; and one cannot ignore the possibility that this was the payment in question and that it was illogically entered also in the paragraph devoted to Hollingbourne and thus made to appear an element in the month's farm though actually peculiar to this manor.

[2] 'Et hoc est in electione prepositi utrum porcos an predictum pretium velit accipere.'

previous history of three of the places entered at the end of the section as paying money only, for one of these paid £16 like Preston, while one paid just half that sum and the third paid £10 like Little Chart—facts which seem to indicate that these payments also were commutations of farms of one or two weeks.[1] All these details are to be found in both the Lambeth and Canterbury texts of the schedule, but the latter in one particular carries the story a little farther, for in it the words *solebat reddere* have been inserted above the word *reddit* in the account of Hollingbourne. Further, some additional indications of change can be discerned if we turn to the descriptions of these monastic manors in Domesday Book and the Domesday Monachorum. To compare these descriptions in detail with those of the schedule would be to embark upon a sea of baffling problems; but two facts deserve notice here. First, the manor of Westwell (*Waelle, Welle*) in Kent, which according to the schedule rendered a three-weeks' farm and a *garsuma* of 100s., appears in Domesday as rendering £40.[2] Secondly, the money renders recorded both in

[1] Since nothing is said about temporal farms in these cases it seems probable that their commutation came earlier and was more definitive than the commutations recorded for Appledore, Preston, and Little Chart. As two of these manors (Monks Risborough and Halton) are in Buckinghamshire and one (Stisted) in Essex, money payments may have been preferred on account of their distance, as they were with the distant manors of Westminster Abbey (see above, p. 131, n. 1). The fourth place entered as paying money only is *Baggeberi* which only paid 21s. Dr. Urry informs me that *Baggeberi* was the name of what is now New Ruttington Lane outside the walls of Canterbury and that the late twelfth-century survey (Canterbury Rental 31) shows that it was then a good deal 'built up', so change in this case may have been due to urbanization. Further support for the argument in the text may perhaps be found in the fact that Ickham, Lawling, and Milton Hall, which rendered farms of a month, 14 days and 7 days respectively, are valued in Domesday at £32, £16, and £8, while Westwell, which owed a 3-weeks' farm, is valued at £24. 0s. 4d. though said to render £40. But we also find more than one example of valuations at rates of £20, £26, and £30 to the month's farm. That the month was one of 28 days is specifically stated in the schedule.

[2] In view of the tendency to commute food farms into money rents, it is tempting to infer that Lanfranc's scheme as represented in the schedule is anterior to Domesday; but Lanfranc apparently intended a greater increase in the number of monks than was actually attained, so it is conceivable that he brought into the scheme of food farms a manor previously let for a money rent. This would be more likely if the rent of Westwell was only xi pounds as stated in the Domesday Monachorum and not xl pounds. At first sight Adisham seems a parallel case: it owes a month's farm according to the schedule while Domesday says that it renders £46. 16s. 4d. But the Domesday Monachorum tells us that Adisham renders £16. 16s. 4d. *de gablo* and is worth (*valet*) £30 *de firma* so perhaps Domesday is merely combining the value of the food farm with the payment *de gablo* and its use of the word *reddit* is here deceptive.

Domesday and the Domesday Monachorum for some of the manors listed in the last section of the schedule differ very considerably from those given in it—some being larger and some being smaller. What the explanation of these differences may be, and which statements represent the earlier condition, it would be hard indeed to say; but at least we have here further evidence that the farm system of the monks of Canterbury underwent a good deal of alteration.

On the whole the evidence for the Priory of Canterbury Cathedral seems to indicate a continuing tendency to commute renders in kind into money payments during the period between the time of Lanfranc and the unknown date of the schedules in their present form, for which a posterior limit is provided by the fact that the relevant portion of Canterbury Register K appears to have been written in the thirteenth century and probably in the first half of it. But one cannot regard these developments as examples of a general economic process in which the royal estates led the way, while an innate conservatism retarded, without preventing, advance in the same direction on the part of the great ecclesiastical corporations. The case of Rochester is a warning against such facile generalization. The schedules of farms in the *Custumale Roffense*, which cannot be earlier in their present form than the last decade of the twelfth century, reveal a system that depended mainly upon renders in kind. The regular month's farm included, it is true, a payment of 60s. *ad coquinam*; and one of the two texts indicates that 5s. might be paid instead of a sester of honey and that 24s. was a possible alternative for a render of twelve 'bacons'.[1] Yet these things are of small account in comparison with the renders of grain—48 quarters of wheat, 60 quarters of barley, 32 quarters of oats, and 9 quarters of peas; while the farm also included 182 lb. of cheese and unspecified quantities of salt, tallow, and firewood. But what makes this Rochester evidence particularly significant is the fact that, of the manors which owed these farms, three, whose renders covered between them four out of the thirteen months provided for, were in 1086 paying rents in money. Southfleet at that time rendered £24 and an ounce of gold. Of Stoke we read that he who holds it pays £13 and 20d. Of Darenth, which then belonged to the archbishop, it is stated that the tenant of the manor renders £18 though it is only

[1] *Custumale*, p. 20, cf. ibid., p. 35.

worth £15. 10s.[1] And this provides occasion for some general reflections.

It is no doubt the business of the economic historian to scan the multitudinous phenomena of human action in the economic sphere with a discerning eye for any general tendencies they may display. If he can rise above the detailed occurrences that form the raw material of his craft, and reveal some pattern in the panorama of history, he will have good reason to feel satisfied with his achievement. But the high pathway which affords these widespread views is beset with pitfalls. It is tempting to look upon recalcitrant facts as if they were obstacles to the march of history rather than to the historian's ready explanation of it. And even when the existence of some general trend has been abundantly proved, there remains a danger that the trend may be mistaken for an operative force. In fact the real forces, though diverse enough, are derived from simple elements—the needs, the aspirations, the intelligence and the energies of individual men. In economic history the great constants are homely things—the need of food and drink, the need of clothing and shelter. And when we consider the recorded facts about the commutation of food rents in Norman England, we should hesitate before postulating a grand movement from natural economy to money economy with the progressive marching in the van and those wedded to the old ways hanging back. Another explanation may be preferred. It was natural that money payments should replace renders in kind on many of the royal estates after the Norman Conquest—or, rather, after the definitive union of England and Normandy under Henry I—for when the king and his court spent much of their time on the

[1] Dd. i, ff. 5b, 3. The Domesday Monachorum describes the payment at Southfleet as *de firma* and says of Darenth that the archbishop 'habet in firma sua xviii libras': op. cit., pp. 96, 88. It may be objected that in the case of Darenth the round sum of £18 might be the money value of a render in kind; but this possibility seems to be excluded by an entry in the schedule of archiepiscopal manors and farms which follows the Domesday Monachorum survey and like it is in a hand of c. 1100. The entry runs thus: 'Derent de firma x et vii libras et x solidos. Gablum xxxi solidos et i denarium. De constumes xv solidos. Et xx solidos archiepiscopo et ij porcos et dimidium' (p. 99). Some light upon the development of the farm system at Rochester is provided by a tradition regarding Haddenham, which in the schedules of the *Custumale* is represented as owing a three-months' farm. The passage in the *Registrum* which embodies this tradition runs thus: 'Tempore Gundulfi episcopi habuimus de firma duos menses, accessit quidem Clemens monachus noster, qui primo habuit custodiam de Hedenham post episcopum, accrevit de firma unum mensem; et secundum vetus rotulum xv dierum plus' (p. 119).

Continent they did not require so much food in England. It was also natural that food rents should often be retained, and in some cases developed, on monastic estates, because the great revival of monasticism meant that there were more monks to be fed. The successive commutations of monastic food farms at Canterbury may well have been due, first, to the fact that under Lanfranc the monks were never as numerous as he had planned, and, secondly, to the great decline in their numbers which took place about the end of the twelfth century.[1] Considerations of need and convenience were the determining factors and not readiness or reluctance to advance from a stage of *Naturalwirtschaft* to one of *Geldwirtschaft*. At Rochester as well as at Canterbury the clothing of the monks seems to have been obtained by purchase in the early Norman period; and perhaps it was the inconvenience of collecting small quantities of grain from a number of places that induced Gundulf to accept sums of money in lieu of various tithes that had been given to Rochester and to devote them *ad vestitum monachorum*.[2]

It is significant that we find different modes of payment definitely mentioned as alternatives in documents that are widely separated in date. When Beonna, Abbot of Medeshamstede, some time between 786 and 796, granted Swineshead in Lincolnshire to a nobleman named Cuthbert, it was stipulated that the rent should be paid either in food or money.[3] In the ninth century, Earl Ælfred, when he bequeathed Chartham to Canterbury, provided that if the community should wish to grant the estate out instead of retaining it in their own hands, they were to grant it to his child or to whichever one of his

[1] For a summary statement of the figures at different dates see R. A. L. Smith, *Canterbury Cathedral Priory*, p. 3.

[2] *Textus Roffensis*, pp. 190–1. Though in this list only one of the payments is described as a tithe and that is not expressed in money, there is clear evidence that five others were tithe commutations (*Ærhetha* = Erith, p. 165; William de Editune and Hunfrith, p. 179; Ralf Pincerna *de Culingis*, p. 164; Osbern de Biliceham, p. 161) and in fourteen more a strong presumption that they were such is created by grants of tithes or of churches at the places or by the persons named: see pp. 153–79 *passim*. As some of the churches are stated to have been given by Henry I, the allocation of these revenues *ad vestitum monachorum* would seem to have been made between 1100 and 1108, the year of Gundulf's death. On the Ely estates a rent apparently adjusted to the needs of the recipients is found early in the twelfth century at Fen Ditton, where a tenement paid a mark to the bishop and three *summae* of flour to the monks: E. Miller, *The Abbey and Bishopric of Ely*, p. 284.

[3] Birch, *Cart. Sax.*, No. 271: 'unius noctis pastum aut triginta [*blank*] ravit siclos'. The grant is cited by Stenton, *Anglo-Saxon England*, p. 477.

kinsmen might wish to have it 'on condition that he makes terms with the community for a rent in money or a food rent ('swæ an feoh swæ an feorme') whichever he may succeed in gaining their consent to'.[1] In the early Norman period Herbert of Gatindene gave to Rochester 'all his tithe or forty pence or their value in eels'.[2]

[1] E. E. Harmer, *Select English Historical Documents of the 9th and 10th Centuries*, No. viii.

[2] *Textus Roffensis*, pp. 176–7.

VI

ESTATE MANAGEMENT II: FARMS,
FARMERS, AND LEASES

WHATEVER form the farm system took, its essential characteristic was the payment to the lord of a fixed rent. Whether the *firmae* were or were not reckoned as providing supplies for a given period of time, and whether they consisted of renders in kind or of sums of money, or were paid partly in kind and partly in money, the amount due was predetermined. And perhaps the most important questions that arise in connexion with this mode of estate management concern the persons who were responsible for these payments, and their relations, on the one hand to the lord, and on the other to the peasantry. Except in the rare cases where there was no manorial demesne, it was not merely a matter of collecting customary rents and dues from the *villani* and other manorial tenants.[1] The demesne was involved. When a manor was put to farm, the farm represented primarily what the lord received from the demesne.[2] The *firmarius* was, in some way or other, in charge of the demesne. But was he a bailiff, closely in touch with the lord who employed him, moved, it may be, from one manor to another, and remunerated with any surplus he could obtain over and above the fixed render? Or was he a lessee, enjoying a large measure of independence, and standing, for a shorter or longer period, between the lord and the peasants? If a lessee, what were the conditions of his lease, and to what extent were the peasants subject to his authority? For the lord of the manor, for the 'farmer' himself, and not least for the village people, it was a matter of intimate concern to which of these types his position approximated. In the fluid conditions of the early Norman period it may well be that intermediate types were not uncom-

[1] As Maitland remarks in connexion with the farms of royal manors described in Domesday Book, the quantity due is one 'which can be expressed by round figures' and 'we do not arrive at these pretty results by adding up the rents due from individuals': *Domesday Book and Beyond*, p. 146.

[2] Cf. N. Neilson, *Customary Rents* (Oxford Studies in Social and Legal History, ed. Vinogradoff, vol. ii, 1910), p. 18.

mon and that individuals might pass, almost insensibly, from the one position to the other; but none the less the bailiff and the lessee represent two essentially different kinds of estate management.[1]

It seems pretty clear from Domesday Book that responsibility for the revenue which the king received from the Crown estates normally lay upon the sheriff of the shire in which they were situated.[2] In a few counties there are definite indications that the arrangements were similar to those obtaining in the next century when the farms of the royal manors were included in the *firma comitatus* which the sheriff rendered to the Exchequer; and a Somerset entry shows that, because Wedmore had been given away by the Confessor, a deduction was made from the sum for which the sheriff was accountable, much as allowance is made for *terrae datae* in the Pipe Rolls of Henry II's reign.[3] Of the sheriff's concern with the royal estates there is also a good deal of sporadic evidence in Domesday in the way of casual allusions to actions taken by particular sheriffs or to events that had occurred during some individual's period of office; and such allusions are just what we should expect to find in the case of usual and familiar arrangements which did not call for description.[4]

[1] The variations and changes in the position of the continental *villicus* (*meier* or *maire*) are instructive in relation to these matters: see Inama-Sternegg, *Deutsche Wirtschaftsgeschichte*, ii (1891), 167–74, 200–2, 267–73; W. Wittich in *Zeitschrift für Social- und Wirthschaftsgeschichte*, ii (1894), 47–50; G. von Below, *Probleme der Wirtschaftsgeschichte* (2nd ed., 1926), pp. 45–46, and his posthumous *Geschichte der deutschen Landwirtschaft des Mittelalters* (1937), pp. 66–70, 74–75; Ph. Dollinger, *L'Évolution des classes rurales en Bavière* (1949), pp. 126, 134; with, for a criticism of earlier views, Dopsch, *Herrshaft und Bauer in der deutschen Kaiserzeit* (1939), pp. 60–78 *et passim*; and, for France, H. Sée, *Les Classes rurales et le régime domanial en France au moyen âge* (1901), pp. 330–7.

[2] For the grounds of this conclusion, and the qualifications to which it must be subject, see W. A. Morris, *The Medieval English Sheriff to 1300* (1927), pp. 28–30, 62–69; cf. R. S. Hoyt, *The Royal Demesne in English Constitutional History, 1066–1272* (1950), p. 11.

[3] See, for Warwickshire, Dd. i, f. 238; for Wiltshire, ibid., f. 164 (sub *Udecestre*, Gloucestershire); for Worcestershire, ibid., f. 172; and for Wedmore, ibid., f. 86. The significance of the Wedmore entry was pointed out by Round, *Commune of London* (1899), p. 73; cf. *V.C.H. Somerset*, i. 396. Round considered it 'highly probable' but not certain that counties were farmed as a whole at the time of the Domesday survey. *V.C.H. Northants.* i (1902), 277.

[4] For example, a loss of plough beasts at Witham in Essex had taken place in the time of Suean and Baignard the (former) sheriffs, Dd. ii, f. 1*b*; at East Bergholt in Suffolk the rents of some *liberi homines* had been raised during the first shrievalty of Roger Bigod and further increased when Robert Malet became sheriff, ibid., f. 287*b*; in Gloucestershire the sheriff had annexed two hundreds (i.e. doubtless, the

Yet the management of the royal estates was far from being co-ordinated in a regular and uniform system.[1] Occasionally a manor is in the custody of the sheriff of a neighbouring shire. In Suffolk, Peter de Valognes who is sheriff of Essex, has charge of Harkstead near the Essex border, and Picot, the notorious sheriff of Cambridgeshire, is custodian of Barrow and Badmondisfield which lie a few miles outside his own county.[2] But departures from the norm went far beyond small adjustments of this kind. Considerable groups of royal manors are found in the charge of royal officials or other persons who do not appear to be sheriffs at all. This is particularly noticeable in the case of estates which were not part of the regular *Terra Regis*, but had come into the king's hands through forfeiture or some other accidental cause. Thus, in Suffolk, the confiscated estates of Earl Ralf are in the charge of Godric Dapifer and the lands which had belonged to the mother of Earl Morkar in the charge of William the Chamberlain and Otho the Goldsmith; while, in Warwickshire, the lands of the Lady Godiva are held at farm of the king by a certain Nicholas whom one suspects to be the same person as Nicholas Balistarius, a tenant-in-chief both in that county and in Devon.[3] Yet even where no special circumstances calling for special treatment can be discerned, some one other than the sheriff might have the custody of a royal manor or manors. Benfleet and Witham which head the list of the king's lands in Essex had both belonged to Harold in the time of King Edward, but the first is in the charge of Rannulf, brother of Ilger, the second in the charge of the sheriff.[4] It is Rannulf, and not the sheriff Eustace, who is entrusted with nearly all the *Terra Regis*

revenue accruing from the hundred courts) to the royal manor of Longborough, Dd. i, f. 163; Milton Regis in Kent was worth £200 by tale *quando Haimo vicecomes recepit*, ibid., f. 2b. In the Exon. Domesday numerous entries relating to royal manors in Devon and Somerset are closely parallel to this Milton entry: see Exon., pp. 84, 85, 98, 99.

[1] Professor Hoyt says: 'The sheriff was normally responsible for the royal revenues within his shire, including the farms of royal manors. But to this condition there were so many exceptions that it cannot be considered a hard and fast rule': op. cit., p. 11.

[2] Dd. ii, ff. 286b, 289b. That Picot took action as sheriff at Freckenham, which is just in Suffolk, appears from the *Textus Roffensis*, pp. 149–50; but the very odd bulge in the county boundary at this point and its sudden divergence from the stream which it follows on both sides of the bulge suggests that Cambridgeshire may have had claims on the place. Picot also held Chesterford, Essex, *in manu regis*: it lies on the Cambridgeshire border: Dd. ii, f. 3b.

[3] Ibid. ff. 284b, 286b; i, f. 239b.

[4] Dd. ii, f. 1b.

in the county of Huntingdon.[1] A considerable group of royal
estates in Suffolk is marked off as 'Terra Regis quam Aluricus
Wanz custodit' and a similar group in Norfolk as 'Terre Regis
quas Godricus servat'; but one can discover no reason why two
men of the conquered nation were given these responsibilities
instead of the Norman sheriff.[2] On the other side of England,
in Gloucestershire, we find that a great officer of the royal
household, Roger d'Ivry the king's butler, has been putting
royal manors out to farm, but perhaps he was sheriff at the time.[3]

In any case it must not be supposed that the functions of the
early Norman sheriff in regard to the royal estates approximated
either to those of the humble *gerefa* depicted in the eleventh-
century *Rectitudines*, or to those of the seneschal or steward of a
thirteenth-century bishop or baron. The Domesday sheriffs cannot usually have been the actual managers even of those estates
for which they were directly responsible. They were men of high
rank, charged with manifold and exacting duties, and must as
a rule have delegated the administration of the royal manors to
subordinates. There is definite evidence of this in Domesday
Book; and it is clear that the sheriff's officers exercised a considerable power of independent action. It was the *ministri* of
Roger Bigod who imposed a new rent upon the free men of the
soke of Bergholt in Suffolk and it was the *ministri* of his successor
Robert Malet who increased it.[4] At Ringsfield in the same
county a group of free men met with similar treatment at the
hand of Aluric the reeve 'in Roger Bigod's time'; an Aluric,
who is doubtless the same person, greatly increased the rent of
the free men of Mutford and its members *sub R. Bigot*; and at
Southmere in Norfolk a certain Brum, the reeve of Roger Bigod,
has taken some action, the nature of which is not quite clear,
in regard to the land of four sokemen.[5] At Ewell in Surrey
the reeves had granted out some land to their friends.[6] Nor is

---

[1] Dd. i, f. 203b: see Stenton, *V.C.H. Huntingdon*, i. 326–7.

[2] Dd. ii, ff. 287, 119b.

[3] Dd. i, ff. 162b (five places in *Dudestan* Hundred), 164 (Beckford and Aston-on-
Carrant). C. S. Taylor asserts that Roger d'Ivry was sheriff of Gloucestershire
(*Trans. Bristol and Gloucestershire Arch. Soc.* xl (1917), 80), but I have found no evidence of this. Roger the Sheriff, father of Walter fitz Roger, was Roger de Pistres:
see Dd. i, ff. 48b, 169, and *Cart. Glouc.*, i. lxxvi.

[4] Dd. ii, f. 287b.

[5] Ibid., ff. 282b, 283, 110; cf. *Haminghelanda* (? Hemingstone), f. 282, and
Herringfleet, f. 284b.

[6] 'Testantur homines de hund quod de hoc manerio subtractae sunt duae hidae

Domesday the only witness in this matter. The Ely chronicler complains not only of the wrongs inflicted upon the abbey by Picot the sheriff, but in particular of the bitter hostility shown towards St. Ethelreda and her possessions by one of his *ministri* named Gervase to whom he 'had committed the business of the whole shire'.[1] And the Abingdon chronicler has preserved for us a writ of William Rufus directing the sheriff of Oxfordshire to see that reparation is made for the injury done to the monks by Eadwi his reeve and his other *ministri*.[2] It is true that action in a matter of agrarian detail may be attributed to a sheriff. According to Domesday it was the sheriff who increased the peasant population at Chedworth in Gloucestershire by introducing 8 *villani* and 3 bordars with 4 plough-teams; but it would be rash to conclude that this indicates his personal intervention in the economy of the village rather than action taken by others under his authority.[3]

If the language of Domesday Book had the legal precision of that employed in documents of the age of Glanvil, the entries which state that the sheriff or some other person *custodit* a particular royal manor or group of manors would have to be understood as meaning that he was actually responsible for the direction of the manorial economy and had to pay over the profits of demesne farming to the king.[4] But in 1086 the word *custodit* was not always used in this strict sense and might cover cases where the manor was rented, either by the 'custodian' or by someone else.[5] Many royal manors were certainly let to tenants; and the

---

et una virgata quae ibi fuerunt T.R.E. sed praepositi accommodaverunt eas suis amicis': Dd. i, f. 30*b*. But this is one of those cases where, as Professor Hoyt remarks, 'it is not clear whether a sheriff's official or an independent royal bailiff is meant': op. cit., p. 11 n. 4.

[1] 'cui dominus ejus jam dictus Picotus . . . totius vicecomitatus negotia commiserat': *Liber Eliensis*, i. 267. We are told that St. Ethelreda and her sister saints appeared unto Gervase and beat him to death—'in quo patet quam mirabilis sit Deus in sanctis suis': ibid., pp. 268–9.

[2] 'Et fac abbati praedicto plenam rectitudinem de Eadwi praeposito tuo et de aliis ministris tuis qui monachis suis injuriam fecerunt': *Chronicon*, ii. 41. This and the preceding case are cited by Morris, op. cit., pp. 53, 54 n. 97.

[3] Dd. i, f. 164, cited by Morris, op. cit., p. 63 n. 188; cf. Slaughter (*Sclostre*), f. 163. Similar action by a reeve (*prepositus regis*) is recorded at Cheltenham (*Chinteneham*), f. 162*b*. At Sparsholt in Berkshire the sheriff had made the lands of three *liberi homines* into a single manor, f. 57.

[4] For the distinction between holding *in custodia* and holding *ad firmam* see Round, *Geoffrey de Mandeville*, Appendix I, pp. 297–8; cf. Stenton, *V.C.H. Derbys*. i. 297.

[5] Of Bergholt in Suffolk, which Aluric Wanz *custodit*, we read: 'Modo reddit ille Aluricus lx libras ad pensum et sic tenet de rege tali conventione quod debet facere

evidence seems to suggest that the sheriffs farmed the farming out of the manors rather than the manors themselves. Occasionally a sheriff will indeed take over one of the king's estates as *firmarius*. For Bromsgrove in Worcestershire, which had rendered £18 of farm in the time of King Edward, Urse d'Abitot, the Norman sheriff, rendered £24 by weight so long as he had the wood.[1] Bradstone in Devon rendered 60s. when Baldwin the sheriff received it at farm.[2] It seems likely too that the sheriff really held at farm some of the manors of which we are only told that they were worth so much, or rendered so much, when he 'received' them. This is suggested by the case of Exning (*Esselinge*) in Cambridgeshire. The *firmarius* of Exning was a man named Godric and not the sheriff Picot; but what is significant is that in Domesday Book the manor is merely described as worth £12 when Godric received it and that only the Cambridgeshire Inquest shows that he was holding it *ad firmam de rege*.[3] Yet in the Exchequer Domesday references to the 'reception' of manors by sheriffs are not very common and in two Kentish cases it seems

regi lx libras de proficuo . . . et dicit etiam quod non remanet in eo quod non facit illud proficuum': Dd. ii, ff. 287, 287*b*. Benfleet in Essex renders £12, though Rannulf, brother of Ilger *custodit hoc manerium*, while the statement 'tamen non est appreciatum nisi viii libras' makes it doubly certain that the £12 was in fact (as the word *reddit* implies) an actual rent and not an estimate of profits: ibid., f. 1*b*. Nor were such uses of the word *custodit* peculiar to the Little Domesday: the three Derbyshire manors of Bakewell, Ashford, and Hope, which William Peverel *custodit*, render £10. 6s.: Dd. i, f. 273.

[1] Ibid., f. 172. The sheriff appears to have rented four other royal estates in Worcestershire, but the abbreviation *vicecom* might conceivably be extended as *vicecomiti*, in which case the rent was paid to and not by the sheriff, though the construction makes this unlikely: ibid., f. 172*b*. On the same folio an entry about Tardebigge tells us that the sheriff of Staffordshire receives the farm of this manor in Swinford, and the words *et reddit* have been inserted above the line after the word *recipit*.

[2] Exon., p. 84: 'reddit lx solidos ad pensum et quando Balduinus vicecomes recepit eam ad firmam reddebat tantumdem.' Hugh fitz Baldric, who had been sheriff in Nottinghamshire, held at farm, on the *Terra Regis* in Leicestershire, Nether Broughton and Croxton Kerrial (with its dependencies Knipton and Harston); and all these places lie very near the Nottinghamshire border, Knipton being within 8 miles of Kilvington in that county, a manor which Hugh held in chief. But then he also farmed the royal manor of Casterton in Northamptonshire (now Rutland) which is separated from Nottinghamshire by the entire breadth of Leicestershire; and it is significant that both this place and the places he farmed in the latter county had formerly belonged to Morkar. See Dd. i, ff. 230, 291*b*, 219*b*; cf. *V.C.H. Leics.* i. 287.

[3] Dd. i, f. 189*b*; I.C.C., p. 4. Round seems to have assumed that *recepit* means 'received at farm': see *V.C.H. Hants*, i. 423; and Professor Hoyt appears to take the same view: op. cit., p. 74 n. 25. For the reasons given in the next note I hold this to be erroneous.

clear that the sheriff was not in fact the *firmarius*; while in the Exon. Domesday, which contains numerous entries of the kind in relation to manors in Somerset and Devon, we also find evidence that the word *recepit* did not necessarily imply that the receiver himself held the manor at farm.[1] When sheriffs 'received' the king's manors, we ought, I think, to understand that they became responsible for their farming out and for paying into the royal treasury whatever was due to the king from them, or, where the royal revenues from the shire were already compounded into a fixed 'farm of the shire', became entitled to treat the renders from the manors as component parts of that farm. They might, and sometimes did, take royal manors at farm themselves; and there is abundant evidence that sheriffs and others often made use of their official positions to feather their own nests.[2] But to what extent they put royal manors to farm to themselves is hidden from us, for Domesday has little to say about the *firmarii*; and, even where names are vouchsafed us, it is often impossible to discover whether or no their bearers were or had been sheriffs.[3] It seems likely that Fulcred who received Oakford in Dorset *ad firmam de rege* had been sheriff in that county, for the way in which he is described in the Exon. Domesday as 'receiving' manor after manor in Dorset is closely parallel to what we read about the sheriffs of Somerset and Devon. But there can be no certainty in the

---

[1] I have noted the following royal manors which are described in the Exchequer Domesday as 'received' by a sheriff or one who was probably sheriff—Maldon and Brightlingsea in Essex (ii, f. 6); Thorney and Blytheborough in Suffolk (ii, ff. 281*b*, 282); Bayford and Hitchin in Hertfordshire (i, f. 133); Eling and Holdenhurst in Hampshire (i, ff. 38*b*, 39); and Dartford and Milton Regis in Kent (i, f. 2*b*). But Dartford was held at farm by a French reeve; and of Milton we are told that it was worth £200 when Haimo the sheriff received it, that he who holds it (*qui tenet*) renders certain sums, and that the reeve (perhaps the same person as the tenant) gives Haimo £12. The clause 'Haimoni vicec' dat prepositus xii libras' makes it almost certain that in the Dartford entry the clause 'Super haec reddit vicec' c solidos' should be understood in the same sense, *vicec*' being extended as *vicecomiti*. In the Exon. Domesday the tell-tale entry is one which informs us that Braunton in Devon 'reddit per annum xvi libras ad pensum et quando Balduinus vicecomes recepit hanc qui tenet eam ad firmam de rege reddebat tantumdem' (Exon., p. 76).

[2] Stenton, *Anglo-Saxon England*, p. 625 and n. 1.

[3] The names of a good many sheriffs are known from charters or casual references in Domesday, but the information is very incomplete and it is only rarely that one can assign even approximate dates to the period of office of any individual. The charter evidence shows that 'sheriffdoms changed hands with some frequency' (Davis, *Regesta*, p. xxx). And that makes it all the more likely that individuals may have served as sheriff without any record of the fact having survived.

matter.[1] It is, however, certain that some royal manors were farmed by people whom there is no reason to regard as sheriffs, and in some counties more than one individual has to be reckoned with, so that even if all of them had at one time or another held the shrievalty and let out a manor to themselves to farm, they evidently continued to hold the farm after they had vacated the office—which means, of course, that it was not *qua* sheriff that they held it. In Cambridgeshire, the royal manor at Litlington is farmed by William the Chamberlain and Otho the Goldsmith, but it is William de Noweres who holds Wood Ditton *ad firmam de rege*, and Godric, as we have seen, is *firmarius* at Exning.[2] In Dorset, besides Fulcred at Oakford, we find a certain Roger who has received Lodres at farm, and, so far as we can tell, still holds it.[3] In Devon, though Baldwin the Sheriff has received Bradstone at farm, Lifton (*Listona*) is held *ad firmam de rege* by a man named Coluin who appears to have been Queen Edith's steward.[4] In Gloucestershire, Roger renders £170 from the manor of Berkeley and its dependencies, Humphrey is paying rent for Thornbury and Fairford, Ralf pays rent for the principal manor at Tewkesbury, Robert d'Oilly holds Shenington *ad firmam*, and, at Barrington, 'Elsi' of Faringdon and Godwin of Stanton each hold a manor *in firma regis*.[5] Occasionally, the statements in Domesday make it clear that someone other than the sheriff is *firmarius*. The manor of Hempstead in Gloucestershire was not at farm when the Earl (William fitz Osbern) had it, but now the sheriff has put it out for 60s.[6] The man who holds Stoke-next-Guildford in Surrey renders £15 by weight and the sheriff has 25s.[7] From the manor of Havering in Essex, Peter the Sheriff receives £80 *de censu* and £10 *de gersuma*; from Hatfield Broadoak he receives £80 and a *gersuma* of £5; from Stanway £33 and a *gersuma* of £3.[8] In Bedfordshire, Ivo Taillebois has

---

[1] Exon. pp. 26–28. 'Aiulfus vicecomes' is mentioned as if he was sheriff in 1086: ibid., p. 29.   [2] Dd. i, ff. 190, 189b; I.C.C., p. 4.

[3] Exon., p. 28.

[4] Ibid., p. 84. See O. von Feilitzen, *Pre-Conquest Names of Domesday Book*, p. 218. He is identified by Feilitzen with the king's thegn named Coluin who retained in 1086 some lands in Devon which he had held before the Conquest.

[5] Dd. i, ff. 163, 163b, 164. Shenington was only transferred to Oxfordshire in 1833. 'Elsi' or 'Alsi' of Faringdon was a king's thegn (ibid., ff. 162b, 170b).

[6] 'Hoc manerium cepit W. comes in dominio et non fuit ad firmam. Sed modo vicecomes posuit eum ad lx solidos': ibid., f. 164.   [7] Ibid., f. 30.

[8] Dd. ii, ff. 3, 2b, 4b. The Peter of the Stanway entry and the unnamed sheriff of the Hatfield entry must be Peter de Valognes, referred to as *Petrus vicecomes* in that relating to Havering.

increased the rents of Leighton Buzzard, Luton, and Houghton Regis, reserving in each case an ounce of gold for the sheriff.[1]

Some great barons held land at farm. In the case of Robert d'Oilly, who, as we have seen, farmed Shenington, a 10-hide estate dependent upon the great royal manor of Tewkesbury, it is possible to guess the reason which led him to take it, for Shenington is only half-a-dozen miles from Hook Norton, the head of his own honour, and his desire to increase his possessions in this neighbourhood is evident from the trouble he took to obtain Tadmarton from the Abbot of Abingdon and the resentment he is reported to have felt when he was made to give it up.[2] But Hugh de Port, the great Hampshire baron, farms some land in Northamptonshire that had belonged to Queen Edith, though, so far as we can tell, he had no other possessions in the Midlands.[3]

A very different type of tenant-in-chief is represented by William, son of Stur, who appears as the farmer of four royal manors in the Isle of Wight. He seems to have been a local man, who held in chief two manors and a number of very small properties in the island, and a small manor at Sopley on the edge of the New Forest, but he played a larger part as a farmer, rendering £60 for the four manors though they were worth less.[4]

One who was not a tenant-in-chief at all might be a *firmarius* on a large scale. Robert Latin or Latimer does not appear among the tenants-in-chief, but may be identified with the Robert Latimier who is described as one of the sheriff's *ministri* in a charter issued by Gundulf some time between 1088 and 1108. As we have seen he farmed several manors in Kent on the fee of Odo of Bayeux. For three he paid a rent in excess of the figures at which they were valued—at Chatham and Boxley greatly in excess. If we assume that the rent was equal to the value where nothing but the value is given, the total amount of rent he had to pay was over £114, and that figure does not include the

---

[1] Dd. i, f. 209, 209b. Ivo's kinsman Ralf Taillebois had been sheriff in Bedfordshire some time before 1086 (ibid., f. 218b) and Ivo's action suggests that he himself held that office. From the *Textus Roffensis* (p. 150) we learn that Picot the Sheriff, acting on the assumption that some land at Freckenham in Suffolk was *terra regis*, granted it to a *regis serviens* named Olchete: this was before 1082, for Odo of Bayeux was acting as justiciar when the land was adjudged to belong to Rochester. The judgement is mentioned in Domesday: *Textus Roffensis*, p. 151; Dd. ii, f. 381.

[2] *Chron. Abingdon*, ii. 7–8: cf. p. 70 above.

[3] Dd. i, f. 219.

[4] Ibid., ff. 52b, 53, 48b.

rent of Lessness (a manor which he also held of Odo) because the language of Domesday Book seems to suggest that he had sublet this estate and was the receiver rather than the payer of the rent, which amounted to £30 as compared with a valuation of £22. It is perhaps significant that Lessness lay apart from Robert's other lands, being near Erith on the Thames, whereas, so far as they can be precisely located, the estates he is described as farming, though not in a compact block, were all situated in the valley of the Medway or its tributaries, within eight miles of Maidstone.[1]

The scale of Robert Latin's farming engagements can be paralleled even in the same county and on the same fee; for an anonymous tenant held the great manor of Hoo for a rent of £113.[2] And if figures quite so large as these are unusual, it is not uncommon to find *firmarii* who have committed themselves to very substantial undertakings. The French reeve who holds the royal manor of Dartford in Kent *ad firmam* has to find more than £87 reckoned in various ways.[3] The archiepiscopal manor of South Malling in Sussex has been held at farm by a man named Godfrey for £90, though the use of the past tense seems to indicate that he was no longer farming it in 1086.[4] Richard fitz Gilbert has let Thaxted in Essex to an Englishman for a rent of £60 and has given Desning (*Deselinga*) in Suffolk to 'a certain reeve' at farm for £65.[5] In most cases only the amount of the render is recorded or we are merely told that the manor is at farm for so much; but where the figure is large it seems probable that an individual *firmarius* was responsible, for it is only small properties that are ever described in Domesday as held at

---

[1] Dd. i, ff. 6*b*, 7, 8, 8*b*, 11*b* and see p. 114 above. For Gundulf's charter see *Textus Roffensis*, pp. 214–15. The Lessness entry runs 'et tamen qui tenet reddit xxx libras' (f. 6*b*). I cannot locate some land 'in Somerden hundred' for which Latin paid a rent of £6. Besides the lands he held of Odo, Latin held a *jugum* worth 5*s*. in the manor of Lenham which belonged to St. Augustine's and lies some 2 miles from Harrietsham, the parish in which the lost hamlet of Harbilton was situated: Dd. i, f. 12 (*Lertham*: for the identification with Lenham see *An Eleventh Century Inquisition*, ed. Ballard, p. 2). If Professor Douglas is right in identifying him with the *Rodbertus interpres* of Domesday Monachorum, p. 87, he also held some land at Otford. According to the *Textus Roffensis* (p. 160) Robert Latimier on his death-bed gave to the monks of Rochester a marsh in the Isle of Grain which he held of Archbishop Anselm and which produced 30*s*. a year. From Gundulf's charter it appears that he had a brother named Ælfwin who was reeve (*praepositus*) of Chatham: perhaps this was the same man as Ælfwine the priest's son who also gave a marsh in the Isle of Grain to Rochester: *Textus Roffensis*, p. 182.

[2] Dd. i, f. 8*b*.
[3] Ibid., f. 2*b*.
[4] Ibid., f. 16.
[5] Dd. ii, ff. 38*b*, 390.

farm by a group of persons. And if this evidence is admitted, we are forced to conclude that over a great part of the south of England *firmarii* were renting large and valuable manors. In Kent, besides the examples already cited, Domesday shows us on the archbishop's estates a render of £101 at Aldington and one of £60 both at Charing and at Lyminge; and we also find Bilsington, a demesne manor of Odo of Bayeux, paying a farm of £70, Elham, another of his manors, paying £50, and Sturry, which belongs to St. Augustine's, paying £54.[1] In Surrey, the rent of Odo's manor of Bramley (*Brunlei*) is only 40d. short of £80.[2] In Sussex, as in Kent, large-scale arrangements seem to have been particularly frequent. On the fee of Earl Roger, Singleton (*Silletone*) renders £120 and a mark of gold, Harting and Trotton together render precisely the same as Singleton, and rents of £50 are recorded for Westbourne and for Stoughton (*Estone*).[3] Further, in the same county, Steyning, which belongs to the abbey of Fécamp, is at farm for £121. 18s.; and on the fee of William de Braose, Washington *was* at farm (*fuit ad firmam*) for £100 and Old Shoreham (*Soresham*) for £50; while the archbishop's manor of Pagham renders £80.[4] Hampshire can also show several examples of this kind of thing—Chalton (*Ceptune*) (Earl Roger) rendering £110 and a mark of gold; Sutton (Count Eustace) rendering £80; Overton (the Bishop of Winchester) at farm for £61.[5] In Dorset, Frampton, which belongs to the Abbaye aux Hommes at Caen, renders £40.[6] Then, in Wiltshire, we have the Glastonbury Abbey manor of Damerham (*Dobreham*) with a farm of £61; and, in Devon, the manors of Ottery St. Mary and Rawridge, which belong to St. Mary of Rouen, are paying each year £70 in Rouen pence.[7] Cornwall, however, can show nothing of the sort; and in Somerset, apart from the *Terra Regis*, one could only cite the Bishop of Winchester's gigantic manor of Taunton, of which it would be hazardous to suggest that its render of £154. 1s. 1d. represents the obligations of a single *firmarius* rather than the sum of a variety of rents and dues that were payable at the centre of this

---

[1] Dd. i, ff. 4, 3b, 4, 10b, 9b, 12. [2] Ibid., f. 31. [3] Ibid., ff. 23, 23b, 24.

[4] Ibid., ff. 17, 28, 16b. Steyning included a borough, so perhaps a collective *firmarius* is in this case less unlikely, but the manor (for such it is called) was mainly agricultural as is indicated by the large number of ploughs—seven on demesne and forty-eight belonging to the peasants.

[5] Ibid., ff. 44b, 40. [6] Ibid., f. 78b.

[7] Ibid., ff. 66b, 104. Damerham is now in Hampshire.

great complex.[1] But farther north, in Gloucestershire, Roger d'Ivry's manors of Tetbury and Upton are jointly at farm for £50; and, on the other side of England, Necton in Norfolk, which belonged to Ralf de Toeni, is, with its dependencies, rendering £60 by weight.[2] If we take account of royal manors the list of counties for which there is evidence of this kind of thing can be somewhat increased, for on the *Terra Regis* one or more examples of farms or renders exceeding £50 are found not only in most of the counties already mentioned, but also in Herefordshire, Worcestershire, Oxfordshire, Berkshire, Buckinghamshire, and Hertfordshire.[3] Domesday Book has, however, nothing to say of such large-scale undertakings in what might roughly be described as the northern half of England. We may perhaps conclude that they really belong predominantly to the south; but it would be rash to infer their entire absence from regions in which direct evidence for their existence is wanting, for as we have seen, rents in Domesday often masquerade as valuations, and one cannot exclude the possibility that here and there a number of small or moderate-sized manors may have been held at farm by the same individual without the fact being recorded.[4]

Occasionally, though very rarely, Domesday shows us a manor held at farm by the peasantry. Willesden in Middlesex, which belongs to the Canons of St. Paul's, is so held, and the valuation of £6. 6s. 6d. no doubt represents the rent that the *villani* paid.[5] In Surrey, on the estates of Chertsey Abbey, *villani* hold East Clandon and pay £6 for it though it is only worth £4.[6] It seems probable that a similar condition of affairs obtained on the Bishop of Winchester's manors of Millbrook and Alverstoke in Hampshire, valued respectively at £5 and £6, for though nothing is said about renders or farms, we are told that the

---

[1] Ibid., f. 87b. Taunton is like Steyning in being a mainly agricultural estate though it included a borough, but it is not like Steyning definitely stated to be *ad firmam* and the Domesday description of it is exceptionally complicated.

[2] Ibid., f. 168; ii, f. 235, 235b.

[3] Leominster (Hereford), Dd. i, f. 180; Droitwich (Worcester), f. 172b; Bensington, Headington, Kirtlington, Shipton-under-Wychwood, Bampton, and Bloxham with Adderbury (Oxford), f. 154b; Sutton Courtenay (Berkshire), f. 57b; Aylesbury (Bucks.), f. 143; Hitchin (Hertford), f. 133.

[4] None of the manors held by Robert Latin was *valued* at more than £35 (though the actual render of Boxley was £55); and it is only the fact that his name is recorded that enables us to discover that his farming undertakings were on a very large scale.

[5] Ibid., f. 127b.

[6] Ibid., f. 34.

villani 'hold' each of these places.[1] A somewhat larger under-
taking is revealed at Blakenham in Suffolk where William de
Scoie's manor is held at farm by *homines* for a rent of £12 a year
and a *gersuma* of an ounce of gold payable every three years; but
one cannot be sure that these *homines* were working peasants,
and in any case they came to grief.[2] Probably there was considerably more farming out of small estates to the peasantry
than is recorded in Domesday Book. It is only from the Exon.
text that we learn the real position on Goscelin of Exeter's
little manor of *Herstanhaia* in Devon: the Exchequer Domesday
says that 6 *villani* have 3 ploughs there and that the estate
renders 20s., but Exon. tells us that the *villani* hold both the land
and the ploughs *ad firmam*.[3] It is again only the Exon. text which
makes it clear that the manor of Lympstone (*Leuestona*) in Devon
was farmed by the peasants for £8.[4] Arrangements of this sort
may well have been in force on a good many estates where there
was no demesne.[5] But if such methods of estate management had
been really common, or had been employed at all frequently on
large and important manors, they could hardly have failed to
leave more traces in the records. In some cases, moreover, it
seems impossible to know whether one ought to think of a small
manor held at farm by a village community or only of a few
peasants paying a rent individually for their holdings. It would
be rash, for example, to draw definite conclusions about the
arrangements on several manors of St. Paul's in Middlesex,
where small groups of *villani* are described as holding the land
sub canonicis: the conditions may or may not have been similar
to those obtaining at Willesden.[6]

The names of *firmarii* are very seldom recorded in Domesday
Book or any of its satellites.[7] But names of native origin form
a remarkably large proportion of the few that are recorded. We

---

[1] Dd. i, f. 41*b*. *Villani tenuerunt et tenent.*

[2] Dd. ii, f. 353*b*: 'homines qui sic ad firmam receperunt omnes fuerunt confusi.'

[3] Dd. i, f. 113; Exon., p. 371.

[4] Exon., p. 425; cf. Dd. i, f. 113. I owe my knowledge of this example to Professor R. S. Hoyt's illuminating article in *Speculum*, xxx (April 1955), 153.

[5] For examples of such estates see Vinogradoff, *English Society*, pp. 396 n. 1 and 2,
and 397 n. 1. Vinogradoff goes so far as to say that 'the absence of hall and demesne
indicates self-governing communities, farming their own dues'.

[6] Dd. i, f. 128.

[7] The tenants of manors let at farm are often named without anything being said
to show whether the named tenant was the *firmarius* who paid the rent or the lord
who received it.

have Coluin in Devon, Brictric and Ulward in Somerset, Alsi of Faringdon in Oxfordshire and Gloucestershire, Godwin of Stanton in Gloucestershire, another Godwin in Leicestershire, the Saxon lady named Bristeva in Oxfordshire, a man named Ailric in Buckinghamshire.[1] There is Godric in Cambridgeshire; and in Norfolk, a Godric, who, bearing such a common name, is probably a different person, has apparently rented Whimpwell some time after the Conquest, but does so no longer.[2] In Essex, as we have seen, 'a certain Englishman' has been given Thaxted *ad censum* by Richard fitz Gilbert.[3] The great Kentish *firmarius* Robert Latin has a brother with an unmistakably Saxon name.[4]

It is perhaps allowable to conjecture that manors let at excessive rents were usually in the hands of English *firmarii*. The bargaining power of the conquered people must have been small; and their desperate desire to retain, or recover a hold upon the land from which they obtained their livelihood would, one suspects, be a stronger inducement to the acceptance of hard conditions than any unjustified optimism on the part of Norman adventurers.[5] Of the twelve people mentioned in the last paragraph, Ailric who farms in a small way and the anonymous farmer of the valuable manor of Thaxted are both described as suffering from excessive rents, and it seems to be implied that Godric at Whimpwell had paid £4 for land that was worth 30s. We remember too that Robert Latin is paying rents greater than their value for three of the manors that he holds. And three of the twelve—Ailric, Brictric, and Ulward—are stated to be in occupation of land that they had held in the time of King Edward.

Throughout a large area of southern and eastern England— in all the seaboard counties, in fact, from Norfolk to Hampshire, as well as in Berkshire and Surrey—frequent reference is made

---

[1] Exon., pp. 84. (Lifton), 453 (*Bochelanda*); Dd. i. ff. 154b, 164 (Langford, Shipton, Barrington), 230b (sub Dishley), 155 (Dorchester), 148b (Marsh Gibbon).
[2] I.C.C., p. 4. (Exning), Dd. ii, f. 220.
[3] Dd. ii, f. 38b.
[4] *Textus Roffensis*, p. 215.
[5] The fact that so many tenants-in-chief were able to enfeoff knights in excess of their *servitium debitum* seems to indicate that at the outset the Normans, if anything, underestimated the resources of the land. As to the recovery of land by the English the tradition preserved in the *Dialogus de Scaccario* is significant: 'Sic igitur quisquis de gente subacta fundos vel aliquid huiusmodi possidet, non quod ratione successionis deberi sibi videbatur adeptus est, set quod solummodo, meritis suis exigentibus vel aliqua pactione interveniente, obtinuit' (op. cit., ed. C. Johnson, p. 54). I am indebted to Professor Galbraith for calling my attention to this passage.

in Domesday to rents which exceed the value of the land or have proved to be oppressive. I have noted 57 examples in Hampshire, 30 in Kent, 17 in Sussex, 15 in Suffolk, 14 in Norfolk, 12 in Berkshire, 10 in Surrey, and 10 in Essex.[1] Within this region evidence of such extortion is found on the royal estates and on the estates of 28 lay and 16 ecclesiastical tenants-in-chief.[2] It is, moreover, possible that the geographical concentration of the references to excessive rents reflects differences in the methods employed by different bodies of Domesday commissioners rather than an actual peculiarity of conditions in this part of England. The eight counties in question coincide with those which Ballard, in agreement with Eyton, judged on stylistic grounds to have formed the areas of two of the commissioners' circuits.[3] On the other hand excessive rents are mentioned sporadically outside this region. I have noticed single cases of this in Derbyshire, Bedfordshire, Buckinghamshire, and Wiltshire.[4] It must, therefore, remain in doubt whether or no the geographical pattern apparent in the Domesday evidence corresponds with the facts of the case. But, for the region for which it is explicit, the witness of Domesday supplies a striking confirmation of what the Saxon Chronicle asserts about the extortionate methods employed by the king on the royal estates and shows that a similar policy was pursued upon other estates both lay and ecclesiastical. The words of the Chronicle are memorable: 'The King gave his land as dearly for rent as he possibly could; then came some other

---

[1] I cannot claim to have made a complete enumeration of all the cases in Domesday, even for the counties mentioned; but the cases I may have overlooked cannot be numerous enough to affect the general truth of the picture suggested by the figures I give.

[2] Odo of Bayeux and Walter the Deacon have been reckoned as ecclesiastical lords: the others are the Archbishop of Canterbury, the Bishops of London, Winchester, Rochester, Chichester, Exeter, and Thetford, and the abbeys of Westminster, St. Augustine's, Chertsey, St. Peter of Winchester, St. Mary of Winchester, Fécamp, and Jumièges. Examples are found on the royal estates in all the eight counties. Among the lay tenants-in-chief is William, son of Stur: his manor of Sopley in Hampshire was let for more than its value, while he himself was paying an excessive rent for four manors in the Isle of Wight; but perhaps we are meant to understand that he also rented Sopley.

[3] Ballard, *The Domesday Inquest*, p. 12. As regards these two groups (Kent, Sussex, Surrey, Hampshire, Berkshire, on the one hand, and Essex, Norfolk, and Suffolk on the other) Professor Carl Stephenson's grouping of the Domesday counties according to the 'language of the record' is in agreement with Eyton and Ballard: *Speculum*, xxii (1947), 3–4.

[4] Melbourne (Derby, *Terra Regis*), i, f. 272*b*; Stotfold (Beds., Hugh de Beauchamp) i, f. 213; Marsh Gibbon (Bucks., William fitz Ansculf), i, f. 148*b*; Damerham (Wilts., but now in Hants, Glastonbury Abbey), i, f. 66*b*.

and bade more than the other had before given; and the King let it to the man who had bidden him more; then came a third and bade yet more, and the King gave it up to the man who had bidden most of all. And he recked not how very sinfully the reeves got it from poor men, nor how many illegalities they did.'[1]

The language of this celebrated passage seems to suit the case of *firmarii* who were independent leaseholders rather than officials; and perhaps the same may be said of the frequent references to excessive rents in Domesday Book. But occasionally the farmer of a manor is described as a reeve (*praepositus*) and such a one may well have held it in a more or less definitely official capacity.[2] A monk was sometimes put in charge of a monastic manor, but did not thereby cease to be a monk owing obedience to his abbot, though his duty in respect of the manor might be merely the payment of a fixed farm. A precious glimpse of the monk as reeve and *firmarius* is afforded by the *Textus Roffensis*. Sometime between 1094 and 1108—probably before 1100—two men who held the manor of Aston in Gloucestershire of Bishop Gundulf surrendered it in exchange for some land at Haddenham in Buckinghamshire; and Gundulf then instructed one of the monks of Rochester, a man named William who was *praepositus* of Haddenham, to take charge of Aston and render therefrom a farm of eight days a year.[3] That this was not an isolated

---

[1] *Anglo-Saxon Chronicle*, sub anno 1086 (really 1087), ed. Thorpe (Rolls Series), i. 354, and for the translation, ii. 187. The paraphrase of the Chronicle in Henry of Huntingdon is worth noting, as it definitely relates the passage in question to 'farming out': 'Rex ipse cum ad firmam terras suas quanto carius poterat, dedisset, alii magis offerenti, et deinde, alii, semper negligens pactum, et ad majora studens, dabat' (Rolls Series, p. 209). This sort of thing is so contrary to traditional views of medieval economy that the reader may be inclined to regard it as an unprecedented outcome of Norman tyranny; and it seems therefore desirable to recall the fact that a grant of the year 902 by which Denewulf, Bishop of Winchester, let Ebbesbourne to his kinsman Beornwulf for a rent of 45*s.*, contains the suggestive proviso 'that no one be permitted by offering a higher rent to turn him out': F. E. Harmer, op. cit., No. xvii. In this connexion it is interesting to note that Ralf de Toeni (apparently the Domesday tenant-in-chief) in the charter of *c.* 1115 by which he granted the soke of Necton in Norfolk to William, son of Estangrin, *in feofirma* to him and his heir, makes the declaration: 'Et si quis voluerit mihi plus crescere in firma non auferam Gullielmo sed teneat honorifice' (D. C. Douglas, *Social Structure of Medieval East Anglia*, Appendix I, No. 57).

[2] See, for example, Dartford (Kent), Dd. i, f. 2*b*, and Bergholt (Suffolk), ii, f. 287*b*, on the royal estates; Newenden (Kent), i, f. 4, on those of the archbishop; and Desning (Suffolk), ii, f. 390, which belonged to Richard fitz Gilbert. In the last three cases, moreover, the rent was definitely excessive.

[3] 'Dum hoc ita fuit, praecepit episcopus domno Willelmo monacho Rofensi

case in the Rochester economy is suggested, if not actually proved, by the account of a dispute about some land near Freckenham in Suffolk which some time between 1077 and 1082 ended in the restoration of this land to the Church. An important witness in the case was a monk named Grim who had long been *praepositus* at Freckenham 'et ex eadem terra servitia et costumas ut de aliis terris de Frackenham susceperat'.[1] Two pre-Conquest examples are provided by the Chronicle of Ramsey Abbey. Some time, it seems, between 1034 and 1049 a certain Lefsius had given the abbey some lands in four Lincolnshire villages along with his son Morker, who entered the abbey school; and we are told that after the father's death Morker, who had become a monk, held these lands *vice firmarii* and paid a yearly rent— 'statutum ex eis censum singulis annis persolvit'—until he was dispossessed by Odo of Bayeux.[2] The Ramsey Chronicle also tells us that 3 hides at Bottisham in Cambridgeshire were given to a monk named Ailric *firmarii vice custodiendum* and that this monk, for many years afterwards until the coming of the Normans, 'dedit exinde Ramesensi ecclesiae censum et firmam constitutam'.[3] Moreover, this Ailric appears in Domesday Book as the former tenant of 2 hides in Bottisham which he could not give or sell without the permission of the Abbot of Ramsey whose man he was.[4] And this is rather significant, for without the information supplied by the chronicler we should not know that Ailric had acted as a *firmarius*, and it seems unlikely that

praeposito de Hedenham curam accipere ejusdem manerii et monachis ecclesiae Sancti Andreae singulis annis firmam octo dierum inde reddere. Et quidem juste, quoniam terrae illae, quae datae fuerunt pro ipsius manerii cambitione, fuerant primum de Hedenham quod penitus erat et est ad victum monachorum': *Textus Roffensis*, p. 220. We also hear of a Rochester monk named Clement 'qui primo habuit custodiam de Hedenham post episcopum', but it is hard to say whether this means after Gundulf's death or after the manor was allotted to the monks: in the latter case Clement was presumably a predecessor of the monk William: *Registrum Roffense*, p. 119.

[1] *Textus Roffensis*, pp. 150–1. As Grim had been *praepositus* for a long time—'ipse enim monachus diu praepositus de Frackenham extiterat'—it is possible that he was not yet a monk when he was appointed, for there were no monks at Rochester when Gundulf became bishop in 1077.

[2] *Chron. Rams.* (Rolls Series), pp. 153–4. The gift was made in the presence of Bishop Ædnoth—presumably Ædnoth II, Bishop of Dorchester 1034–49. It seems just possible that Morker's tenancy began after the Conquest for he is said to have acknowledged the abbey's right to the lands in the presence of Edward of Salisbury, but the dispossession by Odo is stated to have taken place *in permutatione regni*.

[3] Ibid., pp. 144–5.

[4] Dd. i, f. 196.

this common Domesday formula was never employed in the
same sense in other cases where supplementary information of
this kind is not available. Certainly one cannot argue from the
scarcity of direct references to arrangements of this type. At
least in the case of an official who may be ordered from one
place to another, like the Rochester monk William, the instructions given would not need to be recorded like the terms of
a lease. And indirect evidence that it was not uncommon to
employ monks as *firmarii* in the early Norman period is indeed
provided by the fact that in 1102 the practice was forbidden by
the Council of London.[1]

The evidence for leasing is much more abundant. For
centuries before the Norman Conquest this method of dealing
with property had been in use. The great series of Worcester
leases begins with one granted by Bishop Wilfred in the first
half of the eighth century; contains several examples from the
next century; culminates in the great mass of leases—more than
seventy in number—that were granted by St. Oswald between
961 and 992; and includes about a dozen granted by Oswald's
successors down to Ealdred, who held the see of Worcester until
1062 and as Archbishop of York officiated at the coronation of
William the Conqueror.[2] Since most of these leases were for three
lives, or, to speak more exactly, were granted to the original
lessee and two heirs after his day, it is probable that even some
of those dating from Oswald's episcopate were still in being at
the time of the Domesday Inquest. And Domesday Book is witness that leases of this kind were not peculiar to the church of
Worcester. In the time of King Edward, an Abbot of Glastonbury had granted 3 hides at Hannington in Wiltshire to a
certain thegn for three lives; and in the same county a man

[1] 'Ne monachi teneant villas ad firmam': Eadmer, *Hist. Nov.* (Rolls Series),
p. 143. Professor Knowles, who quotes this canon and others of later date to the
same effect (op. cit., p. 443 n. 2), observes, however, that 'what the councils
directly attacked was the leasing of land to monks, who paid an agreed sum to the
monastery and disposed of the profits like any other farmer' (p. 438 n. 2). The
monk Ailric must have held a fairly independent position at Bottisham for Domesday to treat him as a tenant.

[2] For Bishop Wilfred's lease see Birch, *Cart. Sax.*, No. 166: it is a lease for two
lives relating to Bibury in Gloucestershire and is described by Stenton as 'the first
recorded English lease' (op. cit., p. 478). Birch dates it between 721 and 743. We
know of several leases granted by Oswald's successors before 1058 besides those
whose texts have been preserved: altogether Mr. N. R. Ker reckons 28 for the
period between 1016 (? 1003) and 1058: *Studies in Medieval History Presented to
F. M. Powicke*, 1948, p. 69.

named Toti had obtained a hide at *Hiwi* for three lives from the church of Malmesbury.[1] Leases for three lives dating from the Confessor's reign also appear in Worcestershire, where the manor of Selly Oak (*Escelie*) had been leased to Wlwin by the Bishop of Chester and a hide at Wadborough, which belonged to the abbey of Pershore, had been leased to a king's thegn named Godric who paid the monks an annual 'farm' *pro recognitione*.[2] During the same reign, again, the manor of Worthy in Hampshire had been granted out on similar terms.[3] And according to the Abingdon chronicler leases for 'three or two' lives were common on the estates of that house just before the Norman Conquest.[4] In Domesday Book the evidence for leases limited to a single life is perhaps stronger and geographically more extensive; though it is possible that some of the life interests referred to were those of the last holders of leases for more than one life, or originated in bequests subject to a life interest rather than in leases. We have unequivocal examples of life leases granted in the generation preceding the Conquest by Herman, Bishop of Sherborne (or Ramsbury), at Potterne in Wiltshire; by Bishop Alwold (*Ælfweard*), Herman's predecessor in the see of Sherborne, at South Perrott (*Pedret*) in Dorset; by the abbey of Cerne at Cheriton in Somerset; by the Abbot of Evesham at Witton in Droitwich, Worcestershire; by the Bishop of Hereford at Bayston (*Begestan*) in Shropshire; by the Bishop and monks of Winchester at *Svantone* in Hampshire.[5] What seem to be straightforward cases are also found in Suffolk, at *Nocturna* (? Norton), a manor that had belonged to the Abbot of St. Edmunds, and at Little Bealings, where a man named Beorn had obtained a lease for life from the Abbot of Ely; and, though the wording of Domesday is not quite conclusive, we know from the *Historia Eliensis* that the life interest which a certain Gudmund enjoyed in 1066 at Nacton in the same county had been

---

[1] Dd. i, ff. 66b, 72.   [2] Ibid., ff. 177, 175.

[3] Ibid., f. 46b. 'Hoc manerium extra ecclesiam emptum fuit eo pacto et conventione ut post tercium heredem cum omni pecunia manerium ecclesia S. Petri de episcopatu reciperet.' Presumably the Bishop of Winchester was the lessor.

[4] 'Praeterea mos illis diebus futurum ad damnum non parum insoluerat ut offerente quolibet auri vel argenti copiam, trium aut quinque terre portionem hidarum, sive villam integram, diversis abbatiae locis reciperet emptione, quodam subornatu id palliantes, quatinus trium vel duorum vita hominum inde possidendi protenderetur permissio': op. cit., i. 481.

[5] Dd. i, ff. 66, 80, 96b, 177b, 257, 47. Some of these cases are commented on by Freeman, *History of the Norman Conquest*, v, appendix, n. G.

first granted to him by Abbot Wulfric of Ely, who was his brother, and then defined or confirmed by Wulfric's successor Thurstan.[1] It may well be, again, that leases for life are intended by the entries in Domesday relating to *Newetone* (? North Newnton) in Wiltshire, where the lease was held of the Abbess of Wilton; Treyford in Sussex, where it was held of the Abbot of St. Peter's at Winchester; Gaddesden in Hertfordshire, which then belonged to the Abbot of St. Albans; and Milton in Cambridgeshire on an estate of the abbey of Ely which passed after the Conquest into the greedy hands of Picot the Sheriff; but the language employed in relation to each of these places might suit the case of the last life of a longer lease.[2] At Sparsholt in Berkshire, land had been given by a man to his son, who was a monk at Abingdon, subject to a life charge in favour of the donor.[3] An entry relating to Little Melton in Norfolk seems to imply an arrangement of the sort known in continental usage as a *precaria oblata*—a gift of land to the abbey of St. Benet (? of Holme) by a man who has received it back as a life tenant—and Norfolk also supplies more certain examples of the type at Smallburgh, on land belonging to the same abbey, and at Broome, on the lands of St. Edmund.[4] Moreover, we find in Domesday a few cases, which, as Vinogradoff pointed out, are of the nature of a *precaria remuneratoria*.[5] This also was a means by which ecclesiastical landlords increased their estates, but differed from the *precaria oblata* in that the church granted a lease of some of its own land along with that 'offered' to it, so that 'donors', if such they can be called, would be attracted by the prospect of acquiring the temporary use of additional land, while the reversion of both estates was secured to the lessor. Leases of this kind are indicated in Domesday Book at Honing in Norfolk, at Pakenham and Topesfield and Gislingham in Suffolk, and at Conington and Yelling (together with Hemingford) in Huntingdonshire, the churches that granted them being the abbey of St. Benet of Holme, the abbey of St. Edmunds, Canterbury Cathedral,

---

[1] Dd. ii, ff. 286, 373, 406b; *Liber Eliensis*, i. 218–19; cf. E. Miller, *The Abbey and Bishopric of Ely*, pp. 25, 51.

[2] Dd. i, ff. 67b, 23, 139, 201b, cf. also Beechingstoke, Wilts., f. 67b.

[3] Dd. i, f. 59.

[4] Dd. ii, ff. 204b, 219b, 211b. The Little Melton entry runs thus: 'Parvam Meltunam tenuit [*or* tenebat?] Eduuinus T.R.E. de Sancto Benedicto et ita quod eam abbati concesserat post mortem suam.'

[5] *English Society*, p. 229.

Thorney Abbey, and Ramsey Abbey; but only in the case of
Honing is it clear that the ownership of the donor's land passed
to the church before his death and that it was only as a lessee
that he retained the use of it.[1] The Gislingham lease was really
for two lives—those of a man named Alsi and his wife. It had
been granted by Leofstan, who was Abbot of St. Edmunds from
1044 to 1065, and provided that on the death of the surviving
lessee the abbot was to receive a manor of Alsi's named Euston
as well as the reversion of Gislingham. But what makes this
example especially interesting is the fact that this was not the
first time that a lease of Gislingham had been used as a bait to
obtain more land for the abbey. Some time between 1043 and
1047 the Abbot of St. Edmunds had concluded an agreement
with a certain Wulfgeat and his wife and the text of this agreement has been preserved. It too is on the lines of a *precaria
remuneratoria* and provides that the couple in question shall take
over the land at Gislingham on condition that the abbey shall
have possession of it 'after the death of Ælfwine and his wife' and
that an estate at Fakenham which belonged to Wulfgeat shall
also 'pass without any controversy to St. Edmund's after the
death of both of them *(after here bopere day)*'.[2] It is hard to say to
whom the word 'both' in this last sentence refers and the relation between Wulfgeat and Ælfwine is also obscure—though
perhaps they were father and son, as Miss Robertson has suggested.[3] But the significance of the two leases as indications of
the policy pursued by the abbey is not affected by these doubts,
nor by the lack of certainty as to the precise identity of the lands
at Gislingham that were leased in the two cases.

The evidence of Domesday Book as to the prevalence and
nature of leasehold arrangements in the generation preceding
the Conquest can be supplemented to some extent from other
sources. Apart from the Worcester leases, of which something
has been said already, we learn that during this period Burghley
in Northamptonshire, which belonged to the abbey of Peterborough, was granted *ad firmam* for life to a certain Elfgar who
was one of Queen Edith's chaplains; that Ufi, Abbot of St.
Edmunds, had in 1043 or 1044 let some lands at Swanton
Novers and Hindolveston in Norfolk on a life lease to Stigand's
brother Æthelmaer; that Stigand himself had taken a life lease

---

[1] Dd. ii, ff. 219*b*, 361*b*, 372*b*, 444*b*; i, ff. 208, 208*b* (cf. 206*b*).
[2] Robertson, op. cit., No. c.   [3] Ibid., p. 436.

of Tidenham in Gloucestershire from the abbey of Bath and another of Methwold in Norfolk from the abbey of Ely; that the latter abbey had sought a compromise in a dispute about High Easter in Essex by granting it to Esgar the Staller for his life; that at Holcombe—probably Holcombe Rogus in Devon—Ælfwold, Bishop of Sherborne, had in 1045 or 1046 settled a dispute in the same way; that some time between 1046 and 1053 Æthelweard, Abbot of Glastonbury, had leased Uffcombe in Devon for life to a certain Edith, the widow of Hemming.[1] On the estates of the see of Winchester we find a life lease of Adderbury in Oxfordshire granted between 1039 and 1044, another of a newly-acquired estate at Hayling Island which dates from about 1053, and two leases for two lives granted between 1047 and 1057, one of them being a lease of a hide of land at Sparsholt in Hampshire and the other a lease of 3 hides at Alton Priors and Patney in Wiltshire.[2] From St. Albans Abbey, again, we have a lease for two lives relating to a place called *Cyrictuna* and dating from 1050–2, and another, a little later, by which a donor and his wife received back for their lives an estate at Studham in Bedfordshire that they had given to the abbey.[3] From Abingdon Abbey comes an account of a life lease of Leckhampstead in Berkshire which is particularly interesting because it was granted some time between 1030 and 1044 to the brother of a man who had held the same estate as the last life of a lease for three lives granted during the reign of Canute.[4] Yet further examples are

---

[1] *Chronicle of Hugh Candidus*, ed. W. T. Mellows, 1949, p. 67; Robertson, op. cit., No. xcvii, cf. pp. 431–2; ibid., No. cxvii; *Ely Inquest* in I.C.C., ed. Hamilton, p. 138, quoted by E. Miller, op. cit., p. 51 n. 5; *Liber Eliensis*, i. 216–18; Robertson, op. cit., No. cv, cf. pp. 447–8; *The Great Chartulary of Glastonbury*, ed. Watkin (Somerset Record Soc.), vol. i, No. 172, cited and discussed by H. P. R. Finberg in Hoskins and Finberg, *Devonshire Studies*, 1952, pp. 60–62. Croxton (Norfolk) as well as Methwold, was leased to Stigand by the Abbot of Ely and apparently for life, as the Ely Inquest says *et Crochestona similiter*. Stigand had also taken a lease of Snailwell in Cambridgeshire from Abbot Leofsige of Ely, and as Abbot Symeon subsequently laid claim to the manor this too was probably a lease for life: Dd. i, f. 199b; I.C.C., p. 3; Ely Inq. in I.C.C., p. 101. Stigand had further obtained the Ely manor of Wood Ditton but the men of the hundred did not know how: Dd. i, f. 189b.

[2] Robertson, op. cit., Nos. xcviii, cxiv, cvi, cvii. The last of these cannot be later than 1053 as Earl Godwine was one of the witnesses. It seems probable that the land at Alton Priors and Patney was the same as that held in 1086 by William Escudet: perhaps *Wluuardus Belgisone*, William's predecessor, was the second life of the pre-Conquest lease: see above, pp. 108–9.

[3] Kemble, *Cod. Dipl.*, Nos. 950, 945.

[4] Ibid., No. 948; Harmer, *Anglo-Saxon Writs* (1952), No. 3.

supplied by the chronicle of Ramsey Abbey—all of them dating
from the time of Abbot Alfwin, who became abbot in 1043 and
survived the Conquest, but retired from active participation in
conventual business, on account of ill health, some time before
the Confessor's death.[1] We read that when Ædnoth and his
wife dedicated their son to the monastic life they gave Ramsey
some land at *Acleia* (? Oakley, Northamptonshire) but continued
to have the use of the estate on condition that on the death of
the survivor it should pass into the possession of the abbey.[2] We
read again, that Burwell in Cambridgeshire was granted to
a kinsman of the donor of that estate 'in vita sua firmarii vice
tenendam'.[3] And the chronicle also tells us of leases of the
precaria remuneratoria type. One of these related to property at
Yelling and East Hemingford in the county of Huntingdon,
another to Cranfield in Bedfordshire, and a third to Westmill in
Hertfordshire.[4] The last case is closely parallel to that of the St.
Edmunds manor at Gislingham in Suffolk described above, for
Westmill like Gislingham was the subject of two leases of the
kind. The earlier of these, granted apparently between 1020 and
1043, had been a means to the acquisition of a manor at Offord
in Huntingdonshire; but the second ended in disaster as a result
of the Norman Conquest, for the abbey lost Westmill as well as the
prospect of obtaining Wood Walton in Huntingdonshire, which
should have passed into its possession on the death of the lessee.[5]

That it was very common in the generation before the Conquest for people to hold land on a tenancy of one or more lives
is thus certain. The evidence cited above relates to places in
eighteen counties and the estates of twenty ecclesiastical lords;
and there can be little doubt that in this evidence we have
merely the traces, almost fortuitously preserved, of arrangements

---

[1] Harmer, op. cit., pp. 340, 177.   [2] Ibid., pp. 173–4.
[3] Ibid., pp. 174–5.   [4] Ibid., pp. 152–3, 171–2, 145–6.
[5] Westmill was an outlying property—nearly 40 miles from Ramsey—while
Offord was about a dozen miles and Wood Walton only 6 miles away. This would
suggest a method in the policy pursued; but it was otherwise with the Yelling–
Hemingford lease, for the properties it sought to attract were distant. This lease
must be considered along with the other 'remuneratorial' lease relating to Yelling
and Hemingford which was previously referred to as mentioned in Domesday; but
it would seem that these two were not successive leases but concerned different portions of the abbey lands, for both the lessees appear to have survived until the
Conquest. One fell at Hastings: Dd. i, f. 208. The other appears as the (T.R.E.)
possessor of the four estates which Ramsey was to have obtained on his death—
Abington in Cambridgeshire, Ugley and Bumpstead in Essex, and *Walingafella*
(? Waldingfield) in Suffolk: Dd. i, f. 199b; ii, ff. 76b, 77b, 418b.

that must have been far more numerous than the cases mentioned. The conditions of a lease, it is true, would need to be put on record as the instructions given to a reeve would not; and we are not infrequently told that two or three copies were made.[1] But there can have been little motive for preserving such documents once the term of the lease had been reached and the property had reverted to the lessor; and it is surely significant that so many of the cases whose record has come down to us are of leases whose conditions in regard to the reversion of the estate had not been fulfilled—particularly as a result of the confiscations that followed the Norman Conquest—so that in these instances the lessor had good reason for preserving a record which might substantiate a claim to recover the property.[2] Leases for two or three lives would need to be preserved longer and would have a better chance of being entered in a cartulary than leases for a single life; and it may well be that we owe the survival of so many Worcester leases to the stimulus which the preponderance of leases for three lives in the Worcester series gave to the zeal of Hemming's anonymous predecessor. 'Remuneratorial' leases, again, and documents recording a gift of land as well as the donor's life interest, would be more likely to survive than simple leases possessing no permanent evidential value; and for this reason the ratios of the different types in the surviving examples are probably deceptive.[3] The evidence suggests, but cannot be said to prove, that leases for three lives were confined to the west.[4] But no conclusions can be drawn from the dearth of evidence for leasehold arrangements in the north of England or on the estates of lay lords. The scarcity of material relating to

---

[1] For examples see Robertson, op. cit., Nos. xcvii, xcviii, c, cv, cvi, cvii, cxiv.

[2] Ibid., Nos. xcvii, c, cv, cxiv, cxvii, cf. pp. 431, 435, 448, 462, 469; *Liber Eliensis*, i. 217–19, cf. Dd. ii, f. 60; *Chron. Rams.*, pp. 145–6, 152–3, 171–2.

[3] Of tenancies for terms of years Pollock and Maitland say 'the fact that they are hardly ever mentioned in the Anglo-Saxon land-books will not prove that they were practically unknown in England before the Conquest', for 'the solemn "book" would hardly have been used for so humble a purpose as that of creating short tenancies': *History of English Law* (2nd ed.), ii. 111; cf. *Domesday Book and Beyond*, p. 302. For an example of a short tenancy, apparently of early eleventh-century date, see Robertson, op. cit., No. lxxix. Hereward the Wake appears to have held Rippingale in Lincolnshire at farm from the Abbot of Crowland on a yearly tenancy ('sicut inter eos conveniret unoquoque anno'): Dd. i, f. 377, quoted Vinogradoff, *English Society*, p. 378, n. 4.

[4] One must remember that in 816 the Council of Chelsea had forbidden abbots and abbesses to grant out monastic lands 'nisi in dies et spatium unius hominis': Haddan and Stubbs, *Councils and Ecclesiastical Documents*, iii. 582.

lay estates is only what one should expect; and Burton was the most northerly monastery in England at the time of the Norman Conquest.[1]

Although arrangements by which men obtained an estate in land limited by years or lives were common in Anglo-Saxon England on the eve of the Conquest, it is evident that an arrangement of this kind did not necessarily create a rent-paying tenancy. To grant land on lease was not necessarily to put it 'to farm'. The lessee might purchase the lease by paying a lump sum at the outset; or, again, a man might obtain the usufruct of the land in exchange for a loan of money, so that the transaction would involve what lawyers call a 'gage of land' rather than a lease in the strict sense of that term.[2] In such cases what we have

[1] In Earl Æthelred's grant of Stoke Bishop to Cynulf for three lives we have a ninth-century lease of land by a layman to a layman, but its preservation is no doubt due to the fact that the land was to go to the bishopric of Worcester when the lease fell in: Harmer, op. cit., No. xii. Similarly our knowledge of the fact that two estates belonging to Ægelric Bigga were held on life tenancies by two persons, one of whom is described as his *miles*, is derived from a document of 1050–1 declaring that he grants these estates, after his death and the death of the tenants, to St. Augustine's, Canterbury: Kemble, No. 1338, Thorpe, p. 586. The weighty arguments with which Professor Whitelock supports her contention that many Anglo-Saxon wills have perished are mostly applicable *mutatis mutandis* to the case of leases: see *Anglo-Saxon Wills*, p. xli.

[2] For examples of what appear to be out-and-out payments see Birch, *Cart. Sax.*, No. 533 (*c.* 872); Harmer, op. cit., No. xii (? 886–99); *Gloucester Cart.* i. 8 (1022); Robertson, Nos. xcvii (1043–4), cxiv (*c.* 1053). Perhaps such payments are implied in some Domesday entries: e.g. 'Hoc manerium emit Alnod ab episcopo Aluuoldo tantum in vita sua tali conventione ut post ejus mortem restitueretur æcclesiæ' Dd. i, f. 80 (Pedret, Dorset), cf. ff. 72 (*Hiwi*, Wilts.), 96*b* (Cheriton, Somerset), 177 (Selly Oak, Worcestershire), and ii, f. 373 (Little Bealings, Suffolk). It appears to be of leases bought by an initial payment that the Abingdon chronicler complains: see above, p. 160, n. 4. For loans see Heinrich Brunner, *Zur Rechtsgeschichte der römischen u. germanischen Urkunde*, 1880, pp. 193–9, and the cases there cited, which include examples of the conditional conveyance or *Proprietätspfand* (Kemble, Nos. 186, 689, 690) and of two forms of the usufructgage or *Nutzungspfand*—that which corresponds to Glanvil's *vivum vadium* in that the debt is amortized by the usufruct (Kemble, No. 924 = Robertson, No. lxxix), and that corresponding to Glanvil's *mortuum vadium* in which the profit accruing to the gagee from the use of the land only served as interest on the loan (Kemble, Nos. 499, 1237); cf. Brunner, *Political Science Quarterly*, xi, 1896, p. 541; H. D. Hazeltine, *Harvard Law Review*, xvii, 1903–4, pp. 549–57. In these matters, however, legal refinements may easily involve anachronism. The distinction between a lease purchased by an initial payment and a gage of the *vivum vadium* type is somewhat academic, for the rights of the parties would be identical in the two cases. That what appear to be out-and-out payments may in some instances really have been loans is evident from Kemble, Nos. 689 and 690 (expounded by Brunner, *Zur Rechtsgeschichte*, pp. 195–6). The first of these documents tells us that Archbishop Sigeric granted Monks Risborough for two lives to Bishop Æscwig in return for a sum of money, and nowhere suggests that this was a loan; but, in the second, Æscwin [*sic*] declares that he gives back to

is not an instrument of normal estate management by which a landlord secures a steady income instead of the fluctuating gains and losses incidental to direct exploitation of the land, but rather a means of obtaining ready money to meet some exceptional need; and in more than one case we know that the money was required on account of exactions due to the Danish wars.[1] Further, the 'remuneratorial' lease promised a capital gain in the future; and some temporary estates were created by donors, who, when they gave land to a monastery, gave it subject to certain life interests. Nor should we forget that land might be granted as a reward for service or in exchange for some intangible consideration such as the patronage or friendship of a powerful lessee.[2]

Under any of these various types of conditions the grantor might receive sufficient satisfaction without getting any rent; and in the record of some transactions preserved in the *Liber Niger* of Peterborough a 'remuneratorial' lease is sharply distinguished from leases requiring rent to be paid. We are told that some time during the abbacy of Leofric, the last pre-Conquest abbot, three Lincolnshire estates were granted *per conventionem* to Askytel, whose brother Brand, the future abbot, was probably already the 'provost' (that is to say, the prior) of the monastery; and the agreement was that for two of the estates an annual money rent should be paid but that 'pro Malmetun vero aliam terram nomine Thorp post obitum fratris simul et suas (sc. terras?) recipere deberet'.[3] Yet rent or service

---

Archbishop Ælfric (Sigeric's successor) the land at Risborough that Sigeric 'dedit mihi in vadimonium pro pecunia quam a me mutuo accepit'. The life tenancy granted by Bishop Eadnoth of Crediton in 1016–20 was certainly in return for a loan, but whether the debt was being amortized by the usufruct (as Napier and Stevenson seem to suggest) is not at all clear: *Crawford Charters*, pp. 9, 76, 77.

[1] In the reign of Alfred the Great, Werferth, Bishop of Worcester, granted land at Nuthurst, Warwickshire, to a thegn named Eanwulf for four lives in return for 20 'mancuses' of gold 'proxima afflictione et immenso tributo barbarorum eodem anno quo pagani sederunt in Lundonia': Birch, *Cart. Sax.*, No. 534. About 150 years later, Eadric, Abbot of Gloucester, declares that he has granted lands at Hatherley and Badgeworth in Gloucestershire to a certain Stamarcot for his life 'pro xv libris quibus redemi alia praedia monasterii ab illa magna heregoldi exactione quae per totam Angliam fuit'—an evident reference to the heavy Danegeld of 1018: Kemble, No. 1317, and *Gloucester Cart.* i. 8. See also Napier and Stevenson, *Crawford Charters*, pp. 76–77.

[2] For examples see Robertson, Nos. xviii and xix, both granted by Werferth who was Bishop of Worcester from 872 to 915: cf. Maitland, *Domesday Book and Beyond*, p. 303.

[3] Kemble, No. 819, which is from the *Liber Niger* and should be compared with

was sometimes imposed in recognition of the lessor's rights even where the real consideration for the lease seems to have lain in an initial payment. Godric, a king's thegn, is described in Domesday as having 'bought' a lease of three lives at Wadborough; but, as we have seen, he paid an annual farm *pro recognitione*.[1] A widow named Tova pays three marks of gold for a lease of *Cyrictuna*, but every year must give a sextar of honey to the monks of St. Albans *pro cognitione*.[2] When the thegn Osulf and his wife received back a life interest in the land at Studham which they had given to the abbey, and received it back in order that they might build a church there, they none the less agreed to pay the monks 20s. a year *ob istius rei agnitionem*.[3] Moreover, a very substantial rent might be combined with a large initial payment, as we find alike at Swineshead in Lincolnshire in the eighth century and at Tidenham in Gloucestershire in the eleventh century.[4] But on the whole the surviving leases of the late Saxon period tell us singularly little about the payment of rent; and, apart from the general probabilities of the case and such light as can be obtained from post-conquest practice, there is a tantalizing lack of evidence to support the hypothesis that, when land was put out to farm, the farmer was commonly a lessee. Two Peterborough examples already mentioned are, however, quite definite so far as they go, Burghley in Northamptonshire being held by the royal chaplain Elfgar *ad firmam—quamdiu vixit*, and Scotton and Scotter in Lincolnshire,

---

a second account on f. xx *v* (= 25 *v*) of the same manuscript (Society of Antiquaries MS. lx). The estates in question seem to have been given to the abbey, or obtained for it, by Brand: cf. *Chronicle of Hugh Candidus*, pp. 40–41, 71. But according to Domesday two of them were declared by the shire to have been held by Aschill [*sic*] in 1066 'in propria libertate de rege Edwardo', in contrast to *Malmetune* which he held 'de fratre suo Brand in presto': Dd. i, f. 376*b*.

[1] Ibid., f. 175. This was on the estates of Pershore Abbey, and some indication of what 'a farm' meant is afforded by another entry on the same folio which mentions another lessee of the abbey who 'pro recognitione dabat in anno monachis unam firmam aut xx solidos'.

[2] Kemble, No. 950.

[3] Ibid., No. 945 (date 1053–67?). The evidential value of rent payment is forcibly illustrated by the writ of Rufus regarding Isham cited above, p. 132; but at Studham the precaution seems to have been unavailing for, after the Conquest, Studham passed with other lands of Osulf's to Robert de Todeni: Dd. i, f. 215. It seems to be implied that the whole of Studham—'illam terram quae dicitur æt Studham'—was given and received back on lease: if so, the rent was far from representing its value, which in Domesday is stated to have been £8 T.R.E.

[4] Kemble, No. 165 (= Birch, No. 271, cited Maitland, *Domesday Book and Beyond*, p. 303, and Stenton, *Anglo-Saxon England*, p. 477); Robertson, No. cxvii.

for which a rent was to be paid, being evidently granted to
Askytel for his life as well as the estate at Manton (*Malmetun*)
which he held on a 'remuneratorial' lease.[1] It is clear too that
Stigand paid a food rent for the manors he leased from the abbey
of Ely.[2] Nor must one forget the statement of the Ramsey
Chronicle that some land at Burwell was granted by Abbot Alf-
wine to a man named Godwin for life *firmarii vice*.[3] In general too
we are not without evidence which suggests that perhaps the
real function of the written record of leases was to supply proof
of the lessor's right to the reversion of the property, and that
rent, especially in the form of a customary 'farm', might be payable without the obligation being expressed in the document.
The famous letter in which St. Oswald of Worcester informed
King Edgar of the conditions attaching to the leaseholds he had
created on the estates of his church shows that the lessees owed
numerous services and payments of which nothing is said in the
individual leases that have been preserved.[4] And, in the period
immediately preceding the Norman Conquest, it is significant
that when Edward the Confessor gave 'Rutland' to Westminster Abbey, but reserved a life interest therein to his queen,
the writ in which he declared his will provided that during her
life a payment should be made to the abbey, but is curiously
vague as to its nature and amount. The king merely states that
the queen shall have Rutland as long as she lives 'and annually

---

[1] *Hugh Candidus*, pp. 67–68 and n. 13; Kemble, No. 819.

[2] The authority for this is the record of the Ely *placitum* of 1071–5: 'He sunt
proprie ville monasterii insule Ely quas Stigandus archipresul tenebat unde per
annum victum fratribus reddidit tantum quantum pertinet ad hoc. Has vero tenet
rex noster W. post obitum illius Methelwald et Crokestune et Snegelwelle et
dictun' (I.C.C., ed. Hamilton, p. 195).

[3] *Chron. Rams.*, pp. 174–5. Godwin, we read, gave the abbot 'respectum quod
gersume dicunt tanti viri honori conveniens' and had each year to provide hospitality for him. The *gersume* was no doubt a premium for the lease (cf. Robertson,
No. cxiv, for an early use of the word in what appears to be this sense) and the
hospitality was presumably additional to the 'farm' and due perhaps when the
abbot came to collect it. Of such 'rent collecting' we seem to get a glimpse in
the complaint of Hugh Candidus that Ernwy, Leofric's predecessor as Abbot
of Peterborough, exchanged Olney for Stoke (? Stoke Doyle) 'pro nichilo alio
nisi quia proprius (? propius) ei erat ad Stokes ire ad suam firmam quam ad
Holneie': *Hugh Candidus*, p. 65.

[4] Kemble, No. 1287 (= Birch, No. 1136). Holdsworth says: 'We gather from
the letter that all the terms of the loan did not necessarily appear in the written
document. Many of Bishop Oswald's leases have come down to us; but hardly a
word is said in them of the terms under which his tenants held': *History of English
Law*, ii. 70.

enrich the monastery therefrom' ('7 ælce gære þ munster þær of gegodige').[1]

It is against this rather misty background of pre-Conquest usage that we must set the meagre evidence for the early Norman period. After the Conquest, the lands which a man had held on lease were often confiscated along with those he owned; and many of the permanent losses sustained by ecclesiastical landlords were due to the fact that their lessees incurred forfeiture as a penalty for resistance to the invader. In two cases, however, Domesday Book makes it clear that the Norman intruder was deemed to have received his predecessor's leasehold merely for the remainder of the lease. Ralf Mortimer holds Worthy in Hampshire as the *tertius heres* of a lease for three lives; and Urse d'Abitot appears in the same role at Wadborough in Worcestershire.[2] And the evidence, scanty as it is, is sufficient to show that the practice of letting lands on lease was continued by ecclesiastical landlords after the Conquest, and also seems to indicate that the form of lease most favoured at this time was one limited to the life of the lessee. In the last chapter it was remarked that Holme Lacy in Herefordshire and Onibury in Shropshire were in 1085 granted to Roger de Lacy for life by the Bishop of Hereford—the former for knight service, the latter for a money rent; that some time before the Conqueror's death Alton Priors in Hampshire was granted for life to William Escudet by the Bishop of Winchester; that the first Abbot of Shrewsbury—an abbey that was founded in 1083— granted some land for life to a certain Rainer of Thonglands.[3] Again William Hosatus, who in 1086 held Charlecombe in Somerset of the abbey of Bath, was probably a life tenant, for the text of his lease contains nothing that implies any hereditary right, but states that he must pay a rent of £2 a year ('ælce geare ii pund into þa mynstre for ða feorme'), that he must go forth at the king's summons and pay the king's geld and be faithful and obedient to the abbot, and that if he breaks this agreement he shall forfeit the land.[4] From the same cartulary in which this

---

[1] Harmer, *Anglo-Saxon Writs*, No. 94.

[2] Dd. i, ff. 46b, 175. Both cases were cited by Freeman, *Norman Conquest*, v (1876), 778.

[3] See above, pp. 107, 108, 110.

[4] *Two Chartularies of Bath Priory*, ed. William Hunt (Somerset Record Soc., 1893), No. 33, p. 37. That the William of Dd. i, f. 89b was William Hosatus is proved by Exon. Domesday, p. 172.

lease is preserved we learn of another life lease which can hardly have been much later in date, for we are told that some time in the reign of Henry I the Prior of Bath gave evidence in the bishop's court to the effect that the lessee, a certain Grenta of Stoke, had declared on his death-bed that he held the land at Stoke 'vice stipendii non hereditatis lege quoad viverem'.[1] Then between 1071 and 1080 some lands at Thornley and Wingate, within a few miles of Durham, were granted by Bishop Walcher and the community of his cathedral to a woman named Ealdgyth, evidently for her life, is she should wish to retain them so long.[2] Another early example comes from Worcestershire, for Church Lench in that county was granted on a life lease by Abbot Walter of Evesham, who became abbot in 1077 and died in 1104.[3] In Oxfordshire, the Bishop of Lincoln, between 1093 and 1100, granted an estate of 6 hides at Ascot-under-Wychwood to Nigel d'Oilly 'eo tenore quod Nigellus eam in vita sua habeat et deserviat versus episcopum secundam valentiam terre'.[4] In Huntingdonshire, the abbey of Ramsey between 1091 and 1113 granted Dillington to Rannulf, brother of Ilger, for his life, and between 1107 and 1113 granted life leases of Stukely and Ellington.[5] And it was during the reign of Henry I that Pytchley in Northamptonshire, which belonged to the abbey of Peterborough, was granted to Geoffrey Ridel *ad firmam* for his life; that Robert de Boustona received from the abbey of Battle a hide of land at Alciston in Sussex *tenendam in vita sua*; that Pillatonhall and Bedington in Staffordshire were let by the abbot of Burton to a man named Edwin 'ad firmam tenere tota vita sua'; and that Heigham by Norwich was granted by the abbey of St. Benet of Holme to Richard Basset 'habendam ad firmam omnibus diebus vite sue'.[6] Either in that reign or at

---

[1] *Two Chartularies*, pp. 49–50.

[2] Robertson, op. cit., appendix i, No. ii. The identification of the places is not quite certain.

[3] Brit. Mus. MS. Vesp. B. XXIV, f. 8.

[4] *Registrum Antiquissimum of Lincoln*, i, ed. Foster (Lincoln Record Soc.), No. 6, pp. 13–14.

[5] *Cart. Rams.* i. 128, 236, 237.

[6] *Hugh Candidus*, pp. 88–89; Aug. Off. Misc. Bks. (E. 315/18), 18, f. 17; *Burton Cartulary* (William Salt Soc. Hist. Coll. v, pt. l, 1884), p. 35 (cf. Surveys in Hist. Coll. for 1916, pp. 228–9); *Register of St. Benet of Holme* (Norfolk Record Soc., 1932), appendix E, pp. 173–4. Apparently Ridel first obtained Pytchley from his brother Abbot Matthias in 1103–4 (perhaps by an oral agreement?) but a definite lease was granted in 1117. Hugh Candidus represents the original grant as one for a year only, and says that after his brother's death Ridel 'illam villam vi tenuit quamdiu

latest within the first three years of the reign of Stephen, the Dean and Chapter of St. Paul's leased out the manor of Caddington in Hertfordshire to Baldwin the son of Hugh 'tenendum ad firmam toto tempore vitae suae'; between 1126 and 1151 the abbey of St. Augustine gave William de Tichesi a life lease of the *terra de Medegrave* and the *terra Guthwoldi* with two mills; and in 1149 the abbey of Bec granted a life lease of the manor of Dunton in Essex.[1]

Leases for two lives are also found. In 1088 Herbert Losinga, as Abbot of Ramsey, granted Over in Cambridgeshire to William Pecche with reversion to William's wife if she should survive him; and some time between 1075 and 1095 some land that has not been identified was granted in 'fee farm' by the first Abbot of Battle to William de Brutell and his wife 'in vita illius qui supervixerit'.[2] In 1102 part of Twyford in Middlesex was let by the canons of St. Paul's *ad firmam* to a certain Ulf 'in omni vita sua et unus suus heres post eum'.[3] In 1108 the St. Paul's manor of Barnes in Surrey was leased to two brothers for an annual *firma* of £8 and a sextar of wine. This was apparently a joint tenancy, but the survivor was to retain the land on the same terms until his death.[4] In 1114 the canons similarly leased an estate at Twyford to Walter of Cranford and his daughter for their two lives.[5] Again it must have been some time between 1105 and 1119 that Abbot Richard of St. Albans, in the words of the abbey chronicler, 'dedit etiam Gospatrico, filio Consulis Gospatrici et Waldet filio ejus, quamdiu viverent, in feodi firmam Themeslage et totam (terram) Archimorel pro decem solidis annuis'.[6] Then, between 1113 and 1130, the Abbot

vixerit'; but this is scarcely consistent with what he says about Ridel's oath to the next abbot, Ernulf, and the lease granted in 1117 by Abbot John on the same terms. The Alciston lease was granted by Ralph, who became Abbot of Battle in 1107 and died in 1124: I am indebted for my knowledge of this lease and for some other information relating to Battle Abbey to Mr. Aston of Corpus Christi College, Oxford. The lease of Pillatonhall and Bedington must be dated between 1114 and 1135. That of Heigham was granted between 1127 and 1134.

[1] *D.S.P.*, p. 124; *Black Book of St. Augustine*, ed. Turner and Salter, p. 385; M. Morgan, *The English Lands of the Abbey of Bec* (1946), p. 41.

[2] *Cart. Rams.* i. 120–1; Aug. Off. Misc. Bks. (E. 315/18), 18, f. 17.

[3] *Early Charters of St. Paul's*, ed. Gibbs, No. 178, cf. pp. xxiii–xxiv.

[4] *D.S.P.*, p. 127.

[5] Ibid., pp. 127–8. Hale (p. xcv) identifies the property with that held by Durand in 1086: in the meantime it had been held by a man named Reiner.

[6] *Gesta Abbatum*, i. 72. These lands were part of the endowment of Tynemouth Priory which was a cell of St. Albans. The land of Archil Morel, which

of Gloucester grants Brampton in Herefordshire to William Brito
and his wife for their joint lives at a rent of £5 and, in 1125, we
find Westminster Abbey leasing Ockendon in Essex to Henry,
son of Wlured, on condition that he should pay £10 a year, and
that after his death (or if he should become a monk) his heir
(*unus heres*) should have the manor for a rent of £11.[1] And some
time between 1101 and 1106 an estate at Little Melton in Norfolk was let by the abbey of St. Benet of Holme on what was
perhaps potentially a lease for three lives. The lessee was Ralph,
son of Godric Dapifer (who in conjunction with his wife Ingreda
had bequeathed the land to the abbey) and it was provided that
Ralph's wife Letselina should have the estate for her life if she
should survive her husband, that it should pass to Ralph's heir
if an heir was born to him, and that failing such an heir it was
to revert to the abbey when the survivor of the marriage died.
But the words of the deed seem rather to imply that the birth of
an heir would cancel the wife's interest.[2]

Apart from this doubtful case, no lease for three lives has been
noted in this period; and leases for two lives appear to be rarer
than those for a single life, in spite of the fact that the longer
leases would probably stand a better chance of being preserved.
Grants to a man and his heir—*et suo heredi* or *et heredi ejus*—are,
it is true, of frequent occurrence; and if this formula implied a
lease for two lives only, it would be hazardous to regard a single
life as the commoner term. But there is some reason for believing
that the grants in question created a fully hereditary tenure and
were equivalent to a grant made to a man and his heirs in the
plural. They sometimes include words that seem to imply perpetuity; and I have noticed no example of twelfth-century date
in which anything is said about the reversion of the estate or the
stock to the grantor on the heir's death, though in leases which

comprised Bewick and Lilburn in Northumberland, was given by Queen Matilda
probably in 1105 or 1106: see Craster, *Hist. of Northumberland*, viii (1907), 54, cf.
vii, 31 and note. Sir Edmund Craster tells me that *Themeslage* is probably a corruption of *Benelage*, the modern Beanley, which was one of the manors confirmed
to Gospatric by King Stephen and lies within a few miles of Bewick and Lilburn.

[1] *Gloucester Cart.* ii. 113; Westminster Domesday, f. 446 *v.* The church of St.
Alphege, which I have failed to identify, was let for 20s. along with Ockendon:
they were already associated in the time of Abbot Vitalis (1076–82) when the rent
for the two was £12: ibid., f. 129. The value of the manor was in 1086 put at £10,
which is the sum the lessee of 1125 had to pay as rent: Dd. ii, f. 15.

[2] *Register of St. Benet*, No. 119: 'Si vero Radulfus habuerit heredem de muliere
desponsata tenebit ipse heres ipsius Radulfi predictam terram de Medeltone.' That
the heir was to hold the land for life must, I think, be presumed, but is not stated.

are explicitly for a life or two lives a clause referring to the reversion is commonly found.[1] Hereditary rent-paying tenancies granted specifically to a man and his heirs in the plural were of course quite common in the first half of the twelfth century.[2] Nor can it be doubted that there was a tendency for lands, originally let on lease for one or two lives only, to remain in fact in the possession of the same family for generations.[3] On the other hand, leases for terms of years are not unknown, and though the evidence of their existence in the Norman period is extremely scanty, it would be unsound to base any far-reaching conclusions upon its rarity, for one can imagine no practical

[1] For examples of phrases indicating perpetuity see *Register of St. Benet*, No. 121 of 1101–25 ('in feodum et jure hereditario sibi et suo heredi'), No. 126 of 1128–9 ('sibi suoque heredi in feudo et hereditate), cf. Nos. 137, 147; *Burton Cartulary* (Hist. Coll., 1884), pp. 31, 34, three cases of 1114–50 ('et heredi ejus [*or* ipsius] in feudum et hereditatem'). Roger de Mowbray (mid-twelfth century), in a charter granting land to Reginald Poer *et suo haeredi*, provided that the services of the sub-tenant should be due to Reginald *et suis haeredibus*: see *Whitby Cartulary* (Surtees Soc.), p. 225. But one can hardly assume the verbal accuracy of a cartulary text. Sir Frank Stenton suggests that in such cases the singular may have been employed because an individual heir was present at the transaction. Yet Round regarded the Burton grants as leases for two lives only, even (it seems) when the grant included the words *in feudum et hereditatem*: *E.H.R.* xx (April 1905), 279.

[2] See, for example, *Feudal Documents of Bury St. Edmunds*, Nos. 118, 121, 124, 127, 129; Farrer, *Early Yorkshire Charters*, i, Nos. 340, 371, 449, and ii, Nos. 883, 896, 970, 1063; *Gloucester Cart.* i. 268; *Early Charters of St. Paul's*, ed. Gibbs, No. 218.

[3] As we have seen, Roger de Lacy received Holme Lacy and Onibury in 1085 for life only, but in 1177 both places were still held by a De Lacy under the same conditions of rent and service: see above, p. 108. Again, South Walsham, leased for life to 'Nicholas the Clerk' between 1141 and 1149, was between 1175 and 1186 granted *in perpetuam hereditatem* to Geoffrey, son of 'Master Nicholas of Hembling-ton' *sicut . . . pater suus tenuit*; and one can hardly doubt that Master Nicholas was the same person as Nicholas the Clerk (*Register of St. Benet*, Nos. 148, 206). Similarly, the Dean and Chapter of St. Paul's between 1181 and 1202 granted to Roger, son of Morell, *et heredibus suis*, an estate at Twyford which had been leased in 1114 to Walter of Cranford and his daughter Athelais for their two lives and then in 1122 transferred, at Walter's request, to Athelais and her husband Morell (*Early Charters of St. Paul's*, No. 171; *Domesday of St. Paul's*, pp. 127–8; Maxwell Lyte: appendix to *Ninth Report of the Hist. MSS. Com.*, pt. i, p. 65). Another illustration of the hereditary tendency is afforded by the history of an estate at Over in Cambridgeshire, which belonged to Ramsey Abbey. Originally granted in 1088 to William Pecche and his wife for their two lives, it was regranted for life to their son Hamo and again, in 1187, to his son Geoffrey Peche. This last grant, however, was made as a final concord after a trial in the Curia Regis; and the particularity of its insistence upon the abbey's right to the reversion on Geoffrey's death makes one suspect that he had claimed to hold by inheritance. Then, forty years later, we find a second Hamo Pecche, grandson of the first Hamo, making a definite claim to two carucates at Over as the heir of his father Gilbert, the younger son of the first Hamo, on the ground that the latter had given that land 'ipsi Gilberto et heredibus suis'. It was only in 1237, after protracted litigation, that this claim was rejected (*Cart. Rams.* i. 120–7).

purpose that could be served by preserving the documents in which such leases were recorded after the term was reached, and it may well be that no written record was made at all in the case of some short leases for which the testimony of living witnesses might be deemed sufficient. It is perhaps significant that the chief evidence in regard to leases for years in the early part of the twelfth century is provided not by original texts or direct references in cartularies, but by the Burton Abbey surveys which describe the conditions obtaining at the time the surveys were made. They show us that Leigh in Staffordshire and Willington in Derbyshire were both *ad firmam* for a term of sixteen years and that Abbot's Bromley in Staffordshire was held *ad firmam* by the priest and four men *usque ad xx annos*.[1]

On the whole the evidence inclines one to the view that the most usual form of lease in the period under consideration was one for the life of the lessee or for the lives of the lessee and his wife; but there can be no certainty on this point even for the first half of the twelfth century and the relative frequency of the various forms at the time when Domesday Book was compiled must remain still more doubtful. But the material examined in the preceding pages justifies one general conclusion of some importance. During the whole period from the Norman Conquest to the death of King Stephen the leasing of estates for a definite rent was so common, and it is so common to find lands thus leased described as let *ad firmam* or to find the rent described as a *firma*, that we must regard it as probable to the verge of certainty that a large proportion of the estates which were at farm in 1086 were in fact held on lease either for a life or lives, or for a term of years.[2] And this makes it a matter of real importance for the social history of Norman England to ascertain, so far as is possible, the nature of the rights and obligations of the lessees, for those rights and obligations must have had a profound effect upon the economy of a great number of villages and the lives of a great many people.

---

[1] *Hist. Collections* (William Salt Soc., 1916), pp. 226–7, 237–8, 223.

[2] Among the leases of the period which have been cited in this chapter there is some reference to a 'farm' *eo nomine* in Dd. i, f. 175 (Wadborough); *Two Chartularies of the Priory of Bath*, p. 37 (Charlecombe); *Hugh Candidus*, p. 88 (Pytchley); *Register of St. Benet*, p. 174 (Heigham); *Hist. Collections* (William Salt Soc., 1884), p. 35 (Pillatonhall and Bedington); ibid. (1916), pp. 223 (Bromley), 226–7 (Leigh), 238 (Willington); *Early Charters of St. Paul's*, No. 178 (Twyford), *D.S.P.*, pp. 124 (Caddington), 127 Barnes. All these can definitely be dated as anterior to the death of Henry I, with the exception of the Caddington lease which may possibly belong to the early years of Stephen's reign.

VII

ESTATE MANAGEMENT III. LEASEHOLD
CONDITIONS

FOR detailed information as to the conditions on which estates were let on lease in Norman England we are almost entirely dependent upon evidence of twelfth-century date; and sometimes it is even necessary to look beyond the Norman period and, with due caution, to utilize material that comes to us from the reign of Henry II. But now and again, some feature which this evidence reveals can be recognized in Domesday Book, and something of the structure of which it forms a part in the later period can be attributed to the former without much risk of anachronism.[1]

1. In the first place it is clear that money rents were extremely common; but rents in kind also occur, often in combination with rents in money; and a mingling of rent and service was not unknown. In the later of the two surveys of Burton Abbey (both of which date from the first third of the twelfth century) ten estates or pairs of estates are described as held of the abbey *ad firmam*. From each of these a money rent was due, though in one case we are told that the farmer had to pay tithe as well, and in another that he owed suit of court *ad placita Regis* on the abbot's behalf.[2] For two of the estates, moreover, it is possible

---

[1] Confidence in such inferences is of course increased where the anatomy of the later leaseholds resembles that revealed in pre-Conquest sources.

[2] The estates in question are Branston, Abbot's Bromley, Okeover with Ilam, Leigh, Field, Darlaston, Whiston, and Bedington with Pillatonhall in Staffordshire, and Winshill and Willington in Derbyshire. In four cases the land at farm is described as a *manerium* in one or other of the surveys, in a fifth as *terra manerii*, and at Winshill it comprised 'omnia que sunt in manerio' with certain exceptions. The tithe was due from Willington. A deed preserved in the Burton Cartulary shows that the tenant of Field also owed tithe and service, though this is not mentioned in the survey (*Cartulary, Hist. Collections*, 1884, pp. 34–35). Potlock appears in the survey as held by a certain Geoffrey *in fedfirmam*: he owed 40s. rent and tithe and *servicia condecencia corporis*, but according to the deed of grant (*Cartulary*, p. 34) he also had to pay 500 good fat eels from the Trent. Besides the estates described as held *ad firmam*, several others appear in the survey as held by tenants owing a money rent. For the obligations other than a money rent owed by the grantees of Burton lands see Round, *E.H.R.* xx (1905), 279–83.

to reach back to a somewhat earlier date. The farmer of
Whiston, a certain Navenus, had held that land in 1086; and
Field, which Andrew, the farmer of the survey, received in
1116, had been held by a previous tenant on the same conditions.[1] Then from another part of England the Register of
St. Benet of Holme supplies particulars of eight agreements
made in the reign of Henry I and we have the evidence of an
original charter for yet another grant made by this abbey in
the same period. In seven out of the nine a money rent is
stipulated, in one a rent payable in corn; and one, which deals
with lands in several places, provides that some of these shall
owe knight service, that some shall pay a money rent, and that
a holding at Banningham shall make a render of honey.[2] The
last example, however, is the grant made to the *procurator* and
dapifer of the abbey on his appointment to those offices, so that
the duties belonging to them should also be regarded as incumbent upon the land; and in the case of the property demised for
a rent in corn the grantee also owed a general service of maintaining the interests of the abbey—'fortitudinem et auxilium in
omnibus que posset ad placita et ad hundredum et ubicumque
necessarium videret'.[3] It is worthy of remark that in three of
these St. Benet deeds the grantee appears as his father's successor, so that here too we have a link with an earlier generation.
On the other hand, though illustrating in a general way the
nature of the obligations imposed upon monastic tenants in this
period, the evidence from this source is not so directly pertinent
to the problem under discussion as that of the Burton Abbey
surveys, for most of the grants were made to a man and his heir
or heirs, and only the grant of Heigham to Richard Basset for
his life is definitely stated to be made *ad firmam*, while one other
(that of the land at Grenesvill for which the rent in corn was
due) was made 'in feudo et ad firmam'.[4] Additional information
comes to us from Ramsey Abbey. We are told the renders that
were due from 13 estates or groups of estates in the time of
Henry I, and learn that in 9 of these the render consisted of
a money payment; that in 3 a money payment was combined
with the payment of a 'farm' or 'full farm'; and that one group—

---

[1] Dd. i, f. 247*b*; *Burton Cartulary*, p. 34.
[2] *Register of St. Benet*, Nos. 118, 119, 121, 124, 126, 127, 129, 130, and appendix E.
[3] Ibid., Nos. 126, 124.
[4] Ibid., appendix E and No. 124.

the 3 associated and neighbouring vills of Brington, Weston, and Bythorn in Huntingdonshire—rendered a full farm, but that when these vills were *ad denarios sine firma* they paid £21.[1] There can be little doubt that in all these cases we have to do with estates that were 'at farm', and with the payments that the *firmarii* had to make; but unfortunately it is uncertain whether the *firmarii* were lessees or officials.[2] Obscurity also shrouds the nature of the farming-out arrangements on the estates of the abbey of Peterborough, but a preponderance of money rents is clearly revealed in the *Descriptio Maneriorum* which was compiled about 1125. The total of the money rents—'summa in denariis de firmis maneriorum'—is given as £284. 13s. 4d., while the value of the rents payable in grain or grain-products is put at £97. 12s. A majority of the Peterborough manors appear to have paid money only and Fletton alone owed a rent payable wholly in kind.[3] And, as was pointed out in the last chapter, the *Inquisitio Hilberti* shows that on the Glastonbury Abbey estates 29 of the 32 manors which were certainly *ad firmam* in the reign of Henry I were then farmed for money rents.[4]

---

[1] *Cart. Rams.* iii. 257, 261, 266, 274, 277, 279, 285, 287, 301, 305, 307, 311, 314. The surveys supplying the information were evidently made in the latter part of the twelfth century, but tell of conditions under Henry I: they were added to the Rolls Series edition of the Cartulary from Cotton MS. Galba E.X.

[2] At Cranfield 'firmarius in tempore Henrici Regis dedit quindecim libras cum firma' (ibid., p. 301). There are also casual references to the *firmarius* of those days in the surveys of Elton (p. 258) and of Shillington with Pegsdon (p. 308); and in that of Bythorn (p. 313) we read of a service that was owing to the farmer *dudum*. From a document in the Cartulary we know that Girton was held at farm by a man named Robert in the time of Abbot Reginald, who was abbot from 1114 to 1130: ibid. i. 140. Of an official *firmarius* we seem to catch a glimpse in the twelfth-century survey of Burwell in Cambridgeshire, which says (of a tenant of 1½ hides within the manor): 'Et praeter hoc idem Johannes tenuit unam virgatam et dimidiam quando fuit firmarius sine opere' (ibid. iii. 309). This man (John, son of Guy) was a witness to documents of 1114–30, 1148–51, and 1133–60 (*Chron. Rams.*, pp. 262–3; *Cart. Rams.* i. 259, 150–1). The father had been granted a hide at Burwell for himself and his heirs by Abbot Reginald, the arrangement being that he should hold Burwell 'quamdiu abbas Ramesiensisque conventus voluerit ad talem firmam qualem modo habet eam', and that the rent of the hide was to be counted as part of the farm: 'et in ipsa firma per singulos annos pro supradicta hida terrae reddat sibi tenenti firmam vel cuilibet tenenti eam firmam viginti solidos' (*Chron. Rams.*, p. 261). Since the Burwell survey (unlike most of this group of surveys) gives no particulars of the *instauramentum* (a matter especially needing to be noted when a manor was leased) it seems probable that the position of the *firmarius* at this place was exceptional.

[3] *Chronicon Petroburgense* (Camden Soc., 1849), pp. 166–7. The figures cannot be accepted as they stand, for the particulars and totals do not agree.

[4] See pp. 134–5, above.

Further detail is supplied by the twelfth-century leases of St. Paul's Cathedral.[1] In fourteen of those printed by Hale the rent is pretty clearly described. Three (two of which are leases of *Adulvesnasa*) seem to have required a money rent only; in eight a money rent was combined with substantial payments in kind (bread and beer being the outstanding elements in these renders); in one a sextar of wine was due as well as money; in one a money rent was combined with the payment of tithe; and the Sandon lease may perhaps be taken as indicating a rent in kind only. Several of the St. Paul's leases, moreover, contain casual references to former arrangements. The undatable lease of Wickham is evidently a renewal to Robert, son of Ailwin the priest, of that previously held by his father. The land at Twyford granted in 1114 to Walter of Cranford and his daughter has been surrendered by Reiner the former tenant. And Baldwin who receives Cadendon at farm sometime before 1138, has to pay more than his *antecessores*.[2] Additional information about the manors of St. Paul's comes to us from an Inquest relating to twenty estates, which appears to have been taken in 1181.[3] It refers to conditions 'in the time of King Henry I and William the Dean'; but only in a few cases is it clear that the statements it makes about farms or renders are to be understood as belonging to that period rather than to the time of the inquest. Eight manors are described as owing a mixed rent; six paid 'farms' which were presumably paid in kind; and six (including the *maneriolum* of Weeley and a subordinate estate at Luffenhall) appear to have paid money only.[4]

On the whole what we learn about rents from leases of early twelfth-century date seems to be in harmony with the indications of Domesday Book in regard to the farming of manors in the reign of William I. Payments in money are common; but renders in kind and mixed payments are also found; and the farmer sometimes owes service as well as rent. Arrangements

---

[1] *D.S.P.*, pp. 122–39.

[2] *D.S.P.*, pp. 122–3, 127, 124.

[3] Ibid., pp. 140–6. Hale's argument for a slightly earlier date (ibid., pp. ci–cii) rests upon a misapprehension. He unjustifiably assumed that references to arrangements made by certain *firmarii* indicated that these persons were *firmarii* at the time the inquest was taken; but he rightly pointed out that the allusion to Robert Mantel as sheriff (pp. 141–2) shows that the date was subsequent to 1170.

[4] Of the twenty estates, Weeley and Abberton, which paid money only, had been granted on hereditary tenures and were not 'described' for that very reason (p. 146). From this one infers that the farmers of the other manors did not hold them *jure hereditario*.

implying a considerable development of money economy are much more widespread than historians have usually supposed. But now and again we find the word *firma* used, not as a synonym for rent in general, but with the more restricted meaning of a render in kind as distinguished from a payment in money; and perhaps we ought to take this as a hint that natural economy had played a larger part in earlier times and that holding land at farm had once meant, as a rule, holding it for a food rent.[1]

2. An initial payment, distinct from the rent and usually described as a *gersuma*, is sometimes mentioned; and it seems likely that such a payment was made in many cases where nothing is said about it, for there would be less need to record a matter that was over and done with, than to set down in writing the rent which the lessee had to pay in the future. Among recorded examples, two may be cited from the Confessor's reign, for the lessee of some land at Burwell gave the Abbot of Ramsey a *respectum quod gersume dicunt* and Wulfward White paid a *gersuma* to Stigand and the Old Minster at Winchester in order that 5 hides at Hayling might be granted him for his life.[2] Then in 1088, William Pecche, the lessee of Over, pays a mark of gold to Ramsey Abbey *pro nostra concessione*; and just twenty years later the joint lessees of Barnes give 10s. 'in gersumma id est landcept'.[3] A *gersumma* was also paid for another St. Paul's lease which perhaps belongs to the same generation as that of Barnes and provides that some land at Sandon should be held by a man named Galio for his life at an annual rent of 10s.[4] And soon after the middle of the century, if not before, Richard the archdeacon offered the canons of St. Paul's 20 marks *in gersumam* for a lease of *Adulvesnasa*.[5] Moreover, in the light of this evidence, extending as it does on

[1] See, for example, *Cart. Rams.* iii. 257, 279, 301, 311.

[2] *Chron. Rams.*, p. 175; Robertson, op. cit., No. cxiv, cf. ibid., No. xcvii (a mark of gold given by Æthelmær to St. Edmund's Abbey so that he might hold Swanton and half Hindolveston for his life) and Kemble, No. 950 (three marks of gold given to St. Albans Abbey by Tova so that she and her son may hold *Cyrictuna* for their lives).

[3] *Cart. Rams.* i. 121; *D.S.P.*, p. 127.

[4] Hist. MSS. Comm. Ninth Report, pt. i, appendix, p. 65. The lease was subsequently renewed to the lessee's widow for her life and for this concession she paid a *ghersumma* of 6 marks, though that paid by her husband for the original lease had been only 40s. plus half a mark to St. Erkenwald *ad opus sui feretri*: W.D. 4 (liber L), ff. 43v, 44.

[5] *D.S.P.*, p. 129.

both sides of the Norman Conquest, it seems impossible to doubt that the word *gersuma* in Domesday Book usually means 'consideration money paid for a lease', as Round maintained that it did in the case of Essex.[1] In the account of the royal estates in the Little Domesday a *gersuma*, which appears to be distinguished from the rent, is mentioned in some thirty entries; and, outside the royal estates, reference is occasionally made to a payment which was perhaps of the same nature though the word *gersuma* is not used.[2] In the Great Domesday it is very rarely that similar information is given; but two references to a *gersuma* are made in connexion with some royal estates in Worcestershire (entered under Herefordshire); Adisham in Kent is said to owe 100s. *de Garsumnne* to the archbishop; and payments that seem somehow distinct from the render or value, and usually amount either to an ounce or a mark of gold, are mentioned as due from a few lay estates in Cambridgeshire, Hertfordshire, Berkshire, Hampshire, and Sussex, and from two manors of the Bishop of Rochester in Kent.[3] A use of the word *garsuma* which seems closely parallel to that of Domesday is to be found in the Canterbury schedule which describes the scheme of *firme monachorum* attributed to Lanfranc. This mentions a *garsuma* in thirteen cases in terms that imply a money payment distinct from the farms (which are measured in months, weeks,

---

[1] *V.C.H. Essex*, i. 428 n. 6, 578 n. 5. In *V.C.H. Hereford*, i. 316, 318, Round translated *gersuma* as 'fine'. But in his *Geoffrey de Mandeville* (p. 298), while describing the *gersuma* as the excess which a *firmarius* was willing to give for an estate over and above the fixed rental, he says that it might be paid 'either in the form of a lump sum, or in that of an annual payment'. It is not clear whether he supposed that the *gersuma* of Domesday Book might take the latter form.

[2] For example, Weeley (Essex) which belonged to Eudo Dapifer is said to be worth £19 and an ounce of gold (Dd. ii, f. 51) and the St. Paul's manor of *Adulvesnasa* (Essex) is valued at £30 and a mark of silver (ibid., f. 13*b*).

[3] Dd. i, ff. 180*b*, 5; and f. 196*b*: 'Inter totum valet xvi libras et i unciam auri' (Weston, Cambridgeshire): cf. ff. 138 (Miswell, Herts.); 62 (Hanney, Berks.); 44*b* (Ceptone, Hants); 23 (Singleton, Sussex); 5*b* (Southfleet and Stone, Kent). The identification of the payments of ounces or marks with the payments to which the word *gersuma* is applied must, however, be regarded as doubtful—first, because the former appear to resemble the payments of a mark of gold due to the sheriff from three royal estates in Bedfordshire and one of these is described as an annual payment (ibid., f. 209: *Lestone*, i.e. Leighton Buzzard), and, secondly, because in Domesday the latter seem always to be measured in shillings or pounds. On the other hand, the payment which William Pecche made in 1088 for the lease of Over was a mark of gold; and the Canterbury text which professes to set forth the *firme monachorum* as established by Lanfranc shows Monkton as owing two ounces of gold *pro garsuma*, though in every other case the amount of the *gersuma* is given in shillings or pounds (Canterbury Register K, ff. 69*v*–70).

or days) and refers to *Hilleg* (? Monks Eleigh) and to Merstham
with Cheam as paying farms *sine garsuma.*[1]

The *gersuma* was nearly always a round sum; and the ratio
between its amount and the amount of the rent or valuation
varied greatly. For example, Aylsham in Norfolk is valued in
Domesday at £29 blanch and Runham in the same county at
90s. blanch, but the *gersuma* was 20s. in each case.[2] Yet the
figures appear to show a tendency to favour certain simple ratios.
If we ignore the fact that the rent was often paid in blanched
money while the *gersuma* was not, we find that the latter was
one-eighth of the former in 5 out of the 30 cases that have been
noted in the Little Domesday and one-sixteenth in 3 cases.[3]
Further, the Little Domesday provides 4 examples of a *gersuma*
that was a tenth of the rent or value, and 3 others where it was
a twentieth, while in Worcestershire the *gersuma* was one-fortieth
of the render—6d. in the pound—in the 2 cases which are all
that Domesday reveals in that county.[4] Yet it would be rash to
feel much confidence in the apparent implications of these facts.
In a majority of the cases noted in the Little Domesday the
gersuma was 20s. and the rent or value consisted of a certain
number of pounds. And chance can account for much in the
way of coincidence when one is dealing with figures that mostly
consist of neat round numbers.

3. A not uncommon feature of twelfth-century leases is a
provision for an increase of rent after the first few years, or on
the succession of a new life. The Little Melton lease, granted
by St. Benet of Holme between 1101 and 1116, postulates that
the rent shall rise from 10s. to 40s. if and when an heir should
succeed as third life.[5] The rent of Ockendon, which Westminster
Abbey let on a lease for two lives in 1125, was fixed at £10
during the first life and £11 during the second.[6] In five St. Paul's

---

[1] Canterbury Register K, ff. 69v–70.   [2] Dd. ii, ff. 132, 135.

[3] Ibid., ff. 3 (Havering, Essex), 111, 129b, 131, 134 (Hingham, Wickhampton,
Bedingham, and Hempstead in Norfolk), and 2b (Hatfield Broadoak, Essex), 133b
(Happisburgh, Norfolk), 286 (Thurlow, Suffolk).

[4] Ibid., ff. 128b, 131b, 132b (Halvergate, Sall, and Saxthorpe in Norfolk),
285b (Parham, Suffolk), also ff. 5b (Writtle, Essex), 121b, 123 (Cranworth and
Cantley, Norfolk), and Dd. i, f. 180b (Martley and a group of 'six manors' in
Worcestershire, entered in the Herefordshire section of Domesday). The figures in
the last case would be difficult to explain away as a fortuitous coincidence of ratios
between round numbers, being £24 of render with a *gersumma* of 12s. for Martley
and £50 of render with a *gersumma* of 25s. for the six (really five?) manors.

[5] *Register of St. Benet*, No. 119.

[6] Westminster Domesday, f. 446b.

leases which date from the middle decades of the century, provisions of varying degrees of elaboration were made for a gradual increase of rents. The simplest of them is the lease of *Adulvesnasa* to William of Ockendon, which can safely be assigned to the years 1148–50.[1] It stipulates a rent of £35 for each of the first two years of the lease, and one of £45 in each succeeding year of the lessee's life. The Ardeley lease of 1141, and also, it would seem, the Navestock lease of 1152, similarly provided that the rent should reach its maximum in the third year, but the advance was to be made in two stages. Osbert of Ardeley had to pay, in the first year 3 'small farms' in kind and £5 in money, in the second year 4 farms and £7, in the third year and thereafter 4 farms and £8.[2] At Navestock the rent was 2 farms and 2 deliveries of money (*liberationes in denariis*) for the first year, 3 farms and 3 deliveries of money for the second year, and in the third and subsequent years 3 farms and a payment of 40s. with each of them.[3] More complicated arrangements were made at Kensworth in 1152 and at Sandon in 1155. The Kensworth rent started at £5 and rose by £1 each year until the fourth year, but in the fifth year there was to be an increase of £2 bringing the rent up to £10, the figure at which it was to stand for the remainder of the lease.[4] The Sandon rent consisted of farms 'in pane et cervisia et liberatione et elemosina et constantiis pistrini et bracini'. Four of these farms were due in the first year together with a fifth farm of bread only. In the second year 6 'full' farms had to be paid; in the third, 8; in the fourth and subsequent years, 10.[5]

In some cases it is possible to trace the subsequent history of these arrangements. At Little Melton the provisions for an

---

[1] *D.S.P.*, pp. 125–6. The witnesses of the *Adulvesnasa* lease include Edward the priest of St. Augustine's, who received that church in 1148 (Appendix to Ninth Report of Hist. MSS. Comm., pt. i, p. 63), and William the Archdeacon, who as Mr. H. G. Richardson has pointed out, died in 1150 (*E.H.R.*, Jan. 1942, p. 129).

[2] *D.S.P.*, p. 135.

[3] Ibid., pp. 132–3. The amount of the *liberatio* in the first two years is not stated, so it is possible that there was no increase after the second year, but in that case there would have been no need to give particulars for the third year.

[4] Ibid., p. 128. Hale's suggestion (ibid., p. xcv) that the Kensworth rent 'varied in a cycle of seven years' after the pattern of the lease cannot be accepted. For an account of the peculiar circumstances in which this lease was granted see H. G. Richardson, *Law Quarterly Review*, xlviii (1932), 417–19.

[5] Ibid., p. 134. In addition to the St. Paul's leases cited in the text, that for Wickham, which I am unable to date, provided for an increase of rent—in this case after the first year: *D.S.P.*, p. 122.

eventual increase of rent never came into operation. The original lessee evidently left no child to succeed him, for between 1134 and 1140 his second wife was granted the land for life at a rent of 13s. 4d.; and early in the reign of Henry II his brother Hubert de Montchensey, who had seized Little Melton during the civil war, was allowed to have it *in feudo et hereditate* at the original rent of 10s. on acknowledging the abbey's title.[1] On the St. Paul's manors, however, the maximum rents appear to have been maintained in subsequent leases of *Adulvesnasa*, Ardeley, Navestock, and Sandon, while at Kensworth a further increase to £13 had been made by 1181.[2] As regards the 'farms', indeed, the evidence seems to indicate that the maxima to be reached on the estates of St. Paul's under the mid-twelfth-century leases were no more than the sums in force in the early Norman period and that the smaller burdens imposed at the beginning of the leases were of the nature of temporary reductions. Ardeley had owed 'four weeks' in the time of Dean Wulman; and the *Inquisitio Maneriorum* of 1181 describes Sandon as rendering ten full farms 'tempore Henrici Primi et Willelmi Decani'.[3] At Navestock the position is uncertain, but it seems probable that the lease of 1152 covered both *Naastocha Edwini* and *Naastocha Aldwini*, and if so the maximum number of farms that it stipu-

[1] *Register of St. Benet*, Nos. 136, 45, 80, 191.

[2] For *Adulvesnasa* see *D.S.P.*, pp. 129, 142; for Ardeley, ibid., pp. 136, 140, and a lease to Adam, son of Saric, in St. Paul's MS Liber L, f. 42; for Navestock, *D.S.P.*, p. 144, and an original lease to John de Mairegni (who was still *firmarius* there in 1181) in the St. Paul's muniments, A (Boxes 26–40), No. 496; for Sandon, *D.S.P.*, p. 141; for Kensworth, ibid., p. 140. In the *Inquisitio Maneriorum* attributed to the year 1181 the rent of *Adulvesnasa* is given at £50; but this probably includes a rent of £5 for the churches which is distinguished from the rent of the manor in the lease to Richard the archdeacon. I have assumed, perhaps rashly, that the unpublished lease of Ardeley to Adam and that to Master Aubrey are both later than the lease of 1141 to Osbert. The clauses about the stock and buildings in Adam's lease are almost verbally identical with those of Osbert's lease. As the lease to Aubrey differs a good deal from the other two leases as regards both stock and buildings, it was probably separated from them by a considerable interval of time, but, though *Magister Albericus* appears as a witness in mid-twelfth-century documents, close dating is impossible. In Adam's lease the rent is given as four full farms 'et preter hoc xl sol et viid ad elemosinam', but since Osbert's rent rose to four farms and £8 after the second year and Aubrey had to pay 40s. with each farm, I take it that Adam had to do the same (cf. Tillingham, Navestock, and Chingford: *D.S.P* pp. 143, 144). A sum of 7d. due as *elemosina* appears without ambiguity in the lease of Wickham (ibid., p. 122).

[3] Ibid., pp. xxxix, 152, 141. Sandon together with *Roda* (? Roe Green) and Luffenhall owed a farm of 10 weeks and 2 days *tempore Wulmanni*, but Luffenhall was separated from Sandon by 1181: ibid., p. 141.

lated was actually less than had been exacted half a century earlier.[1] Whether the money payments were additions imposed after the early Norman period cannot be determined: nothing is said of such payments in the schedule of farms that were rendered *tempore Wulmanni*, but that schedule merely gives the 'weeks' and 'days' to be supplied by each manor and contains no information about their constituent elements. On some of the St. Paul's manors the number of farms, apart from temporary reductions, remained unaltered for centuries. According to the *Statuta Majora* of *c.* 1300, Ardeley, Barling, Caddington, and Tillingham owed precisely as many 'farms' as they had owed 'weeks' under Dean Wulman.[2] One notes too that at Michaelmas, 1335, Navestock was demised to one of the canons for the same rent as that which fell to be paid, after the initial reduction, under the lease of 1152—three farms and 40s. with each of them.[3] On the other hand, the force of tradition must not be rated too high. In course of time the number of farms was altered a good deal for some of the manors of St. Paul's. But this is not the place in which to consider these developments.

4. Only occasionally do we learn anything about the period of the year at which the leases commenced or about the dates at which the rents were payable. Four of the St. Paul's leases—those of Barnes (1108), Ardeley (1141), Kensworth (1152), and Navestock (1151)—ran from Michaelmas to Michaelmas; and it was clearly the same with the lease of *Adulvesnasa* to William of Ockendon (1148–50) for it contains a provision that after the lessee's death his son should hold the manor until the following Michaelmas. One notes also that the lease of Sandon was granted at Michaelmas, 1155; but the lease of Ardeley to *Magister Albericus*, which I take to be later than that of 1141, could apparently be terminated—after his death, one presumes—either at Michaelmas or on St. Catherine's Day (25 Nov.). Outside the estates of St. Paul's we find two Suffolk manors of St. Edmunds Abbey let on lease for twelve years from Michaelmas, 1160.[4]

---

[1] The two parts of Navestock rendered between them farms of 3 weeks 3½ days *tempore Wulmanni*: ibid., p. xxxix.

[2] Ibid. In the second version of the early schedule of farms (ibid., p. 152) only three weeks are assigned to Tillingham, but the version from the first folio of Liber L is clearly more accurate.

[3] Maxwell Lyte, op. cit., p. 38, No. 1100.

[4] *Feudal Documents*, No. 145.

As regards the payment of rent there was much variety. That owing to St. Benet of Holme under the leases of Heigham (1127–34) and South Walsham (1141–9) had to be paid in three instalments—at the Purification (2 Feb.), Ascension Day, and the feast of St. Peter in Chains (1 Aug.) in the former case, and at the Purification, St. Peter in Chains, and Michaelmas in the latter; but when the abbey granted Little Melton to the widow of Ralph, son of Godric, for her life (as it did between 1134 and 1140) it was arranged that the rent of a mark should be payable half at Easter and half at Christmas.[1] The rent due to the abbey of Gloucester under the lease of Brampton (1113–30) was payable in five instalments—on St. Andrew's Day, Palm Sunday, Pentecost, the Nativity of St. John, and the Nativity of the Virgin.[2] On the estates of St. Paul's there was a tendency to prefer four payments a year. Thus *Adulvesnasa* and Kensworth, which owed money rents only, paid them in four instalments; and the lease of Barling, besides requiring a render of three farms in kind and 40s. with each of them, provided that an additional payment of 20s. should be made at each of the same four rent days that were stipulated in the lease of Kensworth—Michaelmas, Christmas, Easter, and the feast of St. John.[3] On those very dates too the rent of Navestock church was payable, in equal instalments, under a lease of the church and manor that was granted to John de Mairegni (? Marini) some time before 1181.[4] Caddington, again, in addition to a week's farm, owed money that was payable, in unequal amounts, on four feast days.[5] On the other hand, the rent of Barnes, consisting of £8 and a sester of wine, appears to have been paid in a lump sum on St. Paul's Day, but the wording of the lease is ambiguous and perhaps it was only the wine that had to be delivered then; and a similar ambiguity attaches to the lease of Twyford (1114) which provides for a payment of 5s. at Michaelmas and also required the lessee to pay a tithe of corn, sheep, and goats.[6] We must remember, however, that in the case of

---

[1] Register, appendix E and Nos. 148 and 136.

[2] *Gloucester Cart.* ii. 113.

[3] *D.S.P.*, pp. 125–6, 128, 126–7. The 'feast of St. John' was presumably the Nativity of the Baptist (24 June) which would make a natural 'quarter-day' with the other dates and is mentioned without ambiguity as one of the days on which the farm of Wickham was payable (ibid., p. 122).

[4] St. Paul's muniments, A (Boxes 26–40), No. 496.

[5] *D.S.P.*, p. 124.

[6] Ibid., p. 127.

St. Paul's most of the surviving leases provided for the payment of 'farms' representing a week's supplies of bread and beer, and these were no doubt sent up to London in accordance with a traditional routine that was originally arranged to cover the whole year; and it is probably the continued observance of this routine which explains the fact that nearly all the leases fail to stipulate the days on which the farms had to be paid. Exceptionally we are told that the two farms owed by the lessee of Wickham were payable at Martinmas (11 Nov.) and the Nativity of the Baptist (24 June) and that the three farms due from Navestock were payable before the feasts of Christmas, Easter, and St. John.[1] But for further information about the routine of farms we are dependent on the schedule of *c.* 1300 in the *Statuta Majora*, and by then considerable alterations had been made in the ancient system.[2] Yet since the main features of the scheme described in the thirteenth-century schedule are probably derived from the usages of a much earlier period, like the *firmae* themselves, it is not irrelevant to mention them here. Each manor paid a week's farm at a time and none had to supply farms in successive weeks, so that the number of deliveries that had to be made varied with the number of farms due from each manor. This meant that a majority of the thirteen manors made two or three deliveries a year, but Caddington paid only once in the year and Sandon no less than ten times. A majority of the farms became due after the manor owing the payment had enjoyed a respite of ten or more weeks, but the incidence of payment was uneven, and one of the Belchamp farms and four of the Sandon farms were due in the next week but one after a previous farm. In addition to the renders in kind each manor owed a money payment or *dizena* with each farm; and this *dizena* appears to have been payable on the Sunday following the delivery of the produce.[3]

It is instructive to compare these arrangements with those adopted on the estates of Ramsey Abbey and Rochester Cathedral. For our knowledge of the Ramsey scheme we are dependent upon a schedule of uncertain date, but the spelling of place-names in this schedule, which corresponds pretty closely with that of the twelfth-century surveys, is some evidence of its

---

[1] Ibid., pp. 122, 132–3.   [2] Ibid., pp. 158–9.
[3] For the *dizenae* see *D.S.P.*, pp. 154–7. Hales was clearly mistaken in saying that the *dizena* was paid before the produce *firma* (op. cit., p. xlviii).

antiquity.[1] Deliveries were due in each week of the year (which was reckoned to begin on 1 Oct.) and none of the farm manors discharged all its obligations at the same time. Altogether 18 manors were contributory (if we count the constantly associated group of Weston, Brington, and Bythorn as one) and, of these, the 8 which owed a (nominal) 2 week's farm paid 4 times in the year, and the 10 which owed 1 week's farm paid twice, with the exception of Broughton which made a render of bread on a third date.[2] But a payment *in compadio*, which formed an element in the farms and might be paid in money, was in some cases made separately from the rest of the farm. This involved 2 extra pay-days for 6 manors and one extra pay-day for 3 more.[3] As in the St. Paul's scheme, the incidence of payment was irregular. If we include the separate deliveries *ad compadium*, we find that the intervals between payments varied in one case from 2 weeks to as much as 37 weeks on the same manor (Ellington). Even among those manors which paid any *compadium* they may have owed at the same time as the rest of the farm we find Elsworth paying at intervals of 6, 8, 11, and 27 weeks. Ripton discharged all its obligations between 7 January and 18 March and Ellington between 3 June and 16 September. Only in the case of Graveley was the annual burden distributed with approximate evenness, its two payments being made on 12 November and 6 May.

The Rochester 'Ordo maneriorum quomodo firmas facere debent' is also of uncertain date.[4] It incorporates some arrangements which must have been made after 1196 and it attributes to the manor of Haddenham a burden of three months' farm in place of the two months' farm it is said to have owed in the time of Gundulf; but the system may none the less follow the same general pattern as that which obtained before these alterations

---

[1] *Cart. Rams.* iii. 234–6. For the question of date see N. Neilson, *Economic Conditions of the Manors of Ramsey Abbey*, p. 19.

[2] The farms were reckoned as farms of a week or two weeks, but each had been extended to cover twice the nominal period, so that the whole year was covered: *Cart. Rams.* iii. 230, cf. Vinogradoff, *Villainage in England*, p. 302, Neilson, op. cit., pp. 19–20.

[3] A manor paid *compadium* (which is essentially something you eat with your bread) when another rendered only flour, malt, and bread. The money payment *ad compadium* of the Ramsey farms was probably a commuted render of cheese or lard: see *Cart. Rams.* iii. 163 and 231 (where the *et* of *et decem pensae lardi* is clearly a mistake for *aut*). In my attempt to describe the essentials of the scheme I have taken no account of casual dues such as eggs at Easter.

[4] *Custumale Roffense*, p. 12, cf. p. 35.

were made. The Rochester farms were measured in months of twenty-eight days and *quinzanae* (fortnights); and the year from Michaelmas to Michaelmas was exactly divided into such periods—not into weeks as was the case with Ramsey Abbey and St. Paul's.[1] We are not told on what days the various manors had to make their renders, but the periods of the year for which they were severally responsible are precisely stated. Altogether, farms were due from seven manors and the *Cellarium*.[2] The obligations of five of the manors were divided between two distinct periods; but Frindsbury was responsible for three separate months, and Denton and the *Cellarium* were only responsible for a single period each—a month in the one case and a fortnight in the other.[3] There was a tendency to concentrate the burdens of particular manors within the same part of the year. Haddenham answered for one of its three months' farms between 16 February and 16 March and for the other two between 27 April and 22 June. No manor except Haddenham owed more than a month at a time, but Southfleet paid for both its months between Michaelmas and 15 February and the two fortnights owed by Darenth ran from 6 July to 19 July and from 17 August to 30 August. The burden was most widely distributed in the case of Frindsbury, but, though its first month ran from 22 December to 19 January, the second and third months for which it was responsible started on 20 July and 31 August respectively.

These are wearisome details; but the times at which payments fell due must have been matters of intimate concern for those who had to make them; and on the whole the facts seem to suggest that they were determined mainly in the interests of the recipients, though one cannot be sure. Perhaps transport conditions and local facilities for the storage of grain played a part in the temporal allocation of the burdens; but this is mere conjecture.

5. Leases of manors in twelfth-century England were commonly 'stock and land leases'—that is to say, leases under which

---

[1] The odd day was included in the last month (31 Aug. to 28 Sept. inclusive).

[2] The reference to the *quinzana de Cellario* (or *Cellaro*) is puzzling; one can only suppose that it indicates some manor attached to the cellarer's office.

[3] Besides being responsible for one month starting at Michaelmas and a second starting on 19 Jan. the manor of Southfleet according to *one* text of the *Ordo Maneriorum* had to contribute to the farm that was due from Wouldham for the fortnight beginning 22 June: 'debet subvenire firme de Wldeham de centum solidis' (*Custumale Roffense*, p. 35).

much of the stock was provided by the landlord, as it is to this day on hill sheep-farms in the Lake District. This seems to be implied by the author of the *Leges Henrici Primi*; and the evidence of the surviving leases points to the same conclusion.[1] Some leases of the period are known to us only from summary descriptions; but of the few that have been preserved in something like textual integrity a large proportion contain particulars of the stock that must be returned to the lessor at the end of the lease. I have noted thirteen St. Paul's leases which include a statement of this kind; and the Register of St. Benet of Holme provides evidence that the manor of Hardley had been granted with the stock to William the Archdeacon between 1101 and 1125 and furnishes another example in a lease of South Walsham granted between 1141 and 1149.[2] It is the same with the lease of Ingham and Elveden granted by the abbey of Bury St. Edmunds in 1160.[3] But it is from surveys, and not from actual leases, that we learn how common it was in the early part of the twelfth century for stock to be provided by the landlord. For the practice on the royal estates a scrap of information is preserved in the so-called 'Herefordshire Domesday' which, though compiled in the reign of Henry II, is clearly referring to the reign of his grandfather when it enumerates the stock of five royal

---

[1] *Leges Henrici Primi*, c. 56, 3 (*Gesetze*, ed. Liebermann, i. 575): 'querendum est autem in reddicione manerii a pastoribus de animalibus de numero de modo a ceteris servientibus de officio suo si plena singula habeantur et eiusdem valencie; de supplecione in hominibus in pecunia, si deterioratum sit manerium in dominio vel (in) hominibus, in pascuis, in nemoribus, si quis gablum auxerit, si quis injuste tulerit, quid sit in horreis, quid seminatum sit.' The chapter is concerned with the farming of manors.

[2] The 13 St. Paul's leases include 3 of Ardeley, 2 of *Adulvesnasa*, 2 of Navestock and 2 relating to Sandon. Except a lease of land at Sandon to a man named Galio printed by Maxwell Lyte (op. cit., p. 65) a lease of Ardeley to Adam, son of Saric, in Liber L, f. 42, and one of Navestock to John de Mairegni, the original of which is No. 496 in A (Boxes 26–40), all these are printed in Hale's *Domesday of St. Paul's*. In addition, a St. Paul's lease of half a hide at Sandon, though not enumerating the stock, provides that the land shall revert to the canons on the lessee's death 'cum omni vestitura, tam in segetibus quam in bobus, vaccis, porcis, vel ovibus, equis vel equabus'. This lease, which is dated 1101, was a renewal to a widow named Lyveva of a previous lease in Anglo-Saxon to her and her husband, which is vaguely worded, but perhaps implies that the stock went with the land, for it says that the land is granted 'swa hit nu gelogod is'. (Both leases are in Maxwell Lyte, op. cit., p. 65.) Further the Barnes lease of 1108, while similarly containing no enumeration of the stock, provides that on the death of the surviving lessee the canons shall have *quicquid in manerio erit*: *D.S.P.*, p. 127. For the leases of Hardley and South Walsham see *Register of St. Benet*, Nos. 201, 148, cf. No. 27.

[3] *Feudal Documents*, No. 145.

manors in that county and states the sums they respectively rendered *cum tali stauramento*.[1] Whether these renders were the rents owed by lessees, or whether the sheriff farmed these estates in his official capacity and was responsible for the payment of the rents and not merely for their collection, cannot be regarded as certain. But that neither the sheriff nor any one person was the farmer of all the five manors is suggested by the fact that two of them (Linton and Wilton) are described here as having made a joint render of £33, though they are no nearer to one another than Marden and Lugwardine, for each of which a distinct render is recorded. There would seem to be no point in thus linking Linton and Wilton unless they were jointly held by a *firmarius* who was not the farmer of the other manors. And perhaps the casual preservation of the evidence for these five manors affords some ground for regarding them as a sample so far as the royal estates are concerned. That stock went with the land on the English manors of the Abbaye aux Dames at Caen, is made almost certain by some surveys of those manors which have been judged to belong to the reign of Henry I.[2] All the surveys of the series contain particulars of the stock: those of Minchinhampton and Avening in Gloucestershire are unmistakably inventories of what the *firmarii* received; and those of Felsted in Essex and Horsted in Norfolk, though less explicit on this point, indicate clearly that both manors were held at farm.[3] More comprehensive evidence is available for the estates of Glastonbury Abbey and Ramsey Abbey. In the former case, the *Inquisitio Hilberti* not only enumerates the stock on each of the 32 manors which it specifically states to have been at farm in the reign of Henry I, but in regard to 4 of them (Street, Butleigh, Walton, and Shapwick) explicitly says that it was *cum hoc instauro* or *cum tali*

[1] *The Herefordshire Domesday*, ed. Galbraith and Tait (Pipe Rolls Soc., for 1947–8, pub. 1950), p. 75 and f. 39. For Marden, Lugwardine, and Stanford the record also includes figures for seed-corn (wheat and oats)—no doubt the amounts given to the farmers when they took over.

[2] Bibl. Nat. MS. lat. 5650, ff. 26–29. For the date see Jean Birdsall: 'The English Manors of the Abbey of La Trinité at Caen', in *Haskins Anniversary Essays*, 1929.

[3] The two former surveys begin respectively *De hantone receperunt firmari* and *De havelingas receperunt firmarii*. The Horsted survey mentions *Herveus firmarius noster* and that of Felsted states that of the two demesne hides 'debet nobis reddere radulfus ter centum acros terre seminatas': both mention sokemen who *portant firmam ad Wincestre*. The other surveys of the series which give particulars of the stock, but do not tell us whether the manors were at farm, relate to Penbury in Gloucestershire, Tarrant in Dorset, and *Dineslai*.

instauro that they paid the stated rents at that time.[1] For the Ramsey estates particulars of the *instauramentum* are given for 20 of the 22 manors or groups of manors which are described in the surveys that refer specifically to the time of Henry I; and in all but 2 of these 20 cases we either read of the render or farm that was due or find some reference to a *firmarius*.[2] The entries vary somewhat in form and clarity; but there can be little doubt that the enumerated stock is the stock provided for the *firmarii* by their monastic landlord.[3] Probably it is the same with the de-mesne stock recorded in the early twelfth-century surveys of the manors of Peterborough Abbey, for the schedule of rents which forms part of the same document clearly indicates that these manors were at farm. Unfortunately none of these four sets of surveys tells us whether the farmers were lessees or officials. We know, however, that Stukeley and Ellington (two of the eighteen Ramsey manors) had been granted on life leases between 1107 and 1113 and that on the lessee's death these manors were to revert to the abbey with all the *possessio* found in them at that time.[4] And it is perhaps significant that a survey of Burwell in Cambridgeshire, which is one of the two Ramsey surveys with-out any enumeration of the stock, is the only one of the series to contain some indication that the farmer was of an official type.[5]

The *instauramenta* described in twelfth-century leases and sur-veys naturally included plough-oxen, and, as a rule, horses,

---

[1] Trin. Coll. Camb. MS. R. 3.33, f. 115.

[2] The two surveys of the series which contain no information about stock are those of Holywell and Burwell, and these show signs of incompleteness: *Cart. Rams.* iii. 281, 308. The latter part of the text printed as *Consuetudines apud Haliwelle* is really part of a survey of Lawshall in Suffolk: see *E.H.R.* li (Jan. 1936), 104–7.

[3] In the survey of Hemingford the relevant passage runs thus: 'In tempore Henrici Regis erant ibi tres carrucae de duodecim bobus et totidem equis; quisque boum et equorum quatuor solidos. Et centum viginti oves, quaeque quatuor denarios. Et quinque vaccae et unus taurus. Et decem porci perannati. Et cum hoc instauramento dabat tunc quindecim libras.' Of Cranfield we read: 'Apud Cranc-feld sunt decem hidae. Pro quibus firmarius in tempore Henrici Regis dedit quindecim libras cum firma. Et hoc fuit instauramentum curiae in illis diebus. Duo aratra. Quinque vaccae, septem juvencae. Viginti quatuor porci perannati.' See *Cart. Rams.* iii. 277, 301. For Broughton, Wistowe, Upwood, and Lawshall the stock is enumerated as it stood at the time the surveys were made and not for the time of Henry I.

[4] *Cart. Rams.* i. 236, 237. The lease of Dillington, granted to Rannulf, brother of Ilger, between 1091 and 1113, also provided that the vill was to be returned to the abbey of Ramsey on the lessee's death 'cum omni possessione et incre-mento' (*Chron. Rams.*, p. 234); but Dillington is not one of the manors referred to above.

[5] *Cart. Rams.* iii. 309. See above, p. 178, n. 2.

cows, sheep, and pigs, though one or more of the classes may be lacking. Goats are mentioned occasionally and poultry were part of the *instauramentum* at Hardley and Horstead in Norfolk, at Ingham in Suffolk, and at *Adulvesnasa* in Essex.[1] The St. Paul's leases also include grain of various kinds in the *instauramenta* which must be surrendered on the date of termination, or in some cases stipulate that a number of acres shall be sown and a number fallowed. The lease of *Adulvesnasa* to Archdeacon Richard and the Navestock lease of 1152 are particularly comprehensive in the matter of crops and cultivations: the latter provides that on the surrender of the manor the great grange shall be full of winter and spring corn, that all the hay shall be handed over, that the fallow field shall have been cultivated and 40 acres ploughed twice, and that folding and dunging shall have been carried out *secundum facultatem*.[2] An inventory of buildings or of buildings and implements also finds a place in the leases of several of these manors and in the case of *Adulvesnasa* we learn that the details were reported by the canons who had been sent down to 'invest' the lessee.[3]

The historian cannot help wishing that other landlords had resembled the Chapter of St. Paul's in all this careful particularity; but whenever a manor was let on lease there must have been some understanding in regard to buildings, crops, and cultivations, and the survey of Felsted made for the Abbaye aux Dames is an exception to the general rule of silence on such matters in providing that 300 acres must be sown when they are given back to the abbey.[4] Sometimes, however, a lease will contain a general stipulation that all the stock and any improvements shall revert to the landlord; and it seems possible that now and again a lessee had to stock the manor himself at the outset. General provisions for the reversion of all the *possessio* have already been noted in some Ramsey Abbey leases. The life lease of Heigham-next-Norwich which the abbey of St. Benet of Holme granted to Richard Basset between 1127 and 1134 requires the manor to be surrendered on his death 'cum

---

[1] An old cat and two young cats are duly noted on the last of these manors: *D.S.P.*, p. 132.

[2] Ibid., pp. 129–33.

[3] Ibid., p. 130. 'De instauramentis autem illius manerii, qualia Richardus cum manerio recepit, et qualia cum manerio redditurus est, canonici qui ad eum inde investiendum missi sunt, hoc rescriptum in capitulum reportaverunt.'

[4] Bibl. Nat. MS. lat. 5650, f. 26.

omni emendatione et instauramento quod ipse Richardus et sui
posuerint in manerio'.[1] The land at Little Melton in Norfolk,
again, which between 1101 and 1116 was granted to Ralph, son
of Godric, and his wife and after them to their heir, was to revert
to St. Benet's, if they had no heir, 'cum omni emendacione
quam imposuerint'.[2] The manor of Pytchley, too, under the
lease of 1117 to Geoffrey Ridel, had to be returned to the abbey
of Peterborough at his death 'cum omni instauracione que esset
in eo die quo Gaufridus esset vivus et mortuus'; and on the
death of William de Tichesi the lands and mills he had received
from St. Augustine's some time between 1126 and 1151 were to
revert to the abbey 'cum omnibus emendacionibus et restaura-
cionibus quas super easdem facturi erunt'.[3] On the other hand,
when Nigel de Albini some time between 1109 and 1124 gave
Dunton in Essex to the abbey of Bec (by a charter which
possesses unusual interest in that it seems to reveal a stock and
land arrangement on a lay estate) he provided that the abbey
should have the land 'cum illa instauracione cum qua Willelmus de Arch' eam de me habuit' and that William should make
up any deficit *de suo*, but retain any surplus if surplus there
should be.[4] A few more variants may be noted. When the canons
of St. Paul's leased some land at Sandon to Mabel, the widow of
Galiun, they laid it down that half the stock—*omnium instaura-
mentorum dimidietas*—should remain to them on her death.[5]
Under a lease of Potter Heigham granted by St. Benet of Holme
between 1153 and 1168 the lessee on his death had to leave to
the abbey a third of his livestock wherever it might be—'tertiam
partem omnis pecunie sue vive ubicunque fuerit'.[6] And the
lease of Ingham and Elveden granted by St. Edmunds Abbey
for twelve years from 1160 apparently reserves to the lessee both

[1] *Register of St. Benet*, appendix E, cf. No. 148 of 1141–9, which provides for the
return of a specified *instauramentum* (8 oxen, 2 horses, 300 sheep) and also that the
abbey shall have on the lessee's death 'quicquid de propria adquisitione habuerit
in predicta terra'. For a parallel case see *D.S.P.*, p. 126.

[2] *Register of St. Benet*, No. 119.

[3] *Hugh Candidus*, pp. 88–89; *Black Book of St. Augustine*, ed. Turner and Salter,
p. 385.

[4] *Select Documents of the English Lands of the Abbey of Bec*, ed. Chibnall (Camden
Soc. 1951), p. 15, No. xxv: 'et superplus siquid fuerit habeat Willemus de instauracione; si vero minus perficiatur de suo'.

[5] Liber L, ff. 43v, 44. From the list of witnesses it appears that this lease belongs
to the middle of the twelfth century. The Galiun of this lease appears to be the
same as the Galio of that cited on p. 180 above.

[6] *Register of St. Benet*, No. 190.

the crops and any buildings he may have put up—at the end of the twelve years he must leave a specified *instauramentum* to the lessors 'exceptis messibus et edificiis que ibi voluerit facere'.[1]

The stock and land lease was not a Norman innovation. Though the documents in which Anglo-Saxon leases are recorded commonly tell us very little, there are several of early eleventh-century date which reveal conditions of this type, and, all things considered, it seems possible that the lessor's property in some standard equipment of stock was often understood without its being recorded in writing.[2] Further the fact that the stock and land lease is found both before the Norman Conquest and in the early part of the twelfth century greatly increases the significance of the scanty evidence for its use which comes to us from the intervening period. There is first the grant of Thornley made by Walcher, Bishop of Durham (1071–80), to a woman named Ealdgyth. In this we are told that if Ealdgyth dies or leaves the estate 'the terms (*mala*) shall be eight oxen, twelve cows and four men'.[3] Then, far away from this northern region, the abbey of Bath grants Charlecombe in Somerset to William Hosett, the Domesday tenant, with 10 oxen, 60 sheep, and 100

---

[1] *Feudal Documents*, No. 145. A lease of 1186–1200 requires an increment of 200 sheep to be left: *Kalendar of Abbot Samson* (Camden Soc.) p. 120.

[2] See Robertson, op. cit., Nos. lxxiv, lxxix, xcviii: cf. Nos. lxxxi, lxxxvi, and xcvii which mention stock or other equipment to be given up at the end of the lease without stating that this had been provided by the lessor. The return of the lands in a stocked condition—'swa gewered swa hy beon'—is also stipulated in No. lxx. It would be rash to guess just what was implied by the words *mid mete 7 mid mannon* employed in several of these documents, or by the words *cum omnibus utensilibus* which occur in the reversion clause of some pre-Norman Worcester leases (e.g. Earle, *Land Charters*, p. 208 of A.D. 984, and Bond, *Facsimiles*, pt. iv, 22 of A.D. 1038); but the lease of Cutsdean, granted by Oswald of Worcester in 987, contains the clause 'sine detrimento omnium rerum ad se pertinentium, hominum, vel pecorum, seu ciborum, sicut tunc temporis inibi fuerit' (*Hemming's Cartulary*, ed. Hearne, pp. 165–6). It should be noted too that after 1045—perhaps as late as 1065—Abbot Wulfric of Ely, while agreeing that Esgar the Staller should hold High Easter for his life, stipulated that on Esgar's death the estate should revert to the abbey 'cum omnibus quae in ea fuerint' (*Historia Eliensis*, i. 218). That a condition of this kind might be understood without being stated is suggested by a comparison of Robertson, Nos. lxxx and xc. The first document is an agreement between Archbishop Æthelnoth (1020–38) and a man named Toki which provides that Toki shall have an estate at Halton for life and that on his death it shall pass to Christ Church 'with everything that he could produce upon it' ('mid eallum þingum þe he þæron getilian mihte'). The second is a renewal of this agreement by Archbishop Eadsige, Æthelnoth's successor; and it merely says that when Toki dies the land is to go to Christ Church. The recurrence of the alliterative phrase *mid mete 7 mid mannon* perhaps points to a usage that was common and familiar.

[3] Robertson, op. cit., appendix i, No. ii.

acres sown, or perhaps seed for that amount of land (*an c œkera sæd*).[1] In Hampshire, Domesday Book illustrates the continuity of such arrangements by describing Ralph Mortimer as the *tertius haeres* of a lease of Worthy, which had been granted in the time of King Edward and provided that, after the death of the third heir, the cathedral of Winchester should receive the manor *cum omni pecunia*.[2] From Domesday too we learn that Humphrey (probably Humphrey de Anslevill), when he became Eudo Dapifer's tenant in respect of some land in the hundred of Hertford, took over a large amount of stock with the land.[3] In Herefordshire Hugh Lasne gave a member of the manor of Hope to one of his knights *cum una caruca*.[4] According to the Exon. Domesday, the six *villani* of *Herstanahaia* held three ploughs at farm along with a hide and a half of land.[5] It is surely justifiable to conclude that the stock and land lease was a common feature of estate management in Norman England and that, unlike tenure by knight service, we have in it a form of landholding which the conquerors took over from the conquered people.

6. Nothing is more important for the understanding of Anglo-Norman leasehold and its social consequences than to determine the relations between the lessees and the manorial tenants. But this is a matter on which the evidence is very scanty. No doubt the lessee acquired the right to receive such of the customary services as were needed for the cultivation of the demesne. Before the Conquest, the Old English phrase *mid mete*

---

[1] *Two Chartularies of the Priory of St. Peter at Bath*, pp. 37–38; cf. Exon., p. 172.

[2] Dd. i, f. 46*b*. Perhaps a stock and land lease is indicated at Urchfont, Wiltshire, where 2 hides had been held T.R.E. by a reeve who 'postea vero reddidit eas aeclesiae cum omni pecunia sua': ibid. i, f. 68.

[3] Ibid., f. 139: 'cum qua sumpsit Hunfridus quando de Eudone recepit lxviii animalia et cccl oves et cl porcos et l capras et i equam et xiii solidos et iiii denarios de censu regis et inter pannos et vasa xx solidos.' The recording of the details in this exceptional way is perhaps connected with the fact that Eudo is said to have obtained the land without proper authorization (*super regem*). It does not follow that Humphrey was only a lessee. There are references to stock received by a tenant-in-chief at Marks Tey and West Bergholt in Essex (Dd. ii, ff. 57*b*, 89); and a statement which Round took to refer to the sub-tenant at Little Maplestead in the same county ('Tunc nichil recepit modo ii vaccae et xiiii porci et lvii oves': ibid., f. 84) seems to imply that it was unusual not to take over stock with the land: cf. Davis, *Regesta*, No. 399. Land might certainly be granted on an hereditary tenure along with the stock. Abbot Geoffrey of Burton (1114–50) granted to Andrew and his heir in fee farm 'illam partem Leguae quam prius tenuerat Ebrardus clericus et post ipsum Aisulfus presbiter cum hominibus et cum pecunia quam illi acceperant' (*Hist. Collections for Staffs.*, v, pt. i, p. 34).

[4] Dd. i, f. 187.

[5] Exon., p. 371.

and mid mannon, whatever else it may have meant, implied the transfer of a human labour force; and, as we have seen, men as well as oxen are mentioned in the lease of Thornley granted by Walcher, the first Norman bishop of Durham. Yet such expressions cannot properly be taken as proof that the lessee exercised control over the manorial peasantry, for they may refer only to a demesne staff—the people who appear in Domesday as *servi* or *bovarii*. On general grounds, however, it is surely safe to assume that, when a manor was let on lease, the agricultural services of the *villani* and *bordarii* were let along with the demesne, for these services would be needed by the lessee and must have become well nigh useless to a landlord who was not cultivating the demesne directly. Though Domesday Book tells us little about peasant services, it is certain that they were an essential element in the manorial economy, for they figure as heavy burdens both in the pre-Conquest *Rectitudines Singularum Personarum* and in surveys made in the time of Henry I.[1] Probably it was a matter of course for such services to be transferred to the farmer of the demesne and that may be the reason why they are so rarely mentioned in twelfth-century leases; but it is worthy of note that the exceptionally detailed inventory that was made when Richard the Archdeacon took over the manor of *Adulvesnasa* does refer to seventy-nine works per week which *ad curiam illam pertinent*.[2]

The *firmarius* of a manor sometimes had powers that went far beyond the mere utilization of customary services. An interesting, if rather late, example relates to Damerham, a Wiltshire manor of Glastonbury Abbey, now in Hampshire. A certain *Johannes clericus*, who was tenant of a virgate in Damerham and of another in the hamlet of *Stapelham*, took the vill of Damerham to farm and then *propria auctoritate* exchanged his *Stapelham* virgate for a half-virgate in Damerham, 'because it was nearer'. And the exchange meant that the virgate he gave up, though previously held for a money rent, became subject to labour services, while the half-virgate he took in exchange was freed from

---

[1] Week work is recorded, on manors that were evidently at farm, in the Caen, Burton, and Peterborough surveys.

[2] *D.S.P.*, p. 131. The twelfth-century Ramsey Abbey surveys contain a number of references to the rights (and obligations) of the *firmarii* in regard to boon works. Thus some tenants at Ringstead 'si firmarius rogaverit ter arabunt ad cibum firmarii': *Cart. Rams.* iii. 269. At Brington some cotlands 'sunt ad bovarios faciendos vel si firmarius voluerit quaeque earum dabit duodecim denarios': ibid., p. 311.

those it had previously owed.[1] Then from the early twelfth-century surveys of the manors of the Abbaye aux Dames we learn that the farmer of Horsted had established three *villani* who were not there previously.[2] Moreover, when Richard the Archdeacon leased Runwell in Essex from the Canons of St. Paul's (before 1150), it was stipulated that any agreements he might make about the letting of land would be accepted as binding by his landlords.[3] And though a provision of this kind has not been noted in any other lease of the period, the clause was probably inserted in this case, not because it was exceptional for a lessee to have such authority, but because at Runwell it was contemplated that the cultivated area would be increased by assarting.[4] Not only at Runwell, but also at Ardeley, at Belchamp and at Chingford we find manorial tenants who had been put into their holdings by twelfth-century *firmarii*.[5] And that a *firmarius* might have the power to dispose of larger matters than the small tenements involved in the foregoing cases is shown by an example from the

---

[1] *Liber Henrici de Soliaco*, p. 130. We are told that 'de hoc excambio nullum dampnum accidit domino'. As regards the date of this transaction we only know that John was already tenant of the virgates before the death of Bishop Henry (1171) and that he was still a tenant of the manor in 1189 when the matter was reported.

[2] Bibl. Nat. MS. lat. 5650, f. 28*v*: 'habemus iii adhuc villanos quos constituit herueus firmarius noster qui prius ibi non erant.'

[3] 'Et pactiones quas Ricardus cum agricolis de terris ad censum locandis firmabit, ratas et firmas canonici habebunt': *D.S.P.*, p. 125.

[4] 'adquietavit ipse Ricardus adversus regem prefatum manerium in perpetuum de omni exactione et foris factura nemoralis extirpationis quam vulgo sartum vocant': ibid. A writ of King Stephen's is concerned with 240 acres of assarts made at Runwell by Archdeacon Richard: *Early Charters of St. Paul's*, No. 39.

[5] At Runwell, John, son of Walter Ruffus, was in 1222 holding 15 acres *per Ricardum archidiaconum* and another 10 acres *per Ricardum ruffum Archidiaconum*, and several more tenants are said to hold *per Ricardum Ruffum*: *D.S.P.*, pp. 70–71. At Ardeley (ibid., p. 22) Walter de Mora held in 1222 half a virgate 'quam predecessores sui habuerunt per magistrum Albericum' (for whose lease see ibid., pp. 136–7). At Belchamp three tenants mentioned in 1181 had received their holdings *per Ricardum Ruffum* and the labour services on a fourth holding had been commuted for a money rent by the same lessee: ibid., pp. 115–17 and see pp. 138–9 for the lease. At Chingford the survey of 1222 reveals half-a-dozen 8-acre holdings (as well as some smaller tenements) that were held under arrangements made *per Walterum firmarium*—no doubt the Walter who was farmer at Chingford in 1181—and since the joint tenants of one of these holdings also held another 8 acres 'per Mariam relictam Walter firmarii', it seems probable that Walter and his wife had been given a lease of Chingford for their lives: ibid., pp. 88–91. Before Walter's time, 5 acres of demesne and an acre of meadow—or at least the meadow—had been let by a *firmarius* named Ailmar: ibid., p. 144. I take it that the formula '*X* tenet per *Y* firmarium' does not necessarily mean that *X* had himself received the holding from *Y*, but only that the title derived from, or that the conditions depended on, arrangements which *Y* had made either with *X* or a predecessor of *X*.

estates of Ramsey Abbey. Robert the clerk, who was *firmarius* of Hemingford in the time of Abbot William (1160–78), on his own authority—*auctoritate propria*—transferred 2 virgates of the demesne, first to his brother Mathew and then, when Mathew died *sine herede*, to a nephew named Ralph; and the tenancy thus created appears to have become hereditary, for a survey of the manor which was made after 1216 and is the source of all this information, shows the 2 virgates as held by Ralph's grandson in virtue of the grant made by Robert and specifies the rent and boon works, the casual dues and Christmas gifts, that he owed for them.[1]

It was recognized that a farmer's powers were liable to abuse. The author of the *Leges Henrici Primi* seems to include such abuse among the matters to be inquired into when a farmed manor reverts to the lord.[2] In 1152, when the Canons of St. Paul's let the manor of Kensworth *ad firmam* to Humphrey Bucuinte for his life, they stipulated that he should treat and keep the men of the manor in a reasonable way.[3] Half a century later the Constitutions of Hubert Walter for the abbey of Ramsey include a provision that *firmarii* must give adequate security that they will not oppress the men of the abbey subject to them; and, about the same time, two leases granted by Abbot Samson of Bury St. Edmunds record the fact that the lessees took an oath to this effect.[4]

Yet to control the agricultural services of the peasantry and to

---

[1] *Cart. Rams.* i. 381–2.

[2] Op. cit. 56, 3 (*Gesetze*, ed. Liebermann, i. 575): 'querendum est autem in reddicione manerii . . . si quis gablum auxerit, si quis iniuste tulerit.' But perhaps the last words point to peculation by the farmer and not to ill-treatment of tenants.

[3] *D.S.P.*, p. 128: 'et ipse hunfridus homines manerii rationabiliter debet tractare et custodire.'

[4] *Cart. Rams.* ii. 205: 'A firmariis etiam sufficiens cautio recipiatur quod . . . homines monasterii sibi subjectos injuste non gravabunt.' For the St. Edmund's leases see *Kalendar of Abbot Samson*, pp. 120, 128. One lessee swore 'quod homines ad predictas villas pertinentes rationabiliter tractabit et quod eos nouis et indebitis exaccionibus non grauabit, sed tantum statutas et debitas consuetudines ab eis exiget'. The other swore 'quod homines earumden uillarum rationabiliter tractabit et quod non exiget ab eis nisi tantum rationales consuetudines suas'. Another example is the declaration made by William de Amundavill when (in the late twelfth century) he took a life lease from the chapter of Lincoln Cathedral of their 'lay tenement' in Friesthorpe: 'Praeterea sub iuramenti interpositione promisi quod mesagium cum pertinentibus quod Adam de Amundavilla de eis tenuit integre servabo et homines suos moderate et rationabiliter tractabo' (*Registrum Antiquissimum of Lincoln*, ed. Foster and Major (Lincoln Record Soc.), iv, No. 1234).

have the right of sub-letting portions of the demesne did not necessarily mean that the farmer became the substitute of the lord in all respects. Much would depend upon the nature of his relations with the freer classes of tenants; and this is a matter on which it is very hard to obtain information. A ray of light comes to us from an agreement concluded between the Canons of St. Paul's and the two men to whom they leased the manor of Navestock in 1152. A portion of the Navestock land—a portion rated at one hide—had been held by a certain Ralph de Marci, who appears in Domesday as a sub-tenant in Essex and Suffolk; and some time before 1120 the dean and canons granted this land to Ralph's son William and his heirs for a rent of 16s. a year.[1] It subsequently came into the possession of a second Ralph de Marci; but he proved recalcitrant in regard to his obligations, and in consequence the canons agreed that, if Ralph did not pay what he owed, the lessees of the manor should exercise jurisdiction *sicut prepositi*. If they failed to get justice, the canons would step in and take over the case themselves, and if they did not, the amount that Ralph owed was to be allowed as a deduction from the farm which the lessees had covenanted to pay.[2] Clearly the rent of this free tenant was payable to the farmers of the manor; but it looks as if they needed special authorization to exercise jurisdiction to compel payment and were, so to say, appointed as reeves of the lord *pro hac vice*. An earlier and equally striking example of a substantial free tenant owing rent to the *firmarii* of a manor is forthcoming from the estates of the abbey of Burton. Some time between 1114 and 1150—probably before 1127—Abbot Geoffrey II granted to Edda, wife of Nicholas, *et*

---

[1] Hist. MSS. Comm. Appendix to Ninth Report, p. 66; and for the first Ralph de Marci see Round, *Domesday Studies*, ed. P. E. Dove, ii (1891), 553–5. Round points out that the grant to William de Marci is witnessed by Otuel fitz Count who went down with the White Ship in 1120. That the same land is in question throughout and that it was rated at one hide is clear because (i) William was given all his father's land in Navestock, (ii) the survey of 1222 shows William de Breaute 'cum herede et filia Rad' de Marci' holding a hide in Navestock for 16s. a year—the same rent as that fixed for William a century earlier: *D.S.P.*, p. 75.

[2] 'Haec est conventio inter canonicos sci Pauli et Teod' et Robertum de turri; quod ipse Teod' et Rob' facient justiciam de Rad' de Marci sicut prepositi facere debent, si non reddiderit de terra quam tenet de canonicis in Nasestoca quecunque reddere debet tam de censu canonicorum quam de regalibus exactionibus et ministrorum regis. Quod si non potuerint de eo justiciam facere, canonici eam facient. Quam si non fecerint, computabunt eis in firma quodcunque de terra debuerit, tam de censu canonicorum quam de regis exactionibus et ministrorum ejus': *D.S.P.*, p. 133.

heredi ejus, an estate at Dodsleigh in Staffordshire comprising 20 bovates of 'warland', two *culturae* of 'inland' and part of a wood: it was granted *in feudum et hereditatem*.[1] But Dodsleigh was a member of the manor of Leigh; and most of the money rent owed by Edda was payable to Godric and Uluric, the farmers of Leigh, though they only held that manor on a sixteen-year's lease.[2]

On the other hand, when a manor was put to farm, it was quite common for the lord to retain part of the estate in his own hands, or for certain tenants and their holdings to be excluded from the lease. In the case of Leigh just cited, a certain Osbern of Checkley had a house and croft and a bit of wood that were *extra firmam*; and the abbot continued to have a direct interest in the manor, for he retained the right to keep cows and pigs there in the 'custody' of the lessees.[3] Similar reservations were made on some of the other Burton manors. At Bromley none of the wood was included in the farm.[4] At Branston, most of which was held at farm by Edric the monk, the abbot reserved the wood and the land of two holdings comprising 14 bovates, and then, it seems, let these 14 bovates independently.[5] At Winshill, which was also farmed by Edric, a mill and a croft remained in the abbot's hands, and a few rents were apparently paid direct to him.[6] At Willington the mill was included in the farm; but at Potlac it was let separately.[7] On the estates of St. Benet of Holme, again, certain lands were excluded from the life lease of South Walsham (1141–9); and that of Potter Heigham (1153–8) provided that the fines, heriots, and reliefs of five tenants should be reserved to the abbot and that one of them should pay rent to him, though apparently everything else they owed by custom was to go to the lessee.[8] That Westminster Abbey habitually

---

[1] *Hist. Collections Staffs.* v, pt. i, p. 34.

[2] Ibid. for 1916, pp. 226, 227. Edda held Dodsleigh 'pro xx solidis quoque anno ex quibus computantur in firmam Godrici et Ulurici xviii solidi quia et hec terra ad Legam pertinet'.

[3] Ibid., pp. 226, 227.

[4] Ibid., p. 223 (Survey B).

[5] Ibid. v, pt. i, p. 19; cf. ibid. for 1916, pp. 216–17. In Bridgeman's edition of the surveys the facts are obscured by the omission of the words 'et preter terram quae fuit Ormi'.

[6] Ibid., p. 242.   [7] Ibid., pp. 238, 236.

[8] *Register of St. Benet of Holme*, Nos. 148, 190. I differ from the editor's interpretation of one clause in the Potter Heigham lease: 'ceteri que ex consuetudine faciunt sint ad firmam predicti Thome.' The renewal of this lease (No. 257) has *cetera* instead of *ceteri* and this I take to be the correct reading.

reserved certain sources of income can be inferred from the
grant by which Abbot Herbert (*c.* 1121-40) let the manor of
Powick in Worcestershire at farm to the monks of Malvern, for
this stipulates that the abbot shall have those customs 'which he
has in all other manors which are similarly at farm'.[1] As regards
proprietary churches, we find that various arrangements were
made for the payment of rents due from those belonging to
St. Paul's Cathedral. In some cases, though the manors were
farmed, the canons received the church rents directly from the
parish priests, but in other cases they were paid 'through the
farmer' (*per firmarium ecclesie nomine* or *per manum firmarii*), and at
Belchamp, Walton, and Thorp the farmer appears to have been
the actual recipient of these rents.[2] On three of the St. Paul's
manors Peter's Pence was collected by the *firmarii* (two of whom
seem to have kept the money for themselves), but more usually
the parish priest collected it.[3]

The *Inquisitio Ecclesiarum*, from which this information is derived, was probably made in 1181; and it is a far cry from the
reign of Henry II to the generation which witnessed the compilation of Domesday Book. But one suggestive if puzzling
feature is noticeable in the records of both periods. In the inquest
of the manors of St. Paul's which is contemporary with the inquest of the churches, the description of each manor concludes
with a statement of the *summa denariorum*. With three exceptions
this is an odd sum, the figure for Caddington (£7. 6s. 11½d.)
being quite typical; and the three places for which a round sum
is given are Weeley and Abberton, which were not described in
detail because they were let on an hereditary tenure, and Luffenhall, the description of which is distinguished from all the
others by the fact that the figure for the *summa denariorum* is followed by the words *per manum firmarii*. Moreover, in each of these
three cases, the *summa denariorum* equalled the sum that was
rendered to the canons—apparently by way of farm. Elsewhere
there is no correspondence between the two figures: the renders
consisted of whole farms or round sums of money (except at
Runwell, which rendered £6. 12s.); and in places where money

---

[1] *Westminster Domesday*, ff. 293, 293*v*: 'Et illas consuetudines habeat abbas in
eodem manerio quas habet in omnibus aliis maneriis quae similiter sunt ad firmam.'
[2] *D.S.P.*, pp. 146–52. At Belchamp the parson paid a mark a year to the farmer
'non nomine ecclesie sed propter avoeriam'.
[3] At Cadendon and Kensworth the rural dean collected the Peter's Pence and
paid it over to the archdeacon.

payments formed part of the farm these also were in round numbers of pounds or shillings and never ran into odd pence, a delusive appearance of oddness at Caddington being due to the fact that on that manor certain payments were made in marks.[1] Thus everything suggests that the *summae denariorum* were total figures reached by the addition of a number of miscellaneous particulars; and it is hard to see what these can have been if they were not the rents of a group of manorial tenants—an hypothesis which is supported by the fact that the rents of the tenants set forth in the survey of 1222 (the so-called Domesday of St. Paul's) amount on the great majority of the manors to sums of the same order of magnitude as the *summae denariorum* of the earlier inquest.

This contrast between the round sums of the farms or renders and another set of figures which consist of odd sums finds a parallel in Canterbury documents of early Norman date. In the schedule of archiepiscopal demesne manors the *firma* is in almost all cases a sum of pounds or marks, while the *gablum* is generally an odd sum running frequently into pence and sometimes into farthings.[2] And it is much the same with the schedule of the monks' manors. In this the account of the farms as appointed by Lanfranc is immediately followed by a list of places and sums of money headed *Gablum Maneriorum*, and while the farms usually consist of months or weeks or round sums of money, the figures for the *gablum* run into odd pence or fractions of a penny in 19 cases out of 33.[3] Moreover, another Canterbury Register contains a second schedule of the *Gablum Maneriorum* which relates in the main to the same manors as the text just cited, but is apparently of somewhat later date.[4] For a majority of the

---

[1] The Runwell render (£6. 12s.) is just one ore (16d.) short of 10 marks.

[2] *Domesday Monachorum*, pp. 98–99. In 22 out of 26 unambiguous cases the *firma* consisted of whole pounds or (at Malling) whole marks, the figures in the remaining four cases being £52. 10s. (Otford), £32 less a hundred pence (Reculver), £22. 12s. (Sundridge), and £17. 10s. (Darenth). *Gablum* is mentioned in 25 cases and in 14 of these the figures run into odd pence or fractions of a penny; in three only do they amount to whole pounds, and the remaining figures are £29. 10s., £19. 9s., £10. 19s., 116s., 67s., 63s., 35s., and 24s. It should be remembered that the MS. which includes this schedule dates from c. 1100.

[3] Canterbury Register K, f. 69v; Lambeth MS. 1212, pp. 344–5.

[4] Canterbury MS. Lit. D. 4, ff. 5–6. For my knowledge of this text I am indebted to Mr. P. H. Sawyer. The evidence for its later date depends on the assumption that it was drawn up at the same time as the lists of *Redditus Maneriorum* and *Denarii ad coquinam* which immediately follow it in the MS. In the former list the rent of Bocking is stated to be £30 and we are told that this manor used to

manors the figures are identical in the two texts, but there are also many small differences. Thus, for example, the figures for Hollingbourne (£1. 0s. 8¾d.), Kennington (£1. 0s. 3d.), and Westwell (£1. 15s. 5d.) remain the same, but Ickham has changed from £3. 13s. 2¾d. to £2. 12s. 4¾d., Eastrey from £6. 0s. 5¾d. to £5. 6s. 9d., Bocking from £1. 13s. to £1. 11s. 10½d. And this is just what one would expect to find with totals composed of numerous small rents and therefore exposed to alteration with all the changes and chances and casualties incident to a group of small tenants.

Since the amount of the farms appears to have been always considerably greater than the *gablum* or the *summa denariorum*, it is on the face of things possible that the rents in question were payable to the *firmarius*, like the rent owed by Ralph de Marci at Navestock. But even if they were, it must remain significant that the Archbishop and monks of Canterbury in the early Norman period, and the Dean and Chapter of St. Paul's in the reign of Henry II, were sufficiently concerned with the internal affairs of their farmed manors to record the sums obtainable from these rents, and apparently (in the case of the Canterbury monks) to keep the account up to date. The Canterbury evidence, moreover, strongly supports the alternative hypothesis that the *gablum* was additional to the farm and payable to the landlord. In the later of the two schedules of monastic manors the manors are grouped according to the date at which the *gablum* was due and the amounts due as *gablum* from those in each group are added together. This would have an obvious utility if the monks were to be the recipients: they would know how much they could expect on the various rent days. But it is impossible to see what purpose can have been served by this dating and summation of the payments if the *gablum* went to the farmers of the individual manors. Yet another hint which, for what it is worth, seems to point in the same direction, is supplied by the Domesday Monachorum schedule of archiepiscopal manors. Some of its items consist of pairs of manors which rendered a joint farm; but in the case of 2 of these pairs (*Stursete* with Petham and Maidstone with Detling) the *gablum* is given

render the farm of one month; and the *Denarii ad coquinam* are given as £6 for Hollingbourne which 'used to render £8'. The schedule of Register K describes Bocking as owing a month's farm and says that Hollingbourne 'reddit octo libras ad coquinam'.

for each of the 4 places separately.[1] And especially remarkable is some evidence regarding the manors of Cliffe and Adisham, both of which belonged to the monks. In what seems to be the earlier of the two monastic schedules, Cliffe is entered as owing £2 of *gablum* and also appears (in the section of the text headed *Firme in denariis tantum*) as owing a farm of £14. In the later schedule, however, it makes no appearance in the section headed *Redditus maneriorum*, but in that devoted to the *gablum* is represented as owing £5. 6s. 8d. at Easter and again on St. John the Baptist's Day and at Michaelmas. Thus the total amount payable as *gablum* according to this text is the same as the total of the *gablum* and the farm together as given in the other schedule. And further we find that Cliffe is valued at £16 both in Domesday Book and in the Domesday Monachorum. From all this it seems clear, first, that the *gablum* of the earlier schedule was at Cliffe distinct from and additional to the farm, not part of the income that the farmer obtained from the manor, and secondly, that the two payments became combined. But one is left to wonder why the combined payment was classed as *gablum* and not entered under the heading of *Redditus maneriorum*. Perhaps the manor of Cliffe as a whole was let at farm to the same manorial tenant or group of tenants who owed *gablum* for their holdings within it; but there is no knowing whether this was so. As regards Adisham (of which something has been said in a previous chapter) it is clear that the *gablum* was additional to the farm. Accordingly to Domesday Book Adisham renders £46. 16s. 4d. and a *gersuma* of 100s. to the archbishop.[2] According to the Domesday Monachorum it renders £16. 16s. 4d. as *gablum* and is worth £30 *de firma* and 100s. *de gersuma*.[3] It is of course possible that the *gablum* was in this case paid through the farmer; but if so it was none the less additional to the round sum that he owed as farm, and his function in regard to the tenants who owed it can hardly have been more than that of a rent-collector on the landlord's behalf. The alternative supposition—that the exploitation of the tenants in question was handed over to him along with the demesne—is surely ruled out by the fact that alterations in the amount of the *gablum* were recorded in the

---

[1] Domesday Monachorum, pp. 98, 99. 'Stursete et Petham reddunt de firma xl libras. Gablum de Petham c solidos et vi et ii denarios et iii ferd'. Gablum de Stursete lx solidos—Meidestane et Detlinges de firma xl libras. Gablum lx solidos xvi denariis minus . . . Gablum de Detlinges xxx solidos et ix denarios.'

[2] Dd. i, f. 5.   [3] Dd. Mon., p. 89.

cathedral registers. While the Domesday Monachorum, as we have seen, puts it at £16. 16s. 4d., the schedule of Register K gives it as £17. 10s. 8½d. and that of Canterbury MS. Lit. D. 4 as £17. 5s. 6d. But the most decisive evidence comes from the estates of the archbishop and relates to the manors of Boughton under Blean and Charing. Of the first of these places the Domesday Monachorum tells us that in the time of King Edward it was valued at £10 and that the archbishop has [sic] £5. 15s. 3d. de gablo but now 'valet XX libras sed tamen reddit XX et V libras de firma et archiepiscopus habet suum gablum sicut prius'. The entry for Charing is precisely parallel.[1] Yet the gablum was not invariably paid to the archbishop. Croyden was one of his demesne manors; but, according to Domesday Book, Restoldus held 7 hides of its land of the archbishop and Ralph 1 hide, 'et inde habent vi libras et viii solidos de gablo'. There is, however, no ground for regarding these men as firmarii. Restoldus has been identified with one of the archbishop's knights, so probably he held the 7 hides by knight service; and as the manor is stated to be worth £27 to the archbishop and £10. 10s. hominibus ejus, it may be that Restoldus and Ralph had put part of their holdings to farm, and that the gablum on the rest was paid to them and not to the farmer or farmers.[2]

It is only very rarely that Domesday Book throws even a flickering and uncertain light upon these matters; but the casual glimpse it affords suggest that conditions varied from place to place. At Sutton in Norfolk the rents of the liberi homines were evidently included in the farm, and in the same county the rents of some liberi homines at Gillingham were reckoned as part of the rent of £40 'blanch' due from the manor of Ersham.[3] Apparently it was the same with thirteen substantial sokemen who are described as holding 'freely' at South Ockendon in Essex; and seven houses in London which belonged to the Count of Eu's Essex manor of West Thurrock are definitely stated to be included in its firma.[4] On the other hand, at Combs in Suffolk, which belonged to the Count of Mortain, Domesday clearly

[1] Dd. Mon., p. 85.

[2] Dd. i, f. 30b; Dd. Mon., pp. 36, 105. According to the schedule of the Domesday Monachorum (p. 99), Croyden owed a farm of £30. Presumably this refers to the lands retained in demesne, but the figures in the schedule cannot be reconciled with those of Domesday Book.

[3] Dd. ii, f. 180 ('modo totum simul cum liberis hominibus valet x libras . . . et erat ad censatum x lib.'); f. 141b ('additi in censu de ersam'); cf. 138b.

[4] Ibid., ff. 58, 63.

distinguishes the renders of the *liberi homines* from the render of the manor; and the statement *non sunt in firma regis*, made about some *franci homines* at Steeple in Essex, was interpreted by Round to mean that 'the receipts from them were not included in the sum for which the King leased out the estate'.[1] In the Little Domesday freemen and sokemen are often 'valued' separately from the manor to which they are attached; but it is also quite common for the value of such persons to be included in that of the manor. Whether the distinction is at all pertinent to the problem under consideration is very doubtful.

In Norman England the farming-out of manors for a fixed rent was very common, and the farmer was frequently a lessee. But we have no means of knowing whether farming-out was the predominant form of estate management even on the great estates, nor can we discover whether a lessee or a *firmarius* of an official type was the more usual instrument of the system. For this early period, and indeed, for the whole of the twelfth century, evidence in regard to the employment of more direct methods of seigneurial administration is extremely meagre. Yet though the greater landlords were often rent-receivers on a large scale, it would be unwarrantable to assume that they were merely that and played no active part in agrarian life. Scanty as the evidence is, it is sufficient to forbid such a conclusion. The abbey of Ely, at any rate, appears to have exercised a pretty close supervision over its property. A schedule which is appended to the Ely Inquest and must have been compiled in the same generation as Domesday Book, reveals the demesne manors of the abbey divided into numerous groups 'sicut prepositi tenent unusquisque preposituram suam'; and the list shows that the arrangement of these groups was largely, though not precisely, determined by considerations of local propinquity.[2] At Bury

---

[1] Ibid., ff. 291, 4*b*; *V.C.H. Essex*, i. 432 n. 3.

[2] I.C.C., ed. Hamilton, pp. 168–73. The schedule relates to property in 85 vills and gives for each vill the numbers of demesne ploughs and tenants' ploughs 'quos modo habent secundum breves Regis' and also the numbers of *villani*, *bordarii*, and *servi*. The grouping is indicated by the summation of these particulars for 19 groups of vills, but the exact number of *prepositurae* is uncertain, for the 19 totals do not include a group of 3 vills in Essex, 2 pairs of vills, and 5 other vills, and it is impossible to know whether each of these was a separate *prepositura* or whether some totals have been accidentally omitted. Thus one can only say that there appear to have been between 27 and 31 *prepositurae*.

That the schedule is virtually contemporary with the Ely Inquest is made probable by its inclusion in all the three (twelfth-century) manuscripts of the latter and by the way it appears to treat the Domesday figures as current statistics.

St. Edmunds, again, there were in 1086 thirteen reeves—*super terram prepositi*—dwelling in the shadow of the abbey; and it is tempting to connect their number with the division of its food rents into thirteen months.[1] Of activity on the part of Abbot Symeon of Ely (1081–93) there is further evidence. A section of the Ely Inquest is devoted to a statistical summary for the abbey's estates county by county; and, according to this, the demesne manors in Cambridgeshire were 'emendata in manu abbatis Symeonis' by £54, the estates in Essex, including some manors held by the abbey's knights, by £9, those in Norfolk by £17, and those in Suffolk by £7.[2] On the face of it, this might mean nothing more than an increase of rents, but there is reason to think that an increase in ploughing strength was involved. In each case the statement about improvement immediately follows one giving the number of ploughs for which there was land; and it is remarkable that the schedule just mentioned shows plough-teams in excess of those recorded in Domesday at thirty-five places.[3] Perhaps we should see a parallel to this in the work of Abbot Ralph of Battle (1107–24), of whom we are told that he joined unoccupied lands to those already occupied and increased the value of the abbey's estates by about £20 a year.[4] We also read in the Battle Chronicle that, during the five years'

---

[1] Dd. ii, f. 372; Robertson, op. cit., No. civ.

[2] I.C.C., ed. Hamilton, pp. 121, 122.

[3] The demesne ploughs increased at 21 places, 2 of which also show an increase in tenants' ploughs, and an increase in the latter only is found at 14 places. Though some of the differences between the schedule and Domesday Book may, of course, be due to scribal errors, these figures are undoubtedly significant. There are 5 sets of figures in the schedule—2 for demesne ploughs and tenants' ploughs, 3 for villans, bordars, and serfs—and over 200 more digits are employed in the enumeration of the men than in the enumeration of the ploughs. There is therefore more room for error as regards the men. But while the plough numbers differ from those of Domesday for 38 places, showing an increase in 35, the differences in the tenants' numbers are much fewer (on a single count, I find them in 21 places) and they exhibit no preponderant trend either towards increase or towards decrease. Though variations between the different manuscripts of the schedule prevent a concise statement from being quite exact, that is broadly the position. Moreover, in at least 3 cases, discrepancies in the numbers of persons have every appearance of being due to error—an obvious misreading of Domesday (or, rather, of the Ely Inquest) at Stretham and errors of xviii for xxviii and xxvi for xxxvi at Feltwell and Hitcham.

[4] 'Factus est vir agricola, terras habitas instanter coli faciens, non habitas habitis prudenter adjungens, quantitatem adusque pretii librarum per annum plus minus viginti eas multiplicans' (*Chronicon Monasterii de Bello*, Anglia Christiana, 1846, p. 59). Faritius, Abbot of Abingdon (1101–15) was given some waste land at Wallingford *ut eam excolet* (*Chron. Abingdon*, ii. 82).

vacancy which preceded Ralph's appointment, Geoffrey, a monk of St. Carilef, who was put in charge of the abbey, visited the manor of Wye and took drastic action against the *praepositus*, who had wasted it and was unable to give an account of his stewardship (*villicatio*).[1] Allusions such as these are certainly very infrequent; and monastic chroniclers of the period are usually concerned, not with the care or improvement of estates, but with the zeal of abbots in acquiring new property, with improper alienations, or with efforts made to recover what was lost. Yet it was apparently with the object of securing the economic balance of one of the abbey's estates that Abbot Faritius of Abingdon, between 1107 and 1115, got Henry I to grant the meadow of Kingsmead near Oxford to the men of Hinksey at fee farm for a rent of 20s. a year.[2] We must remember, too, that an abbot, and still more a bishop whose duties would involve a good deal of journeying about his diocese, might well visit his estates and consume food rents on the spot. Here and there we find hints suggestive of such personal visits to collect or consume rents. Hugh Candidus complains that Ernwy, who was Abbot of Peterborough in the Confessor's reign, exchanged Olney for Stoke merely because the latter was nearer to go to *ad suam firmam*.[3] Freckenham in Suffolk, which Lanfranc had given to Rochester *ad victum monachorum*, is transferred by Gundulf to the episcopal estates in exchange for Wouldham, because he judges it better that he and his successors should have the long ride into Suffolk *victum ibi longe quaeritare*, than that the monks or the poor folk of the vill should be wearied each year with the transport of the grain.[4] More definite evidence is supplied by the Life of St. Wulfstan. A miracle occurs while the bishop is stopping at

---

[1] Op. cit., pp. 47–49. 'Cumque praecipuum ecclesiae manerium Wi adisset, quod quidam abbatis defuncti serviens procuravit Robertus cognomento de Ciltuna, invenissetque illud undique distractum, coepit causas ab ipso praeposito rationemque requirere villicationis. . . . Tunc [*sc. in the court at Battle to which Robert was summoned*] domino Gausfrido manerii de Wi annullationem praepositumque impotentem villicationis reddere rationem exponente, tandem . . . reus coram communi judicio sistitur Rotbertus. Qui reatum confitens cum veniam flagitaret, decem argenti libris decemque frumenti adjudicatus modiis, cum gratia misericorditer absolvitur.'

[2] *Chron. Abingdon*, ii. 65–66. 'Pratum . . . pernecessarium autem hominibus de villa abbatiae, quae Hangestesi dicitur; pasturarum quippe suorum pecudum indigentes cernuntur.'　　　　　　　　　　　　　　[3] Above, p. 169 n. 3.

[4] *Textus Roffensis*, pp. 143–4. 'Malens quidem sese ac suos successores annuis laboribus equitando victum ibi longe quaeritare quam monachos vel ejusdem villae pauperes homines singulis annis in annonam deportando fatigare.'

Kempsey, one of the episcopal manors, *pro necessariorum oppor-tunitate*.[1] In each of his vills, indeed, Wulfstan had a humble dwelling or cell, to which he used to retire for study and con-templation, but he never built a hall in any of them and instead was diligent in the construction and restoration of village churches. One can hardly mistake the implications of this account. For a bishop to spend time upon his manors is normal; and it is a mark of Wulfstan's exceptional piety that he thought little of his own comfort and was so zealous *in divinis domibus apparandis*.[2] Moreover, the same conclusion is suggested by the very different picture which William of Malmesbury draws of Roger of Salisbury, who, in the next generation, built such splendid houses upon his estates that the historian doubts the ability of future bishops to maintain them.[3] Lanfranc, again, erected many houses for himself and his successors in the archi-episcopal vills, and Anselm appears to have lodged in some of them in 1093 when he was debating with himself whether he should accept the archbishopric.[4] And, though rare, instances are not wanting of monastic leases or grants in fee farm which stipulate that the grantee shall provide lodging and hospitality for the abbot when he comes into the neighbourhood.[5]

Even for the lay estates significant information is not wholly lacking. Ernulf of Hesdin, the lord of Chipping Norton, emerges from the darkness as an energetic landlord, who was prob-ably a real improver. William of Malmesbury, as we have seen, reports that he was a man of wonderful skill in agriculture—*mirus ad agriculturae sollertiam*—and illustrates his pious church-manship by a remark that enables us to catch sight of him inter-vening personally in the operations of the farmyard.[6] And when

[1] *Vita Wulfstani*, ed. R. R. Darlington (Camden Soc., 1928), p. 30.

[2] 'In singulis villis suis, singulas habebat ediculas, in quibus se objectis repagulis a mane post missam includebat': ibid., p. 50. 'Per totam parrochiam in sui juris prediis ecclesias struebat. . . . Nusquam enim in villis suis aulas, nusquam triclinia fecit': p. 52.

[3] *Gesta Regum* (Rolls Series), ii. 558 (*Historia Novella*, bk. ii): 'splendida per omnes possessiones suas construxit habitacula, in quibus solum tuendis successorum ejus frustra laborabit opera.'

[4] Eadmer, *Historia Novorum*, p. 16: 'Super haec in villis ad pontificatum perti-nentibus domos multas atque honestas, partim de lapide, partim de ligno, sibi et successoribus suis aedificavit'; and p. 37.

[5] For examples from the period 1114–50 see *Burton Cartulary* (William Salt Hist. Coll., v, pt. i), pp. 35, 36; and for one belonging to the Confessor's reign see *Chron. Rams.*, p. 175.

[6] *Gesta Pontificum* (Rolls Series), pp. 437–8: 'Ernulfus de Hesding vir inter optimates

we turn to Domesday Book the impression that he was an active
and efficient landlord is emphatically confirmed. Ernulf of
Hesdin was a tenant-in-chief in ten counties. In three of them
—Hampshire, Somerset, and Huntingdonshire—the value of his
property had not changed since 1066; and his one Bedfordshire
manor is worth just what it was when he received it. But in each
of the other six counties there had been a substantial net gain
on Ernulf's estates either since 1066 or since the date when the
manor came into the hands of its new lord. Here and there a loss
had occurred since the days of King Edward, but the losses are
few and comparatively small in amount, and no manor whose
value is given for the date of its 'reception' shows any fall in
value after that time. Altogether the values have increased at
twenty-five places on Ernulf's fee and the total net gain exceeds
£90 of annual value. It is the same story, too, with some manors
in Buckinghamshire and Kent which he held as the tenant of
Odo of Bayeux: on these taken together we find a net gain of
some £23.[1] Particularly remarkable are the indications of recovery after a previous decline. Ruislip in Middlesex, worth £30 in
1066, had declined in value to £12 when Ernulf received it, but is
worth £20 by 1086; and Kingsbury in the same county, though
it too fails to recover its pre-Conquest value of £6, has been
pulled up under its new landlord from £1 to £4.[2] Newbury in
Berkshire (the *Ulvritone* of Domesday), after falling in value from
£9 to £8, was in 1086 reckoned to be worth £24; and Barton in
Buckinghamshire, which Ernulf held of the Bishop of Bayeux,
was worth £3 in 1066 and only £2 when 'received', but is
valued at £14 in 1086.[3] It may be that Ernulf, though commended by William of Malmesbury for his charity to the poor,
was a hard landlord, and that some of his gains were the fruits
of extortion. Chelsfield (*Ciresfel*) in Kent, which he held of Odo,
is valued at £25, but renders £35, and the words of Domesday
seem to imply that this was the rent that Ernulf received from
a *firmarius* and not what he paid to his overlord. But the value of
Chelsfield had itself increased. It had reached £25 after falling

Angliae opinatissimus. Mirus ad agriculturae sollertiam, mirus ad munifice
sollevandam pauperum inopiam. Decimarum ita curiosus ut si horreum non deci-
matum jam intaxatum esset, omnia eici et incunctanter decimari juberet.' See
above, p. 69.

[1] I have had to ignore a few manors on account of the deficiency or obscurity
of the Domesday data.

[2] Dd. i, ff. 129*b*, 130.   [3] Ibid. ff. 62*b*, 145.

from £16 in the time of King Edward to £12; and that is so like what happened at places on Ernulf's own fee, that we are surely justified in crediting this real improvement to him rather than to Odo.[1]

Ernulf of Hesdin was no doubt an outstanding landlord; but one cannot suppose that he was the only baron in Norman England to busy himself with agrarian matters. William of Malmesbury tells us about him not because of his skill in agriculture, but because he could be cited as an edifying example of the healing powers of St. Aldhelm's tomb. And Stenton has argued that Walter de Aincurt should be reckoned 'a discreet and skilful landlord', since his Nottinghamshire estates show an increase in value 'in face of a general depreciation throughout the shire' and 'the value of his lands in Derbyshire and Lincolnshire had also risen since the Conquest'.[2] In his case, however, the gains are much less pronounced than those on the Hesdin estates, and there is nothing to show whether they were due to real improvements or only to an advance in rents. A similar doubt must be felt about Hardwin de Scalers, whose Hertfordshire lands are described in the Ely Inquest as 'emendata de XV libris sub Hardwino'.[3] But we are on surer ground with William Hosatus, the small Somerset landlord who in 1086 held *Tatewiche* in chief and Charlecombe as tenant of the abbey of Bath. Not only had the value of the former place doubled and that of the latter more than doubled since William acquired these modest estates: at Charlecombe a considerable addition had been made to the stock which he received from the abbey when he took the land.[4] And then, at the beginning of Henry I's reign, a great baron's interest in the extension of the cultivated area is revealed by a royal charter granting Simon, Earl of Huntingdon, sixty acres of forest near Kimbolton 'ad essartandum et hospitandum Gosfridum hominem suum super eam'.[5]

---

[1] Dd. i, f. 6b: 'Ernulfus de hesding tenet de episcopo Ciresfel . . . T.R.E. valebat xvi libras et post xii libras et modo xxv libras et tamen qui tenet reddit xxxv libras.'

[2] *V.C.H. Notts.* i. 230–1.

[3] I.C.C., ed. Hamilton, p. 124.

[4] Exon., pp. 430, 172; *Two Chartularies of Bath* (Somerset Record Soc., 1893), pp. 37–38. By 1086 there were two demesne plough-teams, which must mean at least 12 oxen, in place of 10 oxen, and 200 sheep in place of 60.

[5] *Regesta*, ii, ed. Johnson and Cronne, appendix, No. vii.

VIII

VILLAGES AND MANORS

THE Domesday Inquest was planned on the assumption
that the country was divided into village-estates of the type
that is usually called 'manorial'. Though the instructions
given to the several groups of royal commissioners probably
differed to some extent, and scholars have found it possible to
use variations in the phraseology of Domesday Book as a means
of conjecturing the geographical limits of the circuits allotted to
these groups, the range of difference is on the whole so small and
the measure of uniformity and agreement in essentials so remarkable, that the scheme of inquiry preserved in the preamble
to the Ely Inquest may certainly be taken as typical. Something
pretty like it must have been in the hands or minds of all the
commissioners. And its terms enable us to see what the Norman
government expected them to find.

The *Inquisitio Terrarum* was clearly to be made hundred by
hundred and village by village; and it was apparently assumed
that each village would be able to provide a priest, a reeve, and
six *villani* to give evidence.[1] Naturally the first thing to be
noted was the name of the place. But here we find at once that
manorialization is taken for granted. It is the name of the *mansio*
that is asked for; and the only possible translation of *mansio* is
'manor', at least if we understand that word in a sense that is
free from legal technicalities and is sufficiently vague for it to
mean either an estate or a dwelling of some distinction.[2] Yet,
however loose the actual connotation of the word *mansio* may
have been, it is certainly employed in this Ely text for an estate
and moreover for one of a definite type. It is an estate which an
individual owns or, rather, 'holds'; it includes a demesne or

---

[1] 'Hic subscribitur inquisitio terrarum quomodo barones regis inquisierunt,
videlicet per sacramentum vicecomitis scire, et omnium baronum et eorum franci-
genarum, et totius centuriatus, presbiteri, praepositi, vi villani uniuscujusque
ville.' Probably *villani* is a mistake for *villanorum*, as Round suggested.

[2] 'Deinde quomodo vocatur mansio'. In Domesday Book the word *mansio* is often
employed for a house. In the Exon. Domesday it is normally used for estates to
which Domesday Book applies the word *manerium*.

home-farm on which there will be ploughs; there will be 'men' there—*homines*—with ploughs of their own; and it is expected that there will be two main groups of people—the first comprising *villani*, cottars, and *servi*, and the second *liberi homines* and sokemen, this second group being, it would seem, distinguished from the first by a less close association with the demesne and by the possession of property that deserved separate estimation.[1] Woods, meadows, pastures, mills, and fisheries (*piscine*) are mentioned as matters that will need to be recorded.

That the assumptions upon which these articles of inquiry were based failed in many places to correspond with the conditions which the Domesday Inquest revealed, is established beyond question by the text of Domesday Book itself. In particular, the implied identity of manor and village proved to be an illusion. Yet on the whole the brief clauses of the Ely preamble command our respect, for they delineate with masterly simplicity the main features of what was at the time, and was destined for many generations to remain, the most characteristic form of English agrarian organization. Even the coincidence of manor and vill was sufficiently common to make their identification plausible. In the first half of the twelfth century Ordericus Vitalis could regard *villa* and *manerium* as equivalent terms; and at the end of that century the ordinance for the assessment of the carucage of 1198 (the very words of which seem to be echoed in the account of Roger of Howden) presupposes that every vill will have a lord and a bailiff and a reeve.[2] No doubt in this particular matter the Domesday questionnaire was especially at fault; but in other respects its essential realism seems to be vindicated by the fact that practical and experienced men in the thirteenth century, when compiling directions for the valuation of landed property, not only assumed that estates consist of manors, but clearly expected a manor to comprehend all the outstanding elements to which the attention of the Domesday

---

[1] The items proceed from the demesne outwards ('quot carruce in dominio, quot hominum, quot villani, quot cotsethli, quot servi, quot liberi homines, quot sochemani'), and the division between the three first classes of men and the last two is marked by the arrangement in two distinct descending orders of dignity, as well as by the isolation of the latter in the clause 'quantum ibi quisque liber homo vel sochemannus habuit vel habet'.

[2] Orderic iv. 7 (ed. Le Prevost, ii. 223); Roger de Hoveden (Rolls Series) iv. 46 (Stubbs, *Select Charters* (9th ed.), p. 249). Both passages are cited by Pollock and Maitland, op. cit. i. 605, 606.

commissioners had been directed in 1086.[1] A good deal must be allowed, of course, for the spread and intensification of manorialism after the time of Domesday Book. The habit of thinking manorially had practical consequences: it meant that estates of diverse types were moulded into conformity with manorial patterns. Nor must we overlook the fact that there is no evidence which suggests that any of the thirteenth-century texts in question was the work of a man familiar with the regions of Scandinavian settlement or any part of northern England. Yet the remarkable correspondence between the implications of these texts and those of the Ely preamble can only be explained on the assumption that both reflect actual conditions. At both periods the manorial estate must have been an important reality, a common feature of agrarian life. The problem is to know how important and how widespread it was in Domesday England.

There has been much debate among scholars about the meaning of the word *manerium* in Domesday Book; and the most favoured conclusion appears to be that the word was employed in senses that were both vague and various. It looks very much as if the *manerium* was primarily understood to be an estate of the sort presupposed by the terms of the Ely articles, while properties of very different kinds came to be called *maneria* just because men were wedded to the idea that estates must be 'manorial' in type, though sometimes the recalcitrance of the facts led them to abandon such comprehensive uses of the term and to distinguish the 'berewick' and the 'soke' from the 'manor'.[2] For the social historian, however, these questions of nomenclature are rather irrelevant. It is only indirectly that he is interested in the phraseology of the Domesday scribes or even in the conceptions

---

[1] I need only refer to Bracton, bk. ii, c. 34; the *Extenta Manerii*; the *Articuli Visitationis Maneriorum* of St. Paul's (*D.S.P.*, pp. 153–6); *Fleta* (ed. of 1647), bk. ii, c. 71; and Britton, ed. F. M. Nichols, 1865, bk. iii, c. 7, § v. The fact that these texts are not wholly independent of one another scarcely diminishes the significance of their substantial agreement: as the writers' object was practical, their borrowings are good evidence that the matter borrowed was felt to meet real needs and was believed to be in harmony with real conditions. Though in other respects they enter into more detail than the Ely preamble, their classification of the manorial tenants is generally limited to the broad distinction between customary tenants (or villeins) and free tenants. The *Extenta Manerii* and the *Articuli*, however, mention cottagers (*coterelli* or *cotagii*) as well as *custumarii* and *libere tenentes*.

[2] Vinogradoff remarks that the conquerors 'described as manors complexes of property which were in the slightest degree similar to them': *Growth of the Manor*, p. 301.

with which the Domesday commissioners approached their task. His purpose is to ascertain the actual character of agrarian organization in 1086. To what extent was the land of England parcelled out in estates of manorial type? How commonly were whole villages coincident with such estates? What regions, if any, were unmanorial?

It might seem that an answer to the first and third of these questions could be obtained by the simple if laborious process of enumerating for each county, hundred, and wapentake, those entries, on the one hand, in which both demesne ploughs and tenants' ploughs are mentioned, and, on the other hand, those in which ploughs of either class appear in isolation. Or one might, and perhaps with better reason, reckon the ratios, not between the two kinds of entry, but between the ploughs, or the enumerated persons, comprised in each kind. Yet neither of these methods would be satisfactory. Composite entries are an obstacle in the way of such statistical simplification. For example, how should one treat the great royal estate of Leominster in Herefordshire?[1] It contained, we are told, besides Leominster itself, sixteen 'members', the names of which are given and can mostly be recognized as the names of villages on the modern map, round about Leominster, though in some cases about 6 miles away. The statistical data for the whole complex, other than the sub-infeudated portion, are combined: there were 29 ploughs on demesne and the tenants had 201 ploughs. Obviously, if we reckon this as a single manorial entry comparable with the entries for small manors in other counties, we shall make Herefordshire appear much less manorialized than it was. On the other hand, if we assume that we have 17 manors here, or reckon all the 230 ploughs as belonging to one great manorial estate, we shall be giving a highly disputable interpretation to the statements of Domesday and may be grossly exaggerating the manorialization of the county. It is true that the entire estate is called a *manerium*; but one cannot suppose that all its members were closely linked with one central demesne and there is no means of knowing how many of them were estates of manorial type with demesnes of their own. At least $18\frac{1}{2}$ hides out of the total of 80 hides seem to have been sub-infeudated, but the 4 tenants who are named as holding this portion of the Leominster lands had only 3 demesne ploughs between them, so it

[1] Dd. i, f. 180.

is not unlikely that some of them had no demesne at all. On the 60 hides which the king retained in his own hands there were 7 reeves, and perhaps this points to the existence of 7 manorial units, but there can be no certainty in the matter, and even if it were assumed that this was the case, it would still be impossible to say whether these units contained between them all the members of Leominster or whether some of the members were 'unmanorial' dependencies whose only connexion with the central organization lay perhaps in the payment of rents and dues.[1] It is much the same—to take another example—with the estate of Chilcombe in Hampshire which belonged to the church of Winchester.[2] The Domesday description of Chilcombe evidently covers a number of villages, for nine churches are mentioned, but the facts about the ploughs and the peasants are summarized in two totals, one for the lands held by seven named tenants and the other for the lands retained by the monks, and though demesne ploughs and peasants' ploughs are distinguished in both sets of figures, there is nothing to show whether or no the whole area consisted of 'manorial' elements.

The difficulty exemplified by the descriptions of Leominster and Chilcombe is serious and unavoidable, for composite entries are too common to be ignored and usually afford even less information about their component members than is forthcoming in these two cases. Sometimes, as at Melksham in Wiltshire, we have nothing to go upon but a bare reference to the dependencies of the manor.[3] Sometimes, as at Aldington in Kent, we have to infer the composite nature of an entry from the abnormally large number of peasants and plough-teams and the fact that an adjacent area of considerable extent appears to be ignored in Domesday Book.[4]

Frustration meets us again if we attempt to measure the manorialization of a county or any other district by the proportion of its plough-teams that are described as belonging to

---

[1] Vinogradoff (*English Society*, p. 314) interprets the sentence 'Modo habet rex in hoc manerio in dominio lx hidas' as meaning that the *manorial demesne* was reckoned at 60 hides. In fact there can be no doubt that it was the whole manor less the sub-infeudated portions which was so rated: see *Econ. Hist. Rev.* Aug. 1954, pp. 67–70.

[2] Dd. i, f. 41.

[3] Ibid., f. 65. Melksham gelded for 84 hides *cum appendiciis suis*.

[4] Ibid., f. 4. Aldington is credited with 190 *villani* and 50 bordars with 70 ploughs as well as with 13 demesne ploughs and 13 *servi*.

demesne. Even if the numbers of demesne ploughs and tenants' ploughs could be precisely ascertained, they would provide no exact index to the relative areas of the two classes of arable land, for the assistance which the lord received from the ploughing services of the peasants might vary greatly from place to place with the number of those who owed such services or through differences in the amount due from each; and it may be that on some manors no aid of this kind was available. But, further, some entries leave it doubtful whether the teams to which they refer are demesne teams or not; and a yet more serious difficulty springs from the fact that ploughs are often described as being on demesne in the case of estates which seem to have comprised nothing but a home farm and to have been worked entirely by men with no holdings or, at least, no plough-teams of their own. A striking example of this last difficulty is afforded by the county of Cheshire. In Cheshire an exceptionally large proportion of the total number of teams are assigned to demesne—more than 37 per cent. indeed—and yet it was far from being a highly manorialized county, and an outstanding feature of its description in Domesday Book is the number of entries relating to small estates which lacked the co-existence of demesne teams and tenants' teams characteristic of manorial organization and appear to have consisted either entirely of 'demesne' or entirely of peasant holdings.

Since statistical precision in the measurement of manorialization thus appears to be unattainable, the historian is forced to rely upon rougher methods and can scarcely hope altogether to avoid an imputation of impressionism. But there can be no doubt about the general conclusion of Domesday scholars that a large area of north-eastern England was less manorialized than other parts of the country. Nothing but a profound difference in social and agrarian conditions can account for the geographical concentration of the classes described in Domesday Book as sokemen and *liberi homines* and also of the extensive sokeland which in some counties it pointedly distinguishes both from manors and from the outlying members of manors known as 'berewicks'. In Lincolnshire, where the Domesday scribes seem to have made no attempt to distinguish between *liberi homines* and sokemen, the persons they assigned to the latter class amount to about half the enumerated population, and the two classes together form more than 40 per cent. of it both in Norfolk and in Suffolk.[1] In Nottinghamshire and Leicestershire the sokemen have been reckoned at 30 per cent. and 33 per cent. of the population respectively.[2] Northamptonshire and Essex can also show large numbers of sokemen.[3] And what is really significant is that these seven counties form a geographically contiguous series, that sokemen are nowhere else found in such large numbers, and that, with the exception of a small but uncertain number in Kent, the only sokemen existing in 1086 outside this geographical group occur in counties adjacent to one or more of the seven which compose it.[4]

[1] See the figures for the modern areas of these counties in Darby, *Domesday Geography of Eastern England*, p. 379.

[2] Stenton, *Anglo-Saxon England*, p. 509.

[3] Professor Darby reckons 830 in Northamptonshire and 600 in Essex (the modern areas): see *Domesday Geography of Midland England*, p. 453, and *Domesday Geography of Eastern England*, p. 379. Though in these two counties the two classes of sokemen and 'free men' together form a much smaller proportion than in any of the five counties previously cited, the sokemen alone account for a slightly larger percentage in Essex than they do in Suffolk, where the number and proportion of 'free men' was larger than anywhere else.

[4] Outside the group of seven, the only counties whose population included more than a hundred sokemen in 1086 were, according to Ellis's reckoning, Yorkshire with 447, Cambridgeshire with 213, Derbyshire with 128, and Bedfordshire with 107. In addition, sokemen in small numbers are credited to Hertfordshire, Huntingdonshire, Buckinghamshire, and Rutland as well as Kent. The apparent discrepancy between Ellis's figure for Rutland (5) and that given by Darby (112) is clearly due to the large difference between the area of the modern county and that of the *Roteland* of Domesday. Darby assigns six sokemen to Staffordshire, but these must be the six recorded for Winshill which was in Derbyshire until modern times. Ellis credits six sokemen to Gloucestershire, and I have on a previous occasion accepted his authority for this (*Economic Journal*, June 1947, pp. 179–80), but it seems to be an error. Perhaps Ellis misinterpreted an entry relating to *Beceshore* which reads 'un' ho redd vi sochs' (Dd. i, f. 169b). Domesday records the former existence of a handful of sokemen in Surrey and Middlesex (Streatham, f. 34; Wandsworth, f. 35b; Harmondsworth, f. 128b; Hatton and *Ticheham*, f. 129; Eye and Enfield, f. 129b); and this seems to link Kent with the other counties where sokemen occur. The geographical distribution of *liberi homines* in Domesday does nothing to warp the general pattern, for outside Norfolk, Suffolk, and Essex their numbers are negligible and their prominence in these three counties may be due to an idiosyncracy of nomenclature in the Little Domesday. It should be noted, too, that in the northern Danelaw the geographical concentration of the sokemen was in fact closer than appears from the statistics for the counties taken as wholes. Stenton has set forth the position for each wapentake in the Domesday counties of Lincoln, Leicester, Nottingham, and Derby; and the results of his researches are highly significant, for, while they show that in one of the Nottinghamshire wapentakes the sokemen formed little more than 10 per cent. and in one Lincolnshire wapentake less than 20 per cent. of the population, they also reveal the fact that 'within a wide and continuous area, half the population recorded by Domesday consisted of sokemen', *Free Peasantry of the Northern Danelaw*. (*Bulletin de la Société Royale des Lettres de Lund*, 1926, pp. 77–82.)

Moreover it is within the region in which sokemen were most numerous that the territorial soke is a prominent feature in the Domesday map. Again and again we meet here with large estates in which the description of a manor is followed by a list of dependent sokelands in a number of other villages; and we find, too, that the inhabitants of these sokelands generally consist either entirely or predominantly of sokemen. Thus, to name only a few examples, the Bishop of Lincoln's manor of Newark in Nottinghamshire was a manor with two berewicks; but dependent upon it there was sokeland in 16 different villages, and on these sokelands there dwelt 174 sokemen and 14 bordars with 46 plough-teams.[1] In Lincolnshire, again, the sokelands attached to the manor of Folkingham lay in 25 villages, all situated in Kesteven, but extending into 5 different wapentakes; and, with the exception of 10 *villani* at Lavington and a single *villanus* at Scredington, the peasant population of these sokelands consisted entirely of sokemen and bordars—411 of the former and 81 of the latter.[2] In Leicestershire, the *Terra Regis* included 2 large sokes— that of Rothley, with members in 22 places, and that of Great Bowden with members in at least 10 places.[3] On the latter soke the sokemen were quite preponderant, for there were 60 of them and only 2 *villani* and 16 bordars; but the social stratification of the soke of Rothley exhibits a rather different pattern, for, along with 204 sokemen, the enumerated population included 157 *villani* and 94 bordars. Yet on neither of these Leicestershire sokes is there any sign of manorial demesne and even the two manors on which they were dependent can each show only two demesne ploughs.[4] We turn to Yorkshire and find that similar sokes had been common in that county before it was devastated by the Conqueror. Dependent upon the manor of Northallerton in the North Riding (a manor with 11 berewicks and a pre-conquest population of *villani*) there was a soke extending

---

[1] Dd. i, f. 283b. Three groups of sokelands are separately described: one with 26 sokemen, 3 bordars, and 9 teams; one with 77 sokemen, 4 bordars, and 15½ teams; and one with 71 sokemen, 7 bordars, and 21½ teams.

[2] Ibid., ff. 355b, 356.

[3] Ibid., ff. 230, 230b.

[4] As illustrating the relative unimportance of the central manors Stenton remarks that 'Rothley itself brought in yearly £3. 2s., but the men of Rothley soke paid altogether £31. 8s. 1d.' and that 'Great Bowden alone brought in £3.10s., of which £2 represented the profits of the demesne, the remaining 30s. coming from the men of the vill' while the soke rendered £7. 11s. 6d.: *V.C.H. Leics.* i. 287, cf. *Types of Manorial Structure in the Northern Danelaw*, p. 32, n. 2.

into 24 villages. It was all waste in 1086; but the sokelands had formerly been inhabited by 116 sokemen.[1] To the manor of Fals-grave in the same riding there belonged sokeland in 21 places and in this soke there had formerly been 108 sokemen with 46 ploughs; but in 1086 there remained only 7 sokemen, 15 *villani*, and 14 bordars with 7½ ploughs—the rest being waste.[2] Nor are ex-amples wanting in other parts of Yorkshire. In the West Riding, for instance, the sokes of Wakefield and Kippax each included elements in 14 vills; and, in the East Riding, that of Driffield had 10 members and that of Bridlington 14; but Domesday Book tells us nothing about the inhabitants of these sokelands before they fell into a wasted condition.[3] The 'Territorial soke' can also be recognized in Northamptonshire: the royal manor of Rothwell has 10 members occupied only by sokemen; and, on the other side of the county, we find that William Peverel's manor of Higham Ferrers has 8 members, in 5 of which only sokemen are recorded, and that the Countess Judith has a manor at Yardley Hastings with 9 members in which some three-fifths of the enumerated population were sokemen.[4] In Derbyshire, again, the soke of the manor of Mickleover is scattered among 8 villages; but nothing is said about any in-habitants of these sokelands.[5]

It seems probable that the larger sokes in the above-men-tioned counties originated, or at least came into the possession of the lord who first held them, through royal grants either of a wapentake and its court or, in other cases, of 'the king's rights over all the unattached free men dwelling within a given wapen-take'.[6] But many sokemen did not belong to sokes of this type. In Cambridgeshire, where the class had been very numerous and in 1086 still formed a considerable element in the popu-lation, we find perhaps the best examples of sokemen whose condition suggests that it was by individual commendation that they had become dependent upon a lord and hence upon the manor from which he exercised his rights over them.[7] Before the

[1] Dd. i, f. 299.
[2] Ibid. (*Walesgrif*).
[3] Ibid., ff. 299b, 315, 299b.
[4] Ibid., ff. 219b, 225b, 228–228b.
[5] Ibid., f. 273 (*Vfre*).
[6] Stenton, *Types of Manorial Structure*, pp. 43–45.
[7] Of many of the pre-Conquest sokemen of Cambridgeshire we are told that they could give or sell their land: it is often laid down of course that the soke would remain unaffected by such a sale or gift, but the absence of this qualification in other cases may possibly imply that the obligations understood by the word soke

Conquest the sokemen in many Cambridgeshire villages were distinguished one from another by their dependence upon different lords. For example, of the 11 sokemen then to be found in the lost village of Wratworth, 4 belonged to the king, 2 to Edith the Fair, 2 to Robert, son of Wimarc, 1 to Stigand, 1 to Earl Ælfgar, and 1 to Earl Waltheof.[1] But the great mass of the pre-Conquest sokemen of Cambridgeshire, whether they were divided in this way or formed groups dependent upon a single lord, failed to maintain their status under the Normans; and the surviving sokemen were by 1086 generally associated in small groups having the same lord. There were 6 or 7 at one of the Mordens, under Hardwin de Scalers, and also at Snailwell, a manor held by Hugh de Port.[2] There were 7 on Picot's manor of Bourn (*Brune*); and Picot held as many as 26 at Fulbourn, apparently as sheriff on the king's behalf.[3] At Hatley we have a clear example of recent grouping. There had been 8 sokemen there in King Edward's day: 2 were the king's men, 3 the men of Archbishop Stigand, and the remaining 3 were the men respectively of Earl Gyrth, Robert, son of Wimarc, and Ulmar of

(in particular suit of court) could be transferred at the will of the sokeman. Of one of the six sokemen who were at Standon in Hertfordshire before the Conquest we are definitely told that he could sell the soke—'etiam socam suam cum terra vendere poterat' (Dd. i, f. 142*b*). The same liberty is recorded in the case of three men, who are not described as sokemen, at one of the Rodings and at Chignall in Essex (Dd. ii, ff. 40*b*, 59): cf. Maitland, *Domesday Book and Beyond*, p. 100. The silence of Domesday about a right to alienate land in the case of the Lincolnshire and Nottinghamshire sokemen is probably deceptive, for peasants in these counties, who seem to be the successors of Domesday sokemen, are found exercising that right in the twelfth century, and 'these men cannot have acquired during the twelfth century a power of alienation which did not belong to their predecessors in 1086', as the general tendency was for the peasantry to become depressed and for ancient liberties to be lost: see Stenton, *Introduction to the Lincolnshire Domesday*, ed. Foster and Longley, pp. xxvi–xxvii; cf. his *Danelaw Charters*, pp. lxxxviii–xcix and (for his earlier views) *Types of Manorial Structure*, p. 42. But it is probable that the sokemen of Lincolnshire and Nottinghamshire included people who would have been called *liberi homines* in East Anglia and Essex.

[1] I.C.C., pp. 79–81. The prevalence of similar conditions throughout Wetherley Hundred, in which Wratworth was situated, is exhibited in Maitland's table: op. cit., pp. 131–4. The contrast with the region of large territorial sokes must not be exaggerated. In Northamptonshire, William Peverel, the lord of the soke of Higham Ferrers, had also (dependent upon his manor of Coton-under-Guilsborough) a single sokeman in five different vills, and, as Stenton remarks, this suggests that these men 'had severally commended themselves to William Peverel or his unnamed predecessor': op. cit., p. 43 n. 1.

[2] Dd. i, ff. 198, 199. According to Domesday there were 7 at Morden and 6 at Snailwell, but the I.C.C. speaks of 6 in the former case and 7 in the latter (pp. 52, 53).

[3] Dd. i, ff. 200*b*, 190: cf. I.C.C., p. 26.

Eaton. In 1086 there were still 8 of them, but then they all held their land *sub Picoto*.[1]

In other counties beside Cambridgeshire many groups of sokemen appear to have been resident within the manor upon which they were dependent, or, perhaps one should rather say, within the vill in which it was situated. Those in such a position are described by Stenton as 'manorial sokemen'; and he employs the term 'intermanorial sokeland' to distinguish their land from sokeland that was 'geographically separate from the head manor to which it belonged'.[2] In the case of Essex and East Anglia comparison with other counties is made difficult by the modes of exposition that are peculiar to the Little Domesday; but it looks as if most of the sokemen of Essex and very many of the *liberi homines* and sokemen of Norfolk and Suffolk were of this type.[3] Yet conditions within these three counties were so various and intricate that it would be rash to regard any one type as normal; and the summary entries in Domesday are liable to conceal the real state of affairs. The abbey of Ely had, for example, among its Norfolk sokemen, one in Stratton, another in Hardwick, and a couple in Tivetshall, and these are all described in the Ely Inquest as belonging to Pulham, which was a demesne manor of the abbey; but Domesday Book says nothing of this connexion.[4] Similar conditions are sometimes revealed in Domesday itself. Some sokemen in the Norfolk villages of Wroxham, Belaugh, and Hautboys are described either as lying in Hoveton or as included in the valuation of that place; and in Suffolk some 45 *liberi homines* from the villages of Barningham, Hopton, and Weston are said to owe service in Coney

[1] I.C.C., pp. 56, 57. So far as Domesday Book goes we might suppose that there were no longer any sokemen at Hatley in 1086; but their survival is clear from the statement of the I.C.C.: 'Hanc terram tenent et tenuerunt viii sochemanni T.R.E. et modo sub picoto.' In contrast to Hatley, Fen Drayton provides an example of continuing division: 2 of the 10 pre-Conquest sokemen had disappeared by 1086; but the others were still divided among 3 lords, 2 holding of the king as formerly, 5 of Count Alan in succession to Edith the Fair, and 1 of Gilbert de Gand in place of Ulf: Dd. i, ff. 190, 195, 197*b*, 201; I.C.C., pp. 90, 91.

[2] *Types*, pp. 46, 47.

[3] It is in connexion with the subject of sokes that Professor Douglas speaks of 'the confused terminology of the Little Domesday' and of 'the East Anglian soke confusion': *Social Structure of Medieval East Anglia*, pp. 178, 170. Miss Dodwell in her article on 'The Free Peasantry of East Anglia in Domesday', Norfolk and Norwich Arch. Soc., *Original Papers*, vol. xxvii, 1941, p. 146, refers to the 'large numbers of sokemen and free men who do not appear to be attached to any manor'; but throughout this article she appears to be concerned with conditions in 1066 not 1086.

[4] I.C.C., p. 136. The case is cited by Miss Dodwell, *E.H.R.*, July 1948, p. 300.

Weston, while the service of 20 others who appear to live in Hepworth is divided between Coney Weston and Stanton.[1] Moreover in some cases the numbers involved are so large that one can hardly doubt that the group, though recorded in the description of a single manor, was in fact composed of persons dispersed among several villages. Thus we find that 119 sokemen still remained in 1086 appurtenant to the manor of Bergholt in Suffolk, that 115½ sokemen are recorded at Ludham in Norfolk and 80 at Ormesby in the same county, and that 90 *liberi homines* are credited to Rougham in Suffolk.[2] On the whole there is a good deal to suggest that conditions approximating to those of the territorial sokes of the northern Danelaw were of more frequent occurrence in East Anglia than appears on the surface of the Domesday survey; and later evidence affords reason for thinking that there was further development in this direction after 1086.[3] Yet in contrast to the large groups of sokemen whose dependence upon some manor of the lord to whom they all owed service reminds us of the sokes of Lincolnshire or Nottinghamshire, the sokemen of a few East Anglian villages were divided among several lords after the Cambridgeshire fashion. Of the 9 sokemen at Chepenhall in Suffolk, 4 were held by Walter (? Walter de Caen), 3 by Robert Malet's mother, 1 by a man named Humphrey, and 1 by Walter, son of Grip; and the 10 sokemen of Cawston in Norfolk were divided among 6 lords.[4] But division of this kind was not necessarily of old standing. The 87 sokemen who belonged to Stigand's manor of Wymondham had evidently become divided since 1066—probably since 1070, when Stigand was deposed. Only 19 of them were still attached to Wymondham in 1086; and the others had come into the hands of four different lords, William de Warenne having 55, Ralf de Bellofago 10, Count Alen 1, and Roger Bigod a couple.[5]

---

[1] Dd. ii, ff. 158b, 217b, 218b, 365b, 366: cited Dodwell, *E.H.R.*, 1948, pp. 292, 296.

[2] Dd. ii, ff. 287, 220, 115b, 362. It is not clear whether the 119 sokemen were dependent upon Bergholt or upon Shotley. The reference to half-a-sokeman at Ludham probably means that the service of one of the sokemen was divided between two lords, but, as 4½ *liberi homines* are also mentioned in this entry, it seems just possible that we have to do with a man who held half his land by a 'freer' title than the other half.

[3] On all this see D. C. Douglas, *Social Structure*, ch. iv, especially pp. 170–81.

[4] Dd. ii, ff. 329, 329b, 115.

[5] Ibid., f. 137b. The change at Wymondham was thus in the opposite direction to that at Hatley in Cambridgeshire noticed above, pp. 222–3.

Though much remains obscure in regard to the status of the sokemen and *liberi homines* of Domesday Book, and though the rights which members of these classes enjoyed over their holdings varied from one district to another and even between individuals of the same class in the same place, while the condition of many of them had been profoundly affected since the Conquest by forces inimical to their independence, there can still be no doubt that both sokemen and *liberi homines* were distinguished from the regular manorial peasantry by their comparative freedom. The name *liber homo* speaks for itself; and the name sokeman seems to indicate one who was primarily the justiciable of his lord rather than his tenant. The preamble of the Ely Inquest segregates the *liberi homines* and *sochemanni* from the classes intimately connected with the manorial demesne (*villani*, cottars, and *servi*) and expects them to have holdings of their own which ought to be separately recorded.[1] It seems indeed that 'even within the precincts of the manor, the sokemen were regarded as in some sense external to its organization' and that 'the tenements which they occupied were their own property, subject to seignorial exploitation, but co-ordinate with, rather than subordinate to, the lord's demesne'.[2] Of the *liberi homines*—in spite of the wavering uncertainty of the distinction between them and the sokemen and the significant fact that no attempt to distinguish them was made in Lincolnshire or Nottinghamshire—it can at least be said that they were, if anything, more independent than the sokemen and perhaps, in some way or other, of socially superior condition.[3] It would, however, be

[1] Probably this requirement was based on the assumption that they were responsible for the geld upon their land: see Stenton, *Types*, pp. 47–49; *Anglo-Saxon England*, p. 508. In fact Domesday often fails to distinguish the amount (or rather the assessed amount) of their land, and, where it does distinguish it, gives totals and not the quantity held by each individual in accordance with the terms of the Preamble.

[2] Stenton, *Types*, p. 49.

[3] Ballard points out (apparently with reference to conditions in 1066) that on the estates of St. Edmunds in three Suffolk hundreds 126 out of 128 freemen could sell their land and that on the same estates only 5 out of 63 sokemen could do so (*The Domesday Inquest*, 1906, p. 113). Similarly, Mr. Miller remarks that 'so far as the East Anglian manors of Ely abbey are concerned, we can only conclude that, while a sokeman could very often not sell or depart, a free man was very often able to do so': *The Abbey and Bishopric of Ely*, p. 64. Stenton says: 'It has so far proved impossible to explain the distinction which was drawn between these classes, and it is a mere surmise that the free men, although peasants, and often of a meagre sort, may have been able to claim an ancestry which gave them higher rank than sokemen': *Anglo-Saxon England*, p. 509; cf. Douglas, *Social Structure*, p. 110; and see

straying beyond the proper limits of this chapter to discuss the manifold and much debated problems that are presented by the relation of these two classes to their lords, or the question of the extent to which the Danish settlements had contributed to their development or survival.[1] But the outstanding fact which must primarily be emphasized in any attempt to assess the part played by the manor in the life of Domesday England is familiar and beyond controversy. The geographical concentration of the sokemen and *liberi homines*, and the distinctive characters which their presence has given to the forms and vocabulary of the Domesday entries for the region they inhabit, mark that region off from the rest of the country as one that was comparatively 'unmanorial'. Yet the contrast between the two, though profound, must not be exaggerated.

Some villages of the 'unmanorial' area were, it is true, completely free from any manorial element. At Digby in Lincolnshire, for example, all the cultivable land was occupied by 35 sokemen with their 12 plough-teams; and no other inhabitants of this 12-carucate village are recorded in Domesday.[2] Even sokemen mentioned in the descriptions of manors may in some cases have lived in hamlets separate from the manorial village and its complex of fields. Such a condition may well be suspected where their numbers are very large, as in certain examples already cited from East Anglia; and, in an entry relating to Wells in Norfolk, Domesday casually reveals the fact that the 19 sokemen belonging to that manor dwelt in the adjacent village of Warham, where the inhabitants also included a few other free peasants and one bordar but no sign of anything manorial is to be found.[3] No doubt the actual relation of sokemen to the manors to which they were reckoned to be pertinent was much affected by physical distance. The sokeland of the royal manor of Mansfield in Nottinghamshire included elements in a number of places on the other side of Sherwood Forest and some of these places were 20 miles or more from Mansfield. Obviously

also *V.C.H. Suffolk*, i. 405; *V.C.H. Norfolk*, ii. 28 et seq.; B. Dodwell, *Norfolk Arch. Soc.* xxvii. 146.

[1] For recent discussions of the nature of the tie between man and lord involved in 'commendation' see *E.H.R.* lix, 1944, 289–310; ibid. lxiii, 1948, 289–306; E. Miller, op. cit., pp. 59 et seq. For the problem of Danish influence see Appendix III.

[2] Dd. i, f. 369b. Digby was part of the soke of Geoffrey Alselin's manor of Ruskiington.

[3] Dd. ii, ff. 271, 143, 192, 242b.

sokemen who lived thus far away can have had little to do with
the manor to which they were attached, and probably their obligations to it were discharged by payments in money.[1] On the
other hand, Domesday indicates that in East Anglia many sokemen, and *liberi homines* too, were involved in the economy of
their lords' demesnes to the extent of being obliged to fold their
sheep upon them.[2] We know, too, from the record of the Ely plea
of 1072-5 that a large number of sokemen belonging to four
villages in the south-west of Norfolk, and a large number of 'men'
or 'men of the soke' in four Suffolk villages, were liable, when
called upon, to perform a variety of agricultural services, including ploughing as well as harvest work, and further that at Brandon in Suffolk there were six sokemen who might be required to
do some threshing as well as ploughing.[3] Though undefined in
amount, all this, as Maitland remarked, 'seems to point rather
to "boon-days" than to continuous "week-work" '; and he
noted also that these sokemen are commonly assumed to possess
horses which they may have to lend to the abbot if he needs
them.[4] There is nothing, however, in the record to suggest that it
was in any way unusual for sokemen to owe some agricultural
services, though its silence about them in the case of some of the
'sokemen' and many of the '*homines*' whom it mentions should
probably be taken as an indication that these, unlike the others,
were free from such obligations.[5] In any case it would be wholly

[1] Dd. i, ff. 281, 281b; Stenton, *Types*, pp. 36, 45. The 22 sokemen of Leverton
(*Cledretone*), which is one of the villages in question, 'reddebant xx solidos de
consuetudine' and probably we should understand similar payments to be indicated by the values mentioned in the other cases.

[2] Maitland, *Domesday Book and Beyond*, pp. 76-77; Vinogradoff, *English Society*,
pp. 387-90, and the examples there cited. Professor Douglas, however, points out
that in Suffolk fold-soke is only once mentioned in Domesday outside the lands of
St. Edmunds, though on those lands it was 'extremely common' and 'seems to have
been normally incumbent upon the freemen' (*Social Structure*, p. 79). In Norfolk
the references to fold-soke are concentrated in the district south and east of
Norwich and in the hundreds of Clackclose and Smethden which touch the western
boundary of the county (*V.C.H. Norfolk*, ii. 31). The object of fold-soke was of
course to give the lord's land the benefit of the sheep's dung.

[3] I.C.C., pp. 192-5; cf. Round, *Feudal England*, pp. 30-33, 459-61.

[4] *Domesday Book and Beyond*, p. 77. In the early part of the twelfth century four
'sokemans' at Horstead in Norfolk owed a service of carrying the *firma* to Winchester: Bibl. Nat. MS. lat. 5650, f. 28v.

[5] Numerical comparison is not made because in the case of some of the men
whom the record describes as *ejusdem consuetudinis* it is doubtful whether the reference
is to the customs which did include agricultural services or to those which did not.
According to the foundation charter of Blyth Priory in Nottinghamshire, which is
dated 1082, the men of that vill owed their lord unspecified services of ploughing,

wrong to regard even the most unmanorial districts as districts
in which manorial organization was a thing unknown. Even
where the free peasantry formed a large majority of the population, this was not so. If one reads them in isolation, the Domesday descriptions of the territorial sokes may suggest a picture of
large areas occupied only by sokelands and inhabited only by
sokemen, but in fact a good many of the villages in which such
sokelands were situated also contained manorial elements belonging to other lords. The soke of Great Bowden in Leicestershire extended, as we have seen, into some 10 villages, but in 7 of
these there were also estates of manorial type containing both
demesne ploughs and tenants' ploughs.[1] The soke of Newark had
members in 16 villages, in 7 of which we find manors similarly
equipped.[2] The sokeland of Ivo Taillebois' manor of Belchford
in Lincolnshire, again, included elements in about a dozen
places, all within the wapentake of Gartree. But in four of these
vills Ivo himself had one or more demesne teams and in two
others (Hemingby and Cawkwell) we find small manors belonging to other lords.[3] An even sharper warning that we must not

carrying, mowing, reaping, and hay-making; and Blyth is described as 'soke' in
Domesday, but its inhabitants were *villani* or bordars, not sokemen: see Stenton,
Types, pp. 22–23, 92–93. In the reign of Henry I limited agricultural services of
'boon-work' character were recorded in the Liber Niger of Peterborough as due
from the sokemen of several villages, while those of Scotter and Scotterthorpe
(*Scaletorp*) in Lincolnshire even owed week-work (one day a week throughout the
year, but two each week in August). On the other hand the *Descriptio Militum*,
which follows the survey of the demesne manors, states that the sokemen in several
Northamptonshire vills and at Easton in Leicestershire *serviunt cum militibus*, and
that for the land Richard Engaine held of the abbey in Northamptonshire 'soce-
manni faciunt quartam partem militis et ipse iii partes unius militis', *Chronicon
Petrob.*, pp. 173, 172, 169; cf. *Chronicle of Hugh Candidus*, p. 169, also p. 165 where
a fee at Sutton in Northants. is said to owe the service of two knights ('set sokemanni
et alii tenentes totum faciunt'). At Winshill, Derbyshire (now in Staffordshire),
some sokemen owed (temp. Henry I) occasional services both agricultural and in
connexion with hunting: *Burton Abbey Survey B* (Wm. Salt Hist. Collections for
1916), pp. 241–2.

[1] Dd. i, ff. 230b, and 231 (Illston), 232 (Carlton Curlieu and Smeeton), 232b
(Shangton and Galby), 236 (Foxton), 236b (Cranoe).

[2] Ibid., ff. 283b, 284 (Coddington and Barnby-in-the-Willows), 288b (East
Stoke and Cotham, with which both *Cutun* and *Cotes* have been identified), 289b
(Hawton), 291 (Elston), 291b (Syerston). Probably Kilvington should be added,
but in the entry on f. 291b Kilvington and Alverton are lumped together. At
Balderton, besides the sokeland, there was a berewick of Newark.

[3] Ibid., ff. 350b, 351; also (for Hemingby) ff. 349b, 356b, and (for Cawkwell)
f. 361b. At Stixwold there were, beside Ivo's sokelands, two holdings marked as
'manors' in Domesday; but nothing is said about demesne in the one case or about
tenants in the other: see ff. 358, 365.

exaggerate the unmanorial character of Lincolnshire is provided
by the little wapentake of Ludborough in the north riding of
Lindsey. Here sokemen formed a larger proportion of the recorded population than in any other Lincolnshire wapentake.
Yet each of its six vills, with the possible exception of Fotherby,
contained in 1086 one or more properties of manorial character
with a team or teams assigned both to the lord and to the
peasants.[1] And though nothing is more characteristic of all these
north-eastern regions of England than the village of divided
lordship, and a single village, if it contains a manorial element
at all and does not consist entirely of sokelands, will in these
parts commonly include, besides sokelands, several small manors
belonging to different lords, it is none the less true that manors
which seem to represent the 'ideal type' of the manor are here
and there to be found in the midst of this comparatively un-
manorialized area. A few examples, selected from various
counties, will be cited.[2]

In eastern Leicestershire, the 12-carucate village of Noseley
belonged in 1086 entirely to Hugh de Grentemaisnil: he had 2
ploughs with 3 *servi* on the demesne; and 16 *villani*, with a priest
and 8 bordars, had 6 ploughs; but there were no sokemen, and
no sokeland was dependent upon this manor.[3] In the north of
Nottinghamshire, the small village of Bilby was coincident with
a manor held by a certain Ingrann of Roger de Busli: Ingrann
had 1 plough there and the peasants, who consisted of 9 *villani*
and a bordar, had 3 ploughs.[4] In Yorkshire, manors which
appear to be similar in almost all respects to the 'typical' manors
of southern England, occur sporadically in every riding. At
Hessle in the East Riding, all the land (with the exception of
a small berewick dependent upon Ralf de Mortimer's manor of
Ferriby) seems to have been comprised in a manor belonging to
Gilbert Tison, where there was land for 4 ploughs: Gilbert himself had 1 plough; 17 *villani* and 2 bordars had 3; and a priest
and a church are also recorded.[5] In the West Riding, the whole

[1] An entry relating to Fotherby (f. 353) mentions a team belonging to the lord
as well as six peasant teams, but it is a composite entry including some land at
Thorganby in another wapentake.
[2] My examples are confined to manors whose recorded inhabitants included
neither sokemen nor *liberi homines* and thus represent the type that was common
in the south of England rather than that implied in the preamble of the Ely Inquest.
[3] Dd. i, f. 232.   [4] Ibid., f. 285.
[5] Ibid., f. 326b and for the berewick (where there were 4 *villani* with 1 plough)
see f. 325.

village of Spofforth was included in a manor held by William de Perci, and here the demesne evidently occupied a large propor- tion of the land, for while the 9 *villani* and 10 bordars possessed 4 ploughs, their lord had an equal number himself.[1] We turn to the North Riding and find examples in two of the manors which a certain Bodin held as a sub-tenant of Count Alan; and the differ- ence between these two, and between them and the manor of Spofforth, is an apt reminder of the variety that was compatible with regularity in general pattern. Both at Bedale and at Ravens- worth manor and vill were coincident; in both places the peasants consisted of *villani* and bordars; and in both a church is recorded. But whereas 2 of the 7 plough-teams at Bedale belonged to the demesne, Bodin had only half a team at Ravens- worth as compared with 8 teams possessed by the peasantry.[2] In Lincolnshire and in Norfolk 'typical' manors are not easy to find; but at least one can cite Newball in Lindsey, Southorpe in Kesteven, Surfleet in the Parts of Holland, and Horning in Norfolk as manors which were coincident with the vills in which they were situated and contained both demesne teams and peasant teams, but had neither dependent sokelands nor any peasant inhabitants other than *villani* and bordars.[3] And the same may be said of Wicken in Cambridgeshire and Framsden in Suffolk.[4]

That manorialism was spreading under the Normans is notori- ous. The signs of its advance are manifold. There is the decline in the number of sokemen, most evident in Cambridgeshire (where it had been catastrophic), but sporadically discernible in other counties, and perhaps to be suspected wherever Domesday describes the inhabitants of sokelands as consisting entirely of *villani* and bordars.[5] There are the references to *liberi homines* who

---

[1] Dd. i, f. 322. A mill, meadow, and woodland are mentioned. Spofforth was one of several estates in which W. de Perci had succeeded a man named Gamelbar.

[2] Ibid., ff. 312, 310. Ravensworth is within a few miles of the northern boundary of Yorkshire, and the high moorland character of part of the parish of Kirby Ravensworth may explain the smallness of the demesne. Bodin's manor no doubt included Kirby Hill where the church is: it is not mentioned in Domesday. Both this parish and Bedale include hamlets which are separately surveyed in Domesday; but there is nothing to suggest that they were considered as parts of those vills in 1086. It is perhaps evidence of the villar integrity of Bodin's manors that they were assessed at 6 carucates and 12 carucates respectively.

[3] Ibid., ff. 349b (Neuberie = Newball), 368, 369; ii, f. 218b.

[4] Ibid., f. 195b; ii, f. 298b. There were 5 *servi* at Wicken in addition to the *villani* and bordars.

[5] Maitland reckoned that the Cambridgeshire sokemen had numbered more

have been 'added' to this or that manor in King William's time.[1] There are the cases where a demesne team is revealed as an intruder by the fact that without it the peasants' teams exactly equal in number both the carucates at which the land was assessed and the estimated 'teamlands'.[2] And there are the numerous cases of considerable manors formed by the combination of small properties, which Domesday may dignify with the name of 'manors', but which in reality must have differed little from the holdings of substantial sokemen and were perhaps only distinguished from such by the 'thegnly' rank of their possessors.[3]

To recognize the existence of manorial elements in the region just examined is essential to a proper understanding of the agrarian conditions that obtained there.[4] But one must also avoid the mistake of supposing that the rest of England was completely manorialized. The contrast is great; but it can easily

than 900 in 1066 and were reduced to little more than 200 by 1086: *Domesday Book and Beyond*, pp. 62–63; cf. Darby, *Eastern England*, p. 290. An instance of far-reaching decline in Suffolk is provided by Bergholt, where the sokemen had fallen from 210 to 119: Dd. ii, f. 287. Maitland remarks that 'when . . . as is often the case, we find that the occupants of "the soke" are not sokemen but villeins, this seems to point to a recent depression of the peasantry': op. cit., p. 115 n. 3.

[1] e.g. Deopham (Norfolk), Dd. ii, f. 227; Ringsfield and Stonham (Suffolk), ibid., ff. 282*b*, 337*b*. No doubt we must also understand the change to have taken place since 1066 in the numerous cases where similar additions are recorded without any statement about their date.

[2] In 11 of the 17 members of the soke of Bolingbroke in Lincolnshire 'the teams possessed by the men of the respective vills are equal both to the carucates of assessment and to the recorded teamlands', but 'in four out of these eleven entries there appears a demesne team in excess of the estimated number': Stenton, *Types*, p. 20 n. 2. In one case, however, Stenton points out that this demesne team 'seems to descend from a pre-Conquest manerium incorporated in the soke'.

[3] Gringley-on-the-Hill in north Nottinghamshire is a striking example (Dd. i, f. 286*b*). Here, in the old wapentake of Oswaldbeck and in the midst of the sokelands of the distant manor of Mansfield, we find Roger, the man of Roger de Busli, holding a manor which appears to comprise the entire vill of Gringley. Roger has 3 demesne teams and the recorded inhabitants (10 *villani* and 6 bordars) have 8 teams. A church and a fishery and some woodland are recorded. But for the possibility that the next two entries, which relate to sokelands in the neighbouring vills of Misterton, Harwell, and Everton, should be understood as implying that these sokelands were dependencies of Gringley, the manor is of as standard a pattern as any one could find in the south of England. But before the Conquest Gringley had consisted of seven 'manors' held by 7 thegns.

[4] There is nothing novel in this conclusion. Though emphasizing the distinctive character given to the Danelaw economy by the large population of sokemen, Stenton goes so far as to say that in Lincolnshire and Nottinghamshire 'the typical form of estate prevalent in 1066 consisted of a lord's house, the *manerium* of Domesday, with a home farm attached to it, with unfree peasants, the *villani* and *bordarii* of Domesday, living in the same village, and, if later evidence may be followed, assisting in the cultivation of the lord's land' (*Free Peasantry*, pp. 74–75).

be exaggerated. In the first place, allowance must be made for uncertainties resulting from the fact that in the south and west Domesday Book presents us with a not insignificant number of descriptions, which, like that of Leominster already noticed, relate to large agrarian complexes and, though they conform in sum to a manorial pattern, are clearly composite in character and leave us without information about the organization of the subordinate members that are included in the description. Wiltshire, for example, was a highly manorialized county and one in which the village divided between several lords was, as Professor Darlington has remarked, 'the exception rather than the rule'.[1] Yet in Wiltshire three large royal estates are credited with appendages which are not separately surveyed, while, even without any specific reference to such appendages, it is impossible to believe in the unitary character of Calne and Aldbourne and Melksham on the *Terra Regis*, or of Ramsbury on the estates of the see of Salisbury, or Chalke on the lands of St. Mary of Wilton; for well over a hundred *villani* and bordars (or 'cozets') are assigned to each of these places, in addition to *servi* and (except at Ramsbury) some *coliberti*.[2] Nor is it hard to find similar cases in other West Saxon shires. In Dorset, the information relating to the King's lands in twenty-one places is summarized in five composite entries each devoted to a group of villages which combined to furnish a night's farm.[3] And, parallel to the Wiltshire entries whose composite character is betrayed by their large population figures, are those relating to Lambourn, Cumnor, and Barton in Berkshire; to Odiham, Chilcomb, and Sutton in Hampshire; to Somerton, North Curry, Keynsham, Taunton, Wellington, and Walton in Somerset.[4] In each the *villani* and bordars (apart from any other classes) amount to a hundred or more. And then, even in cases where the size of the enumerated population would not necessarily arouse suspicion, we often find references to portions of manors held by named tenants or unnamed knights or thegns and are left pretty much in the dark as to the nature of their holdings. In Wiltshire such references are very numerous on the great ecclesiastical estates; and a few examples will illustrate the uncertainties which ob-

[1] *V.C.H. Wilts.*, ii. 49.
[2] Dd. i, ff. 64*b*, 65 (Amesbury, Chippenham, Corsham); 64*b*, 65, 66, 68.
[3] Ibid., f. 75.
[4] Ibid., ff. 57*b*, 58*b*; 38, 41, 44*b*; 86, 86*b*, 87, 87*b*, 89, 90.

struct their interpretation. On the large manor which the abbey of Glastonbury possessed at Damerham there were 4 demesne ploughs and 14 *villani* and 17 bordars with 19 ploughs. But 'of this same land', Serlo held 5 hides, the wife of Hugh 3 hides, and Roger a hide and 8 acres; and we are only told that there were 3½ ploughs on these tenants' lands.[1] It is the same with the Bishop of Winchester's manor of Enford, with Grittleton and Kington Langley on the Glastonbury estates, with Tisbury and Donhead on the estates of St. Mary of Shaftesbury, with Edington on those of St. Mary of Romsey: the hidage of the free tenants' holdings and the total number of their ploughs are stated; but there is nothing to show whether these ploughs were demesne ploughs or peasants' ploughs or partly the one and partly the other.[2] Still less informing is the description of the great Winchester manor of Downton: here four named tenants, described as *milites*, held respectively 14 hides, 5 hides (in two cases), and 3½ hides, but not a word is said about either ploughs or peasants on these lands, unless we are to make the improbable assumption that they are included in the statistics of the demesne manor.[3] Now in a highly manorialized area such as Wiltshire it may be accounted probable that the larger holdings of the sub-tenants, and also the detached members of great demesne manors, were not uncommonly organized on a manorial pattern and were in fact themselves manors. There is indeed some positive evidence of this. The Bishop of Salisbury's sub-tenants at Ramsbury had on their 27 hides, 11 demesne ploughs, and 31 bordars with 6 ploughs. Yet it would be rash to assume that every one of these tenants' holdings was manorial in character: in the case of the single hide of land held by the 'wife of the reeve' it seems unlikely.[4]

In sum the entries of these various types leave us with a considerable area of land of which we cannot say for sure whether or no it conformed to a manorial pattern; and that some of it did not appears very probable in view of the definitely unmanorial character of some, mostly small, tenements which Domesday reveals here and there in the same area. At Ditchampton in

---

[1] Dd. i, f. 66*b*. Damerham is now in Hampshire.
[2] Ibid., ff. 65*b*, 66*b*, 67*b*, 68.
[3] Ibid., f. 65*b*. Steeple Ashton (f. 68) is another example.
[4] Ibid., f. 66; cf. Bishop's Cannings (f. 66) where also the reeve's wife and a man named Alward had a hide each.

Wiltshire (held by Robert of the Bishop of Bayeux) 18 cottars possessed the 2 ploughs required for the cultivation of the land; and at Hill Deverill in the same county, one of the landlords between whom the vill was divided had a tenement which seems to have been of the same character, for it contained land for a single plough and the recorded population consisted of 'eight *coscez* with 1 plough'.[1] Wiltshire can also show several villages or hamlets where only demesne ploughs are recorded and at least at Stert, Kington St. Michael, and Brigmerston these equal the number judged to be sufficient for all the land.[2] But the Berkshire evidence is more abundant and more remarkable. In this county some thirty Domesday entries reveal peasant ploughs unassociated with demesne ploughs, and a number of these entries relate to estates of considerable size. On the *Terra Regis* there were 35 *villani* and 12 bordars with 25 ploughs at Thatcham, and 32 *villani* and 21 cottars with 20 ploughs at Cookham.[3] On the estates of Abingdon Abbey we find 20 *villani* with 9 ploughs at Winkfield and 16 *villani* and a bordar with 9 ploughs at Whistley.[4] In 8 cases the peasant ploughs numbered from 4 to 8.[5] Moreover the entries which thus record only peasant ploughs are too numerous to be explained away as the result of scribal omissions; and as they occur side by side with entries of a regular manorial type, and relate to lands belonging to a number of different fees and different hundreds, it is impossible to suppose them to be due to any eccentricity of form in the original returns from which they, or their local prototypes, were abstracted.[6] It is noteworthy, too, that on 7 of these estates the

[1] Dd. i, ff. 66, 74b.

[2] Ibid., ff. 70b, 72b. At Stert, where the demesne ploughs were 3 in number, there were 6 *servi*. There was a *servus* at Kington. Apart from a Frenchman with 1½ virgates at Stert, the rest of the recorded population at these three places consisted of bordars.

[3] Ibid., f. 56b. It is perhaps significant that in the thirteenth century Cookham was one of two royal manors in the county 'quae sunt in manibus hominum praedictorum maneriorum': Madox, *Firma Burgi*, p. 54 n. f, quoted Vinogradoff, *Villainage in England*, p. 360 n. 1.

[4] Ibid., f. 59.

[5] Warfield (*Warwelt*), f. 57; Buckland, f. 58b; Tubney, f. 58b; Draycott Moor, f. 59; Easthampstead (*Lachenstede*), f. 59b; Bagshot (*Bechesgete*), f. 60b; Woolhampton (*Ollavintone*), f. 60b; Midgham, f. 61b. At Draycott Moor and Midgham some sub-tenants appear to have had demesne ploughs on their lands.

[6] At Warfield a blank space in the manuscript after the words *Terra est* may possibly mean that demesne ploughs were omitted as well as the number of the teamlands.

number of the peasants' ploughs equals, and on 2 exceeds, the number that was considered sufficient for the area covered by the description, and that in 9 cases it is stated that there was 'nothing in demesne'.[1]

One ought not, however, to assume that *in dominio nil* necessarily means that none of the land was regarded or treated as demesne. The meaning may be merely that the lord had no ploughs of his own at work there.[2] Yet on the whole it seems likely that, where there were no demesne ploughs, there was usually no arable cultivated as a home farm, and that the estate lacked this essential feature of regular manorial organization, though the lord may have kept some things in his own hands— manorial mills for example, or the dairy farm (*wica*) which we find associated with 220 acres of meadow at Buckland.[3] Further, besides the estates on which there were no demesne ploughs, Berkshire can also show about a score of small properties where all the recorded ploughs belonged to the demesne; and in

---

[1] Peasants' ploughs and teamlands are equal at Thatcham, f. 56*b*; Tubney, f. 58*b*; Bagshot and Woolhampton, f. 60*b*; Drayton, f. 61*b*; Earley (*Hurlei*), f. 62*b*; and Swallowfield (*Solafel*), f. 63*b*. At Enborne (*Taneburne*), f. 62*b*, and at *Ebrige*, f. 63, there were 3 ploughs to 2 teamlands. We are told that there is nothing in demesne at Tubney, Earley, and *Ebrige*; and also at Buckland, f. 58*b*, Sheffield (*Sewelle*), f. 60; Midgham, f. 61*b*, and *Burlei*, f. 63*b* (places where the ploughs are fewer than the teamlands); and at *Crochestrope*, f. 60, and Pangbourne, f. 61*b*, where teamland figures are lacking. The variations in the form of the statement—'Ibi nil in dominio', 'In dominio nichil est', and the like—seem insignificant. It should be noted that the statement about the ploughs is usually to the effect that there are so many peasants 'with' so many ploughs; but this form is also usual in the manors where there were demesne ploughs too; and the more precise statement that the peasants 'have' the ploughs is found (among the entries where no demesne ploughs are mentioned) at *Crochestrope*, Earley, *Ebrige*, and *Burlei*. The unidentified *Ebrige* appears to have been demanorialized by Hugolin, who 'transportavit hallam et alias domos et pecuniam in alio manerio'; but his title to hold *Ebrige* was disputed.

[2] As at Ospringe in Kent, where 'in dominio non sunt carucae': Dd. i, f. 10, quoted Vinogradoff, *English Society*, p. 396 n. 2. On the other hand, in the same county, Selling, where there was *nichil in dominio*, is rather significantly described as *manerium sine halla*: Dd. i, f. 12, quoted Vinogradoff, op. cit., p. 362 n. 1.

[3] For Buckland, which is one of the Berkshire estates where there was 'nothing in demesne', see Dd. i, f. 58*b* and Vinogradoff, op. cit., p. 368. Besides the dairy farm, there were 4 fisheries and a mill, and all this may well explain the presence of 7 *servi*. It is true that there was reckoned to be 'land for six ploughs' and that the 9 *villani* and 7 cottars are only credited with 4; but in Berkshire as a whole Maitland's figures show a 16 per cent. excess of teamlands over teams, and in some places where there were both demesne teams and tenants' teams the excess is even greater, in proportion, than it is at Buckland: e.g. Lambourn, f. 57*b*; Burghfield, f. 60*b*; Hartridge, f. 60*b*. Besides Buckland (and some land held by subtenants at Draycott Moor) serfs occur in 8 of these Berkshire cases, but only in 2 of these is no mill recorded.

fourteen of these the enumerated population consisted entirely of bordars, cottars, or serfs.[1]

Conditions in Wiltshire and Berkshire may perhaps be regarded as a fair sample of those obtaining in counties marked by a high degree of manorialization. If so, one may surely draw the general conclusion that, profound as was the contrast between this manorialized area and the Anglo-Danish north and east, estates of unmanorial character, though exceptional, must be allowed a not insignificant place in our picture of its agrarian organization. The manor was here predominant as it was not in the land of sokes and sokemen. But in all England there was probably no considerable area in which all the land and all the rural population were involved in a manorial nexus, nor, on the other hand, any considerable area in which the manor was wholly unknown.

---

[1] The number of ploughs thought to be needed is given in 16 cases in 8 of which it is equalled (or in one case exceeded) by the number on demesne. An omission of peasant ploughs must, however, be suspected at Ardington, where (on the estate which Sawin had held T.R.E.) there were 5 teamlands, but only 1 demesne plough, and 6 *villani* as well as 5 serfs and 2 mills: f. 62.

IX

LOCAL AND REGIONAL VARIETY AND THE 'NORMAL' VILLAGE

LIKE a traveller in a strange country, the inquirer into the
social economy of a remote period tends to be impressed
at the outset by the unfamiliar features which characterize
its general aspect and give a delusive appearance of uniformity
to the things he observes; and when a closer acquaintance reveals important differences between one set of phenomena and
another, he is still apt to regard the differences as the marks of
a contrast between different types and to attribute to those types
a simplicity and self-consistency greater than the facts justify.
To some extent this tendency has affected the historian's conception of the contrast between the manorialized and unmanorial-
ized areas of Domesday England; and though an attempt has
been made in the previous chapter to ascertain the real significance of that contrast, a further examination of local and regional
varieties is required if our picture of the agrarian landscape is
not to be unduly simplified.

The variety of conditions that might be found within the
bounds of a single county may be illustrated by the case of
Derbyshire. In some places there were manors of a very regular
type. At Bolsover in the north-east, for example, and at Bradbourne and Brassington in the west, the manor and the vill were
exactly co-incident, the plough-teams of the tenants were just
twice as numerous as the demesne ploughs in each place, and
the recorded population consisted entirely of *villani* and bordars
at Bolsover and Brassington and of these two classes and a priest
at Bradbourne.[1] But some vills, which were wholly owned by a
single lord, appear to have lacked a demesne farm. At Ockbrook
in the lowlands of the south and at Eyam high up on the
mountain limestone of the north, all the ploughs belonged to the
peasants. In the latter 12 *villani* and 7 bordars had 5 ploughs: in
the former 10 *villani* and 2 bordars had 3, but the population

[1] Dd. i, ff. 276, 274. In all three villages the *villani* were much more numerous
than the *bordarii*.

here also included 4 *censarii*, or rent-paying tenants, who rendered 14*s*.[1] Among villages of divided ownership there were some sharp contrasts. Stapenhill and Edingale, which are now in Staffordshire, were both divided between two lords in 1086; but whereas in the former village the ploughing strength was equally divided between the demesne and the peasants both on the manor which belonged to the abbey of Burton and on that of Nigel de Stafford, at Edingale all the ploughs in each portion of the vill belonged to the *villani*.[2] A more complicated situation is revealed at Breaston. This village was assessed at 6 carucates, but divided tenurially into 5 parts. Three carucates were held by Fulk of Roger de Busli and on this land (which is marked in Domesday as a 'manor') there were no demesne ploughs, but 5 *villani* had a couple. Another 'manor' belonged to the fee of Henry de Ferrers and was held by a certain Herbert as his tenant: this was only assessed at 3 bovates, yet the stock included a demesne plough as well as 5 ploughing oxen in the possession of 2 *villani*. The rest of Breaston consisted of sokeland comprising a waste bovate held by Geoffrey Alselin, a half-carucate which Fulk de Lusoris had wrongfully seized, and 2 carucates which appear to have been dependent upon Gilbert de Gand's manor of Ilkeston and to be occupied by 10 sokemen.[3]

There was not very much sokeland in Derbyshire nor did the sokemen constitute an important element in the population. Sokeland indeed accounts for less than 9 per cent. of the total assessment of the county and less than 5 per cent. of the enumerated population are described as sokemen. Yet members of this class were so grouped that a few villages received a distinctive character from their presence. At Wingerworth and Mosborough in the north-east all the recorded inhabitants were sokemen, there being 14 of them at the former place and 13 at the latter.[4] In the south-east 22 sokemen with 10 bordars under them occupied the bulk of the land at Long Eaton, the next village to Breaston; and at Chaddesden, in the same area, there were 11 sokemen along with 10 *villani* and 5 bordars.[5] Another

---

[1] Dd. i, ff. 273 (*Aiune* = Eyam), 276*b*.
[2] Ibid., ff. 273, 278 (Stapenhill); 274, 278*b* (Edingale).
[3] Ibid., ff. 275, 276*b*, 277*b*, 278.   [4] Ibid., ff. 272, 277.
[5] Ibid., ff. 273, 275. The entries relating to Wingerworth, Mosborough, Long Eaton, and Chaddesden are all marked with the marginal S indicating sokeland; but a village whose inhabitants did not include any sokemen might contain a portion of sokeland: e.g. Beighton and Wessington, ff. 273*b*, 277, 278, 276*b*, 277.

form of agrarian organization is exemplified in Derbyshire by a series of old royal estates which extended, as Stenton says, 'almost without a break across the county from Ashbourne to the Yorkshire border' and were distinguished from the other royal lands by the fact that they were 'farmed' in two groups— one group consisting of Ashbourne, Parwich, Wirksworth, *Mestesforde* (Matlock Bridge), and Darley, and the other more northern group consisting of Bakewell, Ashford, and Hope.[1] There is no reference to sokemen or sokeland in the description of any of these vills or any of their dependencies; but to every one of the eight 'manors' a number of dependent berewicks were attached. No doubt the prevalence of this type of settlement was promoted by geographical conditions, for the region in which these estates were situated is one 'consisting of great tracts of barren limestone rock with slender strips of cultivable soil along the watercourses' and is still characterized by 'scattered hamlets grouped into parishes for purposes of administrative convenience'.[2] But the influence of physical geography must not be over-stressed. To the east of the northern group Newbold, which also belonged to the king, is credited with six berewicks as well as with dependent sokelands, though the places belonging to both these classes lay in a comparatively low-lying district in or about the valley of the Rother.[3] Nor is the evidence in regard to demesne farming quite what one would expect from the nature of the terrain, for in this respect Bakewell with seven demesne ploughs, and its near neighbour Ashford with four, stand out in marked contrast to all the other places including Newbold. There was a single demesne plough at Darley, but otherwise there is nothing to suggest that any demesne farming was carried on either in the central manors or in their berewicks.[4]

Stenton points out that 'not a single sokeman appears west of the Derwent and north of the Trent', with the exception of four 'divided between Trusley, Barrow-on-Trent and Boulton'; and even Trusley, the farthest of these, is less than 6 miles from the Trent. That so large a proportion of the class is found 'on the borders of Notts. and Leicestershire' is, he adds, 'suggestive', as sokemen were so numerous in both these counties: *V.C.H. Derbys.* i. 315.

[1] Ibid., p. 297.   [2] Ibid., p. 312.

[3] Dd. i, f. 272. The berewicks of Newbold are clearly distinguished from the soke; but in the south of the county the royal manor of Melbourne is assigned a number of 'berewicks' which are subsequently described as 'soke': ibid., f. 272b. The Melbourne entry, however, shows signs of confusion: see *V.C.H. Derbys.* i. 331 n. 7.

[4] The entries relating to Bakewell and Ashford lump together the statistics of the manors and their berewicks, so that it is impossible to know whether there was

In Derbyshire demesne ploughs and peasant ploughs are distinguished with great precision and though, for the reasons given in the last chapter, it would be hazardous to draw conclusions about the extent of demesne farming from their relative numbers, some illustration of the variety of conditions may be obtained from the statistics of different types of entry. Of the individual entries which provide information about ploughs, nearly 42 per cent. mention peasant ploughs only; and not quite $1\frac{1}{2}$ per cent. mention only those belonging to the demesne; while in some 13 per cent. the two kinds appear in exactly equal numbers; and the peasant ploughs are a minority in about 9 per cent., but a majority in nearly 35 per cent.[1] Moreover, within the last two groups, the proportions varied a good deal from place to place. For example, the demesne ploughs were more numerous than the others both on the land of Peak Castle and in the unidentified manor of *Bolun*, and were four in number in each case, but in the former there were only 3 *villani* with a single plough and in the latter 8 *villani* and 8 bordars with 3 ploughs.[2] Again, among places with an excess of peasant ploughs it was a matter of 2 to 1 at Kirk Langley and 9 to 1 at Elmton.[3]

The Derbyshire villages also differed from one another in the social make-up and economic condition of their inhabitants. In a few the recorded population, as we have seen, consisted wholly of sokemen. At Duckmanton, a one-manor vill in the Chesterfield area, all the land appears to have been occupied by eighteen *censarii*, and nothing is said of any other inhabitants.[4] Only *villani* are mentioned at several places, and these include villages with demesne ploughs, as well as some where all the ploughs belonged to the *villani* as they did at Edingale.[5] At one

any demesne farming in the latter. It may be noted that at Ashbourne, which is described as 'waste', the priest had a plough of his own and had also 2 *villani* and 2 bordars who possessed half a plough: Dd. i, f. 272*b*.

[1] In Lincolnshire, if we may judge from the classified list of entries printed by Vinogradoff (*English Society*, appendix ix, table ii), 43 per cent. of the entries relate only to peasant ploughs and some 7 per cent. only to demesne ploughs, while about 11 per cent. show equality of numbers, nearly 13 per cent. a minority and 26 per cent. a majority of peasant ploughs. It is important to remember that all these figures relate merely to *entries* and that nothing can be inferred from them as to the number of places or the number of ploughs within the different groups.

[2] Dd. i, ff. 276, 274.

[3] Ibid., ff. 277, 276*b*.

[4] Ibid., f. 277.

[5] Examples are Ash with two demesne ploughs and Sapperton with none: ibid., f. 274*b*.

of the places named Somersall there were only bordars; these
were six in number with a single plough between them, but no
more was needed to cultivate the arable of this little village.[1]
Normally the population of a Derbyshire village seems to have
consisted of both *villani* and bordars, and the former were as
a rule the more numerous, but sometimes their numbers were
equal, as they were, for instance, at Boyleston, and sometimes,
as at one of the Strettons, the bordars were a majority.[2] There
were also, of course, villages in which more than these two classes
were represented. The inhabitants of *Toxenai* (? Trusley) included 5 *censarii* and 2 sokemen as well as 4 *villani* and 5 bordars.[3]
Servi are very rarely mentioned in the Derbyshire Domesday
and a suspicion that the enumeration of this class was incomplete
cannot be wholly excluded, but the fact that in six cases, out of
a total of eight, single individuals only are referred to suggests
that they were not an important element in the society of the
county. On the manor of Duffield, however, the character of
the economy must have been strongly affected by the presence
of the 10 serfs whom we find there along with 32 *villani* and 8
bordars.[4] And on the manor of Morton the co-existence of 4 serfs
and 2 demesne plough-teams suggests that they were ploughmen.[5] Of variety produced by diversity of economic circumstances little can be discovered, but conditions must have been
very different at Ash, where 7 *villani* had 1 plough between
them, from what they were at Sutton-on-the-Hill where 9 *villani*
possessed 7 ploughs.[6] And the mining and working of lead must
have involved some peculiarity in the five places where one or
more *plumbariae* are recorded—Ashford, Bakewell, *Mestesforde*,
Crich, and Wirksworth.[7]

Probably there was some lead-mining in other counties besides Derbyshire. In the Mendips and in Shropshire, which like
Derbyshire had been sources of lead under the Romans, its
production was certainly active in the latter part of the twelfth
century; and it may well be that both in these districts and in

---

[1] Ibid., f. 274b (*alia Summersale*).
[2] Ibid., ff. 275, 277 (*alia Stratone*).
[3] Ibid., f. 274b.
[4] Ibid., f. 275. The manor included five members besides Duffield itself, but
three of them were 'waste' in 1086.
[5] Ibid., f. 276b.   [6] Ibid., f. 274b.
[7] *V.C.H. Derbys.* i. 316. Hope is also mentioned, along with Ashford and Bakewell, as owing a render of lead T.R.E.

some others lead-mining was going on in 1086.[1] In view of the silence of Domesday, however, we can hardly suppose that it was on a sufficient scale to make much difference to the pattern of economic life even in the immediate neighbourhood of the mines. Much the same may be said of the mining of tin in Cornwall, which is also unmentioned. On the other hand, there are references to renders of iron, to iron-workers (*ferrarii*), or to iron-works (*ferrariae*)—references which seem to imply more than a village smithy—in Devon, Somerset, and Wiltshire, in Gloucestershire and Herefordshire, in the West Riding of Yorkshire, in Lincolnshire, Northamptonshire, and Warwickshire, and in Hampshire and Sussex, while a passage in the Cheshire Domesday (relating apparently to land now in the county of Flint) mentions iron-mines (*minariae ferri*)—though the reference here seems to be rather to mines that may be worked in the future than to any actually in operation.[2] Some villages must have received a distinctive stamp from their iron-works. At Hessle in the West Riding the recorded population consisted of six *ferrarii* and three bordars with a single plough.[3] In the Northamptonshire manor of Green's Norton, with its dependencies Adstone and Blakesley, the smiths (*fabri*) had rendered £7 in the time of King Edward though the value of the whole manor was reckoned to have been only £12.[4]

It would be rash to regard the record of iron-works in Domesday as complete; but, among the physical conditions which modified the normal patterns of life in certain localities, those conducive to the production of salt must have exercised a

---

[1] Outside the area covered by Domesday Book a reference to the 'silver mine of Carlisle' in the Pipe Roll of 1130 is interpreted to mean that argentiferous lead was being worked on Alston Moor in the reign of Henry I.

[2] To locate the actual extraction and smelting of iron ore, as distinct from the forges, is in many cases impossible, and Professor Darby has pointed out that none of the three Lincolnshire villages which had one or more *ferrariae* or *fabricae ferri* is situated on an outcrop of iron-stone: *Eastern England*, p. 84. On the other hand, *ferrariae* are mentioned in connexion with Corby in Northamptonshire, which has been an important source of iron-ore in recent times. The association of iron-works with woodland, which one would expect in view of the need for fuel, is well illustrated in Domesday: e.g. Fyfield, Wiltshire, Dd. i, f. 70*b*; Crewkerne and Stanton, Somerset, ff. 86, 86*b*–87, 91*b*; Pucklechurch, Gloucestershire, f. 165; Corby and Gretton, Northants., f. 219*b*; Castle Bytham and Little Bytham, Lincolnshire, f. 360*b*.   [3] Ibid., f. 316.

[4] Ibid., f. 219*b*. The number of these smiths is not stated. Orgrave in Furness, which is mentioned in Dd. i, f. 301*b*, got its name from an ore-pit (Ekwall, *Place-names of Lancashire*, 1922, p. 207). But whether iron was still being obtained there in 1086 (as it was subsequently) is unknown.

stronger influence than those determining the location of metal-
working. The need for salting meat, and in some regions fish,
created a general demand for salt, which could only be met by
a regularly recurring supply, since the utility of salt, unlike that
of metal, is exhausted in a single use. It is therefore not surprising that references to salt-production are of frequent occurrence
in Domesday Book. Salt-pans, where it was no doubt evaporated
from sea-water, are recorded in every sea-board county from
Lincolnshire to Cornwall. They are mentioned in connexion
with 34 places in Lincolnshire, 61 places in Norfolk, 10 in Suffolk, and 22 in Essex.[1] They were very numerous in Sussex and
Kent. It is not uncommon for a single village to be credited with
a large number of salt-pans. Leake in Lincolnshire possessed 41,
Caistor in Norfolk 45; Milton Regis and Chislet in Kent had
27 and 47 respectively; and no less than a hundred are assigned
to *Rameslie* in Sussex.[2] Since some of the entries in question are
clearly composite and cover several settlements, one cannot
assume that all the *salinae* to which an entry refers were actually
in the same place; but, on the other hand, salt-pans are sometimes recorded in connexion with villages lying some miles away
from the coast and such pans must have been situated in outlying parts of the manors to which they belonged and may have
been in the close neighbourhood of those belonging to other
manors. Salt-works evidently formed a very important element
in the economy of some villages. At Lyme in Dorset, a village
whose other recorded inhabitants were 10 villani, 6 bordars, and
an unspecified number of fishermen, there were 27 salt-workers
(*salinarii*).[3] At *Ora* in the same county 13 salt-workers constituted the whole of the recorded population; and at Charmouth
there were, besides 16 *salinarii*, only 3 *villani* and 3 *servi*.[4] Devon
can show a group of 33 salt-workers at Otterton, but Otterton
was a large manor.[5] Usually it is salt-pans and not salt-workers
that are recorded in Domesday and the former varied so much
in value that their numbers afford an insecure basis for comparison; but the 32 salt-pans at Studland in Dorset must have

---

[1] Darby, *Eastern England*, p. 377 and (for their location) the maps on pp. 71, 135,
187, 247, and 370.
[2] Dd. i, f. 348; ii, ff. 134, 221; i, ff. 2b, 12, 17. The large manor which bore the
lost name of *Rameslie* lay in Guestling hundred and must have included several
vills as five churches are mentioned in the Domesday description.
[3] Ibid., ff. 75b, 77b, 85.
[4] Ibid., ff. 78, 80.   [5] Ibid., f. 104.

meant much to the economy of that one-manor village, for they rendered 40s. and the value of the whole manor was put at £8.[1]

The coastal salt-pans appear to have been usually let for a rent to the salt-workers themselves; and it is this which gives the industry its chief sociological interest. Three times in the Hampshire Domesday we read of a *salina sine censu*, as if that was exceptional; and though in this county and also in Sussex and Kent the salt-pans are generally described as being 'of' this or that sum of money, there seems no reason to doubt that the meaning is the same as that expressed by the statement that they 'render' so much, which is common form in Domesday in the counties of Lincoln, Dorset, and Devon and is employed in the only case of *salinae* which it records in Cornwall.[2] Moreover at Lyme and *Ora* in Dorset, and at Kenton, Honiton, and two places called *Holecome* in Devon, the renders are unequivocally described as paid by the *salinarii*.[3]

In contrast to the salt-works scattered round the coast those dependent upon the brine-springs of Cheshire and Worcestershire were highly concentrated—so much so indeed that the places in which they were nearly all situated must be regarded as industrial centres rather than truly rural settlements.[4] Moreover,

---

[1] Dd. i, f. 80. As regards variation in the values or rentals of *salinae* it may be noted that there was one 'of four pence' at Gosberton in Lincolnshire (f. 344b) and one 'of five pence' at Wallop in Hampshire (f. 38b) while there were two 'of 37s. 8d.' at Bedhampton, Hants (f. 43) and one of 14s. 8d. at *Witesfel* in the Isle of Wight (f. 53). At *Flueta* in Devon 11 *salinae* are described as rendering 11d. (f. 104), but, as a rent of 1s. per salt-pan occurs fairly frequently, I suspect a scribal error of pence for shillings. The case is cited by Ellis (*Introduction*, i. 126), whose further statement that one at Ermington yielded £13. 10s. is due to his mistaking the render of the whole manor for that of the *salina* (f. 100b; cf. Exon., p. 78). I have followed the usual practice in translating *salina* as 'salt-pan', but Tait considered that 'salthouse' would be more correct. What seems clear is that it was a unit of salt-making that varied in size.

[2] Dd. i, ff. 38b, 52b (Eling and Watchingwell, Hants); f. 52 (Bowcombe, Isle of Wight); f. 121b (Stratton, Cornwall). In Norfolk, Suffolk, and Essex only the numbers of the *salinae* are given, without any indication of their value.

[3] Ibid., ff. 77b, 78, 100b, 104b, 114, 115b; cf. Exon., p. 196, where the Honiton *salinarii* are described as making their render *per annum*—*de firma*. A combination of salt-making and fishing is indicated at *Holecome* (f. 115b) where 3 *salinarii* owed a *summa* of fish as well as 4s. 9d. in money and 5 *summae* of salt. This *Holecome* is identified in the Victoria County History with Hollowcombe in the parish of Fremington near the north coast and that of f. 114 with Lower Holcombe in Dawlish.

[4] Some account of these centres as they are revealed in Domesday will be found in *The Domesday Survey of Cheshire*, ed. J. Tait (Chetham Soc., 1916), pp. 39–43;

both at Nantwich, Northwich, and Middlewich in Cheshire, and also at Droitwich, a large proportion of the *salinae* belonged to what one might almost describe as 'state demesne', in that two-thirds of the income they produced had before the Conquest gone to the king and one-third to the earl; and the amount of these royal and comital revenues affords some indication of the scale of these inland salt-works. At Droitwich, which was by far the most important of them and was reckoned to be a borough, King Edward had received £52 by way of rent from this source and Earl Edwin £24, while Nantwich had been farmed for £21 and Northwich and Middlewich for £8 each.[1] It is true that the Cheshire salt-works suffered grievously after the Conquest and that in 1086 their rents were still much lower than they had been twenty years earlier. Even at Droitwich, where King William absorbed the comital share, there was some decline, for by 1086 the sheriff was apparently farming both groups for £65 and two *mittae* of salt.[2] But then in addition to those of the royal and comital demesne there were many *salinae* in Droitwich, and some in the Cheshire centres, which belonged to rural manors; and though all these salt-works may fairly be described (in the words which Tait uses of the Cheshire 'wiches') as 'manufacturing *enclaves* in the midst of an agricultural district', their profound and widespread influence upon the life of the countryside must be recognized in any account of rural

---

V.C.H. Worcs. i. 268–70 (by Round); and Darby and Terrett, *Midland England*, pp. 251–6 (by F. J. Monkhouse). A *salina* worth 24s. recorded at *Burwardestone* (Dd. i, f. 264) probably lay at Dirtwich or Foulwich near Malpas and so apart from the main Cheshire centres of the industry, while some of the *salinae* credited to manors near Droitwich may (unlike most of the manorial salt-pans in Worcestershire and its neighbour counties) have been situated in their own villages and not in Droitwich itself. The name of Salt in Staffordshire (*Selte* in Dd. i, f. 248b) suggests that salt was worked, or had formerly been worked there, though nothing is said about this in Domesday. Ekwall remarks that 'there are salt-works within two miles of Salt' (*Dictionary of English Place-Names*, 1940, p. 383).

[1] The Nantwich 'farm' included the profits of the hundred court, subsequently valued at 40s. In all three Cheshire 'wiches' the king had two-thirds and the earl one-third of the 'farm', but at Droitwich the *salinae* themselves had been divided between them, the king having 98 and the earl 51½. The royal *salinae* were somewhat more highly rented, and there can be no doubt that the division was based on the same principle that ruled in Cheshire: from the Droitwich *hocci* (possibly drying sheds?) the king had 13s. 4d. and the earl 6s. 8d. The Droitwich *salinae*, like those of the coastal salt-works, differed greatly in value: of the eight which the manor of Alvechurch possessed in that centre, one rendered 50 *mittae* of salt, and the other seven 70 *mittae*: Dd. i, f. 174, cf. ff. 172 (Bromsgrove), 173b (Northwick).

[2] In an entry for Wellington in Herefordshire 17 *mittae* appear to be valued at 30d. (ibid., f. 187).

England in this period. More than a score of Worcestershire manors are definitely described in Domesday as possessing one or more salt-pans in Droitwich; and similar statements are made about three manors in Gloucestershire, a couple in Hereford-shire and Shropshire, and one in Warwickshire, while Princes Risborough, far away in Buckinghamshire, kept a salt-worker there who supplied that manor with salt. Droitwich is also named as rendering salt to Caynham in Shropshire; Binton in Warwickshire; Thornbury, Sodbury, and Mickleton in Glouces-tershire; Bampton and Rollright in Oxfordshire; and several places in Herefordshire.[1] Moreover a number of Worcestershire villages and one or two in Gloucestershire and Warwickshire are credited with salt-pans which almost certainly were situated in Droitwich though this is not actually stated.[2]

Where a rural manor had only a single salt-pan or part of one, this was no doubt primarily, if not exclusively, a means of providing for its own needs. A *dimidia salina* which belonged to Frodsham in Cheshire is specifically described as 'serving the hall' (*serviens aulae*).[3] Again the earl had a salt-pan appurtenant to his manor of Acton-by-Nantwich from which he used to re-ceive sufficient salt for his house throughout the year. But in this case a toll was payable if any salt from this source was sold.[4] And participation in salt-production as a lucrative industry seems to be indicated wherever a group of *salinae* is credited to

[1] For references see Darby and Terrett, op. cit., pp. 39, 94, 151, 251–6, 298. It is just possible that the '*wych*' of the Shropshire case was one of those in Cheshire, but Droitwich (which is called *Wych* in Domesday) is probably intended. Besides the cases mentioned in the text, five places in Herefordshire possessed 'part' of a *salina* in Droitwich. It is not really clear whether Bampton in Oxfordshire received salt or money *de salinis de Wic* (Dd. i, f. 154*b*).

[2] But, as Mr. Monkhouse remarks, 'the villages near Droitwich probably had their own salt-pans'.

[3] Ibid., f. 263*b*. It was situated in *Wich*—probably Nantwich. Of the seven *salinae* in *Wich* belonging to Weaverham in the same county, six had become waste, but one remained in use and *reddit sal aulae*: ibid., f. 263*b*.

[4] Ibid., f. 268. In view of the tendency to merge private right and public authority which is characteristic of feudalism, this passage is of unusual interest because of the distinction it implies between the earl's own property and the comital share in what I have ventured to call the 'state demesne': 'Tempore regis Edwardi erat in Warmundestrou Hundret unum Wich in quo erat puteus ad sal faciendum et ibi erant viii salinae inter regem et comitem Eduinum ita quod de omnibus exitibus et redditionibus salinarum habebat rex ii partes et comes terciam. Ipse vero comes praeter has habebat unam salinam propriam quae adjacebat suo manerio Acatone. De hac salina per totum annum habebat comes sal sufficientem suae domui. Si quid autem inde venderetur, de theloneo habebat rex ii denarios et comes tercium.'

a manor of moderate extent—perhaps even where we read of a single *salina* rendering a sum of money.[1] Further, the economy of some villages must have been a good deal affected by the demand of the salt-works for fuel. Bromsgrove had been accustomed to provide 300 cartloads of wood in return for the same number of 'mitts' of salt from the 13 *salinae* which this manor possessed in Droitwich; and it appears, too, that 100 cartloads were rendered in return for 100 'mitts' by Northwick and by the *villani* of Martin Hussingtree.[2] Fladbury, though 12 miles away, also supplied wood *ad salinas de Wich*.[3] And besides all these things, the influence of the traffic in salt can be discerned in the ancient salt-ways leading from Droitwich, which are mentioned in a number of Saxon charters and have left their mark upon the map in such names as that of Salford in Oxfordshire.[4] In the customs of the Cheshire 'wiches', moreover, Domesday Book enables us to catch a glimpse of the apparatus by which the traffic was carried on and of the regulations to which it was subject, for we read that various tolls were paid for carts drawn by two or by four oxen, for horse-loads, or for men carrying salt on their backs, and that higher rates were charged in the case of those coming from another hundred or another shire.[5] That similar customs obtained at Droitwich is not unlikely: the wasted condition into which the Cheshire salt-works had fallen (probably through the devastation wrought by the Conqueror in 1070) must have endangered the maintenance of old usages

---

[1] For example, 5 *salinae* belonged to Guiting in Gloucestershire, another 5 (in *Wich*) to Donnington in Shropshire, 7 (in *Wich*) to Tardebigge in Worcestershire: Dd. i, ff. 167, 253*b*, 172*b*. Money rents due from single salt-pans are recorded for Hillborough (Warwickshire), Ditton Priors (Shropshire), and Herford (Cheshire); and a mixed render of money and salt was due from one belonging to Haselor (Warwickshire): ibid., ff. 243*b*, 253*b*, 267, 244.

[2] Ibid., ff. 172, 173*b*, 174*b*. The Hussingtree case seems to imply inter-manorial organization. Hussingtree belonged to Westminster Abbey; and the 100 'mitts' of salt are only mentioned in the next entry which seems to be concerned with the abbey's interests in Droitwich and not specifically with any appurtenances of this particular manor. Further, no woodland is recorded at Hussingtree, while there was a considerable extent of wood on the abbey's demesne manor at Upton Snodsbury, 5 miles away to the south-east. As the abbey appears to have had no demesne farm at Hussingtree, it seems possible this carting service was required from the *villani* there in lieu of agricultural labour.

[3] Ibid., ff. 172*b*–173.

[4] Mawer and Stenton, *Place-Names of Worcestershire*, 1927, pp. 4–9.

[5] Dd. i, f. 268. Peddling in salt is suggested by one of the provisions: 'Homo manens in ipso hundredo si carro ducebat sal ad vendendum per eundem comitatum de unoquoque carro dabat unum denarium, quotquot vicibus oneraret eum.'

and created a need for their being put on record which was not felt in Worcestershire.[1]

In fenland districts, in some river valleys, and on some parts of the coast, fishing played an important part in the economy and must have imposed a special pattern upon the life of a good many villages. Since the instructions embodied in the Ely preamble include a question about the number of *piscine*, it may be presumed that the Domesday commissioners were expected to attempt a complete enumeration of these sources of income; and in fact Domesday Book contains a great many references to 'fisheries' and renders of fish. It is true that it normally mentions *piscariae* and not *piscinae*, but the distinction between these terms which is commonly made by translating the former as 'fisheries' and the latter as 'fish-ponds' cannot be justified, for in the Ely Inquest we frequently read of *piscine* where the Domesday text speaks of *piscariae*. Both terms, however, implied not a mere place where fishing was practised, but an apparatus for the catching of fish—perhaps some sort of weir or hatch like the *cytweras* and *hæcweras* of the pre-Conquest custumal of Tidenham in Gloucestershire and the *fiscwer* mentioned in the manual known as the *Gerefa* which is probably of eleventh-century date —perhaps almost any kind of fixed contrivance for the purpose.[2]

[1] A toll on salt ('theloneum salis quod veniebat ad aulam') is mentioned in the description of Chedworth in Gloucestershire: Dd. i, f. 164.

[2] That a fishery in Domesday means a 'fixed contrivance of some kind', even in the case of sea-fisheries, was in Round's view indicated by such statements as that which records 'four fisheries' at East Mersea in Essex (Dd. ii, f. 46*b*, where the word employed is *piscinae*; *V.C.H. Essex*, i. 424); and it seems impossible to explain in any other way the large numbers of *piscariae* mentioned in some places. Nearly 70 appear to be credited to Tidenham; and 101 *cytweras* and 4 *hæcweras* are assigned to this manor and its dependences in the (probably eleventh-century) statement of its customs: Dd. i, ff. 164, 166*b*, 167*b*; Robertson, *Anglo-Saxon Charters*, No. cix. Further evidence is provided by references in Domesday to 'waste' *piscariae* (Barnby, Yorks, f. 319*b*), to 'sites' of fisheries (Morton, Yorks., and Billinghay, Lincolnshire, ff. 310, 340), to a *nova piscaria* (Monkton, Kent, f. 4*b*), to one which Harold had made (*construxit*) near Mortlake (ff. 30*b*, 31), and to a fishery at Chadwell in Essex which had disappeared *sed potest fieri* (ii, f. 23*b*). For the word *fiscwer* see *Gerefa* 9 (in Liebermann, *Gesetze*, i. 454). Miss Robertson describes the Tidenham weirs as 'basket weirs and hackle weirs'; and Seebohm has illustrated their nature by reference to the constructions employed in modern times for catching salmon in the Severn and Wye: see Seebohm, *English Village Community* (4th ed.), pp. 151–5. The weir-making services of the Tidenham peasants (*geburs*) find a parallel farther up the Severn at Ribbesford, where the *villani* according to Hemming 'captatorias sepes piscium et alias venatorias instaurare debita lege debebant': see *Hemingi Chartularium*, ed. Hearne, i. 256, quoted by Round, *V.C.H. Worcs.* i. 272 n. 2. Fisheries with the significant names of Lotewere, Wlweyewere, Hachenewere, and Tyllingeswere are mentioned in the Ramsey Cartulary: i. 132, 430, 431. Renders

It follows that we cannot expect fishing that was not operated
by such means to be systematically noticed in Domesday; and
this may help to explain the absence of all reference to the subject in some districts where geographical conditions make it
likely that a good deal of fishing was carried on, though no
doubt in this matter as in others Domesday sometimes fails to
record all that it should have recorded.[1] As it is, we read of
fisheries or of renders of eels from mills in almost all parts of the
country. Usually the *piscariae* appear to have been let for a rent
in fish or in money and a Shropshire entry tells of five that were
rented by *villani*; but sometimes one or more of these appliances
would be reserved for the supply of the lord's hall, and the distinction made at Tidenham between the *piscariae in dominio* and
the *piscariae villanorum* may possibly mean that the latter were
appurtenant to the holdings of the peasantry.[2] It was only, however, in a few districts that the fishing was on a scale to make
much call upon the labour-force of the community. The *piscariae*
must have needed repair from time to time, but the actual cap-
ture of the eels or salmon would not be much trouble when thus
assisted, and since there were some village mills which paid a

of eels *de gurgite* are recorded in Domesday at *Eia*, Hoddesdon, and Hailey in
Hertfordshire and at Trumpington in Cambridgeshire: Dd. i, ff. 134*b*, 137*b*, 139*b*,
140, 200.

[1] Professor Darby considers that many fisheries went unrecorded in the fens,
but he does not appear to take account of the restricted sense of the word *piscaria*
in Domesday: *Eastern England*, pp. 68, 367. Domesday certainly seems to ignore the
fisheries in and about Upwell on the Norfolk–Cambridgeshire border where 20
fishermen rendering 60,000 eels a year were said to have been confirmed to Ramsey
Abbey by the Conqueror. Though the charter produced in evidence has been
judged to be spurious or inflated, a detailed rental (probably of early thirteenth-
century date) records eel-rents from this neighbourhood amounting to more than
the traditional figure: *Cart. Rams.* ii. 93; iii. 296–9. At Dartington in Devon two
fishermen owing a render of eighty salmon are recorded by an interlinear insertion
in the Exon. text (p. 346) though unmentioned in Domesday (i, f. 111).

[2] *Piscariae* are commonly described as 'of', or as rendering, a certain sum of
money or a certain number of eels and occasionally (e.g. at Ore in Kent, Mortlake
in Surrey, and Marden in Herefordshire: Dd. i, ff. 10, 30*b*, 179*b*) they are said to
be *sine censu* as if that was unusual. At Kingston, Surrey, there were 'ii piscariae de
x solidis et tercia piscaria valde bona sed sine censu', and at or near Ruyton in
Shropshire 'v piscariae in censu villanorum': ibid. ff. 30*b*, 257*b*. At Swancombe
(*Svinescamp*), Kent, there were 'v piscariae de xxx denariis et sexta que servit ad
hallam', and of two at Eyton-on-Severn (which belonged to the abbey of Shrewsbury) 'una reddit xvi solidos alia est ad victum monachorum': ibid., ff. 6, 252*b*.
A *piscaria ad hallam* (or *ad aulam*) is recorded at Milton, Porchester, and Preston in
Hampshire, and there were *iii piscariae servientes aulae* at Holdenhurst in the same
county and *una piscaria serviens hallae* at Newington near Sittingbourne in Kent:
ibid., ff. 44, 47*b*, 53, 39, 14*b*.

rent of a thousand eels (presumably caught in eel-traps), we can hardly suppose that a fishery which was let for a similar quantity —or, as many were, for much less—can have made any very great difference to the economy of a village or the occupations of its inhabitants.[1] It is true that an odd fisherman or two may be found here and there outside the districts in which fishing was really important. At Dorchester-on-Thames along with 34 *villani* and 22 bordars there was a fisherman (*piscator*) who owed a render of 750 eels and on Richard de Courcy's manor of Nuneham Courtenay, a little farther up the river, the recorded population included 3 fishermen as well as 35 *villani* and 7 serfs.[2] But there is no comparison between this sort of thing and the great herring fisheries which can be discerned on some parts of the coast or the great fisheries of the fens from which Ely, the 'eel district', got its name.[3] Among sea-fisheries the most notable are those of Suffolk and the eastern part of the south coast. In Suffolk, Southwold, Beccles, and Dunwich owed renders respectively of 25,000, 60,000, and 68,000 herrings. From Sandwich in Kent the monks of Canterbury Cathedral received 40,000; and in Sussex the *villani* of Lewes owed a render of 38,500 to the abbey of Hyde at Winchester, while William de Warenne drew one of 16,000 from Iford (*Niworde*) and another of 4,000 came from Brighton.[4] Among fresh-water fisheries those of the eastern fens are pre-eminent. From Wisbech in Cambridgeshire more than 33,000 eels were due to the various lords who had property in that vill, and in the same county Stuntney rendered 24,000 eels and Doddington 27,150, while in Huntingdonshire the fisheries

---

[1] For mills yielding 1,000 eels see Remenham in Berkshire, Horningsea in Cambridgeshire, and Stratford-on-Avon and Wasperton in Warwickshire: Dd. i, ff. 57, 191, 238b, 239. In the village where I am writing (Lower Heyford, Oxfordshire) there is still an eel-trap at the outflow of the mill-pool, and there was a mill here in 1086.

[2] Dd. i, ff. 155, 159.

[3] Modern philology has confirmed Bede's statement: 'Est autem Elge in provincia Orientalium Anglorum regio familiarum circiter sexcentarum, in similitudinem insulae vel paludibus, ut diximus, circumdata vel aquis; unde et a copia anguillarum, quae in eisdem paludibus capiuntur, nomen accepit': *Hist. Eccles.*, iv, c. 17(19). The suffix *ge* 'district' (cognate with the German *Gau*) became confused with *eg* 'island'.

[4] Dd. ii, ff. 371b, 370, 311b–312; i, ff. 3, 17b, 26, 26b. Beccles, Dunwich, Sandwich, and Lewes were not, however, villages, but boroughs, or at least included *burgenses* among their inhabitants; and the same is true of Yarmouth, where there were 24 fishermen: ibid. ii, ff. 118, 283. Yet villages played a part in the Suffolk herring-fishing: in the three north-eastern hundreds of the county there are '18 places for which herrings (*allecti*) are recorded': Darby, *Eastern England*, p. 185.

and meres (*piscariae et marae*) belonging to the abbots of Ramsey, Thorney, and Peterborough were reckoned to be worth £17.[1] Some extensive fisheries are also recorded in Yorkshire. The 20 *piscinae* of Tidworth, which lies between Hatfield Chase and the river Don, owed a render of 20,000 eels; and on the river Hull the fisheries of Leconfield, Beverley, and Cottingham were between them responsible for eel-renders amounting to a total of 21,400.[2] In Lincolnshire, in the marshy lands between the Yorkshire border and the lower Trent, four villages are credited with a total of 62 *piscariae*, but as the total rents of these only amounted to 50s. they can hardly have been very fruitful.[3]

Fisheries of a size sufficient to affect the character of the villages in which they were situated are also recorded in some parts of the west of England. At *Etone* (Eaton Hall), on the Dee above Chester, there was one which rendered 1,000 salmon; and 6 fishermen formed a majority of the recorded inhabitants of the place.[4] In Somerset, the abbey of Muchelney obtained a render of 6,000 eels from two *piscariae* in the neighbourhood, and the Abbot of Glastonbury had 10 fishermen at Meare.[5] The *piscariae* of Tidenham in Gloucestershire were of outstanding importance. In 1086 there were between 60 and 70 of them, a few being in the Wye, but the great majority in the Severn; and though Domesday does not distinguish their value from that of the manor as a whole, we may perhaps see some indication of their productiveness in the fact that the rent which Stigand agreed to pay, when he leased Tidenham from the abbey of Bath, included 6 porpoises and 30,000 herrings as well as a mark of gold.[6] It may well be, indeed, that Seebohm was right in his conjecture that the lease 'was a mutual arrangement whereby the archbishop's table was provided with salmon from the west, and the monks of Bath with herrings from the east'; but this

---

[1] Dd. i, ff. 192, 192b, 193, 196b, 191b, 205.

[2] Ibid., ff. 321, 306b, 322b, 304, 328.

[3] Ibid., f. 369, 369b. The villages are Haxey (*Acheseia*), Epworth, Belton, and Crowle. Farther up the Trent, at Dunham in Nottinghamshire, a single *piscaria* brought in 10s. 8d. (ibid., f. 281).

[4] Ibid., f. 263b.

[5] Ibid., ff. 91, 90. In the case of Muchelney the Exon. text (p. 174) describes the render as made *per annum*; but no doubt the renders mentioned in Domesday were in general annual.

[6] Ibid., f. 164; Robertson, op. cit., No. cxvii. The lease can be dated 1061–5, but Domesday implies that the manor was not leased before this ('Hoc manerium non reddebat censum T.R.E. nisi victum monachis. Stigandus Archiepiscopus tenebat illum quando comes W. accepit eum': i, f. 164).

would still leave it probable that the render bore some relation to the quantity of fish which the abbey had obtained from this manor in the time of King Edward.[1]

Of all the geographical circumstances which affected rural economy as differential factors, the neighbourhood of extensive woodland was probably the most wide-ranging in its influence. A patch of woodland sufficient, or barely sufficient, to satisfy the needs of a village for fuel and fencing material and mast for a few pigs, was a fairly normal concomitant of village life in Domesday England; but the opportunities presented by the really great woods were radically different, and many villages in many parts of the country were near enough to such woods to receive a distinctive mark from their proximity. Domesday Book does not, unfortunately, provide the material for an adequate map of the wooded areas. The untamed forests were not as a rule surveyed; and the income-yielding woods are described by various methods for which no common denominator can be found, their extent being indicated in most counties by extremely baffling linear measurements, but in some by the number of swine that could be fed there, in some by the number that the lord received as pannage rent, and only in Lincolnshire, Devonshire, and Cornwall, for the most part, in acres.[2] In spite of these difficulties the districts that were heavily wooded can be

[1] Seebohm, op. cit., p. 154. I understand that in the opinion of expert biologists it is very improbable that large numbers of herrings ever came as far up the Severn as Tidenham. Some of Stigand's East Anglian estates were near the coast. Burgh Castle and Bungay in Suffolk, and Stockton and Toft Monks just over the Norfolk border, were in the region of the great Suffolk herring-fisheries, but there is nothing in Domesday about fisheries belonging to these places. A render of 2,000 herrings was payable at Stigand's manor of Thorpe-by-Norwich (Dd. ii, f. 138). He also held Snettisham and Hunstanton on the Wash, but is only credited with one fishery at the former and half a fishery at the latter (ibid., ff. 142b, 135b). There were three *salinae* at Burgh Castle and one on his manor at Snettisham.

[2] There is an admirable general account of 'Domesday Woodland' by H. C. Darby in the *Econ. Hist. Rev.*, 1950, pp. 21–43; and detailed summaries of the data, illustrated by excellent maps, will be found in the various volumes of the *Domesday Geography* of which he is editor. Within the various counties the predominant form of 'measurement' is not invariably applied, and even a single entry may employ different methods for different portions of woodland: e.g. at Irnham (*Gerneham*), Lincolnshire, Dd. i, f. 363, cited by Darby. As regards swine-units it must be remembered that a given area of mixed oak and ash would support fewer pigs than the same area under oak alone; and Domesday hardly ever tells us anything about the species of the trees. Exceptionally attempts were made to estimate 'forest' areas: see Dd. i, ff. 154b (Oxfordshire), 286b (Cheshire). For a brief but useful account of the forest areas of Saxon England see P. Hunter Blair, *An Introduction to Anglo-Saxon England*, 1956, pp. 248–50.

distinguished pretty clearly; and it is possible to discern something of the influence exercised by these woodland areas upon social and economic conditions in the neighbourhood. Obviously they presented special opportunities for development in the way of 'home colonization'; and something has been said in a previous chapter about the form which such development took in the Weald, where 'denes' or swine-pastures, established at a distance from the manors to which they belonged, were in some cases able to grow through 'assarting' into considerable agricultural settlements.[1] It is true that the word 'dene' (*dena*) is hardly to be found in Domesday Book outside the county of Kent; and though it records about fifty 'denes' in that county, and indicates the nature of some of them by employing the term *denae silvae* and by referring to the swine-rents that they owed, it merely includes them in the descriptions of the manors to which they belonged and throws no light upon their geographical location.[2] The combined evidence of Saxon charters and thirteenth century surveys, however, makes it clear that the Kentish denes were in fact commonly isolated from their parent manors or vills and that there were many more of them than are enumerated in Domesday.[3] Thus, in the case of Lenham, Domesday says nothing about any dependent denes, though it credits the manor with *silva XL porc'* (which we may assume to mean woodland yielding a pannage rent of forty swine); but the charter which records the gift of Lenham to St. Augustine's in the year 804, names thirteen denes in the Weald (*tresdecim denberende on Andrede*) among the appurtenances of the estate, and several of these can be identified with places situated in the Staplehurst–Cranbrook area—from 8 to 13 miles distant from Lenham—and were still recognized as dependencies of that manor in the thirteenth century.[4] Again, though it does mention four denes in its description of Leeds, a near neighbour of Lenham, the fact

---

[1] Above, pp. 14–15.

[2] Outside Kent, a *dena silvae* is recorded at Ewell in Surrey and there is a reference to the third part of a dene in the description of Windsor: Dd. i, ff. 30b, 56b.

[3] Above, p. 14.

[4] Dd. i, f. 12; Birch, *Cart. Sax.*, No. 316; Wallenberg, *Kentish Place-Names* (Uppsala, 1931), pp. 93–100; *Black Book of St. Augustine*, ed. Turnei and Salter, pp. 250–3. In Birch, op. cit., No. 507 (an original charter of the year 863) reference is made to 'pascua porcorum que nostra lingua saxhonica denbera nominamus' and several proper names ending in *denn* follow: cf. ibid., No. 496. In the word *denbera*, *denn* appears to be compounded with *bearo*, a grove or wood, so that it is really equivalent to the *denae silvae* of Domesday.

that these were not in Kent at all, but in Sussex, is only revealed by one of the 'satellite' texts.[1] On the other hand, Domesday Book itself tells us of numerous small settlements in the woodland region of northern Sussex which were members or former members of manors in the south of that county.[2] These outlying hamlets are not called 'denes' and nothing is said to suggest that they were still devoted to pig-farming; but, among the very few that are named and not merely described as anonymous appurtenances of their parent manors, Hazelden and Standen bear names that betray their origin, and in Shoyswell Hundred, where a number of the unnamed settlements were situated, half a dozen place-names are now to be found which appear to incorporate the suffix *denn*. A similar number of such names also occur today within the bounds of Loxfield Camden Hundred, which marches with that of Shoyswell and comprises the northern portion of the ancient hundred of Malling. This district, being covered by the obviously composite entry relating to the great archiepiscopal manor of South Malling, appears as a blank space in the Domesday map; but it can hardly be doubted that it was in fact at outlying members of the manor in this part of the hundred that much of the woodland pig-farming was carried on which yielded a pannage rent of no less than three hundred swine.[3] And if place-names with the suffix *denn* become scarce and finally disappear as one moves into the north-western part of Sussex, some of the denes that are recorded in the tenth century as appurtenances of Washington and Annington in the south can be indentified with places in this region.[4]

Of the manner in which the denes were exploited in the eleventh century very little can be discovered.[5] Until they had

---

[1] Dd. i, f. 7*b*; A. Ballard, *An Eleventh-Century Inquisition of St. Augustine's, Canterbury* p. 2. It is some 14 miles from Leeds to the nearest point on the Sussex border.

[2] See Dd. i, ff. 19, 19*b*, 22*b*.

[3] Ibid., f. 16.

[4] Birch, *Cart. Sax.* Nos. 834, 961. Among the Washington denes were Horsham, Crockhurst (a lost place in Horsham), and Hazelwick (in Worth), while another was probably Gotwick (in Rusper); but of those belonging to Annington it can only be said that two of them are possibly represented by Strudgwick Wood (in Kirdford) and Lydwicke (in Slinfold): see *Place-Names of Sussex*, pp. 225, 226, 281, 233, 107, 160. It is remarkable that five of the denes mentioned in these two charters bear names ending in *wic*. In place-names the word *denn* is sometimes indistinguishable from *denu*, 'a valley'. There is a valuable discussion of the forinsec denes of Sussex in J. E. A. Jolliffe, *Pre-Feudal England: The Jutes*, pp. 82 et seq.

[5] Some rather miscellaneous evidence of later date is discussed in N. Neilson, *The Cartulary and Terrier of Bilsington* (British Academy Records, 1928), pp. 2–39.

undergone some development through assarting, their use as swine-pastures was presumably based upon seasonal trans-humance, and an alternation between the woodland denes and pastures in the neighbourhood of their parent manors is perhaps reflected in the distinction not infrequently drawn between swine-rents paid as pannage and those paid *de herbagio*.[1] More-over, as it is of the rents received from the woods that we normally read in Domesday, it is clear that pig-farming in the Weald was largely, if not exclusively, in the hands of farmers or peasants and was not a mere branch of demesne economy.[2] Nor can it be doubted that by 1086 some of the denes had developed into small agricultural settlements where peasant independence is likely to have been fostered both by the need for providing the pioneers with adequate incentives and by the isolation of the settlements from the manorial centres. In the Sussex hundred of Hawksborough the outlying members of southern manors appear to have been mostly without demesnes; and the *villani* in some of them were a good deal richer in plough-beasts than those of the parent manors.[3] One is reminded of a remark made by Flach: 'il peut être vrai de dire que la liberté est sortie du fond des bois.'[4]

Though isolated swine-pastures of the kind to which the word 'dene' was applied were perhaps peculiar to the wealden area, extensive pig-farming was a normal feature of districts in which there was much glandiferous woodland, and in some of

[1] Besides 300 swine *de pasnagio* the income of the manor of South Malling included 'de herbagio xxxviii sol. et vi den. et ccclv porc' herbag'': cf. Sheffield, Sussex ('De silva et herbagio xxxii porc'': Dd. i, f. 22*b*); Hooe, Sussex ('silva x porc' de pasnagio. De herbagio vii porc'': f. 18); Dorking, Surrey ('Silva l porc' de pasnagio. De herbagio xxxviii porc'', f. 30*b*).

[2] Of peasant pig-farming we get a glimpse (but in connexion with pasture, not woodland) at Titsey in Surrey ('pro pastura septimus porcus villanorum': Dd. i, f. 36*b*) and at Pagham in Sussex ('De herbagio unus porcus de unoquoque villano qui habet vii porcos': ibid., f. 16*b*). According to a marginal note to the Pagham entry it was *similiter per totum Sudsex*, and that would mean that nearly 2,500 pigs grazed the pastures of South Malling. The same rate was in force at Ferring, Wittering, and Elsted (ff. 16*b*, 17, 17*b*). But the marginal note was not quite true. On the same folio herbage of one pig in three is recorded at Bishopstone, and herbage of one in six at Aldingbourne. At Battersea (*Patricesy*) *villani* paid one pig in ten, probably as pannage (f. 32): cf. Leominster (f. 180), and Mickleover in Derbyshire in the next century (Burton Abbey Survey B, p. 230).

[3] On an outlying member of West Firle 9 *villani* had 8 ploughs, while on the parent manor there were 80 with 34 ploughs: at Laughton (*Lestone*) there were 14 villani and 3 bordars with 10½ ploughs, but on one of its outlyers in Hawks-borough Hundred 15 *villani* had 15 ploughs: Dd. i, ff. 19, 21, 22*b*.

[4] *Les Origines de l'ancienne France*, ii (Paris, 1893), 155.

these must have played a really important part in the economy.[1] Especially notable is the region between the escarpment of the Chilterns and the London area—roughly south-west Hertfordshire and the adjacent parts of Bedfordshire, Buckinghamshire, and Middlesex. Within a circuit of 13 miles round King's Langley no less than twenty places were credited in 1086 with wood for a thousand swine or more.[2] And not very far to the east the swine-bearing woods of Cheshunt, Enfield, and Edmonton, together with those of their near neighbours Waltham and Chingford in Essex, were reckoned to be sufficient for a total of 8,582.[3]

Such large figures (almost invariably expressed in round numbers) cannot be taken to represent the actual number of pigs that were turned out in the woods at the time the survey was made; but there can be little doubt that they are rough estimates of the extent to which these sources of income were in fact exploited, and not mere indications of their potential capacity.[4] It seems clear, too, that most of the swine in question, like those of the weald, did not belong to the manorial demesnes. In the case of Norfolk, Suffolk, and Essex we have proof of this in the statistics of demesne stock preserved in the Little Domesday,

[1] Jolliffe regards the forinsec dene as a Jutish peculiarity: op. cit., p. 87. Outside Kent, Sussex, and the adjacent parts of Surrey there seems to be no certain case of a place-name incorporating the element *denn*, as distinct from *denu* (see *Place-Names of Sussex*, p. 550; *Place-Names of Surrey*, p. 350; Ekwall, *Oxford Dictionary of English Place-Names*, sub. *denn*). But this might indicate peculiarity in regional vocabulary rather than in economic usage.

[2] Among these places, Luton, Hatfield, Harrow, and Wendover each had wood for 2,000 swine: Dd. i, ff. 209, 135, 127, 143*b*.

[3] Dd. i, ff. 137, 129*b*; ii, ff. 15*b*, 12*b*, 64. The numbers given are all round numbers with the exception of that for some wood belonging to the sokemen at Waltham—wood for 182 swine.

[4] Several considerations point to this conclusion: (1) Domesday Book is primarily concerned with actual conditions; and, though it often mentions the ploughs that might be employed as well as those actually employed, always enumerates the latter and makes the distinction clear. (2) It is the actual use of the woods as swine-pastures that is reflected in the swine-rents which are reported, instead of swine totals, in some counties. (3) The scale of things agrees fairly well in general with that of the swine-rent counties, if the rent is assumed to have been about a tenth. (4) If the figures only represented possibilities, the absence of all reference to the potentialities of the woods as sources of timber would be strange. (5) Actual exploitation is suggested by the form of some entries: e.g. Sawbridgeworth, i, f. 139*b* ('Silva ccc porc' et de reddita earum iiii sol'), Hendon, f. 128*b* ('Silva mille porc' et x sol'). Maitland, though he thought that many woods would be understocked, considered that 'this mode of reckoning the capacity of woodland would only occur to men who were accustomed to see large herds' (*Domesday Book and Beyond*, p. 443 n. 1). The ninth-century ealdorman Alfred, whose property lay largely on the north downs in Surrey and Kent, bequeathed 2,000 swine to his wife and daughter: F. Harmer, *English Historical Documents*, pp. 13, 47.

for the numbers of the demesne swine never approach the magnitude of the swine-unit figures for the larger woods. At Waltham in Essex the demesne herd only numbered 40, though the
manor included wood for 2,200 pigs, besides wood for 182 pigs
on the lands of the sokemen. Thorpe-next-Norwich had wood
for 1,200 pigs, but there were only 13 on demesne. East Bergholt
in Suffolk, with wood for a thousand, had a demesne stock of 29.
And though we have no means of applying this test to the great
beech-woods of the Chilterns, the Ely Inquest does tell us that
there were only 60 demesne pigs at Hatfield, where there was
wood for 2,000.[1] Moreover the evidence of the Exon. Domesday
justifies a similar conclusion with regard to pig-farming in
Devonshire. Like the Little Domesday, this precious text has
preserved the statistics of demesne stock which the scribes of the
Great Domesday omitted, and though the woods of the south-
western counties which it covers are not described in swine-
units and it is therefore impossible to compare the numbers of
the demesne swine with those of the herds which the woods were
reckoned to sustain, everything suggests that, in Devon at least,
the demesnes played a minor part in this branch of stock-farming. The numbers of the demesne swine are usually quite small.
Only six manors in the whole of Devon had a demesne herd
exceeding 30.[2] That of Otterton, which was the largest of all,
numbered 60. Yet it is certain that extensive pig-farming was
practised in this county, for no less than 366 *porcarii* are distinguished as such from the rest of the rural population, and
there were four manors where the annual swine-rents due from
a group of them amounted to a hundred pigs or more.[3] In these

[1] Dd. ii, ff. 15*b*, 138, 287; I.C.C., p. 125. The Waltham figures are for the
Bishop of Durham's manor. In places with comparatively little glandiferous wood,
demesne pig-farming might be predominant. At Acton in Suffolk, for example,
there was wood for 40 swine and a demesne herd of 160—the largest in the county;
and Belchamp Walker in Essex with wood for 20 can show a hundred on demesne.
Dd. ii, ff. 416, 77. In Cambridgeshire, where the swine-bearing woods were much
smaller, the demesne swine tended to be relatively more important than they were,
as a rule, in the other counties; but there were only 43 on Aubrey de Vere's
manor at Camps which comprised wood for 500: I.C.C., p. 29. The total number
of demesne swine recorded in the three counties of Norfolk, Suffolk, and Essex
taken together is 22 per cent. of the number for which there is said to be wood.
For the totals of woodland swine-units I am indebted to Professor Darby.

[2] Exon., pp. 85 (*Hertitona* = Hartland), 107 (Crediton), 177 (Otterton), 192
(Bratton Fleming or Bratton Clovelly?), 266 (*Dondritona* = Dunterton), 390
(Buckland).

[3] Exon., pp. 107 (Crediton), 108 (Tawton), 324 (Bampton), 353 (Torrington).
Except at Bampton these rents are specifically stated to be paid *per annum*.

rent-paying *porcarii* one can hardly fail to recognize the fellows of the gafol-paying swine-herd who figures in the *Rectitudines*. Sharply distinguished from the serf swine-herd who kept the 'in-herd', the gafol-paying swine-herd is there described as paying (on many estates) an annual due of 10 old pigs and 5 young ones and as retaining for himself any others he might breed.[1] The rents of the Devon *porcarii* were, however, lower than this; and though it may well be that some individuals of the class acted as herdsmen for the villagers, as Liebermann conjectured to have been the case with the *gafolswane* of the *Rectitudines*, there can be little doubt that many of them were independent farmers primarily devoted to the breeding and rearing of pigs.[2] They often occur in groups, and in 13 places the group included from 10 to 30 individuals. At Chittlehampton, where there were 22, they formed a large majority of the enumerated inhabitants.[3] There were similar groups in Somerset and Wiltshire, the only other counties in which any considerable number of persons are assigned to this class. All the 87 *porcarii* recorded in Wiltshire, and 52 out of the total of 84 or 85 recorded in Somerset, belonged to such groups.[4] It is impossible to suppose that in these cases we have to do with mere village herdsmen appointed to look after the pigs of the ordinary peasants.

The question inevitably arises whether the prominence of *porcarii* in the Domesday survey of these three south-western counties reflects an actual peculiarity in the regional economy

---

[1] Liebermann, *Gesetze*, i. 448–9.

[2] In 21 cases, involving 104 *porcarii*, the rents are not stated; and at Ottery St. Mary and Kenton money rents were due. The rents of the remaining 253 *porcarii* averaged scarcely more than 5 pigs per man, but at Coldridge 3 of them paid a total of 50 (Dd. i, f. 102b). Of the 6 isolated individuals whose rents are given, 4 paid 10 pigs each, one 6, and one 5: the corresponding figures for Somerset *porcarii* are 12 (2 cases), 10 (2 cases), and 5 (1 case). For Liebermann's suggestion see *Gesetze*, ii. 645.

[3] Exon., p. 448; Dd. i, f. 118. Besides the *porcarii* there were 7 *villani* and 8 *servi*.

[4] In the case of Devon and Somerset the figures in the text are considerably larger than those given by Ellis. He overlooked some that are recorded in Domesday Book and took no account of those that are recorded only in the Exon. text, of whom there were, according to my reckoning, 70 in Devon and 28 in Somerset. The omission of so many by the scribes of the Exchequer text is understandable if one remembers that they were deliberately omitting the livestock figures and that a misreading of *porcarii* as *porci* is only too easy: I have had to omit from my figures *ii porc'* recorded at Paorda (Exon., p. 297) because it is uncertain whether they were swine or swine-herds. It follows that in Wiltshire, where we have only the Domesday figures, the *porcarii* may well have exceeded 87. That there was a good deal of pig-farming in this county is suggested by the fact that an annual render of 130 swine and 32 'bacons' was due to the sheriff: Dd. i, f. 69.

or is merely due to idiosyncrasy in the terminology employed by
the Domesday commissioners for this part of England. It would
certainly be rash to assume that there were no pig-farmers
similar to the *porcarii* of Devon among the men who owed swine-
rents in the Weald, or among those whose pigs wandered about
the beech-woods of the Chiltern hills; but on the whole it seems
probable that it was because of a real difference in conditions
that a different classification was adopted in the west, and that
actual specialization in this branch of stock-farming was commoner and more noticeable in Devon, and to a less degree in
Wiltshire and Somerset, than it was in other swine-feeding
regions. The alternative hypothesis is less acceptable for two reasons. In the first place no *porcarii* appear to be recorded in Cornwall or Dorset, though both these counties are included, or in the
case of Dorset partly included, in the area covered by the Exon.
Domesday. Secondly, outside that area (and apart from Wiltshire which is usually thought to have been included in the same
Domesday circuit) we find a few persons, but only a few, who
are described as *porcarii* and appear to be of the same type as
those of Devon. At Hanley Castle, now in Worcestershire, there
were 6 who owed a render of 60 pigs.[1] At Forthampton on
the border of Worcestershire and Gloucestershire there were 4
owing a render of 35 pigs.[2] A Herefordshire entry tells of a half-
hide of land which a certain *porcarius* had held in the time of
King Edward.[3] This last case perhaps points to a combination
of arable farming with pig-breeding; and the Hanley *porcarii*
evidently practised such mixed farming on a considerable
scale, for they possessed four whole plough-teams. They must
have been men of some substance and must have possessed
fairly large herds of swine to justify their being distinguished
by a classification which emphasizes this aspect of their
affairs.[4]

Both at Hanley and at Forthampton there were woods which
appear to have been extensive. But though the association of

[1] Dd. i, f. 180b.
[2] Ibid. At Minchinhampton in Gloucestershire 2 *porcarii* rendering 20 pigs are
recorded in the early twelfth-century survey of that manor: Bibl. Nat. MS. lat.
5650, f. 27v. There is a clear distinction between these and the *porcarius* who held
a virgate *per servicium suum* at Felsted in Essex, where there was a demesne herd of
200 pigs: ibid., f. 26v.
[3] Ibid., f. 179b.
[4] The four *porcarii* of Forthampton had one plough between them.

pig-rearing with woodland is an outstanding fact in the economic geography of Domesday England, it would be wrong to overlook the evidence which points to the use of ordinary pasture for this purpose—perhaps in many cases as a seasonal alternative to the use of the woods. As we have seen, 'herbage' as well as 'pannage' was a source of swine-rent on certain manors in Sussex and Surrey. It is remarkable, too, that in Somerset and Devon some of the larger groups of *porcarii* are to be found in places with more pasture than woodland, and that at North Perrott, in the former county, where there were twenty *porcarii* and 'two leagues' of pasture, no wood at all is mentioned in either of the Domesday texts.[1] Yet no certain conclusion can be based upon such evidence, for the total amount of wood and pasture recorded is in some cases so obviously inadequate that the land utilized by the *porcarii*, whatever its nature, cannot have been included in the description.[2] The name of Swindon in Wiltshire perhaps originated in the use of downland pasturage for pig-feeding, but one cannot be sure, for in place-names of this type, as Ekwall observes, 'it is generally impossible to decide whether wild or domestic swine are referred to'.[3]

Sheep were no doubt to be found almost everywhere. The outfit of the typical *gebur*, as described in the *Rectitudines*, includes half-a-dozen sheep, and the payment of a young sheep or 2*d.* is mentioned as one of the obligations he will owe to his lord, while in the section of the same tract which is devoted to the duties of the reeve, and is commonly known as the *Gerefa*, sheep-shearing and the setting-up of sheep-hurdles appear among the tasks that have to be performed in the summer months.[4]

---

[1] Dd. i, f. 86: cf. Exon., p. 80, which gives the additional information that the North Perrott *porcarii* paid 100*s.* a year. On Odo fitz Gamelin's manor at Torrington, where there were 25 *porcarii* paying 110 pigs as rent, the pasture is described as 2 leagues long by 1 league broad and the wood as 300 acres: Dd. i, f. 116*b*. At Taunton, where there were 17 *porcarii*, we are told that the pasture was 2 leagues long by 1 league broad and the wood 1 league each way: ibid., f. 87*b*.

[2] At Tawton in Devon where 22 *porcarii* paid a rent of 100 pigs, only 100 acres of pasture and 12 acres of *silva minuta* are recorded, while Paignton, with a swine-rent of 50, is credited with only 40 acres of pasture and 41 acres of wood: Dd. i, ff. 101*b*, 102.

[3] *Oxford Dictionary of English Place-Names* (2nd ed.), p. 435 *sub* O.E. *swin*. At Lambourn in the Berkshire downs, less than 12 miles from Swindon the priest had free pasture for 40 pigs 'in wood and open country'—*on wude on feolde*—(Robertson, *A. S. Charters*, appendix i, No. v, a document witnessed by a Domesday tenant).

[4] R.S.P. 4 (1, 3); *Gerefa* 9 (Liebermann, *Gesetze*, i. 446, 447, 454). But the reference to a vineyard shows that the allusions of the *Gerefa* are not limited to things of common occurrence.

Throughout both the regions for which the Domesday census of demesne livestock has survived—virtually four contiguous eastern counties and a similar block of four counties in the south-west—it is unusual to find a demesne without sheep except in cases where no livestock at all are recorded besides the ploughing-oxen.[1] Yet some districts were especially devoted to this branch of farming. Round's remark that 'sheep are associated with marshlands' is applicable to more than one part of the country. In Essex pasture for sheep is frequently mentioned in Domesday Book in just the same way as woodland for swine; but the villages to which these sheep-pastures are assigned lay in 'a belt parallel with the coast', and it is clear that the pastures in question consisted for the most part of coastal marshes and, in the case of villages situated a few miles inland, formed detached portions of the manors to which they belonged, like the woodland denes of Kent and Sussex.[2] Some of the largest sheep-bearing marshes in the county lay between the estuaries of the Blackwater and Crouch, where the map today is dotted to the seaward side of the parochial centres with minor place-names ending in 'wick'.[3] Southminster, which is one of these centres, is credited in Domesday with pasture for as many as 1,300 sheep; but as a rule the numbers associated with the Essex sheep-walks are smaller than those of the woodland swine-units of this and other heavily wooded counties, and a comparison between them and the demesne flocks suggests that a much larger proportion of the sheep-rearing was carried on as a branch of demesne farming than was the case with the pigs. At Southminster the demesne flock numbered 696; at Tillingham, its near neighbour, there was pasture for 400 sheep and a demesne flock of 340; and at

[1] Of the counties in question (Norfolk, Suffolk, Essex, Cambridgeshire, Somerset, Devon, Cornwall, Dorset) the returns are incomplete for Cambridgeshire and Dorset. Outside these counties, such fragments of the census as are preserved exhibit the same characteristic. Sheep are mentioned among the demesne stock at Sutton, which is the one Wiltshire manor included in the Exon. Domesday (p. 41), and at Haddam, Hatfield, and Kelshall (*Chyllesella*) in Hertfordshire and Spaldwick, Colne, Bluntesham, and Somersham in Huntingdonshire, these being the only places in those counties for which information is supplied by the Ely Inquest (I.C.C., ed. Hamilton, pp. 124–5, 166–7). There was a flock of sheep, too, on the unnamed estate in the hundred of Hertford which Humphrey de Anslevill held of Eudo Dapifer and an *ovile* of 662 sheep at Eynesbury in Huntingdonshire (Dd i, ff. 139, 206*b*).

[2] Round, *V.C.H. Essex*, i. 369–73; Darby, *Eastern England*, pp. 241–4, with maps which should be compared with the one for demesne sheep on p. 257 and with that for woodland on p. 238.

[3] For the sense of the term 'wick' in Essex see Round, op. cit., pp. 372–3.

several places in the county the numbers of the demesne sheep exactly equal those for which there is said to be pasture.[1] Equality between the numbers is also found in Norfolk on a manor held by one Aldit at Wells-next-the-Sea, and they had formerly been equal on one of the manors at Wheatacre, but on the other hand, at Houghton St. Giles in this county, no demesne flock is recorded though there was pasture for a thousand sheep.[2] Except in Essex, however, references to sheep-pasture are rare and the Domesday evidence is mostly limited to the records of demesne sheep and the counties for which such records have survived. On or near the Norfolk coast a considerable development of this branch of farming is discernible both in the neighbourhood of the Wash and, to a less extent, in the region between the Broads and the Waveney. In the latter area, Halvergate, a village separated from Breydon Water by the Halvergate Marshes, is credited with 700 sheep for which rent was received, in addition to a demesne flock of 260; and its near neighbours Tunstall and Cantley possessed flocks of 318 and 400 respectively.[3] On the edge of the Wash, west of Wells, there were flocks of 600 or a little more at Heacham, at Brancaster, at one of the Burnhams and apparently at Dersingham, while half a dozen other places had flocks ranging from 300 to 520, and, in the fenland between King's Lynn and Wisbech, Terrington possessed 515 and West Walton no less than 2,100.[4] Arable farming indeed played a comparatively insignificant part in the economy of some of the manors in this area. Terrington, Burnham apart from its berewicks, and the Ely Abbey manor at West Walton (to which 1,300 of the West Walton sheep belonged) had each more than a hundred sheep to a plough as compared with an average for the whole of Norfolk of little more than nine. It can hardly be doubted that there were similar developments of sheep-farming in the geographically similar fens of south Lincolnshire, though the Little Domesday with its statistics of livestock is here no longer available and the only positive evidence is of much later date—in particular a record of c. 1160 which informs us that Crowland Abbey had then over 2,000

[1] Dd. ii, ff. 10, 13, and, for equality between the numbers, ff. 43, 43b, 77b (Thundersley, Hockley, Dovercourt). At West Thurrock, where there was pasture for 500, the demesne flock numbered 550: ibid., f. 63.

[2] Ibid., ff. 271, 250, 113 cited Darby, op. cit., p. 131.

[3] Ibid., ff. 128b–129, 239b, 262, 268b, 123.

[4] Ibid., ff. 163, 215b, 128, 256, 206b, 251b, 160b, 213.

sheep, besides lambs, at Monklode and nearly as many at Langtoft.[1]

Sheep-farming on a large scale was far from being confined to salt-marsh and fen. On or adjoining the East Anglian 'Breckland' and extending into the upland region of Cambridgeshire, there was a remarkable series of manors with large demesne flocks. Methwold in Norfolk had 800 sheep in 1086; Santon Downham, just over the Suffolk border, had 900; and farther to the south we find Eriswell with 800, *Cocklesworda* (an unidentified berewick of Eriswell) with 880, Mildenhall with 1,000, Icklingham with three flocks containing 934 between them, and *Deselinga* (which is represented today by Desning Hall in Gazeley) with a flock of 960, while the series is continued in Cambridgeshire by the flocks of Wood Ditton (520), Carlton (630), Weston Coville (765), and West Wratting (767).[2] At most of these places the ratio of demesne sheep to total ploughs was high, reaching a hundred or more per plough at Eriswell, Santon Downham, and Wood Ditton. But adjacent fenland may have been utilized for the grazing of some of these sheep, as a certain amount of such land is included within some of the Breckland parishes in Suffolk and, among these, Mildenhall, which had more sheep than any other in 1086, has given its name to a large stretch of fen.

For extensive sheep-farming on upland pastures in the west of England we have unequivocal evidence. In Dorset, though the demesne flocks recorded in the Exon. Domesday at Abbotsbury (600) and at Little Bredy (550) may well have got part of their sustenance from coastal marshes, and one cannot dismiss that possibility in regard to the 900 sheep which it assigns to the Isle of Portland, the Cranborne flock of 1,037 and the Ashmore flock of 826 must have been downland sheep, and it is worthy of note that at both these places there were more than a hundred of them to each plough.[3] In Somerset there was some farming of the same sort on parts of the Mendips.

[1] M. Wretts-Smith in *Journal of Economic and Business History*, iv (Nov. 1931), 182.

[2] Dd. ii, ff. 136, 359, 402b, 403, 288b, 289, 416, 434, 390; I.C.C., pp. 10–11, 20–24.

[3] Exon., pp. 37, 35, 27, 30. The ratio of sheep to ploughs was markedly lower at Abbotsbury, Little Bredy, and Portland. At Cranborne and Ashmore the ploughs were as many as those stated to be sufficient for the land. The largest demesne flock recorded in Dorset was one of 1,600 belonging to Puddletown, the *Piretone* of Domesday (Exon., p. 26), but as this manor had a distant member in the Isle of Purbeck one cannot say where the sheep were kept. For the identification with Puddletown I am indebted to Dr. W. G. Hoskins.

To the south-east of the range, the demesnes of Doulting, Shepton Mallet, Charlton, Croscombe, and Pilton, which are near neighbours to one another, carried a total of 1,760 sheep, with the number of sheep per plough varying from 25 at Pilton and Croscombe to 100 at Shepton and 106 at Charlton.[1] On the northern side of the hills, Chewton Mendip had a flock of 800.[2] And outside the region for which the Exon. Domesday supplies statistics, we have, for the early part of the twelfth century, some information about certain manors in Wiltshire and Gloucestershire. According to the survey of the Glastonbury Abbey estates, which was drawn up by Hilbert the Precentor in or about the year 1171 but records their condition in the time of Henry I, the abbey in that reign possessed a demesne flock of a thousand sheep at Monkton Deverill which lies high up on the Wiltshire plateau, one of 700 at Idmiston on the eastern edge of Salisbury Plain, and one of 2,500 at Damerham, which is only a few miles distant from Cranborne.[3] And in the southern Cotswolds the early twelfth-century survey of the English lands of the Abbaye aux Dames at Caen reveals a flock of 1,012 (including lambs) at Avening and another of 467 at Minchinhampton.[4]

Compared with the factors already discussed, other causes of variety in the direction and balance of economic activities were, it would seem, of minor importance. In some places an exceptional amount of meadows may have put an emphasis upon cow-keeping and made the cow a competitor with the ewe and the goat as a source of milk and cheese. Both in the Vale of the White Horse and beside the upper reaches of the Thames a

---

[1] Exon., pp. 153–5.

[2] Ibid., p. 106. But Chewton had 28 ploughs. The large numbers of sheep recorded at Keynsham and Taunton are deceptive, for these were huge complexes with a great many ploughs. On the other hand, the ratio of sheep to ploughs was high on some small manors. Wilmington in Priston, which lies between the Mendips and Bath, had 3 ploughs and a flock of 300: Exon., p. 171.

[3] Trin. Coll. Camb. MS. R. 3. 33, f. 116v. Damerham was transferred from Wiltshire to Hampshire in modern times.

[4] Bibl. Nat. MS. lat. 5650, ff. 29v, 27v–28. There seems to be no justification for the statement that 'the nuns had flocks numbering 1,700 grazing on Minchinhampton common': E. Power, *The Wool Trade in English Medieval History* (1941), p. 33. That there were large flocks elsewhere in the Cotswolds is likely enough; but I cannot agree with Dr. W. G. Hoskins in thinking that place-names incorporating the word 'sheep' point to any special development of sheep-farming either in this or other districts (see W. G. Hoskins, *The Making of the English Landscape*, 1955, p. 80). Such names occur in twenty-six counties; and in Oxfordshire we have Gosford (the goose-ford), Swinford (the swine-ford), and Oxford itself, within a few miles of Shipton-on-Cherwell and of one another.

number of Berkshire villages had meadows containing from 100 to over 300 acres; and in the former district Domesday reveals the existence of a *vaccaria* or dairy-farm of cows at Sparsholt, where the meadows comprised a total area of 366 acres.[1] That there was a notable development of cheese-production on these Berkshire meadow-lands cannot be doubted. From Shellingford, 4 miles to the north of Sparsholt, the abbey of Abingdon received dues of cheese which were reckoned in 1086 to be worth £4. 16s. 8d. or more than half the total value of the demesne manor; and a generation later the Abingdon Chronicle has a good deal to say about various Berkshire 'wicks' and the cheese to be obtained from them. But it seems to associate these 'wicks' with sheep and not cows.[2] In any case it is rare to find a *vaccaria* mentioned in Domesday, and meadow-land was, in general, scarce.[3] Moreover cows are seldom distinguished from other *animalia ociosa* in the livestock statistics and appear in very small herds where they are specifically mentioned, the largest number recorded at any one place throughout the whole area covered by the Exon. Domesday being thirteen at *Stafort* in Dorset.[4] Even the unspecified *animalia* are not usually very numerous—though there were a hundred on the large manor of *Tauetona* (? South Tawton) in Devon—and on the whole one can hardly suppose that the subject of cow-keeping in Domesday England would have remained in such obscurity if considerable cow-dairies had been at all common and cows had been much valued for their milk as well as for the breeding of plough-oxen.[5]

---

[1] Round, *V.C.H. Berks.* i (1906), 307; Dd. i, ff. 57, 57*b*, 59, 63.

[2] See the references in Round, op. cit., p. 306 nn. 6 and 7. Perhaps both cows-milk and ewes-milk were used: on several Glastonbury Abbey manors in the thirteenth century, 12 cows and 50 *oves matrices* appear to have been the standard stock of the *wikarii* or tenants of a *wika*: see Maitland, *Domesday Book and Beyond*, p. 115 n. 1.

[3] At Langwith near York a vaccary which is not mentioned in Domesday is known to have been in existence in the time of Count Alan Rufus who died in 1089: Clay, *Early Yorkshire Charters*, iv, No. 13, cf. p. 86. In some counties meadow is not uncommonly described as sufficient for the plough-beasts, or even for a smaller number of them than were in fact employed: see G. H. Fowler, *Bedfordshire in 1086* (Beds. Hist. Rec. Soc., 1922), p. 62; cf. Darby, *Eastern England*, p. 300. The great extent of meadow which Domesday attributes to some places in Lincolnshire—reaching 700 or 800 acres in certain cases—is a great puzzle and creates a suspicion that in this county land was classed as meadow which would not have been entered as such in other counties.

[4] Exon., p. 49. At Winscombe in Somerset (ibid., p. 148) there were eight and not sixteen as stated by Round: *V.C.H. Somerset* i. 424.

[5] Cows may occasionally have been included in the plough-teams: at Penbury in Gloucestershire, the early twelfth-century Caen survey describes 22 oxen and

There were places here and there in which horse-breeding was a feature in the economy. The Conqueror granted Westminster Abbey the tithe on a stud of 200 horses at an unidentified place in Surrey, and it seems likely that these were the 'forest mares of the King' which Domesday mentions in the hundred of Kingston.[1] In Suffolk, 40 *equae silvaticae* are recorded at Long Melford and 31 at Mildenhall.[2] There were 60 *equae indomitae* at Long Ashton in Somerset, and half a dozen other places in that county had 20 or more.[3] The total numbers recorded are larger in Somerset and Cornwall than in any other county for which figures are available; but Devon is not far behind with particularly large groups at Brendon (104) and at Lynton (72). Those at Brendon are described as *equae indomitae*, those at Lynton as *equae silvestres* but there can be little doubt that they were all alike 'Exmoor ponies'.[4] One cannot suppose, of course, that manors in which horse-breeding was especially developed were limited to the area for which Domesday livestock figures are available or to places where it casually alludes to the matter; and indeed it is known that at Burton-on-Trent the abbey possessed a 'haraz' or stud-farm which contained 70 horses, including the foals, in the time of Abbot Nigel (1094–1114).[5] Yet all this seems to have been a matter of sporadic local developments: and in any case the sort of horse-breeding that is suggested by the term 'forest-mares' would not, one imagines, call for much diversion of human labour from normal agricultural tasks. And though there were no doubt many districts in which hunting interests were important and involved the peasantry in special obligations such as the maintenance of 'deer-hedges',

2 cows as forming 3 plough-teams and records 6 other cows *cum vitulis* and 4 yearling calves: Bibl. Nat. MS. lat. 5650, f. 27. In the early Peterborough surveys, cows are commonly recorded, but the numbers are small—the largest being 17 plus 2 bulls and 4 calves at Eye, a fenland vill in the soke of Peterborough: *Chron. Petr.* (Camden Soc., 1849), p. 165. The earlier of the Burton Abbey surveys mentions somewhat larger herds on four manors, mostly near the abbey, though the largest was 16 miles away at Leigh, where there were 33 (not 23) cows, 2 bulls, and 11 calves: *Hist. Collections for Staffs.* (for 1916), pp. 212, 215, 219, 226; cf. p. 287.

[1] Davis, *Regesta*, No. 166 (xx); Dd. i, f. 36.

[2] Dd. ii, ff. 359, 288*b*.   [3] Exon., p. 134.

[4] Ibid., pp. 316, 374. Both terms are common in the Exon. Domesday and perhaps in some cases a distinction was intended. The county totals for both are, accord ng to my reckoning, Somerset 391, Cornwall 388, Devon 321; but it is not always clear whether the reference is to mares or horses.

[5] *Hist. Collections for Staffs.*, 1916, p. 212 (Survey B). Perhaps we should also understand that there were 95 mares at Whiston (ibid., p. 228), but the text is doubtful at this point.

or the erection of a temporary hunting-lodge, these occasional duties can have done little to alter the ordinary tenor of village life.[1] Again, a vineyard, where there was one, would call for a good deal of labour of a most unusual character, but vineyards were so rare that their influence is negligible.[2]

The lives of men cannot have been as much affected by minor differences in the direction and mode of economic activity as by differences in the form of their settlements. The distinction between settlements in nucleated villages and those which consisted of scattered hamlets or isolated farmsteads can no longer be regarded as marking the contrasted habits of Germanic and Celtic peoples, but there is no denying its sociological importance, since the character of social relations must have varied a good deal with the degree to which human dwellings were concentrated or dispersed. It is, however, impossible to determine with any precision the geographical distribution of the various forms of settlement in Domesday England. Some districts are indeed revealed as districts in which hamlets and scattered farmsteads were very common; but even in Devon, where Domesday records an abundance of tiny settlements and the existence of some which it fails to mention is attested by Saxon charters, there is reason for thinking that 'compact villages of considerable size' were to be found in various parts of the county.[3] Moreover it would be quite unsafe to assume that the compact or 'nucleated' village was the only form of settlement in regions where Domesday gives no hint of the existence of dependent hamlets, for, as we have seen, large manors are often described in composite entries which fail to reveal the nature of their component parts.[4] Detailed topographical investigation,

[1] For the duty of maintaining the 'deer-hedge' see R.S.P. *passim*; for that of assisting in 'drives' (*stabilitio venationis*) see Dd. i, f. 56*b*; cf. ff. 179, 269*b*. Neilson notes a wealden obligation to erect a '*sumerhus*' (temp. Will. I?), which is perhaps a southern parallel to that of making a hunting-lodge (*aula episcopi in foresta*) which was incumbent upon the *villani* of 'Auklandshire' a century later (*Cartulary of Bilsington*, Introduction, pp. 11, 15; *Bolden Buke* (Surtees Soc., 1852), p. 26).

[2] Darby reckons that there are 38 references to vineyards in Domesday (*Hist. Geography of England*, 1936, p. 196 n. 1). They were dispersed among 13 counties, but 9 of them were in Essex, 5 in Middlesex, 4 in Suffolk and in Wiltshire. Several are described as new (Dd. i, ff. 128, 129, 138*b*, 175*b*) or as not yet fully bearing (Dd. ii, ff. 73*b*, 74, 77). Among those whose measure is given the largest seems to be one of 12 'arpents' (at most perhaps 15 acres) at Bisham in Berkshire (Dd. i, f. 60*b*): that at Lacock in Wiltshire was only half an acre (f. 69*b*).

[3] W. G. Hoskins and H. P. R. Finberg, *Devonshire Studies* (1952), pp. 289 et seq.

[4] With reference to such Domesday descriptions Maitland judged that 'when

combined with a critical study of later evidence, will perhaps eventually lessen the obscurity in which these matters are shrouded; but there must always be some doubt about the antiquity of places that are not actually named either in Domesday Book or in charters of contemporary or earlier date; and the process of arguing from the known to the unknown is hampered as regards this problem by the fact that a hamlet might grow into a substantial village, or decay overtake a village, without any record surviving of the time or manner of the transformation.[1] In the present state of knowledge, all generalization must be tentative and vague. The Domesday evidence affords little precise guidance; but it is on the whole compatible with the conclusions which are suggested as probable by the facts of physical geography. In the bleak and narrow valleys of the Highland Zone, at least in the north, small settlements must have tended to preponderate. In the heart of woodland areas, the clearances, in many cases, can hardly have got beyond an initial stage in which they were insufficient to maintain more than a tiny group of families. In marshland regions, much would turn upon the extent of the patches of dry ground, and where these were very small, the individual settlements would almost necessarily be limited to isolated homesteads or hamlets of very modest dimensions. It can scarcely be doubted, moreover, that the universal need for water made the level of the water-table an important factor and that, even in districts where steep and closely folded hills might seem to make for dispersal, easy access to a river would tilt the balance in favour of village aggregations if the alternative would involve the necessity of

more than five-and-twenty team-lands or thereabouts are assigned to a single place, we shall generally find reason to believe that what is being described is not a single vill': *Domesday Book and Beyond*, p. 17 n. 1.

[1] If Ekwall's interpretation of the place-name element *stoc* is accepted, evidence for the early transformation of dependent, and probably only seasonal, settlements is to be found in the early appearance of villages with names embodying that word, for in Ekwall's view 'it is probable that in their origin the *stocs* were outlying pastures, where the cattle were kept during part of the year': *Studies on English Place-Names* (Stockholm, 1936), pp. 39, 42. Perhaps most of our Suttons, Nortons, Westons, and Astons, whose names imply relation to some other place, were originally hamlet or farmstead members of discrete vills. On the other hand, where parishes bearing Old English names contain hamlets with names ending in 'thorpe' (as often in Yorkshire), this seems to point to a creation of dependent members within the territory of a compact vill as a result of Danish colonization. A good example from the North Riding is Terrington with its hamlets Ganthorpe, Mowthorpe, and Wigganthorpe, all mentioned in Domesday.

sinking wells of considerable depth. Yet it is one thing to recognize the constraining influence of physical obstacles which
cannot readily be surmounted in an age of simple techniques
and quite another to suppose that the shape of the settlements was always appropriate to the nature of the terrain. A
geographical fatalism which rests upon the assumption that
imperfect skill is consistently applied with perfect intelligence
stands self-condemned. Ignorance, prejudice, 'historical' factors
connected with the local circumstances of land-ownership,
accidents of various kinds, and mere inertia, must all be allowed
a part in determining both the form of settlement and the direction of economic activity in individual cases. And, though the
exaggerated theories of Meitzen and his school must be repudiated, the traditions of different peoples may still have counted
for something both in the Celtic west and in the regions of
Scandinavian colonization.[1]

The variety that marked the landscape of Domesday England
can hardly be described without some risk that its nature will be
misunderstood. For though the differences between place and
place, and between one district and another, were indeed manifold, their range was restricted. In many important matters
there was a large measure of uniformity.

The contrast between life in hamlets or solitary farmsteads
and life in the nucleated villages was reduced by the general
prevalence of a social organization which had the village for its
norm. Those whose dwelling-places were scattered appear to
have been usually associated for certain purposes in groups
similar to that of the compact village, so that even where very
small settlements predominated, it would be truer to speak of
a system of dispersed villages than of a system of hamlets. In
ordinances of tenth-century date it seems to be assumed that all
men belong to a village (*villa* or *tunscipe*); a division of the
country into counties, hundreds (or wapentakes), and vills was
'the geographical basis' of the Domesday survey; and in the later
Middle Ages 'the hamlet seems always to have lain within the

---

[1] On all this see Maitland, *Domesday Book and Beyond*, pp. 9–16; Vinogradoff,
English Society, pp. 264–73; W. G. Hoskins in Hoskins and Finberg, *Devonshire
Studies*, pp. 289–333. The importance of the water-table as a determinant of settlement forms is strongly emphasized by G. Des Marez (*Le Problème de la colonisation
franque et du régime agraire en Belgique*, Brussels, 1926); but he acknowledges that 'des
contingences historiques, seigneuriales, par exemple, ou militaires, peuvent avoir
contrarié l'application logique des lois de la géographie' (p. 188).

boundaries of a vill'.[1] In the apportionment of the geld it is normally the vill which is assessed in units of 5 hides or 6 carucates; and, if villages were in many cases combined to make up these units, the smaller settlements would of necessity be grouped in this way. Then the rule that every male over twelve years old must be in a 'tithing' for police purposes, if he is to enjoy the legal rights of a free man, drew men together whether their dwellings were isolated or not.[2] Ecclesiastical obligations, again, were similar for all men and linked them all with particular churches. And though neither the police group nor the ecclesiastical *parochia* was coincident with the vill, the pervasive influence of the village organization is apparent in the history of both, for village churches tended more and more to take the place of the old collegiate 'minsters', and in some parts of England the tithing appears in later days in a territorialized form and is either identified with the vill or treated as a subdivision of it.[3]

In agriculture we have to reckon with a general uniformity of certain basic conditions. This needs emphasis for two reasons. In the first place a description of local and regional variations, such as that attempted in the preceding pages, is of necessity lengthy, and just for that reason is liable to give the reader an exaggerated impression of their importance. Secondly, the evidence for variety in the matter of stock-farming depends to a great extent upon the statistics of demesne livestock provided by the Little Domesday and the Exon. Domesday. But it is almost certain that the economy of the demesnes was more varied than that of the peasant-holdings. The lord or *firmarius* who controlled the management of a number of demesnes could achieve a degree of specialization which was impossible for the peasant. On those which were adjacent to his places of residence special attention might be given to products whose bulk or perishable nature made their transport particularly difficult, while on distant manors, if conditions were favourable, the balance could be modified in favour of horse-breeding, wool-production, or

---

[1] III Edmund, 6; IV Edgar, 8; Maitland, *Domesday Book and Beyond*, p. 10; Pollock and Maitland, i. 562.

[2] II Cnut, 20. The tithing was not created by Cnut; the existence of the 'tithing-man', its official head, is taken for granted in Edgar's Ordinance of the Hundred, 2 and 4.

[3] On the territorial tithing see Pollock and Maitland, i. 569. The history of the village churches is discussed in the next chapter.

cheese-making. More than that. He might be entitled to carrying services from manorial tenants, so that the transport of produce, which is an essential prerequisite of agricultural specialization, would be as it were subsidized, with the result that a degree of specialization which transport costs would otherwise have rendered uneconomic—and which was uneconomic if judged by the ratio of effort to satisfaction that it involved—might for this reason be well worth while for him. Yet even on the demesne farms it is abundantly clear that tillage—which of course meant corn-growing—had almost everywhere an important place in the economy. And though it is not unlikely that particular branches of production were developed to a modest extent on some of the larger peasant holdings, and at least possible that it was by the sale of surplus produce, rather than from the earnings of members of their families as wage-labourers, that the peasants obtained the means of paying such money dues as they owed and of purchasing salt or any other necessaries that they were unable to produce for themselves, there can be no shadow of doubt that as a rule their little family farms were in all parts of the country primarily devoted to production for subsistence and closely resembled one another, because food and drink and clothing, and fodder for the plough-beasts, were the common needs of all. The villagers of the Conqueror's day, like their successors a few generations later, may well have received an occasional meal in return for their 'boonworks', and herrings from a distance, and perhaps cheese that had been made on some other manor of their lord, may have formed part of their diet when they were thus employed, while the clothing they wore and the implements they used may not improbably have been fashioned in part out of materials which were not strictly local products; but we may feel sure that, from one year's end to another, the bread and beer, the meat and eggs and cheese which sustained them, were almost entirely derived from grain that was grown, and from animals and hens that were reared, within the bounds of the village where they lived. A core of common agricultural practices directed to the attainment of these things was a prerequisite of the particular developments which distinguished one locality from another.

The 'normal village' is a conception closer to reality than that of the 'typical manor'. Yet very little is known about the nature of its organization. A village reeve (*tunesgerefa* or *tungravius*) is mentioned more than once in the Laws of Æthelred II as concerned with the enforcement of certain secular and ecclesiastical obligations, and in regard to the latter is associated with a priest and with the tithingmen (*decimales homines*), very much as priest and reeve were to be associated with six *villani* of each village in the Domesday Inquest, and as priest and reeve and four of the better villagers (*iiii de melioribus ville*) are described in the *Leges Henrici Primi* as competent to attend the shire-court as substitutes for the lord or his steward.[1] In Domesday Book local reeves are rarely mentioned and its Herefordshire section is quite exceptional in recording thirty-six. Yet entries which unmistakably reckon a reeve among the village population occur here and there in a good many counties and give one the impression that the existence of such an official was taken for granted. In some he is described as *prepositus villae*.[2] In some he is mentioned along with the priest.[3] In nearly every case (notwithstanding the lack of a definite article) it is made clear that we have to do with 'the' reeve and not merely with 'a' reeve, for, like the priest, he is almost invariably mentioned without the word *unus* which is generally employed in the case of *villani*, bordars, serfs, Frenchmen and radmen where an isolated member of any of these classes is recorded.[4] Entry after entry shows

---

[1] IV Æthelred, 3; VII Æthelred, 2(5); VII Æthelred (Anglo-Saxon), 2(3); *Leges Henrici Primi*, 7(7).

[2] Dd. i, ff. 30 (Guildford, Surrey); 133, 138*b* (Bayford, Stanstead Abbots, and Ware, Herts.); 149 (*Evreham* = Iver, Bucks.); 182 (Frome, Herefordshire); cf. f. 32 (*prefectus villae*, Battersea, Surrey).

[3] Ibid., ff. 167*b* (Quenington, Gloucestershire); 174 (Hanbury and Alvechurch, Worcestershire); 181*b*, 184*b*, 186, 187 (Holme Lacy, Weobley, Pyon, *Cuure* = Cowarne, and Wellington, Herefordshire); 253, 253*b*, 254 (Hodnet, Lydham, and *Catinton* = Chetton, Salop); also the three Hertfordshire cases cited in the previous note: cf. Robertson, *Anglo-Saxon Charters*, appendix i, No. v (Lambourn, Berks.).

[4] In the composite description of Leominster the reference to seven reeves is not surprising, though why there were two at Christleton in Cheshire is far from evident (Dd. i, f. 264). Perhaps it was because there were two there that the next entry employs the very exceptional term *unus prepositus* for the local reeve. That term also occurs in the entry relating to Bartestree, Herefordshire (f. 183), but on that little manor, apart from its berewick, the only other recorded inhabitants were three *servi*, so perhaps this *prepositus* was not an ordinary local reeve but like the one mentioned in connexion with Hindringham, Norfolk (*quidam prepositus Willelmi episcopi*, Dd. ii, f. 198*b*; cf. Desning, Suffolk, ibid., f. 390, and Freshwater, Isle of Wight, i, f. 53*b*). For examples of the usage described in the text see Mathon, now in Herefordshire (*presbiter et unus villanus et iij bordarii et prepositus*, i, f. 175*b*); Mansell, Herefordshire (*prepositus et ij francigenae et unus bordarius*, f. 184*b*); Bayford, Herts. (*Presbiter et prepositus hujus villae cum xxii villanis—Ibi ix cotarii et i servus*, f. 133); Holme Lacy, Herefordshire (*presbiter et prepositus et unus*

him associated with the plough-owning peasants. He is never classed with the serfs and in a few places there are indications that he was superior to the bordars and cottars.[1] At Sawbridgeworth in Hertfordshire, where the *villani* are described as holding either virgates or half-virgates, the reeve has half a hide; and both at Bromyard and at Cradley in Herefordshire he is mentioned as one of a group of manorial tenants who possess teams 'in demesne' and have 'men' or 'bordars' under them.[2] At Frome in the latter county it is the *prepositus villae* who holds the mill, seemingly for a rent of 32*d*.[3] Some scraps of additional information are available for the early part of the twelfth century. In one or other of the Burton Abbey surveys a reeve, who is clearly one of the peasants and in most cases holds two or more bovates, is mentioned in the description of eleven of the abbey's manors.[4] Some casual references to local reeves in the Liber Niger of Peterborough cast a little light upon their functions. We are told that the wives of the *bovarii* at Castor in Northamptonshire winnow the demesne corn 'when the reeve bids them'; that at Fiskerton in Lincolnshire the land of twelve full *villani* is waste 'quam praepositus ville adquietat de bursa sua et

francigena, f. 181*b*); Orleton, Herefordshire (*prepositus et unus radman*, f. 183*b*); cf. Aston, Cheshire (*i radman et i bordarius et i servus*, f. 266). It looks as if the tendency was to omit the word *unus* where only a single individual would be expected (e.g. *bedellus*, *vaccarius*, *daia*, *forestarius*, all at Bushley, Worcestershire, though under Herefordshire, f. 180*b*); and in the case of smiths Domesday wavers between *faber* and *unus faber*. But one must not expect a consistently followed principle, though with the *prepositus* it seems pretty clear.

[1] For example see Ware, Herts. ('Ibi xxxviii villani cum presbitero et preposito villae et cum iii francigenis et ii anglicis hominibus habent xxvi carucas et dimidiam et ibi sunt xxvii bordarii et xii cotarii et ix servi': Dd. i, f. 138*b*), cf. Aldenham and Stanstead, Herts.: i, ff. 135, 138*b*.

[2] Dd. i, f. 139*b* (Sawbridgeworth); cf. Northwick, Worcestershire, where the reeve and a radman are credited with 3 virgates each, while the holdings of the *villani* are not stated (f. 173*b*). For Bromyard see f. 182*b* ('De hoc manerio tenent iii milites episcopi ix hidas et unam virgatam et ii presbiteri i hidam et unus capellanus i hidam et iii virgatas et prepositus unam hidam et unus radman i hidam. In dominio habent xi carucas et dimidiam et homines eorum habent xx carucas. Unus eorum habet ii servos et iii acras prati'). For Cradley see f. 182 ('De hoc manerio ten' presbiter unam virgatam et dimidiam et prepositus dimidiam hidam et ii milites i hidam et unam virgatam et dimidiam et unus radman dimidiam hidam. Hi habent in dominio v carucas et bordarii eorum vi carucas').

[3] Ibid., f. 182. The sum = $\frac{1}{5}$ mark, or 2 'ores' of 16*d*.

[4] Op. cit., pp. 215 (Branston), 217 (Stretton), 221 (Wetmore), 229 (Mickleover), 232 (Littleover), 234 (Finderne), 237 (Willington), 238 (Stapenhill), 241 (Winshill), 245 (Appleby), 246 (Austrey). The case of Mickleover is puzzling, for Survey B (p. 231) describes three of the *censarii* as *prepositus*, though Survey A (p. 229) gives only one *prepositus* and he has two bovates *ad opus*.

locat prout melius poterit'; that similarly at *Esctona* there are two and a half vacant virgates 'quas praepositus locat pro iii solidis'.[1] Then a Suffolk charter which was issued between 1121 and 1148 reveals the reeves of Fornham, Chevington, and Saxham each acting as a rent-receiver on behalf of St. Edmunds Abbey, and in a charter of *c.* 1115 relating to some land at Downham in the same county *Frodo prepositus ville* appears as one of the witnesses.[2] Like Domesday Book these documents seem to take the reeve for granted and their evidence is especially noteworthy because the places with which they are concerned lie in parts of the country for which Domesday itself has little or nothing to say about local reeves.

Both the Saxon word *gerefa* and the Latin *praepositus* were employed for officials of many types and various ranks, and confusions and misunderstandings due to this fact are not easy to avoid. Yet there can be little doubt that the evidence cited in the last paragraph relates to officials who were concerned with the local affairs of a small community and, for the most part, only with such; and further that the form of rural organization in which important functions were discharged by a reeve of this sort was normal in Domesday England. It would be rash of course to assume that a grouping of manors under a single *praepositus*, such as obtained on the Ely estates, can in no case have meant their combination for all the purposes of reeveship; but an arrangement of that kind would obviously involve practical difficulties, and on the whole it seems likely that each place would normally have its own local reeve and that the Ely *praepositi* were like the bailiffs or serjeants of the thirteenth century who often supervised the administration of several manors while each of these had at the same time a resident reeve.[3] The question arises, however, whether the reeves whom we find in the villages of Norman England were actually reeves of the village or officials of the manor. The tract which describes the duties of the *gerefa* treats him unmistakably as the servant of a lord and as concerned with an estate of manorial character, and, though we are told that he must know the things that belong to a 'tun' and

---

[1] *Chron. Petroburg.* (Camden Soc., 1849), pp. 163, 164, 162.

[2] *Feudal Documents from the abbey of Bury St. Edmunds*, ed. Douglas, Charters Nos. 121, 174.

[3] N. Denholm-Young, *Seignorial Administration in England*, 1937, pp. 32, 156; H. S. Bennett, *Life on the English Manor*, 1937, pp. 162, 166. For the Ely arrangements see above, p. 207.

he is once referred to as the reeve of a 'ham' (*hames gerefa*), it has been held that both words in this context have the meaning of a lord's homestead or demesne farm rather than a village.[1] Then Domesday Book in a Gloucestershire entry refers to the reeves of two 'manors' (*horum ii maneriorum prepositi*) and in its description of Thorney in Suffolk states that the *prepositus hujus manerii* holds 26 acres in the king's soke.[2] We find, too, that between 1035 and 1044 a lady named Leofgifu bequeathed to 'Godric my reeve at Waldingfield' (in Suffolk) the 30 acres she had previously let to him, that some time between 1109 and 1131 the Bishop of Ely granted 3 virgates at Fen Ditton in Cambridgeshire 'Alurico preposito meo de Ditton' and that the witnesses to a grant of land at Brocklesby in Lincolnshire, which was made by a certain Gilbert, son of Nigel, between 1143 and 1147, include a man named Berewold 'qui eo tempore prepositus erat mee terre'.[3] And we remember that in the time of Bishop Gundulf one of the Rochester monks had been *praepositus* of Haddenham in Buckinghamshire and another *praepositus* of Freckenham in Suffolk; that Gundulf transferred the former to the manor of Aston in Gloucestershire and charged him with the duty of rendering thence a 'farm of eight days'; and that the latter had acted as receiver of the 'services and customs' of all the lands of Freckenham.[4] It is thus clear that the word *praepositus* could describe a manorial official who had charge of a single manor and whose position was really that of an official *firmarius*. Yet one cannot suppose that such was the case with all those *praepositi* who in Domesday Book and in the Burton Abbey surveys appear among the ordinary villagers and in possession of ordinary peasant holdings.[5] And after all, though the distinction

---

[1] Skeat took the words 'ðæs ðe to tune belimpd, ge on tune ge on dune' as referring to things 'that concern a homestead, both in the farmyard and on the down' and Liebermann renders them 'was zum Landgute gehört, sowohl im Dorfbezirk wie auf dem Hügel', while *hames gerefa* is 'reeve of a household' for Skeat, and 'Gutsamtmann' for Liebermann. See Cunningham, *Growth of English Industry and Commerce during the Early and Middle Ages* (4th ed.), pp. 573, 575; Liebermann, *Gesetze*, i. 453, 455; cf. C. M. Andrews, *The Old English Manor* (Baltimore, 1892), p. 131; and, for the various senses of 'ham' and 'tun', A. H. Smith, *English Place-Name Elements* (Eng. Place-Name Soc., 1956), pt. i, 226–31, pt. ii, pp. 188–98.

[2] Dd. i, f. 164 (Chedworth and Arlington); ii, f. 281b.

[3] D. Whitelock, *Anglo-Saxon Wills*, No. xxix; E. Miller, *Abbey and Bishopric of Ely*, p. 284 (appendix No. vii); Stenton, *Danelaw Charters*, No. 247, cf. pp. cvi–cvii.

[4] Above, pp. 157–8.

[5] Most of the Burton Abbey *praepositi* are described as holding their land *ad opus* or as owing week-work, while at Findern and Willington the more substantial peasants as well as the reeves owed money rents.

between a village head-man and a manorial official seems sharp and important in the eyes of a modern legal theorist, it would be rash to assume that it was consciously made in the minds either of the manorial lords or of the village folk in the eleventh century, or indeed that it was bound to have practical significance. In so far as the reeve was concerned with the observance of customary routines, the source of his authority might be undefined. The lord and the peasants may well have regarded him and his office somewhat differently, and not improbably their relations with him would in practice depend a good deal upon his economic position and his temper as an individual. One would like to know whether in a vill which comprised more than one manor there would usually be a separate reeve for each or one reeve for the whole village, but positive evidence for the Norman period has not been found, and even the discovery of cases revealing the latter condition would still leave it possible for a legal purist to speculate unprofitably whether they really implied a village reeveship or only a concentration of distinct offices in one man's hands. In general it is important to remember that a manorial stamp was given to the Domesday material when it was rearranged in Domesday Book, that our other sources of information are manorial in nature, and that the relations and obligations with which manorial documents are concerned do not necessarily constitute the most important factors in the lives and social circumstances of all the persons involved in them.[1]

Within a small community various functions are likely to be discharged by the same man and little occasion may arise for the delimitation of distinct offices. Yet the simplicity of conditions must not be over-rated. The eleventh-century *Rectitudines*, which refers to the beadle, the hayward and the woodward, is probably describing an ideally elaborated organization rather than one of common occurrence. But the beadle (*bedellus*) makes an occasional appearance in Domesday Book. Since there were 8

---

[1] Thus the description of certain people as 'riding-men' indicates the nature of the services they owed their lord, but does not tell us how they were mainly occupied. If I may illustrate the matter by a modern analogy, a parish magazine today may refer to the vicar, the churchwardens, and the members of the parochial church council, and will perhaps report the news that some member of the congregation has been elected a parish councillor. It will not tell us that only the vicar holds a paid, whole-time office, nor reveal the fact that the parish council and the parochial church council are wholly distinct bodies.

reeves and 8 beadles on the great Leominster estate in the time
of King Edward and 7 of each of these officials in 1086, and
since the beadle is mentioned immediately after the reeve in the
description of 5 places in Worcestershire, it seems likely that he
was in some way an assistant of the reeve, though at *Pevne* and
at Boddenham in Herefordshire only a beadle is recorded.[1] That
the beadle's primary function was one of summoning people to
fulfil their obligations—that he was in fact a sort of petty constable—is suggested by the connotation of the Old English word
bydel and by the duties which the *bedellus* of later centuries
appears to have performed in connexion with the manorial
court.[2] But it can hardly be supposed that an officer of this kind
was to be found in many English villages in 1086, for, apart
from a royal beadle (*quidam bedellus regis*) who was holding half
a virgate at Milton Ernest in Bedfordshire and another named
Alwin Coc who appears as tenant of a similar amount at Abington in Cambridgeshire, the fourteen beadles already mentioned
as belonging to eight places in Herefordshire and Worcestershire appear to be the only ones recorded in Domesday Book;
and it is perhaps significant that (except the two who are not
associated with a reeve) they all occur on royal manors.[3] On the
other hand, there is no reason for thinking that the institution
was in any way peculiar to these two counties, for all the entries
in question, except that relating to Bromsgrove, are included in
the Herefordshire section of Domesday and that section is unusually detailed in its occupational analysis of the population.[4]

[1] Dd. i, ff. 180, 172, 180b, 182, 184. The Worcestershire beadles were at Bromsgrove, Martley, Feckenham, Holloway (*Haloede*), and Bushley; but the last four
of these places were surveyed under Herefordshire.

[2] Liebermann, *Gesetze*, ii. 339 (sub Büttel); C. M. Andrews, op. cit., pp. 142–3;
H. S. Bennett, op. cit., pp. 178–82; G. C. Homans, *English Villagers of the Thirteenth
Century* (Harvard Univ. Press, 1942), p. 292.

[3] Dd. i, ff. 218b (Milton Ernest), 190 (Abington). That Alwin Coc was *bedellus
regis* is revealed by the I.C.C. (p. 61). Two named *bedelli* are recorded as former
tenants of land at Holme in Bedfordshire (Dd. i, f. 218b) and we also read of three
men of King Edward who had formerly been *bedelli* in Kingston on Thames or the
hundred of that name (f. 32b). But it seems doubtful whether any of these people
were ordinary local beadles. Ellis gives a total of 22 beadles for the whole of
Domesday—21 in the Herefordshire section and 1 in that for Worcestershire. He
must have added the 8 former beadles of Leominster to those recorded for 1086.

[4] From Ellis's tables it appears that more than half of the total number of reeves
recorded in the whole of Domesday and three-eighths of the total number of smiths
are recorded in the Herefordshire section, while it alone mentions cowmen
(*vaccarii*) or a carpenter other than the two *carpentarii regis* who appear as tenants-
in-chief in Cambridgeshire.

Of the rural churches there is so much to be said that the discussion of this topic must be left to the next chapter. But the water-mill, which figures so prominently in the traditional lore of the English village, is a subject that demands some consideration here. The articles of inquiry preserved in the Ely preamble included a question about the number of mills; and mills are in fact so frequently mentioned in Domesday Book that one can almost say it was normal, throughout the greater part of the country, for a village to contain one or more if water-power was available. The figure of 5,624 given by Miss Hodgen as the total number of Domesday mills is almost certainly too low: the figures which Professor Darby has published for fifteen counties, though hard to interpret and confessedly imprecise, seem to indicate that the number in this area was appreciably larger than Miss Hodgen's total of 2,628 mills at 1,600 places.[1] In spite of this defect, however, and in spite of uncertainties due to the variable and inadequate information which Domesday affords in regard to the towns, there is no reason to doubt the truth of her conclusion that the ratio of mills to the enumerated population 'varied widely from county to county and from region to region'.[2] The ratio between mills and plough-teams was also very unequal. In Norfolk and Lincolnshire it was apparently twice what it was in Herefordshire. Within the modern area of Northamptonshire there was a mill to every 10 or 11 ploughs, but in the adjacent county of Huntingdon only one to about $27\frac{1}{2}$.

Yet one cannot properly infer from such figures either that the Domesday record is seriously incomplete or that in many

---

[1] See Margaret T. Hodgen, 'Domesday Water Mills' in *Antiquity*, xiii (1939), 261–79. Though inexact, this article contains much valuable information which may be compared with that collected in Richard Bennett and John Elton, *History of Corn Milling* (1899), vol. ii, ch. ix. Any attempt to enumerate the Domesday mills is complicated by frequent references to fractions of mills when the ownership of them was divided; but Miss Hodgen and Professor Darby appear to have dealt with this difficulty in much the same way. Nor can the discrepancy between them be due to the fact that the latter's figures are for the modern counties while those of Miss Hodgen's tables (apart from an unfortunate inconsistency in regard to Rutland) appear to relate to the Domesday counties. This can make very little difference to the totals, for the fifteen counties in question are contiguous, so that changes due to altered boundaries must to some extent cancel each other out. Outside this area, Fowler enumerates $102\frac{1}{2}$ Domesday mills in Bedfordshire as compared with Miss Hodgen's 93; and in Derbyshire, Wiltshire, and Berkshire I have myself noted more mills than she credits to those counties.

[2] Op. cit., p. 272. Whether we include the unsatisfactory statistics of the 'urban population' or confine ourselves to the 'rural population', the figures for the fifteen counties given in Darby's *Domesday Geography* support this conclusion.

counties a large proportion of the grain was ground by hand querns. River boundaries tend in some cases to make the county an unsatisfactory unit for calculations of this nature. In Miss Hodgen's tables, Surrey is credited with a mill for every 35·6 recorded 'households' and Middlesex with only one mill for 63·9. But there were seven mills at Battersea reckoned to yield a revenue of £42. 9s. 8d., or corn of that value; and one can hardly suppose that they ground nothing but corn grown in Surrey or that none of the flour they produced was taken across the Thames to consumers in London.[1] Still more to the point is the fact that mills varied greatly in value and presumably in capacity. Their value or rent may not have been closely proportionate to the amount of corn they could deal with; but mills as valuable as those of Battersea must obviously have done much more work than those worth only a few shillings. And the inadequacy of statistics in which no account is taken of this factor is clearly shown by the evidence for Northamptonshire and Huntingdonshire. As regards the number of their mills, these counties, though contiguous, stand in sharp contrast to one another. In proportion to its plough-teams Northamptonshire, as we have seen, possessed two and a half times as many mills as its neighbour; and it had a mill for (roughly) every 32 units of recorded population while there were nearly 76 such units to every mill in Huntingdonshire.[2] But the mills of the latter county had an average value of 23s. 3d. while the average for the Northamptonshire mills works out at little more than 8s.[3] Both in proportion to the plough-teams and in proportion to the population figures the value of the mills was actually somewhat greater in Huntingdonshire than it was in Northamptonshire.

[1] Dd. i, f. 32.

[2] The population figures are calculated from those given in Darby's *Domesday Geography* for the modern county areas. I have included the 'urban' population and taken the 204 *mansiones* in the town of Northampton as equivalent to 204 population units. If the calculation were based only on Darby's totals for the 'rural population', it would show 31 units per mill in Northamptonshire and nearly 66 in Huntingdonshire. 'Fractional' mills are not here a serious trouble: there are only half a dozen in the former county and in the latter only two 'halves' of the same mill. If one assumed that the recorded serfs are individuals and not heads of households the contrast would be sharpened, for 696 serfs are recorded for Northamptonshire and only one for Huntingdonshire: but perhaps serfs were omitted from Domesday in the latter county, the single serf recorded being at Winwick which was surveyed under Northamptonshire: see Darby, *Eastern England*, pp. 328, 331.

[3] A few eel rents in Northamptonshire preclude exactness; but they total only 1515 eels.

Considerations of this kind cannot, however, explain the extra-ordinary character of the Domesday data in regard to Devon and Cornwall. Devon, according to Miss Hodgen's reckoning, had only one mill for every 200 'households' and Cornwall only one for more than a thousand 'households', though in no other county does her table show as many as a hundred per mill. In the whole of Cornwall only six mills appear to be recorded and these had an average value of less than 10s.[1] One is bound to conclude either that Domesday has in these two counties been guilty of omissions on an unparalleled scale or that water-power was but little employed for the grinding of corn in this part of England. To make a definite choice between these alternatives is impossible, but there is some reason for thinking the latter the more probable. Large numbers of mills are recorded in Somerset and Dorset, which apparently formed part of the same Domesday circuit as the two south-western counties, and the contrast between the former pair and Devon, and between Devon and Cornwall, would be hard to account for on the assumption that the commissioners followed different methods in each of these three cases, and yet even in Cornwall did not wholly exclude mills from their purview; while, on the other hand, if the contrasts reflect real differences in conditions, the extreme scarcity of mills in Cornwall as compared with Devon would be natural enough if the use of water-power for grinding, though still unusual in both counties, was in process of being introduced from the east.

The mills of Domesday England varied greatly, not only in value, but also in the relation of their values to the values and the ploughing strength of the manors to which they belonged. The total value of the manor of Battersea was £75. 9s. 8d. and its seven mills contributed no less than £42. 9s. 8d. to this sum; but in the same county the two mills of *Cherchefelle* (? Reigate) produced only 11s. 10d. though the manor was worth £40.[2] In Huntingdonshire, Hartford, with 12 plough-teams, had 2 mills worth £4, while Kimbolton, with 30 teams, had 1 mill worth 5s.[3] These may be extreme cases; but sharp contrasts in both ratios are of such frequent occurrence in Domesday Book that

---

[1] Miss Hodgen has overlooked one of the Cornish mills and puts the number in Devon at 87, while Bennett and Elton give a list of 94½. The larger figures and Maitland's team totals yield mill–plough ratios of $\frac{1}{58}$ (Devon) and $\frac{1}{197}$ (Cornwall).

[2] Dd. i, ff. 32, 30.   [3] Ibid., ff. 203*b*, 205*b*.

one is bound to suppose, either that it was common for much of the corn to be ground by hand, or that many mills did work for other people besides the inhabitants of the places in which they were situated. Perhaps both these practices combined to produce the puzzling pattern of the statistics; but until the evidence has been subjected to exhaustive investigation it will be wise to refrain from confident assertions. At the same time there is reason for thinking that it was not only at an exceptional place like Battersea that some extra-manorial milling was done. Mills with a value amounting to half, or more than half, the value of the estate cannot have been wholly employed on corn grown within its bounds. And such mills are to be found here and there in various parts of the country.[1] Perhaps, too, it is not irrelevant to note the fact that when Cecily de Rumilly, sometime between 1131 and 1140, gave the mill of Silsden in Yorkshire 'cum omni moltura eiusdem wille' to Embsay Priory, she not only denounced the use of hand-mills, but also thought it necessary to threaten severe penalties against any who should evade the suit they owed to Silsden mill by sending a horse-load of corn to some other mill.[2]

Occasionally mills are described as 'serving the hall' and probably those that were unrented were also, for the most part, occupied in grinding demesne corn.[3] At Leeds in Kent there

[1] For examples of mills or groups of mills with values amounting to at least half the values attributed to the manors or properties to which they belonged (as distinct from the villages in which they were situated) see Dd. i, ff. 43b (Longstock, Hants), 70b (Little Horningham, Wilts.), 199b (Swaffham, Cambridgeshire), 207 (Hemingford, Huntingdonshire), 231b (Aylestone, Leicestershire), 239b, 241b (Milverton and Myton, Warwickshire), 256b (Sheinton, Salop), 281, 289b, 290 (Tilne, Epperstone with Woodborough, and Gamston, Notts.). At Old Sleaford, Lincolnshire (f. 344b) there were 8 mills worth £10 which is half the value of the manor T.R.E., but by 1086 that had risen to £25. That the value assigned to a mill was not always included in the total (as it obviously was at Battersea) is shown by the case of West Drayton, Notts., where there were 3 mills rendering 50s. and the values given for the manor are 30s. T.R.E. and 17s. 4d. modo (f. 285).

[2] Early Yorkshire Charters, ed. C. T. Clay, vii. 55–56 (No. 4): 'Si quis autem de predicta willa renuerit venire ad predictum molendinum ego et heredes mei compellemus eum illud sequi ita quod si repertus fuerit veniens ab alio molendino saccus et bladus erunt canonicorum et equus et forisfactum erunt mea et heredum meorum.' For a similar penalty in thirteenth-century Worcestershire see Register of Worcester Priory (Camden Soc., 1865), p. 32a: cf. H. S. Bennett, op. cit., p. 131.

[3] For examples of mills described as ad aulam, ad hallam, ad hallam serviens, ad aulam molens, serviens aulae, or serviens curiae see Dd. i, ff. 18 (Catsfield, Sussex), 30b (Dorking, Surrey), 43 (Bedhampton, Hants), 94b (Raddington, Somerset), 103b (Tavistock, Devon), 174b (Powick, Worcestershire), 252b (Burton, Salop), 263b (Macclesfield, Cheshire). Seven cases have been noted in Cheshire. At Boarhunt in Hampshire there were 'molinus de xlii denariis et alter ad aulam' (f. 44b), and of two mills at Bellingham in Cambridgeshire 'unus reddit vi solidos et alter molituram

were five mills in the possession of the villagers (*v molini villa-norum*).[1] But as a rule mills were let for a fixed rent. Except in the Little Domesday, a sum of money is named in an overwhelming majority of the entries: the mills are generally described as mills 'of' that amount or are specifically said to render it. Nor can it be doubted that these sums represent rents and not estimates of value: no values are put upon mills which 'served the hall' or upon those *sine censu*. It may be that the actual payments were sometimes made in kind rather than in coin: at Battersea, as we have seen, corn of equal value was recognized as an alternative to the money rent. But the very fact that payments in corn or other commodities are not infrequently mentioned, and are in a good many cases mentioned as additional to a sum of money, is some indication that payment in money was commonly expected where nothing is said to the contrary. Eels were of course the most usual supplementary due and at Huntington in Shropshire the whole rent appears to have taken this form.[2] Apart from eels we hear most about renders in kind in the west midlands. In Domesday Shropshire, which is quite exceptional in this respect, fifteen places are described as having mills whose renders consisted entirely of grain.[3] One or two similar cases occur in Herefordshire, Worcestershire, and Gloucestershire, and other examples are to be found far away from this region, at Arundel in Sussex and at Dover.[4] These grain

de dominio' (f. 195b). For mills *sine censu* see Dd. i, ff. 5 (Preston, Kent), 28 (Steyning, Sussex), 35 (Tolworth, Surrey), 53b (Sheat in Gatcomb, Isle of Wight), 62b (Stratfield Mortimer, Berks.), 96, 99 (Willet in Elworthy, Torweston in Sampford Brett, *Come*, and Nether Stowey, Somerset), 173b (Grimley, Worcestershire). At Barton in Abingdon, Berkshire, there were two mills 'of forty shillings' and two others 'in curia abbatis sine censu' (f. 58b) and at Shepton Montague, Somerset, 'ii molini unum [*sic*] sine censu alterum reddit vii solidos et vi denarios' (f. 92b). In the Somerset cases, where Domesday says *sine censu*, the Exon. text says that the mill grinds the lord's corn (*molit annonam suam*) and it employs the same phrase for the Raddington mill which Domesday describes as *ad aulam molens*. Whether the statement *nil reddit* which Domesday makes about some mills is ever merely the equivalent of *sine censu* is doubtful: a mill at Shillington, Bedfordshire, of which this is said, is described as 'broken' (f. 210b).

[1] Dd. i, f. 7b.

[2] Ibid., f. 256b, cited Darby (*Midland England*), p. 147.

[3] Ibid., ff. 253 (*Membrefelde* = Morville), 253b (*Archelov* = High Ercall, and Donnington), 255 (Aston), 255b (Worthen and Pontesbury), 256 (Sutton), 257 (*Asnebruge* = Isombridge), 257b (Ryton), 259b (*Udevertune* = Wotherton), 260 (Burford, Ashford, and Cleobury Mortimer), 260b (Stokesay and Wistanstow).

[4] Ibid., ff. 183, 184b (Clifford and Marcle, Herefordshire), 175, 176b (Comberton and Kyre Magna, Worcestershire), 170b (Rudford, Gloucestershire), 23 (Arundel), 11 (Dover).

renders were nearly always for definite quantities—usually a given number of *summae*, though other measures occur occasionally. At Marcle in the county of Hereford, however, and at Pontesbury in Shropshire, the amount is unspecified, and at Rudford in Gloucestershire the mill 'reddit annonam quantum potest lucrari'. It is rare for Domesday to indicate that any particular kind of grain was required, but the Arundel mill had to pay 'x modia frumenti et x modia grossae annonae' with four unspecified *modia* in addition, and probably we should understand that the render consisted of wheat at Stokesay, Aston, and Wotherton in Shropshire, at Kyre Magna in Worcestershire, and at Dover, as the word *frumentum* is used instead of *annona* in these cases, while at Ryton in Shropshire the mill paid eight 'sesters' of rye, which is a remarkable fact since the name Ryton is interpreted by Ekwall to mean 'rye-farm'. It may seem odd that mill-rents should consist of corn rather than flour, but the miller or farmer of the mill no doubt took as 'multure' a proportion of the corn brought to the mill to be ground, and this with the eels from his eel-trap would normally constitute the revenue out of which his rent had to be found whatever form it took. There are indeed two places—Bledlow in Buckinghamshire and Yockleton in Shropshire—where the mill-rents were paid in *summae* of malt.[1] But entries which tell of such things are very few in number. Except in the Little Domesday, it is of sums of money that we read in all but a small minority of cases, and the Little Domesday merely fails to provide information on the point and gives no indication that conditions were peculiar in this respect in the counties which it covers.[2]

About the men who occupied the mills Domesday Book tells us practically nothing. In something like half a dozen entries there is a bare reference to a miller; a *custos molini* is mentioned

---

[1] Dd. i, ff. 146, 255b. R. H. Kinvig takes the *annona* which formed part of a mill-rent at Binton, Warwickshire (f. 243), to be flour and not grain: see Darby (*Midland England*), p. 299. Among the more unusual cases cited in that volume are Wasperton, Warwickshire (f. 239), where the rent included four *summae* of salt as well as 20s. and a thousand eels; Lydham, Shropshire (f. 253b), where the render took the form of a pig; Cleeve Prior, Worcestershire (f. 174) with a rent payable in honey; and Marcle, Herefordshire (f. 179b), where one of the mills 'nil reddit nisi victum ejus qui eum custodit'.

[2] No renders are given for mills in Norfolk or Suffolk (though a value is assigned to one Suffolk mill); and only one valuation and one render (a money render) have been noted in Essex (Darby, *Eastern England*, p. 377: cf. Bennett and Elton, op. cit. ii, 108, 171–180).

in connexion with a manor in Derbyshire; and we learn quite casually that a Frenchman has the mill at Wistanstow in Shropshire, that it is the reeve who has one mill at Frome in Herefordshire, and that a sokeman named Kip has half-a-hide of land and 'a mill of twenty shillings' at Sawbridgeworth in Hertfordshire.[1] The early twelfth-century surveys are a little more informing. In particular they suggest that it was not unusual for the miller to be a peasant who combined an agricultural holding with his occupation of the mill. The Liber Niger of Peterborough mentions mills in connexion with 14 manors and on 6 of these they were let along with a virgate.[2] In the earlier of the two Burton Abbey surveys, the miller—or one who bears the same name—appears as a tenant of one, two, or four bovates at Burton, Stratton, Littleover, and Stapenhill.[3] The Shaftesbury Abbey survey, which is believed to date from c. 1130, tells much the same story. At Bradford-on-Avon, Tisbury, and Hatch in Wiltshire and at Iwerne Minster, Melbury Abbas, and Fontmell in Dorset it reveals mills let with holdings ranging from 2 acres to more than a hide.[4] If arrangements of this kind were common a generation earlier, it would go far to explain Domesday's failure to distinguish the millers from the other villagers.

It was with mills as sources of income for the landlords that the royal commissioners were concerned in 1086; and it is in regard to ownership as distinct from occupation that both groups and fractions of mills are recorded. The same miller might no doubt rent a couple as Lepsi did at Burton-on-Trent

[1] Dd. i, 276b (Morton), 260b, 182, 139b.

[2] *Chron. Petr.* (Camden Soc.), pp. 158 (Oundle), 159 (Cottingham), 160 (Warmington and Alwalton), 161 (Pytchley), 166 (Stanwick); cf. p. 162 (*Escetona*).

[3] Op. cit., pp. 213–15, 217–18, 232–3, 239. At Burton, Lepsi 'tenet ii molendina pro l solidis a festo omnium sanctorum primi anni Galfridi abbatis [sc. 1114] usque ad iiii annos et debet gratis molere frumentum et brasium dominicum et reddere pisces qui ibi capiuntur et molendina tam bona restituere cum novis molis quando deseret sicut erant quum accepit'. He is probably the same as *Lepsi pistor* who held a bovate for 12d. and some boon works. At Stapenhill, the mill was held, along with 4 bovates and a croft, by Leuing the goldsmith for 6s. 3d. 'et operatur opus monasterii sine mercede ad cibum abbatis dum operatur'. In the later survey of Stapenhill a second mill is mentioned which 'debet molere totum wintercorn de curia': it was held by Turold the carpenter 'pro xx solidis quoque anno et pro solidatis suis ut faciat omnia opera ecclesie que pertinent ad officium suum et de ligno et de plumbo'.

[4] Brit. Mus. Harl. MS. 61, ff. 37, 40, 43b, 46b, 48, 50b, 51. Identity of names suggests that the tenants of some of the smaller holdings also held other land in the same manor in addition to that mentioned along with the mill. But both this and the later Shaftesbury survey still await critical analysis.

and a man named Edwin at Stratton in 1114, but the later Burton survey shows that the two mills which the abbey owned at Stapenhill were in different hands, and the list of manorial tenants in the Shaftesbury survey of Fontmell includes the names of four men each of whom rented a mill.[1]

Some of the mill clusters recorded in Domesday seem surprisingly large. In the case of a great manorial complex such as Leominster, which comprised 16 members, the mills were probably dispersed among the dependent villages; and some notable clusters occur in towns such as Louth and Thetford.[2] But here and there we find a number of mills credited to a manor which appears to be quite rural and not outstanding in extent. Ham in Essex has 8.[3] Blockley in Gloucestershire has 12.[4] And even more strongly suggestive of development in response to local opportunities is the condition of certain villages of divided lordship. At Meldreth in Cambridgeshire three lords had 2 mills each and each of two others had one.[5] At Tealby in Lincolnshire, out of a total of 14 or 15 mills, 3 belonged to Ralph Paynel, 3 to Godard as tenant of Gozelin, son of Lambert, and 4 to Roger a tenant of Roger of Poitou.[6] Yet the impression which such numbers give is very deceptive. No value is stated in the case of Ham, but the average value of the Meldreth mills was only 6s. 6½d., and those at Blockley and Tealby were worth less than that. At Nettleton in Lincolnshire 9 mills are recorded, but their total value was only £1.[7]

Fraction of mills, which imply divided ownership, are recorded sporadically in many counties, but occur with exceptional frequency in Lincolnshire and Norfolk.[8] Sometimes the fractions can be added together and a village mill divided between two or three owners is clearly revealed. Thus, at Coleshill in Berkshire, St. Mary of Winton, William, son of Richard, and Turstin, son of Rolf, had each a third share in the mill; and both at Compton Bassett in Wiltshire and at Bullingham in Herefordshire the ownership of a pair of mills was similarly

---

[1] Above, p. 284 n. 3, and for Fontmell, Harl. MS. 61, ff. 50b, 51. By the time the later Burton survey was made, Lepsi was renting three mills. There were three mills at Fontmell in 1086 (Dd. i, f. 78b).

[2] Ibid., ff. 180, 345; ii, ff. 118b, 119, 173.

[3] Dd. ii, f. 64.

[4] Dd. i, f. 173, surveyed under Worcestershire.

[5] Ibid., ff. 191, 193b, 194b, 198b, 199b.

[6] Ibid., ff. 342b, 350, 352, 357b, 359, 362b, 364.

[7] Darby, *Eastern England*, p. 75.　　　　　　　　　[8] Ibid., p. 377.

divided into three shares of equal value.[1] In these cases all the
owners had other property in the village; but such sharing was
not always 'intra-villar'. Occasionally the evidence suggests that
distinct villages had an interest in the same mill. Thus Ringsfield and Barsham in Suffolk are adjoining villages and each is
credited with half a mill.[2] Half-mills again are recorded at
Rivenhall and Great Braxted in Essex, and here we reach certainty in the matter, for Domesday tells us that there was
formerly a mill at Rivenhall, but that Richard de Sachevilla took
away half of it ('medietatem molini abstulit Ricardus de Sachevilla') and Round was able to demonstrate that the Richard who
held Great Braxted in 1086 as the tenant of Eudo Dapifer was
in fact Richard de Sachevilla.[3] But sometimes the ownership of
a mill was split into fractions a good deal smaller than halves or
thirds and intricacies occur which almost anticipate the sub-
divisions and tangles that developed in regard to knights' fees
and liability to scutage. A manor at Fetcham in Surrey includes
a fifth part of one mill and a third part of another.[4] At *Lang-
hedana*, an unidentified place in Suffolk, a *liber homo* named
Wlbolt (? Wulfbeald), who held a tiny manor there, had a fourth
share in a mill every third year.[5] In Norfolk, we read of eighths
more than once, and Blickling possessed seven-eighths, while at
Tasburgh one small owner had an eighth part of a mill and another a third part.[6] In many of the simpler cases the division was
probably due to the partition of an estate between heirs or
heiresses. At Coleshill, Compton Bassett, and Bullingham alike
this is almost proved by the equality or virtual equality in
hidation and value of the properties sharing the mills.[7] And the

---

[1] Dd. i, ff. 59*b*, 61, 63, 70*b*, 71*b*, 74, 184, 186, 186*b* (*Boniniope, Boninhope* = Bullingham). The last example is cited by C. W. Atkin in Darby, *Midland England*,
p. 100. Fractions which cannot be related to one another are of course common:
see Darby, *Eastern England*, pp. 74, 136, 188, 248; *Midland England*, p. 407. This
makes one suspect omissions in the Domesday enumeration, but it is perhaps
possible that shares were sometimes entered as if they were whole mills.

[2] Dd. ii, ff. 282*b*, 335*b*, cited Darby, *Eastern England*, p. 188.

[3] Dd. ii, ff. 27, 49; *V.C.H. Essex*, i. 379; Darby, op. cit., p. 248.

[4] Dd. i, f. 32.

[5] Dd. ii, f. 404*b*, cited Maitland, *Domesday Book and Beyond*, p. 144.

[6] Ibid., ff. 196*b* (Blickling), 202, 225*b* (Tasburgh). Darby incorrectly gives one
of the shares at Tasburgh as a twelfth instead of a third. For other examples of
eighths see ff. 154, 239*b* (Saxlingham and Rockland).

[7] At Bullingham there is complete identity; at Coleshill the T.R.E. figures are
identical, but the hidage in one case and the value in another had become different
from that of the other two manors by 1086; at Compton two of the estates were

same conclusion suggests itself when we find rights in the church divided into the same fractions as rights over the mill—a state of affairs exemplified at Elkington and Linwood in Lincolnshire, at Taverham in Norfolk, and at Flixton in Suffolk.[1] But the less simple cases are not easily accounted for in this way; and where a mill is divided into many shares we may, with Maitland, feel 'tempted to think that this mill has been erected at the cost of the vill'.[2] We should, however, remember the possibility that work of this kind might be undertaken through the co-operative enterprise of individuals rather than by corporate action on the part of a village community.[3]

assessed at 6 hides each and each was worth £5, but the third comprised 5½ hides and was valued at £4. 10s.

[1] Dd. i, ff. 365; ii, ff. 157b, 158, 434b. At Flixton, however, a fifth of another mill is recorded in connexion with another holding (f. 380), and Darby points out that fifths are also recorded at Elmham and Linburne which are near to Flixton (op. cit., p. 188).

[2] Op. cit., p. 144.

[3] In this connexion it is relevant to consider Professor Hoyt's arguments about the farming of manors by *villani*: see *Speculum*, xxx. 147–69 (Apr. 1955).

X

THE VILLAGE CHURCHES

I

THE village church was already a common feature of the English countryside at the time of the Domesday Inquest.[1] It is true that for county after county one may scan the pages of Domesday Book without discovering any evidence that this was so. But the fact is beyond dispute as regards Suffolk and Huntingdonshire. In these two counties the Domesday scribes seem to have attempted something like a complete enumeration of the churches, though that was far indeed from being their usual practice. Within the modern bounds of the county of Huntingdon, Professor Darby has reckoned that 'approximately 83' places are mentioned in Domesday and that churches are recorded at 53 of them.[2] For Suffolk he concludes that 'churches are mentioned in connection with 345 villages' and puts the total number of places mentioned (including towns and mere hamlets as well as villages) at 'approximately 639'.[3] Thus,

---

[1] In what follows I have received much help from the material collected in H. Boehmer, *Das Eigenkirchentum in England* (in *Texte und Forschungen zur englischen Kulturgeschichte: Festgabe für Felix Liebermann*, Halle, 1921, pp. 301–53) and in William Page's essay in *Archaeologia*, lxvi (1915), 61–102. Some of Boehmer's conclusions seem to me disputable; and I have found still more to disagree with in Page's article; but, in spite of rather serious inaccuracies, both writers supply very valuable references.

[2] *Eastern England*, pp. 317, 346.

[3] Ibid., pp. 190, 156. Where two or more adjoining villages today have the same name Darby has counted them as one, unless there is 'specific mention' of distinct settlements in Domesday. In particular South Elmham is reckoned as one, though today six parishes bear that name (S. Elmham St. James, S. Elmham St. Michael, &c.); but in this case at least the restriction does not weaken the argument in the text, for Domesday assigns a number of churches to Elmham—apparently six or seven (ibid., p. 191). Besides those of the 345 villages, churches are recorded for Ipswich, Dunwich, Beccles, Clare, Eye, and Sudbury; and Bury St. Edmunds had its abbey. All Darby's figures are for the area of the modern county. Some Suffolk villages besides Elmham are credited with more than one church; and the total number recorded in Domesday for the Domesday county is put at 364 by Ellis, at 398 churches and two chapels by Cox, at 422 churches and chapels by Boehmer: see Ellis, *Introduction*, i. 287; *V.C.H. Suffolk*, ii. 9–10; Boehmer, op. cit., p. 309. References to fractions of churches make enumeration a difficult problem and help to explain these discrepancies.

of the villages mentioned in Domesday, those which possessed
a church outnumbered those without one to a considerable degree in both counties. It does not follow, of course, that this was
the case in all parts of their area. If we may regard the record as
virtually complete for Suffolk, some districts in that county were
decidedly less well provided than others.[1] Round Stowmarket
almost every village had a church: besides that of Stowmarket
itself, more than fifteen churches are recorded within a radius
of 4 miles.[2] On the other hand, in a similar area round Saxmundham, there is no reference to a church in the descriptions
of a majority of the villages. Even here, however, Domesday
records the existence of a church at Saxmundham itself and at
five other places, which clearly means that opportunities for
public worship were accessible to all the inhabitants of the
district.

It is impossible to determine with certainty whether the rest of
England was as well supplied with village churches as Huntingdonshire and Suffolk. In proportion to its area the county of
Suffolk was apparently one of the most populous and fully cultivated in the whole country, so it would not be at all surprising
if the churches there were, in proportion to the area, more
numerous than in less well developed regions. Social conditions
may possibly have favoured the multiplication of churches in
this part of England, for it is arguable that the *liberi homines* and
sokemen, who formed so large an element in the population of
East Anglia and Lincolnshire, were for the most part people
with locally restricted interests, who would feel the need for a
church in their own village and had, at any rate before the Conquest, sufficient independence and control of resources to meet
that need for themselves, while, on the other hand, in more
manorialized counties, a thegn who was the lord of several vills
might be satisfied with the erection of a church in his chief place
of residence. The suggestion has even been made that the ob-
literation of the older ecclesiastical order by the Danish conquests
actually promoted the growth of a parochial system in place of

---

[1] The record was not quite complete. Cox cites a church at *Horepole*, mentioned
in the Ely Inquest, but omitted from Domesday Book: I.C.C., p. 147; *V.C.H.
Suffolk*, ii. 9.

[2] Shelland is the only Domesday village I have noted in this area where no
church is recorded; but Needham Market, Gipping, and Stowpland appear not
to be mentioned in Domesday at all. Exact numbering of the churches is precluded
by uncertainties in the Stonham entries.

that based upon central minsters serving many villages.[1] But these hypotheses are open to grave objections.

In the first place, the argument based upon the comparative freedom of the population, though consonant with the fact that a large number of churches are recorded in Lincolnshire and Norfolk, will not suit the case of Huntingdonshire, where sokemen were very few and *liberi homines* wholly lacking in 1086. The same may be said of the subdivision of rights in village churches, which is a notable feature in East Anglia and Lincolnshire, and in some cases may have originated in the establishment of a church through co-operative effort on the part of the peasantry such as is exemplified at Stonham in Suffolk, where the land attached to the church had been given by nine 'free men' for the good of their souls.[2] In Huntingdonshire the only divided church of which Domesday tells us was at Sibson on the northern edge of the county; and here the fact that the mill was divided between the same two lords as the church suggests the conclusion that, when Domesday refers to some fraction of a church, this may well reflect the division of the village between several manors rather than the co-operation of peasants.[3] In some places such division was probably due to the partition of an estate among several heirs.[4]

As regards the behaviour of church-building thegns in other parts of England, there are certainly a good many instances of a church being recorded at only one village on the estates of thegns who held many villages; but this can readily be explained by the casual nature of the references to churches in Domesday Book, and there is usually no evidence to show whether the village with the church was the place where the thegn resided.[5] No

---

[1] W. Page, op. cit., p. 85. Miss Deansley has made a similar suggestion about the effect of Danish incursions in Kent: *Trans. Royal Hist. Soc.*, 4th series, xxiii (1941), 52; cf. Douglas, *The Domesday Monachorum*, p. 11.

[2] Dd. ii, f. 438, cited by Maitland, *Domesday Book and Beyond*, p. 144.

[3] For Sibson see Dd. i, f. 205 cited Darby, *Eastern England*, pp. 344, 346. On the whole question see Stenton, *Danelaw Charters* (1920), pp. lxxv–lxxvii.

[4] Cf. Stenton, *The Lincolnshire Domesday*, ed. Foster and Langley (Lincoln Record Soc., 1924), Introduction, pp. xxi–xxii. The church of Kingston Bagpuize in Berkshire, which is not mentioned in Domesday, was founded between 1078 and 1097 by the co-operation of the two Domesday sub-tenants who held manors there: *Chron. Abingdon* (Rolls Series), ii, 30–31, 120–1; Dd. i, ff. 60b, 61.

[5] Page (op. cit., pp. 98–101) has collected much valuable material about churches on the estates of pre-Conquest thegns, but is inclined to make unwarranted assumptions about their places of residence, and seems sometimes to treat the silence of Domesday as an indication that no church existed.

doubt three Hertfordshire thegns—Æthelmar of Bennington, Wlwin of Eastwick, and Anschil of Ware—lived at the villages after which they were named; and there was a priest at each of these places; while neither church nor priest is mentioned elsewhere on their estates, apart from a clerk (*clericus*) whose presence is indicated on Æthelmar's land at Sacombe.[1] But then in Kent three churches are recorded by Domesday in the entry relating to Norton which had belonged to 'Osward of Norton', and this Osward may clearly be identified with the former possessor of Tonge and Allington-in-Hollingbourne, both places with churches.[2] In Surrey there was a church or chapel at three out of the four villages which are said to have been held before the Conquest by a man named Erding.[3] In Hampshire and Berkshire, Domesday witnesses to the existence of a church in six of the vills in which Ralf de Mortimer succeeded to the property of Cheping.[4] And, though it comes from East Anglia, striking evidence of a thegn showing an interest in a number of village churches is provided by the will of a certain Edwin, who was a king's thegn under the Confessor, for he bequeathed land to a dozen churches, of which all but one were in Norfolk.[5]

On general grounds it would be hard to believe that the religious needs of the people can have been better provided for in the regions that had suffered most at the hands of the pagan Danes than they were in the counties south of Thames and west of Watling Street which had escaped the worst destructions.[6] And it is impossible to suppose that the real condition of affairs can be gauged from the occasional references to churches and priests which for many counties are all that Domesday Book affords in the way of guidance on this matter. Nothing but an assumption that the Domesday scribes acted on different principles in different counties can explain the apparent contrast between Suffolk and Huntingdonshire, on the one hand, and the neighbouring county of Cambridgeshire, in which (apart from

---

[1] Page, op. cit., p. 98.

[2] Osward was succeeded by Hugh de Port at Norton, Tonge, and Allington (Dd. i, ff. 10, 9, 7*b*–8) and is referred to as *Osward de Nordtone* on f. 1*b*.

[3] Dd. i, ff. 34*b*, 35; Page, op. cit., p. 101. Page overlooked Erding's tenure of *Cisendone*, where no church is mentioned.

[4] Dd. i, ff. 46*b*, 47, 62*b*; Page, op. cit., p. 99. Page overlooked the church recorded at Baddesley.

[5] Whitelock, *Anglo-Saxon Wills*, No. xxxiii. The will never took effect, as the testator evidently incurred forfeiture after the Conquest (ibid., p. 200).

[6] Cf. D. M. Stenton, *English Society in the Early Middle Ages* (1951), p. 205.

the abbeys of Ely, Thorney, and Chatteris and the priory of Swavesey) we are told only of 'minsters' at Shelford and Meldreth, of a village church (*æcclesia illius villae*) at Teversham, and of land-holding priests who may not have been parish priests at all, at some eight other places.[1] A similar conclusion must be drawn from the statistics of Warwickshire, Oxfordshire, and Berkshire. In Oxfordshire, which had an enumerated population somewhat greater than either its northern or southern neighbour, references to priests or churches are even more scanty than in Cambridgeshire; but priests are recorded at 66 places within the area of the present county of Warwick and Ellis reckoned that 59 churches are mentioned in Domesday Berkshire.[2]

There is, moreover, positive evidence, not only that the Domesday scribes acted very differently in different counties, but that complete enumeration was scarcely ever attempted, except, it would seem, in Huntingdonshire and Suffolk. In Cornwall only collegiate churches appear to have been thought worthy of notice. Eleven of these are recorded, while nothing at all is said of any village churches or village priests.[3] But, though it is not unlikely that conditions in Cornwall were rather archaic and that the erection of village churches had done less there than elsewhere to supplant the old system of central minsters, Domesday Book indirectly reveals its own deficiency by mentioning 'about seven places, named after saints mostly Celtic, twenty-four places whose names begin with "Lan", one beginning with "Eglos", and one ending in "Circa" '.[4] Even in

---

[1] For Shelford, Meldreth, and Teversham see Dd. i, ff. 198, 198*b*, 201*b*. Priests are mentioned at Chesterton (f. 189*b*), Oakington (f. 191*b*), Babraham and Harston (f. 194), Papworth (f. 196*b*), Great Abington (f. 199*b*), Pampisford and Tadlow (f. 202). In four cases they are named, which perhaps suggests that they were merely landowners who happened to be priests; and the same conclusion is probably justified in regard to three other people—Ralf who had more than 2 hides at Whaddon, Robert who had over a hide at Haslingfield, and Turbert who held some land as a sokeman at Whaddon—for it is only from the I.C.C. that we learn that they were priests: Dd. i, ff. 194*b*, 198*b*; I.C.C., pp. 64, 72, 62. The I.C.C. mentions a priest at Kennett who seems to be mingled with the *villani* in Domesday, and the Ely Inquest mentions a church at Cambridge which Domesday appears to ignore: I.C.C., pp. 1, 121.

[2] Dd. iii, *Index Rerum*: *Æcclesiae*; Ellis, *Introduction*, ii. 428, 477; Darby, *Midland England* (1954), p. 303.

[3] Canons are mentioned either in Domesday or in Exon. in connexion with eight of the eleven Cornish churches, but the status of those of St. Michael's Mount and St. Constantine is left in doubt (though they were clearly not village churches), and at St. Neot's we read, not of *canonici*, but of *clerici* (*presbiteri* in Exon.).

[4] Page, op. cit., p. 68. His suggestion that these sites were perhaps only open-air

counties where the number of churches recorded in Domesday is far from being impossibly small, there is clear evidence of omission. According to Darby 'churches are mentioned in connexion with 217 villages in Norfolk apart from those of Norwich, Thetford, and Yarmouth'; and this means that a church (or in a few cases more than one church) is recorded for some 30 per cent. of the places that are referred to at all. But it is surely significant that about fifteen of the Norfolk churches appear only in interlinear insertions, as if noted by an afterthought, and that not one is mentioned from folio 119*b* to the end of folio 131. Further, in seven Norfolk villages the Ely Inquest witnesses to the existence of churches which Domesday ignores.[1] The decisive proof comes, however, from Kent. Boehmer reckoned that about 175 country churches are mentioned in the Kentish section of Domesday Book.[2] But the existence of a much larger number is proved beyond cavil by the lists of churches preserved in the Domesday Monachorum of Canterbury, the Textus Roffensis, and the White Book of St. Augustine.[3] Those in the first of these texts record the results of a reorganization of chrism-money and other dues that was made by Lanfranc, apparently at the beginning of his pontificate. The Rochester list is of the same character and, though the manuscript in which it is preserved was not compiled until about 1115, probably belongs to much the same date as the Canterbury lists and seems to represent a similar arrangement made for the diocese of Rochester, either by Lanfranc himself or perhaps by Gundulf who became bishop of that see in 1077. The White

places of worship marked by a cross seems far fetched. For the existence of such places he cites Bede (*Hist. Eccles.* iii, c. 2) and the eighth-century Life of St. Willibald (*Mon. Germ. Hist. Scriptores*, xv. 88). But it is a far cry from these to the Domesday period. Moreover, Bede says that a church was subsequently built on the site of Oswald's cross, and the *Vita Willibaldi* seems to imply that thegns' churches were not unknown: 'mos est Saxanice gentis quod in nonnullis nobilium bonorumque hominum predibus non aecclesia, sed sancte crucis signum . . . in alto erectum ad commoda diurni orationis sedulitate habere solent.'

[1] I.C.C., pp. 136, 137, 137 n. 9 (*Dereham, Torp, Puleham, Felteuuella, Nortuvalda, Waltona, Terintona*). The argument for omissions in Norfolk employed by Ellis (*Introduction*, ii. 291) and by Boehmer (p. 309 n. 1) depends on the erroneous assumption that the description of Tovi's estate only refers to churches in the concluding statement: 'Omnes ecclesie sunt in pretio cum maneriis' (Dd. ii, f. 265). In fact churches are recorded at Stoke and Swainsthorpe.

[2] Op. cit., p. 307.

[3] *Domesday Monachorum*, ed. Douglas, pp. 77–79; *Textus Roffensis*, ed. Hearne, pp. 228–31; Gordon Ward in *Archaeologia Cantiana*, xliv (1932), 39–59; xlv (1933), 60–89; cf. Douglas, op. cit., pp. 5–15.

Book of St. Augustine cannot claim the same antiquity as the other texts and is judged to have been written *c.* 1200; but the list of the abbey's churches occurs in connexion with some documents of the eleventh century, and Dr. Gordon Ward, who has made an intensive study of all the lists, considers that it is based on 'an original list contemporary with those of Rochester and Canterbury', though the scribe to whom we owe the copy in the White Book brought it up to date, adding to it at least the church of St. Laurence's hospital in Canterbury which is said to have been founded in 1137. All the lists present difficult problems of identification; but Dr. Gordon Ward reckons that those of the Domesday Monachorum and the Textus Roffensis give the names of 365 churches 'while the White Book adds others which bring the number up to 407'; and he argues that, if a few in the White Book may be later insertions, there were some ancient churches in the city of Canterbury which 'find no place in these records'. His general conclusion is that there were in the county over 400 churches of pre-Norman origin.[1] And this would mean that in proportion to the population, so far as that is enumerated in Domesday Book, Kent was even better provided with churches than Suffolk itself.[2] Even if we restrict ourselves to the lists in the Domesday Monachorum, which unquestionably belong to the eleventh century, the grave insufficiency of the Domesday record is still apparent.[3] More than half of the 212 churches comprised in those lists appear to be unnoticed in Domesday Book, and though some probably lie concealed among the unnamed churches that are mentioned in certain composite entries, not more than 26 at the most could be accounted for in that way.[4]

---

[1] *Archaeologia Cantiana*, xlv. 89.

[2] I assume that in Suffolk the Domesday record of churches is virtually complete, and one cannot be sure of that: see *V.C.H. Suffolk*, i. 402, and Darby, *Eastern England*, p. 190. Douglas aptly points out that even in 1904 there were only 427 parishes in Kent: op. cit., p. 15.

[3] Though the existing manuscript of the lists was written after the death of Lanfranc (1089), the arrangements must have been made before 1086, for Domesday shows that the church of Milton Regis had by then passed into the possession of St. Augustine's.

[4] Nine of the 10 churches listed (Dd. Mon., p. 78) as dependent on Milton may well be included among the unnumbered churches which Domesday assigns to that manor; and other possibilities of concealment are the 5 (or 8?) churches which Domesday mentions in connexion with Folkestone, the 6 of Hoo, and the 3 of Norton.

II

Though the village church, in the broadest and least technical sense of that term, was a familiar element in the life of
Domesday England, it would be going too far to affirm that the
whole country was as yet divided into parishes normally comprising the territory of a single village, or a couple of villages,
and served by their own parish priest, as appears to be assumed
in the preamble of the Ely Inquest. For a village to contain
a church was no unusual thing, and in some districts only
a minority of the villages were without one. But such churches
were the outcome of a long process which was still incomplete.
If the beginnings of the development can be discerned in the
first quarter of the eighth century and perhaps even earlier than
that, much still remained to do, and much was in fact being
done, in the later years of the eleventh century. If in the pages
of Bede we read of miracles performed by St. John of Beverley
when he went to consecrate two north-country churches which
the thegns Puch and Addi had apparently built on their estates,
the biographer of St. Wulfstan, whose episcopate lasted from 1062
to 1095, can tell us of similar incidents that occurred when Wulfstan consecrated churches at Wycombe in Buckinghamshire, at
Longney-on-Severn in Gloucestershire, and at Ratcliffe-upon-
Soar in Nottinghamshire, and further indicates that these
churches owed their erection to three men, two of whom were
king's thegns, and all of whom can be identified with individuals
mentioned in Domesday as holding land in 1086.[1] Yet another
of King Edward's thegns, Oswulf, son of Frane, was, along
with his wife Æthelith, responsible for building the church of
Studham in Bedfordshire which was consecrated by Wulfwig,
Bishop of Dorchester between 1053 and 1067.[2] It is probable,

---

[1] Bede, *H.E.* v., cc. 4, 5; *Vita Wulfstani*, ed. Darlington (Camden Soc., 1928),
pp. 32, 40, 45. Puch and Addi are called *comites* in Bede, but are 'gesiths' in the
Alfredian version. That they built the churches is implied, for Puch invites the
bishop to consecrate the one and the other is described as 'Addi's church' (*ecclesiam
comitis vocabulo Addi*). For Longney also we depend on inference from the statement:
'Eielsius quidam qui minister regis Edwardi fuerat, ad villam suam Langene . . .
evocavit antistitem ad consecrandam ecclesiam'; but that Swertlin had built the
church at Wycombe and Sewy that at Ratcliffe is clearly stated. A church at
Osingadun was consecrated by St. Cuthbert who died in 687: if this was a village
church it is an earlier example than those consecrated by St. John of Beverley:
Vita Sancti Cuthberti Auctore Anonymo, iv, c. 10 (*Two Lives of St. Cuthbert*, ed. B. Col-
grave, 1940, p. 126).

[2] Kemble, *Cod. Dipl.*, dccccxlv (Thorpe, *Diplomatarium*, pp. 374–5); Dd. i,
ff. 215, 138, 149. According to a late twelfth-century charter (ante 1173) the

again, that Alsi and Blacheman, who respectively held Eastbridge and Blackmanstone in Kent in the time of King Edward,
were, as Professor Douglas has suggested, the founders of two
churches mentioned in the Domesday Monachorum among
those dependent upon Lympne, for the churches are called
Ælsiescirce and *Blacemannescirce*, and Eastbridge and Blackmanstone are less than 5 miles distant from Lympne.[1] But beside
these examples of church-building by men of native English or
Anglo-Danish stock—examples which may in some cases belong
to the years preceding the Conquest—we find a church at Kingston Bagpuize in Berkshire built between 1078 and 1097 by
combined action on the part of the two lords of the place (*ejusdem loci domini*), one of whom was certainly a Norman; and we
learn that between 1084 and 1097 a church was consecrated at
Peasemore in the same county, and that the owner, and presumably builder, of this church was a certain Richard, the lord
of the vill, whose name, in conjunction with that of his son
Philip, suggests a continental origin.[2] Ecclesiastics as well as
laymen played a part in these developments. Wulfstan is said to
have built churches on his own manors, and to have pressed for
their erection on the estates of others, in all parts of his diocese.[3]
One was built by his archdeacon Ailric.[4] We hear too of a
church at Whistley in Berkshire founded by Abbot Athelelm of
Abingdon some time between 1078 and 1084.[5] And Lanfranc
built a church at Harrow shortly before his death.[6] Of general
activity in church-building we have evidence, not only in the

---

church of Lower Heyford in Oxfordshire was also consecrated by Wulfwig:
Eynsham Cartulary, ed. Salter (Oxford Hist. Soc., 1907), i. 109.

[1] *Domesday Monachorum*, ed. Douglas, pp. 13, 78. Churches at Eastbridge and
Blackmanstone are mentioned in Dd. i, f. 13. But one cannot wholly exclude the
possibility that the churches were named after owners who were not their founders.

[2] *Chron. Abingdon*, ii. 30–32, 120–1. In the second entry about Peasemore we
read: 'Ricardus et filius ejus Philippus de Pesimari ecclesiam habent in eadem
villa quam dedicare et coemiterium illic benedici per domnum Osmundum
episcopum fecerunt tempore Rainaldi abbatis.' In the first entry Richard is
described as *ejusdem tunc dominus villae*. To a somewhat earlier and possibly pre-
Conquest date must be attributed the church of Leckhampstead in Berkshire, for
it was consecrated by Bishop Herman, who died in 1078: ibid. i. 475.

[3] *Vita Wulfstani*, iii, c. 10 (p. 52): 'Per totam parrochiam in sui juris prediis
ecclesias struebat: in alienis ut struerentur instabat'; cf. i, c. 14 (p. 21).

[4] Ibid., iii, c. 15 (p. 55). At *Frantone* in Gloucestershire, which lay within
Wulfstan's diocese, Domesday records a church *quae non fuit*—presumably built
since 1066 (Dd. i, f. 169).

[5] *Chron. Abingdon*, ii. 18–19.

[6] Eadmer, *Historia Novorum* (Rolls Series), p. 45, cf. pp. 361–2.

assertions made by Orderic and William of Malmesbury from the standpoint of the second generation after the Conquest, but also in the buildings themselves, which incidentally show that it was not so much a matter of Norman innovation as those historians imply.[1] It may be impossible to date examples of the early Norman style sufficiently closely to distinguish work of the eleventh century from that which belongs to the reign of Henry I; but there is no gainsaying the relevance of the surviving remnants of building in that late Saxon style which Baldwin Brown regarded as characteristic of the epoch of Edward the Confessor, but as 'running on for some decades after the Conquest', and, according to the same authority, examples of this style can be discerned in more than a hundred churches distributed among twenty-four counties.[2] Yet the work praised by the twelfth-century historians, and exemplified in the stones of so many village churches today, must have been largely a matter of rebuilding, and as evidence for the development of the parochial system it is important only because the zeal from which it sprang can hardly have failed to stimulate new foundations as well as the improvement and enlargement of churches inherited from the past. The real proof, both that the parochial map was still incomplete and that it was being filled in during this period, is to be found in concrete examples of newly founded village churches such as those already cited.[3] They are in various ways more significant than appears at first sight. In the first place, the case of Whistley throws a vivid light upon the sense of need which was urging men to action. The inhabitants of Whistley had previously belonged to the parish of Sonning, 3 miles away on the other side of the Loddon; and one of the reasons given for the new foundation is that in winter it was difficult for the

<hr />

[1] Orderic says of the Conqueror: 'Ecclesiae nempe quae sub eo vel ab eo ad laudem Dei in Neustria vel Anglia factae sunt, devotionis ejus, largitatisque in Dei cultu laudabile testimonium asserunt, bonique studii exemplum imitabile posteris pariunt': iv. i (ed. Le Prevost, ii. 162). Of England after the Conquest, Malmesbury says 'videas ubique in villis ecclesias, in vicis et urbibus monasteria, novo aedificandi genere consurgere': see *Gesta Regum* (Rolls Series), ii. 306.

[2] G. Baldwin Brown, *The Arts in Early England: Anglo-Saxon Architecture* (1925), pp. 437–89. Of the examples in his list, 28 come from Lincolnshire, 11 from Norfolk, and 10 from Yorkshire (exclusive of the county towns), but Sussex supplies 8 and Gloucestershire 7. Beyond the range of Domesday Book, the list includes 4 cases from Northumberland and 2 from Durham.

[3] It may be doubted whether Lanfranc's church at Harrow was a new foundation, for it was still unconsecrated when he died in 1089 and there was a priest with a hide of land there in 1086: Dd. i, f. 127.

Whistley people to get to church across the fords. Secondly, the recorded examples are recorded incidentally, so that nothing can be inferred from the fact that so few have been noted. Only four concrete cases of new churches consecrated by Wulfstan are mentioned by his biographer, but each of these is referred to merely because the consecration provided the opportunity for an edifying display of the saint's prophetic or wonder-working powers. The building of Studham church, again, is recorded in a charter because it was the occasion of an agreement between the founders and St. Albans Abbey about the payment of a rent during the founders' lives and the reversion of the land and the church to the abbey. Probably Eadmer would never have mentioned the church of Harrow if Anselm's right to consecrate it had not been contested by the Bishop of London in whose diocese it lay, and if a theft committed at the time of the consecration had not been discovered in a marvellous manner. And alike at Kingston Bagpuize, at Peasemore, and at Whistley the Abingdon chronicler had a special reason for telling how the new churches came to be established. It was the same reason with all three— a sequel of disputes about the rights of the mother churches which were affected by the new foundations and the fact that in one way or another the interests of the abbey were involved.[1]

The references to these disputes, and the chronicler's use of the words *capella* and *ecclesia* as alternative descriptions of these new Berkshire churches, are highly significant. They remind us that the parochial system was as yet incompletely developed, not only in the sense that the number of village churches was only gradually approaching the total that the country was to possess in the later middle ages, but also in regard to the status of the churches. The simplification which was to end by making the village church, whether a rectory or a vicarage, into a parish church such as we ordinarily understand by that term, was a long and gradual process and it is doubtful how far it had gone by the end of the eleventh century. That every man owed tithes and various dues to some particular church or other had long been recognized; and no doubt the fact that a person lived in a particular place would determine at what church he should

---

[1] The consecration of Leckhampstead church is probably mentioned because the abbey's property there had been the occasion of much dispute and Bishop Herman at the consecration pronounced a curse upon all who should infringe the abbey's rights: *Chron. Abingdon*, i. 475.

seek a priest to baptize his children and to what graveyard his body should be carried for burial. Thus in a sense everyone belonged to some ecclesiastical *parochia*. But the old system under which numerous villages were served by the group of clergy attached to a central minster was not wholly superseded; and in some villages the churches were minsters rather than village churches in a strict sense. An enactment of Æthelred II, attributed to the year 1014, had distinguished four different types or ranks of churches—the 'head minster' or principal church, that of medium rank (*medemra mynster*), the lesser church with a graveyard, and the 'field church' or country chapel.[1] Apparently this was an elaboration of the distinction, made more than half a century earlier in a law of Edgar's, between the 'old minster to which obedience is due', a thegn's church with a graveyard, and a church without a graveyard.[2] And, in legal compilations of Norman date, churches were still classified on similar lines. The enactment about tithe being due to the old minster appears in the Latin of the *Quadripartitus* as requiring payment 'to the mother church to which the parish appertains' ('ad matrem ecclesiam cui parochia adjacet') and the so-called *Instituta Cnuti* requires payment 'to the old churches to which the parishioners properly belong' ('antiquis ecclesiis ad quas juste parrochiani pertinent'), while the *Leis Willelme* recognizes three grades of churches, the highest rank being that of a 'mother church' which is a cathedral, abbey, or *iglise de religiun*, the second that of the 'mother church of a parish' (*mere iglise de parosse*), and the lowest that of a chapel (*chapele*).[3] It is, however, noteworthy that the clause of the *Leis Willelme* in which these distinctions are made, though derived from the law of Æthelred II, presents us with a somewhat simplified version of the older scheme and unmistakably treats as a parish church every ordinary church which is more than a mere chapel.[4]

[1] VIII Æthelred, 5, i (Liebermann, *Gesetze*, i. 264; A. J. Robertson, *Laws*, pp. 118–19), repeated in I Cnut, 3, ii (Liebermann, p. 282; Robertson, pp. 156–8), which further characterizes the church of the third class as one where there is little divine service (*þær lytel þeowdom sig*).

[2] II Edgar, 1 and 2 (Liebermann, p. 196; Robertson, pp. 20–21).

[3] Liebermann, p. 197; *Leis Willelme*, I. i (Liebermann, p. 492; Robertson, p. 252). The terms used in the Latin version of the *Leis* are (i) 'cathedralis—ecclesia vel cenobium vel quecunque religiosorum ecclesia', (ii) 'matrix ecclesia parochialis', (iii) 'capella'.

[4] The clause concerns penalties for violation of sanctuary, and Miss Robertson has shown that the penalty in the case of the *mere iglise de parosse* was (though

The grading of churches was thus remembered, and there were places where for centuries to come it might affect such matters as the payment of church-scot; but everything goes to show that the contrast between the ancient minsters and the manorial churches was losing its significance for the organization of pastoral functions.[1] The multiplication of local churches must have deprived the old system of most of its utility before the Norman Conquest; and thereafter we have to reckon with new forces tending to accelerate and intensify the processes of change. Under the old law the thegn who possessed a church of his own had been required to pay two-thirds of his tithe to the central 'minster' even if a graveyard was attached to his church. But the Norman landowners exercised a large discretion in the disposal of their tithes and very commonly gave the two-thirds to a monastery either in Normandy or England.[2] It is probable that, as a result, a good many minsters became too poor to support a college of canons. Some, like Shrewsbury, became engulfed in the rising tide of Anglo-Norman monasticism.[3] In other cases, a transformation of the canons into ordinary parish clergy may have been promoted by Lanfranc's legislation about clerical celibacy, for the Council of 1076 required married canons to put away their wives, but was more merciful to parish priests who were already married. Domesday Book, it is true, contains numerous references to what Stenton aptly describes as 'collegiate foundations representing "old minsters" of the Anglo-Saxon time'.[4] Though many of the entries which tell of clergy in the plural probably do so only because they summarize

miscalculated) intended to be equivalent to that for the lesser church with a graveyard in the laws of Æthelred and Cnut (op. cit., p. 365).

[1] The case of Fawsley in Northamptonshire, cited by Stenton, provides a striking example of the long persistence of usages anterior in origin to the development of the parish in the ordinary sense of that term. Before the Conquest church-scot had been paid to Fawsley church from two hundreds which were attached to the royal manor at that place, and as late as the fourteenth century the priory of Daventry, to which the church had been given by Henry I, 'was still receiving church-scot from nine separate parishes in virtue of his gift' (*Anglo-Saxon England*, p. 154).

[2] Stenton, *Anglo-Saxon England*, p. 156. It is significant that a writ of Henry I (1100–15) provides that five churches in the *Terra Regis* in Yorkshire shall not lose their old 'parishes', 'propter socas quas inde dedi quibusdam baronibus meis set . . . habeat unaquaque mater ecclesia de istis et capellas suas et decimas per omnes soccas' (Farrer, *Early Yorkshire Charters*, i, No. 428)—not less so that he gave these churches to York Minster (ibid., Nos. 426, 427, 429).

[3] 'In Sciropesberie Civitate facit Rogerius comes abbatiam et eidem dedit monasterium Sancti Petri ubi erat parochia civitatis': Dd. i, f. 252b.

[4] Op. cit., p. 660.

the statistics for several villages, churches of undoubtedly collegiate character are revealed in many parts of the country, and
it is unlikely that every minster was recorded when so many
village churches were ignored. But where something of their
history in this critical period can be discerned, the minsters
usually prove on examination to be either in a state of decay or
to be undergoing some process of transformation. In one way or
another they were losing their old character. It is surely significant that the church at Morville in Shropshire, which had been
served before the Conquest by eight canons and apparently
retained something of its collegiate character in 1086, is none
the less described in Domesday Book as a manorial church
(*ecclesia hujus manerii*).[1] There were no doubt exceptions. In a
region where men dwelt for the most part in scattered hamlets,
too small to maintain a parish church and its priest, the cure of
souls may well have continued to be attached to a central collegiate foundation. This seems to have been the case at Hartland
in Devon, where there were twelve canons in 1086, for the later
history of Hartland is that of a gigantic parish with numerous
hamlets and numerous dependent chapels which never split
off to become the churches of separate parishes.[2] On general
grounds one suspects that some of the collegiate churches in
Cornwall may still have exercised pastoral functions in the old
way. Perhaps the 'priests of Taunton', of whose existence we
learn from the Exon. Domesday, still ministered in 1086 to the
inhabitants of an ancient *parochia* which stretched away to the
north-west for more than 10 miles; but all one can say for
certain is that more than a dozen places owed church-scot to
Taunton and that the lords of these places had to be brought
there for burial; and it seems not unlikely that some loosening
of the collegiate bond lies behind the fact that when regular
canons were introduced about 1120, and an attempt was made
to convert the seculars to the new way of life, these last proved to
be incorrigible—'eorum mores in mala consuetudine inveterati

[1] Dd. i, f. 253. For further details about Morville and other old minsters see
Appendix III.
[2] Exon., p. 421 (*Nistenestoc* = Stoke-in-Hartland), cf. Dd. i, f. 117; W. G.
Hoskins and H. P. R. Finberg, *Devonshire Studies*, 1952, p. 306. In the reign of
Henry II the church of St. Nectan of Hartland, hitherto a foundation for secular
canons, was converted into one for regulars, being made over for that purpose
'cum capellis et terris et decimis et omnibus pertinentiis suis' (*Mon. Ang.* vi. 436).
In the thirteenth century we find a vicar established in the parish church, but the
canons still had to provide suitable priests to minister in the dependent chapels.

novellam sancte conversationis gratiam aspirare non valebant.'¹
In some other places the lineaments of an ancient *parochia*
can be discerned. At Mottisfont in Hampshire, for example,
Domesday Book tells us that the Archbishop of York had a
church and six chapels 'cum omni consuetudine vivorum et
mortuorum', and the location of the chapels indicates a *parochia*
extending from the Test to the Wiltshire border.² But there is
nothing to suggest the presence of a group of priests at the
mother church of Mottisfont and the very existence of the
chapels witnesses to a process of disintegration, which in this
case was not permanently arrested as it was at Hartland.³ And
though one may be sure that many village churches besides
those actually described as *capellae* or *æcclesiolae* in Domesday
were dependent upon older mother churches to the extent of
owing some payments to them, the mother churches in question
must often have been themselves parish churches in the ordinary
sense and not minsters of the ancient type; and, so long as the
inferior status of the daughter churches was maintained as a
ground for the payment of dues, there can hardly have been
much will or power to resist local desire to make them independent in all that related to the cure of souls. Very significant facts
are revealed by the Abingdon Chronicle about the three Berk-

---

¹ Exon., p. 67; Dd. i, f. 87*b* (cf. Exon., p. 162 for some differences in the list of
places); and the passages quoted from B.M. Royal MS. 8 E IX, f. 93 in J. C.
Dickinson, *The Origins of the Austin Canons* (1950), pp. 118 n. 8, 242 n. 1. One
wonders why only the *domini* of the dependent places are mentioned in regard to
sepulture. Perhaps it was taken for granted that all residents in the district had to
be buried at Taunton and Domesday records the obligation in the case of the lords
because they might not be resident. Or can it be that local graveyards already
existed and that the rights of the old minster were only maintained in respect of
those whose burial fees were most worth having? Churches at *Lydyard, Legha,* and
Hilla, which are among the dependent places, are mentioned in a confirmatory
charter of 1154–62 (*Mon. Ang.* vi, pt. i, p. 166), and there are said to be Norman
fonts in the churches of Bradford and Halse. And it should be noted that between
1174 and 1191 the Prior and Canons of Taunton agreed that (with a few exceptions)
all their churches and chapels and the canons ministering in them should be
answerable to the bishop: *Hist. MSS. Com. Wells; Dean and Chapter MSS.,* i. 38.
² Dd. i, f. 42.
³ Evidence that five of the six dependent chapels of Mottisfont had become
regular parish churches is forthcoming from the first decade of the fourteenth
century: *Registrum H. de Woodlock,* ed. A. W. Goodman (Canterbury and York Soc.,
1940–1), i. 239, 255, 281; ii. 848, 889–90. A generation earlier the same conclusion
is suggested though perhaps not proved by the fact that each of the five is described
as an *ecclesia* in a list of *ecclesiae* and *capellae* which is believed to date from *c.* 1270:
Registrum J. de Pontissara (Canterbury and York Soc.), ii. 604. In none of these
documents is there any hint that the development was recent.

shire churches, built in the last quarter of the eleventh century, to which reference has already been made. The words *capella* and *ecclesia* are indifferently employed for all three. At Whistley, which was in the old parish of Sonning, it was agreed that the Abbot of Abingdon (to whose monastery the manor of Whistley belonged) should have his own priest—'suum clericum, officiorum Dei curas agentem, omnesque oblationes, quae ad ipsam ecclesiam ab quibuslibet oblatae sunt, recipientem et ad usum suum deserviendo ecclesiae reservantem'—but that half a mark should be paid annually to the Bishop of Salisbury who was the lord of Sonning and that the church of Sonning should have all the dues (*consuetudines*) which it used to receive from the vill of Whistley in the time of King Edward.[1] At Kingston Bagpuize and at Peasemore the rights of the respective mother churches were commuted for fixed annual payments; and it is especially noteworthy that a cemetery was attached to the new church in both these places.[2]

On the whole it seems fair to assume that the churches recorded in Domesday were parish churches of a more or less ordinary kind unless the contrary appears, and that the differences between them were tending to have little more meaning for those who worshipped within their walls than the difference between a rectory and a vicarage in modern times. Over against the legal grading to which appeal might be made in regard to economic obligations or the scale of penalties for violation of sanctuary, we have to reckon with the imponderable influence of a feeling that all churches were equal in holiness—a feeling that had found overt expression in one of the laws of Æthelred II.[3]

III

Though certainty is precluded by the dearth of evidence for many counties, there can be little doubt that the village churches of Domesday England were usually served by a resident priest. The parson was already a familiar figure in village society. The assumption made in the Ely Preamble—that every village would be able to furnish a priest as a member of the Domesday jury—

---

[1] *Chron. Abingdon*, ii. 18–19. The date of the agreement is 14 Mar. 1089.

[2] Ibid., pp. 30–32, 120–1.

[3] 'Ne syn ealle cyrcan na gelicre mæðe worldlice wirðe, þeah hi godcundlice habban halgunge gelice': VIII Æthelred, 5 (Robertson, op. cit., pp. 118–19), repeated in I Cnut, 3a (ibid., pp. 156–7).

cannot of course be accepted in view of the unwarranted character of its assumption that the manor and vill were coincident.
None the less the fact that such expectations were entertained
is a fact to be reckoned with. And more reliable evidence is
supplied by Domesday Book. When, on the one hand, we find
in Surrey over 60 churches recorded without a village priest
being mentioned anywhere, and, on the other hand, find a
priest, or in a few cases a couple of priests, included among the
inhabitants of some 60 villages in Warwickshire and some 40
villages in Leicestershire though nothing is said of any village
church in either of these counties, we have some reason for
thinking that the two forms of statement were roughly equivalent and that a church normally implied a priest and a priest a
church.[1] And when we read that at Houghton in Huntingdonshire and at Easington in the North Riding of Yorkshire the
church was without a priest, we infer that this was an unusual
state of affairs.[2] In Huntingdonshire the matter is beyond doubt,
for the presence of a priest is specifically indicated in connexion
with 49 of the 57 churches recorded in the Domesday county.[3]
It is much the same with Derbyshire, where we find a priest, or
in two instances two priests, at 38 out of the recorded total of
some 44 village churches.[4] A considerable bulk of relevant evidence is also available for a few other counties, and this, though
less compelling, points in the same direction. In Yorkshire, Ellis
and Boehmer both reckoned that 166 churches are mentioned

[1] Cf. Ellis, *Introduction*, i. 289–90. The only churches mentioned in Leicestershire
and Warwickshire are those of the county towns. The entry relating to Tachbrook
in Warwickshire: 'haec terra est de aecclesia S. Cedde' (Dd. i, f. 238b) probably
only means that the land belonged to the church of Lichfield, though it is true
that Tachbrook church, which is a prebend of Lichfield, is dedicated to St. Chad.

[2] Dd. i, ff. 204b (cited Darby, op. cit., p. 346), 305 (cited Ellis, op. cit. i. 296).

[3] Of the eight churches for which Domesday gives no information about a priest,
one was at Sawtrey St. Andrew and may well have been served by the priest of
Sawtrey All Saints whose presence is recorded, another is only noted in an interlinear insertion where lack of space may have led to the omission of reference to a
priest, a third (Fletton) was little more than a mile from the abbey of Peterborough
to which it belonged, a fourth (Stibbington) was probably served by the priest of
Sibson (the two places being associated in Domesday Book and now forming the
parish of Sibson-cum-Stibbington), and a fifth (Perry) was perhaps only a chapel
dependent upon the church of Great Stoughton where there was a priest, for West
Perry, with which the *Pirie* of Domesday has been identified, is now a hamlet of
that parish.

[4] The remaining 6 churches include 2 at Weston and 2 at Sawley with a priest
for each pair: Dd. i, f. 273. A priest is also recorded at 5 places where nothing is
said about a church (viz. Stainsby, South Wingfield, Eckington, Newton, and
Lullington: ibid., ff. 273b, 277, 278b).

and a rough count shows a priest associated with 111 of them.[1]
The same may be affirmed in regard to more than 40 per cent.
of the Domesday churches of Lincolnshire and about half of
those in Nottinghamshire.[2] And though evidence on this scale is
confined to the north-eastern part of England, there is no reason
to think that this reflects a geographical contrast in conditions
rather than differences in the methods employed by the compilers of different sections of Domesday Book. Priests are as
rarely mentioned in Norfolk and Suffolk and Cambridgeshire
as in Wiltshire and Somerset and the counties of the south coast.
Moreover, the Herefordshire folios of Domesday afford a little
information which harmonizes, in the main, with the statistics
already cited. Only 19 churches are recorded, but there appears
to have been a priest at 13 of them and one of the others was
served by 2 priests, though, on the other hand, there was apparently only one priest for 3 churches in the castlery of Ewyas.
Further, the presence of a priest, or in 2 places a pair of priests,
is noted in 17 villages where nothing is said about the church.[3]
At Frome (? Bishops Frome) which is one of these Herefordshire villages, and also at Windsor, at Farndon in Cheshire, and
at Fulletby in Lincolnshire, the priest is specifically described as
the priest of the vill (*presbyter villae*); and probably we have in
these cases only a more precise indication of the normal status
of the priests mentioned in connexion with villages in Domesday,
for, except at Fulletby, the particularity of the description is obviously due to the need of distinguishing the village priest from
other ecclesiastics who held land in the same place.[4] Now and

---

[1] H. J. Reid reckoned that in the wapentake of Skyrack in the East Riding
thirty places are mentioned as having churches and remarks that 'no less than
twenty-five of these are said to have a presbyter also': *Domesday Studies*, ed. P. E.
Dove, ii (1891), 442.

[2] Boehmer reckons 92 Domesday churches in Nottinghamshire and about 260
in Lincolnshire (op. cit., p. 308); but the frequent reference to fractions of churches
is an obstacle to exact enumeration.

[3] I have taken no account of about a dozen cases where we read of one or more
capellani or *clerici* holding land. It looks very much as if these were prebendaries of
Hereford cathedral, but whether they officiated as priests in the villages is uncertain.
The priests recorded in the description of Leominster are also excluded from the
figures in the text as one cannot say for sure whether they were the priests of
dependent members of that great manor or not.

[4] Dd. i, ff. 181b, 56b, 263, 349b: cf. Boehmer, op. cit., p. 306. Perhaps a parallel
to the case of Fulletby should be seen in an entry relating to Berrington in Shropshire ('Hujus villae aecclesiam et presbyterum tenet S. Petrus in Sciropesberiae'
[*sic*], f. 254b), for here too no other priest is mentioned. At Potterne in Wiltshire,
Hinton (? Hinton Martell) in Dorset, and Bedminster in Somerset, we read of the

again we find a priest who is apparently serving two village churches, and there was one with three churches at Hackness in the North Riding of Yorkshire as well as at Ewyas in Hereford-shire.[1] But churches with two priests also occur, and sometimes the description of a manor will include a reference to two priests, though the existence of a church has to be inferred.[2] With entries of these two types, however, it is not always certain that we have to do with the staff of a village church rather than with the remnants of a collegiate minster; and it is possible that, in some of the villages in question, one of the priests was only a land-holder and did no duty in the church. Yet the parson and his curate seem to be unmistakably revealed in the priest and deacon (*presbyter cum diacono*) recorded at Market Bosworth in Leicester-shire.[3]

IV

In any inquiry into the economic condition of the village churches and their clergy it is necessary at the outset to recog-nize, first, that Domesday Book, being essentially a survey of land and agricultural resources, has rarely anything to say about tithes or other ecclesiastical dues such as church-scot or burial fees, and, secondly, that it is only for Suffolk and, to a less degree, for Norfolk that it provides comprehensive information about the parson's glebe. In Suffolk it was certainly normal for a village church to possess an endowment of land; and about half a dozen churches in that county are specifically stated to be without land as if this was an unusual condition.[4] But the

---

priest of the manor (*presbyter hujus manerii*: ff. 66, 76, 86*b*): at Hinton he had to be distinguished from other priests.

[1] Ibid., ff. 323, 185. Examples of 2 churches to a priest are Hartford (Hunting-don), f. 203*b*; Chirbury (Salop), f. 253*b*; Weston-on-Trent and Sawley (Derby-shire), f. 273; Collingham and Hawton (Notts.), ff. 284, 289*b*; and Kyme (Lincolnshire), f. 337*b*. Two priests and 3 churches are mentioned in the entry for Ridlington in Rutland, f. 293*b*, and the description of Newark and its dependencies refers to 10 churches and 8 priests, f. 283*b*.

[2] For churches with two priests see Hope (Herefordshire), ibid., f. 187; Burford and Stanton Lacy (Salop), ff. 260, 260*b*; Bakewell and Repton (Derbyshire), f. 272*b*; Ossington (Notts.), f. 281*b*; and Topcliffe (Yorkshire), f. 323. Examples of entries recording two priests without any reference to a church are found in other counties: e.g. Cheshire (Acton and Halton, ff. 265*b*, 266), Leicestershire (Melton Mowbray, f. 235*b*), and Warwickshire (Stoneleigh, Upton, Kingsbury, Monks Kirby, Long Itchington, ff. 238, 239*b*, 243*b*, 244).

[3] Ibid., f. 233.

[4] Dd. ii, ff. 286*b* (Cornard), 355 (Worlington), 382 (*Lundale* = Undley), 386 (Brightwell), 390*b* (Denham). At Dagworth (f. 409*b*) there were two churches, one

amount of the glebe varied greatly from place to place. The church of Hinderclay, for example, had only one acre, while that of Long Melford had two whole carucates, or 240 acres.[1] Irregular areas, which bear no simple relation to any standard unit like the bovate or the carucate, but might well result from an accumulation of small gifts, are of frequent occurrence. On the other hand the figures compiled by Boehmer show that about half the total number of churches recorded in Suffolk possessed a holding of land which clearly reveals itself as a recognized agrarian unit or a simple fraction or multiple of such a unit. Thus he reckoned that there were 25 churches with 15 acres, 46 with 30 acres, 10 with 60 acres or half a carucate, and 8 with 1 or more carucates. Twelve churches possessed 10 acres, while 28 had just twice and 28 just four times that amount. There were also 11 churches with 6, 27 with 12, and 19 with 24 acres.[2] Thus we may say that the pattern of the glebe lands of Suffolk was in general similar to that of the peasant holdings of Domesday, at least in this respect—that it combined a large range of difference, and a great number of individual irregularities, with a marked tendency for most of the holdings to fall into definite classes. In scale too the lands of the village churches were usually similar to the holdings of the peasantry—often approximating to those of the *villani*, but in a substantial minority of cases resembling those of the humbler class of bordars or cottars. The church of Long Melford, however, though apparently an

of which was without land; and two churches (or chapels?) without land were dependent upon the well-endowed church of Blythburgh (f. 282).

[1] Ibid., ff. 364b, 359. Boehmer puts the number of Suffolk churches which had 5 acres or less at 47, op. cit., p. 312.

[2] Ibid., pp. 312–13. Entries relating to fractions of churches, which are fairly common in this county, are assumed by Boehmer to relate to similar fractions of their property: the assumption is reasonable and is supported by the entry 'quarta pars æcclesie et quarta pars ex hoc quod ecclesiae pertinet' Dd. ii, f. 422, but one cannot be certain of its correctness, so that it introduces an element of doubt. Apparently Boehmer put a different interpretation upon the entry relating to Mendham which mentions an eighth part of a church of 40 acres and the fact that more land belonging to it is entered under Norfolk: ibid., f. 379b. The relevant Norfolk entry relates to 43 acres of 'ecclesiastical land' (f. 195b). It is rather puzzling to find 13 Suffolk churches with 16 acres, but, apart from this, the areas mentioned in the text are the only areas (greater than 5 acres) which, if we accept Boehmer's figures, are represented by more than 5 examples. He lumps together areas of 5 acres or less. Among them I have noted 7 cases of 3 acres and 7 of 5. More than a dozen churches possessed a little meadow in addition to the arable (e.g. an acre at Thorndon, Badingham, and Strickland, ff. 323, 328b, 335, and half an acre at Buxhall, f. 350b). Apparently Boehmer's figures are for the arable only.

ordinary village church, had an estate which might properly be described as a small manor. As we have seen, it comprised, or rather was rated at, two carucates; and it evidently contained both a home farm and dependent tenant-lands, for we are told that there were 2 ploughs belonging to the church and 2 belonging to its 'men', who were 13 in number—4 being *villani* and 9 bordars.[1] No other village church in the county was as well endowed with land as Long Melford, but it was not the only one with dependants of this kind. That of Framlingham had a *villanus* and 4 bordars, and the churches of Badingham and Shimpling had each a bordar.[2] At Hadleigh the church appears to have possessed one of the mills as well as a whole carucate of land.[3]

The county of Norfolk presents a similar picture. The village churches are generally credited with glebe, and the lack of it is noted in a few cases.[4] As in Suffolk, it might amount to as little as an acre, but at one of the Barshams, and also at Langley, there was a church with a hundred acres, and the churches of Carleton St. Peter and Burnham Thorpe each possessed 80 acres.[5] Some poorly endowed churches, and some that were comparatively well endowed, possessed holdings of irregular size—an acre and a half at Swanton Morley, for example, 11 acres at Caister St. Edmunds, 17 acres at Pickenham, 53 acres at Stow Bardolph.[6] But about a hundred Norfolk churches had holdings of one or another of the same standard sizes that were

---

[1] Dd. ii, f. 359.

[2] Ibid., ff. 302b, 328b, 415b. Each of these three churches had 60 acres of land, and in addition Badingham had an acre and Shimpling half an acre of meadow.

[3] Ibid., f. 372b. Of the churches named by Boehmer as possessing as much as a carucate, only Long Melford and Hadleigh can be regarded as village churches—apart from Eriswell to which he attributed a hide in error.

[4] The churches at Croxton, Houghton, Calthorpe, Witchingham, Hunstanton, and Hellesdon are stated to have no land: ibid., ff. 169, 169b, 218, 224b, 265b, 271b.

[5] See ibid., ff. 168b (Barsham), 196b (Langley), 233b (Carleton St. Peter), 169 (Burnham Thorpe). There are today three parishes called Barsham—East Barsham, West Barsham, and North Barsham—and three churches are recorded in Domesday. As these had 100 acres, 12 acres, and 8 acres respectively, it is tempting to conjecture that the mother church had once possessed a carucate, from which small portions had been detached for the endowment of two chapels or daughter churches. There were churches with a single acre of glebe at Paston (f. 159), Hempton (f. 170), and Sloley (f. 229b). Altogether I have noted thirteen churches with glebe amounting to 5 acres or less. In all these Norfolk figures no account has been taken of entries relating to fractions of churches or of those which give a combined acreage for the glebe of two churches.

[6] Ibid., ff. 226b, 210, 235, 206b.

frequent in Suffolk, the commonest sizes being, in Norfolk, 30, 20, and 12 acres, which are almost equally well represented and together furnish over 50 examples. Dependent bordars are very occasionally mentioned—one at Swafield, one and a half at Swainsthorpe, two at North Burlingham—and a somewhat ambiguous entry seems to credit the church of Stockton with 3 bordars and a half-share in a mill, perhaps also with a superiority over 12 sokemen.[1]

Outside East Anglia direct information about parochial glebe is scanty. But though regional variations may well have been great, there is reason for thinking that in this matter the conditions revealed in Norfolk and Suffolk were not abnormal to any significant degree, and that what is peculiar to these counties is the fullness with which the facts are recorded rather than anything in the nature of the facts themselves. Domesday Book, as we have seen, often fails to mention village churches or priests, and often refers to a church without saying anything about a priest, and to a priest without recording the existence of a church, so it would be strange if it never failed to distinguish the glebe. It might be argued, perhaps, that social conditions in East Anglia were unusually conducive to the endowment of village churches; but then in Lincolnshire, where the social structure was similar, Domesday has little to say about glebe, and if we are to suppose that in Lincolnshire its record is incomplete, we cannot assume that elsewhere it gives us the whole story. Such an assumption would, moreover, involve a contrast too sharp to be credible. In proportion to the enumerated population the county of Huntingdon was almost as well supplied with churches as Suffolk; but, whereas nearly all the Suffolk churches are credited with some land, Buckworth and Bottlebridge are the only villages in Huntingdonshire whose churches are described as possessing any at all, and it is possible that the property was thought worthy of record in these two cases because in each of them it exceeded an ordinary peasant holding in amount.[2] That

---

[1] Dd. ii, ff. 193, 265, 199b. The Stockton entry (f. 141b) runs thus: 'et in eadem i æcclesia lxv acr' et iij bor et dim' mol et xii soc' xxv acr' semper iij car' et vi ac' prati.' As a mill and bordars and sokemen have all been mentioned earlier in the description of Stockton, there is some ground for thinking that the whole of this sentence refers to the possessions of the church. The 'half-bordar' at Swainsthorpe no doubt means a right to half the rent or services that a bordar owed.

[2] Dd. i, ff. 205b, 206. At Buckworth half a hide with 2 villani and a plough belonged to the church: at Bottlebridge 2 priests held St. Mary's church with 2 hides and 2 ploughs and 3 acres of meadow.

it was in fact common for a village church to possess a small amount of land, where nothing is said about it, seems to be a legitimate inference from the way in which Domesday in some counties associates priests with the peasantry. Even this indirect light is often excluded by the *formulae* of reference. In Yorkshire, Lincolnshire, Nottinghamshire, Derbyshire, and Huntingdonshire, though the presence of a priest is frequently noted, the information generally takes the form of a mere statement that there is a priest, or a priest and a church, in the village, so that we are left without anything to indicate his relation to the other inhabitants and their possessions. But this practice was not followed for the other counties in which considerable numbers of priests are recorded. In Leicestershire, Northamptonshire, Warwickshire, Staffordshire, Gloucestershire, Herefordshire, and Hertfordshire it is usual for the priest to be included in the enumeration of the manorial tenants and their teams, and entries of the same type occur in Cheshire, Shropshire, and Worcestershire, while a scarcely less significant *formula* is found in Essex, the only county of the Little Domesday with frequent references to village priests.[1] Some forms of entry almost compel the conclusion that the priest was possessed of one or more ploughbeasts and therefore of land on which to employ them. Thus at Welham (*Walendeham*) in Leicestershire 'seven *villani* with the priest have two teams'; at Therfield (*Ferreuuelde*) in Hertfordshire '27 *villani* with the priest and one Frenchman have eleven teams'; at Longdon in Worcestershire there are 'ten *villani* and seventeen bordars with the priest having six teams'; at Brockworth (*Brocowardinge*) in Gloucestershire there are 'eight *villani* and six bordars and the priest and two *liberi homines* and the reeve' and 'between them all they have fifteen teams'.[2] At Clifton-on-Teme in Worcestershire doubt is altogether precluded, for the enumeration of *villani*, bordars, and oxherds is followed by the sentence 'Inter omnes cum presbytero habent VI carucas.'[3]

[1] Ellis unaccountably omitted to include any priests in his abstract for Staffordshire, where in fact I have noted 27. For the other counties mentioned above Ellis gives totals ranging from 29 for Cheshire (including the lands between Ribble and Mersey) to 136 for Yorkshire. After these the next largest numbers he gives are 18 for Middlesex and 12 for Kent. According to Tait 32 priests are recorded in Cheshire: *Domesday Survey of Cheshire* (Chetham Soc., 1916), p. 30.

[2] Dd. i, ff. 234, 136, 174*b*, 169. For comparable examples in other counties see Hartwell, Northamptonshire (f. 220); Fillongley, Warwickshire (f. 242*b*); King's Pyon, Herefordshire (f. 184*b*); Leyland, now Lancashire (f. 270); Lydham, Shropshire (f. 253*b*). [3] Dd. i, f. 176*b*.

But a slight element of uncertainty hampers the interpretation of two forms of statement which are very common. Ross in
Herefordshire provides an example of the first: 'Ibi XVIII
villani et VI bordarii et presbyter cum XXIII carucis.'[1] This
might be regarded as fairly conclusive were it not for the fact
that in Domesday Book the preposition *cum* sometimes appears
to be used as a mere conjunction.[2] Secondly there are the entries
which begin the enumeration with the priest, like that in the
description of Aston in Hertfordshire—'Ibi presbyter et XI
villani cum V bordariis habent V carucas'—for the grammatical
usages of Domesday make it possible to translate this: 'There is
a priest there; and eleven *villani* with five bordars have five
teams.'[3] Yet on the whole it seems probable that we ought to
consider all these statements as creating at least a presumption
that the priest possessed some of the oxen. The Domesday
scribes, as Round so often insisted, loved to express the same
meaning in different words; and we have also to reckon with
regional differences in the phraseology employed. To take a
case in point, statements about men 'with' teams are extremely
common in the Worcestershire folios, while in those devoted to
Hertfordshire we find that they nearly always 'have' teams. As
regards enumeration starting with the priest it is noteworthy
that the Aston entry just quoted is supplemented by a distinct
statement: 'Ibi VI cotarii et IIII servi'; and this separation of
the cottars from the team-owning group (a very common
feature of the Hertfordshire Domesday) surely increases the
probability that the priest had a share in the total of teams.[4] In
any case there is no need to seek any special reason for the
precedence accorded to the priest in these entries, which only re-
produces that of the *Forma Inquisitionis* preserved in the Ely preamble. Sometimes indeed the priest is linked with the reeve in
Domesday Book much as he is in that document.[5] Perhaps there
was also a slight tendency to associate priests with the radknights
or radmen of the west, or with the occasional French settler; but

---

[1] Ibid., f. 182.

[2] e.g. Wheathampstead, Hertfordshire: 'Ibi presbyter cum xv villanis habent
[*sic*] v carucas' (ibid., f. 135).

[3] Ibid., f. 134.

[4] With these Hertfordshire entries one may compare that for Cowarne (*Cuure*)
in Herefordshire: 'In dominio sunt ii caruce et presbyter et praepositus et xxvi
villani et viii bordarii. Inter omnes habent xxxii carucas. Ibi iiii servi et faber'
(ibid., f. 186).

[5] Above, p. 272 n. 3.

it would be attributing too much precision to the methods of the Domesday scribes to see much, if any, significance in the variable order in which the different classes of persons are mentioned.[1] In Essex, however, the *formulae* employed by the Little Domesday enable us to see the priest definitely ranked with the *villani*, as distinct from the bordars, in eight cases, and less clearly in a few more, while only at Braxted and Chickney does he seem to be classed with the bordars rather than the *villani*.[2] The priest of Braxted appears indeed to be sharing the poverty which had overtaken the peasantry of that manor since the Conquest, for whereas there had formerly been two tenant plough-teams, they were wholly lacking in 1086, and in place of 4 *villani* and 3 bordars there were only 8 bordars and the priest. In other counties too we occasionally find an entry which suggests that the priest did not possess any plough-beasts. At Minchinhampton in Gloucestershire the enumeration of the peasants and their teams is followed by the statement: 'Ibi presbyter et X servi.'[3] At Abberley in Worcestershire the priest and a serf; at the unidentified *Ruuenore* in Herefordshire 4 serfs, the priest, and the smith; at Bishop's Stortford in Hertfordshire the priest, 2 knights, and 12 cottars, are similarly isolated from the team-owning group.[4] And then we find a Gloucestershire manor where 'there are two ploughs on the demesne and the priest and one *villanus* and four serfs *sine caruca*' and read of Nafford in Worcestershire (where the land was apparently uncultivated) that there is a priest without either plough or stock.[5] But clearly these exceptional entries strengthen the case for thinking that in the villages where priests are included in the group of team-owning peasants, they did possess some plough-beasts and hence some glebe land. Nor must it be forgotten that, while plough-beasts imply land, the priest, like many a bordar or cottar, might

---

[1] For examples of priests placed next to radknights in the enumeration see Alveston, Gloucestershire (Dd. i, f. 165); Ombersley, Worcestershire (f. 175b); Bodenham, Herefordshire (f. 186b); Cleobury Mortimer, Shropshire (f. 260); and Barthomley, Cheshire (f. 265b).

[2] See, for example, Takeley: 'Tunc iij villani modo v et i presbyter. Tunc iii bordarii post et modo x' (Dd. ii, f. 50). At Braxted the entry runs: 'Tunc iiii villani modo nullus. Tunc iii bordarii modo viii et i presbyter' (ibid., f. 12; cf. f. 72b for Chickney).   [3] Dd. i, f. 166b.

[4] Ibid., ff. 176, 186b, 134. There are parallels to the Abberley entry at Eckington and Barlborough in Derbyshire (f. 277); but in that county the priests are usually mentioned separately and not grouped with the peasants, so it would be rash to regard these two entries as significant.

[5] Ibid., ff. 167b (*Scipetune*), 175.

well have a little land without having any oxen. At Hampstead Norris in Berkshire the priest apparently possessed no stock though he had as much as half a hide of land.[1]

From the actual statements which Domesday Book makes about the lands of churches and priests one might easily conclude that in some counties the village churches were much better endowed than those of East Anglia.[2] Churches possessing a hide or more are recorded in considerable numbers. In Berkshire there were churches thus well equipped on perhaps a dozen of the royal manors, and among them that of Shrivenham had no less than 5 hides.[3] In Wiltshire too the royal demesne was notable for rich churches, and outside the *Terra Regis* we find in this county a church with 4 hides at Downton.[4] At Godalming in Surrey there was one with 3 hides.[5] At Wellingore in Lincolnshire there was 'a church and a priest having two carucates and two bovates'.[6] But if in some villages the parochial glebe exceeded that recorded for any village in Norfolk or Suffolk, it would be rash to assume that a higher scale of endowment was general. Where glebe is rarely noted at all, the cases most likely to be judged worthy of record are those of churches

[1] Ibid., f. 63 ('De hac terra tenet presbyter æcclesiæ in elemosina dimidiam hidam et nichil ibi habet').

[2] Boehmer says: 'Wenn wir auch keine Statistik aufstellen können, so gewinnen wir doch den Eindruck, daß sowohl in Wessex wie in Mercia die Widme häufig ½ oder eine ganze Hufe Landes umfaßte, also zwei oder viermal so groß war, wie die besseren ostenglischen Pfarren; nicht selten erreichte oder überschritt sie aber auch die Normalgröße eines Adelsgutes (5h)': op. cit., p. 314.

[3] Dd. i, f. 57b (Shrivenham). I say 'perhaps' because some of the other entries are equivocal.

[4] Ibid., f. 65b.   [5] Ibid., f. 30b.

[6] Ibid. f. 337b. Wellingore church also possessed 14 acres of meadow. Ellis's statement that it 'had 129 acres of meadow, beside 14 acres of other land' is due to a manifest misinterpretation of Domesday (op. cit. i. 295). Godalming and Wellingore were both royal manors: Shrivenham, Downton, and Godalming all gave their names to hundreds. Yet all the examples cited were to all appearance village churches to the exclusion of churches in boroughs, those of market towns like Luton and Leighton Buzzard in Bedfordshire and Crewkerne and Frome in Somerset, and those with more than one priest. Though a village church might have two priests the combination of a large endowment with a reference to two or more priests creates a suspicion that the church was or had been collegiate. Entries which mention a couple of priests but say nothing about a church may possibly relate to two parishes even when not obviously composite like those for Ripple *cum uno membro Uptun* in Worcestershire and Chaddesley *cum viii Bereuuiches* in the same county (ff. 173, 178). It should be noted that Boehmer has invented a 5-hide church at an imaginary place in Gloucestershire called 'Levenot': he mistook the name of a pre-Conquest landowner for a place-name: op. cit., p. 315; cf. Dd. i, f. 166b.

whose possessions were unusually extensive. Moreover entries which merely state that a priest holds a certain amount of land often leave it doubtful whether they relate to parochial glebe or to personal property.[1] And the casual references to glebe which we find in most counties ought probably to be understood as standing out against a background of conditions similar to those which we have seen to be implied in many sections of Domesday Book by the association of the priest with the *villani* and bordars.

It is at least clear that in many parts of the country besides East Anglia the glebe varied in extent from one village to another, but commonly consisted of some regular agrarian unit. The Middlesex data are particularly informing, for, though Domesday only records 18 priests in this county, it states the holdings of all of them. Three had half a virgate or 15 acres, 6 a virgate, 5 half a hide, one 3 virgates, and 3 a whole hide. And even if we exclude equivocal statements which may possibly refer to collegiate minsters or to the private property of priests rather than parochial glebe, we find evidence of variety in a good many counties. In Gloucestershire the range of the recorded cases was much the same as in Middlesex—from 12 acres to a hide.[2] In Wiltshire and Lincolnshire it was greater, for in the former county the church of *Haseberie* (now Hazelbury House in Box) had only half a virgate, while that of Downton, as we have seen, possessed 4 hides, and in Lincolnshire several churches with a bovate of glebe stand out in contrast to the richly endowed church of Wellingore.[3] In Devon, Colyton church had half a virgate while that of Woodbury is credited

---

[1] At Warfield (*Warwelt*) in Berkshire, for example: 'Presbyter Goisfridi de magna vile habet inde i hidam quæ semper fuit de isto manerio sed iste misit in manerio domini sui' (Dd. i, f. 57). Again, at Bibury (*Becheberie*) in Gloucestershire there was a 'presbyter habens iii hidas et cum suis iiii carucas' (ibid., f. 164b). At Chippenham in Wiltshire, where we are told that Bishop Osbern holds the church of the manor with 2 hides, the position is made clear by the statement: 'Una ex his hidis est tainlande altera pertinet æcclesiæ' (ibid., f. 64b), cf. Long Ashton, Somerset (f. 88b); but similar distinctions may well have passed unnoticed elsewhere.

[2] Dd. i, ff. 164 (Dymock), 165 (Bishop's Cleeve).

[3] Ibid., f. 65b, and, for Lincolnshire, ff. 337b (Coleby), 342b (Middle Rasen), 363b (Syston), 371 (Thorpe-in-the-Fallows or Aisthorpe), 337b (Wellingore). Intermediate cases occur in both counties: e.g. (in Wiltshire) Burbage with a virgate (f. 65b), Collingbourne with half a hide (f. 65), Pewsey with a carucate, Avebury with 2 hides (f. 65b), and (in Lincolnshire) Wilsford with 2 bovates (f. 366), Willoughby-in-the-Marsh with a half carucate (or half a team) (f. 355), and Potter Hanworth with a carucate (or a team) (f. 361).

with a hide and a virgate and half a 'ferlin'.[1] Both Somerset and Sussex afford examples of glebe amounting to a virgate, to half a hide and to $1\frac{1}{2}$ hides respectively; and virgates, half-hides, and hides occur in Hampshire.[2] In Berkshire, along with the rich churches already noted, there were several with half a hide and one (at Letcombe Regis) which apparently possessed only a virgate.[3] Endowments ranging from 15 acres to ten times that amount are found in Essex.[4] And, scanty and casual as the data are, differences of some degree or other can also be discerned more or less clearly in the village church endowments of Yorkshire, Nottinghamshire, Cheshire, Shropshire, Worcestershire, Herefordshire, and Surrey.[5]

The difference between a 'fat living' and a 'lean living' was not of course determined solely by the amount of glebe. The revenue from tithe would vary with the extent and resources of the parish, and the yield of other dues such as plough-alms and burial fees would also depend upon these factors. It would be rash indeed, in view of the manifold uncertainties involved, to attempt to gauge the relative importance of these various sources of income.[6] But it is at any rate certain that the village priest frequently received only a portion of the tithe; and it may be that in some places the whole of it was still paid to a central mother church. A good many rich churches were, moreover, held by wealthy ecclesiastics who must have employed a chaplain or vicar to discharge the duty of the cure. And even where the village priest was in a full sense the incumbent of the living, it appears that he might have to pay a rent for the use of the glebe to the owner of the church,

[1] Ibid., f. 100*b*. In the Exon. text, however, the land of Woodbury church is given as *half* a hide and a virgate and half a ferlin (p. 88).

[2] See (for Somerset) Long Ashton (Dd. i, f. 88*b*), Chewton Mendip (f. 87), Carhampton (f. 91*b*); also (for Sussex) *Wilesham* (f. 18*b*), North Mundham (f. 24), Stoughton (*Estone*, f. 24); and (for Hampshire) Ann (f. 49), Ringwood (f. 39), Whitchurch (f. 41). The church of Singleton (Sussex) possessed $3\frac{1}{4}$ hides (f. 23); but the reference to *clerici* suggests that it was, as Page says, 'a small minster'.

[3] Ibid., f. 57*b*.

[4] Ibid., ii, ff. 26*b* (Horndon-on-the-Hill), 2*b* (Hatfield Broadoak). A reason for the special mention of a small endowment can sometimes be discerned. Several churches which had only a virgate had different owners from the manors to which they otherwise belonged. At *Wilesham* the church virgate was not part of the 15 hides at which the manor was rated. Leatherhead church, which had 40 acres, belonged to the manor of Ewell (f. 30*b*).

[5] For cases in Staffordshire see *V.C.H. Staffs.* iv (1958), 19.

[6] How various they might be is shown by the recorded rights of the church of Lambourn: Robertson, *Anglo-Saxon Charters*, appendix i, No. v.

whether it was owned by the lord of the manor or by a monastery to which it had been given.

As regards the diversion of tithe to monasteries Domesday Book tells us little. The abbey of St. Michael's Mount in Normandy has the church and tithe of Basingstoke; the abbey of Lyre has several churches and tithes in the Isle of Wight; both the abbey of Lyre and that of Cormeilles are described as possessing the tithes and in some cases the churches of several manors in Gloucestershire and Worcestershire and (in the case of Cormeilles) in Herefordshire.[1] But this form of benefaction cost the donor nothing and the charter evidence shows that it was widely favoured by the baronage of Norman England. Thus, during the Conqueror's reign, Hugh de Grentemaisnil gave two-thirds of the tithe on all his manors to the abbey of St. Evroult; Geoffrey de Wirce gave tithes in a number of villages, along with Monks Kirby Priory, to St. Nicholas of Angers; Ralf de Toeni the elder gave tithes to the abbey of St. Peter of Castellion; Hugh de Gournay, Henry de Ferrers, Richard fitz Gilbert de Clare, and others gave tithes to the abbey of Bec.[2] English foundations were also enriched in the same way. Walter de Lacy, who died in 1085, gave or bequeathed two-thirds of the tithe of ten vills to the church of St. Peter in Hereford which he had founded; the founder of Belvoir Priory, Robert de Toeni, who died in 1088, similarly gave to that house two-thirds of the tithe in ten vills; and Geoffrey de Mandeville the first, when he founded Hurley Priory towards the end of the Conqueror's reign, gave it one-third of the corn tithes and two-thirds of the tithe of livestock on all his manors.[3] But the great extent to which tithes were appropriated by monasteries is most fully revealed by confirmation charters and similar material of twelfth-century date. To take one example, the possessions which Henry II confirmed to the abbey of St. Mary's, York, in 1156–7, included tithes in at least thirty-eight different places.[4] It is probable that these gifts of

[1] Dd. i, ff. 43, 52b, 164, 179b, 180b. That it was St. Mary of Lyre and not St. Mary of Cormeilles that possessed the tithe at Forthampton in Gloucestershire seems clear from the confirmatory charter of Henry II: *Mon. Ang.* vi, pt. ii, pp. 1092–3.

[2] Ordericus Vitalis, *Hist. Eccles.* vi, c. 5, ed. Le Prevost, iii. 19–29; *Mon. Ang.* vi, pt. ii, p. 996; ibid., p. 995 (cf. ibid., p. 1026, and Round, *Calender of Documents Preserved in France*, No. 416); H. E. Salter, *E.H.R.* xl. 73–78.

[3] *Gloucester Cart.* i. 85; *Mon. Ang.* iii. 289; J. Armitage Robinson, *Gilbert Crispin* (1911), pp. 132–4.

[4] Farrer, *Early Yorkshire Charters*, i, No. 354.

tithe were very often confined to that due from the manorial
demesne, but even so they must have meant that much less than
might otherwise appear was available for the remuneration of
the village priests.[1]

That well endowed churches were made a source of income
for ecclesiastics who had served the king in his writing office or
otherwise and whose pluralism was incompatible with personal
discharge of the parochial duty, is clear from Domesday Book,
though in this matter also it fails to reveal the full extent of the
practice.[2] The classic case is that of Rainbald or Reginbald, the
king's priest, who was described by Round as 'the first great
pluralist' and probably held the office of chancellor at some time
or other under William I.[3] In Domesday he is credited with the
possession of seven rich churches—two in Somerset, Wiltshire,
and Berkshire and one in Gloucestershire—but according to
a rather suspect charter which is attributed to Henry I, and is
concerned with the lands and churches formerly held by Rainbald, he also possessed (presumably at the time of his death)
eight or nine other churches, together with some dependent
chapels.[4] Frome in Somerset, which was the richest of all his
churches, he had obtained before the Conquest; and it was also
before the Conquest that Osbern, the future Bishop of Exeter,
who belongs to the same group of royal clerks and chaplains and

---

[1] The limitation to demesne tithes is sometimes pretty clearly indicated, and
probably should often be understood where it is not; but H. E. Salter's assertion
that 'it was only the tithes of the demesne that might be transferred' seems to overlook the case where the donor was owner of the church and not merely a tithe-
payer (*Newington Longeville Charters* (Oxfordshire Record Soc., 1921), p. xiv). The
abbey of Cirencester received 'duas partes decimae de toto dominio Cirencestriae
et totam decimam totius parrochiae': *Mon. Ang.* vi, pt. i, pp. 177–8.

[2] Boehmer says: 'Diese reichen Pfarreien waren auch hier meist königliche
Pfarreien und natürlich in der Regel nicht in den Händen simpler clerici rustici,
sondern in Besitze von Leuten, die dem König amtlich oder persönlich nahe
standen und eben darum nie selber den Pfarrer spielen wollten und konnten':
op. cit., pp. 314–15.

[3] Round's belief that he was chancellor in the Confessor's reign, rested on doubtful foundations, as Miss Harmer has shown (*Bulletin of the John Rylands Library*,
1938, pp. 341–2); but the interlinear description of him as *canceler* in Domesday
(i, f. 180b) deserves respect.

[4] Dd. i, ff. 86b, 91 (Frome and Milborne Port), 65b (Pewsey and Avebury), 56b,
57 (Cookham and Bray), 162b (Cheltenham); *Mon. Ang.* vi, pt. i, pp. 177–8.
Among the churches mentioned in the charter are two in Northamptonshire, one
in Buckinghamshire, and the outstandingly rich church of Shrivenham in Berkshire; it also includes churches at three places (Hagbourne, Berkshire, and Latton
and Eisey, Wiltshire) where Domesday shows Rainbald as holding land but says
nothing about any churches.

was possibly chancellor about 1070, received a well endowed church at Chippenham in Wiltshire and the extremely rich church of Bosham in Sussex, both of which he still retained in 1086.[1] And among the pluralists of Domesday Book we also find two undoubted chancellors of the Conqueror's reign—Osmund, who was rewarded with the bishopric of Salisbury in 1078, and Maurice, who succeeded him as chancellor and became Bishop of London in 1085 or 1086. Osmund held a hide of land with the church of Faringdon in Berkshire, half a church with a half-hide at some place in Wiltshire, and some of the lands belonging to the exceptionally wealthy church of Grantham in Lincolnshire.[2] Maurice had two 3-hide churches in Somerset (North Curry and St. Andrew's, Ilchester), a church with half a hide at Congresbury in the same county, and more than a hide and a half of the land of Wimborne church in Dorset.[3] There can be little doubt that similar provision was made, on a smaller scale, for royal clerks of less exalted station, but certainty is precluded by the darkness which shrouds the careers of these humbler folk and the hazards which attend attempts to identify individuals bearing common names.[4]

It is impossible to determine the precise relation of the rich pluralists to their churches. They may have been proprietors rather than incumbents. We are told indeed that Rainbald was the priest at Frome (*Reinbald ibi est presbyter*) and the Exon. text seems to assert that he 'served' the church of Milborne Port (*qui servit ecclesie*); but the statement that Bishop Osmund holds half a church savours of proprietorship.[5] One suspects that the

[1] Dd. i, ff. 64b, 17, cf. f. 43. That Rainbald held the church of Frome T.R.E. is stated in Exon., p. 83.   [2] Dd. i, ff. 57b, 65b, 343b.

[3] Ibid., ff. 86b, 91 (two entries), 87, 76. It should be noted that the examples cited in this paragraph are not confined to village churches.

[4] It seems likely that Bristuard the priest who as one of the *elemosinarii regis* held the churches of Dorchester and Bere in Dorset (with more than a hide and the tithes) was the same person as the priest Bristoard described as holding the church of Bedwyn (with 1½ hides) in the list of persons holding churches which concludes the account of the *Terra Regis* in Wiltshire and includes churches held by Rainbald and by the Bishops Osbern and Osmond (ibid., ff. 79, 65b).

[5] Ibid., ff. 86b, 65b; Exon., p. 84. In the later Middle Ages, however, a church might have two incumbents, presented by different patrons and each receiving half the emoluments. Lower Heyford in Oxfordshire is an example of this, each incumbent being *rector medietatis ecclesie* (*Rot. Hund.* ii. 827). It seems possible that some of the churches with two priests mentioned in Domesday were divided in this way. In view of the fact that half the church of Wetherden in Suffolk belonged in 1086 to St. Edmunds Abbey and the other half apparently to Hugh de Montfort, it is interesting to find that in 1198 Abbot Samson and Robert de Scales each

distinction was often left in obscurity. The same man might, no doubt, be both proprietor and incumbent. But, in any case, an absentee, whether he was the one or the other, would draw an income from the church and less would be left for the resident priest.

The rights exercised by the owners of churches, whether laymen or ecclesiastics, are a matter on which sharply opposed opinions have been held by historians. Vinogradoff maintained that 'although subject to patronage, and occasionally to exploitation, the township churches and their lands never became the property of the manorial lord in the same way as mills or fisheries', but at the same time he held that 'all parish churches had to contribute to the farm of their manors' and that 'the insufficiency of parochial churches, the rise of private jurisdictions, and the spread of private religious bequests, led to the foundation of many private churches and chapels, which collided, in respect of revenue, with the mother churches of the parishes'.[1] Boehmer, on the other hand, came to the conclusion that every church in England was a proprietary church and had an owner.[2] Vinogradoff's language is not very clear, but there can be no doubt that the proprietary church was far from being the unusual thing he seems to imply. In Domesday Book churches are commonly associated with mills and other sources of manorial income; and now and again we find statements which clearly indicate the proprietary rights of the lord without in any way suggesting that such rights were exceptional. Thus Turold the priest holds the church of West Hanney in Berkshire of Walter Giffard; Osbern d'Eu holds that of Farnham of the Bishop of Winchester; Robert the Cook, who holds Ninfield in Sussex as a tenant of the Count of Eu, has in demesne there one plough and a church and one bordar; and several times in Norfolk we are told that the churches have been included in the valuation of the manors.[3] Particularly significant are some

---

quitclaimed to the other not half the advowson, but the advowson of half the church—*advocationem medietatis ecclesie*: Dd. ii, ff. 360, 409; *Kalendar of Abbot Samson*, (Camden Soc.), No. 118, p. 145.

[1] *English Society*, pp. 374, 373.

[2] 'Wie auf dem Kontinente, haben damals auch in England alle Kirchen einen Eigentümer. Alle Kirchen sind *propriae ecclesiae*, Eigenkirchen': op. cit., p. 317. But he judged that the owner's rights were less extensive than on the continent: 'Der Kirchherr hatte hier nicht mehr, sondern stets weniger Rechte, als anderwärts': ibid., p. 327.

[3] Dd. i, ff. 60, 31, 18 (*Nerewelle*); ii, ff. 116, 172, 208, 219*b*, 234*b*, 265.

entries which show that property in the church has been divided along with property in the mill. At Linwood in Lincolnshire Durand Malet has the third of a church and the third of a mill.[1] At Elkington in the same county there is half a church and half the site of a mill.[2] A manor at Taverham in Norfolk includes a quarter of a mill and a quarter of a church.[3] At Flixton in Suffolk half a church and half a mill are held by a certain Geoffrey as tenant of Eudo, son of Spirewic, while the other halves of both appear to have belonged to the Bishop of Thetford.[4] Comparable with these entries is that associating the third part of a church and the third part of a fair at Aspall in Suffolk.[5] But whether the division of rights in a church originated in the partition of an estate or in the co-operation of two or more lords in its foundation, a property right is clearly implied whenever a fraction of a church is recorded as belonging to some manor. And references of this kind are numerous. Boehmer reckoned that 187 churches are described in fractional terms in Domesday Book; and if a large proportion of these were in Lincolnshire or East Anglia, and division into such small fractions as a fifth, an eighth, or a twelfth is hardly to be found elsewhere, this is not surprising in a region where the vills commonly contained a plurality of manors, where sokemen and *liberi homines* were especially numerous, and where traces of a custom of partible succession can be found. Outside Lincolnshire and East Anglia occasional references to half-churches, quarter-churches, and the like have been noted in eight counties from Yorkshire in the north and Cheshire in the west to Berkshire and Wiltshire in the south. Even more decisive and far-reaching evidence is provided by the frequency with which churches were given to monasteries, for it was the churches and not merely the advowsons that were given, so that the proprietary right of the donor is presupposed by the gift. By 1086 more than a hundred English churches had, according to Boehmer, come into the possession of religious foundations on the other side of the

---

[1] Dd. i, f. 365.   [2] Ibid., f. 351*b* (*Archintone*).

[3] Dd. ii, ff. 157*b*, 158.

[4] Ibid., ff. 434*b*, 380, 381; cf. the case of Newton near Folkingham in Lincolnshire: Dd. i, f. 341*b*.

[5] 'In eadem tercia pars æcclesiæ et tercia pars feriæ': Dd. ii, f. 418. The entry concludes the description of the Suffolk lands of Rannulf Peverel. The rest of the church appears to have belonged to Robert Malet (ibid., f. 321); but there is no further reference in Domesday to the fair: H. C. Darby, *Eastern England*, p. 203.

channel; and charters of the early Norman period bear witness to the freedom with which laymen disposed of churches in this way.[1] But besides being transferred by gift, churches could be bought and sold, given in pledge, or let at farm. Hugh fitz-Baldric has bought the church of St. Andrew in the city of York.[2] About St. Mary's, Huntingdon, there is a conflict of claims: according to the local jury the church and its land belonged to the abbey of Thorney and had been given in pledge to the burgesses by the abbot, but King Edward gave it to two of his priests, and they sold it to Hugh the king's chamberlain who resold it to two priests of the town.[3] The church of Grantham was at farm, formerly for £8 and now for £10 but is only worth 100s.[4] These were not village churches; but the village churches cannot have been more sacrosanct than they were.

That the owner of a church was commonly paid a rent can scarcely be doubted.[5] Occasionally, we find direct reference to such a payment in Domesday Book. The rich church of North Curry in Somerset, which Bishop Maurice holds with 3 hides of land, renders 60s.[6] That of Corfham in Shropshire renders 18s. to the monks of Shrewsbury.[7] At Godalming in Surrey, Rannulf Flambard holds a church which renders 12s. a year, and at Streatham in the same county there is a chapel which renders 8s.[8] There are five churches rendering 64s. on the Abbot of Fecamp's unidentified manor of *Rameslie* in Sussex, and a church in Chichester which belongs to the archiepiscopal manor of Pagham renders the same number of pence.[9] A church at Sherborne in Hampshire pays 20s., one at West Meon in the same county 50s., and one at Pershore in Worcestershire 16s.[10] An entry relating to a church in York, which belonged to Richard son of Erfast, tells us that he got 30s. from the church and its land.[11]

---

[1] Boehmer, op. cit., p. 345. In donations of the period it is not unusual for the lands or appurtenances of the churches to be specifically mentioned: see, for example, Ralph Paynel's charter of c. 1090–1100 refounding the priory of Holy Trinity, York, in which the formula 'ecclesiam de X et quicquid ad eam pertinet' is repeated ten times: *Early Yorkshire Charters*, ed. C. T. Clay, vi, No. 1. For an illuminating discussion of the later survival of such phrases and the gradual limitation of ownership to the advowson see Stenton, *Danelaw Charters*, pp. lxxii–lxxiv.

[2] Dd. i, f. 298.   [3] Ibid., f. 208.   [4] Ibid., f. 337b.
[5] Cf. Boehmer, op. cit., p. 318.   [6] Dd. i, f. 86b.
[7] Ibid., f. 253b.   [8] Ibid., ff. 30b, 34b.   [9] Ibid., ff. 17, 16b.
[10] Ibid., ff. 45, 40b, 174b.
[11] 'De ecclesia et terra habet xxx solidos': Dd. i, f. 327; and for the identification of the church with Holy Trinity in Micklegate see ibid., f. 298, and *V.C.H. Yorks.* ii. 176, 192.

Three churches which belonged to the Bishop of Winchester's manor of Alresford in Hampshire used to pay £6 a year but were unable to sustain the charge.[1] On the other hand, the church of Luton in Bedfordshire, though it possessed 5 hides of land and is apparently valued at £3, is only paying £1.[2] In three cases the parish priest is indicated as the rent-payer. At West Wickham in Kent he pays 40s. a year; at Thanet in the same county, 20s. a year; at *Ladgvern* (? Llanwarne) in Herefordshire, 2s.[3]

From such casual references as these it would be rash to draw any general conclusion. But they help us to interpret the indirect evidence afforded by the Domesday valuation of churches and their glebe. Like mills in some counties, many churches in East Anglia, and a few elsewhere, are along with their glebe lands specifically valued. Alternatively the Norfolk Domesday, as we have seen, will sometimes tell us that all the churches on the lands of a certain tenant-in-chief have been valued with the manors; and thus appears to imply that the value of a church means its value for the manorial lord who owns it, and not what it is worth to the parish priest.[4] Further, where the area or assessed area of the glebe is recorded, the value has often an obvious relation to its acreage.[5] In Suffolk, out of some 97 entries giving both areas and values, there are more than 40 in which the value is precisely 2d. an acre, 10 in which it is 1d. an acre, and 7 in which it works out at 1½d. an acre. In Norfolk, out of 106 cases that have been noted, 41 show values of 1d. an acre and 8 of 2d. an acre, while in 9, 1s. was reckoned for every 10 acres. In other counties information is scanty, but a correspondence between the valuation and the assessed area of the

---

[1] 'Ibi iii aecclesiae de iiii libris. Hae reddebant vi libras per annum sed pati non potuerunt': Dd. i, f. 40; cf. f. 41b (Hinton Ampner, Hampshire): 'Ibi aecclesia de xl solidis. Reddit tamen l solidos.'

[2] Dd. i, f. 209. Perhaps the glebe, or some of it, was in this case retained for his own use by William the Chamberlain who held the church with its land of the king.

[3] Ibid., ff. 9, 12, 181b.

[4] Dd. ii, f. 172 ('Omnes ecclesiae de terra Willelmi de Warena appreciate sunt cum maneriis'); cf. ff. 208 (Hermer), 219b (St. Benet of Holme), 234b (Reginald, son of Ivo), 265 (Tovi). The churches of Walsingham and Melton are individually described as *in pretio manerii*: ibid., f. 254, 254b.

[5] At Shouldham in Norfolk two churches with 73 acres appear to be valued at 6s. 1d. and at Coddenham in Suffolk a church with 12½ acres is valued at 25d.: ibid., ff. 250b, 338. At Bungay in Suffolk the value was apparently 2d. per arable acre, no allowance being made for 2 acres of glebe meadow (ibid., f. 300, cf. Loddon, Norfolk, f. 211b); but Boehmer's statement that glebe meadows are frequently mentioned and ignored in this way in the rent (op. cit., p. 318) is unjustified.

glebe is sometimes clearly discernible—especially in Wiltshire.[1]
One cannot exclude the possibility that rates of 2d. or 1d. an
acre were estimates based on a rule of thumb which treated the
carucate or hide as worth either £1 or 10s.; but even so it is
hard to see what they can have been except estimates of the
rents that owners of churches might expect to receive. Moreover,
in the case of manors, the Domesday 'values' are often the
actual rents at which the manors were put to farm, so it would be
only natural if a similar practice was followed in the valuation of
churches.[2] Nor is positive evidence altogether lacking. For three
churches in Somerset—Congresbury, Milverton, and Frome—
the Exon. text employs the words *reddit per annum* where the
Exchequer Domesday says merely *valet*; and a priest at Bridg-
ham in Norfolk, who is described in Domesday as 'worth two
shillings', appears in the Ely Inquest as a 'priest of ten acres'
who 'renders' that sum.[3]

Although the proprietary church with glebe for which rent
was due was of common occurrence, it should not be assumed
that all the village churches of Domesday England were of this
type. In the folios devoted to East Anglia, besides entries recording the area and value of the parochial glebe, there are many
which give the area without referring to its value and many
which describe the glebe as 'free land'. The first of these two
methods of description was obviously employed where the value
of the church was merged in that of the manor; but churches
which in fact possessed 'free land' might also be mentioned in
this summary way, as is shown by the cases of Barham and
Brihtoluestana in Suffolk, for the Ely Inquest here supplements
Domesday Book by describing the glebe at these two places as
libera terra.[4] In Domesday Book itself well over a hundred Suffolk
churches are credited with the possession of 'free land'; and

---

[1] On the *Terra Regis* in Wiltshire glebe is valued at £1 per hide (or in one case
per carucate) at Rushall, Aldbourne, Wootton Rivers, Pewsey, Avebury, and
Heytesbury; at £2 a hide at Britford, Combe, Melksham, and Bedwyn; at £4 a
hide at Burbage and *Haseberie*: Dd. i, ff. 65, 65b. For examples of glebe valued at
£1 per hide in other counties see *Wilesham* (Filsham Farm in Hollington), Sussex,
ibid., f. 18–18b; Sparsholt, Berkshire, f. 57; Carhampton, Somerset, f. 91b; Finhoe,
Devon, f. 101; *Nedreham* (Haddenham), Buckinghamshire, f. 143b; Leighton
Buzzard, Bedfordshire, f. 209; and Mersea, Essex, ii, f. 22.

[2] For manorial rents entered as values see above, Chapter V.

[3] Dd. i, ff. 87, 91b, 91, and Exon., pp. 98, 179, 180; Dd. ii, f. 213b, and I.C.C.,
ed. Hamilton, p. 133.

[4] Dd. ii, ff. 383b, 406; I.C.C., pp. 159, 143.

though no other county can show more than a few whose glebe is thus described, the contrast is perhaps due rather to peculiarity in the practice of the Domesday scribes than to an actual difference in conditions. Even in the Norfolk Domesday only about half a dozen cases have been noted; but here, besides the inherent improbability of so sharp a contrast between such similar counties, a warning against the *argumentum ex silentio* is provided by the fact that six Norfolk churches which appear to be altogether ignored by Domesday are entered as possessing 'free land' in the Ely Inquest.[1]

Unfortunately the meaning of 'free land' in this connexion is obscure. It has been suggested that the term may refer to 'exemption from the geld or from military services'.[2] But it may well bear more than one sense in Domesday and imply different or more extensive exemptions than these, and it is possible that the glebe thus described was in many cases rent free.[3] In Suffolk —the only county for which the evidence is abundant—Domesday very rarely assigns a value to churches possessing free land, while of the churches with land that is not so described more than a third are valued.[4] The problem is complicated by the fact that a number of the Suffolk churches are stated to hold their free land *pro elemosina* or *in elemosina*, while the church of Woolpit in this county and some five churches in Norfolk appear as holding land *in elemosina* though nothing is said about the land being 'free'. We must not, however, assume that the term *elemosina* as here employed bears a technical meaning and necessarily implies a tenure of the kind known later as frankalmoin. In Domesday Book the word 'is used in various senses and contexts', and sometimes seems merely to refer to the charitable intentions of a donor.[5] If freedom from secular burdens

---

[1] I.C.C., pp. 136, 137, 137 n. 9 (*Dereham, Torp, Felteuuella, Nortuualda, Waltona, Teritona*).

[2] B. A. Lees in *V.C.H. Suffolk*, i. 403. In the late twelfth-century inquisition of churches belonging to St. Paul's, churches with 'free land' seem to be contrasted with those whose land was geldable: *D.S.P.*, pp. 147–51.

[3] Boehmer (op. cit., p. 329) says: 'Libera terra bedeutet in Domesday, wie es scheint, auch oft soviel wie zinsfrei . . . in der Regel aber wohl, das auf der Widme nur die trinoda necessitas lastet.'

[4] Domesday assigns no value to the churches with free land in Norfolk, but this cannot be regarded as significant, for in this county the values of churches are often included in the manorial values, and the Ely Inquest does assign a value to each of the six Norfolk churches with free land which it records: see above, note 1.

[5] Pollock and Maitland, i. 241. At *Tuanatuna* (? Swanton) in Norfolk the church had 60 acres of free land *elemosina plurimorum* (Dd. ii, f. 189b). Pollock and Maitland's

is suggested by a Gloucestershire entry stating that the church of Cirencester holds of the king 3 hides *in elemosina* which it had held of King Edward *quietas ab omni consuetudine*, we find on the other hand that, of three estates in Sussex which three Norman abbeys hold *in elemosina* of Earl Roger, two are said to 'defend' themselves for 2 hides and the third for 11 hides.[1] Of definite spiritual service attached to lands held *in elemosina* there are two examples in Norfolk. A priest at Hevingham with 40 acres and another at Witton with 30 acres have each to sing three masses; but none the less the land of the former is valued and that of the latter is stated to be liable to geld.[2] And though the expression *libera terra in elemosina* employed in the Suffolk entries seems to bring us close to the *libera elemosina* of the next century, even that did not always mean exemption from all secular burdens, while the concentration of all the Suffolk entries in a few consecutive folios of the Little Domesday creates a suspicion that we have to do with the idiosyncrasy of a particular scribe and need not regard glebe described in these terms as different in character from that of which we are merely told that it is *libera terra*.[3]

contention that the words *in elemosina* sometimes implied a precarious tenure is hardly sustained by the examples they cite, op. cit. i. 241 n. 2.

[1] Dd. i, ff. 166*b*, 25 (Climping), 25*b* (Eastergate and Runcton).

[2] 'In Heuincham i liber homo presbyter xl acras terrae in elemosina et cantat unaquaque ebdomada tres missas semper i caruca et i acra prati silva x porc(orum) et valet v solidos et iiij denarios' (Dd. ii, f. 133); 'In Wittuna i presbyter xxx acras in elemosina semper ix soc(emani) de xii acris terrae semper ii carucae et ii acrae prati ex hoc cantat iiij missas pro rege et regina et tunc redd[ebat] ii solidos et totum habet i leugam in longitudine et dimidiam in latitudine et x d[enarios] de gelto quicunque ibi teneat' (ibid., f. 133, 133*b*). The word *tunc* in the latter entry shows, I think, that the rent was no longer due.

[3] The Suffolk entries referring to *elemosina* all relate to lands of St. Edmund's; but that seems to be irrelevant. The description of the abbey's estates extends from the beginning of f. 356 (verso) to the end of f. 372 (recto) and the entries in question all occur between the beginning of f. 361 (verso) and the end of f. 366 (recto). In this section 25 churches and one fraction of a church are credited with free land 'in' or 'for' alms, 2 churches with free land not so described, one with land in alms, not characterized as 'free', and 3 churches and one fraction of a church with glebe merely described as 'land' or 'acres'. On the rest of the abbey's land in Suffolk we find, on the other hand, 23 churches with 'free land', 18 churches and 7 fractions of churches with 'land' or 'acres' and not a single case in which the word *elemosina* is used. The whole description is arranged hundred by hundred, but the 'elemosinary' section ends in the middle of Blackbourn Hundred. The hypothesis of scribal idiosyncrasy is not invalidated by the fact that the manuscript of the Little Domesday shows no change of handwriting at the beginning or end of the section, for it is probably a fair copy of a preliminary draft as Professor Galbraith has suggested.

For examples of secular services due from lands held in frankalmoin see Pollock and Maitland, op. cit. i. 245 n. 2, 246 n. 1; cf. Farrer, *Early Yorkshire Charters*, ii, No. 822, quoted by A. L. Poole, *Obligations of Society* (1946), p. 6.

For counties other than Suffolk the evidence bearing upon the problem is scanty; and little that is definite can be discovered beyond the fact that conditions varied from place to place. At Londonthorpe in Lincolnshire land belonging to the church of Grantham is described as 15 bovates *ad geldum*, but none the less is *quieta ab omnibus servitiis*; and similarly we read that two churches in Salford used to hold a carucate in Manchester which was free of all dues except the geld—'quietam ab omni consuetudine praeter geldum'.[1] On the other hand, the land of the church at *Ladgvern* in Herefordshire does not pay geld, but, as we have seen, the priest pays a rent for it—*reddit ii solidos inde*.[2] In Berkshire, glebe free of geld is recorded at Wantage and Sparsholt, but geld is paid on the glebe at Thatcham and at West Hanney.[3] In Wiltshire, in a list of ten churches belonging to the *Terra Regis*, the amount of the glebe and the value are given for each, but among them Highworth seems to be distinguished by the fact that geld was not paid; and in the same county one of the 5 hides belonging to the church of Alderbury is definitely marked off from the others by its freedom from this burden.[4] Yet of 2 hides at Bitton in Gloucestershire we are told that one used to pay geld and that the other belonged to the church, as if this implied exemption.[5] Here and there glebe is said to be held *in elemosina*. This was the case at Stoke-by-Guildford in Surrey, at Eling and Ringwood in Hampshire, at Hampstead Norris in Berkshire.[6] At Horndon-on-the-Hill in Essex there were 15 acres *ad elemosinam ecclesiae*.[7] And probably one should see a reference to glebe in such entries as those which state that the priest at Brompton Regis in Somerset holds a hide *elemosina de rege*, that at Childwall in Lancashire there used to be a priest with half a carucate *in elemosina*, and that in the time of King Edward a priest had held 30 acres *in elemosina* at Wethersfield in Essex.[8] But there is no knowing what precisely these expressions mean; while the statement that a hide at Tottenhall in Staffordshire 'est elemosina regis ad ecclesiam ejusdem villae' was perhaps intended merely to indicate that the endowment

---

[1] Dd. i, ff. 343b, 270.   [2] Ibid., f. 181b.

[3] Ibid., ff. 57, 56b, 60. Values are given for Wantage, Sparsholt, and Thatcham, but not for West Hanney unless its valuation is included in that of the manor.

[4] Ibid., ff. 65b, 68b. I have reckoned as one of the ten churches the half of a church (unnamed) which Bishop Osmund held of the king *in elemosina*.

[5] Ibid., f. 170b.   [6] Ibid., ff. 30, 38b, 39, 63.

[7] Dd. ii, f. 26b.   [8] Dd. i, ff. 86b, 269b; ii, f. 4.

was a royal gift.[1] And who can say what differences of condition,
if any, there were between the half-virgate of glebe at Lymn in
Cheshire which was *quieta*, the hide which was *libera* at Aldington in Worcestershire, and that which 'never paid geld' at
Droitwich?[2]

Darkness and doubt thus inevitably obscure much that we
should like to know about the social and economic position of
the village clergy; and but few general conclusions can be
drawn from the evidence. The recorded facts about the glebe,
even if taken to be a fair sample, afford no certain means of
measuring the prosperity or poverty of the parish priests. Their
other sources of income—tithe and burial fees and the rest—
must have varied greatly from place to place. Moreover, rent
was often paid for the glebe; the tithe, or some portion of it, was
in many cases diverted to the maintenance of a monastery; and,
in spite of the increasing disrepute of 'simony', it cannot be
doubted that the incumbent of a living sometimes made an
initial payment to obtain it. Of these deductions and payments,
however, we know so little that it is impossible to estimate at all
surely even the range of difference in worldly fortune which
separated the poorest of the country clergy from the richest.
Perhaps some feeling that a moderate standard was fitting for
this class of men may have facilitated the diversion of tithe to
extra-parochial purposes and clothed with propriety the use of
very rich livings as endowments for absentees who served the
king as clerks in the administration of government. At the same
time it is clear that considerable differences remained. Occasionally Domesday Book affords a glimpse of a country parson with
glebe approximating in scale and character to a small manor. At
Ashbourne in Derbyshire the glebe was assessed at a carucate
and the priest possessed a whole plough-team of his own and
had as tenants 2 *villani* and 2 bordars with half a team between
them, besides another tenant described as a 'man' (*unum hominem*) who paid a rent of 16d.[3] At Brompton Regis in Somerset,
again, the priest had one team and his 4 villan tenants another, while his estate as a whole was assessed at a hide and
valued at 20s.[4] At Shrivenham in Berkshire the scale of things
was yet larger, for the glebe was assessed at 5 hides and, besides

[1] Dd. i, f. 247b.   [2] Ibid., ff. 267b, 175b, 174b.   [3] Ibid., f. 272b.
[4] Ibid., f. 86b. The land here included 3 acres of meadow and was held *in* (?) *elemosina de rege.*

a demesne plough, we read of 4 *villani* and 5 bordars with 2 ploughs and are told that 'what the priest has' is worth £4.[1] And in spite of the absence of any reference to teams possessed by his tenants there can be no doubt about the generally 'manorial' character of the property held by the priest of the manor (*presbyter hujus manerii*) at *Hinetone* (? Hinton Martell) in Dorset, which comprised 2 ploughs, 4 *villani*, and 2 bordars, a mill rendering 5*s*., 11 acres of meadow, a considerable piece of woodland, and 11 houses in Wimborne.[2] In a few cases where the village priest appears as enjoying a generous endowment of glebe there is nothing to indicate whether or no it was divided in 'manorial' fashion between a home farm and peasant holdings. Thus at Aldbourne in Wiltshire the glebe amounted to 2 hides worth 40*s*. and the priest (*presbyter ejusdem aecclesiae*) has 2 ploughs, while in the same county the priest at Bishop's Cannings similarly holds a couple of hides, and the holding of the priest at Potterne (*presbyter hujus manerii*) is valued at 40*s*. like the glebe at Aldbourne.[3]

That in some villages the resident parson occupied a position markedly superior to that of the ordinary villager is thus quite clear; but no such conclusion can be drawn in respect of a good many places where Domesday reveals a rich church or mentions a priest possessed of a considerable estate. As we have seen, fat livings were often held by absentees and pluralists; and, besides that, some of the more affluent clergy appear to have been just landowners who happened to be in orders and, for all that we can tell, exercised no pastoral functions in the parishes where their property lay. Among these last we must certainly include two priests who were reckoned to be tenants-in-chief—Alfred, the tenant of Wolverton in Hampshire, and Osbern who held three small manors situated in different wapentakes in Lincolnshire—but outside the ranks of the tenants-in-chief there were others occupying very similar positions;[4] and, though it is often hard to know whether Domesday is referring to glebe or to the property of an individual, a suspicion that we have to do with the latter can hardly be avoided in cases where the name of the

[1] Dd. i, f. 57*b*. The demesne plough is not actually described as *in dominio*, but that it belonged to a rectorial home farm is clearly shown by the language of the entry: 'ibi i caruca et iiij villani et v bordarii cum ij carucis.'

[2] Ibid., f. 76.   [3] Ibid., ff. 65, 66.

[4] e.g. Gilbert the priest who as tenant of the Countess Judith held 2 hides at *Cotes* and another 2 hides at Eynesbury in Huntingdonshire: ibid., f. 206*b*.

priest is recorded.[1] When St. Wulfstan went into Nottinghamshire to consecrate the church of Ratcliffe-on-Soar, he encountered a wealthy and quarrelsome priest, who had been corrupted
by the love of riches, but, in the account of the incident
which William of Malmesbury extracted from the lost biography
by Wulfstan's chaplain Coleman, there is nothing to show that
this truculent fellow was a village parson or derived his wealth
from ecclesiastical endowments.[2] On the other hand, a rich
living could be regarded as an opportunity of advancement. It is
noted as a mark of virtue in Wulfstan that as a young man he
chose to become a monk rather than accept such a living when it
was pressed upon him by his bishop.[3]

Taken as a whole the evidence of Domesday Book leaves one
with the impression that the village priest was usually reckoned
to be a member of the peasant community. His glebe can rarely
have exceeded the scale of the larger peasant holdings; and in
some places it was so small that, but for the income he received
from tithe and other dues, his lot would have resembled that of
a bordar or cottar rather than a *villanus*. With glebe rated at half
a hide—a figure of frequent occurrence—he might be a fairly
substantial farmer without out-distancing the more prosperous
of his rustic parishioners. A generation or so later, an illustration of this is afforded by the early survey of the estates of
Shaftesbury Abbey. At Berwick St. Leonard in Wiltshire,
Wulfric the priest had half a hide belonging to the church, and
we get some idea of the amount of stock that was reckoned to
go with such a farm from the numbers for which he enjoyed
free pasturage—15 cattle, 60 sheep, 3 horses, and 15 pigs.[4] But

[1] For Alfred (*Alured*) and Osbern see Dd. i, ff. 49, 366*b*. At Long Ashton in
Somerset a priest named Guy had 3 hides of land with 2 ploughs and 2 serfs besides
3 *villani* and 2 bordars with ploughs of their own; but the land belonging to the
church of this manor amounted only to a virgate and the Exon. text states that
'a priest' (*i presbyter*) held this: ibid., f. 88*b*, Exon., p. 134. At Powick in Worcestershire a priest has a plough and 2 *bovarii* and 2 bordars with 2 ploughs, but one
suspects that he was not the parish priest since he is referred to as *unus presbyter*,
which is quite contrary to the usual practice in this county: Dd. i, f. 174*b*; contrast
Wolverley (*Ulwardelei*), f. 174: 'Ibi presbyter habens dimidiam carucam et unus
liber homo habens i hidam.' The entry relating to the lands of priests at *Hinetone*
(? Hinton Martell) in Dorset is very complicated and puzzling: ibid., f. 76.

[2] *Vita Wulfstani*, ed. Darlington, ii, c. 22 (p. 45).

[3] Ibid. i, c. 3 (p. 8). But it was not, it seems, a village church that the bishop
offered: William of Malmesbury calls it *ecclesiam suburbanam*, which Peile translates
as 'a church near the city'.

[4] B.M. MS. Harl. 61, f. 43*v*: 'Wilfricus presbiter habet ecclesiam et dimidiam
hidam adjacentem ecclesie et decimam omnium rerum de dominio et decimam

while this clearly marked him off from the virgaters and half-virgaters and the numerous men with 5 acres who formed the majority of the abbey's tenants at Berwick, there were two others in the village besides Wulfric who held half a hide of land. At about the same date one of the Burton Abbey surveys shows us something of the manner in which a village priest of the Norman period might be implicated in the peasant economy. At Abbot's Bromley in Staffordshire, 2 bovates belonged to the church and Aisculf the priest had these, apparently free of rent; but besides them he held 30 acres of the abbot's 'inland' for a rent of 2s. He was evidently an enterprising man and one able to co-operate with his fellows, for he subsequently gave up his holding of inland and joined with four other tenants of peasant holdings to take the whole manor, bar the woodland, at farm on a twenty years' lease at a rent of 100s.[1] But while here we find a parson associated with the more aspiring of the peasantry in a farming venture of some magnitude, at Wetmore, some 10 miles away in the near neighbourhood of Burton itself, the priest appears to have had only a house and a croft of inland and, like the cowman (*vaccarius*) who had a similar holding, owed labour service one day a week.[2]

The Wetmore case throws a vivid light upon the social standing of the humbler members of the village clergy. But it cannot properly be taken as showing that the parson's glebe might owe labour services like other peasant holdings, for the croft at Wetmore is described as inland and was probably not glebe at all but should be classed with the inland rented by Aisculf of Abbot's Bromley which the survey sharply distinguishes from the land belonging to his church.[3] The Shaftesbury Abbey

villanorum et xv animalia quieta de herbagio et lx oves et iii equos et xv porcos et habet de nemore unum lignum ad nutrimentum foci et ad alia necessaria.' Perhaps we should understand the words *quieta de herbagio* as applying only to the cattle, in which case the other figures must represent the actual stock belonging to Wulfric.

[1] *Hist. Collections for Staffs.*, *1916* (pub. 1918), Survey A, pp. 222–3.

[2] Ibid., p. 220; cited by A. L. Poole, *From Domesday Book to Magna Carta*, 1951, p. 60.

[3] It may well be that there was only a dependent chapel at Wetmore and that it had no glebe: two-thirds of the demesne corn tithes were paid in nearby Burton to one Recelbert who was probably the parish priest in that place: op. cit., p. 214. Like Aisculf of Abbot's Bromley, one Wulfric, who was priest at Cheselbourne in Dorset, appears (in the Shaftesbury survey of c. 1130) as holding a virgate for a money rent in addition to half a hide of (apparently rent-free) glebe: Harl. MS. 61, ff. 44v, 45.

survey, however, shows that a small amount of ploughing and carting was due from a virgate at Atworth in Wiltshire which was held by the priest along with the church and thus appears to have been glebe.[1] Yet on the Shaftesbury estates even this exiguous burden was exceptional. The same survey mentions land that seems to be glebe at half a dozen places without saying anything about either service or rent, though the recording of such obligations was evidently part of the surveyor's purpose.[2] Domesday Book gives little help in regard to this matter. We are told, indeed, that in the largely Welsh district of Archenfield, in southern Herefordshire, the priests of three churches which belonged to the king were obliged to carry royal messages into Wales as well as to say two masses a week *pro rege*.[3] But courier service is very different from agricultural service: it seems to be in harmony with the association of priests and 'rad-knights' which has been noticed in some Domesday entries in the mid-western counties, and it was the one form of secular service permitted to priests in Normandy by the decrees of the council held at Lillebonne in 1080.[4] On the other hand to conclude that even these Archenfield priests owed no other services than those which are mentioned would be rather rash; and in general this is not a topic on which anything can be inferred from the silences of Domesday, for it is almost completely silent both about knight service and about the labour services of the ordinary peasantry. There can be little doubt that the owners of proprietary churches would expect some kind of service from the priests and that the Normans were inclined to make increased claims upon them. References in Domesday to 'half-priests'

---

[1] 'Et apud Attewidam habet ecclesiam et unam virgatam terre et totam decimam de dominico et totam decimam hominum ipsius ville et debet unam (acram) arare et unam waretare et prestabit suum carrum in Augusto una die et habebit ad festum S. Johannis Baptiste usque ad festum S. Michaelis in diversis pascuis viii boves et iiii vaccas et duos herciatores': ibid., f. 37. Edwy, the priest who had this church, was also, it seems, the incumbent of Bradford-on-Avon and Limpley Stoke—places in the immediate neighbourhood.

[2] Ibid., ff. 38*v*, 39 (Tisbury, Wiltshire), 43*v* (Berwick St. Leonard, Wiltshire), 44*v* (Cheselbourne, Dorset), 45*b*–46 (Iwerne Minster, Dorset), 50 (Fontmell, Dorset), 52 (*Stokes* = ? Beechingstoke, Wiltshire). It is intriguing to find that at Fontmell and also at Melbury Abbas and Compton Abbas in the same county (ff. 47*v*, 49) the priest is said to have 'what the *villani* are willing to give him': it was the same at Handley in Dorset according to a survey on f. 54*v* which is perhaps a little later than the others.

[3] Dd. i, f. 179.

[4] Ordericus Vitalis, op. cit., bk. v, ed. Le Prevost, ii. 317.

at Laythorpe by Kirby in Lincolnshire, at Langley in Norfolk, and at Middleton in Suffolk, seem to imply an obligation of personal service that was due partly to one lord and partly to another.[1] And it is highly significant that in 1076 the Council of Winchester laid it down that no clerk should render from his benefice any service beyond that which he had performed in the time of King Edward.[2]

There is, however, no reason to think that the services demanded consisted of agricultural labour on the lord's demesne, though here and there that may have been the case. Whether or no he had any clerkly skill, a priest could be useful in many ways—if only by acting as a complacent private chaplain. Among the scandals which William of Malmesbury reports as signs of English decadence on the eve of the Conquest was the practice by which great persons, instead of going to church in the morning, would get a priest to hurry through the offices for them in their bedchambers.[3] But without being committed to anything that could be regarded as improper or derogatory, a parson was bound to feel under some obligation if he regularly took his meals in the lord's hall as Wulfric of Haselbury did during the years he served as parish priest at Compton Martin.[4]

V

Of the village clergy themselves, and what manner of men they were, we know but little. They must have been almost entirely of English stock, though probably, as time passed, the younger sons of Norman patrons would here and there be found among them. After as before the Conquest they were quite commonly married; and the campaign in favour of clerical celibacy failed to make the condition disreputable in common opinion.[5] The charge of illiteracy or semi-literacy which William of Malmesbury brings against the pre-Conquest clergy in

---

[1] Dd. i, f. 357: 'dimidia aecclesia et [sic] cum dimidio presbytero'; ii, f. 196: 'In eadem i presbyter integer et ii dimidii tenent c acras liberae terrae et jacent in ecclesia sancte andree'; f. 400: 'huic manerio sunt additi v liberi homines et dimidius presbyter.'

[2] 'Ne aliquis clericus civilis vel rusticus de beneficio ecclesiae aliquod servitium reddat praeter illud quod fecit T.R.E.': quoted Boehmer, op. cit., p. 323 n. 1.

[3] Gesta Regum (Rolls Series), lib. iii, § 245 (ii. 305).

[4] Wulfric of Haselbury, by John, Abbot of Ford, ed. Dom M. Bell (Somerset Record Soc., vol. 47, 1933), p. 14.

[5] For the state of opinion see D. M. Stenton, op. cit., p. 211.

general, could no doubt be largely justified as regards the *clerici rustici* throughout the Norman period; and that it was no rare thing for a parson to be given to tippling on festive occasions is suggested by one of the decrees issued by the Council of Westminster in 1102, which says that priests must not attend drinking parties nor 'drink to pegs'.[1] Yet Brichtric, who was the parish priest of Haselbury in Somerset about the year 1135, is represented in John of Ford's Life of Wulfric as a man of simple-minded piety and unswerving devotion to the duties of his office, though he was painfully conscious that his inability to speak French made him seem a dumb dog in the presence of the bishop and the archdeacon. So far as the other work of his ministry allowed, Brichtric gave himself constantly to psalmody and prayer, and used to ride a horse when he went home to dinner, so that he might waste as little time as possible away from his church. He was succeeded at Haselbury by his son Osbern, whose mother Godida, when she makes her single appearance in the narrative, is engaged in sewing a linen alb for the anchorite Wulfric. Osbern, who as a boy acted as server both for his father and for Wulfric when they said mass, appears to have acquired something of Brichtric's fervour: he was probably unmarried, for after he became the parish priest he usually slept in the church.[2] These are precious details because they relate to fairly ordinary men. Yet neither before the Conquest nor afterwards were all the village clergy undistinguished folk. St. Wulfstan himself had for a while held the post of parish priest at Hawkesbury in Gloucestershire during the third decade of the eleventh century. It is true that he soon relinquished this cure, and, as a monk in the cathedral priory of Worcester, entered upon the career which led to his becoming bishop of the diocese in 1062.[3] But after the Conquest clergymen of English blood virtually ceased to be eligible for great positions in the Church, so it may well be that, until the expansion of monasticism afforded an alternative to pastoral work for increasing numbers,

---

[1] W. of Malmesbury, op. cit. ii. 304; and for the decree ('Ut presbyteri non eant ad potationes nec ad pinnas bibant') see Eadmer, *Hist. Nov.* (Rolls Series), p. 142. St. Dunstan was reputed to have had pegs introduced into drinking-cups, so that when the cup went round each man could tell when he had drunk his share; but they appear to have promoted a custom of 'allowing no heeltaps', as Stubbs puts it: W. of Malmesbury, op. cit. i. 166; Stubbs, *Historical Introductions to the Rolls Series*, pp. 24–25.

[2] Op. cit., pp. 29, 30–31, 52, 53, 102, 109.

[3] *Vita Wulfstani*, iii, c. 2 (p. 47); i, c. 3 (pp. 8–9).

some men, whose abilities and zeal would otherwise have marked them out for promotion, remained country parsons to the end of their days. If such there were, they have joined the company of those which have no memorial. But in the reign of Henry I we find in Wulfric of Haselbury and Gilbert of Sempringham two incumbents of country livings whose sanctity was destined to win them lasting renown. Both practised the austerities demanded by medieval conceptions of holiness and both were supposed to possess thaumaturgic powers; but the contrast between their lives is remarkable.

Wulfric was born in Somerset, and, like St. Wulfstan, came of a family of English stock and moderate station.[1] Though we hear nothing of his being sent to school—as St. Wulfstan in former days had been sent first to Evesham and then to Peterborough—he evidently acquired some clerkly skill, for the copying of books was among the occupations of his later years. He was ordained before he had reached the canonical age and became parish priest at one of the villages in Wiltshire which bear the name of Deverill; but at first he took his duties lightly and spent part of his time hunting with hawk and hound. It was while he was thus engaged that the crisis of his conversion is said to have occurred through an encounter with a beggar who correctly guessed the amount of money he had in his purse (apparently two silver pennies and a halfpenny) and, on receiving an alms, blessed Wulfric and foretold his future. Soon after this, William FitzWalter, who was the lord of Compton Martin, Wulfric's native place, invited him to become the parish priest of that village. He remained there some years; but, getting his meals as he did in FitzWalter's hall, he found it difficult to satisfy the desire for extreme austerity that now possessed him; and eventually he left Compton for Haselbury, a village belonging to the same lord near the southern border of Somerset, and passed the rest of his life as an anchorite in a cell adjoining Haselbury church. He thus ceased to be a parish priest; but in so far as it reveals more of the character of the former parson of Deverill and Compton, the story of these later years is not irrelevant. Wulfric maintained a close friendship with the local priest Brichtric and his successor Osbern, and his relations with

---

[1] St. Wulfstan's parents were 'nec tenues censu nec natalibus abjecti' (*Vita*, i. c. 1, p. 4): Wulfric is described as 'de mediocri Anglorum gente originem ducens' (*Wulfric of Haselbury*, p. 13).

other neighbours appear to have been friendly. But he gave himself to intense self-mortification and was clearly obsessed with a disordered imagination, though the unchronological form in which John of Ford's biography is cast prevents our knowing whether this was a gradual development. It cannot, however, have been many years before the prophetic and miraculous powers with which he was credited made him famous throughout the length and breadth of England. Henry I and Stephen and Stephen's queen were among the visitors to his cell; and St. Bernard sent a message asking for his prayers. Probably the Haselbury villagers felt proud of their anchorite; but one may perhaps doubt whether they were as favourably impressed as his biographer supposed, when, one Easter Day, he came out of his cell into the midst of the congregation and 'sparing neither his own shame nor the modesty of the bystanders' publicly confessed that his sleep had been disturbed by a sexual dream. The anonymous priest to whom he made confession on another occasion seems to have thought that his conscience was a little morbid. Wulfric in a moment of temper had cursed a mouse for nibbling some of his clothing. The mouse straightway fell dead and thus, as John of Ford says, 'by its death gave glory to God and peace to his saint'. But Wulfric felt remorse. He sent for a priest and confessed what he had done. The priest—it was probably Brichtric—said that he only wished Wulfric would curse all the mice of the district in the same way.[1]

A very different picture is presented by the biography of Gilbert of Sempringham which was written by one who knew him. Gilbert was the child of a mixed marriage. His father, Gocelin, a knight of Norman origin, appears in Domesday Book as holding land of Alfred of Lincoln in about half a dozen Lincolnshire villages, while his mother is described as an Englishwoman of lower rank.[2] The boy had some physical deformity;

---

[1] John of Ford's Life of Wulfric, from which all these details are obtained, was written some thirty years after the anchorite's death which occurred in 1155. The author carefully collected information from people who had known Wulfric and from others who had heard reports from Wulfric's friends, and his naïve belief in the miraculous makes him all the more faithful as a reporter of the stories told him. Dom Bell's Introduction and notes are full and informing, but not always accurate. On p. 141 he says that Haselbury is 'as John of Ford remarks, almost exactly twenty miles from Exeter as the crow flies'. In fact John gives the distance as 30 miles (p. 15), and it is really nearer 40 than 30.

[2] *Mon. Ang.* vi, pt. ii (insertion following p. 945), p. v^x; Dd. i, f. 358, 358b. In the Dugdale text of the biography which is based on a Cottonian MS., the mother is

and perhaps that is why he was given a clerkly education, first at home where he is said to have made slow progress, and afterwards in France where he studied with so much success that he obtained 'the name and degree of a master'.[1] When he came back to Lincolnshire he began to teach the country children, both boys and girls. This phase in his life is charmingly depicted in the fifteenth-century prose of Capgrave's version of the original biography: 'For first was he a maystir of lernyng to the smale petites, swech as lerne to rede, spelle and synge. Tho childryn that were undyr his disciplyne he taute not only her' lessones on the book, but be-side this, he tawt for to pley in dew tyme, and here playes taute he that thei schuld be honest and mery with-outen clamour or grete noyse.'[2] Gilbert's father appears to have provided the means for this enterprise and eventually presented his son to the livings of Sempringham and West Torrington to be held in plurality. The young rector was not yet in priest's orders, if indeed he was ordained at all; and no doubt that is why he had a chaplain to live with him at Sempringham. Probably another chaplain or vicar acted as parish priest at West Torrington, for that village lies between 30 and 40 miles away to the north. There was evidently no priest's house at Sempringham, and, to begin with, the rector and his chaplain lodged in the village. But Gilbert found that the charms of their host's daughter were attracting his fancy, so he fled from temptation and together with Geoffrey the chaplain went to live in a parsonage house which they built in the churchyard.[3] Some time

described as *non inferioris tamen conditionis*; but Miss Rose Graham points out that in that manuscript the word *non* is an interpolation in a later hand, and that it does not occur either in the Harleian MS. or in that in the Bodleian: *St. Gilbert of Sempringham and the Gilbertines* (1901), p. 3 n. 9. Miss Graham is in error in making Gocelin a tenant of Gilbert de Gant.

[1] 'Institutus est itaque tam diu liberalibus et spiritualibus studiis donec magistri nomen mereretur et gradum.' As a witness to charters he is sometimes described as *magister*: see Farrer, *Early Yorkshire Charters*, ii, No. 1233; iii, No. 1895.

[2] *John Capgrave's Lives of St. Augustine and St. Gilbert of Sempringham*, ed. J. J. Munro (E.E.T.S., 1910), p. 64. According to the original biography the teaching was imparted *pueris et puellis provincialibus*; and as regards the discipline we are told that Gilbert taught them 'ita quod pueros a jocandi et vagandi libertate cohercitos, cogeret secundum statuta monasteriorum silere in ecclesia, cubitare simul, quasi in dormitorio, non nisi locis statutis loqui et legere, et alia honestae vitae experiri insignia' (op. cit., p. vi[x]). One can only hope that Capgrave's imagination did not deceive him as to what this really meant.

[3] Perhaps, as Miss Graham thinks (op. cit., p. 6), their first dwelling-place, after leaving their lodgings, was a room over the church porch (*in atrio ecclesiae*), but the text is not quite clear on this point.

after this he became a clerk in the household of Robert Bloet, Bishop of Lincoln, and when Bloet died in 1123, continued to serve his successor in the same capacity. He retained both his livings, however, but, taking only enough to live on (*stipendia vitae*) from the income of Sempringham and nothing at all from Torrington, gave everything that could be spared to the poor and turned the Sempringham parsonage for the time being into an almshouse for the needy. While still attached to the episcopal *curia* he was ordained priest and offered an archdeaconry, but he refused this and returned to Sempringham, where he established a little nunnery for seven of the village maidens alongside the church. This was the beginning of the religious order that was destined to perpetuate his name. The story of its development lies outside the sphere of village affairs, but witnesses to the originality, energy, and organizing skill of its founder. When Gilbert died in extreme old age in 1189, the order comprised thirteen houses, of which four were houses of regular canons and the rest primarily nunneries, to which canons were attached as chaplains. And his influence as a parish priest was evidently remarkable. All the original nuns seem to have been his parishioners; and we are told that the village became singularly well-behaved and that if any Sempringham people went into another church they could be recognized at once by their devout demeanour. Their rector knew how to enforce a salutary lesson in a memorable way. Though abounding in charity he insisted that what was due to the church should be duly paid, and when one of his parishioners failed to pay tithe, made the man turn all the corn out of his barn and count out the correct number of sheaves. But then Gilbert maintained that what had been stolen from God was unfit for human use and publicly burnt the tithe sheaves on the village green. The general impression one receives from his biography is of a man living by a strict ascetic code, but kindly and cheerful and much loved by those who knew him. And though a plentiful supply of miracles was forthcoming after his death and it was said that even in his lifetime men had been cured of various ailments by contact with an old stocking he had worn or a cup from which he had drunk, Gilbert himself seems as a rule to have played no part in such marvels. Occasionally some natural event—an opportune change of weather or the arrest of a London fire before it reached his lodging—seemed to occur in answer to his prayers;

and he may well have believed himself that such was the case. But to believe in the efficacy of prayer is not the same thing as to suppose oneself distinguished from other Christians by the possession of miraculous powers.[1] And it is remarkable that Gilbert's biographer adopts an almost apologetic tone in regard to this topic, as if the wonders that happened in the saint's lifetime were fewer than his readers would expect. In the words of Capgrave, who here closely follows the Latin original:

> And thoug it be so that these dayes benot used with myracles as the former dayes were, in whech wer doo many myracles, for as the Psalme saith, we se now no toknes, now is there no profete for to telle us what schal befall; and thoug it be so that Seynt Gilbert be mor worthi to be in worchep for his merytory dedes than for doyng of myracles, yet on-to the wytnesse of his good werkys, be-side the grete bysynesse he had in wynnying of soules, whech is of mor vertu than curyng of bodies, yet were there, thorw the grete merit of his holy lyf, doo many toknes thorw whech his doctrine was commended and his holyness confermed.[2]

---

[1] For the miracles belonging to his lifetime see R. Foreville, *Le Livre de S. Gilbert de Sempringham* (Paris, 1943), pp. 74–82. The account of No. 15 (cures effected by bread which he had blessed) ends significantly: 'Ipse tamen non modo signorum gloriam non quesivit, sed tota intentione fugit, ita ut cum multociens a devotis aliquibus sanis vel egris peteretur benedictionem, vix dare consensit tali se munere vel tanto honore reputans indignum vel suam potius ab hominibus abscondens dignitatem.'

[2] Op. cit., p. 74. The words of the original are as follows: 'Licet enim non sunt haec tempora signorum, juxta illud, "Signa nostra non vidimus, jam non est prophetia" (*sic*); et ipse magis moribus studuerit quam miraculis, in attestationem tamen piorum operum, et confirmationem sermonum, praeter multarum quae fecit lucra animarum, quae praejudicant miraculis, quaedam per eum divinitus facta sunt signa, quibus et sanctitas vitae ejus, et sinceritas doctrinae commendatur' (*Mon. Ang.* vi, pt. ii, p. xxii[x]). It should be noted that Capgrave goes beyond his authority's *quaedam signa* when he speaks of 'many toknes'.

XI

THE PEASANTS AND THEIR HOLDINGS

I

Norman England, though a land of great estates, was also a land of peasant farms. In the manorial units of which the great estates were so largely composed, the holdings of the peasants were an essential element; and, where manorial organization was lacking, the land was usually occupied by men who appear to be of peasant type. But in all parts of the country the rustic population was regarded by the Domesday commissioners as consisting of distinct classes of persons and as a rule a village included members of more than one class among its inhabitants. The preamble to the Ely Inquest shows that at least one group of the commissioners were instructed to ascertain the numbers of *villani*, *cothcethle*, *servi*, *liberi homines*, and *sochemani*; and a classification similar to this, as regards the first three classes, but varying in the degree of its elaboration, was in fact adopted everywhere. Yet in spite of much scholarly debate on the subject, the precise significance of these distinctions is not wholly clear. Part of the trouble is due to the employment of two discrepant criteria, that of legal status and that of economic condition; and the social historian has also to avoid the peril of assuming that differences which were important for the purposes of the Norman government had equally important consequences for the lives of the persons concerned. A valuable aid to our comprehension is provided by the brief account of the Domesday Inquest which Robert, Bishop of Hereford, wrote in the very year the survey was made. In it he tells us that the description of England comprised (along with the possessions of the great) the *homines*, both serfs and free men, and as well those dwelling in cottages as those possessing homesteads and lands.[1] The twofold classification, legal and economic, is here

[1] 'Hic est annus xx^{mus} Willelmi, regis Anglorum, quo jubente hoc anno totius Angliae facta est descriptio in agris singularum provinciarum, in possessionibus singulorum procerum, in agris eorum, in mansionibus, in hominibus tam servis quam liberis, tam in tuguria tantum habitantibus, quam in domos et agros possidentibus, in carrucis, in equis et caeteris animalibus, in servitio et censu totius terrae omnium': Stubbs, *Select Charters* (9th ed.), p. 95.

clearly displayed; but the economic distinction between cottagers and farmers is remarkable and helpful in its simplicity.
It looks as if Bishop Robert thought that the village folk belonged in the main to one or other of these two classes. And in
Domesday Book some 72 per cent. of the total enumerated
population (exclusive of tenants-in-chief and burgesses) are
accounted for under the terms *villanus*, *bordarius*, and *cotarius* or
coscet, of which the first seems on the face of it to imply a regular
or typical 'villager', while the others are derived from words
meaning a cottage.[1] *Villani* and *bordarii* are indeed the two
largest classes in nearly all the Domesday counties and in most
of them are far more numerous than any other.

The employment of discrepant criteria in Domesday Book
has made its classification of the peasantry at once too simple
and too complicated. Men with very similar holdings appear
in some counties to have been allotted to different classes on
account of differences in their legal position and their relation
to the manorial lords; but on the other hand where differences
in these matters lacked the challenging prominence which they
had in the Danelaw, they tended to be concealed through a less
discriminate application of the term *villanus*.[2]

Legal distinctions and the baffling problems connected with
the degrees of freedom enjoyed by various elements in the
population have in the past received a disproportionate amount
of attention from historians and some change of emphasis may
be justified, for it is not unduly materialistic to believe that
what mattered most to the peasant was the size and character
of his holding.[3] Unfortunately direct information about the
amount of land occupied by individuals is very rarely provided
by Domesday Book. Its description of Middlesex, however, is
exceptionally rich in detail and thus affords a starting-point for
inquiry.

In Middlesex, the basis of classification was economic. Virtually 90 per cent. of the enumerated rural population are

[1] The figure in the text is based upon the rough but comprehensive statistics
compiled by Ellis. The word 'bordar' appears to be derived from a Frankish word
borda which O. Bloch (*Dictionnaire étymologique*) defines as 'cabane de planches'.

[2] See Stenton, *Anglo-Saxon England*, pp. 469–72, where the 'deceptively simple'
character of the Domesday terminology is strongly emphasized as regards the
villani.

[3] The question whether men were free to 'withdraw' and seek another lord
('recedere—recedere quo voluerunt—recedere ad alium dominum') may well have
had more practical importance for the lord than for his men.

described as *villani*, *bordarii*, or *cotarii*, and a further 5 per cent. were *servi*.[1] The terms cottar and bordar, though identical in primary meaning and often treated in Domesday as synonymous, are here distinguished on economic grounds, the former term being usually employed for persons possessing little or nothing beside their cottages and the latter for those who were, in a modest way, what we should call 'smallholders'.[2] In this county indeed we are given abundant information about the holdings of all classes, and though the hides, virgates, and acres of which they are said to consist cannot be regarded as exact measures based upon an acre corresponding to our statute acre, there is reason to think that they were intended to represent real agrarian units and not merely fiscal assessments and that they can at least be taken to indicate the relative position of the various groups.[3]

Certain features stand out clearly:

1. The holdings of the Middlesex *villani* consisted almost invariably of standard units—hides, half-hides, virgates, or half-virgates. For more than 900 individual cases, or something like 78 per cent. of the total number in the county, the information is free from ambiguity; and of these cases over 47 per cent. were virgates and over 42 per cent. half-virgates, while only three holdings were of irregular extent.[4] It is true that many of the examples come from entries which include other items of uncertain meaning, but the preponderance of virgates and half-virgates is no less evident if such examples are eliminated from the statistics.[5]

---

[1] The figures are based on those of Ellis and are percentages of his total less the numbers he gives for tenants-in-chief, mesne lords, and burgesses.

[2] On the frequent interchangeability of the terms bordar and cottar see *Economic Journal*, lxi (June 1951), 342–4, 352–4. In one Middlesex entry a bordar and cottar seem to be distinguished on other than economic grounds, each being credited with 5 acres: the cottar was apparently associated with the priest's glebe: Dd. i, f. 130 (West Bedfont).

[3] Cf. Maitland, *Domesday Book and Beyond*, pp. 477–8; Vinogradoff, *English Society*, pp. 167–8. As the figures for the tenants' holdings added to those of the demesne sometimes equal, sometimes exceed, and sometimes fall short of the geld assessment for the manor as a whole, and often differ considerably from the 'teamland' figures, it is difficult to see what they can be except estimates of actual areas.

[4] There was a *villanus* with 8 acres at one of the Bedfonts, and at Stepney one with 12 and another with 14 acres: Dd. i, ff. 129, 130.

[5] Entries quite free from ambiguities and showing no signs of corruption in the text show that, of 454 villan holdings, 216 were virgates and 196 half-virgates: see *Economic Journal*, lvi (June 1946), 254.

2. The holdings of the bordars (whose total number was less than a third of that of the *villani*) are most often expressed in acres. Precise information is given about 101 individual cases, which is some 29 per cent. of the total, and 71 of these were 5-acre holdings; but statements which credit a group of bordars with a given area without indicating whether that is what each individual possessed or the total amount possessed by the group, make it hazardous to attempt more comprehensive statistics, though it is noteworthy that a majority of such statements would admit of interpretations suggesting that the holdings to which they relate contained 5, 7½, 10, or 15 acres.[1]

3. Of the 464 cottars, 243 are not credited with any land and 49 others appear to have possessed nothing but gardens.[2] A cottar at West Bedfont and another at Westminster had a 5-acre holding, and there were 5 cottars at Staines with 4 acres apiece.[3] No other individual cottar holdings are clearly described; but among all the statements that are made in ambiguous terms there is only one which necessarily indicates the existence of holdings as large as 6½ acres while four will at most only allow from an acre to 2½ acres for any of the 11 cottars to whom they refer.[4]

4. Groups of individuals with equal holdings were common both among the *villani* and the bordars. At Isleworth no less than 51 *villani* had a virgate apiece: at Tottenham each of 12 bordars had 5 acres.[5] Such grouping in fact occurs so frequently that, when we read of 'six *villani* of six virgates' at Tottenham and of 'twelve bordars who hold half a hide' at Hendon, it seems very probable that here too we have to do with virgate holdings and 5-acre holdings respectively.[6] There is less evidence of this sort of thing and more evidence of irregularity among the cottars, but, besides the 5 at Staines who had

---

[1] Some of these cases depend on the assumption that the virgate was the usual virgate of 30 acres.

[2] At Fulham there were 'viii cot' de suis hortis'; at Westminster 41 paid 40s. *pro ortis suis*: Dd. i, ff. 127b, 128.

[3] Ibid., ff. 130, 128.

[4] In some cases the meaning of an ambiguous entry is made clear by the context: thus in the statement 'Ibi i villanus de i virgata et viii bordarii quisque de dimidia virgata et iiii cotarii de xix acris' (Stepney, f. 130b), the particularity of the entry relating to the bordars and the descending order of magnitude indicate that the cottars had 19 acres between them.

[5] Ibid., ff. 130, 130b.

[6] Ibid., ff. 130b, 128b.

4 acres each, several small groups are credited with areas which
if they are taken to be the total amounts possessed by groups
imply an average of 1, 2, or 3 acres per cottar.

5. Though a virgate or half-virgate would appear to have
been the normal holding of a *villanus* and 5 acres the normal
holding of a bordar, a good many *villani* had more than a virgate and a considerable number of bordars more than 5 acres.
Among the former we find 1 at Hanwell with 2 hides, 2 at
West Bedfont whose holdings averaged that amount, another at
Greenford who had a hide and a virgate, and altogether 14 who
had a hide each and 72 with half a hide.[1] And this means that
of the total number whose holdings are clearly distinguished
nearly 10 per cent. possessed 2 virgates or more, while only
3 individuals had less than half a virgate. Among the bordars
there were 4 at Hampton and 8 at Stepney who had a half-
virgate each, and it seems likely that the 16 bordars at Hayes
who are credited with 2 hides were in a similar position.[2]

6. Peasants of various classes, or groups of peasants of the same
class with holdings of different sizes, occur together in almost
every vill in the county. Indeed the diversity of conditions involved in this association of groups belonging to distinct grades
was as marked a feature of the agrarian economy as the equality
obtaining between members of the several groups. Lisson (*Lile-
stone*) where there were only 4 *villani* with half a virgate each,
3 cottars of 2 acres, and a single slave, was exceptional in the
simplicity of its social structure.[3] As a rule conditions were more
or less similar to those obtaining at Harewell where the recorded
population consisted of 5 *villani* and the priest with a virgate
each, 5 other *villani* each of whom had half that amount, 7
bordars with 5 acres each, another bordar who had 3 acres,
3 apparently landless cottars and 3 slaves.[4] Some of the
larger manors such as Edmonton, where the grading of holdings
was more elaborate than this, may indeed have included hamlets in which the stratification was simpler than that exhibited
in the statistical summary of the whole; but Harewell was a

[1] Ibid., ff. 128*b* (Hanwell), 130 (West Bedfont), 128*b* (Greenford). In all these
figures no account has been taken of *villani* who are described as holding (presumably at farm) the whole of certain small estates such as that of 4 hides at St. Pancras
which 4 *villani* held of the Canons of St. Paul's (*sub canonicis*, f. 128).
[2] Ibid., ff. 130, 130*b*, 127. A bordar with only 3 acres is recorded at Harefield:
f. 130.
[3] Ibid., f. 130*b*.   [4] Ibid., f. 130.

manor of moderate size in which 5 plough-teams sufficed for
the cultivation of its arable land, so there is no reason to doubt
that its virgaters, half-virgaters, bordars, cottars, and slaves
dwelt together as neighbours in a single village. And 4 or more
ranks of peasant holdings are discernible in nearly a score of
places, while the holdings specifically assigned to *villani* fall into
two or more classes in some 35 out of the 60 odd vills that
Domesday distinguishes by name. In a fair number of cases it
was only a matter of some *villani* possessing virgates and others
half-virgates, but in 8 villages we find, along with *villani* who
had only a half-virgate 1, 2, or (at Fulham) 5 others who had
a whole hide and were thus, on the face of things, 8 times as
well off as the poorer members of their class.

Outside Middlesex only scraps of information of similar
character are provided either by Domesday or by any of its satellite texts. In Hertfordshire, Domesday itself describes the large
manor of Sawbridgeworth in unusual detail and reveals features
that have a general resemblance to those observed in Middlesex.[1] The priest has a hide, the reeve half a hide. Each of 14
villani holds a virgate, each of 35 half a virgate.[2] There are 46
bordars with 8 acres apiece, 2 bordars 'of ten acres' (probably
5 acres each), 20 cottars 'of twenty-six acres', 30 cottars to
whom no land is credited and 30 slaves. There are also said to
be 4 sokemen who have 7 cottars 'under' them, but the account
of the sokemen is obscure. One Asgar holds 2 hides and has
2 *villani*, 7 bordars, 3 cottars, and 4 slaves under him. A man
named Kip has half a hide and a mill, and another sokeman
pays, it seems, a rent of 5*s.* 4*d.*[3]

Three other Hertfordshire manors—Haddam, Hatfield, and
Kelshall—are included in the Ely Inquest; and in each of them
it discloses a stratification of peasant holdings which is ignored
in Domesday Book.[4] Of the 15 *villani* at Haddam we learn that

---

[1] Dd. i, f. 139*b*.
[2] The *villani* also rented a virgate and a half and 9 acres.
[3] 'alter sochs de v sol et iiij den'.' Whether there were really only 3 sokemen or
whether an account of the fourth has been omitted remains in doubt. That the
prosperous Asgar was reckoned to be one seems probable: of the pre-Conquest
sokemen one had 2 hides, 2 a virgate each, and 2 others half a hide, though the
context fails to indicate whether or no each of them had that amount. It is noteworthy that these sokemen's holdings had varied so widely in size and that the
man with two hides was not free to sell his land though his poorer fellows were.
[4] I.C.C., pp. 124, 125; Dd. i, f. 135.

one had a virgate and the others half a virgate each. At Hatfield, where Domesday says that the priest with 18 *villani* and 18 bordars have 20 ploughs, the Ely Inquest tells us that the priest has half a hide, that the *villani* have a virgate each, and that 12 of the bordars have half a hide and 6 of them another half-hide, which one guesses to mean 5 acres each and 10 acres each respectively. At Kelshall Domesday reports that 12 *villani* with 9 bordars have 6 ploughs, but the Ely Inquest shows that 2 of the *villani* were virgaters, 10 half-virgaters, and that the bordars had a virgate—probably 3⅓ acres each on an average. It also gives some account of the holdings in 18 Cambridgeshire manors, all in the district known as the Isle of Ely.[1] There were *villani* and cottars in every one, slaves in all but 4, and sokemen in 8. As in Middlesex and Hertfordshire, the *villani* occur in groups, each member of which is credited with the same amount of land, but it is here most unusual for a manor to contain more than one such group.[2] Ostensibly the villan holdings were smaller than in the other two counties, being described as 10 acres or less in the case of 13 manors and nowhere exceeding half a virgate; but these figures cannot be regarded as estimates of actual area, for many of them exhibit a close correspondence with the assessments for geld and seem impossibly small in comparison both with the number of ploughs that the *villani* possessed and with the 'teamland' figures.[3] On all the 8 manors on which sokemen are recorded, the sokeman appears as a person who has more land, on an average, than a *villanus*, and though the figures in some cases point to sokeman holdings of irregular extent, standard units are clearly recognizable at Doddington where the *villani* had 7½ acres each and 8 sokemen had a hide between them, and again at Wentworth where, along with *villani* holding

---

[1] I.C.C., pp. 115–20; cf. Dd. i, ff. 191*b*, 192, which provides the same information (with slight discrepancies) for ten of these manors.

[2] At West Wickham where the Ely Inquest records 2 *villani* who had 15 acres each and a third with 10 acres, Domesday only records 2 with 10 acres apiece. On the other hand, at Whittlesey, where all the *villani* on the Ely manor had 12-acre holdings, those on the Thorney Abbey manor had 8 acres each according to Domesday (f. 192*b*).

[3] For example, at Little Downham, which was assessed at 4 hides, there were 2½ hides on demesne and 15 *villani* had 12 acres each or a total of just 1½ hides; but there was said to be land for 8 ploughs and there were in fact 8 there, 4 of which belonged to the *villani*: I.C.C., p. 119; Dd. i, f. 192. It must be noted, however, that at Haddam and Kelshall in Hertfordshire, where the holdings were virgates and half-virgates, these also are more nearly related to the assessments than to the other figures.

10 acres each, there were 2 sokemen with a hide between them and a third who possessed a virgate.[1] In most places the cottars are not credited with any land at all, but at Littleport 'eight cottars of one acre' and at Stretham 10 with an acre each are recorded, while on 3 of the manors bordars are distinguished from apparently landless cottars—bordars with 5-acre holdings at Haddenham and West Wickham, and a single bordar with 4 acres at Linden End.[2]

These last cases imply a distinction between bordars and cottars similar to that which is drawn in Middlesex, but it is significant that in the summary which follows the main body of the Ely Inquest the term bordar is exclusively employed; and in the Cambridgeshire Domesday the absence of all reference to cottars in a compact block of six hundreds in the south-east of the county is evidently due to a difference of nomenclature. In this part of Cambridgeshire all members of the bordar–cottar class are called 'bordars', as they are throughout most of Domesday England, while in the rest of the county the term 'cottar' is applied to more than 700 individuals, being used, perhaps, sometimes as a mere synonym for 'bordar', but often as a means of distinguishing those who had little or nothing besides their cottages.[3] Domesday Book, the Cambridgeshire Inquest, and the Ely Inquest tell us, between them, a good deal about these humble denizens of the county, outside as well as inside the Isle of Ely; but because of the inconsistencies of terminology it is only if we treat the bordar–cottar class as a whole, both in Cambridgeshire and in Middlesex, that a fair comparison can be made between the two counties. If we do this, a striking resemblance becomes apparent. In both, a large proportion of those for whom information is available are described as holding 5 acres each; but also a large proportion were people with merely an acre, or a garden, or with no land that was thought worthy of mention. Again Cambridgeshire can show one bordar and Middlesex a dozen who possessed as much as 15 acres, while a fair number with 10-acre holdings in

[1] I.C.C., pp. 116, 120. At Wentworth 9 *villani*, who had 10-acre holdings, are described as 'under' the two more prosperous sokemen.

[2] Ibid., pp. 116, 117, 118, 120. At Chatteris a couple of bordars, who had 8 acres each, appear to be equal in this to the *villani*, but the form of the entry 'vi villani iib quisq. de viii ac' makes one suspect that the particulars of the villan holdings have dropped out of the text.

[3] *Economic Journal*, lxi (June 1951), 352–4.

the former county can be paralleled by those who averaged that amount in the latter. In both counties we find some holdings of various sizes intermediate between 1 and 10 acres, and in both members of the bordar–cottar class are frequently associated in groups in which each member had an identical holding, though at the same time it is by no means unusual for a village or a single manor to contain, along with such a group, other members of the bordar–cottar class whose economic position was different.[1] For other parts of England neither Domesday nor any of its satellites provides more than casual references to the holdings of bordars, but altogether there are a considerable number of such references, especially from East Anglia and from Somerset, and their evidence, so far as it goes, is in harmony with that already considered.[2] It would indeed be absurd to assume that the bordar who is credited with 5 acres on the *Terra Alwini* in Somerset had precisely the same amount of land as the 5-acre bordar recorded at Buxhall in Suffolk.[3] Acres, if measured at all, varied with the length of the rod employed in the locality, and rough estimates must often have sufficed in place of measurement. Yet even if the Domesday figures were intended to be taken as fiscal assessments rather than as areas, it is likely that in regard to the holdings of bordars and cottars they were closely related to agrarian realities. It would be easy for the village jurors to ascertain how many local 'acres' these people had, and if the lord was responsible for the geld on these small tenements, as it is probable that he was, there would be little point, as well as some difficulty, in working out separate assessments for them. The data lack precision but are far from being worthless. If we read in a modern biography that a man was born and reared in a farm labourer's cottage, the significance of that information is not much affected by the fact that such cottages vary in size and character.

Statements about the holdings of sokemen are very frequent in some sections of Domesday Book. But they are baffling in character. There can be little doubt that sokemen were responsible for the geld due from their lands; and evidently it is as a rule the geld assessments which Domesday records in these cases. Unfortunately it is also evident that the relation between these assessments and the extent of land to which they applied varied

[1] Ibid. 354–5.   [2] Ibid. 356 (table III).
[3] Exon., p. 396; Dd. ii, f. 382*b*.

unaccountably from place to place, so that no general conclusions can be drawn from them in regard to the size of the
sokemen's holdings.[1] There are, however, certain places
where we find a close correspondence between the assessment
figures for the land, the number of the estimated teamlands,
and the number of ploughs actually employed there, and if we
assume that this relation held good for the lands of the sokemen
referred to, their assessments can in these cases be taken
to indicate the scale of their holdings. The evidence is meagre
and perhaps not wholly unexceptionable, but, so far as it goes,
suggests that sokeman holdings were very various in extent, and
cannot be said to support the view that they were normally
larger than the holdings of *villani*, as they appear to have been
on the eight Cambridgeshire manors mentioned above. In
Bedfordshire, for example, though 7 sokemen had 3 hides between them at Sharnbrook, the same number held only 7 acres
at Stanford.[2] Again, in Lincolnshire, a carucate of land at
Dunham belonged to 4 sokemen and half that amount to 4
others at Kirkby Underwood, while at Fulsby in the same
county one of the sokemen had, it seems, a whole carucate and
the other 3 half a carucate between them.[3] The inhabitants
of several Lincolnshire villages included 1 or 2 sokemen who
appear to have possessed only a 'toft'.[4]

To draw any general conclusions from the statements of
Domesday about the holdings of the persons described as *liberi
homines* is impossible. Like those concerning the sokemen they
are evidently fiscal assessments which bear no constant relation
to the size of the holdings.[5] Nor can the *liberi homines* be regarded

[1] For the discrepancy between assessments and the plough-team statistics in
Suffolk see *Economic Journal*, lvii. 189–90. The baffling nature of the figures in
Nottinghamshire can be appreciated if one compares those for Marnham (Dd. i,
f. 285*b*), Morton (f. 287*b*), Aslockton (f. 288*b*), and Ossington (f. 290).

[2] Ibid., ff. 210, 212*b*.

[3] Ibid., ff. 362*b*, 358*b*, 339.

[4] e.g. Cockerington, Coleby, and Great Limber: ibid., ff. 358, 362*b*, 364. A sokeman at Beesby (or Maltby) had four tofts: f. 359*b*. One at Gosberton had, it seems,
only a garden: f. 344*b*.

[5] The plough-team figures provide a rough test. An intelligible correspondence
between assessment and area is indeed suggested where there was just one plough
per carucate (e.g. Anmer, Barwick, and Stanhoe in Norfolk: Dd. ii, ff. 151*b*, 161*b*,
167; Little Waldingfield and Cornard in Suffolk: ibid., ff. 392*b*, 428*b*) or just
double that ratio (e.g. Kirkby Bedon, Scottow, and Crimplesham in Norfolk:
ibid., ff. 124*b*, 229*b*, 230*b*; Rushbrooke, Hunston, and Eleigh in Suffolk: ibid.,
ff. 363*b*, 367, 392*b*). But then we find a whole plough-team on holdings rated
respectively at 20, 14, 12, and 8 acres (*Watlingsete*, Norfolk: ibid., f. 114; Brome,

as a definite economic class. The distinction between them and the sokemen, like that between bordars and cottars, is ignored in some counties, and, where it is made, appears to indicate some difference in social or legal standing which had little or nothing to do with the extent of their property.[1] About 96 per cent. of all those to whom the appellation is applied are found in East Anglia, and unfortunately the Little Domesday often leaves it doubtful whether it is recording pre-Conquest conditions only or a state of affairs that still obtained in 1086; but in spite of this and other obscurities it seems clear that people of widely various economic position were included. Some *liberi homines* held small manors and had a few tenants.[2] Some were themselves 'under' others so described.[3] At Raveningham in Norfolk there was one credited with 'three acres' worth 6*d.*, while at Stanhoe in the same county another had land assessed at a whole carucate and valued at 20*s.*[4] In Suffolk, the inhabitants of Westhorpe included a *liber homo* with a single 'acre' worth 2*d.*; but the estate which a *liber homo* had possessed, and apparently still possessed, at Syleham comprised 'two carucates' worth 60*s.*: it included a mill, 5 acres of meadow, and woodland for 60 swine, and there were 2 demesne plough-teams there besides 2 (formerly 4) teams belonging to a dozen bordars.[5]

A further source of information about the holdings of the Domesday peasantry is provided by the plough-team statistics. It is available for a much larger part of the country than the data hitherto examined. But it has serious defects. In the first place, the statements which Domesday makes about the teams of the manorial tenants usually lump different classes together, and, since bordars sometimes did and sometimes did not possess plough-beasts, a mere statement that *x villani* and *y* bordars have

---

Suffolk, f. 282; Plumstead and Irmingland, Norfolk, ff. 172, 158*b*) and 6 ploughs on 'forty acres' at *Thurketeliart* in Norfolk (f. 230).

[1] Four men at Methwold in Norfolk are called *liberi homines* in Domesday and sokemen in the Ely Inquest (Dd. ii, f. 136*b*; I.C.C., p. 138, cited Darby, *Eastern England*, p. 114); and in Suffolk the Feudal Book of Abbot Baldwin employs the latter term in several cases where Domesday employs the former (Great Barton, Pakenham, Rougham, Bradfield, Fornham St. Martin, West Stow, Stow, Uggeshall; op. cit., ed. Douglas, pp. 5–7, 11; Dd. ii, ff. 361*b*, 362, 364, 365, 371*b*).

[2] e.g. Weston, Suffolk, ibid., f. 282*b*.

[3] e.g. Shelton and Keningham, Norfolk, ibid., ff. 189*b*, 265.

[4] Ibid., ff. 279, 167.

[5] Ibid., ff. 371, 379*b*.

n ploughs leaves it uncertain whether or no all the ploughs belonged to the former.[1] For this reason it is necessary to limit the inquiry to cases in which the teams of a single class of peasants are enumerated, and such limitation both reduces the size of the sample and reduces it very unevenly throughout the country, so that for some counties the data are much less adequate than they are for others. Secondly, even the admissible cases generally give only the total number of teams belonging to a group of persons, and, though holdings of equal standard sizes were certainly very common, the evidence previously cited has shown that a village sometimes contained persons of the same class who possessed holdings of very different extent. Hence we can, for the most part, only draw conclusions about the average number of plough-beasts possessed by the members of the group. Again the relevance of the figures is limited to arable land: they cannot measure the economic condition of peasants who depended to any unusual extent upon stock-farming. This is not indeed so serious a defect as appears at first sight, for it can scarcely be doubted that in most districts the great majority of the peasants were mainly arable farmers and that their sheep and pigs tended to be roughly proportionate to their arable holdings. As Round has remarked: 'The realm described by Domesday is a realm in which the plough is King.'[2] At the same time it cannot be supposed that there was everywhere an exact correspondence between the number of a peasant's plough-beasts and the extent of his arable land. Maladjustments of ploughing strength must have occurred and would probably be harder to avoid on the smaller holdings. On such holdings, again, spade labour or cultivation with the aid of some sort of digging-stick may have played a considerable part; and it is not unlikely that, in some places, those who served as the lord's ploughmen, or as his shepherd or swineherd, were allowed the use of a demesne plough on their own land, for usages of this kind were fairly widespread in the later Middle Ages and are recorded on some of the manors of

---

[1] At Soham, Isleham, and Horningsea in Cambridgeshire, where the Domesday entries are thus ambiguous, the I.C.C. makes it clear that the bordars possessed at most only gardens: I.C.C., pp. 7, 8, 28. Even where the numbers given in entries of the type make it virtually certain that some of the teams belonged to the bordars (as at Tardebigge, Worcestershire, where 2 *villani* and 28 bordars are credited with 12 teams: Dd. i, f. 172b), there is no means of knowing how many did so.

[2] *V.C.H. Warwicks.* i (1904), 291.

Shaftesbury Abbey in the early part of the twelfth century.[1] Finally a man would require more ploughing strength in proportion to the size of his holding if he owed ploughing services on his lord's demesne, and we know far too little about the prevalence and the amount of such services to make precise allowances for this factor. It has been argued indeed that this really deprives the plough-team statistics of all validity as a source of information about the scale of the peasants' holdings.[2] But such scepticism is surely excessive. The ploughing services owed by the *gebur* of the *Rectitudines* did not prevent the author of that manual from regarding a pair of oxen as the concomitant of a yardland. Plough-beasts cannot normally have exceeded the number that could be fed from the resources of the holding and the common rights belonging to it. And it would require a more effectively pervasive power than manorial lords or their *firmarii* can conceivably have possessed to compel the peasants to go on feeding beasts that were wholly supernumerary to their needs, when a useful hide and carcass could be obtained by an easily contrived 'accident'.

Unquestionably the plough-team data for 1086 can yield only very rough and inexact conclusions. But in spite of their limitations they tell us a good deal.[3]

1. The groups of *villani* for which the record of teams has been judged free from ambiguity comprise 10,733 persons, or rather more than 10 per cent. of the total number of *villani* as summed by Ellis for the 32 counties to which they belong.[4] Of this number, 6,758 or nearly 63 per cent. occur in groups whose members had on an average more than a quarter of a team, which in the case of an 8-oxen team means more than the pair of oxen usually reckoned as the complement of a typical virgate

---

[1] For example, at Hatch in Wiltshire, one Leofric, who has 4 acres, 'tenet carucam et ex ea arat suam terram'; two others hold *similiter*; and the cowherd, as well as the shepherd, has 4 acres and 'arat suam terram de carruca abbatisse': Harl. MS. 61, f. 43: cf. ff. 40v (Tisbury), 44 (Berwick St. Leonard), 45v (Cheselbourne, Dorset). At Bradford-on-Avon 7 *bubulci*, who have half a virgate apiece, *habent carucas ii dies*: ibid., f. 38.

[2] See E. Miller, op. cit., pp. 45–48. Though I cannot accept Mr. Miller's conclusions, I have received much help from his criticism.

[3] The paragraphs that follow are largely based upon my articles in the *Economic Journal* for June 1946, June 1947, and June 1951, in which further details and some discussion of critical points will be found.

[4] Cornwall, Middlesex, and the land between Mersey and Ribble are excluded for the reasons given in the *Economic Journal*, June 1946, pp. 247–9. The figures are (with negligible exceptions) for the Domesday counties.

of 30 acres. Nearly 24 per cent. indeed averaged half a team or more, while less than 28 per cent. were in groups with an average of less than a quarter team.

2. Perhaps the best means of making some comparison between the *villani* and the sokemen is afforded by the statistics for a block of four counties—the counties of Lincoln, Nottingham, Leicester, and Northampton. Apart from Norfolk and Suffolk, these are the only counties in which Domesday enumerates more than a thousand sokemen, and the problem is not complicated here, as it is in Norfolk and Suffolk, by the presence of numerous *liberi homines*.[1] Moreover, in the four taken together, the plough-teams are separately recorded for groups comprising 17 per cent. of the sokemen and 10 per cent. of the *villani*. And the figures show that 47 per cent. of the sokemen in these groups and 28 per cent. of the *villani* had on an average more than a quarter of a team, while 45 per cent. of the former and 58 per cent. of the latter averaged less than a quarter of a team. Thus the sokemen seem to have been rather better off as regards plough-beasts than the *villani* were in this particular group of counties, but both classes were on the whole worse off than the *villani* elsewhere. It should be recognized, however, that these figures conceal important differences between the four counties, and that the pattern of the statistics is largely determined by the numbers involved in the case of Lincolnshire which for both *villani* and sokemen far exceed the combined totals for the other three. The differences are shown in the following table which gives for each county the average number of plough-beasts per sokeman and per villan of those whose teams are separately stated, eight being reckoned to a team:

	Lincolnshire	Leicestershire
Plough-beasts per sokeman . .	1·8	2·3
Plough-beasts per villan . .	1·5	(2·5)[2]

	Nottinghamshire	Northamptonshire
Plough-beasts per sokeman . .	3·0	3·4
Plough-beasts per villan . .	2·7	2·5

It should be noted, however, that the average per villan works out at 2·9 for the 32 counties taken as a whole, and at 3·0 or

[1] According to Ellis three *liberi homines* in Northamptonshire are the only persons so described in all the four counties, but he overlooked about half a dozen in Domesday Leicestershire, and there was one *francus homo* in Lincolnshire. Such numbers are negligible.

[2] This figure is based on a total of only 82 *villani*—a 3 per cent. sample.

more for 6 of the 11 counties for which a 10 per cent. sample is available. But sokemen are more likely than *villani* to have been free from ploughing services.

3. *Liberi homines* are, with negligible exceptions, recorded as such only in the Little Domesday and its frequent ambiguities are an obstacle to statistical presentation of the evidence regarding their plough-teams. It is, however, clear that persons of very various condition were thus described. In Norfolk it is fairly common to find a *liber homo* who has half a team; but groups to whom no plough-beasts are assigned and groups with an average of less than an ox per man are also of pretty frequent occurrence. That grave losses had befallen many members of the class since the Norman Conquest is revealed by entry after entry. But there were some for whom poverty was no new thing. Thirty-two *liberi homines* at West Dereham, for example, had 'always' had only two plough-teams between them.[1] Similar heterogeneity is also discernible among the *liberi homines* of Suffolk, who far outnumber those of any other county. If anything the contrasts were even sharper than in Norfolk. On the one hand, the appellation is given to men who had held—and, so far as one can tell, still held in 1086—small manorial estates with one or two demesne ploughs and a few tenants with plough-beasts of their own.[2] On the other hand, there were some groups with no plough-beasts at all, and some whose members averaged less than an ox apiece.[3] In both counties a diversity of conditions sometimes obtained within the bounds of a single vill.[4]

4. Among the counties in which no cottars are recorded and the term bordar was apparently employed to cover the whole bordar–cottar class, there are five in which more than 10 per cent. of the persons so designated are either mentioned in isolation in a way which suggests that they had no plough-beasts, or are included in groups whose teams are separately

---

[1] Dd. ii, f. 274. The text may possibly mean that the teams belonged to twenty-five of them.

[2] See, for example, ibid., ff. 379b (*Seilanda* = Syleham), 396 (Depden).

[3] For *liberi homines* clearly said to be without plough-beasts see ibid., ff. 386b (Rushmere St. Andrew), 404 (Thorney or Finborough?); but a lack of them may be presumed in the numerous cases where they are not mentioned, especially as negative statements seem to be confined to people who had formerly possessed some. At Gedding (f. 363) thirteen *liberi homines* had half a team *inter omnes*.

[4] e.g. at Seething, Norfolk (ibid., ff. 186, 186b, 264), and Ashfield, Suffolk (f. 439).

enumerated.[1] And, of the three thousand odd who constitute this sample, nearly 40 per cent. appear to be without plough-beasts; but some 214, or nearly 7 per cent., belonged to groups with an average of at least a quarter of a team per bordar, and a further 499, or more than 16 per cent., averaged more than an eighth though less than a quarter of a team. Wide differences within the class are also revealed in other counties. In nearly all there were some, and in some there were many, who are markedly separated from the plough-owning peasantry in the enumeration; but bordars who pretty evidently possessed 2 or more oxen can be discerned in 24 counties besides the 5 already mentioned.[2] In Herefordshire there were 40, and in Worcestershire 26, who averaged half a team or more.[3]

5. Little can be learnt from team statistics about the 'cottars' as distinct from the 'bordars'. In Wiltshire, where *coscez* and *cotarii* together far outnumber the cottars of any other county, they are usually mentioned in conjunction with other classes, so that inferences about their possessions are precluded. A considerable number are, however, mentioned in a context which suggests that they were without plough-beasts, while, on the other hand—notwithstanding the fact that the Wiltshire Domesday definitely distinguishes 'bordars' from both types of cottar—some occur in separate groups to which teams or portions of teams are assigned, and these cottars include thirty-six who averaged exactly one ox apiece and two at Codford who are between them credited with a whole plough-team.[4]

6. Some points of general significance stand out from the mass of details. Though there is nothing in the team statistics that really conflicts with the conclusion that a virgate was regarded as the normal holding of a *villanus* and something like 5 acres as the normal holding of a bordar or cottar, it is clear

[1] The counties are Norfolk, Suffolk, Bedfordshire, Hampshire, and Gloucestershire.

[2] See table IV, *Economic Journal*, June 1951, p. 364. I have not included Nottinghamshire among the twenty-four, though a single bordar with half a team is recorded there.

[3] A bordar at Hampton in Herefordshire appears to have possessed a whole team: Dd. i, f. 180.

[4] Ibid., ff. 69, 70b, 72, 74b (Ludgershall, Somerford, Whaddon in Alderbury, Deverill), and 71b (Codford). In Berkshire, I have noted 8 cottars with a plough-team at Sparsholt, 12 with half a team at Hanney, and 11 with half a team recorded under Ardington (ibid., ff. 60b, 61b, 62); but a team credited to 6 cottars at Witham in Somerset (f. 97b) really belonged to 3 *villani* whom Domesday omits to notice: cf. Exon., p. 357.

that large divergences from such norms were both common and widespread. As regards the *villani*, the evidence, though limited to about one-tenth of their total number, enables us to infer the existence of at least one member of the class who possessed a whole plough-team or more in 98 villages distributed over 20 counties, and on the other hand we can discern one or more *villani* who cannot have possessed more than a single ox, and may not have had one at all, in 150 villages distributed among 10 of the same counties and 10 others.[1] Among the sokemen, who in general do not appear to have differed much from the *villani* in economic condition, there were certainly some who had a whole team in 9 of the 11 counties in which the enumerated population included more than a hundred persons so designated in 1086; and in 10 of them there were some who had less than a pair of oxen. In Norfolk, where the data cover more than half the total number of sokemen recorded as dwelling there, we find 17 averaging a team apiece and 772 who averaged less than an ox per man.[2] In Lincolnshire there are instances of individual sokemen possessing a single ox, 2 oxen, 3 oxen, half a team, 6 oxen and a whole team.[3] Of the differences in economic condition that obtained within the bordar–cottar class enough has been said already. Though general impressions in regard to Domesday are liable to be deceptive, one does receive an impression that the range of differences was greatest amongst these people and amongst those who had the distinction of being described as *liberi homines*. Nor would it be surprising if this were indeed the case. 'Freedom' may mean freedom for the enterprising or the fortunate to prosper and obtain more land and stock; but it also means freedom to become indebted, freedom to sell one's land, freedom to sink into poverty. And the bordar

---

[1] *Economic Journal*, June 1946, pp. 260–1. Individual *villani* with two teams are recorded at *Haingurge* (? Hawkridge Farm, Hellingly) in Sussex, at Gillingham in Dorset, and at either Barnsley or Keresford (it is not clear which) in the West Riding of Yorkshire: Dd. i, ff. 21*b*, 80*b*, 317. There were little groups of *villani* who averaged more than one whole team apiece at *Curemtone* in Devon, at Lyde and Moore in Herefordshire, at Clapham, Astwick, and Clophill in Bedfordshire: the Bedfordshire groups contained a total of twenty-five individuals: ibid., ff. 118, 182*b*, 212, 213*b*, 214.

[2] *Economic Journal*, June 1947, table II, p. 184.

[3] Ibid., p. 185. Individual sokemen possessing one ox only (one-eighth of a team) occur at Rothwell, Cleatham, Beckering, Markby, and Lobingham: Dd. i, ff. 342, 346, 359, 359*b*, 360. There was a sokeman with an entire plough-team at Fulsby, Ashby in Bottesford, Ulceby by Alford, Burgh-in-the-Marsh, and Scopwick: ibid., ff. 339, 346, 355*b*, 360, 369.

or cottar whose regular holding was very small must have been free for a good deal of his time, for neither the tillage of 5 acres, nor in many cases the services imposed upon their tenant, can have occupied very much of it, so that, for the bordar, wage-earning labour might provide a means of adding to his holding. The hesitations and inconsistencies of Domesday Book in regard to the use of the terms 'bordar' and 'cottar' would be readily intelligible if the class to which they belonged was, so to say, a class in motion—a class tending to split into branches distinguished by economic divergence.

A remarkable regional difference is also perceptible in the plough-team statistics. Holdings appear to have been particularly small in the counties on the east coast south of the Humber and especially large in Herefordshire, Gloucestershire, and Worcestershire. For some classes of peasants the contrast is in some of the counties obscured by the smallness of the sample, but if account is taken of the evidence as a whole there can be little doubt of its reality, and in all the three western counties bordars as well as *villani* were unusually well furnished with plough-beasts, while in Norfolk, where team figures are available for over 10 per cent. of the bordars, nearly 15 per cent. of the *villani*, and more than 59 per cent. of the sokemen, each of these classes appears to have been exceptionally ill-provided.[1] On the other hand, in Bedfordshire, where we have a 67 per cent. sample for the *villani* and one of 54 per cent. for the bordars, there was a striking contrast between the two. The Bedfordshire *villani* were, it seems, among the most prosperous in England, having an average of 3·7 oxen per man of the sample, but more than half the bordars in the county had apparently no plough-beasts at all.[2]

The evidence of Domesday Book can be supplemented to some extent by that of the small group of estate surveys which date from the early part of the twelfth century. If due caution is exercised there is no serious risk of anachronism in using them

[1] For details see *Economic Journal* as cited above. From the team statistics for the *villani* of Essex and Suffolk we should not gather that their holdings differed much from the average for the whole country, but the sample in each case is inadequate, being only 1·0 per cent. and 1·6 per cent. respectively, and the much more adequate information which is available for the sokemen and bordars indicates both counties as regions of small arable holdings.

[2] No cottars as distinct from bordars are, I think, recorded in Bedfordshire. Ellis gives a total of 107 sokemen: of these the 31 whose teams are separately stated had on an average just half a team (4 oxen) apiece.

for this purpose. The earlier of the two Burton Abbey surveys is less than a generation and the first section of the Peterborough survey little more than a generation later than Domesday; and the earliest Shaftesbury and Caen surveys also appear to belong to the reign of Henry I.[1] Changes had no doubt occurred since 1086; but, apart from the evaporation of slavery, there is little reason to suppose that they were as rapid or far-reaching as those of the first twenty years after the Conquest. In many respects the surveys confirm and deepen the impression we receive from Domesday. The fundamental distinction between the more substantial peasant farmers and the cottagers—a distinction similar to that which the author of the *Rectitudines* had made before the Conquest between the *gebur* with his yardland and the *kotsetla* for whom 5 acres was deemed a fitting allotment—is a clearly marked feature of the agrarian organization on 20 of the 28 manors described in the Liber Niger of Peterborough, on some of the Burton Abbey manors, and on nearly all those covered by the earliest of the Caen and Shaftesbury surveys. The grouping of holdings in standard units—virgates or bovates with their multiples and fractions—is also common on the estates of these 4 monasteries.[2] Both the contrast between villan and cottar and the standardization of holdings are, however, familiar characteristics of English manorial economy and conspicuous throughout the greater part of medieval history; and it is by their revelation of the inequalities that obtained within the bounds of many manors in various parts of the country that the surveys in question contribute most to our knowledge of peasant holdings in the early feudal age. There is no knowing, indeed, whether differentiation had increased since 1086; but as Domesday itself exhibits marked inequalities in Middlesex, where its descriptions are exceptionally detailed, and nearly everywhere else employs a summary method which must have concealed any that existed, it seems likely that in this respect the agrarian pattern which obtained at the end of the

---

[1] These four contain surveys of manors in Staffordshire, Derbyshire, and Warwickshire (Burton); the counties of Northampton, Nottingham, Lincoln, and Huntingdon (Peterborough); Norfolk, Essex, and Gloucestershire (Caen); Wiltshire and Dorset (Caen and Shaftesbury).

[2] Several Anglo-Norman donations of tithe include the gift, in each village to which they apply, of a peasant tithe-collector who has a virgate or, in some cases, a half-virgate, and thus seem to imply the normality of such holdings: see *E.H.R.* lxix (1954), 580–96, and the references there given.

Conqueror's reign was not very different from that which is discernible in the time of Henry I.[1] In any case the early twelfth-century surveys are significant for the generation to which they belong.

On the Burton Abbey estates the normal holding of a *villanus* was 2 bovates or a virgate, but only at Field is it clear that all the peasant farms were of that amount.[2] On 8 manors such holdings are found together with others of half their size and of double their size. At Winshill, in addition to 10 2-bovate holdings, there were 16 others measured in bovates and these were of 5 different sizes ranging from 1 bovate to 5½.[3] In general, variety is less notable in the Liber Niger of Peterborough; but on 15 of that abbey's manors the *villani*, as distinct from other classes, were divided into full *villani* and half-*villani*, and at Tinwell we find virgaters and half-virgaters. Groups of sokemen are also recorded on a number of the manors and enough is said about their possessions to make it clear that the members of these groups had on an average more than the *villani* in some places and less in others.[4] The early Shaftesbury survey presents some puzzles; but almost everywhere it reveals holdings which fall into groups according to their size and differ a good deal from one another though composed, in varying numbers, of standard units. A striking example is furnished by the manor of Cheselbourne in Dorset. At the time of the survey, which Stenton dates about 1130, it contained one holding of 2 hides, one of a hide, and one of 3 virgates, together with 7 half-hide holdings, 15 holdings of a virgate, and 2 of half a virgate, one of which was combined with a mill. In addition there were at least 13 5-acre holdings, and 1 of 4 acres held in conjunction with a mill. In the same manor Domesday merely records 21 *villani* and 10 bordars with 8 plough-teams, together with 5 slaves.[5]

---

[1] It will be remembered that the contemporary Ely Inquest records holdings of different sizes on three Hertfordshire manors where Domesday fails to reveal any such stratification: above, pp. 344–5.

[2] *Hist. Collections for Staffs.* (William Salt Soc. for 1916), p. 227 (Field). Holdings also appear to have been equal at Darlaston and Whiston (pp. 227, 228), but the account of these places is rather obscure. In the later survey (Survey A) men with 2 bovates, or a virgate, are sometimes distinguished as *villani plenarii* from *villani dimidii* who had half that amount (pp. 241, 244, 246); and in one entry 12 acres (at Horninglow) are equated with a bovate (p. 222).

[3] Ibid., pp. 240–2.

[4] *Chron. Petr.* (Camden Soc., 1849), appendix, *passim*. For the relative position of the sokemen cf. Pilsgate, *Estona*, and Warmington, ibid., pp. 158, 160.

[5] Harl. MS. 61, ff. 44*v*, 45, 45*v*; Dd. i, f. 78*b*. The identity of the hidation points

As regards the especially free peasantry of East Anglia, the impression of their widely varying condition which we get from Domesday is confirmed by the so-called 'Feudal Book' of Bury St. Edmunds. The third section of that document is composed of lists of named peasants in a number of Suffolk villages, with the number of 'acres' held by each and the payments due from them; and, though the discrepancies between these lists and the summary statistics of Domesday are too great to admit of their being actually contemporary, they were probably compiled before the death of Abbot Ailbold which occurred in March 1119.[1] Further, the close correspondence between the area assigned to some of the villages and that described in Domesday Book as occupied by *liberi homines* justifies the conclusion that the peasants of the lists were the successors of those persons, while the difference in their numbers is in some cases so small that one can hardly suppose conditions in these particular places to have been radically altered since 1086. The 'acres' to which the document refers were no doubt fiscal assessments, but these may not have differed much from the agrarian reality, at least where the smaller holdings are concerned, and, however inexact the correspondence, the great variety in the assessments within each village must roughly reflect actual differences in the scale of the tenements. Of that variety the account of the first two villages affords striking examples. At Great Barton, the 61 holdings recorded were of 26 different sizes, ranging from 3 roods to 81 acres. At Pakenham there were 36 holdings of 18 different sizes varying from 1 acre to 26 acres.[2] Altogether the lists cover 34 villages and some degree of variety is apparent in all but two of them. Yet traces of standard holdings are not lacking. There

to the coincidence of the areas covered. In contrast to the Shaftesbury surveys, those of the Caen Cartulary are uninforming about individual holdings, but one can at least discern both virgates and half-virgates in its account of *Dineslai*: Bibl. Nat. MS. lat. 5650, ff. 28*v*, 29.

[1] *Feudal Documents from the Abbey of Bury St. Edmund*, ed. D. C. Douglas, pp. 25–44. On the problem of dating see ibid., pp. xlvi–lxvii; Galbraith, *E.H.R.* lvii (1942), 168 n. 1; R. H. C. Davis, *Kalendar of Abbot Samson* (Camden Soc., 1954), p. xxxviii n. 4. The first two sections of the Feudal Book are based on Domesday material; but the editor's contention that the third section contains the actual 'names, estates and rents of the Domesday freemen and sokemen' is quite unacceptable, and there is really no evidence that even the first two sections were compiled by or for Abbot Baldwin, who is constantly referred to by name as one would hardly expect him to be in his lifetime.

[2] *Feudal Documents*, pp. 25–27. A few holdings were shared by two or more persons, who are sometimes described as brothers.

were 11 3-acre tenements at Great Barton; and at Pakenham there were 4 of 3½ acres and 3 of 7 acres, as well as 3 of 5½ and 3 of 11 acres.[1] It is possible that some of the peasants who possessed these holdings had other land as well; but the diversities exhibited in this section of the 'Feudal Book' suggest that the freedom they enjoyed had opened the way to manifold changes, which, whether they came about through partible succession or through freedom of alienation, were probably, in many cases, either the cause or the consequence of poverty.[2]

The early estate surveys, together with a few charters, also supplement the witness of Domesday Book about the bordar–cottar class, and, more particularly, the *bovarii* or *bubulci*, who may possibly be the successors of Domesday *servi*, but appear to have become merged with the bordar–cottar class by the time of Henry I.[3] On the whole these documents show that the fluidity of conditions must not be exaggerated. The smallholders of which they tell occur mostly in groups whose members have equal allotments, so that we are reminded not so much of the more prosperous bordars who appear here and there in Domesday Book, as of the cottager described in the *Rectitudines*, of whom we are told that he ought to have 5 acres, but may have more or less than that according to the custom of the estate. When Aubrey de Vere the elder founded the priory of Colne in Essex, between 1101 and 1111, the endowments provided by him and his men included tithes in nine villages and in each of them 'a man with five acres', no doubt as a tithe-collector.[4] When Geoffrey de Mandeville founded the priory of Hurley in

---

[1] There were also at Great Barton 5 holdings of 6, 2 of 9, and 3 of 12 acres. Of 10 holdings at Whelnetham (p. 34) 1 was of 60, 2 of 30, and 4 of 7½ acres.

[2] Cf. *Kalendar of Abbot Samson*, p. xxxiii. Mr. Davis considers that the very small holdings of some of the socage tenants recorded in that late twelfth-century document cannot have been the only land they had; and these socage tenants were clearly the successors of those of the 'Feudal Book'. But Ballard's contention that many of the *liberi homines* of Domesday Suffolk had land in more than one place was based on identity of names, and is invalidated by the commonness of names in this period: Ballard, *Domesday Inquest* (1906), p. 144: cf. B. Dodwell, *Norfolk Archaeology*, xxvii (1941), 157; and my article in *Economic Journal*, lvii (1947), 193–5. For instances of partible inheritance in Suffolk see G. C. Homans, *Econ. Hist. Rev.* viii (1937), 53 n. 2.

[3] That slaves were replaced by *bovarii* in the twelfth century, and to some extent before that, is argued by M. M. Postan, *The Famulus* (*Econ. Hist. Rev.* Supplement No. 2), pp. 6–13. 'Bordiers', *boverz*, and *serjanz* are mentioned together in *Leis Willelme*, 17a (A. J. Robertson, *Laws*, p. 260). In the Latin version the word *boverz* is rendered *bubulci*.

[4] *Chron. Abingdon* (Rolls Series), ii. 57–59.

Berkshire, apparently between 1085 and 1087, he similarly gave in each of his manors, along with certain tithes, 'unum rusticum qui octo acras terre habeat'; and one of the manors involved was Sawbridgeworth, where, as we have seen, there were according to Domesday 46 bordars who had 8 acres apiece.[1] On the other hand, bordars with only 2 acres were associated with the widespread donations of tithe which Eudo Dapifer and two of his men made to the abbey of Colchester, and it was also a 2-acre bordar that the Bishop of Lincoln gave, between 1094 and 1109, to Eynsham Abbey along with the tithe of Thame in Oxfordshire.[2] Some of these examples seem to imply either an expectation that men with identical holdings would be found on many of the manors of a fee, or else an intention to create such, probably on manorial demesne.[3] But there is no evidence of any general tendency for conditions to be moulded by a custom that was uniform for all the manors of a great estate. Four-acre holdings were certainly common on a majority of those belonging to Shaftesbury Abbey as recorded in the earlier survey of that house; but the same survey shows that 5 acres were the normal complement of the smallholders at Berwick St. Leonard in Wiltshire and at Cheselbourne in Dorset and that there were six 3-acre holdings at *Tortelega*. At some places there were divergences from the local norm. Thus the abbey tenants at Berwick St. Leonard included one with 4 acres, another with a 'curtilage' and 3 acres, and a third who is credited with a 'curtilage' only; and at Iwerne Minster in Dorset, where 4-acre holdings were numerous, 2 of the 4 *bubulci* possessed 5 acres, a carpenter had 2 curtilages and 2 acres, and several people appear to have had merely a curtilage.[4] The Liber Niger of Peterborough is much less detailed than the Shaftesbury survey and rarely mentions the extent of the smaller holdings; but it reveals groups of *bovarii* whose holdings were

---

[1] J. Armitage Robinson, *Gilbert Crispin*, pp. 132–4; Dd. i, f. 139*b*. No 8-acre bordars are recorded on any of De Mandeville's estates in Middlesex; but at Ebury (*Eia*) 4 had a virgate between them, and at Enfield 20 had a hide and a virgate—figures which point to an average of 7½ acres per bordar.

[2] *Cart. Mon. de Colecestria* (Roxburghe Club, 1897), pp. 4–10, 11–14; *Eynsham Cart.*, i. 36, No. 7. Probably we should understand that the bordars which the Bishop of Lincoln gave with the tithe of Banbury and Cropredy also had 2 acres.

[3] For some Domesday examples of bordars who seem to have held portions of demesne see *Economic Journal*, lxi. 361; cf. Postan, op. cit., p. 12.

[4] Harl. MS. 61, ff. 44 (Berwick), 45, 45*v* (Cheselbourne), 42*v* (*Tortelega?*), 46–47 (Iwerne Minster).

equal within the same manor but differed from one manor to another. At Fiskerton in Lincolnshire they had 5 acres; and at Glinton, Castor, and Pytchley in Northamptonshire they had respectively 9 acres, 10 acres, and half a virgate. At Kettering the survey records 8 *cotsetes* who held 5 acres each and a *porcarius* who seems to be in possession of 8 acres.[1] The early surveys of the Abbaye aux Dames at Caen are singularly uninforming on these matters except in regard to *Dineslai*, a place which has sometimes been identified, on insufficient grounds, with Tilshead in Wiltshire. At *Dineslai* 5 *bovarii* held 30 acres *de dominio*, and we are told that 3 of them were free and the other 2 slaves. There were also 3 men who held respectively 2 acres with a close, an acre and a half with a close, and 2 acres.[2] On the estates of Burton Abbey standard holdings were common, but at the same time there was a good deal of variety and there is some evidence that conditions were changing. Groups of *bovarii* who held a bovate each are recorded in the earlier survey at Burton, Mickleover, Littleover, Findern, Stapenhill, and Winshill. At Stretton every *bovarius* had 2 bovates; and at Branston there were 2 with that amount of land and a third who possessed a single bovate. Holdings such as these seem to put the ploughmen into much the same class as the *villani*, who on the Burton manors normally held 2 bovates. At Appelby and Austrey, however, all the *bovarii* had 5 acres; and some with 5-acre holdings appear, along with those who had a whole bovate, at Littleover and Findern. *Cotseti* are referred to among the inhabitants of 10 manors, including some where Domesday mentions only *villani*. Most of them seem to be just cottagers, holding merely a *cortillagium* or, according to the later survey, a house (*domus*); but 3 at Appelby had 3 acres each; 1 at Austrey had 5 acres like the *bovarii* at that place; and at Stapenhill, where each *bovarius* held a bovate *de terra cotsetorum*, there were 4 other cotsets (*alii cotseti*), of whom 1 had 5 acres of inland and the others only a house and garden. At Littleover a *cotsetus* named

---

[1] *Chron. Petrob.*, pp. 164, 163, 162, 157. As there were four demesne ploughs at Kettering it seems likely that the *cotsetes* were ploughmen like the others. Those at Pytchley are called *bubulci*.

[2] Bibl. Nat. MS. lat. 5650, ff. 28*v*, 29. At Felsted, 19 bordars held 4 virgates (f. 26); but it seems that these were fiscal virgates and that the actual area was a good deal larger, though my former conjecture about it (which I described as 'extremely hazardous') must be abandoned, as it was partly based on a crude arithmetical error of which I was guilty: *Economic Journal*, lxi, 369 n. 2.

Aluric seems to have risen above the norm of his class, for we are told that he holds a bovate 'et facit dimidium opus villani'; and it is perhaps significant that in the later survey an Aluric, who holds the same amount of land and was presumably the same person, is no longer described as a *cotsetus*.[1] Signs of change can be discerned in several places. For example, at Wetmore some holdings of from 1 to 4 bovates look as if they had been formed by an amalgamation of smaller units, for they are described as *de terra cotsetorum*; and Survey 'A' (the later of the two surveys) reveals a clear case of engrossing at Stapenhill, where a certain *Alwinus Fretecorn* held a house and 3 acres of inland *sicut cotsetus*, in addition to 2 bovates which he held *sicut villanus*.[2] At Mickleover, where the earlier survey appears to credit 6 *bovarii* with a bovate each, Survey A records 5 who held 10 bovates between them.[3] At Stapenhill it shows how the holdings of the *bovarii* had lost their former regularity, for, in place of 4 who had a bovate each, we are told that 1 holds 22 acres—described as the land of 2 *bovarii*—for the care of 1 plough, and that 2 other *bovarii* hold respectively 9 acres and 6 acres *pro custodia alterius aratri*.[4] Such cases suggest that the lot of some peasants was improving. But both on the Burton estates and the Shaftesbury estates some men were virtually landless or had at most a croft or perhaps a couple of acres. One or more individuals who were in this position are recorded in one or other of the Burton surveys on eleven of that abbey's manors, and in the early Shaftesbury survey on a majority of the manors of which it gives a detailed account. On the large Shaftesbury manor of Tisbury in Wiltshire, where there had been 40 *villani* and 50 bordars in 1086, that survey records 41 tenants who possessed or shared holdings ranging from half a virgate to 2 virgates, and, among some 40 others who were less well provided

---

[1] Op. cit., p. 232. Round's dates are 1114–18 for Survey B and 1116–33 (probably 1116–27) for Survey A.

[2] Ibid., pp. 220, 238.

[3] Ibid., pp. 229–31; cf. Littleover (pp. 232, 234), where perhaps the *bovarii* advanced by two stages, as Survey B after recording 4 5-acre *bovarii* ends with a statement, which may be a later addition, about 4 who have a bovate each, and Survey A credits the same number with 8 bovates; but, since there were 4 demesne ploughs, it is possible that there were really 8 *bovarii* at first, and that subsequently the work of the 5-acre men (perhaps *fugatores*?) was taken over by the families of those with 2 bovates, as happened in respect of one of the demesne ploughs at Stapenhill.

[4] Ibid., pp. 238–9.

than these, 22 with only 4 acres each, 2 with 4 acres and a bit more (*particula terre*), and 12 who appear to have had only a 'curtilage' or, in one case, a curtilage and 2 acres.[1]

II

Of the services and payments that the peasants owed, little can be learnt from sources of earlier date than the first half of the twelfth century. The pre-Conquest *Rectitudines* does indeed tell us a good deal about three classes of persons inferior to the thegn, before describing the conditions attaching to special manorial offices.[2] In the section devoted to the *geneat*, who is obviously superior to the other two and has been described as a 'peasant with some of the characteristics of a mounted retainer', it certainly fails to say anything about the size of his holding and merely indicates, without in any way measuring, the obligations to which he might be subject—rent, it may be, and riding on errands, and casual services such as carting, reaping, mowing, and hedging. But the accounts of the *gebur* and the *kotsetla* are more definite; and in them we clearly recognize members of the two main classes of the English peasantry—the regular peasant farmer and the cottar or bordar with a smallholding—for the *gebur* is credited with a yardland (the virgate of post-Conquest documents) and we are told that the *kotsetla* ought to have not less than 5 acres. Yet typical as was the character of their holdings, it would be unsafe to assume that the tenurial conditions ascribed to them were really typical of the classes to which they belong. The author of the *Rectitudines* is describing the organization of a highly manorialized estate and the obligations of which he writes are those which he judged to be properly, and not unusually, incumbent upon the peasants attached to such an estate.[3] Even so he repeatedly emphasizes the fact that customs are diverse and that the rights and duties

---

[1] Harl. MS. 61, ff. 38v–41. The figures are not quite free from doubt as some names occur more than once. They are exclusive of holdings by knight service and other larger holdings.

[2] A critical edition of the Anglo-Saxon text and the Latin version, together with a German translation, is in Liebermann, *Gesetze*, i. 444–53; for a commentary see ibid. iii. 244–52. There is an English translation in Bland, Brown, and Tawney, *English Economic History: Select Documents* (1914), pp. 5–9. Liebermann considered that the *Rectitudines* and its companion the *Gerefa* were probably written in Wessex or south-central Mercia *c.* 1020–30.

[3] Cf. Liebermann, op. cit. iii. 245–6, § 6; Stenton, *Types*, p. 53.

of men vary from place to place. Moreover, if the *geneat* plays a less important part than the *gebur* in the cultivation of the lord's demesne, he is none the less clearly regarded as a normal denizen of the manor; and though it may well be that as a result of the Norman Conquest many persons of his class suffered a loss of status similar to that which befell many of the sokemen in eastern England, there can be little doubt that successors of the *geneats* as well as successors of the *geburs* are included among the *villani* of Domesday Book.[1] It is indeed the *geneat* and not the *gebur* who is identified with the *villanus* in the Latin version of the treatise which was made in the early part of the twelfth century.[2] And while *geneats* and *geburs* appear side by side in the survey of Tidenham, which is usually judged to be of mid-eleventh-century date, Domesday records only *villani* and *bordarii* upon that manor.[3]

For all these reasons it is impossible to form any estimate of the proportion of the peasantry that were in the eleventh century subject to burdens resembling those incumbent upon the *gebur* and the *kotsetla* of the *Rectitudines*. Yet in general character those burdens have so much in common with the obligations of *villani* and cottars recorded in various parts of the country in the next century that a consideration of their nature is an essential preliminary to the study of the concrete evidence provided by the surveys.

The *gebur* is represented as owing both regular week-work and casual services, as well as payments in money and payments in kind. He has to work three days a week in harvest and from Candlemas (2 February) to Easter, and two days a week

---

[1] Cf. Stenton, *Anglo-Saxon England*, p. 471. The resemblances between the *geneats* and the radmen or radknights of Domesday and between the *geburs* and the Domesday *bures* and *coliberti* cannot mean that all their successors were so described. Vinogradoff judged that the *coliberti* were only distinguished by 'the casual resolve of several sets of jurors' (*English Society*, p. 468); and the same may be true of the radmen. Both are in Domesday confined to western England The *coliberti*, though more numerous on the whole, are outnumbered by the radmen in four counties.

[2] Maitland thought the author of the Latin version so ignorant of the old English language that on such a matter his testimony 'is of no value': *Domesday Book and Beyond*, p. 329. But the fact that he does not attempt to translate certain words (e.g. *scorp*, which Maitland cites, and *gebur*) suggests that he was cautious where knowledge failed him. Liebermann describes the translation as 'im ganzen sorgsam und treu gefertigt': op. cit. iii. 310.

[3] Robertson, *Anglo-Saxon Charters*, No. cix; Dd. i, f. 164. The 38 *villani* of Tidenham recorded in Domesday were unusually prosperous, having on an average a whole plough-team apiece: the 10 bordars are not credited with any teams and so cannot well be identified with the *geburs* who owed ploughing services.

throughout the rest of the year; but, if he does any carrying, he is excused from week-work while his horse is so employed. Among his other services the most important appears to be ploughing, for he has to plough an acre a week from the first ploughing until Martinmas (11 November) and a further 8 acres besides (2 of which are in payment for pasturage), so that altogether he might well be required to plough something like 18 acres of his lord's demesne. In addition he pays 10*d.* as rent; he pays 'hearthpenny' (which probably means Peter's Pence); and he renders 23 (or 24?) 'sesters' of barley, 2 hens, and a young sheep, and provides seed-corn for 3 acres.[1] Every *gebur* must moreover give 6 loaves to the lord's swineherd when the pigs are driven to get mast in the woods. On the other hand, at the outset of his tenancy he ought to receive 7 acres of his yard-land already sown and be given stock, implements, and household utensils (all of which must revert to the lord on his death); and we are told that in some places it is the custom for people to be given meals on certain occasions and to have small perquisites.

Of the *kotsetla* it is said that on some estates he must work every Monday in the year and three days a week in harvest.[2] He may also be called upon to assist in the discharge of his lord's obligations in such matters as *Saewearde* (coast-guard duty or perhaps the repair of a sea-wall) and work in connexion with the deer-hedge for the king's hunting. He ought not to pay any rent for his land; but he pays hearthpenny 'as it befits every free man to do', and also church-scot. Two pre-Conquest documents, which in all probability do not differ widely in date from the *Rectitudines*, provide a little supplementary evidence. The first is the survey of Tidenham already mentioned.[3] It deals with two classes of persons whom it distinguishes as *geneats* and *geburs*. Like the *Rectitudines* it describes the obligations of the former in general terms, but the emphasis upon riding and carrying services is here unmistakable. Like the *Rectitudines* it is more precise about the *gebur*. The Tidenham *gebur*, however, owed as week-work only half an acre's ploughing, and though

---

[1] Twopence could be paid in lieu of the sheep.

[2] The Latin version adds that on some estates he works every day in harvest and receives a perquisite sheaf.

[3] Robertson, op. cit., No. cix. Liebermann thought that it may have been drawn up by the author of the *Rectitudines* or by someone acquainted with that work (*Gesetze*, iii. 245): in two places verbally identical expressions are employed.

one cannot assess the burden involved by his duties in the making of fish-weirs and in fencing work, his other services were far from heavy.[1] Payments in kind (other than rods which might be given in lieu of weir-building) were apparently limited to a 'half-sester' of honey, 6 sesters of malt, and a ball of net yarn; but every yardland on the estate had to pay 12*d.* and, it seems, 'four pence as alms'; and the *gebur* also paid 6*d.* at Eastertime. A man who kept pigs had to give 3 for the first 7 and 1 for every 10 in excess of that number.[2]

The other document is a memorandum of dues and services owed by the peasants (*ceorlas*) of Hurstbourne Priors in Hampshire.[3] They included a payment of 40*d.* per hide of land and payments in kind comprising 2 ewes with 2 lambs at Easter, 4 loads of split wood, and some specified, but, in Stenton's judgement, now indeterminable quantities of ale, wheat, and barley. By way of labour services the Hurstbourne peasants owed an unspecified amount of work in every week except three throughout the year; and in addition they had to plough 3 acres and sow them with their own seed, mow half an acre of meadow and stack the hay, stack the split wood, wash and shear the lord's sheep, and put up sixteen pole-lengths of fencing.[4]

In neither document is anything said about cottars; nor does the Hurstbourne document make any distinction between different classes of the peasantry.[5] But the resemblances between the obligations of the Hurstbourne *ceorlas*, the Tidenham *geburs*, and the *geburs* of the *Rectitudines* are remarkable. As we have seen, all three owed labour services—both week-work and services of the kind usually known as boon-works—and all three owed money payments and payments in kind. In some details too there was a close correspondence. The money payment of 40*d.*

---

[1] He had to plough an acre as church-scot and supply seed for sowing it and he had also to 'reap an acre and a half and mow half an acre and work at other kinds of work, always in proportion to the work'. Perhaps the last clause implies such things as sowing and haymaking on the areas reaped and mown.

[2] Perhaps the pig rent was paid for the use of pasture (herbage as distinct from pannage), for an additional payment was apparently due if mast was available. The pig rent, the money rent, and the alms payment were presumably due from *geneats* and well as *geburs*.

[3] Robertson, op. cit., No. cx.

[4] Though the money payment is assessed on the hide, this does not necessarily imply that the *ceorla* was assumed to have that amount of land. At Tidenham we are given the rate per yardland, but in 1086 the *villani* there evidently had much more than a yardland: see above, p. 365 n. 3.

[5] In 1086 there were bordars as well as *villani* at Hurstbourne.

a hide at Hurstbourne corresponds exactly with that of 10*d*. a yardland which the *Rectitudines* postulates for the *gebur*, and is not very different from the rate per yardland at Tidenham. The 3 acres of ploughing and sowing owed by the Hurstbourne *ceorla* is matched by the 'gafol-earth' service which forms a distinct item among the ploughing obligations of the *gebur* in the *Rectitudines*. Both at Tidenham and at Hurstbourne the boon-works (if so we may call them) included the mowing of half an acre and an almost identical amount of fencing. Yet the differences were considerable. Though no precise comparison is possible, the burdens of the peasants at Tidenham and Hurstbourne seem to have been definitely lighter than those recounted in the *Rectitudines*. The Tidenham *gebur* was exempt from most of the week-work which the *Rectitudines* assigns to his namesake, nor can it be supposed that the vaguely described week-work at Hurstbourne was really comparable with that owed by the latter.[1] And only slight ploughing services are mentioned in the Hurstbourne memorandum.

In Domesday Book references to the obligations of the peasantry are very rare and generally of a casual nature. The most notable are contained in the descriptions of certain manors in Herefordshire and Worcestershire. On the great demesne manor of Leominster the peasants plough and sow 125 acres, provide seed for the sowing, and make various payments amounting to £12. 4*s*. 8½*d*., while every *villanus* who has 10 pigs gives one of them as pannage.[2] We cannot tell how these burdens were distributed among the various classes of the manorial tenants; but, as they possessed 201 ploughs, the ploughing service meant little more than half an acre per plough, and the money payments seem light for an enumerated population of 331 persons excluding the slaves. Obligations of different types are also associated in one or two other entries. At King's Caple, 5 Welshmen, who had 5 ploughs, rendered 5 sesters of honey, 5 sheep with their lambs, and 10*d*.[3] At *Lene* (Eardisland) the *villani* gave 13*s*. 4*d*. *de consuetudine*; and the

---

[1] Cf. Vinogradoff, *Growth of the Manor*, p. 286 n. 59.

[2] Dd. i, f. 180. The payments included lxv *solidos de melle*, which perhaps means honey worth that amount, and not a commuted render as I have assumed in the text. It should be noted that the services and payments said to have been formerly due at Leominster were similar to those obtaining in 1086, but we are told that the radknights used then to give 14*s*. 4*d*. and 3 sesters of honey.

[3] Ibid., f. 181.

coliberti, of whom there were 6, rendered 3 sesters of wheat and barley, 'two and a half' sheep with their lambs, and $2\frac{1}{2}d$.[1] At Eckington (*Aichintune*) 6 *coliberti* paid 11s. 2d. and ploughed and sowed 12 acres.[2] But more often only a single item is recorded. Renders of honey are prominent (especially where the tenants were Welsh), and sometimes, as at King's Caple, these appear to be related either to the number of persons owing them or to the number of their ploughs.[3] In several cases it is a money rent of which we read.[4] In a few the only obligation mentioned is a service of ploughing and sowing. At Marcle the *villani* had to plough and sow with their own seed 80 acres of wheat and the same amount of oats.[5] This was a large contribution to the cultivation of the demesne, for the demesne ploughs were only 4 in number; but the peasants had 40 ploughs, and 4 acres per plough is not a hard burden. Similar but lighter services are mentioned at Bricklehampton and Defford in Worcestershire. The peasants possessed 6 ploughs on both these manors and they were bound to plough and sow 6 acres at Bricklehampton and 4 at Defford.[6]

Yet relatively abundant as these details are, they afford no basis for any general conclusion even about the two counties concerned. It may be that the facts are recorded because they were exceptional. References to Welshmen and Welsh law in the Herefordshire folios remind us that we are in a region where unusual features might occur. There is no knowing, too, whether the obligations that are described represent the sum of those owing at each place or whether they should be understood as supplementary to an assumed background of normal usage.

[1] Ibid., f. 179b. Presumably two sheep and three sheep were given in alternate years.

[2] Ibid., f. 174b.

[3] See Westwood (f. 181) and Ewias Harold (f. 184).

[4] For example, at Baysham, Letton, and *Avretone* (ff. 181, 184b, 185). At Risbury (f. 180) an isolated *villanus* paid 10d., like the *gebur* of the *Rectitudines*.

[5] Ibid., f. 179b. For 9 acres of the oats the service appears to have been due to the tenants of two half-hides which had been severed from the demesne manor: cf. ff. 182b, 185b.

[6] Ibid., f. 174b. There were 8 *villani* and 10 bordars at Defford, so perhaps each *villanus* had to plough half an acre. It is conceivable, though very unlikely, that each *villanus* had to plough 4 acres there, and 6 at Bricklehampton. On several Worcestershire manors 'radmans' or *liberi homines* had before the Conquest owed a single day's mowing and such service as they might be ordered (f. 174b). As Vinogradoff points out, the vagueness of the latter obligation is 'not a mark of special servility', but due to the fact that riding on errands, &c. had to be 'according to circumstances' (*English Society*, p. 387).

B b

The most remarkable fact about these entries is the absence of any reference to week-work, with the one exception that twelve bordars at Ewias Harold are said to work one day a week.[1] Round considered that the specified ploughing and sowing services were in lieu of work on 'a certain number of days'; but Vinogradoff was confident that the Leominster peasants must have owed a considerable amount of week-work in addition. In fact each of these judgements rested upon an unsure foundation.[2] Where Domesday describes certain peasants on a manor as subject to particular obligations, it is indeed unlikely that they owed any other services or payments of the same kind as those specified. A stipulated area of ploughing surely implies that no other ploughing services were required. But anything more than that would be mere conjecture; and the one thing that one can safely say about this Herefordshire and Worcestershire material in general is that it confirms the statement of the *Rectitudines* that conditions varied from place to place.[3]

Of predial services in other counties nothing definite can be learnt from Domesday. We read of some radknights at Deerhurst in Gloucestershire who, though they were *liberi homines*, used in King Edward's time to plough and harrow and reap and mow *ad opus domini*—of others, connected with the manor of Tewkesbury, who used to plough and harrow for their lord's *curia*.[4] At Alfriston in Sussex the *villani* and bordars *arant ad medietatem*, whatever that may mean.[5] Of greater significance are some casual references in which it seems to be taken for granted that *villani* owe labour services. Eight burgesses who belong to the manor of Drayton in Staffordshire *operantur sicut*

---

[1] Dd. i, f. 186. No other reference to week-work has been noticed in the whole of Domesday Book; and this one entry shows that an exceptional statement need not point to an exceptional condition, for later evidence makes it certain that members of the bordar–cottar class very commonly owed work on one day a week like the *kotsetla* of the *Rectitudines*.

[2] Round, *V.C.H. Hereford*, i. 291; Vinogradoff, *English Society*, p. 314. If Round was thinking of week-work he must have failed to notice that even 4 acres per plough would be no equivalent for the smallest amount of week-work; and Vinogradoff's argument is based upon a confusion between the two senses of *dominium*: see *Econ. Hist. Rev.* (2nd series), vii (Aug. 1954), 67–68.

[3] An entry about Almeley in Herefordshire ('Alterius villae homines laborant in hac villa et reddunt xxxvii solidos et viii denarios': Dd. i, f. 182*b*) suggests that the Domesday descriptions of peasant obligations were not exhaustive.

[4] Dd. i, ff. 166, 163. Both passages are quoted by Vinogradoff (*English Society*, p. 69), but he omits the significant word *tamen* in the former ('Radchen' idest liberi homines T.R.E. qui tamen omnes ad opus domini arabant').

[5] Ibid., f. 21*b*.

alii villani.[1] Of Broadholme in Nottinghamshire we are told that the *opus villanorum* belongs to Saxilby, just over the Lincolnshire border.[2] At Steyning in Sussex the occupiers of certain tenements used to work *sicut villani* in the time of King Edward.[3] But a statement that Eudo Dapifer worked the demesne at Barley in Hertfordshire with the demesne ploughs of his nearby manor of Newsells perhaps indicates that the Barley *villani* did not owe very much in the way of ploughing services.[4]

Money payments are more frequently recorded, perhaps because they were rather abnormal. Over 30 entries have been noted in which *villani* are described as rendering a sum of money. They occur sporadically in 11 counties from Yorkshire to Hampshire and from Herefordshire to Middlesex, but nearly half the total are supplied by Devon and Kent. Most of them concern isolated individuals and the sums in these cases range from 8*d.* to 10*s.*[5] Bordars and cottars also appear as paying money, unlike the *kotsetla* of the *Rectitudines*. Examples have been noted in 29 places distributed over a dozen, mostly southern, shires; and the sums payable by individuals, or, on an average, by the members of groups, vary from less than 4*d.* to 2*s.* 8*d.*[6]

It is the same with members of those special classes which in some counties are distinguished from the ordinary peasantry. In Shropshire, people rendering money are found among Welshmen, 'radmans', *hospites*, and *homines*.[7] At Clere in Hampshire 2 *coliberti* pay 13*s.* and at Pucklechurch in Gloucestershire another pair pay 34*d.*[8]

[1] Ibid., f. 246*b*.

[2] Ibid., f. 291*b*.

[3] Ibid., f. 17. Contrast a tenant at Wolverton in Worcestershire who rendered 'omnes consuetudines firmae sicuti reddebant antecessores sui excepto rustico opere' (f. 172*b*) and those who, at several places in that county, 'sicut alii liberi homines serviebant' (f. 175 *passim*).

[4] Ibid., f. 139 ('laborat cum propriis carucis de Nuesselle').

[5] *Villani* paying 5*s.* or more occur at Buckland and a place in Bewsborough Hundred in Kent (ibid., ff. 10*b*, 11*b*); Cheverton in the Isle of Wight (f. 52*b*); Stonehouse and Cullompton in Devon (ff. 113*b*, 117*b*: cf. Exon., p. 435); and Stepney in Middlesex (f. 127). At Oare in Kent 3 *villani* paid 20*s.* for a *jugum* which they held at farm (f. 10).

[6] In 16 cases, involving 55 individuals, the payment was, or averaged, 1*s.* or more.

[7] Dd. i, ff. 254*b* (Maesbrook), 256 (Priest Weston), 259*b* (Leaton), 260 (Leintwardine). It is not clear whether the *hospites* held any agricultural land.

[8] Ibid., ff. 39, 165. Perhaps the Pucklechurch *coliberti* really lived in Gloucester, and there is nothing to show whether they or those at Clere had land, but elsewhere in both counties groups of *coliberti* are credited with plough-teams.

The payment of rent does not of course imply exemption from labour services; but it is unlikely that regular week-work was due from *villani* or others who paid as much as 5*s.*, or indeed from bordars paying something like 2*s.*, unless their holdings were abnormally large. Some peasants, moreover, are specifically described in Domesday Book as 'rent-payers'—*censores* or *censarii.*[1] These terms occur almost exclusively in the north—in the counties of York, Derby, Nottingham, and Lincoln—but, since all these counties were judged by Eyton and Ballard to belong to the same Domesday circuit, this may be due to the adoption of a peculiar nomenclature by the commissioners of that circuit and not to peculiar conditions in the region, though in other circuits Dorset can show 2 *censores* at Askerswell (*Oscherwille*) and 9 at Allington, and there was a group of 36 *censarii* on the great manor of Waltham in Essex.[2] Perhaps some of the people thus described were not really peasants, but *firmarii* of manors, or tenants unconnected with agriculture; but many are credited with plough-teams or portions of plough-teams, or are unmistakably associated with other classes of the peasantry; and in such cases it cannot be doubted that they were distinguished by the fact that they held their land mainly, if not wholly, for a money rent.[3] Within the class considerable differences in economic position are discernible. At Bugthorpe in Yorkshire the rent of 2 *censarii* produced 20*s.* 4*d.*, but at *Toxenai* (? Trusley) in Derbyshire there were 5 who rendered 5*s.*, which probably means 1*s.* each.[4] It is worthy of note that at Duckmanton in Derbyshire and at Bishop Wilton and Acomb in Yorkshire all, or nearly all, the peasantry belonged to this rent-paying class.

The evidence of Domesday Book regarding the obligations

---

[1] According to Ellis 159 persons are thus distinguished in Domesday.

[2] Dd. i, ff. 78*b*, 80*b*; ii, f. 15*b*.

[3] In Yorkshire a *censorius* at Skelton had some land formerly held *cum halla* by a certain Torber 'et sunt ibi duae caruce et vi villani', and 2 *censores* at Carnaby 'habent ix villanos cum iii carucis': Dd. i, ff. 298*b*, 331. There is nothing to suggest that those in Dorset or Essex occupied any agricultural land. A difference in tenure (other than mere rent-paying) is perhaps implied by the entry: 'Ibi v censarii reddunt v solidos et ii sochemanni v solidos': ibid., f. 274*b* (*Toxenai*, Derbyshire).

[4] Ibid., ff. 303, 274*b*. Individual *censarii* who had a whole plough-team are found at Palterton and Swadlincote in Derbyshire and South Witham (*Widme*) in Lincolnshire; but 5 at Broughton (*Bertone*) in Lincolnshire had 1 team between them and at Duckmanton in Derbyshire 18 possessed a total of 5 teams: ibid., ff. 277, 278, 371, 362*b*, 277.

[5] Ibid., ff. 277, 302*b*, 303*b*.

of sokemen and *liberi homines* is puzzling. There are occasional references to escort, guarding, or carrying services which certain sokemen owed, or had formerly owed, to the king or the sheriff; and we are told of small payments that were due if these services were not required.[1] Sporadically both sokemen and *liberi homines* are said to render sums of money; but the rationale of these renders is generally obscure, and statements implying some distinction between a *census* and a *consuetudo* serve rather as a reminder that conditions might be complex than as a clue to their explanation.[2] Even where the payments are obviously related to the area at which the land was assessed, the figures are remarkably various. On the Countess Judith's land in Northamptonshire 5 consecutive entries record small groups of money-paying sokemen and in 3 of these cases the sums they render work out at just 12 ores of 16*d*. for each hide of land, but in the other 2 the rates are 6 ores per hide and 4 ores per hide respectively.[3] And then at Fulbourn in Cambridgeshire there are 26 sokemen who have 4 hides and pay £8 ('viii libras arsas et pensatas'), which is 30 ores per hide; and at Castor in Norfolk we find a sokeman who used to pay 5*s*. 4*d*. (4 ores), though his land is only assessed at 10 acres.[4] Statements such as these are, moreover, infrequent as well as puzzling; and Domesday is particularly disappointing in Lincolnshire, the classic land of the sokemen. On the other hand, in the counties covered by the Little Domesday volume it is not uncommon for the freer classes of the peasantry or their lands to be valued separately from the manors to which they are attached; and (though the details are in many ways so baffling that one is reminded of Round's warning against 'the vain attempt to obtain definite conclusions from the bewildering morass of figures contained in Domesday Book') there is some reason for thinking that the values in question represent actual payments, as we have seen was the case with many of the Domesday valuations of manors.[5] It is sometimes

---

[1] Ibid., ff. 134, 140 (*Sutreshele* and Lilley, Hertfordshire), 190, 190*b* (Fulbourn and West Wratting, Cambridgeshire).

[2] Dd. ii, f. 130*b* (Fersfield, Norfolk); but cf. f. 6*b* (Lawford, Essex) where the terms seem to be treated as synonymous.

[3] Dd. i, f. 228; cf. f. 220 (5 sokemen who seem to be paying 4 ores for a hide at Stoke Albany, Northants.), and ii, f. 289*b* (12 *liberi homines* at Badmondisfield, Suffolk, who pay at the rate of 12 ores per carucate).

[4] Dd. i, f. 190; ii, f. 110*b*.

[5] Above, chapter V, especially pp. 118–23.

unmistakably the *liberi homines* themselves who are 'valued'.[1] And if, for example, we compare a statement which is made about Thurlow in Suffolk—'Tunc val(uit) manerium IX libras modo XVI et liberi homines XX solidos'—with one about Badmondisfield in the same county—'Tunc val(uit) manerium VII libras modo X et liberi homines reddunt XL solidos'—we can hardly doubt that the free men of Thurlow were money-payers like the others.[2] A similar conclusion is suggested by a comparison of some Northamptonshire entries concerning soke-men. In each of the villages in which the Countess Judith had the sokemen mentioned above, Robert de Buci is also credited with land occupied only by sokemen. In his case, however, it is of values, not renders, that we read; but in four out of the five villages these values come to precisely the same number of ores per hide as the sums rendered by the countess's sokemen.[3] As Professor Douglas says, 'there seems no doubt of the wide-spread existence of a money-paying peasantry in East Anglia at the time of Domesday'; and probably it was much the same in most of the counties in which *liberi homines* and sokemen formed an important element in the population.[4] It does not follow that all the payments in question should be regarded without qualification as rents. Some may represent ancient customary obligations of a public nature—tribute in money or in kind, which was originally due to the king, but had become payable to the peasants' lord as the result of a royal grant.[5] Such payments might come to be treated as rents or to be merged with rents; and it seems possible that the baffling differences in the ratios between the renders or 'values' and the assessed areas of the peasants' holdings may in part be due to the imposition of

---

[1] See, for example, Castle Acre and Deopham, Norfolk (Dd. ii, ff. 160*b*, 227); and Chilton near Sudbury, Suffolk (f. 304).

[2] Ibid., ff. 286, 289*b*.

[3] Dd. i, ff. 225, 228. The correspondence relates to the present values. The entries for Sutton Bassett illustrate the interlocking of the two estates. That for Robert runs: 'Idem tenet i hidam et ij partes dimidiae hidae in Sutone. Terra est ii carucis et dimidiae. Has habent ibi viii sochi. Valuit v solidos. Modo xxi solidos et iiii denarios'; and that for the countess: 'In Sutone est dimidia hida et tercia pars dimidiae hidae et ibi iiii sochi habent i carucam et dimidiam et reddunt per annum x solidos et viii denarios.' Except at Dingley (the one place where the values and renders fail to correspond) the combined areas form complete hides, and one therefore suspects a textual error in the Dingley entry which the complexity of the fractions may explain.

[4] Douglas, *Social Structure*, p. 99.

[5] Ibid., pp. 99–106; cf. R. H. C. Davis, *Kalendar of Abbot Samson*, p. xlvii.

additional rents in some cases but not in others.[1] The commutation of services and renders in kind probably played a part
in the development of money rents, and it may be that a good
many of the freer peasants discharged all or most of their obligations by means of such payments, as Douglas maintains; but the
record of the Ely plea of 1071–5 cited in a previous chapter
shows that there were sokemen both in Norfolk and Suffolk who
owed miscellaneous agricultural services of boon-work character, and, as Round pointed out, the similarity of those incumbent upon the people in question in the two counties suggests
that we have to do with a custom 'of wide prevalence', while
Domesday Book itself frequently refers to the obligation of fold-
soke in the same region.[2]

Neither Domesday Book nor any document of approximately
contemporary date gives a complete account of the obligations
of any individual peasant or the means of measuring the relative importance of labour services, money payments, and renders
in kind for any class in any part of the country. The Domesday
Monachorum and the contemporary schedules of Canterbury
Cathedral manors, discussed in a previous chapter, do indeed
provide grounds for the belief that peasant money rents were
much more common on those estates than one would gather
from Domesday Book, for the sums entered in these documents
as *gablum* are largely odd sums running into pence or fractions
of a penny, and can hardly be anything else than the totals of
numerous small payments due from humble folk. But evidence
that mostly relates to Kent cannot safely be taken as a guide for
other regions.[3]

With the reign of Henry I more detailed evidence becomes
available—especially that of the surveys which were compiled
for the abbeys of Burton, Peterborough, and Shaftesbury. These
surveys have the merit of being concerned with different parts
of the country, but their value as a sample is limited by their
monastic origin, for it is impossible to know how far conditions
on lay estates were similar to those they describe. They are rich
in detail, but, for that reason, do not lend themselves to a

---

[1] The payment of £8 by the sokemen of Fulbourn used not to be made before
the Conquest: Dd. i, f. 190.
[2] Douglas, *Social Structure*, p. 97; Round, *Feudal England*, p. 33; and, for references to fold-soke, Vinogradoff, *English Society*, p. 387 n. 7.
[3] For Kentish peculiarity see Vinogradoff, op. cit., pp. 92–94; Neilson *Cambridge Econ. Hist.* i. 454–6.

summarization of their contents. Yet at the outset one general observation may be made. On all three estates the obligations of the peasantry appear to be compounded, as it were, of the same elements. In the surveys of all three we find frequent reference to two types of labour services—on the one hand, regular week-work, and, on the other hand, occasional services of various kinds, including ploughing. In each case, again, money payments play an important part; and in each renders in kind are also mentioned. To those familiar with English manorial economy in the later Middle Ages all this may seem trite and obvious. It is not, however, without significance that these early twelfth-century documents show that, alike in the north, the east, and the south-west of England, monastic land-lords were receiving from the manorial tenantry services and dues of the same types as those described a century earlier in the *Rectitudines*.

The elements were the same, but they were employed and combined in a bewildering variety of ways; and the surveys reveal, not only differences between the estates of the three abbeys, but, even more notably, differences between different manors of the same abbey, and between some peasants and others on the same manor.

In the Burton Abbey surveys a sharp distinction is drawn between tenements let for a money rent and those 'at work'; and, in spite of some uncertain details, it is clear that more than half the area covered by substantial holdings, measured in bovates, virgates, or carucates, belonged to the former class.[1] This does not mean that a majority of the peasants were rent-payers, for the rented lands included larger holdings and a few of these were occupied by tenants who can scarcely be regarded as peasants. In the case of Leigh, for example, the earlier survey records 24 working bovates held by 12 *villani* and 40 rented bovates held by 8 tenants, one of whom had *villani* of his own.[2] Yet many ordinary peasant holdings were rented. At Burton itself nearly half the occupiers of 1 or 2 bovates paid rent, and at Field almost all the tenanted land consisted of 2-bovate holdings occupied by *censarii*.[3] The proportion between the

---

[1] This is true of both surveys. Exact comparison is prevented by the difficulty of isolating later additions.

[2] Op. cit., pp. 226–7. In this comparison carucates are reckoned as 8 bovates.

[2] Ibid., pp. 212–15, 227.

two classes of land varied greatly from manor to manor. At
Mickleover the working bovates were twice as numerous as those
ad malam when the later survey was made; but at Findern only
1 bovate was then *ad opus*, while 31 bovates were *ad malam*.[1]
On the manor of Abbot's Bromley a notable change took place
during the interval between the surveys. At the earlier date
10 bovates out of a total of 30 were held for works, but at the
later date the triumph of money rents was complete.[2] There
seems to have been a small movement in the same direction on
some other manors; but it would be strange if the surveys
revealed extensive changes, for the earliest possible date for
Survey B is 1114 and the latest possible date for Survey A is
1133.[3] Transition from one class to the other was evidently easy
and changes were made in both directions, sometimes without
a change of tenant. The later survey of Mickleover, for example,
mentions 4 rented holdings which had previously been *ad opus*,
and 2 others which had been transferred from rent to works.
Of 3 rented holdings on that manor and 2 at Littleover, Survey B
says that 'they can be put at work if the abbot wishes'; but
perhaps this implies more stable conditions on the others.[4] At
Leigh a tenant of 2 working bovates is described as paying rent
hoc anno.[5] There were a few individuals who had both rented
and working land.[6]

The working holdings on the Burton estates owed week-work,
which was everywhere 2 days a week for 2 bovates, and 1 day
for holdings half that size. Besides this, the tenants *ad opus* owed
miscellaneous services of boon-work nature, such as fetching
salt and fish. These varied to some extent from manor to manor,
but had the same general character. They included a little
ploughing, but this was at most a matter of 2 or 3 days in the
year and an additional acre or half-acre. In some places the
tenants had also to fallow an acre *propter faldam*, which no doubt
means that it was a price paid for freedom from the obligation
of putting their sheep in the lord's fold.[7] At Bromley fold-soke
was commuted for 7*d.*; and in general the only money payments

---

[1] Ibid., pp. 229–30, 234–5.   [2] Ibid., pp. 222–3.
[3] This was proved by Round in 1906, but needs emphasis, because since then
the second survey has been erroneously described as 'a generation or two later'
than the first: *Trans. Royal Hist. Soc.*, 4th series, xx (1937), 190.
[4] Op. cit., pp. 230, 231, 232.   [5] Ibid., p. 226.
[6] Ibid., pp. 241 (Edric at Winshill), 245 (Godwin and Algar at Appelby).
[7] Ibid., pp. 238, 246.

made by the working tenants on the Burton manors seem to have been a few pence in commutation of some service or other.[1] A couple of Christmas hens and the making of a 'sester' of malt were very common obligations. Pannage also appears to have been due on a good many manors and at Mickleover was defined as a tithe of the pigs.[2]

The sums paid by the tenants *ad malam* varied a good deal. A shilling a bovate and 18*d*. a bovate were very common rates. But variations occur in the same manor. Thus, at Burton, Survey B mentions holdings of 2 bovates that were rented respectively for 2*s*., 2*s*. 6*d*., and 3*s*.; and at Leigh, though 1*s*. per bovate was normal, one holding of 4 bovates was let for 2*s*. and another of a carucate (i.e. 8 bovates) for 6*s*.[3] Services of an occasional character were usually due in addition to the money rent. A few *censarii* seem to be distinguished from the rest by their liability to go on errands or attend the courts of shire and wapentake. To plough twice or thrice, to reap for 3 days in August, and to do some fencing were very common services. But the rent-payers in general owed no regular week-work, though Survey A tells of some tenants at Willington who paid at a uniform rate of 16*d*. a bovate and yet did a normal amount of week-work for several months.[4]

The *cotseti* on the Burton estates are commonly said to owe a day's work, which evidently means a day a week, as is specifically stated in the account of some manors.[5] But many people, whose position appears to have been similar to theirs, paid a money rent. Among those described as holding a *domus* at Burton, ten were subject to the usual cotset's obligation of work, but a rather larger number were rent-payers.[6]

On the Peterborough estates described in the *Liber Niger* the burdens of the *villani* were heavier than on those of Burton Abbey.[7] Of the 283 *villani* or virgaters whose week-work is clearly recorded, a majority had to work 3 days a week and

[1] Op. cit., p. 222. [2] p. 230.

[3] pp. 213, 226–7.

[4] p. 237. The week-work was due 'a festo sancti Petri post festum sancti Johannis' (? 29 June or 1 Aug.) until 11 Nov.

[5] pp. 235, 241, 246.

[6] pp. 212–14 (Survey A). One of those who worked is called a *cotsetus*; and the *domus* of Survey A seems to be equivalent to the *cortillagium* which each cotset held according to Survey B. The rents paid for a *domus* ranged from 6*d*. to 18*d*.

[7] In what follows the last sections of the survey (beginning *In Stanfort*) are ignored as the data they contain are either irrelevant or inadequate.

most of the *dimidii villani* are found on manors where that was the amount required from the full villan holding.[1] On 6 manors 2 days of week-work was the standard rate, but 46 of the 116 peasants owing it had extra work to do in August.[2] At Collingham and at Alwalton only a single day's week-work is mentioned, but the Collingham villans paid an unusually heavy money rent and the work at Alwalton was teamwork involving the use of the peasants' ploughs and a vague reference to *operationes . . . secundum consuetudinem manerii* may possibly mean that they did ordinary week-work as well.[3] Only at Eye does it seem clear that there was no week-work, and all the peasants on that manor are described as *dimidii villani*.[4]

Ploughing services were in some places heavier than on the Burton manors. But both the burden upon the tenants and the part their ploughs played in the cultivation of the demesne varied from manor to manor. At Kettering each of the 40 virgaters had to plough 4 acres and in addition their 22 ploughteams had to be employed on the demesne on 7 occasions. At Wermington, where the *villani* and *semi-villani* held $34\frac{1}{2}$ virgates, they were only required to plough approximately 2 acres per virgate and to do 3 ploughing boons (*praecationes cum carrucis*) with their 16 teams. As there were 4 demesne ploughs on each of these 2 manors, the tillage of the demesne must have depended less upon the services of the peasants at Wermington than it did at Kettering.[5]

Renders of hens and eggs were made on most of the Peterborough manors and other minor renders are mentioned in some cases. Besides such things, certain payments in kind were due on fifteen manors *ad caritatem* (or *ad festum*) *Sancti Petri*.[6]

---

[1] The total of 283 does not include 25 *homines* at Oundle who had 20 virgates and owed 3 days of week-work per virgate. Half-villans usually worked *secundum tenaturas suas* or *quantum ad eos pertinet*.

[2] For the extra August work see op. cit., pp. 159 (Cottingham), 160 (*Estona* and Thurlby); cf. p. 161 (Pytchley).

[3] Ibid., pp. 159, 160. The Alwalton villans 'habent vii carrucas unde operantur semel in ebdomada'. Unspecified *operationes* are also recorded on three manors where no week-work is mentioned and at Fletton, where the statement that the *villani* worked once a week from Michaelmas to Easter may refer to ploughing.

[4] Ibid., p. 165.

[5] There were eight sokemen at Wermington whose obligations are not recorded, but even if they owed ploughing services similar to those of the *villani*, the statement in the text would still be true.

[6] The omission of these words in the case of Alwalton is clearly accidental. In two cases a money payment was an alternative.

A few sheep or a cow formed a part of these deliveries in each place, and in some places they included specified numbers of loaves, of ells of cloth (*de panno* or *de lineo panno*), and of *disci*, which may mean, not actual dishes, but small measures—perhaps of flour, butter, or salt.[1] The quantities varied; and only on seven manors are all the items found in combination. It seems possible that the liability really lay upon the manors as wholes, including their demesnes, though it is sometimes implied that it was discharged by the *villani*.[2] That it was in one or another sense a collective obligation is suggested by the inadequate divisibility of some of the components.

Apart from their liability to this mysterious *consuetudo beati Petri*, the most remarkable difference between the Peterborough villans and those of Burton is that the former everywhere owed money payments as well as services. These payments varied greatly. Among the peasants bound to 3 days' week-work, those at Kettering paid 2s. 1½d. a virgate (or about 3·9s. per plough), while those at Oundle paid 1s. (or 2·2s. per plough).[3] The *villani* of *Estona*, who owed 2 days of week-work and 3 August boons paid only 10d. a virgate (or 1s. 5½d. per plough); but at Thurlby, where the villans owed a similar amount of week-work, the rate appears to have been no less than 3s. a bovate. The *Estona* villans, however, seem to have been more heavily burdened with occasional services and had to sow the land they ploughed with their own seed.[4]

The *Liber Niger* tells of other manorial tenants besides the villans. Sokemen—to the number of 205—are recorded on 13 manors; and at Collingham in Nottinghamshire and Pilsgate in Northamptonshire they far outnumbered all other classes.[5] But the account of them lacks fullness and clarity, and in some cases fails to separate their obligations from those of the villans.

[1] The word *scutella* employed at Thorpe has the same meaning: *Chron. Petr.*, p. 159; cf. p. 168 n. For the suggested sense of *disci* see *Cart. Rams.* i. 408, and the Glastonbury *Rentalia* (Somerset Record Soc., 1891), pp. 63, 65, 145.

[2] At three places the loaves are said to be *de curia*, though but for the order of the words (*de curia cc panes*) one would think this referred to their quality: cf. *Cart. Rams.* ii. 134 ('unum panem album de aula et unum panem militis').

[3] *Chron. Petr.*, pp. 157, 158. The figures suggest that the virgate was larger at Kettering. Ploughing services appear to have been rather heavier at Oundle.

[4] Ibid., pp. 159, 160. The rate per occupied bovate would be even higher at Thurlby, but the words *isti debent reddere* (in contrast to the *reddunt* of all parallel cases), together with the neatness of the arithmetic, indicate that the three waste bovates were included in the total.

[5] Ibid., pp. 159, 158.

They were evidently less subject to labour services. Only on the Lincolnshire manor of 'Scotter and Scalthorp' are sokemen said to do any week-work, and there it was limited to one day a week with an extra day during August, while the full villans had to work two days every week.[1] It seems that the sokemen usually paid more money than the villans. Yet they cannot be regarded as a specifically rent-paying class, distinguished as such like the Burton *censarii*. At *Estona* they paid not quite 1s. a virgate, while the *villani*, as already noted, paid 10d.; and there was a man named Toli in this village whose rent for the virgate he held was 5s.[2] At Collingham a money rent was a main obligation for both classes—the sokemen paying not quite 4s. 10d. each on an average and the villans just 4s.—but the sokemen's holdings appear to have been smaller than the others.[3] Certainly a payment of 12d. is the only recorded liability of an isolated sokeman at Cottingham; but then there was a villan at Adwalton who paid 18d. *pro omnibus consuetudinibus*, and a sokeman at Thorpe is merely said to do service 'with his horse'.[4] In the case of some sokemen, however, the survey of the manors evidently tells only part of the story. Three at Castor, whom it names and describes as owing some small reaping services and (in one case) a little ploughing, appear again in the *Descriptio Militum*, which follows the *Descriptio Maneriorum*, and in it are said to serve *cum militibus*.[5] In general nothing definite can be said about the named tenants recorded in the survey. They include priests, millers, and tenants by military service, and there is no telling whether any were really peasants. They were mostly rent-payers; but the rents are of baffling variety. On the manor of 'Scotter and Scalthorp', for example, the sons of Tochi paid 3s. for 3½ bovates, while Acche paid 10s. for 2½ bovates.[6]

---

[1] Ibid., p. 164.

[2] Ibid., p. 160.

[3] Ibid., p. 159. The stated areas work out at 9 acres per villan and 6 acres per sokeman, if the carucates in which they are expressed contained 120 acres. That these were fiscal assessments and that the actual areas were much larger is evident from the high rents and the high ratio of ploughs to carucates.

[4] *Chron. Petr.*, pp. 159, 161.

[5] Ibid., pp. 163, 173. Some other sokemen mentioned in the *Descriptio Militum* as owing military service (at *Estona*, Werrington, Walton, and Pilsgate) were possibly identical with some included in the manorial survey. That a tenant's villans might do work for their lord's lord appears from the survey of Thorpe, for a tenant there named Godric 'habet iii villanos et quisquis metit abbati dimidiam acram in Augusto' (p. 159).

[6] Ibid., pp. 164–5.

Like the Burton *cotseti*, the cotsets and bordars on the Peter-borough manors were usually obliged to work one day a week, but on some they were rent-payers (the rents ranging from 7*d.* per man at Alwalton to 15*d.* at Fletton), and at Glinton and Castor they appear to have owed both rent and week-work.[1] It is a curious point of resemblance between the *Liber Niger* and Burton Survey B that each mentions labour services as due in a few places from the wives of the *bovarii*. On the Peterborough manors they consisted of winnowing or reaping, or a combina-tion of those tasks. On the five Burton manors the wives worked one day in every week.[2]

Of all the early twelfth-century surveys that of Shaftesbury Abbey is the most detailed. But it is rather ill-arranged; its statements are sometimes ambiguous; and the existing text con-tains some obvious errors.[3] Yet a few general conclusions are possible in spite of these doubtful elements. Nearly every manor included some people who owed three or more days of week-work. Only at Orchard in Dorset is no week-work recorded, and the villans there paid a uniform rent of 3*s.* 4*d.* a virgate, and had also to give 4 'sesters' of oats per half-hide and do a little ploughing.[4] Sedgehill was also exceptional in that a single day of week-work, combined with *opus Augusti*, was the rule on that manor for holdings of various sizes.[5] But even where the week-work was comparatively heavy, the virgaters and half-virgaters bound to such work usually paid money too. In some cases the

---

[1] *Chron. Petr.*, pp. 161, 165, 162, 163.

[2] Ibid., pp. 163, 164, 165; Burton Survey B, pp. 231, 234, 235, 246, 247. The Caen survey (f. 29) similarly describes the wives of *bovarii* at *Dineslai* as working each Monday. Perhaps it was a relic of servile condition: from the same survey it appears that the wives of the *servi* at Felsted worked a day a week (f. 26*v*). For a later example of Monday work owed by ploughmen's wives see *Red Book of Worcester* (Worc. Hist. Soc., 1934), pt. i, p. 37; cf. *Register of Worcester Priory* (Camden Soc., 1865), p. 66*a*.

[3] B.M. Harl. 61, ff. 37–52*v*, 54*v*–55*v*. The arrangement of the sections leaves it doubtful how many manors are covered. Including the account of Handley (ff. 54*v*–55*v*), which may be slightly later, the survey deals with over 600 holdings. Though the context makes it likely that the vague *opus* of some entries means *opus cotidianum*, there can be no certainty about it; and there is ground for suspecting that references to week-work have been omitted from some entries on f. 45. A scribe capable of writing *semper* for *septem* in the sentence 'de semper [*sic*] porcis semper dabit unum' (f. 48*v*) may well have made mistakes that cannot now be detected.

[4] ff. 51, 46*v*. Apparently the ploughing was done on the neighbouring manor of Iwerne Minster.

[5] f. 43*v*.

amounts mentioned are so large, and have so little relation to the extent of the holdings or the other burdens to which they were subject, that one is led to suspect error in the text; but a normal rate of $7\frac{1}{2}d.$ a virgate and $3\frac{3}{4}d.$ a half-virgate is clearly discernible on several manors and one of just double that amount at Compton Abbas.[1] An additional payment, distinguished as *lignagium*, was also a very common obligation. It was due on most of the manors, and was due both from working holdings and from those that were rented. It was charged at the rate of 10*d.* per virgate, and is never mentioned in connexion with smallholdings that were measured in acres. The name implies that it had to do with wood; but whether it was paid for the privilege of taking wood or in commutation of a carting service does not appear. Church-scot was due from the tenants of many holdings of different sizes. Some paid four hens; others an 'amber' of grain or flour.[2] It was evidently a personal tax, for it did not as a rule vary with the size of the holding, though on several manors the virgaters and half-virgaters paid in grain and the tenants of 4 acres in hens. Only a few of the rent-paying tenants appear to have been liable. Holdings that paid rent and owed no week-work were not rarities on the Shaftesbury estates and they included some virgates and half-virgates; but the ambiguities of the text and its apparent omissions of relevant detail are here especially baffling; so that the proportion which the rented holdings bore to the total cannot be determined. The rent-payers were commonly liable to some boon-works or errands, and some of the larger tenements were held by knight service. A few men occupied both a rented and a working virgate.[3] Smallholdings of 4 or 5 acres mostly owed works; but some were rented. In either case the burden was heavy in

---

[1] These payments look as if they were based on the acreage of a 30-acre virgate and invite comparison with the Bury St. Edmunds hidage dues (Douglas, *Feudal Documents*, pp. cxxii–cxxvii; cf. R. H. C. Davis, *Kalendar of Abbot Samson*, pp. xxxvii–xxxix).

[2] A church-scot of four fowls was rather common. There is later evidence that it was payable on many Glastonbury Abbey manors: *Liber Henrici de Soliaco* (Roxburghe Club), pp. 28, 83, 110, 117, 121, 129; *Rentalia et Custumaria* (Somerset Record Soc., 1891), pp. 65, 78, 101. For examples on other estates see *Custumals of Battle Abbey* (Camden Soc., 1887), pp. 60, 63, 80; *Chron. Abingdon* (Rolls Series), ii. 301, 309; N. S. B. Gras, *Economic and Social History of an English Village* (Harvard Univ. Press, 1930), p. 236; and, for a general discussion of church-scot, N. Neilson, *Customary Rents* (Oxford Studies, vol. ii, 1910), pp. 193–6.

[3] At Melbury Abbas, for example: 'Boie de una virgata iiii s. et de alia v d. . . . et opus iii dierum in ebdomada' (f. 48).

comparison with the conditions obtaining on the Burton and Peterborough estates. Those at work were bound to 2 or, in some places, 3 days a week; and some 4-acre holdings owed a rent of 2s. as well as *opus Augusti*.[1] But the ploughmen, shepherds, and swineherds, who usually held 4 acres in return for their services, had their land ploughed by the demesne ploughs and were, as a rule, entitled to some additional perquisites.

No other source is so rich in information about early twelfth-century conditions as the three surveys just examined. But additional evidence of some importance is provided by the early survey of the English lands of the Abbaye aux Dames at Caen, which is roughly contemporary with them, and by the retrospective references to the reign of Henry I contained in the surveys of Ramsey Abbey manors that were compiled in the latter part of the century.[2]

The Ramsey material is rather intractable for in the statements it contains, those relating to 'the time of King Henry' cannot always be distinguished from those that were intended to apply only to the date at which the surveys were made. There can be little doubt, however, that, except in Norfolk, the prevailing system on these estates had been one of labour services based on week-work. For eleven manors the number of virgates that were *ad opus* before 1135 is stated without ambiguity, and altogether some 236 virgates are accounted for in this way. In a few of these cases it is definitely indicated that the working virgates comprised all the regular peasant holdings, and in some others the evidence makes the same conclusion probable.[3] Of the services whose nature is described, only those at Stukeley

---

[1] At *Acclega* two men appear to have paid a shilling each in lieu of *opus Augusti* (f. 42v); and at Handley a man held 4 acres for 12d. or 2 days of (week-) work (f. 55).

[2] Bibl. Nat. MS. lat. 5650, ff. 26–29v; *Cart. Rams.* iii. 257–89, 301–14. These Ramsey surveys cannot be precisely dated. A few pre-1135 tenants were still living when they were made (pp. 258, 261), but a good many had been succeeded by their sons. Unless the references to Abbot William (pp. 258, 262, 272) are later insertions, these indicate a date later than 1160 and probably later than 1177 or 1178 when he ceased to be abbot. The fact that Henry I is generally referred to simply as 'King Henry' is no reason for regarding the surveys as anterior to the accession of Henry II: there are parallels in the Glastonbury *Inquisitio Hilberti* made after the death of Henry of Blois (1171) and in the 'Domesday of Ralph de Diceto' of 1181 (*D.S.P.*, p. 112). The expression 'post mortem Henrici Regis Senioris' occurs once (*Cart. Rams.* iii. 306), but the passage may be a later addition.

[3] In this and in what follows I have taken no account of lands held by the free tenants, usually described as *libere feudati*.

and Ellington in Huntingdonshire are specifically stated to have
been due in the earlier period, but a like antiquity should probably be ascribed to the others. At Stukeley and Ellington the
obligations of a working virgate were, in their main features,
virtually identical: they included 2 days of labour and 1 day of
ploughing every week from Michaelmas to the beginning of
August (with the exception of certain holidays) and 5 days work
each week during the harvest season.[1] But since very similar
amounts of week-work were due at the date of the survey on
13 other manors (of which 9 were in Huntingdonshire, 2 in
Cambridgeshire, and 2 in Bedfordshire) it seems clear that this
was an established norm on the estates of the abbey in these
counties. Rented holdings were certainly not unknown in this
region in 'the time of King Henry'. On the manor of Shillington-
with-Pegsdon in Bedfordshire the $32\frac{1}{2}$ working virgates were
indeed a minority, for there were 35 *ad censum*—the rent being
22*d*. a virgate for 30 of these, and 50*d*. for each of the remainder.[2]
But elsewhere—in the few places where an exact comparison is
possible—the working virgates greatly outnumbered the others.
At Girton in Cambridgeshire 16 virgates had been *ad opus*, and
one *ad censum* for 5*s*., while all the rest of the land was demesne:
'totum reliquum erat in dominio'.[3] In general, references to
rented holdings are scanty, except in Norfolk. There, however,
the Ramsey surveys reveal a very different pattern, and though
it is impossible to disengage the data that should be attributed
to the period before 1135 from those belonging to the latter
part of the century, that scarcely affects the main issue. Apart
from minor differences in the matter of boon-works, the survey
of Brancaster and Burnham Deepdale, that of Hilgay-with-
Snore, and that of Wimbotsham and Downham Market, all
exhibit the same features. They contain no reference to regular
week-work and virtually all the tenants are described as paying
money.[4] The survey of Ringstead-with-Holme is the only one
of the Norfolk series that tells of tenants owing week-work, and,
except in August, this was limited to one day a week. Moreover,
on this manor money rents were paid by all but six of the

---

[1] *Cart. Rams.* iii. 275, 306.
[2] Ibid. 307. Virgates paying 22*d*. were subject to public burdens: each
'defendebat erga regem'.   [3] Ibid. 313.
[4] Ibid. 261–6, 285–9. By an unfortunate error Brancaster was included among
manors where regular week-work was customary in N. Neilson, *Economic Conditions*,
p. 51.

seventy-odd tenants; and the rent-payers included the tenants *in landsetagio* who were liable to week-work.[1]

The Caen survey covers only seven manors, but it throws a little light upon conditions in some parts of the country from which no other evidence of the kind is available for this early date, and it is remarkable for the variety it reveals on the estates of a single landlord. Moreover, the account of the one manor which the Abbaye aux Dames possessed in Norfolk is in striking agreement with the Ramsey data for that county. Both at Horstead in Norfolk and at Felsted in Essex it had some sokemen who paid rent and had to carry the 'farm' to Winchester; but on the former manor the villans and bordars also were rent-payers, whose only agricultural service appears to have been 16 days of reaping due from the villans, while at Felsted the virgaters had to work 4 days a week and owed ploughing and other boons as well, and the bordars owed, some 1 day, some 2 days, and some 3 days of week-work.[2] In Gloucestershire, the *villani* worked 5 days a week, and the cottars (*cocez*) 3 days a week, at Penbury; but at Minchinhampton and Avening only some two-thirds of the virgates were *ad opus* and the rest *ad gablum*, though what this meant in detail is not stated.[3] At Tarrant in Dorset the bordars worked thrice a week and the villans twice, but the latter had also to pay a rent which works out at just over 18*d.* apiece.[4] On the remaining manor—the unidentified *Dineslai*—a combination of week-work and rent was also common, but some of the tenants paid rent only and there were others who paid even higher rents than these and yet were bound to do a day's ploughing.[5]

---

[1] *Cart. Rams.* iii. 266–9. Only later surveys are available for the abbey's estates at Walsoken and Wells: these make no reference to week-work: ibid. 290–9; cf. ii. 318–20. Lawshall, the only Ramsey manor in Suffolk, does not conform to the Norfolk pattern: week-work was there customary: ibid. iii. 282–5. For the attribution of this survey to Lawshall see *E.H.R.* li (Jan. 1936), 104–7.

[2] Bibl. Nat. MS. lat. 5650, ff. 28–28*v*, 26–26*v*. The reaping at Horstead is paralleled by the 16 days of August work owed by each toft *de lansetagio* on the Ramsey manor of Wimbotsham: *Cart. Rams.* iii. 287. A ferrying service (? *naviculum*) appears to have been due at Horstead.

[3] ff. 27, 27*v*, 28, 29–29*v*. In the later series of surveys, contained in the same manuscript, rent-payers at Avening appear as owing some boon-works as well as a rent of 4*s.* or 5*s.* a virgate, while the *operarii* had to work 'qua die ebdomade sine sabbato' (5 days a week?) for a virgate, or that number of days in alternate weeks for a half-virgate: ff. 47*v*–48*v*.

[4] f. 27*v*.   [5] ff. 28*v*–29.

Of all the monastic estates covered by these early surveys those of the Abbaye aux Dames were the most widely dispersed; but it would be rash to regard the contrasts between its manors as indications of regional diversities. In Norfolk such a conclusion is indeed suggested by the similarity of conditions at Horstead and on the Ramsey Abbey manors in that county; but though heavy week-work is recorded in Dorset on several of the Shaftesbury manors as well as at Tarrant, we are warned against making too much of its prevalence in this part of the country both by the fact that no week-work was due on the Shaftesbury manor of Orchard in Dorset and by the evidence of a brief text which records the customs observed by the men of Portswood in Hampshire before Henry I gave that manor to the Priory of St. Denis in the adjoining town of Southampton. From this it appears that the normal holding at Portswood was a 'virgate' and that the tenant of a virgate paid a rent (*gablum*) of 5*s.* and owed certain *operationes*, but these works, which are specified in great detail, included no ploughing and nothing that can properly be called week-work, though from 24 June to 1 August some weeding had to be done every day.[1]

III

An inquirer who ventures into the field of Anglo-Norman social history is like a man exploring the darkness with a searchlight, who discovers much that does not greatly concern him and finds that the searchlight is jammed when he attempts to turn its beam upon some object he particularly wishes to illumine. It is on record that in the year 1086 Count Eustace of Boulogne had four goats and four beehives on his manor of Coggeshall in Essex.[2] There is good evidence that when the Canons of St. Paul's granted a lease of Ardleigh in the same county in 1141, the largest of the three manorial barns was filled partly with wheat and partly with oats.[3] But the historian cannot well say whether it was usual, or rare, or wholly unknown for the rustic inhabitants of Norman England to have a village ale-house to which they could resort for gossip and refreshment. And whether or no meetings in such a place were

---

[1] C. H. Haskins, 'The Manor of Portswood', in *Mélanges d'Histoire offerts à M. Charles Bémont* (Paris, 1913), pp. 77–83. The manor was given to St. Denis about 1127.

[2] Dd. ii, f. 26*b*.   [3] *D.S.P.*, p. 136.

possible, it is only the human nature which he shares with them that can inform his imagination in regard to the thoughts they tried to express when they encountered one another, either at work or when work was done. He can feel sure that they grumbled at the weather, that they complained of aches and pains, that they sometimes quarrelled and spoke ill of their neighbours. He will not readily suppose that they were less prone to drunkenness and violence than their thirteenth-century successors, of whom he reads, for example, in the 'Pleas of the Crown for the County of Gloucester'.[1] He may suspect that, along with sufferings due to hunger and sickness and 'the furious winter's rages', they had experience of others that were the outcome of sullen hatreds, fierce passions, and brutal lusts. Yet something within him compels the belief that kindliness and comradeship and lasting affections had a part in the lives of these village folk, and that laughter and song were not wanting. Of village sports he is vouchsafed, as it were, an actual glimpse; for the biographer of Wulfstan describes the future saint as a lad competing against other lads in a Warwickshire village before a crowd of applauding spectators. That was in the early part of the eleventh century; but the account seems to imply that such things were not uncommon in the writer's day, and both the *Vita Wulfstani* and its Saxon original belong to the Norman period.[2]

Imagination can help the historian; but it can easily betray him; and the distorting lights of anachronism are perhaps most likely to affect his vision in relation to some of the questions to which modern curiosity most urgently desires an answer. Were the villagers of those distant generations class-conscious? Subjected as they were in greater or less degree to the lordship of barons and knights and churchmen, who spoke for the most part in a foreign language and were distinguished in dress and equipment, did they look upon their lords with resentment? Were they cowed—fearing at every turn 'the frown o' th' great'? Did they think of their subjection as a yoke that might perhaps be thrown off?

[1] ed. Maitland (1884).
[2] *Vita Wulfstani*, ed. R. R. Darlington (Camden Soc., 1928), p. 6 ('Conuenerat in campum frequens cetus adolescentum; cuinam letius ludo uacans non diffinio. Cursitabatur ut fieri solet in talibus uirentis graminis equore; plausui et fauore adortantium respondebat stridulus aer. Emicat inter alios Wlstanus; communique cunctorum iudicio illius ludi triumphum reportat. Agrestium multitudo in laudes acclamat').

One can scarcely ask such questions without falling into the anachronism of reading back into the early feudal age the sentiment of Wat Tyler and John Ball and of trying to interpret it in the light of Marxian doctrines based upon the circumstances of nineteenth-century industrialism. It is certainly true that, long before the Norman Conquest, the learned Ælfric represented the slave ploughman as living in fear of his master and lamenting the unfreedom to which he felt that the hardness of his life was due. But in Norman England slavery was passing away, as the *bovarius*, who was a smallholder, took the place of the slave as the typical demesne ploughman. It is true that this was part of a process which merged slave and free peasant alike in a condition of serfdom, and the prevalence of that condition is exemplified by the fact that the word *villanus* was becoming a synonym for 'serf', but it would be ludicrous to suppose that the peasants themselves appreciated the nature of a change which the modern historian discerns with difficulty as the consequence of a protracted development. That the Norman Conquest had brought suffering and loss to innumerable Englishmen, and that this produced a sense of outrage can hardly be doubted. But, as Stenton observes, 'it is probable that, as a class, the peasants had suffered less than those above them'.[1] And though it was as landlords, and harsh landlords, that the Normans established themselves in England, hatred of a foreign conqueror is not the same thing as hatred of a landlord. If we turn away from conjecture to the record of peasant obligations in the early monastic surveys, it is not of men subject to a lord's caprice that we read, but of men following a routine of custom, which limited the services to which it bound them; and it is the superior and freer villagers who seem liable to be called upon at any time to go on their lord's errands, as indeed the Norman knight might at any time be summoned to follow his lord in war. It would be an anachronism to suppose that the *villani* of the early Norman period were as sharply distinguished from freemen as their successors were after the great development of royal justice under Henry II and those fateful decisions which subsequently determined that the royal courts should not concern themselves with the relations of a lord and his 'villeins'. It was in a much later generation that Bracton found it possible to say that the villein, and even the freeman who held land by villein tenure, ought

[1] *Anglo-Saxon England*, p. 677.

not to know in the evening what he must do on the morrow 'et semper tenebitur ad incerta'.[1]

'Were the English peasants in the early feudal age class-conscious?' If the modern questioner is insistent, the historian's first observation must surely be that those peasants did not really constitute a class. Men who were alike in economic condition differed in legal and social status. Men who seem to have been equal in the degree of their subjection to the manorial lord differed greatly in the size of their holdings. Even in those regions where Domesday Book appears to reveal a uniform class of *villani*, and says nothing of sokemen, radknights, or *liberi homines*, it almost always draws a distinction between the *villani* and the bordars or cottars who lived beside them. Moreover, the evidence adduced in the earlier part of this chapter strongly suggests that the appearance of uniformity which the summary statements of Domesday give to the *villani* in most parts of the country is more or less delusive, and that among the *villani* of the same village there might be differences in economic standing similar to those which Domesday itself discloses within the villages of Middlesex. It would be wrong too to think of the manorial lords either as a uniform class or as individuals who were constantly resident, flaunting their wealth and their pride day after day in the eyes of the village folk. In many, probably in most, villages there was no resident lord; and throughout the vast area covered by the demesne manors of the great monastic estates the lords were certainly absentees, whose infrequent visits might be occasions for exaction, but would also, one suspects, cause a not unwelcome flutter of excitement. The arrival of an abbot's splendid retinue may well have been regarded by many in much the same way that country people today usually regard a meet of the hounds. And though it is not always true that a man's enemies are those of his own household, perhaps we shall not be deceived if we imagine the villagers of Domesday England as more often animated by envious feelings towards the more prosperous of their fellow villans, or by hostility against the men of the next village who had intruded upon pastures they considered to be their own, than stirred by the sentiments which a Marxist would think it proper for them to cherish.

Yet anachronism of the kind just considered is not so inimical to truth as that which would paint the eleventh and twelfth

[1] *De Legibus*, lib. iv, f. 208*b* (ed. G. E. Woodbine, iii. 131).

centuries in colours borrowed from an imaginary golden age and represent the peasants of those days as devout and happy Christians, loyal to their lords and contented with their lot. If the concepts of 'class consciousness' and 'class war' must be exorcized for a crudity which makes them misleading as aids to the interpretation of the period, it should none the less be recognized that the sufferings of the common people, though largely due to factors that had nothing to do with their subjection, were aggravated by the weight of the obligations they owed their lords; that in most villages there were groups of peasants whose equality gave them a common interest; and that the changes which were in progress, along with the emergence of fortunate individuals from the rut, must have tended to foster hopes of improvement. In one direction too it seems clear that arbitrary action on the part of the lords had the paradoxical consequence of putting one—or, in some cases, two or even three—of the peasants in a position of peculiar independence. It was not uncommon, when a donation of tithe was made to a monastery, to accompany the gift with the grant of a villan or bordar to act as a tithe-collector. But the individuals whose services were thus transferred became accountable only to a distant lord—perhaps an abbey on the Continent—and in the service of that lord would be required to extract the tithe, undeterred by the farmer of the demesne or the bailiff of the local lord, and (where the usual practice was observed) to prevent the local priest from taking more than one-third of the tithe sheaves. If the donation of tithe was limited to that due from the manorial demesne—as it probably was in most cases—there would be nothing to bring these tithe-collectors into conflict with their fellow peasants and their independence would be some qualification for the role of a village Hampden.[1] Nor are we altogether without concrete evidence of discontent. The runaway peasant was not peculiar to the later Middle Ages. A precept of William Rufus enjoins the sheriffs to compel the return of fugitives who had fled from the lands of the abbey of Ramsey; and more than a generation later Stephen issued similar instructions.[2] The same sort of trouble appears to have

[1] For the evidence regarding peasant tithe-collectors see *E.H.R.* lxix (Oct. 1954), 580–96. Cases are recorded for more than 130 villages, distributed over 20 counties; and there is reason to think that many more cases than these have gone unrecorded.
[2] *Chron. Rams.*, p. 212; *Cart. Rams.* ii. 62. The latter precept was witnessed by

occurred on the estates of Abingdon Abbey during the reign
of Henry I, for in three separate documents—issued respectively
at Woodstock, at Wallingford, and at Westminster—that king
ordered sheriffs and others to see that the fugitives of the abbey
were recovered with all their *pecunia*.[1] And then we have the
significant fact that when William de Roumara founded the
abbey of Revesby in Lincolnshire in 1142, and, in order that
the ground might be cleared for the Cistercian monks who were
to be established there, gave the *rustici* of Revesby and two
neighbouring villages a choice of receiving other land from him
or departing in freedom, only seven chose to remain under his
lordship, while thirty-one refused that alternative and were
allowed to go their way 'cum domibus et omnibus bonis suis'.[2]
The historian would give much to know where they, and others,
went and how they fared. But the searchlight here fails him.

Aubrey de Vere, apparently the chamberlain of that name who was killed in 1141.
It covers the chattels of the fugitives as well as the men themselves.

[1] *Chron. Abingdon*, ii. 81–82; *Regesta*, ii, Nos. 726, 856, 1799. Two of these pre-
cepts belong to the first decade of the century: one is concerned with the men of
the abbot 'qui de terra sua exierint de Walingeford propter herberiam curiae
meae, vel propter alias res'; and the other alludes to a man who was on the land
of Robert de Ferrars, one of the addressees. In the third (issued at Woodstock) the
phrase used is 'cum tota pecunia et catallo suo', which the editors of the *Regesta*
translate as 'with all their money and chattels', but I think it more probable that
pecunia means cattle or livestock. Along with the evidence cited in the text, note
should be taken of a passage in the so-called *Leis Willelme* in which it is said that
no one must retain *naifs* who leave the place where they were born and go *a autri
terre*: c. 30 (Robertson, *Laws*, p. 268).

[2] *Facsimiles of Early Charters from Northamptonshire Collections*, ed. Stenton
(Northants. Record Soc., 1930), pp. 1–7. Those who departed, though classed
with the *rustici*, included one *Willelmus medicus* and *Alwinus homo Willelmi*. The seven
who accepted an exchange were established in neighbouring villages.

APPENDIX I

The Arable Area in 1086

THE twenty-eight counties referred to in the text are those of Nottingham, Lincoln, Norfolk, Suffolk, Essex, Cambridge, Huntingdon, Northampton, Rutland, Leicester, Warwick, Worcester, Hereford, Gloucester, Somerset, Devon, Cornwall, Dorset, Wiltshire, Hampshire, Sussex, Kent, Surrey, Berkshire, Oxford, Buckingham, Bedford, and Hertford. For these—if we take Darby's figures where they are available and Maitland's elsewhere—we have a total of 71,785 Domesday plough-teams. At the traditional figure of 120 acres per team this would mean 8·6 million acres of arable, while the official Agricultural Statistics give the arable area on 4 June 1914 as 7·7 million acres. It is true that Maitland's figures were for the Domesday counties, not the modern counties; but over a wide area the differences between these would largely cancel out. There are, however, serious objections to the assumption that every Domesday plough implies the tillage of 120 acres. But if we reckoned only 100 acres per plough, we should still be left with 7·2 million acres of arable which is 93 per cent. of the 1914 area.

The calculation has been confined to twenty-eight counties on account of the virtual exclusion of the four northern counties from the Domesday survey, the jejune character of its Lancashire section, the abnormal conditions produced by devastation in Yorkshire, Derbyshire, Cheshire, Shropshire, and Staffordshire, and the modern growth of London which would vitiate any comparison in the case of Middlesex.

APPENDIX II

Subordinate Holdings on the Winchester Estates

I T is a familiar problem of Domesday interpretation to know whether figures for subordinate holdings described under the heading of a demesne manor are additional to those given for the latter or included within them. I have treated them as additional to the Winchester estates because:

1. The values for 1086 are often distinguished without ambiguity: e.g. Farnham (Surrey), Stoke (Hants), Downton (Wilts.): Dd. i, ff. 31, 40*b*, 65*b*.
2. The total figures for one or more items on the subordinate holdings sometimes exceed the corresponding figures for the demesne manor: e.g. Fareham, Hurstbourne Priors, Crondall (Hants), Calbourn (Isle of Wight), and Taunton: ibid., ff. 40*b*, 41–41*b*, 52*b*, 87*b* (cf. Exon., pp. 161–3). Since subordinate holdings are comparatively small, this kind of proof is naturally not available in many cases.

In Wiltshire, though the values are in general clearly distinguished, some doubt attaches to the other statistics, for no peasants are enumerated for the subordinate holdings and in some cases nothing is said about any ploughs upon them. But even if these were included in the statistics of the demesne manors (though there is some evidence to the contrary at Enford, f. 65*b*), the round numbers given in the text perhaps allow a sufficient margin of error. Apart from Hampshire, Wiltshire, and Somerset the problem of subordinate tenements is negligible on the Winchester estates.

APPENDIX III

Peasant Freedom and the Danes

THE orthodox theory according to which the remarkable freedom of the peasantry in East Anglia and the northern Danelaw was a result of the Danish conquests and settlements has been powerfully assailed by Mr. R. H. C. Davis on the basis of the East Anglian evidence.[1] It is, however, one thing to suppose that the free peasantry were of Scandinavian race and enjoyed a freedom introduced by their ancestors, and another thing to see in Danish influence the chief factor which checked manorialization in this part of England and preserved in some measure the social conditions of an earlier age from transformations such as occurred elsewhere. Mr. Davis shows that there is strong reason for thinking that sokemen and socage dues are a survival from pre-Danish times.[2] Vinogradoff was of much the same opinion and could describe the soke as 'an Old English institution'.[3] But some of the arguments urged by Mr. Davis against extensive Danish settlement in East Anglia are open to objection. Scandinavian personal names, even if borne by people who were not, or not wholly, of Scandinavian blood, are yet a mark of Scandinavian influence; and in view of the change of Guthrum's name at his baptism and the widespread abandonment of Scandinavian names by Norman families in Normandy, it is surely likely that there were more Danes with English names than Englishmen with Danish names.[4] As regards place-name evidence, one must remember that, if Norfolk and Suffolk were already well populated when the Danes came (as it seems likely they were), a large amount of immigration might well take place without leading to the foundation of new villages and the consequent appearance on the map of village-names in the newly-prevalent language. Under such conditions the presence of immigrants might only reveal itself in minor names such as field-names; and these have not yet, I think, been studied in East Anglia. In the Wirral peninsula villages with Anglo-Saxon names have been found to possess fields bearing Scandinavian or partly Scandinavian names.[5] Even a single name, if it includes a Danish common noun or adjective, and not merely a Danish personal name, implies a Scandinavian influence sufficient to modify the vocabulary of the neighbourhood.

[1] *Trans. Royal Hist. Soc.*, 5th series, v, 1955, 23–39.
[2] *Kalendar of Abbot Samson*, pp. xliii–xlvii.
[3] *Growth of the Manor*, p. 303; cf. *English Society*, pp. 134, 322, 441.
[4] See Stenton, *Trans. Royal Hist. Soc.*, 4th series, xxvii, 1945, 6–7.
[5] See F. T. Wainwright, *Antiquity*, June 1943, pp. 59–60.

APPENDIX IV

Some 'Minsters' and Collegiate Churches

THOUGH the history of the old Anglo-Saxon 'minsters' in the early Norman period is very obscure, the following notes will, I trust, be sufficient to justify the statement made on page 301 that they 'usually prove on examination to be either in a state of decay or to be undergoing some process of transformation'.

1. The church of St. Gregory at Morville in Shropshire had possessed 8 hides of land in the time of King Edward and was then served by 8 canons. By 1086 there were only 3 priests (*presbiteri*) there and the church with 5 hides was held by the abbey of Shrewsbury of its founder Earl Roger, to whom Morville and its 18 berewicks belonged. The remaining 3 hides were held by the earl's chaplains (*capellani comitis*) and occupied by 5 men as their tenants.[1] So much is revealed by Domesday Book; but of the chaplains and the nature of their tenure we get a further glimpse a little later, for, when one of them died (apparently before 1114), his son claimed to have the deceased man's prebend, and it was maintained that this claim was invalid because Earl Roger had provided that as the clerks died off their prebends should be appropriated by the abbey.[2] Later again, we find Robert de Bethune (Bishop of Hereford 1131–48) ordering that certain chapels should still be subject to the mother church of Morville, that the people should attend that church on the great festivals, and that its priest—for there was now, it seems, only one priest—should have the disposal of any lands or tithes given to the chapels, and could if he wished require all burials to take place at the mother church.[3] Clearly St. Gregory's had by then ceased to be collegiate and much of its property had been transferred to the abbey; but it still retained some of the rights belonging to a central minster, though perhaps the bishop's intervention may indicate that they were not undisputed.

2. A variation on the same theme is afforded by the story of another Shropshire church—that of Bromfield. The manor of Bromfield had been held in the Confessor's reign by twelve canons, but one of these was a rich priest named Spirtes or Spirites, who had been highly favoured by Harold I and Harthacnut and was a landowner in half a dozen counties. At Bromfield this man had obtained

[1] Dd. i, f. 253.
[2] *Collectanea Topographica et Genealogica*, i. 25; R. W. Eyton, *Antiquities of Shropshire*, i. 32; see also *Regesta*, ii, No. 1051.
[3] Eyton, op. cit., pp. 36–37.

10 out of the 20 hides at which the manor was assessed; but he fell from favour and was banished, with the result that his Bromfield holding came into lay hands and was lost to the church.[1] There is nothing in the Domesday account to suggest that the church was still serving as the active centre of an extensive *parochia*; and on two of its manors a priest is mentioned. It continued to be collegiate, however, until eventually the canons decided to take monastic vows and it became a priory of the abbey of Gloucester. There seems to be some doubt about the date of this change; but according to the Gloucester *Historia* it took place in 1155.[2] Of the antecedent condition of the college we get a glimpse from a charter of Henry II which appears to indicate that some of the 'prebends' of the church had been held by parish priests since the time of Henry I, and safeguards the life interests of these people and the other canons.[3]

3. At Cullompton in Devon the old order of things appears to have been swept away at a much earlier date. The church there with its five prebends ('cum praebendis quinque ad eandem pertinenti-bus') was given by William I to Battle Abbey and the abbey trans-ferred it with its endowments ('cum quinque terris praebendarum, scilicet Uppetona, Colebroche, Hinelande, Waevre, Esse, et omni-bus ad eam pertinentibus') to the new priory of St. Nicholas in the city of Exeter, no doubt with the result that Cullompton church ceased to be collegiate and became virtually indistinguishable from an ordinary parish church. That it had previously been a house of canons is suggested by the reference to prebends; and though the chronicler who tells us of these things speaks of Cullompton *ubi prius habitaverant monachi*, he may mean only that the monks who came from Battle had dwelt there until the priory of St. Nicholas was completed.[4]

4. A similar fate befell Stow St. Mary in Lincolnshire. Founded

[1] Dd. i, f. 252*b*; *Hemingi Chartularium*, ed. Hearne, p. 254; cf. Round, *V.C.H. Worcs.* i. 289 n. 3. Most of the estates of Spirtes passed to Nigel the Physician, and this man appears as possessing a rent of 16*s.* at Bromfield in 1086; but the 10 hides were given by the Confessor to Robert fitz Wimarch *sicut canonico*, and then given by him to his son-in-law.

[2] *Gloucester Cart.* (Rolls Series), i. 19, 66; cf. Eyton, op. cit. v. 210.

[3] *Gloucester Cart.* ii. 213–14. Henry II gave to the prior and monks, along with the church, 'omnes praebendas quas Fredericus clericus de Bureford, et Robertus Colemon de Pautesburi, et Edricus presbiter de Brumfeld, et Robertus presbiter de Feltuna et alii canonici tenuerunt in Brumfeldehernesse tempore Henrici regis avi mei vel meo tempore, scilicet omnes terras et villas de Haverford, et de Dodinghopa, et de Efford, et de Feltuna, et de Burhheia, et de Ledewich, et tres praebendas in Brumfeld et tres in Halhtuna, salva tamen tenura praedictorum canonicorum quamdiu vixerint. Qui omnes has praenominatas terras et villas tenuerunt in elemosinam de praedicta capella mea' (i.e. the church of St. Mary of Bromfield, which the monks were to hold *sicut meam dominicam capellam*).

[4] *Chronicon Monasterii de Bello*, pp. 31–33.

by one of the bishops of Dorchester in the first half of the eleventh century, it appears to have been a college of priests, and it is tempting to conjecture that it was intended to serve a large *parochia* in a part of the diocese which was remote from the bishop's see and had seen the ancient order of things overwhelmed by the flood of Danish conquests and settlements.[1] Not long before the Norman Conquest we find it adding to its possessions by purchase; but in Domesday Book a single priest is recorded in connexion with the church; and in 1091, when Remigius, the first Norman bishop of the diocese, decided to make it monastic, he described it as 'quondam prolixo temporis spatio presidentium incuria desolatam'.[2] A little later his successor transferred the abbot and his monks to Eynsham in Oxfordshire, and thereafter we find the church of Stow forming one of the prebends of Lincoln Cathedral and functioning as an ordinary parish church.[3]

5. The ancient and richly-endowed church of Bosham in Sussex, which must have been an important 'minster', appears in Domesday in a state of something like disintegration. Its estate, which before the Conquest was rated at 112 hides and was reckoned to have been worth £300, had been largely secularized. Thirty hides were held by Hugh, son of Rannulf, 17 by Ralf de Chesney. The rest belonged to Osbern, Bishop of Exeter; but 12 hides of this, comprising the manor of Thorney, were held by Malger and yet another hide by Ralf. The remnants of a clerical community may perhaps be recognized in a certain clerk (*quidam clericus*) who had a hide of land and four other *clerici* who held a hide *communiter*. The *clerici* had the tithe of the church valued at 40*s*.; but a separate statement that there is a church and a priest there suggests either that a village church had been established on a subordinate manor or that the landholding clerks did not exercise the cure of souls.[4]

6. The canons of Holy Trinity, Twinham (i.e. Christchurch), appear in Domesday among the Hampshire tenants-in-chief; and we are told that all the tithe of Twinham and one-third of the tithe

---

[1] *Cartulary of Eynsham*, i. x; cf. Whitelock, *Anglo-Saxon Wills*, p. 212. It is doubtful which bishop was the founder. The evidence that it was, or became, a house of secular priests is a grant of 1053–5 in which Leofric and Godiva state that they have 'furnished' it with priests and wish to have there 'such service as is had in St. Paul's within London': *Eynsham Cart.* i. 28–30; Robertson, *Anglo-Saxon Charters*, No. cxv. There is difficulty, however, about a Domesday entry which says that 'Robert the priest' 'effectus est monachus in S. Mariae Stou' (i, f. 345); but the word *monachus* is an interlinear insertion. In the index to Foster and Longley's edition of the Lincolnshire Domesday the *canonici in S. Maria* mentioned in connexion with Redbourne (f. 345) are assigned to Stow, but the reference is surely in fact to the canons of St. Mary of Lincoln.

[2] Dd. i, f. 376; cf. Whitelock, op. cit., pp. 96, 212; Dd. i, f. 344; *Eynsham Cart.* i. 33.

[3] Ibid., Nos. 6 and 7 (pp. 35, 36), cf. p. xi. For information about the later prebend of Stow I am indebted to Miss Major.

[4] Dd. i, ff. 17, 17*b*.

at Holdenhurst (*Holehest*) belongs to their church; while within the section covered by the canons' rubric two priests named Alnod and Alsi are recorded as holding *Bortel* and *Bailocheslei* of the king. Further, in the description of the royal manor of Holdenhurst, an *aecclesiola* in that place is mentioned.[1]

It seems possible that Twinham was a collegiate minster of the old type and that traces of its original *parochia* are to be found in a list of churches and chapels described as belonging to it in a charter of Richard de Redvers to whom Christchurch (as it was by then called) was given by Henry I. This list comprises the church of Hordle with the chapel of Milford, the church of Boldre with the chapel of Brockenhurst, the chapel of Holdenhurst, and the chapel of Sopley (all places within 10 miles of Christchurch), while a 'prebend' at *Pideleton* is also among the possessions confirmed by the charter.[2] But the existence of all these churches and chapels points to the disintegration of the old *parochia* (if such it was); and in 1150 the charter by which Henry of Blois, Bishop of Winchester, provided for the introduction of regular canons at Christchurch, seems to indicate the status of the separate parishes by its reference to the 'personae ecclesiarum vel capellarum ad Christi Ecclesiam pertinentes (? pertinentium)'.[3] That this process had begun before 1086 is suggested by Domesday's reference to an *aecclesia* at Brockenhurst (as well as to the *aecclesiola* at Holdenhurst); and that it had continued since the date of Richard de Redvers's charter may perhaps be inferred from the fact that in 1150 the church of Boldre was credited with a chapel at Lymington in addition to that at Brockenhurst.[4] At Christchurch itself there was much change before the secular canons were replaced by regulars. From the involved account in the *Historia Fundationis* it would appear that Flambard, who rebuilt the church, did not fill up prebends which fell vacant, so that the number of canons fell from 24 to 13, and that when Henry I granted the church to Gilbert de Dousgunels, only 5 were left.[5]

7. In Kent, as Professor Douglas has shown, several of the ancient 'minsters' and their dependent districts can be recognized in one of the lists of churches in the Domesday Monachorum; but it is of dependent churches not dependent vills that we read, and this surely implies that the districts had already been cut up into parishes served by ordinary village churches. Professor Douglas indeed says that 'the ecclesiastical region served by a community attached to a minster church survived in Kent until after the Norman Conquest'; but I can find no evidence of such a survival of pastoral functions, nor anything

---

[1] Ibid., ff. 44, 39.   [2] *Mon. Ang.* vi, pt. i, p. 304.   [3] Ibid., p. 305.
[4] Dd. i, f. 51*b*; *Mon. Ang.* vi, pt. i, p. 305. It is perhaps worth noting that in 1150 the term *ecclesia* is used instead of *capella* for the churches at Milford and Sopley.
[5] Ibid., p. 303.

to suggest that the dependence of the Kentish village churches upon a minster amounted any longer to much more than an obligation to obtain the 'chrism' or consecrated oil there rather than at the cathedral. Some of the churches may well have ranked as prebends of the minster; but the legislation of 1076 must have made married prebendaries anxious to be reckoned as ordinary parish priests. At St. Martin's, Dover, which heads the list of central churches in the Domesday Monachorum, some loosening of the collegiate bond is suggested by the statement of Domesday Book: 'T.R.E. erant prebendæ communes et reddebant LXI libras inter totum. Modo sunt divisæ per singulos per episcopum Baiocensem.'[1]

8. The church of St. Peter at Leominster in Herefordshire is a case of considerable interest but much obscurity. It formed part of the endowment of the abbey founded by Henry I at Reading; and the confirmatory charter issued by the Bishop of Hereford in 1123 indicates that it was given 'with all the parishes belonging to it' ('cum omnibus ad ipsum pertinentibus parochiis') and proceeds to specify these.[2] The list contains thirty-eight names, and all except some half-dozen of them are easily recognizable on the modern map.[3] They lie round about Leominster on all sides, running up to the county border on the north and north-east and to places from 10 to 12 miles away to the westward and south-westward. The charter further states that 'ancient and trustworthy men' have vouched for these places, but have abstained from giving evidence about many others, which of old were part of the *parochia* of Leominster, because they were too antiquated.[4] It seems probable that all this relates to the *parochia* of an ancient minster distinct from the suppressed nunnery of Leominster which a probably spurious charter (professing to have been issued by Henry I in 1125) mentions in connexion with the donation to Reading.[5] But if the episcopal charter can be trusted it would

---

[1] Dd. i, f. 1b.   [2] *Mon. Ang.* iv. 56.

[3] I say 'names' not 'places', for the name *Forda* occurs twice and pairs of villages bearing the same name are mentioned in several cases.

[4] 'Haec antiqui et autentici viri in praesentia mea attestati sunt et plurima quae antiquitus de parochia Leominstre fuerunt, pro vetustate nimia se tacuisse dixerunt.' *Mon. Ang.* iv. 56.

[5] Professor Knowles quotes the authority of Sir Frank Stenton for the judgement that the existing text of this charter cannot be regarded as a genuine document of Henry I's reign: *The Monastic Order in England,* p. 281 n. 1. The suppression of the Leominster nunnery is generally supposed to have followed upon Swein's seduction of the abbess in 1046; but in 1086 the manor was at farm *praeter victum monialium,* and an abbess (presumably of Leominster) was holding Fencote, which is one of the places described as formerly appertaining to Leominster: Dd. i, f. 180. Freeman's contention that Domesday is referring to provision made for former inmates of the nunnery after its dissolution seems rather bold, but was accepted by Round. Perhaps before the nunnery was suppressed a minster of clerks had acted like the Kentish minsters which Miss Deansley describes as

appear that by 1123 the bounds of the old *parochia* were fading from memory and that some of the dependent vills could be regarded as separate parishes. How things stood in 1086 must remain doubtful. Of the place-names mentioned in the charter of 1123 a majority appear in Domesday either as members of the manor or as lands which appertained to Leominster in the time of King Edward and used to render dues there. But there is nothing to suggest that the dues in question were ecclesiastical, and the language of Domesday seems to imply that they were no longer paid in 1086.[1] It is true that six priests are included among the inhabitants of that portion of the manor that was retained in demesne (as well as two others on the sub-infeudated lands), but it would be rash indeed to take this as evidence for the survival of a collegiate foundation still fulfilling its ancient functions. Leominster is described in Domesday in a composite entry covering 16 outlying members of the manor; and on the face of things there is no more reason to assume that the 6 priests were the clergy of a central minster and not for the most part the parish priests of dependent vills, than there is to suppose that the 7 reeves and 7 beadles and all the other inhabitants dwelt in Leominster itself.[2]

9. The case of Aylesbury church is also puzzling. Its rights are thus described in Domesday: 'De VIII hundredis qui jacent in circuitu Elesberie unusquisque sochemannus qui habet i hidam aut plus reddit unam summam annonæ huic æcclesiæ. Adhuc etiam de unoquoque sochemanno i acra annonæ aut iiii denarii solvebantur huic æcclesiæ T.R.E. sed post adventum regis W. redditum non fuit' (Dd. i, f. 143*b*). That the first sentence relates to church-scot is indicated by its close correspondence with the Pershore church-scot (*circset*) which was due from an area of 300 hides 'scilicet de unaquaque hida ubi francus homo manet unam summam annonæ in die festo S. Martini et si plures habet hidas sint liberæ' (f. 175*b*). But was Ragg right in translating the words *adhuc etiam* in the second sentence 'besides this also', thus making the due of an acre's crop (or 4*d*.) additional to the *summa* and perhaps implying that only this additional payment ceased at the Conquest (*V.C.H. Bucks.* i. 233)? Miss Neilson took it that the Aylesbury church-scot ceased altogether (*Customary Rents*, p. 194). And it seems possible that *adhuc etiam* should be understood in the sense 'still, too', and that the old payment was 'still' made

'sustaining the charge of a nunnery': *Trans. Royal Hist. Soc.*, 4th series, xxiii (1941), 52.

[1] 'Inter totum sunt xxxii hidae et omnes geldabant T.R.E. et reddebant consuetudinem ad Leofminstre': Dd. i, f. 180*b*.

[2] At Chilcomb in Hampshire Domesday records nine churches (*Ibi ix aecclesiae*), but no one can suppose that these were all situated in the village which was the centre of that great manorial complex: ibid., f. 41.

T.R.E. but only in a modified form. Vinogradoff remarks that 'soc-men holding hides would be difficult to find in Buckinghamshire, either T.R.W. or even T.R.E.' (*English Society*, pp. 441–2). Within what I take to be the 8 hundreds in question, Domesday records the presence T.R.E. of 30 sokemen, of whom 4 certainly and possibly some 9 others had a hide or more; but I only find 5 T.R.W., of whom 3 had less than a hide, while 2 may or may not have had so much. But perhaps some of the T.R.E. tenants who are named but not de-scribed, or who are unnamed and described as *homines*, ranked as sokemen. In any case the area in question seems a very large one to be the *parochia* of a 'minster', and contained before the Conquest at least three other churches besides that of Aylesbury—one at Haddenham (*Nedreham*, Dd. i, f. 143*b*) which in 1086 was held with the tithe by a priest named Gilbert, one at Wing where much of the pre-Conquest building survives, and one, as its name shows, at Whitchurch. Perhaps the churches of Bradenham, Little Missenden, and Hardwick should be added to these for the naves of the former two are 'possibly of the eleventh century' and that of Hardwick is 'probably of pre-Conquest date' (*Report of Royal Commission on Historical Monuments: Buckinghamshire*, i. xxiv, ii. 141).

10. At Damerham in Wiltshire (now transferred to Hampshire) there was a collegiate church of which nothing is said in Domesday Book. Its condition in the latter part of Henry I's reign and its sub-sequent history is thus described by Henry of Blois who was ap-pointed Abbot of Glastonbury in 1126: 'Nec præteream quod in manerio de Domerham (quod praecipuum videbatur juris Glas-toniæ) inveni sex qui dicebantur canonici singulas praebendas possi-dentes.... Singulis canonicis deinde vicissim moriendo cedentibus nec prece nec precio vinci vel flecti volui, quo ab ipsis habita ad aliud quam ad unum idemque dominium concederem. Sic singula ad unum collegi, jamque ibidem per me, Dei gracia, renovata ecclesia et ecclesiasticis ornamentis per omnia melius solito reparatis, capel-lanum, qui ecclesiæ jura suppleat, convenienter locavi' (*Adam de Domerham*, ed. Hearne, ii. 313). The contemptuous reference to 'so-called canons' is significant.

11. Though the term *monasterium* could be used in the twelfth century for almost any kind of church, it is probable that the element 'minster' in place-names such as Leominster generally indicates the site either of a monastery or of an old 'minster' of the kind which exercised the cure of souls over an extensive *parochia* through a group of priests. It is therefore remarkable that no reference either to church or clergy can be found in the Domesday entries relating to Bea-minster, Charminster, Iwerne Minster, Lytchett Minster (Lichet), Sturminster, and Yetminster in Dorset, or in those relating to Ex-minster in Devon, Pitminster in Somerset, Warminster in Wiltshire,

Minster Lovell in Oxfordshire, Kidderminster in Worcestershire, Emstrey (*Eiminstre*) and Minsterley in Shropshire, Misterton (*Minstretone*) in Leicestershire, and Southminster in Essex. For though Domesday often passes over churches in silence, it is difficult to suppose that all these would have been ignored if they were still exercising the important functions belonging to a central minster of the old type. In Nottinghamshire and Sussex, counties in which Domesday is comparatively generous in its notice of churches, we find bare references to the existence of a church (*Ibi aecclesia*) at Misterton (*Minisstretone*) in the former county and at Lyminster (*Lolinminstre*) and *Nonneminstre* in the latter, but there is nothing to suggest that these were other than ordinary village churches; and though the church of Axminster in Devon is referred to in the Exon. Domesday as if it were important, its land was only valued at 20*s*.[1] At Bedminster in Somerset we are carried beyond mere probabilities by a definite reference in Domesday to the *presbiter hujus manerii*; and at Ilminster in the same county the Exon. text seems to indicate the presence of a single priest named *Liuric*, while the Exchequer Domesday has nothing to say about either church or clergy.[2] For Iwerne Minster a scrap of further evidence is forthcoming from the Shaftesbury Abbey survey of *c*. 1130 which shows 'Keineward the chaplain' holding three churches (apparently *Prestentun* and Hartgrove as well as Iwerne). On another folio of the same manuscript an entry relating to Iwerne (which may be a little later) refers to the *presbiter illius ville*.[3] As regards the antiquity of the above-mentioned 'minster' names it may be noted that Sturminster, Exminster, and Lyminster occur in the will of Alfred the Great and that seven of the others appear in ninth- or tenth-century texts. Finally, it is perhaps significant that so many of the vills in question belonged in 1086 to bishops or monasteries. Beaminster, Charminster, and Yetminster belonged to the Bishop of Salisbury, Pitminster to the Bishop of Winchester, Southminster to the Bishop of London, while Ilminster belonged to Muchelney Abbey, Iwerne to Shaftesbury Abbey, *Nonneminstre* to the abbey of Almeneches, Emstrey to the abbey of Shrewsbury, and Upminster to the Canons of Waltham.[4] It is tempting to think that these

---

[1] Dd. i, ff. 286*b*, 24*b*; Exon., p. 77. *Nonneminstre* is described as being held before the Conquest mainly by a priest named Esmund, partly by another named Esmeld; but Feilitzen regards them as identical, Esmund being an error for Esmeld: op. cit., p. 367. The name *Nonneminstre* may mean, not a minster of nuns, but one belonging to, or founded by, Nunna—possibly the seventh-century king of that name: *Place-Names of Sussex* (English Place-Name Soc.), i. 169 n.

[2] Dd. i, f. 86*b*; Exon., p. 173. In the Geld Rolls (Exon., p. 74), we read of land 'quam tenent presbit' et vill de illeminstre' which suggests 'the priest and *villani*', but the contraction might be for the plural *presbiteri*.

[3] Harl. MS. 61, ff. 45*v*, 46, 53*v*.

[4] The bishops and monasteries were not in all cases the sole lords.

facts may point to transfers similar to those which took place at Morville and Cullompton.

12. References in Domesday to 'minsters', canons, or small groups
of priests are by no means confined to the cases already mentioned.
Apart from cathedral canons and the clergy situated in boroughs
(such as Oxford, Dover, and Clare), there were, for example, canons
at Plympton in Devon (Dd. i, f. 100b), at South Malling in Sussex
(f. 16b), at Wolverhampton (f. 247b); while priests or clerks in the
plural are mentioned at Yealmpton (*Elintone*) in Devon (f. 100b),
at Singleton and Boxgrove in Sussex (ff. 23, 25b), at Cheltenham
in Gloucestershire (f. 162b), at North Lydbury and Wroxeter in
Shropshire (ff. 252, 254b); and casual references to a *monasterium*
are found at Stanway, Gloucestershire (f. 163b), Hitchin, Hertfordshire (f. 132b), North Crawley, Buckinghamshire (f. 149), Staines in
Middlesex (f. 145b, unless Stone in Buckinghamshire is intended),
and Long Sutton in Lincolnshire (f. 377b). But the 'canons of St.
Andrew' mentioned in the Exon. Domesday (p. 71) and assigned
by Page to the church of St. Andrew at Ilchester, which he in consequence regarded as a 'minster' (op. cit., pp. 70–71) were undoubtedly the canons of Wells Cathedral. The distinction between
canonici, *presbiteri*, and *clerici* must not be stressed: all three terms are
employed for the clergy of Wolverhampton (Dd. i, ff. 247b and 249b
sub *Segleslei*). The terms *monasterium* and *aecclesia* are used indifferently
for the church of Withcall in Lincolnshire (ff. 364, 375).

APPENDIX V

Village Ale-Houses

PENALTIES for breach of the peace in an ale-house (*eala-hus*) were imposed in the reign of Æthelred II (iii. i. 2), but the enactment may only relate to towns and not villages. Walter Map, in one of his stories, refers to houses 'quales Anglici in singulis singulas habebant diocesibus bibitorias', and Tupper and Ogle in their translation render this as 'such a house as the English have in each parish for drinking'.[1] But such a translation of *diocesis* is highly questionable; and in any case this evidence belongs at the earliest to the last quarter of the twelfth century. About the same time, however, a glimpse of village folk drinking together is afforded by William of Newburgh, in his account of a man named Ketell—*homo quidem rusticanus*—who lived at the village of Farnham in Yorkshire, but had died before William wrote. Ketell, we are told, had the gift of seeing devils if any were present, and, among other marvels, used to relate that he once entered a *domus potationis* and saw a little devil sitting on each man's drinking-cup, but when prayers were said 'as the custom is', the devils flew away and only returned when the rustics resumed their seats and their drinking ('Cumque inter potandum preces ex more indicerentur, et nomen Salvatoris insonaret, exterriti exsiliebant, virtutem sacri nominis non ferentes, sed mox residentibus ad phiales rusticis, rursus introibant sessionem priorem cum motibus solitis repetentes').[2] Yet even here one cannot be sure whether *domus potationis* stands for 'the' ale-house of a village or 'an' ale-house in, perhaps, a market town. The subject deserves further investigation.

[1] *De Nugis Curialium*, ed. M. R. James, in *Anecdota Oxoniensia*, 1914, p. 75; ibid., translated by F. Tupper and M. B. Ogle, 1924, p. 94.
[2] *Chronicles of the Reigns of Stephen, Henry II and Richard I* (Rolls Series), i. 151–4.

INDEX

Abbaye aux Dames (Caen), English estates of: holdings of peasants on, 362; obligations of peasants on, 386.

Agriculture, tendency to uniformity in basic conditions of, 270–1.

Ale-house, village, problem of, 387, 405.

Arden, Forest of, 15–16.

Beadles, 276–7.

Bordars and Cottars, 232–3, 237–8, 240–1, 273, 308, 309 n. 1, 339–41, 357; holdings of, 342–7, 354, 355–6, 360–4; plough-beasts of, 353–4, 356; obligations of, 366, 370, 371, 378, 382, 383–4, 386.

Bovarii and *Bubulci*, 329 n. 1, 360, 361, 362, 363, 384; wives of, 382.

Brichtric of Haselbury, 333, 335.

Burton Abbey, estates of, 91–94: demesne and peasant ploughs on, 93; holdings of peasants on, 357, 358, 362–3; obligations of peasants on, 376–8, 382.

Caen, *see* Abbaye aux Dames.

Castellaria, the, 30–32.

Censarii or *Censores*, 238, 240, 372, 376, 378.

Censores, *see* Censarii.

Chapels, 298, 299, 302, 397, 399.

Cherwell Valley, condition of in 1086, 5–8; not untypical, 8–9.

Church-building, eleventh century, 295–8.

Churches: in Suffolk, 288–9; in Huntingdonshire, 288, 290, 304; in Cambridgeshire, 291–2; in Oxfordshire, Berkshire, and Cornwall, 292; in Norfolk, 293; in Kent, 293–4; in Derbyshire and Surrey, 304; in Yorkshire, 304–5; in Lincolnshire, Nottinghamshire, and Herefordshire, 305; casual nature of references to in Domesday Book, 292–4; thegns as builders of, 289–91; proprietary, 319–23; endowments of, 306–27.

Church-scot, 300, 366, 383, 401.

Coliberti, 232, 365 n. 1, 369, 371.

Cotseti, *see* Bordars and Cottars.

Cottars, *see* Bordars.

Courts, honorial, 35; hundred, 36–38.

Dairy-farms, 264–5.

Danes, influence of, 226, 395.

Denes, 14–15, 253–5.

Derbyshire, variety of conditions in, 237–41.

Domesday Book: limitations of, 3–4; deceptive omissions and composite entries in, 9, 10, 12, 13, 14, 16, 17, 21 n. 1, 232.

Estates, intermixture of, in Oxfordshire, 56–60; consequences of, 61–62; with lands of the Church of Winchester, 78–80; with lands of Ramsey Abbey, 85–88; with lands of Eudo Dapifer, 101.

Estates, preponderance of great, 25–26; obstacles to precise statistics of, 26–27; compact, 30–32; great and moderate in Oxfordshire, 40–44; small in Oxfordshire, 44–45; royal, management of, 128–30, 143–50, 153.

Estates, scattering of, 28, 33, 45–47; before the Norman Conquest, 29–30, 46–47; far-reaching influence of, 33–39.

Eudo Dapifer, estates of, 99–104: subinfeudation on, 101–2; demesne and peasant ploughs on, 103; increase of after 1086, 103–4.

Farming-out of manors, evidence for widespread, 113–28.

Fee-farms, as tenures for life, 111–12.

Fens, the, 18, 250–1.

Firmarii: of royal estates, 147–50; sheriffs as, 147–9; barons as, 150; peasants as, 153–4, 287 n. 3, 330; monks as, 157–9; of native origin, 154–5; official, 157; on a large scale, 150–3; powers of in relation to peasants and free manorial tenants, 196–207.

Fisheries, 18, 248–52.

Fold-soke, 227, 377.

Food-rents, 128–39; modification and commutation of, 129–30, 133–40.